The series Lecture Notes in Computer Science (LNCS), including its subseries Lecture Notes in Artificial Intelligence (LNAI) and Lecture Notes in Bioinformatics (LNBI), has established itself as a medium for the publication of new developments in computer science and information technology research, teaching, and education.

LNCS enjoys close cooperation with the computer science R & D community, the series counts many renowned academics among its volume editors and paper authors, and collaborates with prestigious societies. Its mission is to serve this international community by providing an invaluable service, mainly focused on the publication of conference and workshop proceedings and postproceedings. LNCS commenced publication in 1973.

Masaaki Kurosu · Ayako Hashizume
Editors

Human-Computer Interaction

Thematic Area, HCI 2024
Held as Part of the 26th HCI International Conference, HCII 2024
Washington, DC, USA, June 29 – July 4, 2024
Proceedings, Part V

Editors
Masaaki Kurosu
The Open University of Japan
Chiba, Japan

Ayako Hashizume
Hosei University
Tokyo, Japan

ISSN 0302-9743 ISSN 1611-3349 (electronic)
Lecture Notes in Computer Science
ISBN 978-3-031-60448-5 ISBN 978-3-031-60449-2 (eBook)
https://doi.org/10.1007/978-3-031-60449-2

This Springer imprint is published by the registered company Springer Nature Switzerland AG
The registered company address is: Gewerbestrasse 11, 6330 Cham, Switzerland

Foreword

This year we celebrate 40 years since the establishment of the HCI International (HCII) Conference, which has been a hub for presenting groundbreaking research and novel ideas and collaboration for people from all over the world.

The HCII conference was founded in 1984 by Prof. Gavriel Salvendy (Purdue University, USA, Tsinghua University, P.R. China, and University of Central Florida, USA) and the first event of the series, "1st USA-Japan Conference on Human-Computer Interaction", was held in Honolulu, Hawaii, USA, 18–20 August. Since then, HCI International is held jointly with several Thematic Areas and Affiliated Conferences, with each one under the auspices of a distinguished international Program Board and under one management and one registration. Twenty-six HCI International Conferences have been organized so far (every two years until 2013, and annually thereafter).

Over the years, this conference has served as a platform for scholars, researchers, industry experts and students to exchange ideas, connect, and address challenges in the ever-evolving HCI field. Throughout these 40 years, the conference has evolved itself, adapting to new technologies and emerging trends, while staying committed to its core mission of advancing knowledge and driving change.

As we celebrate this milestone anniversary, we reflect on the contributions of its founding members and appreciate the commitment of its current and past Affiliated Conference Program Board Chairs and members. We are also thankful to all past conference attendees who have shaped this community into what it is today.

The 26th International Conference on Human-Computer Interaction, HCI International 2024 (HCII 2024), was held as a 'hybrid' event at the Washington Hilton Hotel, Washington, DC, USA, during 29 June – 4 July 2024. It incorporated the 21 thematic areas and affiliated conferences listed below.

A total of 5108 individuals from academia, research institutes, industry, and government agencies from 85 countries submitted contributions, and 1271 papers and 309 posters were included in the volumes of the proceedings that were published just before the start of the conference, these are listed below. The contributions thoroughly cover the entire field of human-computer interaction, addressing major advances in knowledge and effective use of computers in a variety of application areas. These papers provide academics, researchers, engineers, scientists, practitioners and students with state-of-the-art information on the most recent advances in HCI.

The HCI International (HCII) conference also offers the option of presenting 'Late Breaking Work', and this applies both for papers and posters, with corresponding volumes of proceedings that will be published after the conference. Full papers will be included in the 'HCII 2024 - Late Breaking Papers' volumes of the proceedings to be published in the Springer LNCS series, while 'Poster Extended Abstracts' will be included as short research papers in the 'HCII 2024 - Late Breaking Posters' volumes to be published in the Springer CCIS series.

I would like to thank the Program Board Chairs and the members of the Program Boards of all thematic areas and affiliated conferences for their contribution towards the high scientific quality and overall success of the HCI International 2024 conference. Their manifold support in terms of paper reviewing (single-blind review process, with a minimum of two reviews per submission), session organization and their willingness to act as goodwill ambassadors for the conference is most highly appreciated.

This conference would not have been possible without the continuous and unwavering support and advice of Gavriel Salvendy, founder, General Chair Emeritus, and Scientific Advisor. For his outstanding efforts, I would like to express my sincere appreciation to Abbas Moallem, Communications Chair and Editor of HCI International News.

July 2024 Constantine Stephanidis

HCI International 2024 Thematic Areas and Affiliated Conferences

- HCI: Human-Computer Interaction Thematic Area
- HIMI: Human Interface and the Management of Information Thematic Area
- EPCE: 21st International Conference on Engineering Psychology and Cognitive Ergonomics
- AC: 18th International Conference on Augmented Cognition
- UAHCI: 18th International Conference on Universal Access in Human-Computer Interaction
- CCD: 16th International Conference on Cross-Cultural Design
- SCSM: 16th International Conference on Social Computing and Social Media
- VAMR: 16th International Conference on Virtual, Augmented and Mixed Reality
- DHM: 15th International Conference on Digital Human Modeling & Applications in Health, Safety, Ergonomics & Risk Management
- DUXU: 13th International Conference on Design, User Experience and Usability
- C&C: 12th International Conference on Culture and Computing
- DAPI: 12th International Conference on Distributed, Ambient and Pervasive Interactions
- HCIBGO: 11th International Conference on HCI in Business, Government and Organizations
- LCT: 11th International Conference on Learning and Collaboration Technologies
- ITAP: 10th International Conference on Human Aspects of IT for the Aged Population
- AIS: 6th International Conference on Adaptive Instructional Systems
- HCI-CPT: 6th International Conference on HCI for Cybersecurity, Privacy and Trust
- HCI-Games: 6th International Conference on HCI in Games
- MobiTAS: 6th International Conference on HCI in Mobility, Transport and Automotive Systems
- AI-HCI: 5th International Conference on Artificial Intelligence in HCI
- MOBILE: 5th International Conference on Human-Centered Design, Operation and Evaluation of Mobile Communications

List of Conference Proceedings Volumes Appearing Before the Conference

1. LNCS 14684, Human-Computer Interaction: Part I, edited by Masaaki Kurosu and Ayako Hashizume
2. LNCS 14685, Human-Computer Interaction: Part II, edited by Masaaki Kurosu and Ayako Hashizume
3. LNCS 14686, Human-Computer Interaction: Part III, edited by Masaaki Kurosu and Ayako Hashizume
4. LNCS 14687, Human-Computer Interaction: Part IV, edited by Masaaki Kurosu and Ayako Hashizume
5. LNCS 14688, Human-Computer Interaction: Part V, edited by Masaaki Kurosu and Ayako Hashizume
6. LNCS 14689, Human Interface and the Management of Information: Part I, edited by Hirohiko Mori and Yumi Asahi
7. LNCS 14690, Human Interface and the Management of Information: Part II, edited by Hirohiko Mori and Yumi Asahi
8. LNCS 14691, Human Interface and the Management of Information: Part III, edited by Hirohiko Mori and Yumi Asahi
9. LNAI 14692, Engineering Psychology and Cognitive Ergonomics: Part I, edited by Don Harris and Wen-Chin Li
10. LNAI 14693, Engineering Psychology and Cognitive Ergonomics: Part II, edited by Don Harris and Wen-Chin Li
11. LNAI 14694, Augmented Cognition, Part I, edited by Dylan D. Schmorrow and Cali M. Fidopiastis
12. LNAI 14695, Augmented Cognition, Part II, edited by Dylan D. Schmorrow and Cali M. Fidopiastis
13. LNCS 14696, Universal Access in Human-Computer Interaction: Part I, edited by Margherita Antona and Constantine Stephanidis
14. LNCS 14697, Universal Access in Human-Computer Interaction: Part II, edited by Margherita Antona and Constantine Stephanidis
15. LNCS 14698, Universal Access in Human-Computer Interaction: Part III, edited by Margherita Antona and Constantine Stephanidis
16. LNCS 14699, Cross-Cultural Design: Part I, edited by Pei-Luen Patrick Rau
17. LNCS 14700, Cross-Cultural Design: Part II, edited by Pei-Luen Patrick Rau
18. LNCS 14701, Cross-Cultural Design: Part III, edited by Pei-Luen Patrick Rau
19. LNCS 14702, Cross-Cultural Design: Part IV, edited by Pei-Luen Patrick Rau
20. LNCS 14703, Social Computing and Social Media: Part I, edited by Adela Coman and Simona Vasilache
21. LNCS 14704, Social Computing and Social Media: Part II, edited by Adela Coman and Simona Vasilache
22. LNCS 14705, Social Computing and Social Media: Part III, edited by Adela Coman and Simona Vasilache

23. LNCS 14706, Virtual, Augmented and Mixed Reality: Part I, edited by Jessie Y. C. Chen and Gino Fragomeni
24. LNCS 14707, Virtual, Augmented and Mixed Reality: Part II, edited by Jessie Y. C. Chen and Gino Fragomeni
25. LNCS 14708, Virtual, Augmented and Mixed Reality: Part III, edited by Jessie Y. C. Chen and Gino Fragomeni
26. LNCS 14709, Digital Human Modeling and Applications in Health, Safety, Ergonomics and Risk Management: Part I, edited by Vincent G. Duffy
27. LNCS 14710, Digital Human Modeling and Applications in Health, Safety, Ergonomics and Risk Management: Part II, edited by Vincent G. Duffy
28. LNCS 14711, Digital Human Modeling and Applications in Health, Safety, Ergonomics and Risk Management: Part III, edited by Vincent G. Duffy
29. LNCS 14712, Design, User Experience, and Usability: Part I, edited by Aaron Marcus, Elizabeth Rosenzweig and Marcelo M. Soares
30. LNCS 14713, Design, User Experience, and Usability: Part II, edited by Aaron Marcus, Elizabeth Rosenzweig and Marcelo M. Soares
31. LNCS 14714, Design, User Experience, and Usability: Part III, edited by Aaron Marcus, Elizabeth Rosenzweig and Marcelo M. Soares
32. LNCS 14715, Design, User Experience, and Usability: Part IV, edited by Aaron Marcus, Elizabeth Rosenzweig and Marcelo M. Soares
33. LNCS 14716, Design, User Experience, and Usability: Part V, edited by Aaron Marcus, Elizabeth Rosenzweig and Marcelo M. Soares
34. LNCS 14717, Culture and Computing, edited by Matthias Rauterberg
35. LNCS 14718, Distributed, Ambient and Pervasive Interactions: Part I, edited by Norbert A. Streitz and Shin'ichi Konomi
36. LNCS 14719, Distributed, Ambient and Pervasive Interactions: Part II, edited by Norbert A. Streitz and Shin'ichi Konomi
37. LNCS 14720, HCI in Business, Government and Organizations: Part I, edited by Fiona Fui-Hoon Nah and Keng Leng Siau
38. LNCS 14721, HCI in Business, Government and Organizations: Part II, edited by Fiona Fui-Hoon Nah and Keng Leng Siau
39. LNCS 14722, Learning and Collaboration Technologies: Part I, edited by Panayiotis Zaphiris and Andri Ioannou
40. LNCS 14723, Learning and Collaboration Technologies: Part II, edited by Panayiotis Zaphiris and Andri Ioannou
41. LNCS 14724, Learning and Collaboration Technologies: Part III, edited by Panayiotis Zaphiris and Andri Ioannou
42. LNCS 14725, Human Aspects of IT for the Aged Population: Part I, edited by Qin Gao and Jia Zhou
43. LNCS 14726, Human Aspects of IT for the Aged Population: Part II, edited by Qin Gao and Jia Zhou
44. LNCS 14727, Adaptive Instructional System, edited by Robert A. Sottilare and Jessica Schwarz
45. LNCS 14728, HCI for Cybersecurity, Privacy and Trust: Part I, edited by Abbas Moallem
46. LNCS 14729, HCI for Cybersecurity, Privacy and Trust: Part II, edited by Abbas Moallem

47. LNCS 14730, HCI in Games: Part I, edited by Xiaowen Fang
48. LNCS 14731, HCI in Games: Part II, edited by Xiaowen Fang
49. LNCS 14732, HCI in Mobility, Transport and Automotive Systems: Part I, edited by Heidi Krömker
50. LNCS 14733, HCI in Mobility, Transport and Automotive Systems: Part II, edited by Heidi Krömker
51. LNAI 14734, Artificial Intelligence in HCI: Part I, edited by Helmut Degen and Stavroula Ntoa
52. LNAI 14735, Artificial Intelligence in HCI: Part II, edited by Helmut Degen and Stavroula Ntoa
53. LNAI 14736, Artificial Intelligence in HCI: Part III, edited by Helmut Degen and Stavroula Ntoa
54. LNCS 14737, Design, Operation and Evaluation of Mobile Communications: Part I, edited by June Wei and George Margetis
55. LNCS 14738, Design, Operation and Evaluation of Mobile Communications: Part II, edited by June Wei and George Margetis
56. CCIS 2114, HCI International 2024 Posters - Part I, edited by Constantine Stephanidis, Margherita Antona, Stavroula Ntoa and Gavriel Salvendy
57. CCIS 2115, HCI International 2024 Posters - Part II, edited by Constantine Stephanidis, Margherita Antona, Stavroula Ntoa and Gavriel Salvendy
58. CCIS 2116, HCI International 2024 Posters - Part III, edited by Constantine Stephanidis, Margherita Antona, Stavroula Ntoa and Gavriel Salvendy
59. CCIS 2117, HCI International 2024 Posters - Part IV, edited by Constantine Stephanidis, Margherita Antona, Stavroula Ntoa and Gavriel Salvendy
60. CCIS 2118, HCI International 2024 Posters - Part V, edited by Constantine Stephanidis, Margherita Antona, Stavroula Ntoa and Gavriel Salvendy
61. CCIS 2119, HCI International 2024 Posters - Part VI, edited by Constantine Stephanidis, Margherita Antona, Stavroula Ntoa and Gavriel Salvendy
62. CCIS 2120, HCI International 2024 Posters - Part VII, edited by Constantine Stephanidis, Margherita Antona, Stavroula Ntoa and Gavriel Salvendy

https://2024.hci.international/proceedings

Preface

Human-Computer Interaction is a Thematic Area of the International Conference on Human-Computer Interaction (HCII). The HCI field is today undergoing a wave of significant innovation and breakthroughs towards radically new future forms of interaction. The HCI Thematic Area constitutes a forum for scientific research and innovation in human-computer interaction, addressing challenging and innovative topics in human-computer interaction theory, methodology, and practice, including, for example, novel theoretical approaches to interaction, novel user interface concepts and technologies, novel interaction devices, UI development methods, environments and tools, multimodal user interfaces, human-robot interaction, emotions in HCI, aesthetic issues, HCI and children, evaluation methods and tools, and many others.

The HCI Thematic Area covers four major dimensions, namely theory and methodology, technology, human beings, and societal impact. The following five volumes of the HCII 2024 proceedings reflect these dimensions:

- Human-Computer Interaction - Part I, addressing topics related to HCI Theory and Design and Evaluation Methods and Tools, and Emotions in HCI;
- Human-Computer Interaction - Part II, addressing topics related to Human-Robot Interaction and Child-Computer Interaction;
- Human-Computer Interaction - Part III, addressing topics related to HCI for Mental Health and Psychological Wellbeing, and HCI in Healthcare;
- Human-Computer Interaction - Part IV, addressing topics related to HCI, Environment and Sustainability, and Design and User Experience Evaluation Case Studies;
- Human-Computer Interaction - Part V, addressing topics related to Multimodality and Natural User Interfaces, and HCI, AI, Creativity, Art and Culture.

The papers in these volumes were accepted for publication after a minimum of two single-blind reviews from the members of the HCI Program Board or, in some cases, from members of the Program Boards of other affiliated conferences. We would like to thank all of them for their invaluable contribution, support, and efforts.

July 2024

Masaaki Kurosu
Ayako Hashizume

Human-Computer Interaction Thematic Area (HCI 2024)

The full list with the Program Board Chairs and the members of the Program Boards of all thematic areas and affiliated conferences of HCII 2024 is available online at:

http://www.hci.international/board-members-2024.php

Human-Computer Interaction Thematic Area (HCI 2024)

HCI International 2025 Conference

The 27th International Conference on Human-Computer Interaction, HCI International 2025, will be held jointly with the affiliated conferences at the Swedish Exhibition & Congress Centre and Gothia Towers Hotel, Gothenburg, Sweden, June 22–27, 2025. It will cover a broad spectrum of themes related to Human-Computer Interaction, including theoretical issues, methods, tools, processes, and case studies in HCI design, as well as novel interaction techniques, interfaces, and applications. The proceedings will be published by Springer. More information will become available on the conference website: https://2025.hci.international/.

General Chair
Prof. Constantine Stephanidis
University of Crete and ICS-FORTH
Heraklion, Crete, Greece
Email: general_chair@2025.hci.international

https://2025.hci.international/

Contents – Part V

Multimodality and Natural User Interfaces

Challenges and Opportunities Designing Voice User Interfaces for Emergent Users

Pankaj Doke[(✉)] and Sunil Kumar Kopparapu

TCS Research, Tata Consultancy Services Limited, Thane, India
{Pankaj.Doke,Sunilkumar.Kopparapu}@tcs.com

Abstract. Human Computer Interfaces and Interaction has been a topic of research for many decades. In the case of voice-based interactions, the earlier investigations were based on Plain Old Telephone System (POTS) systems. Developed country-originated research was also about Western, Educated, Industrialized, Rich, Democratic (WEIRD) users. However, the past few decades have seen the rise and deployment of wireless telecom and data networks with better capabilities even in developing countries such as India. This has also been supported by the ease of availability of smart devices such as smartphones and smart speakers. The deployment of these technologies has also concerned a very large number of Emergent Users (EU). Voice being a very natural and easy-to-use mode of interaction for EU, we believe it merits an independent investigation especially since Adoption of Graphical User Interface (GUI) designs, for EU, has been challenging beyond the initial phase of Availability. Today, designers are adapting GUI designs to Voice User Interface (VUI) design and hence we feel that VUI designs for EU may be riddled with the same issues as GUI design for EU. Additionally, voice as a medium has distinctive design implications as compared to visual display units. Along with these aspects, the design contexts of EU are vastly different from those of WEIRD users. In this paper, we highlight potential challenges we foresee for VUI for EU and the opportunity for developing design artefacts such as frameworks, tools, design patterns, models, and theories for increasing adoption of VUI by EU.

Keywords: Voice User Interfaces · Emergent Users · Interaction Design

1 Introduction

Developing countries such as India, which are also contemporarily referred to as the Global South (GS) [14] has seen a significant deployment of wireless telecom and data networks [28, 38, 42, 54] along with affordable smart devices. This has led to significant research from both industry and academia, towards explorations of contextual design for the Users in these countries, termed as "Emergent User" (EU) [3, 17]. However, barring a few studies involving voice-based interactions [72, 73, 58, 67, 74] the dominant HCI investigations have been in the area of mobile GUI based applications and their adoption by EU [3, 17].

M. Kurosu and A. Hashizume (Eds.): HCII 2024, LNCS 14688, pp. 3–16, 2024.
https://doi.org/10.1007/978-3-031-60449-2_1

While these smartphones offer both visual and voice modalities of input and output, it should be noted that given the dominant daily-life context and abilities of EU, voice as a modality ranks as the most preferred natural modality [26, 47, 79]. In fact, novel designs with input and output using voice as a modality rank as one of the grand challenges of HCI [71]. Also, as the use of AI/ML models rapidly permeate into everyday computing-based interactions, they would impose novel implications and challenges on the EU. Thus, users would have to negotiate with ever evolving (and imperfect) technologies to achieve their goals [66] under the umbrella of human-environment interactions [75].

In this context, we would like to argue that VUI for EU offers exciting challenges and opportunities for research and innovation. Apart from the grand challenge posits, the challenges posed by EU are themselves significantly complex and need deep research investigations [35] making the work impactful especially given the billions of EU lives impacted across several continents.

Voice based interactions have been studied in the past which have resulted in voice based interactive systems such as Avaaj Otalo [57], Spoken Web [1], GappaGoshti™ [37], CGNet Swara [45], Tamil Market [60, 61] amongst others which ranged from purely POTS based IVR systems to enabling web based systems with voice-enablement to native low-resource mobile applications with voice features. However, for varied reasons their success in terms of adoption has been limited [12, 20, 34]. Further, HCI work carried out in the Global North (GN) [14] for its WEIRD users [11, 29, 36, 76] are less likely to be adaptable to the Global South (GS) EU archetypes users [12, 34, 36].

Figure 1 captures the relationship between modalities of interaction between an EU and interaction affordances of the artefact. It further highlights that if the interface is a GUI, it demands that the user be proficient in text input mechanisms such as a foreign language or local language, which is very challenging for an EU [35] or reading and cognitive abilities [17, 28]. Hence, we argue that for EU, VUI offers a better premise of more usable and adoptable contextual design concerning smart devices. Further, Fig. 1 depicts the senses, (a) Speech {Speech Impaired}, (b) Vision {Vision Impaired}, (c) Hearing {Hearing Impaired} on the left side. It also depicts the combination of these senses and their Impairments using AND logic gates. The output of the AND gates indicate the preferred UI (GUI or VUI or TUI). Further, the dotted lines at the top indicate the Demands of the UI on the EU. For example, a GUI would demand that the EU have better literacy and the ability to input text using a virtual keyboard. A VUI, as can be seen in Fig. 1, would not have any such demand on the EU. Note that demands are a barrier to the adoption of an interface or technology by the user.

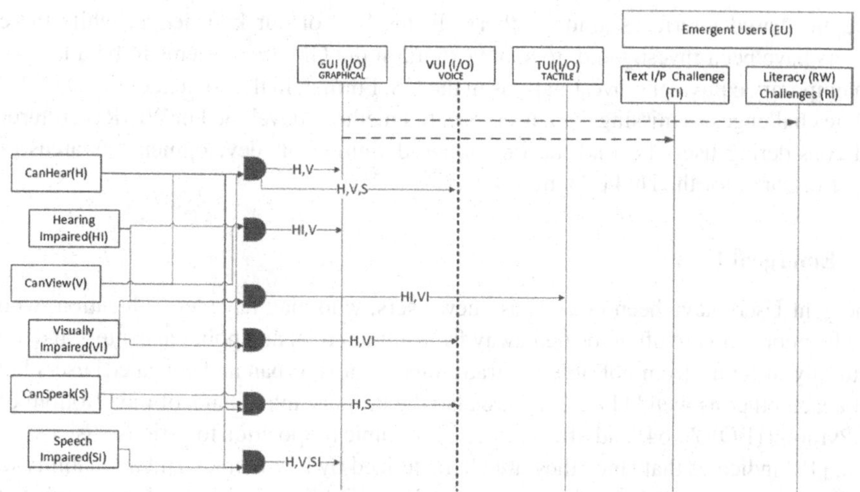

Fig. 1. Opportunity scope for voice user interfaces (VUI) for emergent users (EU).

2 Problem Statement

India is undergoing a significant technological revolution in terms of access to internet, mobile apps and data consumption. Statistics indicate that the per month 4G data traffic is 12, 640 Petabytes, about 10 million 5G devices, 17 GB data consumption per user with a growth rate of 31% [38, 56]. The statistics also indicate that 90% of the users prefer to consume information in local languages and in addition smartphone penetration is increasing rapidly in rural areas. Despite these impressive statistics, users face challenges in adoption of government's digital touchpoints due to low digital literacy and the applications user engagement especially in local languages due to users' conceptual models of digital services and the way apps are constructed [31]. Studies also show that by 2025, 56% of new internet users would be from Rural India [32]. This can be interpreted to indicate that the migration of internet access from mobile to smart devices is happening rapidly via smart devices such as smart TV, smart speaker et cetera.

Additionally, data from education surveys shows that many Government school students of standard 8, could not read English Sentences in Rural India. This is just one of the many dimensions of an EU context [17, 40].

User and User Contexts has been a significant driver of investigations in the "Second Wave" of HCI theories and practice [6] while the 'Third Wave" would try to bring in the focus on culture, emotion, and user experience.

One of the dominant themes which arose was the (a) acceptance of Global North (GN) and Global South (GS) and (b) that the methods and techniques developed for GN cannot be directly transplanted and at best there is a need to adapt and in many cases developed afresh [9, 14, 20, 30, 33, 55, 76]. Qualitative methods, based on ethnographic studies, also need to be repurposed for the varied contexts of EU [68]. As [35] highlights, the challenges which relate to EU are in the space of conceptual models of the digital world, cognitive issues such as abstractions, digital identity, trust, cultural variations, metaphor-based interfaces among others. To the best of our knowledge, while these aspects have been investigated, to some extent, in the GN, there seems to be a lack of contemporary equivalent investigations in the GS. Further, in the context of the GS, [33] list the challenges as missing data, user research methods developed in WEIRD cultures and considering users beyond the immediate definition of 'development' as areas of future research for the HCI community.

2.1 Emergent User

Emergent Users have been defined as "new users, who may have less education, who may be poor, who are often located away from commercial and political centers and are culturally different from not only the traditional (that is, urban and educated) users but from each other as well" [17]. They are also the primary inhabitants of the "Bottom of the Pyramid (BOP)" [64] and offer a unique economic proposition to various businesses. Also, [19] indicates that since they are characterized by low literacy and an inability to handle text-based digital interfaces, traditional paradigms of design need to be revisited to address their needs. Similarly, [77] highlighted that the barriers for EU are small screen size, virtual keyboards, poorly designed apps. They also highlighted that on one hand reading based activity led to anxiety and confidence issues but on the other hand features such as spoken search and natural language delighted the users and familial settings in which the devices got used. Similarly, [40] highlights that textual interfaces are unusable or error-prone while speech-based systems give a higher degree of comfort to the user while also being natural and time efficient with the users. In a study conducted in rural India by [13] the users preferred speech as their mode of interaction and as the study quotes, one of the users said, "I was concentrating on what was being said and if I had started looking for pictures my mind would have been diverted". This indicates that the presence/availability of a facility/interface with GUI + VUI need not necessarily imply that the GUI would be adopted. Despite (a) system glitches and (b) not having access to the best of speech technology, most of the users were willing to use speech. The study further noted that the users were very enthusiastic about talking to the device and hearing it speak back to them confirming that speech is perceived as a natural way of interaction even with machines! Similar findings were also reported by [70] that users preferred speech-based access to information as compared to text interfaces or touch tone interfaces. In another context of investigation for ICT for banking, [39] found users needed less assistance and less time to complete their task when voice was used compared to text-based user interfaces. In an interesting exercise across two continents, using multiple workshops with EU, [34] engaged in the creation of design artefacts to probe design directions using EU lens. Their recommended directions for design are (a) un-noticeable interactions, (b) speech interfaces that go beyond utility and simple task completion or question answering and (c) interactions that qualify to be mindful and explore the 'quantified other'.

We observe two notable perspectives in the context of using VUI or designing with VUI. In Perspective One, the preference is for combining GUI with VUI [73], and in the other, it is preferably VUI [28]. The GUI + VUI perspective relies on theories of information theory, general model of human information processing, semiotics, dual coding theory, and the gestalt theory. The authors in [73] take the view that the interaction between the user and the GUI + VUI artefact is a communication exercise anchored in information theory. With this lens, the communication happens over the channel manifested in the modalities of the interface. The messaging over this channel is then driven by the general model of human information processing where the "message passing" on the channel is governed by the processes of stimuli identification, response selection and response programming. They observe that there are references of mapping between stimuli-response in GUI to increase user performance but is notably absent in VUI. It should be noted that they constrain the VUI to an IVR which is used in a typical Telephony/POTS context as compared to a voice-bot such as Amazon Echo, Apple Siri, Google Assistant. Due to this constraint, in which an IVR audio prompt maps an action to a particular key on the telephone keypad, they introduce a concept of "directedness" in the IVR/VUI. Such a directedness hence 'directs' or influences the user behaviour and nudges the user towards task completion.

They subsequently move to the Content of the voice prompts, while still anchored in the overall umbrella of communication and in this case, interpret it via Semiotics. They argue that the designer created representations (voice messages) and the users engage in 'interlocution'. Herein, the meaning of the message is interpreted by the user via a negotiation. While they cite Pierce, this also is along the lines of the theory articulated about common ground by H.H. Clark [10].

They then steer towards the Dual Coding theory to combine the Audio and Video (GUI) channels of communication. Since the theory argues that the auditory and visual subsystems are independent (but connected), employing them together increases the capabilities of the user and (indirectly) the user's performance.

By using the 'temporal' dimension of the GUI and aligning it with the temporality of VUI, they use Gestalt theory to argue that the GUI + VUI can hence be presented (and perceived) as a singular entity than as disparate entities, especially since GUI is spatial and VUI is temporal. From a design synthesis this would mean synchronising the GUI element with the VUI element so that both are perceived as one. They tested their hypothesis with an Android tablet and 36 EU belonging to 5 different villages in Madhya Pradesh.

However, in our observations, EU are likely to use small form-factor smartphones or feature phones (such as keypad-based JioPhone in India) as compared to Tablets in their daily lives. In such a context, the form factor introduces constraints on the GUI interface design. This is likely to influence the "logical information content" to be spread across more than one screen. In this situation, the working memory constraints of the EU would be challenged as the user would have to navigate back and forth between screens. Further, due to lesser textual literacy the GUI interface would need to skew towards non-textual elements for communication and hence building a 'semantic whole' between the VUI messaging and the semiotics of the GUI element could increase the design challenges for an 'average' designer. Apart from this, the current findings were for an IVR context as compared to a broad-based VUI context which encompasses smart devices such as speakers or newer devices such as the "AI Pin" device from Humane [80]. In such cases, the input modality is Speech/Voice of the User as compared to touch/tap on the device. Thus, a modality in the experiment where Speech was input (along with GUI as input) could have shed more light on the performance metrics of the modalities for the EU.

In Perspective Two, [41] shared that bimodal audio-visual information can be confusing for EU, however their tests were conducted with computers. In a recent study, [28] highlighted that prior work on voice based interfaces are simple as compared to text-based alternatives and inclusive of users which less literacy. Their key finding was the use of smartphone based inbuilt voice input features to navigate media and communication apps by EU. These usages were for voice-based search and messaging. Their findings indicate that there is merit in NLP/LLM based work for low resource languages so that users can speak comfortably in their local languages, thus indicating a basis for VUI.

We thus note that there is a variety in perspectives and a need for significant research required in VUI, both as an input as well as output modality and the noted contemporary research findings support the need for it.

3 Similar Work

We would like to discuss two themes here. In the first theme, the focus is on implications of combining the Visual channel (GUI) along with the audio channel (VUI). In the second theme, the focus is on studying the implications of situating smart devices in the context of EU.

3.1 GUI2VUI and GUI + VUI

Machines use varied I/O mechanisms to interact with the users. Since the technology for visual display unit and tangible input devices developed earlier, the Output mechanism has been primarily Graphical leading to development of theories and tools for GUI. Similarly, input has been primarily via Keyboards either as tangible or virtual keyboards (VKB). Primarily, there are two contemporary contributions. (1) GUI2VUI where the current principles and guidelines of GUI are being adapted to voice as a medium for WEIRD users [46, 48–50]. Similarly, [24] identified the need for and synthesized 11 usability heuristics for VUI. (2) GUI + VUI where the investigation is in complementing VUI with GUI to overcome the challenges posed by voice as medium [73]. We note complementary observations in two studies involving India-based WEIRD and EU users, namely by [16] about use of voice based conversational AI in banking by India-based WEIRD-like users and by [56] comparing GUI and VUI for task completion by EU; [56] noted that GUI-VUI based tasks were performed faster than VUI based tasks and within VUI hierarchical navigation was faster while [16] noted that WEIRD-like users found VUI as intuitive, attractive and usable. We hence would like to consider if these studies can be replicated for EU.

3.2 A "Smart Device" Hole-In-The-Wall

Motivated by an early work of installation of a computer in a socio-spatial context of EU called the "Hole in the Wall" experiment [15, 43, 44, 58] conducted an experiment by setting up two devices to be freely used by EU in their contexts. One of the devices was powered by Google software and the other was powered by Human assistance [78].

They compared a human (understanding) powered speech system with a data driven AI powered one (Google) on the dimensions of efficacy, use and adoption so that the findings could be used to improvise AI systems. The researchers highlighted that when basic speech recognition accuracy was low, the system responded with an "I don't know" answer. They also shared that as the users got to know their systems, they adjusted their questions accordingly. This corresponds to the findings by [51] of users deploying tactics to negotiate the technology state-of-art and the need for it [66]. Further, as the users' spoken language has evolved in a space which houses people from different regions of India, it has words from those languages (code switch). Hence, one would need a robust multi-lingual, code-switch speech engine to factor these real-world aspects. We feel one research question which arises could be theories of self-repairing VUI4EU based on the work of [69]. A key factor highlighted is the implication of a canned answer of "don't know" as a response because of speech recognition errors even though it might potentially have the desired answer in its information base or language model. Hence, they propose investigating directed-dialogue with the system surfacing the 'actual output of the speech recognition' to the user. What is currently not known is the format of communication to be adopted for EU. Similarly [63] observing the poor performance of the smart speaker shared that future work should focus on request/response design as compared to a conversation. Another study by [5] highlighted that for oral cultures, there are fundamental differences in which users perceive and operate artefacts while contemporary designs are influenced by 'writing (WEIRD) cultures' and hence we need newer ways of situating VUI in local ways of saying and doing.

4 Discussion and Suggestions

We would like to highlight a few observations on certain themes which are under consideration by the HCI/Design community. These can serve as beacons to help researchers to explore topics and areas of contribution.

4.1 Theme: Conversational User Interface

While the work by [22] is predominantly in the context of WEIRD, it highlights important issues which are unanswered, such as, (a) what is the impact of CUI/IUI on user behaviour and perceptions, (b) what are the issues of ethics and privacy, (c) what is the role of personalization, and (d) which design guidelines can be used for creation of the interfaces and designing the interactions. Some of the topics explored by [62] were collaboration and cooperation, access to and access through CUI and supporting health and well-being.

One of the areas under active investigation is to evolve heuristics [53] for VUI design from existing GUI design principles [49]. Then there are other aspects such as (i) confounding the near-human voice-quality with the capability to meet user expectation about task closure, (ii) impact of accessibility on use of interface, (iii) learnability of the VUI involving what can be said, error recovery processes or recallability of various commands, and importantly (iv) absence of standards or heuristics for evaluation of a VUI. Apart from highlighting the mapping between GUI heuristics and the challenges faced by user, the authors also highlight two new categories, namely, (a) security and privacy, and (b) social interactions. One interesting area of research could be exploring these two categories. For instance, does use of throat microphone lower risk associated with publicly voicing the passwords. The throat microphones intervention seem closer to what EU created interventions might look, as indicated by [34]. As highlighted by [8] users' tradeoff on the utility-privacy spectrum in the use of technology in favour of Privacy as is expected in Individualistic cultures. In the EU cultural context of communitarian/collectivism, Privacy, which has its amalgamated legal origin in the US, is interpreted differently [4]. And if viewed from a value-driven lens, could have different ramifications since EU are value-conscious users. Hence, it would be interesting to investigate this perspective in the EU context. Again, it would be interesting to verify this hypothesis in the EU context. In terms of conversations, Grice's maxims [27] have been explored in the design of VUI by [52], we propose that they could be analysed for the contextual applicability for EU. For example, the User-Usage model of [17] highlights different sub-archetypes within the EU archetype; an interesting research question would be "what would be the least number of contextualised voice-archetypes needed while interacting these sub-archetypes instead of a single voice persona". Would a famous personality voice persona have higher efficacy as compared to a family member's voice? Would the user become a reflective person if the VUI mimicked the user's person? Could social hierarchy be reflected via the use of family member's voice persona?

4.2 Theme: Technology Negotiation and Patterns

Often, technology progress is on a continuous trajectory while it is still in use. In such cases users try to negotiate their way with the existing technology and achieve their goals [7, 18, 51, 66]. Such obstacle categories to be negotiated were noted by [51] as Unfamiliar Intent, Speech recognition and NLP Error, Failed Feedback and System Error. The 10 tactics employed were Hyperarticulation, Simplification, New Utterance, User More Info, If Available Rely on GUI, Settling, Restarting, Frustration Attempts, Quitting and Recall. Such Patterns of tactics need to be created for VUI for EU (VUI4EU) and documented with their corresponding solutions, not unlike [2, 25]. While cataloguing patterns is important, it would also be worthwhile to investigate the use of Conversation Analysis [21, 23] method for EU. Thus, from a research and deployment perspective, it would be important to have a catalogue of patterns which articulate the design challenge, design interventions and a mechanism to analyse the challenges and interventions. While human-human communication uses Explanation as tool to arrive at a "shared understanding", it may not be so between users and VUI. In this context [59] found that users never took steps to resolve their misunderstanding with VUI so that they could be avoided in the future. They were more forgiving and accepting of the VUI behaviour. When WEIRD users engage with a VUI, they have a shared common ground in terms of language skills such as correctness, articulation, tonality et cetera. This can be viewed as a plausible social power construct, wherein the WEIRD users 'forgives' VUI for its errors. However, in case of EU, if the VUI has a large language model and if it speaks with authority, would the EU be able to discern that the VUI is incorrect. Would the user be able to negotiate the task closure on an equal footing with the VUI. These are interesting research questions which can be investigated.

When [65] investigated the role of users' English in using a VUI with Google Home smart speaker, they found that English language proficiency has a profound influence on ease of learning and usability while using the VUI and hence recommend that these factors be addressed. In a vast country like India which has a traditional oral culture and where languages and their dialects change every few kilometres, one could investigate if an optimal or least-effort mechanism can be designed to overcome these challenges of English proficiency and subsequently for local language dialects with VUI.

5 Summary

The foreseeable future as per Industry reports and ground observations, (i) proliferation of smart devices and smart apps within India, (ii) the deployment of increasingly powerful AI/ML models, and (iii) better-faster-cheaper telecom/data infrastructure is predicted. Hence, the question of interest is "will this scenario lead to large-scale adoption of these devices", "will the devices become an integral part of the user's lives"? Historically, the adoption of any product is dependent on the design of the product as well as the user of the product. The domains of HCI and Design which deal with these aspects have been biased towards WEIRD users. As a result, much of the body of work, till date, has been about such users. It is only of late that EU' have become central to the discourse within the community. There is an increased awareness and criticism that the knowledge bases generated for WEIRD users and their contexts cannot be transplanted for the contexts of EU.

Ergo, a lot of methods, techniques, tools, datasets, user models, evaluation models, guidelines and artefacts need to be created when it comes to VUI for EU as they are simply not present. These artefacts would be of immense help to the design community in creating VUI's which would not only be useful but also usable for EU. Today, in the absence of such artefacts, the designers are forced to repurpose the GUI skills developed for WEIRD users for EU, this mismatch could potentially compound the challenges for EU. While there are case studies and research available for GUI and IVR based systems for EU, the same cannot be said for VUI for smart devices. Some studies over a period have clearly indicated that the users prefer and are happy when the modality of interaction is Voice. Hence, it is critical that the community develops such artefacts at the earliest else poorly designed experiences and products would potentially raise the barrier to adoption.

References

1. Agarwal, S.K., et al.: The spoken web: a web for the underprivileged. ACM SIGWEB Newslett. **2010**(Summer), 1–9 (2010). https://doi.org/10.1145/1796390.1796391
2. Alexander, C.: The Timeless Way of Building. Oxford University Press, New York (1979)
3. Balkrishan, D., et al.: Making and breaking the user-usage model: whatsapp adoption amongst emergent users in India. In: Proceedings of the 8th Indian Conference on Human Computer Interaction, pp. 52–63 Association for Computing Machinery, New York, NY, USA (2016). https://doi.org/10.1145/3014362.3014367
4. Basu, S.: Privacy protection: a tale of two cultures * Masaryk University. J. Law Technol. **6**, 1–34 (2012)

5. Bidwell, N.J., Siya, M.J.: Situating Asynchronous Voice in Rural Africa. In: Kotzé, P., Marsden, G., Lindgaard, G., Wesson, J., Winckler, M. (eds.) INTERACT 2013. LNCS, vol. 8119, pp. 36–53. Springer, Heidelberg (2013). https://doi.org/10.1007/978-3-642-40477-1_3
6. Bødker, S.: When second wave HCI meets third wave challenges. In: Proceedings of the 4th Nordic Conference on Human-Computer Interaction: Changing Roles, pp. 1–8 ACM, Oslo Norway (2006). https://doi.org/10.1145/1182475.1182476
7. Budiu, R., Laubheimer, P.: Intelligent assistants have poor usability: a user study of Alexa, Google Assistant, and Siri. Nielsen Norman Group (2018)
8. Burbach, L., et al.: "Hey, Siri", "Ok, Google", "Alexa". Acceptance-relevant factors of virtual voice-assistants. In: 2019 IEEE International Professional Communication Conference (ProComm), pp. 101–111 (2019). https://doi.org/10.1109/ProComm.2019.00025
9. Chetty, M., Grinter, R.E.: HCI4D: HCI challenges in the global south. In: CHI '07 Extended Abstracts on Human Factors in Computing Systems, pp. 2327–2332 Association for Computing Machinery, New York, NY, USA (2007). https://doi.org/10.1145/1240866.1241002
10. Clark, H.H.: Context and common ground. In: Encyclopedia of Language & Linguistics, pp. 105–108 Elsevier (2006). https://doi.org/10.1016/B0-08-044854-2/01088-9
11. Coney, L.: Why you being WEIRD to me? Reflections of a black researcher on WEIRD-ness in HCI. XRDS. **28**(4), 12–17 (2022). https://doi.org/10.1145/3538541
12. Corbett, E., Weber, A.: What can I say? Addressing user experience challenges of a mobile voice user interface for accessibility. In: Proceedings of the 18th International Conference on Human-Computer Interaction with Mobile Devices and Services, pp. 72–82 (2016)
13. Cuendet, S., et al.: VideoKheti: making video content accessible to low-literate and novice users. In: Proceedings of the SIGCHI Conference on Human Factors in Computing Systems, pp. 2833–2842 Association for Computing Machinery, New York, NY, USA (2013). https://doi.org/10.1145/2470654.2481392
14. Dados, N., Connell, R.: The global south. Contexts **11**(1), 12–13 (2012). https://doi.org/10.1177/1536504212436479
15. Dangwal, R., et al.: A model of how children acquire computing skills from hole-in-the-wall computers in public places. Inf. Technol. Int. Dev. **2**(4), 41–60 (2005). https://doi.org/10.1162/154475205775249319
16. Deka, C., et al.: Assessing a Voice-Based Conversational AI prototype for Banking Application (2021).https://doi.org/10.1109/NICS54270.2021.9701536
17. Devanuj, J.A.: Technology adoption by "emergent" users: the user-usage model. In: Proceedings of the 11th Asia Pacific Conference on Computer Human Interaction, pp. 28–38 Association for Computing Machinery, New York, NY, USA (2013). https://doi.org/10.1145/2525194.2525209
18. Devillers, L., et al.: Spoken Language Interaction with Virtual Agents and Robots (SLIVAR): Towards Effective and Ethical Interaction
19. Dhaygude, M., Chakraborty, D.: Rethinking design of digital platforms for emergent users: findings from a study with rural Indian farmers. In: IndiaHCI'20: Proceedings of the 11th Indian Conference on Human-Computer Interaction, pp. 62–69 (2020)
20. Donner, J., et al.: Stages of design in technology for global development. Computer **41**, 34–41 (2008). https://doi.org/10.1109/MC.2008.203
21. Dourish, P.: Embodied Interaction: Exploring the Foundations of a New Approach to HCI
22. Doyle, P.R., et al.: CUI@IUI: theoretical and methodological challenges in intelligent conversational user interface interactions. In: 26th International Conference on Intelligent User Interfaces – Companion, pp. 12–14 Association for Computing Machinery, New York, NY, USA (2021). https://doi.org/10.1145/3397482.3450706

23. Frohlich, D., Luff, P.: Applying the technology of conversation to the technology for conversation. In: Luff, P. et al. (eds.) Computers and Conversation, pp. 187–220 Academic Press, London (1990). https://doi.org/10.1016/B978-0-08-050264-9.50014-2
24. Fulfagar, L., Gupta, A., Mathur, A., Shrivastava, A.: Development and Evaluation of Usability Heuristics for Voice User Interfaces. In: Chakrabarti, A., Poovaiah, R., Bokil, P., Kant, V. (eds.) ICoRD 2021. SIST, vol. 221, pp. 375–385. Springer, Singapore (2021). https://doi.org/10.1007/978-981-16-0041-8_32
25. Gamma, E., et al.: Design patterns: elements of reusable object-oriented software. Addison-Wesley, Reading, Mass (1995)
26. Garg, R., et al.: The last decade of HCI research on children and voice-based conversational agents. In: Proceedings of the 2022 CHI Conference on Human Factors in Computing Systems, pp. 1–19 Association for Computing Machinery, New York, NY, USA (2022). https://doi.org/10.1145/3491102.3502016
27. Grice, H.P.: Logic and conversation (1975)
28. Gupta, M., et al.: Sophistication with limitation: understanding smartphone usage by emergent users in India. In: ACM SIGCAS/SIGCHI Conference on Computing and Sustainable Societies (COMPASS), pp. 386–400 Association for Computing Machinery, New York, NY, USA (2022). https://doi.org/10.1145/3530190.3534824
29. Henrich, J., et al.: Most people are not WEIRD. Nature **466**(7302), 29 (2010)
30. Ho, M.R.: Human-computer interaction for development: the past, present, and future. Inf. Technol. Int. Dev. **5**, 4 (2009)
31. Indian Cellular and Electronics Association: Contribution of Smartphones to Digital Governance in India, a study by India Cellular & Electronics Association July 2020. https://icea.org.in/blog/wp-content/uploads/2022/06/ICEA-Digital-Governance-in-India-Report-2020.pdf
32. Internet and Mobile Association of India: Internet in India (2022). https://www.iamai.in/sites/default/files/research/Internet%20in%20India%202022_Print%20version.pdf
33. Jain, P., et al.: From the margins to the centre: defining new mission and vision for HCI research in South Asia. In: Extended Abstracts of the 2021 CHI Conference on Human Factors in Computing Systems, pp. 1–6 ACM, Yokohama Japan (2021). https://doi.org/10.1145/3411763.3441327
34. Jones, M., et al.: Beyond "yesterday's tomorrow": future-focused mobile interaction design by and for emergent users. Personal Ubiquitous Comput. **21**(1), 157–171 (2017). https://doi.org/10.1007/s00779-016-0982-0
35. Kant, V., Joshi, A.: Challenges in Supporting the Emergent User. In: Proceedings of the 9th Indian Conference on Human Computer Interaction, pp. 67–70 Association for Computing Machinery, New York, NY, USA (2018). https://doi.org/10.1145/3297121.3297131
36. Linxen, S., et al.: How WEIRD is CHI? In: Proceedings of the 2021 CHI Conference on Human Factors in Computing Systems, pp. 1–14 Association for Computing Machinery, New York, NY, USA (2021). https://doi.org/10.1145/3411764.3445488
37. Lobo, S., et al.: GappaGoshti™: a social networking platform for information dissemination in the rural world. In: Proceedings of the 6th Nordic Conference on Human-Computer Interaction: Extending Boundaries, pp. 727–730 Association for Computing Machinery, New York, NY, USA (2010). https://doi.org/10.1145/1868914.1869015
38. McKinsey: Mckinsey Global Institute Report on Digital India Technology to transform a connected nation March 2019. https://www.mckinsey.com/~/media/mckinsey/business%20functions/mckinsey%20digital/our%20insights/digital%20india%20technology%20to%20transform%20a%20connected%20nation/mgi-digital-india-exec-summary-april-2019.pdf
39. Medhi, I., et al.: A comparison of mobile money-transfer UIs for non-literate and semi-literate users. In: Proceedings of the SIGCHI Conference on Human Factors in Computing Systems, pp. 1741–1750 Association for Computing Machinery, New York, NY, USA (2009). https://doi.org/10.1145/1518701.1518970

40. Medhi, I., et al.: Designing mobile interfaces for novice and low-literacy users. ACM Trans. Comput.-Hum. Interact. **18**(1), 1–28 (2011). https://doi.org/10.1145/1959022.1959024
41. Medhi, I., et al.: Optimal audio-visual representations for illiterate users of computers. In: Presented at the 16th International World Wide Web Conference, WWW2007 May 8 (2007). https://doi.org/10.1145/1242572.1242690
42. MEITY, G.O.I.: India's trillion dollar digital opportunity. https://www.meity.gov.in/writeread data/files/india_trillion-dollar_digital_opportunity.pdf
43. Mitra, S.: The hole in the wall: self organising systems in education. (2006)
44. Mitra, S., Dangwal, R.: Limits to self-organising systems of learning-the Kalikuppam experiment: Self-organising systems of learning. Br. J. Edu. Technol. **41**(5), 672–688 (2010). https://doi.org/10.1111/j.1467-8535.2010.01077.x
45. Mudliar, P., et al.: Emergent practices around CGNet Swara, voice forum for citizen journalism in rural India. In: Proceedings of the Fifth International Conference on Information and Communication Technologies and Development, pp. 159–168 Association for Computing Machinery, New York, NY, USA (2012). https://doi.org/10.1145/2160673.2160695
46. Munteanu, C., et al.: Conversational voice user interfaces: connecting engineering fundamentals to design considerations. In: Extended Abstracts of the 2021 CHI Conference on Human Factors in Computing Systems, pp. 1–3 Association for Computing Machinery, New York, NY, USA (2021). https://doi.org/10.1145/3411763.3445008
47. Munteanu, C., et al.: Speech-based interaction. Course, ACM SIGCHI. 2012, 2013, 2014 (2011)
48. Murad, C., et al.: Finding a new voice: transitioning designers from GUI to VUI design. In: Proceedings of the 3rd Conference on Conversational User Interfaces, pp. 1–12 Association for Computing Machinery, New York, NY, USA (2021). https://doi.org/10.1145/3469595.3469617
49. Murad, C., et al.: Revolution or evolution? Speech interaction and HCI design guidelines. IEEE Pervasive Comput. **18**(2), 33–45 (2019). https://doi.org/10.1109/MPRV.2019.2906991
50. Murad, C., et al.: Voice-first interfaces in a GUI-first design world: barriers and opportunities to supporting VUI designers on-the-job. In: Proceedings of the 4th Conference on Conversational User Interfaces, pp. 1–10 Association for Computing Machinery, New York, NY, USA (2022). https://doi.org/10.1145/3543829.3543842
51. Myers, C., et al.: Patterns for how users overcome obstacles in voice user interfaces. In: Proceedings of the 2018 CHI Conference on Human Factors in Computing Systems, pp. 1–7 (2018)
52. Nass, C., Brave, S.: Wired for Speech: How Voice Activates and Advances the Human-Computer Relationship. The MIT Press, Cambridge (2005)
53. Nielsen, J., Molich, R.: Heuristic evaluation of user interfaces. In: Proceedings of the SIGCHI Conference on Human Factors in Computing Systems Empowering People - CHI '90, pp. 249–256 ACM Press, Seattle, Washington, United States (1990). https://doi.org/10.1145/97243.97281
54. Nokia MBit2022 Report, Mb. 2022: India Mobile Broadband Index 2022 by Nokia. https://www.nokia.com/sites/default/files/2022-03/nokia-mbit-2022.pdf
55. Oreglia, E. et al.: Designing for emerging rural users: experiences from China. In: Proceedings of the SIGCHI Conference on Human Factors in Computing Systems, pp. 1433–1436 Association for Computing Machinery, New York, NY, USA (2011). https://doi.org/10.1145/1978942.1979152
56. Padhi, D.R., et al.: Hierarchy or List? Comparing menu navigation by emergent users. In: Proceedings of the 9th Indian Conference on Human-Computer Interaction, pp. 29–34 Association for Computing Machinery, New York, NY, USA (2018). https://doi.org/10.1145/3297121.3297125

57. Patel, N., et al.: Avaaj Otalo: a field study of an interactive voice forum for small farmers in rural India. In: Proceedings of the SIGCHI Conference on Human Factors in Computing Systems, pp. 733–742 Association for Computing Machinery, New York, NY, USA (2010). https://doi.org/10.1145/1753326.1753434
58. Pearson, J., et al.: StreetWise: smart speakers vs human help in public slum settings. In: Proceedings of the 2019 CHI Conference on Human Factors in Computing Systems, pp. 1–13 Association for Computing Machinery, New York, NY, USA (2019). https://doi.org/10.1145/3290605.3300326
59. Pins, D., Alizadeh, F.: Without Being Asked: Identifying Use-Cases for Explanations in Interaction with Voice Assistants
60. Plauché, M., Nallasamy, U.: Speech interfaces for equitable access to information technology. Inf. Technol. Int. Dev. **4**(1), 69–86 (2007). https://doi.org/10.1162/itid.2007.4.1.69
61. Plauché, M., Prabaker, M.: Tamil market: a spoken dialog system for rural India. In: CHI '06 Extended Abstracts on Human Factors in Computing Systems, pp. 1619–1624 Association for Computing Machinery, New York, NY, USA (2006). https://doi.org/10.1145/1125451.1125746
62. Porcheron, M., et al.: CUI@CSCW: collaborating through conversational user interfaces. In: Conference Companion Publication of the 2020 on Computer Supported Cooperative Work and Social Computing, pp. 483–492 Association for Computing Machinery, New York, NY, USA (2020). https://doi.org/10.1145/3406865.3418587
63. Porcheron, M., et al.: Voice interfaces in everyday life. In: proceedings of the 2018 CHI Conference on Human Factors in Computing Systems, pp. 1–12 (2018)
64. Prahalad, C.K., Hammond, A.: Serving the world's poor, profitably. Harv. Bus. Rev. **80**(9), 48–59 (2002)
65. Pyae, A., Scifleet, P.: Investigating the role of user's English language proficiency in using a voice user interface: a case of Google Home smart speaker. In: Extended Abstracts of the 2019 CHI Conference on Human Factors in Computing Systems, pp. 1–6 (2019)
66. Rao, P.V.S., Kopparapu, S.K.: Friendly Interfaces Between Humans and Machines. Springer, Singapore (2018). https://doi.org/10.1007/978-981-13-1750-7
67. Robinson, S., et al.: Revisiting "Hole in the Wall" computing: private smart speakers and public slum settings. In: Proceedings of the 2018 CHI Conference on Human Factors in Computing Systems, pp. 1–11 Association for Computing Machinery, New York, NY, USA (2018). https://doi.org/10.1145/3173574.3174072
68. Rüller, S. et al.: Messy Fieldwork: a natural necessity or a result of western origins and perspectives? In: Companion Publication of the 2020 ACM Designing Interactive Systems Conference, pp. 185–190 Association for Computing Machinery, New York, NY, USA (2020). https://doi.org/10.1145/3393914.3395864
69. Schegloff, E.A., et al.: The preference for self-correction in the organization of repair in conversation. Language **53**(2), 361–382 (1977). https://doi.org/10.2307/413107
70. Sherwani, J.: Speech interfaces for information access by low literate users. Carnegie Mellon University (2009)
71. Shneiderman, B., et al.: Grand challenges for HCI researchers. Interactions **23**(5), 24–25 (2016). https://doi.org/10.1145/2977645
72. Shrivastava, A.: Spoken dialog system: gaining insights into developing a model from a game of cards. In: Proceedings of the 3rd International Conference on Human Computer Interaction, pp. 111–114 Association for Computing Machinery, New York, NY, USA (2011). https://doi.org/10.1145/2407796.2543128
73. Shrivastava, A., Joshi, A.: Directedness and persistence in audio-visual interface for emergent users. In: Proceedings of the 10th Indian Conference on Human-Computer Interaction, pp. 1–12 Association for Computing Machinery, New York, NY, USA (2019). https://doi.org/10.1145/3364183.3364191

74. Shrivastava, A., Joshi, A.: Effects of visuals, menu depths, and menu positions on IVR usage by non-tech savvy users. In: Proceedings of the 6th Indian Conference on Human-Computer Interaction, pp. 35–44 Association for Computing Machinery, New York, NY, USA (2014). https://doi.org/10.1145/2676702.2676707
75. Stephanidis, C., et al.: Seven HCI grand challenges. Int. J. Hum.-Comput. Interact. **35**(14), 1229–1269 (2019). https://doi.org/10.1080/10447318.2019.1619259
76. Sturm, C., et al.: How WEIRD is HCI? Extending HCI principles to other countries and cultures. In: Proceedings of the 33rd Annual ACM Conference Extended Abstracts on Human Factors in Computing Systems, pp. 2425–2428 Association for Computing Machinery, New York, NY, USA (2015). https://doi.org/10.1145/2702613.2702656
77. Summers, K., Alton, N., Haraseyko, A., Sherard, R.: Bridging the Digital Divide: One Smartphone at a Time. In: Marcus, A., Wang, W. (eds.) DUXU 2018. LNCS, vol. 10919, pp. 653–672. Springer, Cham (2018). https://doi.org/10.1007/978-3-319-91803-7_49
78. Uliza: Uliza: Local language services. https://www.uliza.org. Accessed 22 Jul 2023
79. Zamora, J.: Rise of the Chatbots: finding a place for artificial intelligence in India and US. In: Proceedings of the 22nd International Conference on Intelligent User Interfaces Companion, pp. 109–112 Association for Computing Machinery, New York, NY, USA (2017). https://doi.org/10.1145/3030024.3040201
80. Humane Ai Pin. https://hu.ma.ne. Accessed 20 Dec 2023

Assessing Perceptions and Experiences of an AI-Driven Speech Assistant for Nursing Documentation: A Qualitative Study in German Nursing Homes

Drin Ferizaj(✉) and Susann Neumann

Department of Geriatrics and Medical Gerontology, Charité – Universitätsmedizin Berlin, corporate member of Freie Universität Berlin and Humboldt-Universität Zu Berlin, Reinickendorfer Straße 61, 13347 Berlin, Germany
{drin.ferizaj,susann.neumann}@charite.de

Abstract. In addressing the critical need for efficient nursing documentation amidst rising workloads and skilled worker shortage, this study investigates the adoption of AI-based speech assistants within German nursing homes. The necessity for innovative support solutions like digitization through speech technology is underscored by current, time-consuming documentation processes prone to errors. Highlighting the urgency for innovative digital solutions, our qualitative research delves into caregivers' perceptions, usage experiences, and factors influencing acceptance of an AI-based speech assistant. Findings indicate substantial work facilitation and improvements in daily tasks, including immediate information access, elimination of unnecessary movement, reduced process interruptions, and timely, mobile documentation, which collectively lead to significant time savings and notable reduction in caregiver workload. Furthermore, the integration of speech assistants fosters transparency and interactivity in resident care. Despite these benefits, key barriers such as technical challenges, the need for accuracy with dialects and accents, and data privacy concerns highlight the complexity of widespread adoption. Addressing these issues through enhanced technical support, training, and infrastructure improvements is crucial for leveraging the full potential of speech recognition technology in nursing documentation. This study contributes to the discourse on digital healthcare solutions, emphasizing the importance of a comprehensive approach to overcome technical and acceptance barriers. Further investigation into the broader impacts on care recipients and documentation quality is necessary to fully understand and optimize the use of AI-based speech assistants in nursing practice.

Keywords: Speech Assistant · Artificial Intelligence · Nursing Documentation · User Acceptance · Healthcare Technology Adoption

M. Kurosu and A. Hashizume (Eds.): HCII 2024, LNCS 14688, pp. 17–34, 2024.
https://doi.org/10.1007/978-3-031-60449-2_2

1 Introduction

To ensure needs-based and safe care, precise and understandable nursing documentation is crucial. Nurses are responsible and accountable for creating and planning this documentation, significantly contributing to targeted communication in healthcare. Essential requirements include sufficient time and effective tools for documentation [1].

Currently, nurses spend a considerable portion of their working hours on documentation, with international estimates between 25% and 35% [2–5].

Nurses also report challenges and workloads such as time and staff shortages, high bureaucratic documentation efforts, insufficient knowledge of documentation standards, and limited time for patient care [6–8].

Moreover, studies indicate that documentation deficiencies are common in both paper-based and electronic health record (EHR) systems, including incomplete, missing, or non-compliant entries, posing significant risks to patient safety [2, 9, 10].

Speech recognition (SR) technology offers a potential solution to overcome challenges and barriers in the documentation process by transcribing spoken words into an electronic patient record or word processing program in real time [11]. This facilitates a more seamless and efficient documentation process, presenting several advantages over traditional methods such as dictation or self-typing. A primary benefit of SR technology is its time efficiency, significantly reducing documentation tasks and streamlining the process [12].

However, findings remain mixed regarding whether SR technology is superior to text entry. Technical issues, such as high error rates in speech recognition, have led to decreased acceptance and negatively affected the use of SR technologies [12, 13]. For nursing documentation, both the benefits and acceptance issues identified by nurses highlight various barriers to usage [12, 14]. Thus, there is a need for research on the integration of SR into existing infrastructures, its deployment and effects in different nursing settings [12], or the enhancement of SR performance and usability [15].

In the context of healthcare technology adoption, the Unified Theory of Acceptance and Use of Technology (UTAUT-2) [16] provides a comprehensive framework by incorporating key constructs such as perceived usefulness, ease of use, social influence, and facilitating conditions [17]. Perceived usefulness evaluates the anticipated benefits of technology use, while ease of use focuses on the user's expected effort. Social influence reflects the impact of others' opinions on the individual's decision to use the technology. Facilitating conditions refer to the organizational and technical support available to the user.

In German nursing homes, the adoption of AI applications has been limited, partly due to insufficient digital infrastructure, which is not yet universally available across all care sectors. Additionally, the lack of stable networks, adequate devices, or necessary interfaces for data exchange poses significant challenges [18].

Therefore, the aim of this study is to analyze the perceptions and experiences of caregivers in nursing homes where an AI-based speech assistant for nursing documentation has been implemented. The study focused on a) analyzing the functional, ethical, usability and security aspects of the speech assistant and b) contextualizing the findings within the Unified Theory of Acceptance and Use of Technology (UTAUT-2), with conceptual adjustments and expansions of the model to derive insights into the acceptance of speech assistants in nursing practice.

2 Methods

2.1 Study Design and Data Collection

The study was conducted as part of the "PYSA - Nursing Documentation with Hybrid Speech Assistant" project, funded by the German Federal Ministry of Education and Research. The research design adopted an exploratory, descriptive, and interpretative approach, utilizing content and thematic qualitative analysis. Semi-structured interviews and non-participating observations of caregivers were carried out between August and October 2022.

Before the interviews, non-participating observations were conducted in two nursing facilities to gain an initial impression of the research field and identify relevant aspects for the interview guide creation. Using a self-developed guide, observed aspects included commonly used functions, technical errors of the speech assistant, other barriers in the current documentation process, and the process of dictating various documentation entries. Observations lasted about 4 h, with researchers shadowing three individuals (two nursing professionals and one caregiver) during morning shifts, staying in the background to avoid disrupting interactions between caregivers and residents.

Participants for the interviews were recruited through a stakeholder of the project consortium, using purposive sampling to ensure a variety of user roles of the speech assistant, including at least one representative per user role and caregivers with varying years of professional experience.

The one-on-one interviews, conducted by the authors, lasted between 45 to 120 min, mostly online via MS Teams and for two participants in person. All interviews were recorded. The interview guide, developed in coordination with the project consortium, covered four thematic areas: caregivers' usage experiences, communication and interaction with the speech assistant, application scenarios, and the speech assistant's functionality and operation.

2.2 Setting and Participants

The interview participants comprised nursing and care personnel from three residential care facilities in Baden-Württemberg, Germany.

Eligibility criteria included being ≥ 18 years old, roles encompassing nurses, nursing assistants, social service caregivers, and nursing trainees, and the use of the "voize" speech assistant within their facility.

The study included 10 participants (mean age = 40.33 years; age range = 28–58 years; standard deviation = 9.93 years; gender distribution: 2 males, 8 females; roles: 3 nurses, 1 nursing assistant, 1 trainee, 1 caregiver, 2 nursing service managers, 2 residential area managers). Notably, two participants had prior experience with personal speech assistants, such as Google Assistant or Siri.

2.3 Speech Assistant Description

The utilized speech assistant “voize” is a software-based application that incorporates AI models to process voice inputs offline on a smartphone and automatically generate the correct structured documentation entries. These entries are confirmed by the nursing staff and integrated into the existing documentation system via an interface.

The underlying SR models are regularly trained with voluntarily submitted documentation data, enabling continuous improvement and customization to the linguistic characteristics and professional vocabulary of the nursing staff.

2.4 Data Analysis

The study’s authors transcribed all recordings in full using the F4 software, adhering to the simple transcription rules of Dressing and Prehl [19].

Data analysis was also conducted by the authors, initially through structured content analysis according to Mayring [20], complemented by thematic analysis to gain deeper insights into the caregivers’ experiences and attitudes.

Additionally, the thematic analysis was enhanced by employing the UTAUT-2 model as a conceptual framework. The process was iterative, allowing for the refinement and integration of both a priori and a posteriori categories and codes, enabling a thorough exploration of the data.

2.5 Ethical Considerations

Necessary approvals from nursing homes were obtained for observations and interviews. Before the study began, the nursing homes’ works councils were asked for permission by submitting the interview guide and observation protocol for co-determination. Subsequently, permission was granted by the management of each nursing home and the nursing staff working there.

During the observations, the study’s authors informed the residents about their role as observers.

Interview participants were provided with written information about the study and its purpose and were briefed accordingly. All participants gave their written consent before the interviews.

3 Results

The qualitative analysis yielded 91 codes, which were organized into 16 categories. These categories corresponded to seven themes, primarily derived from the UTAUT-2 framework. The main themes are Facilitating Conditions, Social Influence, Performance Expectancy, Effort Expectancy, Habit, Privacy Concerns and Use Behavior. An overview of the extracted themes and categories is shown in Fig. 1, with example quotes for each provided in the appendix.

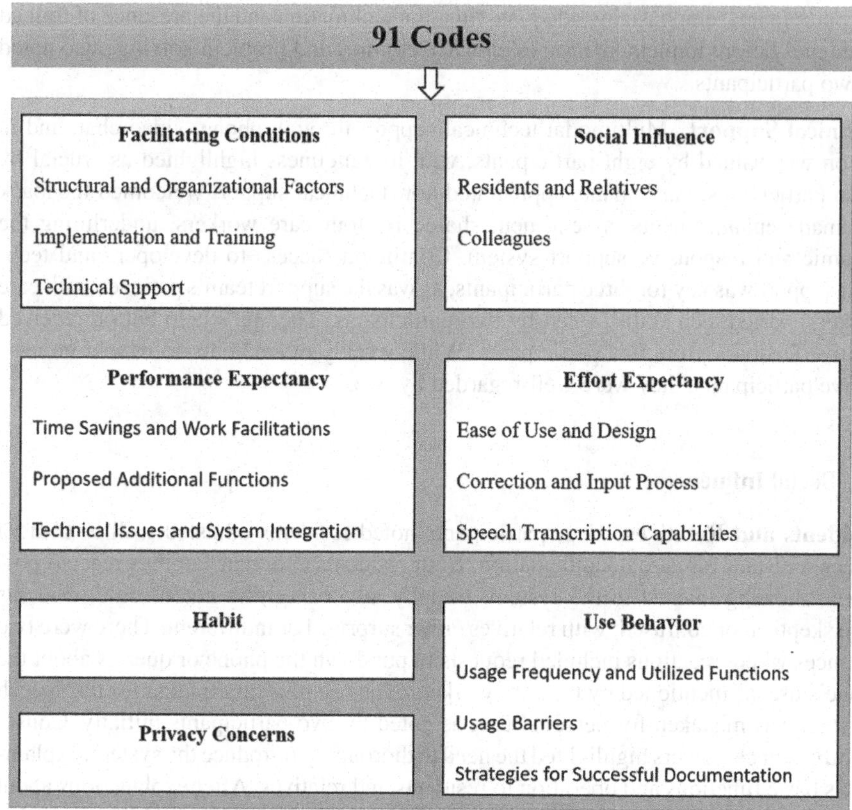

Fig. 1. Illustration of extracted Categories (regular font) and Themes (bold).

3.1 Facilitating Conditions

Structural and Organizational Factors. Participants favorably viewed Wi-Fi access in resident rooms for connectivity, with four noting Wi-Fi speed issues that led to delays. The offline functionality of speech assistants was emphasized. Several participants highlighted the adequate number of smartphones for staff documentation, with three finding this preferable to the limited PCs in the office. Furthermore, there was an interest in integrating the voice system with the ward's phone to minimize the necessity of carrying multiple devices.

Implementation and Training. The training, conducted in small groups and individually, was deemed beneficial by four participants, with a minimum duration of two days suggested by the same number of participants for grasping the speech assistant's functions. Videos and guides within the app were particularly valued by three participants. It was positively noted by three caregivers that during training, care workers' questions were answered and an environment of encouragement was fostered to freely ask additional questions. Extended or refresher training was recommended by two participants for those less tech-savvy. Team support, crucial for system familiarity, was highlighted by two participants, emphasizing adequate time for acclimation and the presence of trained colleagues before implementation to enhance comfort and problem-solving, also noted by two participants.

Technical Support. Multimodal technical support through phone, video chat, and in person was valued by eight participants, with its timeliness highlighted as crucial by seven participants. Participants appreciated how technical support welcomed feedback and made enhancements, a sentiment shared by four care workers, underlining the dynamic and responsive support system. Continuous access to developers and technical support was key for three participants, as was the support team's patience with care workers' varied tech skills, noted by two participants. The app's help button received positive feedback from two participants. While weekly office hours were seldom used by five participants, they were well-regarded by two.

3.2 Social Influence

Residents and Relatives. Four participants noted residents adjusted well to using a speech assistant for care documentation. Both residents and their families reacted positively, showing interest in the system. Initially, two caregivers noted some residents were skeptical or confused, with relatives either surprised or indifferent. There were two instances where reactions included requests to put down the phone or queries about the phone's use, as mentioned by the care workers. The use of a smartphone for the speech assistant was mistaken for personal use, as noted by two participants initially. Consequently, four caregivers highlighted the need to thoroughly introduce the system, explaining its basic functions and operation to residents and relatives. After explanations about the speech assistant's role in nursing, four participants reported that families responded positively, showing understanding and interest. The relationship between carer and resident varied, with three participants noting improvements from involving residents in the documentation process, while another three saw no change. Three participants suggested that for successful onboarding, it was important to allocate time for educating residents and relatives, using methods like posters/flyers, information evenings, and personal discussions. Four carers underscored the value of actively engaging residents in the documentation process.

Colleagues. Two interviewed care workers recommended that new team members be introduced to the speech assistant from the outset. They stressed the importance of addressing concerns and seeking further clarification from developers as needed. It was suggested by two participants that team leaders act as pioneers and points of contact for initial troubleshooting, while another two emphasized that the head of nursing should exemplify the technology's use. The importance of peer support and cooperation was underlined by two caregivers, with a call for collective assistance among colleagues. Additionally, two participants noted the risk of demotivation from inadequate guidance and social support.

3.3 Performance Expectancy

Time Savings and Work Facilitations. The theme of performance expectancy includes codes reflecting care workers' expectations that speech assistants would improve their job performance. Notably, time savings and workload reduction were highlighted as central benefits by seven participants each. Specifically, mobile documentation was praised for its ability to save time by allowing on-site recording of information, eliminating the need to return to a computer station, as noted by six participants. Another five care workers found that speech input improved report completion speed and efficiency, enhancing overall documentation processes. Flexibility in documenting from any location and at any time, particularly through offline functionality, was identified as a time-saving feature by four care workers, who appreciated the elimination of unnecessary trips for filing reports. This flexibility extended to documenting in various locations, as observed with caregivers documenting in hallways, residents' rooms, and other areas, supporting the convenience of mobile documentation.

Immediate access to resident information without needing to visit a computer station was valued by four participants, directly contributing to reduced movement and more efficient workflows. The speech assistant's ability to provide access to crucial patient information, including (wound) photographs, was especially helpful for managing residents with conditions like dementia.

Integration of speech assistants was seen to streamline documentation and administrative tasks, reducing reliance on paper records, as noted by three participants. Additionally, the speech assistant helped prevent the accumulation of undocumented care work at the end of the shift, as remarked by three participants. The use of the speech assistant and its photo function for wound documentation, highlighted for its accuracy and usability by four care workers, represented a significant improvement over traditional methods.

Another aspect tied to performance expectancy was work facilitation, where six care workers felt speech assistants enhanced transparency and integrated residents into the documentation process more effectively. The ability to document directly at the bedside, especially in critical situations like falls, was seen as invaluable, allowing for immediate and accurate record-keeping. This capability, along with digital note-taking, was recognized for reducing information loss and improving the reliability of care documentation, as emphasized by four participants.

Proposed Additional Functions and Improvements. Three care workers found the app's current functionalities adequate, yet others identified areas for enhancement, highlighting limitations in information accessibility. Key areas for improvement include easier sharing and editing of care plans and prescriptions, noted by five participants. Four participants suggested enabling prescription modifications directly within the app. Efficiency gains were targeted through proposals for standard text snippets and synonym use, as well as features for reclaiming accidentally dismissed tasks, each mentioned by two participants. Unique suggestions encompassed automated spelling and grammar checks, multi-language support with translation, integrated checklists with voice commands, alerts for improbable vital signs, customizable font sizes, direct print options, task reminders, and batch documentation capabilities for multiple residents. These suggestions, though varied and less frequently mentioned, point to a broader desire for a more comprehensive and efficient documentation tool.

Technical Issues and System Integration. Several benefits of using the speech assistant were acknowledged, but technical challenges that could affect performance were also identified. Five participants reported malfunctions in the system, while six care workers faced app hanging or freezing issues. Delays were specifically mentioned by two care workers when marking multiple items like medications simultaneously. Three mentioned log-in difficulties, and two experienced synchronization problems with the care management program. Additionally, three reported automatic categorization errors. Hardware constraints, such as the smaller screens of handheld devices compared to computers or tablets, were noted by four participants, leading to a preference for using larger station computers for tasks requiring extensive visibility, like shift delivery or entering detailed documentation. Nevertheless, the speech assistant proved beneficial during major system issues at one participant's site, allowing for offline documentation up to three days.

3.4 Effort Expectancy

Ease of Use and Design. The usability and design of the speech assistant emerged as a critical theme, with emphasis on ease of use and intuitive navigation. Three caregivers found the interface straightforward, labeling it as simple enough for beginners after a minimal learning phase. Clarity and organization were frequently praised, with five care workers appreciating the well-organized interface and the ease of accessing reports, patient names, and clinical details directly from the home screen or via search functionality. Issues related to an initially complex system with excessive options were noted but have been addressed through software updates, enhancing usability. The software's navigation was commended for its intuitive flow and logical menu structure by two participants.

Correction and Input Processes. The error correction functionality in speech assistants was generally regarded as low-effort and intuitive by eight participants. The primary correction methods include tapping words for deletion and re-speaking, or double-tapping for re-input, complemented by manual typing for minor adjustments or full re-entries by six care professionals. Despite overall positive feedback, resistance to speech recognition in favor of typing was noted among some users, particularly for those with language barriers who opt for subsequent manual corrections. Observational data confirmed the use of these correction strategies in practice.

Additionally, the utility of a dedicated button to prevent accidental audio recording was appreciated by four care workers, with its operation deemed acceptable. However, suggestions for improvement were made, including the potential replacement of the button with a wake-word system, which, despite its advantages, was also flagged for possibly causing confusion. The correction workflow was praised for its simplicity and intuitive design by two care workers.

Speech Transcription Capabilities. Five participants were pleased with the speech assistant's accuracy in capturing speech promptly, noting minimal need for corrections. Additionally, six care workers observed the system's improvement in recognizing individual speech patterns over time. Speech clarity and slow pacing enhanced transcription accuracy, as five care workers noted, with two also commending its ability to accurately capture whispered speech. Despite these positives, challenges were reported: four users encountered incorrect transcriptions necessitating time-consuming manual corrections, especially with lengthy inputs, specialized terminology, and names. Accents or dialects posed accuracy issues for five care workers, necessitating careful transcript review. Background noise handling was mixed, with three participants noting effective noise exclusion, while three others faced issues with unwanted background sound transcription. Delays in recording, mentioned by two care workers, also led to transcription errors.

3.5 Habit

Initially, six participants found speech-based documentation unfamiliar, requiring adjustment. However, seven reported it becoming ingrained in their routine with consistent use, with the adjustment period ranging from one week to six months, depending on technical proficiency. Effective adoption was facilitated by practices such as joint dictation exercises, exploring the app's capabilities, gradually increasing usage, and starting with simple tasks like vital sign dictation before progressing to complex ones. Employing varied documentation styles and terminology also supported habit development.

3.6 Privacy Concerns and Anxiety Linked to Speech Assistant Usage

Seven participants reported to be positive about technology and competent in its use, yet the introduction of the speech assistant raised several concerns. Four staff members feared surveillance, including unwarranted monitoring and data misuse, worrying about voice recordings being used to assess their work stress and interactions with residents, and timing of care tasks. Additionally, three staff members feared increased company control, while another three faced technical anxieties, leading to a temporary withdrawal from using the speech assistant. This issue was addressed through team meetings led by the facility manager, clarifying the speech assistant's role in easing documentation tasks rather than monitoring performance, which normalized its adoption and alleviated surveillance concerns. Efforts to clarify misperceptions and ensure data privacy were instrumental. Following initial staff education, four users felt more at ease with the technology, and most users felt unbothered by potential risks. This comfort was bolstered by discussions with workplace representatives, clear explanations of data flows, and assurances that data would not be shared inappropriately, further diminishing apprehensions.

Other reservations included misunderstandings by two care workers about the assistant's use and shyness among five participants when using the app, with four managing to overcome this by practicing in private. Two care professionals expressed concerns about incorrect voice input. Additionally, there were single instances of uncertainty regarding word choice, worries about being interrupted during documentation, beliefs about the overemphasis on technology in care, and fears of damaging the mobile device.

3.7 Use Behavior

Usage Frequency and Utilized Functions. Nine out of ten care workers and all participating observers reported regular use of the speech assistant, with only one mentioning minimal use. Additionally, nine expressed trust in the app, and an equal number would recommend it. Usage varied among caregivers, with three using it intensively for all documentation, three adopting it for specific tasks, and two utilizing certain functions only. Four nurse assistants highlighted the app's mobility advantage, eliminating the need for a computer for documentation.

The app was primarily used for documenting daily care activities such as hygiene, bowel movements, and dietary intake, each noted by six care workers. Other key functions included wound documentation with photos, nursing reports, marking completed tasks for shift delivery, checking medication lists, and taking notes. Despite its wide usage, complex shift deliveries still required PCs. One participant estimated the app's use between 15 and 23 times per shift, underscoring its integral role in daily nursing documentation.

Usage Barriers. Several factors impeded the speech assistant's consistent adoption. Notably, older colleagues and night shift workers found it challenging, as mentioned by three participants. These barriers were attributed to both usability and implementation, with a noted absence of leadership endorsement deterring some staff. Morning shifts, characterized by higher stress, presented particular obstacles to usage. Additionally, dissatisfaction with the time required for corrections further hindered adoption, whereas managerial presence enhanced commitment but was offset by the lack of guidance, diminishing motivation. Long dictations and early performance issues were minor but noted barriers. Individual reluctance also stemmed from perceptions of prolonged documentation or increased stress.

Proposed Strategies for Successful Speech-Based Documentation. Participants shared effective strategies for adopting speech-based documentation, emphasizing respectful communication that involves residents in the process. They stressed the importance of mentally organizing reports before dictation to minimize corrections. Privacy concerns led to avoiding dictation in front of residents, especially when entries might spark discussions or justify actions, noted by four participants. Documentation involving sensitive topics, like bladder or bowel function, was also conducted away from residents, as reported by four participants. Special consideration was given to residents with dementia, preferring private spaces for dictation to avoid making them feel discussed, a concern for two participants. The decision to dictate in a resident's presence was influenced by their mood and condition, with two participants noting that resident mood and privacy laws further influenced choosing locations without additional individuals or in single-occupancy rooms, also highlighted by two participants. Additionally, some chose to use the assistant post-care to ensure privacy and respect, a practice adopted by two participants.

4 Discussion

The integration of SR technologies in healthcare settings, particularly in nursing homes, signifies a notable shift towards digital healthcare solutions aimed at improving efficiency and care quality. Crucially, the UTAUT-2 model has played a key role in our study for organizing essential factors that shape SR adoption in these contexts. Our studies, along with further findings [17, 21], suggest a conceptual expansion to include "Privacy Concerns," particularly relevant in healthcare domains where data security is crucial. In the following, the key findings and their implications for the adoption of SR technologies in nursing environments will be explored.

The pronounced time savings and workload reduction reported by care workers, as highlighted by the utilization of speech assistants in care documentation, are in concordance with existing literature, underscoring the potential work-related benefits [13, 14, 22–24]. This alignment with prior research emphasizes a noteworthy reduction in the time dedicated to documentation tasks, underscoring that care documentation, typically a time-intensive aspect of caregivers' daily workload, can be substantially mitigated through technological solutions [12, 13, 22]. By enabling direct and mobile documentation, speech assistants not only positively influence care workers' time management but also enhance the immediacy of care reports while minimizing the risk of information loss [22].

Moreover, our findings on the flexibility offered by the speech assistant for care documentation in various settings - hallways, residents' rooms, and outdoors - highlight the potential of this technology to adapt healthcare practices to the dynamic nature of care environments. Adding to this, the temporal efficiency of speech recognition for care documentation is highlighted, with previous evidence already indicating that speaking documentation is significantly faster than typing [12, 13, 22].

Although this study highlights the time savings and workload reduction benefits of speech assistants, improvements in documentation quality and completeness were less pronounced, diverging from previous findings [23, 25]. While an improvement in quality of care documentation was not directly noted, speech assistants functions such as photographic wound documentation were vastly appreciated as useful for accurate documentation.

The technical challenges identified - app malfunctions, system integration issues, and hardware limitations - negatively impacted the rating and perception of the speech assistant. These barriers, which are consistent with previous studies [12, 14, 26], highlight the critical need for addressing and updating software issues as well as network infrastructure to unlock the full potential of speech assistants for care documentation.

Our studies' findings elucidate the multifaceted nature of facilitating conditions necessary for the successful implementation of speech recognition technology in healthcare settings. Several research articles have highlighted the importance of sufficient facilitating conditions to ensure seamless integration of innovative technologies in the medical field [12, 14, 24]. Especially training and consistent technical support mechanisms play a crucial role in facilitating the adoption of the speech assistant [12, 14]. The successful implementation of speech recognition technology in healthcare settings hinges on addressing both structural and human factors comprehensively. Key infrastructure elements like reliable Wi-Fi and access to necessary hardware form the backbone for deploying these digital tools effectively. In this context, it is necessary to provide ongoing multimodal technical support as well as training programmes to enable care workers to effectively work with SR technologies [27]. While the significance of training and technical support is well-established within the literature, this study uncovers a less discussed but equally vital aspect: the role of mutual support and internal experts within teams in fostering technology acceptance and continuous learning.

Additionally, we found that the ease of use and usability is central to the adoption of SR technology for care documentation. This aspect aligns with findings from existing literature [23, 26, 28]. However, several barriers of speech assistant integration into healthcare documentation were identified that are consistent with the literature. Apart from technical issues, the accuracy of the SR system, while substantially improved, still falls short with differing user accents, background noise, medical terminology, and names. This can lead to errors in documentation, which demand additional time for correction and could potentially compromise patient care [22, 27–29]. Furthermore, our study, alongside others [29], has identified initial barriers, including skepticism among residents and caregivers, as well as data privacy concerns, which have led to resistance among care workers. Therefore, in the critical initial phase of introducing and implementing speech-assistant technologies, it is paramount to proactively address and attentively listen to any concerns raised by the staff. Echoing Ronquillo and colleagues [30], it's crucial for nursing to take an active role in AI, particularly in understanding AI technologies and their involvement in AI's lifecycle, to mitigate such barriers effectively.

4.1 Practical Implications

- Ensure an adequate number of smartphones for staff documentation.
- Conduct training in small groups and individually, with a minimum duration of two days.
- Use videos and guides within the app for training.
- Foster an environment of encouragement and support during training.
- Provide extended or refresher training for less tech-savvy individuals.
- Offer continuous technical support through phone, video chat, and in-person assistance.
- Provide timely technical support and welcome feedback for enhancements.
- Educate residents and relatives about the speech assistant's functions and operation.
- Involve new team members in using the speech assistant from the outset.
- Actively engage residents in the documentation process.
- Allocate time for educating residents and relatives about the system.
- Emphasize time savings and workload reduction as central benefits of using the speech assistant.
- Design the speech assistant interface to be easy to use and with intuitive navigation.
- Provide correction and input processes that are low-effort and intuitive.
- Facilitate habit development through joint dictation exercises and gradual usage increase.
- Address privacy concerns and anxieties related to speech assistant usage.
- Promote regular use of the speech assistant and its recommended functions.

- Ongoing and proactive identification of barriers to consistent adoption of speech-based documentation.
- Implement effective strategies for successful speech-based documentation, including respectful communication and privacy considerations.

4.2 Limitations

Our study is constrained by a limited sample size, and observations confined to two nursing facilities may not capture the full spectrum of healthcare environments. Importantly, the rapid evolution of SR technology during the study period necessitates consideration, as it could affect the applicability of our findings over time.

We propose a refinement to the UTAUT-2 model, though this does not infer causal relationships. Additionally, while we omit a detailed cost analysis, this aspect warrants further exploration to elucidate the broader economic implications of SR technology in nursing settings [23]. Acknowledging varied user experiences, the call for longitudinal studies becomes apparent, underlining the need to track SR technology's long-term utility and integration within healthcare practices [23, 26]. Our findings align with trends of enthusiasm for SR potentially not translating into sustained adoption, indicating the importance of addressing both the benefits and challenges for consistent use [26].

5 Conclusion

Our study delves into the experiences and factors influencing the acceptance among caregivers of the AI-powered voice assistant 'voize' within German nursing homes, demonstrating the capacity of SR technology to streamline care documentation and alleviate administrative tasks. Key insights reveal that immediate access to information and mobile documentation integration via an AI-based speech assistant significantly improves nursing documentation and elevates care quality. Future advancements in SR technologies will be pivotal in encouraging acceptance, highlighting the continuous need for system enhancement. Ethical, privacy, social, and technical considerations, coupled with extensive training, are crucial for the technology's seamless adoption and broad acceptance. Utilizing SR to afford care professionals more time presents an opportunity to foster improved patient relationships. This study emphasizes the urgent need for further investigation into SR technology's influence in nursing contexts, focusing on enhancing SR performance for diverse dialects and accents and assessing its impact on patient care and documentation accuracy.

Acknowledgments. The Authors would like to thank all the caregivers of this study who dedicated us her precious time. We further like to thank Corina Burkhardt-Herdtle for their assistance in recruiting participants.

Disclosure of Interests. The authors have no competing interests to declare that are relevant to the content of this article.

Appendix. Example Quotes of Qualitative Main Themes and Their Categories.

Main Themes/Categories	Example Quotes
1. Facilitating conditions Structural and Organizational Factors Implementation and Training Technical Support	"…so far, there hasn't been any shortage, like if something was taken and I had to wait, I wanted to mention that right away, that we have enough cell phones and that's much better than the two or three PCs we have in the office, always waiting for others. That's obviously a big advantage,…there's always one or two left over, then you can access them." (P03) "We tried a few things together, then each person was allowed to try on their own… we continued our work as usual and every now and then… Someone would look over our shoulder and be right there for questions or if we didn't know something. They really took a lot of time for us and explained it well, I must say." (P7) "…as soon as I have a problem, I let them know and then it works wonderfully, that they simply fix the error… And they also get in touch with us relatively promptly, on the same day, usually within the same hour." (P9)
2. Social Influence Residents and Relatives Colleagues	"…it was initially an 'aha' moment for the family members. On one hand, now they're also walking around on duty with their personal cell phones. We then posted a flyer and also informed them again during the family evening that we are now also using cell phones, that it is not for our personal use, but rather our work phone, so to speak, where we simply do the documentation." "…we exchanged information with each other, which was included in the bi-weekly duty meetings, where the whole team, a large number of people, was present. If any questions had arisen by then, they were generally addressed there. Otherwise, everything was discussed or communicated on the day of the shift if there were any issues, and then efforts were made…" (P6)

(*continued*)

(*continued*)

Main Themes/Categories	Example Quotes
3. Performance Expectancy Time Savings and Work Facilitations Proposed Additional Functions and Improvement Technical Issues and System Integration	"So definitely a time-saving aspect, organizationally, there isn't as much information lost anymore, because you either record or note down a lot more right away… The flow of information isn't as significantly interrupted." (P1) "Not quite there yet, it's still a bit expandable. That is… With the categories for gymnastics, looking at them individually, and also the fact that, for example, I can make a collective entry." (P5) "…there should still be functions like font enlargement." (P07) "…sometimes there were also issues with the connection, where the report entries, stool entries, and such were not transferred to the computer. Then one still had to double-check to ensure that everything was entered correctly." (P8)
4. Effort Expectancy Ease of Use and Design Correction and Input Processes Speech Transcription Capabilities	"…when you log into the screen, the reports come first, and there's the resident's name at the top. If you click on that, you get the list of all residents, all rooms. On the left side, you can then select everything from hygiene entries, care reports, today's measures, wounds, and everything else. You can click on that, there is also a plus sign, and then you enter new information. Absolutely no problem. I find the app quite good." (P4) "Yeah, we try to speak as clearly as possible so that he really understands every word correctly, so that we wouldn't have to correct him." (P8)
5. Habit	"It was unusual at first, the actual transition from the PC to the phone… When it's stressful, today you also tend to occasionally go faster to the PC and write with the keyboard, especially for long texts." (P1) "From unusual to indispensable." (P6)

(*continued*)

(*continued*)

Main Themes/Categories	Example Quotes
6. Privacy Concerns and Anxiety linked to Speech Assistant Usage	"…with everything new that comes, I always fear, are we being listened to more, are people somehow getting other data from us that we don't even know about, what that device can do and this artificial intelligence…. It's all a bit scary to me. It's more control for the company, even whether we're stressed, then during care, then when we speak a sentence, you can hear whether we're stressed or whether we're calm." (P2)
7. Use behavior Usage Frequency and Utilized Functions Usage Barriers Proposed Strategies for Successful Speech-Based Documentation	"…for me, voize is sufficient for what I have to enter. As I said, care reports, bowel movements, hygiene measures, everything that comes as an option for us to document… I enter through voice and also as (Intv: voice recording?). Yes, mostly yes."(P3) "…app use on average per shift theoretically 15 to 23 times for all residents" (P5)" "Older colleagues didn't manage well with the app, so we had to explain a few times." (P4) "…some are still cautious, but everyone now takes their cell phone with them - sometimes more, sometimes less. When I'm not there, it's immediately less that has to become second nature." (P9) "…for those who are actually bedridden, then I approach things a little differently. But then I also go to people nearby and respectfully say what I have done and not do something over someone's head." (P1) "It's also very individual, and not every day is the same. I cannot tell you, I always do it now in the room or always in front of the door or always in the staff room; every day is different, we work with people and everything is very individual. That's why I use the app very individually too, but I make sure I do it very promptly, otherwise it won't help me much." (P7)

References

1. Grogan, L., Reed, A., Fennelly, O.: Nursing documentation in digital solutions. Introd. Nurs. Inform. 175–201 (2021). https://doi.org/10.1007/978-3-030-58740-6_7
2. Akhu-Zaheya, L., Al-Maaitah, R., Bany Hani, S.: Quality of nursing documentation: paper-based health records versus electronic-based health records. J. Clin. Nurs. **27**, e578–e589 (2018). https://doi.org/10.1111/jocn.14097
3. Schenk, E., Schleyer, R., Jones, C.R., Fincham, S., Daratha, K.B., Monsen, K.A.: Time motion analysis of nursing work in ICU telemetry and medical-surgical units. J. Nurs. Manag. **25**, 640–646 (2017). https://doi.org/10.1111/jonm.12502
4. Yen, P.-Y., Kellye, M., Lopetegui, M., Saha, A., Loversidge, J., Chipps, E.M., et al.: Nurses' time allocation and multitasking of nursing activities: a time motion study. AMIA Annu. Symp. Proc. **2018**, 1137–1146 (2018)
5. Roumeliotis, N., Parisien, G., Charette, S., Arpin, E., Brunet, F., Jouvet, P.: Reorganizing care with the implementation of electronic medical records: a time-motion study in the PICU*. Pediatr. Crit. Care Med. **19**, e172 (2018). https://doi.org/10.1097/pcc.0000000000001450
6. Kebede, M., Endris, Y., Zegeye, D.T.: Nursing care documentation practice: the unfinished task of nursing care in the University of Gondar Hospital. Inform. Health Soc. Care **42**, 290–302 (2017). https://doi.org/10.1080/17538157.2016.1252766
7. Tasew, H., Mariye, T., Teklay, G.: Nursing documentation practice and associated factors among nurses in public hospitals, Tigray. Ethiopia. BMC Res. Notes. **12**, 612 (2019). https://doi.org/10.1186/s13104-019-4661-x
8. Scharfenberg, E.: Was beschäftigt Pflegekräfte? Online-Umfrage, Berlin (2016)
9. Hertzum, M.: Electronic health records in Danish home care and nursing homes: inadequate documentation of care, medication, and consent. Appl. Clin. Inform. **12**, 27–33 (2021). https://doi.org/10.1055/s-0040-1721013
10. Considine, J., Trotter, C., Currey, J.: Nurses' documentation of physiological observations in three acute care settings. J. Clin. Nurs. **25**, 134–143 (2016). https://doi.org/10.1111/jocn.13010
11. Koivikko, M.P., Kauppinen, T., Ahovuo, J.: Improvement of report workflow and productivity using speech recognition—a follow-up study. J. Digit Imaging **21**, 378–82 (2008). https://doi.org/10.1007/s10278-008-9121-4
12. Joseph, J., Moore, Z.E.H., Patton, D., O'Connor, T., Nugent, L.E.: The impact of implementing speech recognition technology on the accuracy and efficiency (time to complete) clinical documentation by nurses: a systematic review. J. Clin. Nurs. **29**, 2125–2137 (2020). https://doi.org/10.1111/jocn.15261
13. Zuchowski, M., Pashayeva, A., Wohlrab, M.: Medizinische Spracherkennung im stationären und ambulanten Einsatz – Eine systematische Übersicht. Gesundheitsökonomie Qual. **25**, 83–90 (2020). https://doi.org/10.1055/a-1115-6980
14. Dinari, F., Bahaadinbeigy, K., Bassiri, S., Mashouf, E., Bastaminejad, S., Moulaei, K.: Benefits, barriers, and facilitators of using speech recognition technology in nursing documentation and reporting: a cross-sectional study. Health Sci. Rep. **6**, e1330 (2023). https://doi.org/10.1002/hsr2.1330
15. Blackley, S.V., Huynh, J., Wang, L., Korach, Z., Zhou, L.: Speech recognition for clinical documentation from 1990 to 2018: a systematic review. J. Am. Med. Inform. Assoc. JAMIA **26**, 324–338 (2019). https://doi.org/10.1093/jamia/ocy179
16. Venkatesh, V., Thong, J.Y.L., Xu, X.: Consumer acceptance and use of information technology: extending the unified theory of acceptance and use of technology. MIS Q. **36**, 157–178 (2012). https://doi.org/10.2307/41410412

17. Slade, E.L., Williams, M., Dwivedi, Y.: An extension of the UTAUT 2 in a healthcare context. In: UK Academy for Information Systems Conference Proceedings, pp. 55 (2013)
18. Budde, K., et al.: KI für Gesundheitsfachkräfte. Chancen und Herausforderungen von medizinischen und pflegerischen KI-Anwendungen. Whitepaper aus der Plattform Lernende Systeme (2023). https://doi.org/10.48669/pls_2023-2
19. Dresing, T., Pehl, T.: Praxisbuch Interview, Transkription & Analyse: Anleitungen und Regelsysteme für qualitativ Forschende, 8th edn. Eigenverlag, Marburg (2018)
20. Mayring, P.: Qualitative Content Analysis: Theoretical Background and Procedures. In: Bikner-Ahsbahs A, Knipping C, Presmeg N, Publisher. Approaches Qual Res Math Educ Ex Methodol Methods. Dordrecht, pp. 365–80. Springer, Netherlands (2015). https://doi.org/10.1007/978-94-017-9181-6_13
21. Palau-Saumell, R., Forgas-Coll, S., Sánchez-García, J., Robres, E.: User acceptance of mobile apps for restaurants: an expanded and extended UTAUT-2. Sustainability **11**, 1210 (2019). https://doi.org/10.3390/su11041210
22. Suominen, H., Zhou, L., Hanlen, L., Ferraro, G.: Benchmarking clinical speech recognition and information extraction: new data, methods, and evaluations. JMIR Med. Inform. **3**, e4321 (2015). https://doi.org/10.2196/medinform.4321
23. Saxena, K., Diamond, R., Conant, R.F., Mitchell, T.H., Gallopyn, G., Yakimow, K.E.: Provider adoption of speech recognition and its impact on satisfaction, documentation quality, efficiency, and cost in an inpatient EHR. AMIA Summits. Transl. Sci. Proc. **2018**, 186 (2018)
24. Lyons, J.P., Sanders, S.A., Fredrick Cesene, D., Palmer, C., Mihalik, V.L., Weigel, T.: Speech recognition acceptance by physicians: a temporal replication of a survey of expectations and experiences. Health Informatics J. **22**, 768–778 (2016). https://doi.org/10.1177/1460458215589600
25. Blackley, S.V., Schubert, V.D., Goss, F.R., Al Assad, W., Garabedian, P.M., Zhou, L.: Physician use of speech recognition versus typing in clinical documentation: a controlled observational study. Int. J. Med. Inf. **141**, 104178 (2020). https://doi.org/10.1016/j.ijmedinf.2020.104178
26. Alapetite, A., Boje Andersen, H., Hertzum, M.: Acceptance of speech recognition by physicians: A survey of expectations, experiences, and social influence. Int. J. Hum.-Comput. Stud. **67**, 36–49 (2009). https://doi.org/10.1016/j.ijhcs.2008.08.004
27. Kumah-Crystal, Y.A, Pirtle, C.J., Whyte, H.M., Goode, E.S., Anders, S.H., Lehmann, C.U.: Electronic health record interactions through voice: a review. Appl. Clin. Inform. **9**, 541 (2018). https://doi.org/10.1055/s-0038-1666844
28. Fratzke, J., Tucker, S., Shedenhelm, H., Arnold, J., Belda, T., Petera, M.: Enhancing nursing practice by utilizing voice recognition for direct documentation. J. Nurs. Adm. **44**, 79–86 (2014). https://doi.org/10.1097/nna.0000000000000030
29. Vogel, M., Kaisers, W., Wassmuth, R., Mayatepek, E.: Analysis of documentation speed using web-based medical speech recognition technology: randomized controlled trial. J. Med. Internet Res. **17**, e247 (2015). https://doi.org/10.2196/jmir.5072
30. Ronquillo, C.E., Peltonen, L.-M., Pruinelli, L., Chu, C.H., Bakken, S., Beduschi, A., et al.: Artificial intelligence in nursing: priorities and opportunities from an international invitational think-tank of the Nursing and Artificial Intelligence Leadership Collaborative. J. Adv. Nurs. **77**, 3707–3717 (2021). https://doi.org/10.1111/jan.14855

Conversation Summarization System Emphasizing Recent Context for Supporting Seamless Rejoining of a Group Chat After Temporary Absence

Jotaro Hori(✉), Masayuki Ando, Kouyou Otsu, and Tomoko Izumi

Ritsumeikan University, Kusatsu 525-8557, Shiga, Japan
is0578iv@ed.ritsumei.ac.jp, {mandou,k-otsu, izumi-t}@fc.ritsumei.ac.jp

Abstract. This study focuses on a specific issue that emerges when a member temporarily leaves a group face-to-face chat. In such a situation, the leaving member often struggles to understand the conversation context when they return to the conversation. We propose a system that presents a summary of the conversation content after the user has left to facilitate a smooth rejoining of the chat in such a situation. In our system, an original summarization method, recent conversation summarization, which focuses on the conversation content just before rejoining, is incorporated to provide a suitable summary for rejoining the conversation. We conducted experiments to assess the proposed concept and its summarization method. From the results in the preliminary experiment for testing the effectiveness of the recent conversation summarization in controlled conversation settings, it is found that users were able to understand conversation content easily and rejoin conversations early in the case of using recent conversation summarization. From the results in the main experiment for evaluating the support of the system in a real conversational context, it is suggested that the proposed method can support understanding of the conversation context and early rejoining.

Keywords: Conversation Rejoin support · Conversation Summarization system · Face-to-Face Communication · Group interaction

1 Introduction

Face-to-face chats are an essential part of our daily lives, allowing us to share information and express our feelings with each other. Particularly, in workplaces, several articles suggest that casual chats have effects on enhancing positive social emotions [1] and face-to-face communication improves team performance [2]. Face-to-face chats do not have specific tasks unlike structured and formal conversations such as meetings. Specifically, differences from the formal conversations exist, such as conversational properties (timing or agenda) are not fixed in advance [3]. Therefore, conversational topics are changed quickly during a chat. These chat features sometimes make it difficult for members to

M. Kurosu and A. Hashizume (Eds.): HCII 2024, LNCS 14688, pp. 35–50, 2024.
https://doi.org/10.1007/978-3-031-60449-2_3

understand the conversation context. A typical example is a situation in which a member leaves the conversation temporarily for reasons such as receiving a phone call or using a restroom. In such a situation, because the conversation is continued by the remaining members, when the leaving member returns, the topic of the chat has often changed from the time they left. Thus, it is difficult for them to grasp the context of the missed conversation and rejoin the conversation. In such situations, the rejoining member often interrupts the chat to ask others, "What were you talking about?" to understand the conversational context. However, this interruption stops the ongoing chat and sometimes stresses both the active and rejoining members.

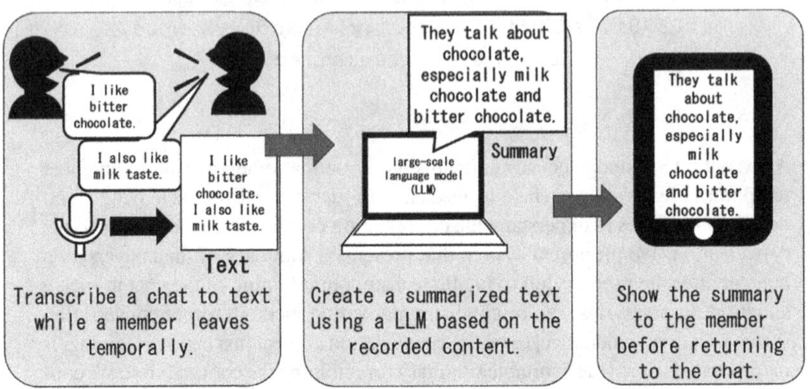

Fig. 1. Overview of the proposed system

Our study aims to find a design that assists in rejoining a conversation early for members who temporarily leave a chat. To achieve this, we propose a system that transcribes conversational content in real-time while a member leaves the chat and provides it to the leaving member as a summarized text mainly focusing on recent content (Fig. 1). This mechanism enables a leaving member to request a summary of the ongoing conversation by other members, such that they can obtain a quick overview of the ongoing discussion topic before returning to the conversation. However, the ease of rejoining the conversation may depend on the system's quality of the provided summary text. Therefore, this paper also discusses the summary information that should be provided to leaving members in the process of designing the proposed method. In particular, we hypothesized that focusing the summary on recent conversational content could support easier understanding and early rejoining of the conversation. In our proposed method, an original summarization method, called recent conversation summarization, which focuses on the conversation content just before rejoining, is incorporated.

In this study, we examine the following two research questions (RQs):

- RQ1: Is the summarization method focusing on the most recent content more useful for users to rejoin the conversation than the normal summarization method focusing on all content equally?
- RQ2: Can the proposed system using the large language model (LLM) support users rejoining conversations?

To verify RQ1, we conducted preliminary experiments under controlled settings with the fixed conversational scenarios, members, and the presented summary text. Based on the results of the preliminary experiments, we implemented a prototype system using a LLM to verify RQ2. We conducted a user test as the main experiment for evaluating the prototype system in a real group conversational context. In this paper, we report these experimental results and discuss the design for providing appropriate information in supporting rejoining conversations.

2 Related Research

Several studies on communication support for users who participate in the middle of a conversation exist. These studies focus on supporting smooth joining of discussions in electronic conferencing or understanding in bulletin board systems (BBSs). For instance, Matsuo et al. [4] mentioned that reading many messages on BBSs is difficult task, and they proposed an approach of characterizing messages on BBSs. In the method, BBS messages are characterized by three indices, degree of inclusion of given provided information, degree of inclusion of new information, and degree of effect for the successive messages. They also proposed a prototype system using these indices.

These studies targeting online communication suggest that presenting information of the previous conversation context to users makes it easier for them to participate in the conversation. This finding can be applied to support participation in the middle of a face-to-face conversation. However, when returning to a face-to-face chat after temporarily leaving, it is important not only to grasp the context but also to allow users to participate in the conversation seamlessly, just as they would have done before leaving. Hence, it is necessary to consider how to summarize the conversation to allow users to grasp the conversation context in less time.

Regarding the summarization of conversation, some studies that consider summarization methods for making it easier to understand the previous conversation content exist [5, 6]. For instance, Yamashita et al. [5] used previous conversation summaries to assist operators in intervening when problems occur in automatic conversation systems. In their study, they compared seven types of dialog summaries to find the most useful summary for a smooth handover, and they showed that the best summaries were an abstractive summary along with one utterance immediately before the handover and an extractive summary comprising five utterances immediately before the handover. This suggests that a summary emphasizing recent information may contribute to make it easier for person to join a conversation in the middle. Therefore, using conversational text immediately before rejoining may be effective in providing summary-based support for a temporarily leaving member, which is the problem addressed in this study. In contrast to previous studies focusing on joining in the middle of conversations, we address the communication problems in rejoining in real group chats. In addition, we also discuss the type of summary that should be provided to increase the ease of rejoining.

3 Proposed Method

3.1 Proposed Concept

In this study, we propose a system that transcribes conversational content in real-time when a member has left a chat and provides it to the leaving member as a summarized text upon their return. The overview of our proposed concept is shown in Fig. 1. In our assumed use case, a microphone is installed at the conversation locations to record the remaining members' conversation when a member leaves temporarily. The person who leaves the chat can request a summary from their smartphone to grasp the ongoing conversation while they are away. The person can check the contents of the conversation while leaving from the summary on their device. This mechanism enables leaving members to request a brief summary of the ongoing conversation by other members, such that they can obtain a quick overview of the present topic before returning to the conversation. In addition, the leaving members are expected to smoothly rejoin the conversation.

3.2 Recent Conversation Summarization

To realize the proposed concept described earlier, summaries provided to leaving members should have suitable information for their return to the conversation. A crucial aspect to consider for such information is ensuring that they can understand the topic and context of the ongoing conversation upon their return. This suggests that simply providing a normal summary of the conversation for their time out may not make it easier to rejoin the conversation. For instance, because conversational topics change frequently in chats, presenting a summary that treats "all" conversation contents evenly might increase user's confusion for understanding the current conversational context. As suggested from a related study [5], summaries focusing on the most recent conversation may help reduce the cost of understanding the conversation content and of returning to it. Therefore, we consider a novel summarization method called recent conversation summarization, which focuses on recent conversational content to support the ease of early rejoining of the conversation and use it for realizing our proposed concept.

In this section, we describe the recent conversation summarization method; this is a summarizing method that emphasizes the latest conversation topics while maintaining a description of the overall content using LLM-based text summarization. In this paper, we call the generated summary by the method as the recent conversation summary.

To generate a summary that places emphasis on the most recent part of a conversation and allows users to grasp the entire conversation context, this summarization method creates a summary by dividing the conversational text as an input source into a recent part and a front part. After dividing the input source into a front part and a recent part, the LLM text summarization method is applied to each. The summary of the front part is created with fewer characters than the recent part. Thereafter, the final summary is created by concatenating the summaries of each part, which contains more of the recent part. By creating the recent conversation summary in this way, preparing a summary sentence that stably contains a large amount of the contents of the most recent conversation is possible. An example summary used in the preliminary experiments described below is provided in Table 1. Unlike the normal summarization procedure where all input sources are applied directly to the LLM, our method emphasizes the most recent content to the summary text.

Before developing a system implementing the concept, we performed a preliminary validation of the usefulness of the recent conversation summary. This is presented in Sect. 4. Thereafter, a prototype system that implements the concept based on the results of the preliminary experiments is presented in Sect. 5. Finally, the results of the validation experiment using the system in are provided Sect. 6.

4 Preliminary Experiment

We conducted a preliminary experiment to evaluate the effectiveness of the recent conversation summarization and the intrinsic validity of the proposed concept before implementing our proposed method as a prototype system. The main purpose of this preliminary experiment is to clarify whether the summarization method focusing on the recent conversation content helps users to rejoin conversations, as shown in RQ1. Experimenting in open settings with a fully implemented prototype system with a summary generation mechanism is one way to evaluate our concept. However, in such a setting, chat contents and the precision of the LLM's summary could potentially affect the quality of summarization presented and evaluation of the validity of our concept. Therefore, prior to a system evaluation experiment, verifying the effectiveness of the recent conversation summarization is beneficial, which may affect the usefulness of the proposed system directly, under controlled settings. In this section, we describe a preliminary experiment under a controlled situation to verify the effectiveness of the proposed summarization method, emphasizing recent contents.

4.1 Experimental Settings

In this experiment, participants were asked to leave the conversation during a group conversation, and thereafter asked to view a summary of the conversation on their smartphones before returning to the conversation. The participants were asked to repeat this experience with two different patterns of summary sentences and evaluate the ease of rejoining the conversation and understanding the conversational context. In this experiment, we compared the case presenting the summarized text generated by the normal summarization procedure using LLM (baseline condition) and generated by the recent conversation summarization (proposed condition).

The experiment was conducted under a special setting to control the content of the participants' experiences. Specifically, we prepared the conversation content and summary sentences used in the experiment in advance and the participants were asked to chat with two staff members prepared by the experimenter on a specific topic. When the participant returns to the conversation after temporarily leaving, the two staff members continue talking with a prepared scenario that corresponds to the summary sentences presented to the participant. Using these settings, a controlled situation was set up in which the participants could not know the topics the other members were talking about.

In this experiment, 12 people in their 20s acquainted with the experimental staff participated.

Table 1. Example summary texts of the difference between normal summarization (left) and recent conversation summarization (right). They are created by LLM (Chat GPT-3.5, Open AI Inc.) based on the scenario we created manually. (These texts are a translated version from the original one in Japanese presented in the experiment. In the original texts, the number of characters is set as approximately same between these texts.)

Normal summarization that treats "all" conversation contents evenly	Recent conversation summarization that emphasizes recent conversation contents
A and B are discussing snacks for movie watching at home. They mainly prefer sweet foods, and they particularly enjoy talking about chocolates. As beverages to go well with it, B chooses coffee and A chooses milk. The combination of green tea and chocolate is unpopular, and the conversation turns to Daifuku. A introduces a recommended shop, and B also reveals preference for fruit Daifuku. Finally, a friendly conversation ensues in which opinions are exchanged about fruits in fruit Daifuku. (80 words)	A and B discuss food and beverages when watching a movie, particularly exchanging opinions on beverages that go well with chocolate, and then discuss their preference for fruit Daifuku. A likes Muscat best and finds strawberries a little sour, while B argues that strawberries are favorite and is the first in his ranking. Their opinions are divided on the question on whether this muscat or strawberry ranks higher. (68words)

4.2 Scenarios and Summary Text

In this preliminary experiment, the participants experienced two summary presentation patterns; recent conversation summary and normal summary. We prepared two different scenarios and summary texts to avoid experiencing the same topic when they returned to the conversation under each experimental condition. The scenario themes are "fruit daifuku (Japanese mochi dessert with fruit)" and "trend colors of clothes." We designed these two scenarios to avoid direct topic words that could indicate their discussion topic.

When using the scenario regarding fruit daifuku, the two staff and a participant were initially asked to talk about interesting movies. After the participant had left the room, the remaining staff began to change the topics from interesting movies to watching movies at home. In this scenario, the conversational topic transitions to a discussion about snacks they eat when watching movies at home, and finally to a discussion about their preferences for the flavor of fruit daifuku. In this case, the staff proceed the conversation as the conversation topic (flavor of fruit daifuku) is withheld for the participant, for instance, "Muscat is good, but strawberry is the best." The experimental staff acted out the scenario as if they were talking about the last topic of the predefined conversational scenario when the participant returned to the room. Therefore, the scenario is difficult for the participant to understand the context by only listening to the ongoing conversation.

The summary text for each scenario was created from the scenario sentences using ChatGPT [7]. The summarized text in normal summarization was generated by ChatGPT from the entire sentences of the scenario. In contrast, the summarized text in recent conversation summarization was made by combining the generated summaries by ChatGPT from the recent and front parts of the original text. The recent part was assigned from the part of each scenario in which fruits daifuku or trend colors are mentioned.

Each summarized text was adjusted to be approximately 200 characters in Japanese. For the prompts, we attempted to use several types for both the two summaries with the aim of generating a reasonable summary and selected the one we considered suitable. We mainly generated them based on the prompt, "Summarize this conversation between two people in XX (in Japanese)" after writing the content of the conversation (XX denotes the number of characters or lines.) Table 1 summarizes the two summary texts about fruit daifuku.

4.3 Procedure and Evaluation Items

At the beginning of the experiment, the participant was instructed on the overview of the experiment and signed a consent form. Next, the participant was asked to chat with two staff prepared by the experimenter in the laboratory. During the chat, the experimenter called the participant's smartphone, which was given to them in advance, and asked them to leave the laboratory and come to another room where the experimenter was waiting. In the room, the experimenter instructed them on the experimental application to observe the preset summary text and its usage on the smartphone.

While the participant left, the two staff pretended to chat following the prescribed scenario, and thereafter continued the conversation after the participant returned. After the participant read the summary text displayed to understand the content of the chat before entering the laboratory, they took the seat and rejoined the conversation by speaking up. After the participant rejoined the chat, they were asked to answer a questionnaire that two staff members handed to them. The questionnaire had nine questions and asked the same questions under the two conditions (Table 2). These questions were composed by a 7-point Likert scale (7 is the most positive score). The participants underwent this procedure twice by changing the summarized text displayed on the smartphone and conversation content. We compared the results under the two conditions applied to each summarization. In this process, the order of the case using recent and normal summaries were also swapped for each participant. During the experiment, we recorded the laboratory using a video camera.

4.4 Results and Discussions

Figure 2 shows box-and-whisker diagrams representing the means and distributions of responses for the questionnaire items, along with the results of the two-tailed t-test.

First, we show the results of Q2, 6, and 7 on the usefulness of the summary for rejoining the conversation. In Q2 and Q6, the average values are more positive in the case of using the recent conversation summary than in that of the normal summary. In Q7, the average values are the same in both summaries. From the results of a two-tailed t-test, a marginally significant difference is observed only in Q2 ($p = 0.09$), and statistical differences are not observed in the other two questions. From the marginally significant result in Q2, it is suggested that he recent conversation summary makes it easier to grasp information for rejoining the conversation than the case of the normal summary. In addition, the average values of these three questions are equal or more positive when the recent conversation summary is used, and these results demonstrate that the recent

Table 2. Question items in the questionnaire of the preliminary experiment

ID	Question
Q1	By reading the summarized text about conversation content that took place during temporarily leaving, I felt easier to rejoin the conversation
Q2	I easily grasped the conversation content that took place during temporarily leaving from the provided summarized text
Q3	It took a long time to grasp the conversation content that took place during temporarily leaving from the provided summarized text
Q4	I felt it is useful to know the conversation content that took place during temporarily leaving from the provided summarized text
Q5	I felt it is troublesome to read the summarized text about the conversation content that took place during temporarily leaving
Q6	After I returned to the laboratory, I could understand what the others were talking about
Q7	After I returned to the laboratory, I needed to listen to the others' conversation to understand what they were talking about
Q8	After I returned to the laboratory, I felt the summarized text I read before was useful to understand what the others were talking about
Q9	After I returned to the laboratory, I felt I could rejoin the chat early

conversation summary tends to provide more useful information to rejoin a conversation than a normal summary.

Next, we show the results of Q3 and 9 on the sense of time when rejoining the conversation. Q3 is the question where a lower score suggests that participants did not perceive the process as time-consuming. In Q3 and 9, the average responses are more positive in the case of using the recent conversation summary than that of the normal summary. From the results of the t-test, a significant difference is observed only in Q3 ($p = 0.01$). This result suggests that the recent conversation summary can allow users to grasp the conversation content during their time out within a relatively short time.

Q1, 4, 5, and 8 ask about the impression of rejoining a conversation after reading the summarization. From the t-test results, there are no significant differences among all questions. In Q1, 5, and 8, the average values are slightly positive in the case of using the recent conversation summary, that is, the recent conversation summary can be regarded as similar or more positive than the normal summary in terms of ease of rejoining (Q1), troublesomeness (Q5), and usefulness for understanding the conversation content (Q8). In contrast, in the Q4 result, the average value for the normal summary is more positive than that of the recent conversation summary without statistical significance. However, the average values of both conditions are greater than 5 in Q4. Therefore, knowing content from the summary could be useful regardless of the difference between the recent conversation summary and the normal summary.

In the preliminary experiment, it is found that the recent conversation summarization was effective in grasping the conversation content during temporary leaving easily and

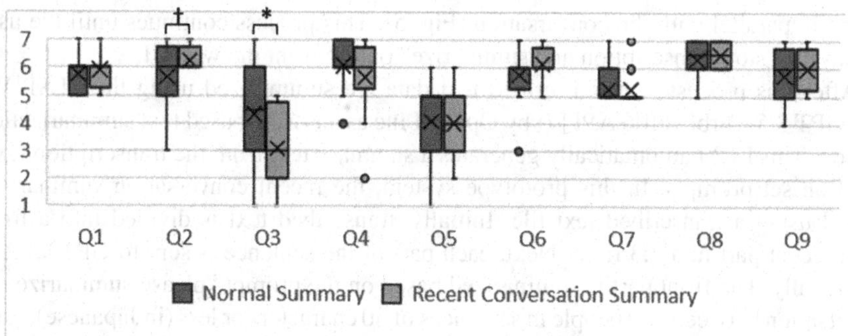

Fig. 2. Box-and-whisker diagrams of mean scores under each condition in Q1–9 of the preliminary experiment. (†: $p < 0.1$, *: $p < 0.05$)

quickly from the results of Q2 and 3. Furthermore, regardless of the summarization method, the scores of the questions asking the ease of rejoining (Q1) and the sense of comprehension of conversational content (Q2 and Q6) are positive, scoring more than 5. These facts suggest that our idea to present conversational text summaries after temporarily leaving is effective in supporting rejoining the conversation and grasping the context.

5 Prototype System

In Sect. 4, we evaluated whether the recent conversation summary or the normal summary was more useful for understanding the conversation content in rejoining the conversation after temporarily leaving. The results demonstrated that the recent conversation summary is more useful regarding assistance in grasping the conversation content and reducing the feeling about the time taken to rejoin the conversation. Therefore, to verify the effectiveness of our proposed concept described in Sect. 3, we developed a prototype system enabling real-time recent conversation summarization using LLM while group face-to-face chatting and presenting the generated summary to leaving users. With this system, a leaving user can request the recording to start and transcribe a conversation in a conversational environment and generate a summary via the web UI (Fig. 3). The leaving user can obtain a recent conversation summary of the discussion topic of the others while away.

Figure 4 shows the overall configuration and processing flow in the prototype system. The prototype system comprises a microphone for recording the voice in group chatting, a processing PC for transcription from a recorded voice and text summarization using LLM, and the user's PC for providing a web UI for users to check the summary. The prototype system starts transcription by pressing the start button on the user's PC. Simultaneously, voice recording starts on the side of group chatting. The recording is transcribed as an audio file in 5-s increments. For the transcription process, we used the faster-whisper [8]. The transcription process is asynchronous to the voice recording, and the text file in which the transcription is saved is designed to contain 5 s of recorded content per line. This parallel processing mechanism allows for real-time processing of speech in parallel with the conversation (Fig. 5). This process continues until the user presses the "stop transcription and summarize" button from the web UI.

After this process, the transcribed text data are summarized using the LLM. We used GPT-3.5-Turbo-1106 API [7] by OpenAI Inc as an LLM-based text summarization method. This LLM automatically generates a summary text from the transcription texts based on set prompts. In this prototype system, the recent conversation summary is created using a transcribed text file. Initially, transcribed text is divided into a front and a recent part in a 7:3 ratio. Next, each part of the sentence is sent to GPT3.5 API individually. The front part is summarized based on the prompt "please summarize the conversation between two people in sentences of 50 characters or less (in Japanese)," and the recent part is summarized based on the prompt "please summarize the conversation between two people in sentences of 150 characters or more (in Japanese)."

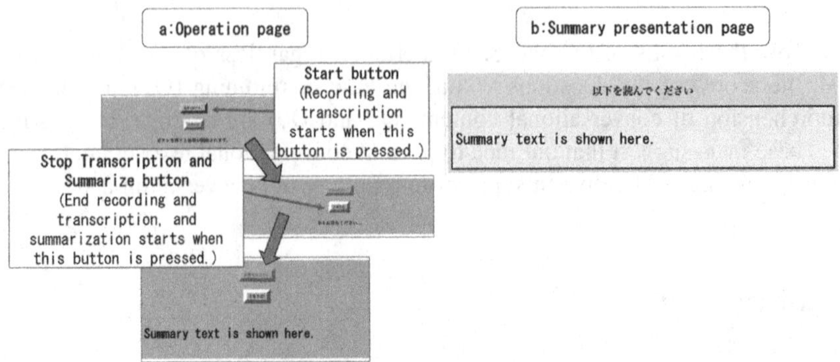

Fig. 3. Example view of the web-based operation interface in the prototype system. (a) Operation page, (b) Summary presentation page.

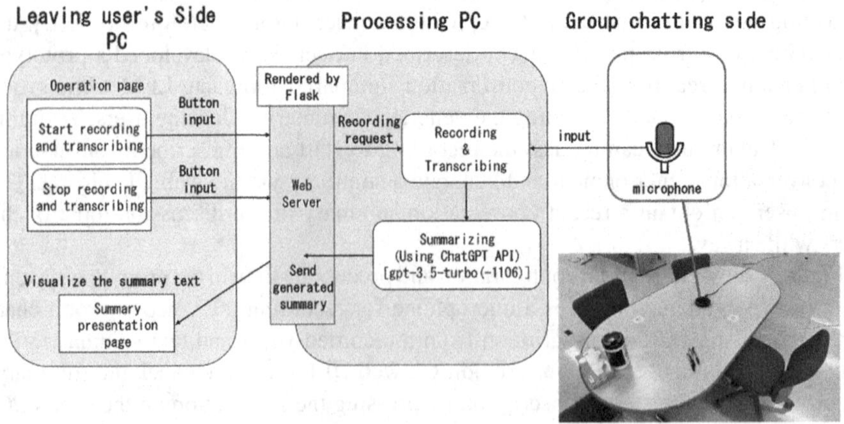

Fig. 4. Overview of the prototype system

In this system, we consider a situation in which three members of a group join a chat and one of them leaves the chat, as in the experiment described in the next section. Finally,

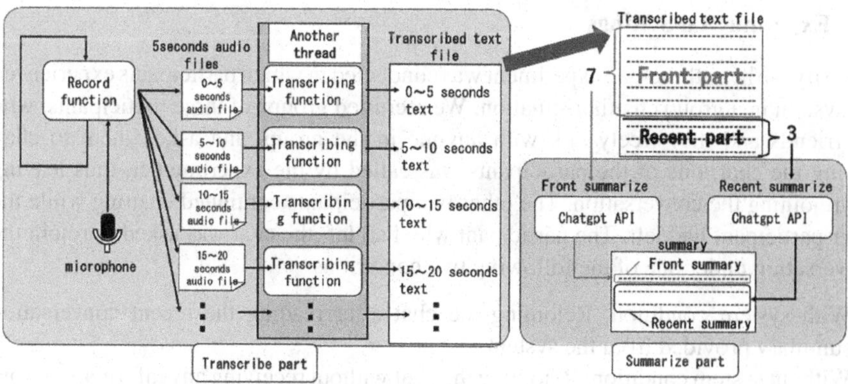

Fig. 5. Overview of transcription and summarization

the final result text is created by connecting both summary texts and showing them to the leaving user-side web UI. This prototype enables the summary text generation focusing on the recent content (Fig. 5).

6 Experiment

6.1 Purpose and Hypotheses

This experiment aimed to verify the effects of the proposed system using recent conversation summarization on rejoining a conversation after a member temporarily leaves. We conducted an experiment using the prototype system described in Sect. 5. In this experiment, we set the following three hypotheses:

H 1. It is easier to understand a conversation flow in detail when using the proposed system than when not using the system (understanding of a flow of conversation).

H 2. It is easier for a member who leaves temporarily to rejoin a conversation earlier when using the proposed system than when not using the system (earlier, smoothness to rejoin).

H 3. A temporarily leaving member is less likely to feel that the conversation progress has been stopped when using the proposed system than when not using the system (effect on conversation progress).

It is expected that when using the system, more amount of information about the conversation content during temporary leaving can be obtained in advance, such that a user can understand the conversation context in detail (H1). This leads to the feeling that the user can rejoin the conversation earlier after leaving (H2). In addition, it is possible that a temporarily leaving user may not need the conversational contents to be explained to them by other members when using the system, thus reducing the feeling of stagnation in the conversation (H3).

6.2 Experimental Settings

To verify the hypotheses, an experiment was conducted in which participants experienced the system in a group chatting situation. We recruited groups of three participants, who are friends and they freely talk with anyone in the group, and asked them to chat. During the chat, one of the participants was called by the experimenter, thus leaving and rejoining the conversation. The other two participants continued chatting while the other participant had left. The participant who had left the chat was asked to rejoin the conversation under one of the following two conditions:

- With system condition: Rejoining the chat after reading the recent conversation summary provided from the system.
- Without system condition: Rejoining the chat without receiving any information from the system.

After the leaving and rejoining the conversation under one of the conditions, the participants are experienced again the flow of the chatting, leaving, and rejoining under the other condition. We compared the impression of the participants under the two conditions.

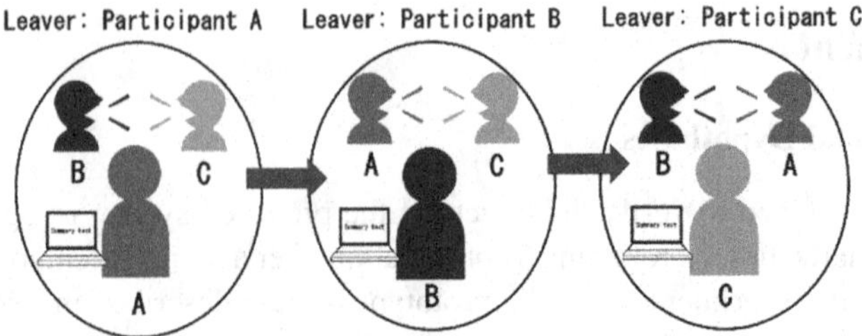

Fig. 6. Experimental procedure

Each participant was asked to temporarily leave and rejoin the conversation under the two conditions and this process was repeated while changing the leaving participants (Fig. 6). Therefore, the participants chatted six times in one group.

6.3 Experimental Procedure and Evaluation Items

At the beginning of the experiment, the participant was instructed on the overview of the experiment and signed a consent form. After the informed consent, the participants were informed that there were two roles in the experiment; a user who experiences the system and the remaining participants who continue with the conversation. They were also informed that one of them was assigned in turns to be the user of the system. Thereafter, we explained to every participant what the two remaining participants in the chat would do when the leaving member returns to the laboratory. In particular, it was required that the remaining participants explain the topic of their conversation at that time in a few words (e.g., "We were just talking about…") to the returning member. This explanation is necessary to allow for rejoining under the without system condition. Subsequently, the participants were given the phone and informed that they would be contacted during the conversation. When the participants could not find a starting topic for conversation, we prepared some topic cards and asked them to use them freely if necessary. The experimenter then exited the laboratory, and the participants were asked to start a conversation.

The experimenter called one of them 3 min after leaving the laboratory on the phone and asked them to leave the laboratory. Under the with system condition, when they reported having left the laboratory, the experimenter pressed the start button to start recording and transcribing the contents of the conversation in the laboratory. The participant who left the chat was instructed to meet the experimenter along the corridor, and thereafter, was required to perform a simple calculation task for approximately 4 min after leaving the laboratory. Next, we provided instructions on the procedure for returning to the laboratory, and asked the leaving participant not to inform the other participants anything that happened outside the laboratory, including information that they received and tasks that they performed. Thereafter, 5 min after leaving, the leaving participant was asked to return to the laboratory and rejoin the chat. Under the with system condition, a laptop was placed as a monitor in front of the room to present the summary text, which was checked by the leaving participant. Meanwhile, the remaining participants in the laboratory continued with their chatting freely. When the leaving member returned to the laboratory, the two remaining participants explained the ongoing topic in a few words.

Table 3. Question items in the questionnaire

No	Hypothesis	Questionnaire items
1	H1	When I rejoined the conversation, I felt I was able to follow it with others
2		When I rejoined the conversation, I needed to ask for more details to understand its content
3		After rejoining the conversation, I felt that it was difficult to understand its content
4	H2	After returning to the laboratory, I felt that I was able to rejoin the conversation early
5		After returning to the laboratory, I felt that it was easy to rejoin the conversation
6		When rejoining the conversation, it took time to understand the context of the conversation during temporarily leaving
7	H3	When rejoining the conversation, I felt I stopped an ongoing conversation

Two minutes after the leaving participant entered the lab again, the experimenter returned to the laboratory and provided them with a questionnaire to answer. Table 3 summarizes the questionnaire that asked for the leaving participant to answer on a 7-point Likert scale (7 is the most positive). The questionnaire has seven questions and asks the same questions under the two conditions.

This leave and rejoin process was experienced by one participant under two conditions. In addition, the process was repeated with the three participants as shown in Fig. 6, changing roles as all of them experienced the system's user. Therefore, the participants group experienced six leave and rejoin processes. During the experiment, we recorded the chat scene in the laboratory using a video camera.

6.4 Results and Discussion

A total of 18 university students participated in the experiment. Figure 7 shows box-and-whisker plots of the questionnaire results and the results of a two-tailed t-test.

The results of all questions show that the average responses are more positive under the with system condition than without system condition. The results of a two-tailed t-test indicate that significant differences (Q1, 2, and 4, and 7 with $p < 0.05$, and Q3, 5, and 6 with $p < 0.01$) are observed in all of them.

In this section, we discuss the hypotheses set in Sect. 6.1 based on the experimental results. First, we discuss hypothesis H1, "It is easier to understand a conversation flow in detail when using the proposed system than when not using the system." Q1–Q3 were set in response to hypothesis H1, and all of them achieved significantly more positive scores under with system condition than without system condition. From these results, it is found that the proposed method supports following the conversation when rejoining the chat and faces less difficulty in understanding the content without the need to ask for details. Therefore, it is suggested that using the system leads to a better understanding of the conversation content. These results support hypothesis H1.

Next, we discuss hypothesis H2, "It is easier for a member who leaves temporarily to rejoin a conversation earlier when using the proposed system than when not using the system." Q4–Q6 were set in response to hypothesis H2, and all of them exhibit significantly positive scores under the with system condition than without system condition. From these results, it is found that the proposed method supports early and easy rejoining of the conversation and quick understanding of the conversation content. Therefore, hypothesis H2 is supported. It is considered that the factor allowing early rejoining and quick understanding of conversations is a reduced need to ask for further details of the conversation. In fact, Q2; "When I rejoined the conversation, I needed to ask for more details to understand its content" is significantly positive in the case of using the system.

Finally, we discuss hypothesis H3, "A temporarily leaving member is less likely to feel that the conversation progress has been stopped when using the proposed system than when not using the system." The related question to hypothesis H3 in the questionnaire is Q7. In this question, a significant difference is observed. It suggests that the leaving participants are less likely to feel that they had stopped the ongoing conversation by using the system to rejoin a conversation. From this result, hypothesis H3 is supported. The reason of this is considered that the process of asking for more details of the ongoing conversation was reduced when participants rejoined the conversation using the system, as shown in the results of Q2.

In summary, these results suggest that using the system that provides the recent conversation summary may help leaving members to easily and early rejoin a conversation and understand its context.

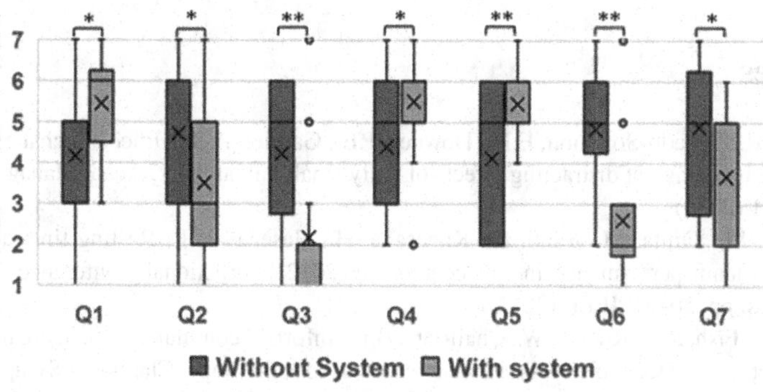

Fig. 7. Box-and-whisker diagrams under each condition in Q1–7 (*: $p < 0.05$, **: $p < 0.01$)

7 Conclusion

This study focused on a specific issue that emerges when a member temporarily leaves a group face-to-face chat and we proposed a design that assists in rejoining a conversation early for temporarily leaving members. We proposed a system that provides a text summary of the conversations during the time out for the user to facilitate a smooth rejoining of the chat in such a situation. In our system, an original summarization method, recent conversation summarization, which focuses on the conversation content just before rejoining, was incorporated to provide a suitable summary for returning to the conversation.

The preliminary experiment evaluated whether the recent conversation summary was more useful than the normal summary in rejoining the conversation after temporarily leaving. From the preliminary experiment, the results suggested that presenting the recent conversation summary would be useful to rejoin a conversation. Specifically, the recent conversation summary was more useful regarding assistance in grasping the conversation content and reducing the feeling about the time taken to rejoin the conversation.

Based on the preliminary experimental results, we developed a prototype system for presenting summary sentences using the recent conversation summarization. Thereafter, we conducted the main experiment to evaluate whether the proposed system could support rejoining of the conversation for leaving members by comparing the case with/without the system. The results of the main experiment suggest that it would be useful to use the system for users who temporarily left. Specifically, using the system, the participants made it easier to understand other people's conversations, and felt they could follow the conversation without asking for details. In addition, they tended to feel to need less time to understand the content, easily rejoined the conversation, and felt less likely that they had stopped an ongoing conversation in the case of using the system.

In future studies, we will consider a mechanism supporting not only the leaving member but also the remaining members in the chat. In addition, verification of whether the proposed method is useful for conversations with more than three people and in situations where more than one person leaves at a time is necessary.

References

1. Methot, J.R., Rosado-Solomon, E.H., Downes, P.E., Gabriel, A.S.: Office chitchat as a social ritual: The uplifting yet distracting effects of daily small talk at work. Acad. Manag. J. **64**(5), 1445–1471 (2021)
2. Watanabe, J.I., Fujita, M., Yano, K., Kanesaka, H., Hasegawa, T.: Resting time activeness determines team performance in call centers. In: 2012 International Conference on Social Informatics, pp. 26–31. IEEE (2012)
3. Kraut, R.E., Fish, R.S., Root, R.W., Chalfonte, B.L.: Informal communication in organizations: form, function, and technology. In: Human reactions to technology: Claremont Symposium on Applied Social Psychology, pp. 145–199 (1990)
4. Matsuo, Y., Ohsawa, Y., Ishizuka, M.: Mining messages in an electronic message board by repetition of words. In: The Second International Workshop on Chance Discovery, Pacific Rim International Conference on AI (2002)
5. Yamashita, S., Higashinaka, R.: Optimal summaries for enabling a smooth handover in chat-oriented dialogue. In: Proceedings of the 2nd Conference of the Asia-Pacific Chapter of the Association for Computational Linguistics and the 12th International Joint Conference on Natural Language Processing: Student Research Workshop, pp. 25–31 (2022)
6. Sood, A., Mohamed, T.P., Varma, V.: Topic-focused summarization of chat conversations. In: Advances in Information Retrieval: 35th European Conference on IR Research, ECIR 2013, Moscow, Russia, March 24–27, 2013. Proceedings 35, pp. 800–803. Springer Berlin Heidelberg (2013).https://doi.org/10.1007/978-3-642-36973-5_88
7. Introducing ChatGPT. https://openai.com/blog/chatgpt. Accessed 15 Dec 2023
8. faster-whisper. https://github.com/SYSTRAN/faster-whisper. Accessed 15 Dec 2023

Designing a Serious Game with Natural Interaction to Support the Learning of Chinese Sign Language and Deaf Social Etiquette

Ruhan Li, Beibei Miao, Mengting Jiang, and Min Fan(✉)

School of Animation and Digital Arts, Communication University of China, Beijing, China
mfan@cuc.edu.cn

Abstract. Sign language is an important communication means among deaf community or between deaf and non-deaf people. This paper presents a serious game (called "Finger Burger") that utilizes natural interaction, situated learning, animation and narratives aims to teach both deaf and non-deaf individuals Chinese Sign Language (CSL) and deaf social etiquette. In order to explore the role of natural interaction on CSL learning gains and game experiences, we conducted a preliminary evaluation with 12 young adults who used both our natural interaction (NI) game and a similar version but with a mouse-click interaction (MCI). We mainly used quantitative methods to analyze the data, supplemented by qualitative results. The results demonstrated our games could significantly improve users' learning gains on CSL and deaf social etiquette. Although the MCI version exhibited slightly better performance in CSL learning, the NI version excelled in executing complex sign tasks. The NI version also yielded superior learning gains in social etiquette. Participants in the NI reported a generally more positive game experience compared to those in the MCI condition. We discuss the affordances and challenges in designing natural interaction for sign language learning.

Keywords: Natural Interaction · Serious Game · Chinese Sign Language · Deaf Social Etiquette · Learning gain · Game Experience

1 Introduction

There are approximately 27.8 million people in China who suffer from various levels of hearing impairments (also referred to as "Deaf people"), which have caused significant communication difficulties. Most deaf people also suffer from speaking problems, making it even harder for them to express themselves [1]. Sign language, as a unique form of communication that utilizes gestures and hand movements, not only plays an essential role in communication among deaf people but also fosters mutual understanding between the deaf community and non-deaf people. As languages are rooted in culture, learning sign language can benefit non-deaf people by helping them to develop a better understanding of the Deaf community and its culture (also referred to as "Deaf Culture"), which includes its own language, values, rules of behavior and traditions [1] (e.g., sign language, deaf social etiquette). An increasing number of non-deaf people are devoting

M. Kurosu and A. Hashizume (Eds.): HCII 2024, LNCS 14688, pp. 51–66, 2024.
https://doi.org/10.1007/978-3-031-60449-2_4

a significant amount of time on social media to learn sign languages and deaf social etiquette [2]. However, since sign languages and deaf social etiquette are completely different from the languages and social etiquette used by non-deaf individuals in daily life, acquiring them can be challenging, especially for non-deaf individuals who lack contextual usage.

Previous research has shown that sign language learning can be enhanced through contextualized and multi-sensory (hands-on) approaches. Traditional instruction relies on experienced teachers (or recorded videos) to demonstrate sign languages and their meanings [2]. With the widespread use of portable devices such as smartphones and tablets, sign language learning has transited from the traditional classroom to online platforms [2]. Many apps employ drill-and-practice tasks, such as daily challenges, to support repetitive sign language learning (gestures), or simply provide explanations on certain sign language and their meanings [3–5]. However, these apps mainly utilize graphics or videos as demonstration materials, without capturing or evaluating users' accuracy in imitating these actions and learning sign languages, thus rendering the learning experience unengaging or ineffective.

Recent HCI research has focused on exploring the use of natural interaction to enhance the effectiveness of sign language learning (e.g., SignTown[1]) [6–8]. Natural interaction refers to human-computer interaction that leverages users' existing skills and knowledge, aiming to achieve easy understanding and natural interaction outcomes [9]. The frequently used forms of natural interactions include gesture-based, expression-based, movement-based interactions [9]. While several studies have presented natural interaction design for sign language learning [7, 11], few have specifically focused on Chinese Sign Language (CSL) (with an exception of SignTown) and evaluated the effects of natural interaction on sign language learning effectiveness and experience. Moreover, most of the designs have overlooked the cultural and social aspects that are important when using sign languages in contexts.

In this paper, we present the design of Finger Burger, a serious game employing natural interaction to facilitate the learning of CSL and deaf social etiquette for both deaf and non-deaf individuals[2] (see Fig. 1a). In the game, a player plays a role of a restaurant manager and completes a series of tasks using hand gestures in a burger store, collecting various sign language cards. We outlined the design rationale, key design features, and technique solutions employed in the game. Specifically, we used *natural interaction*, *animations, situated learning*, and *gamification* to promote an engaging and effective of CSL and deaf social etiquette learning experiences. To gain a better understanding of how natural interaction influences the learning effectiveness and game experience (NI condition), we also designed a similar game using mouse-click interaction (MCI condition) (see Fig. 1b). We conducted a preliminary evaluation with 12 participants (non-deaf young adults) who used both systems, comparing their deaf culture learning gains and game experiences. We discuss (1) the affordances of different interaction modes, particularly natural interaction, in supporting learning and game experiences; (2) the design challenges and trade-offs in designing sign language learning systems with natural interaction; and (3) the limitations of our research.

---

[1] https://sign.town/

[2] The demonstration video of the game can be accessed from https://tny.im/WG8X8.

Fig. 1. (a) a participant played with the natural interaction version; (b) A participant played with the mouse-click version.

Our work has three main contributions. First, we present the design of a serious game employing natural interaction to support the learning of CSL and deaf social etiquette. Second, we present empirical results on non-deaf users learning gains and game experiences with natural interaction compared to the mouse-click interaction. Third, we discuss the affordances and challenges associated with using natural interaction to support the learning of CSL and deaf social etiquette.

2 Literature Review

2.1 Sign Language Learning Methods

Sign language is the primary mode of communication for deaf people. Similar to spoken languages, sign languages contain a rich vocabulary and grammatical rules, and are capable to express emotions and intentions [11]. However, the expressions of sign language heavily rely on the mobilization of the body and hand gestures [2]. Embodied learning is a method of enhancing learning through physical involvement, and this method has been applied to sign language learning by previous researchers [11, 13, 14]. For example, Hyeon-Jun and Baek proposed a wearable glove design that allows students to receive feedback through visual images and vibration motors as they imitate sign language with the device [11]. Rho et al. designed a virtual reality-based system for the New Zealand Sign Language (NZSL) alphabets learning, which provides a multi-sensory and immersive learning environment. It effectively increases users' NZSL learning effectiveness and confidence [12]. Morett investigated the role of embodied action and mental imagery in sign language learning in two specific experiments with hearing adults learning American Sign Language (ASL). The first experiment compared 4 different methods of sign language learning and found that enactment (+ embodied action, + mental imagery) improved sign language memory and recall better than the other three methods, especially for symbolic sign language [13].

Integrating situated learning method with sign language learning can also enhance the learning effectiveness. Herzig and Allen designed an SBA, an app based on a bilingual storybook in ASL and English. Deaf children could watch, read and interact with the contextual elements in the app, which improved their language and literacy skills [3]. Novaliendry et al. designed a VR system to provide deaf children with an immersive and interactive learning environment. Children could learn and practice sign language in virtual environments based on everyday scenarios, which helped to improve their engagement and confidence in using sign language [4].

2.2 Natural Interaction and Gesture Recognition Technology

Gesture interaction is a typical example of natural interaction based on gesture recognition technology that allows users to interact with devices in an intuitive and seamless way using their hands. Gesture recognition can be implemented based on a set of applications such as Leap Motion, RealSense, Kinect, and MediaPipe.

Gesture recognition technology has been widely applied into virtual reality, automotive user interfaces and biomedical and educational fields, which can provide embodied and multi-sensory experiences. Bangaru et al. designed a training system based on gesture recognition that can automatically assess the performance of construction workers while wearing earplugs and provide timely feedback to help them learn how to wear them correctly through body movements [14]. Joy et al. developed SignQuiz, a web application based on gesture recognition that works in two modes to support the learning of finger spelling in Indian Sign Language. In the learning mode, the user clicks to view the material, and in the test mode, the user imitates the sign. The system would automatically recognize and provide feedback. Research indicates that imitating and practicing gestures effectively increases users' sign language vocabulary [7].

Gesture recognition technology can also lead to accessibility design, providing more convenient and user-friendly services for disadvantaged groups. For example, Mehra and Pandey developed a translation tool based on gesture recognition. Applying deep learning, the tool recognizes sign language and converts it into audio and text. This design takes into account the special needs of the hearing impaired and enables them to communicate more easily with others, thereby improving their quality of life and social participation [8]. Ullah et al. developed a body-worn system based on the recognition of complex sign language of children with autism spectrum disorder (ASD) to help children with ASD to communicate with normal children [6].

2.3 Serious Games in Sign Language Learning

Serious games emphasize the balance between functionality and entertainment, which makes them widely used in education and learning [15]. Research has shown that serious games can provide immersion and a sense of achievement in sign language learning, by increasing students' enthusiasm and supporting better learning outcomes [5, 17]. Economou et al. compared the learning effects of British Sign Language (BSL) alphabet learning between the traditional video instruction and a serious game approach. The research showed that students who used the serious game felt more satisfied and performed better in terms of correct identification [16].

Meanwhile, there are serious games for learning sign language that are designed to incorporate other knowledge, expanding the design possibilities. Pontes et al. developed an educational game called MatLIBRAS Racing. The game presents Arabic numerals and BSL symbols, allowing players to learn and memorize sign language symbols while solving mathematical problems. The game increases the difficulty and challenge by gradually hiding Arabic numerals, thus promoting cognitive development in players [5]. SignTown is a real-time, web-based sign recognition game where users take control of an avatar in a fictional world. It allows users to learn and express themselves in Hong Kong Sign Language or Japanese Sign Language (also known as Shuwa in Japanese). It also provides information about deaf social etiquette in different regions.

3 System Design

3.1 Learning and Design Goals

The learning goal of the design was to assist individuals in acquiring CSL proficiency and deepening their understanding of deaf social etiquette, with a specific focus on the words and social culture in restaurants. Our design objective was to create a serious game as a research instrument to explore the advantages of natural interaction in facilitating deaf culture learning gains and enhancing game experiences (Fig. 2a).

Drawing from sign language learning theories and the research on natural interaction, we established four distinct design goals: (1) Natural Gesture-based Interaction: designing gesture-based natural interaction to support CSL learning and main interaction process (e.g., selecting) (see Fig. 2a); providing real-time feedback using gesture recognition technology to determine whether the user was signing correctly or not (see Fig. 2c); (2) Animations with Color Cues: designing 2D animations for each sign to demonstrate the signing process; designing specific color cues to aid users in differentiating between hands and distinguishing between the palm and back of each hand (see Fig. 2b); (3) Situated Learning: incorporating social situations and role-playing elements and narrative to facilitate CSL and deaf social etiquette learning within the context of dining out; and (4) Gamification: adding simple game mechanisms (collecting cards as the user learns) to motivate the learning process.

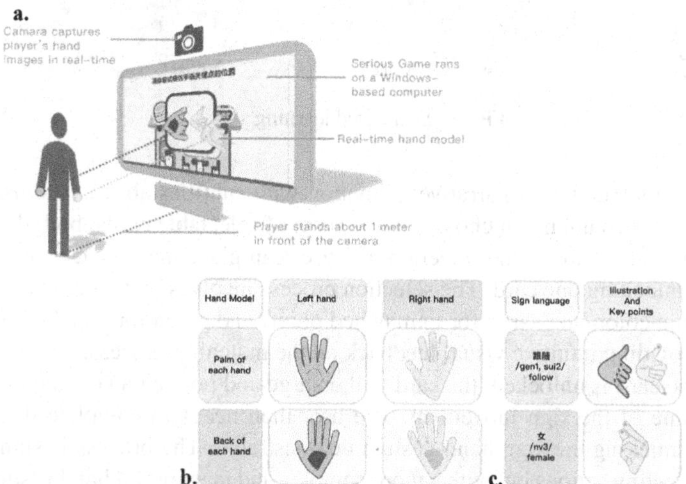

Fig. 2. (a) Finger Burger: the natural interactive serious game; (b) color cues for hands; (c) illustrations and color cues of key points in sign language.

3.2 The Serious Game of Finger Burger

Finger Burger is a serious game that utilizes gesture-based interaction to support both deaf and non-deaf individuals in learning CSL and deaf social etiquette. The main interaction involves the user playing the role of a restaurant manager and serving customers dining out in the burger restaurant. The user must make choices using hand gestures, such as selecting serving the customer on the left card (male) or on the right card (female) at the beginning of the game. He/she then proceeds to complete a series of hand gesture imitating tasks to learn signs (see Fig. 3). Finally, the user can check and view all the collected cards. The game ran on a Windows-based computer.

The game contains three progressive narrative scenes: the outside of the restaurant, the inside of the restaurant, and the kitchen. Throughout the entire process, the user can learn a total of 15 signs and gain knowledge about five aspects of deaf social etiquette. We selected the commonly used signs in restaurants and daily scenarios, based on teaching materials in China, encompassing both simple one-handed signs and more complex two-handed signs. In addition, by selecting associated objects in the game scenes, the user can explore five important aspects of deaf social etiquette related to dining out (e.g., removing all table decorations or irrelevant objects while eating in a restaurant allows better use of sign language for unobstructed communication).

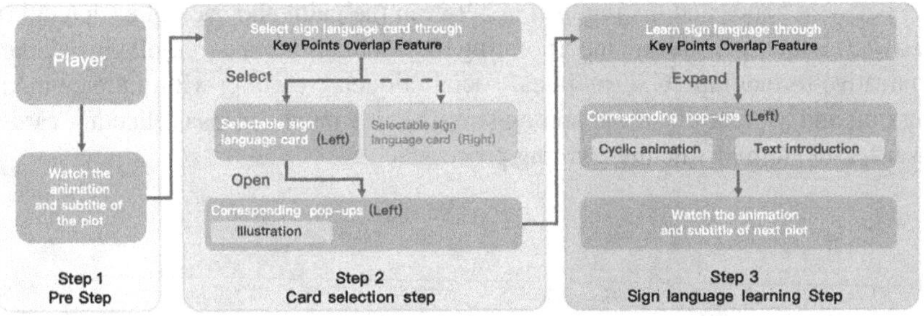

Fig. 3. Structured learning steps.

The game starts with a narrative animation with subtitles above. The user is then presented with two unknown choices in the form of selectable cards, both displaying a white palm icon. To make the selection, the user can place their hand on either left or right side, unlocking one card. The selection process involves matching five key points, with dynamic color cues—red for unmatched points and green for matched points (see Fig. 4)—providing intuitive visual feedback on the matching process.

Once the card is unlocked, the card will enlarge and pop out a sign icon that shows the key frame of the sign movement. The user then needs to complete the imitation tasks by mimicking the sign hand gesture demonstrated. The process is similar to the previous selecting actions but with a more complex and meaningful hand gesture. As the users completed the task, the pop-out window would expand with a clip that shows the hand movement process. The explanation of the sign and the movement is also provided beside the animation. The user then knows the meaning of the selected card.

Then the game narrative will continue until the end of the game. Since each of the interactive plots provides two options, the user needs to play at least two full rounds of the game to learn and unlock all the signs. If any card has been unlocked and learned, it will display the corresponding sign language illustration (see Fig. 4). During the game, besides selecting the cards displayed on the left or right side, the user can also place their hand on the associated objects to trigger pop-out cards for deaf social etiquette.

At the end of game, players can view the currently learned signs in a sign language library (see Fig. 5). Each learned sign can be touched to open the pop-out to help the user review the words.

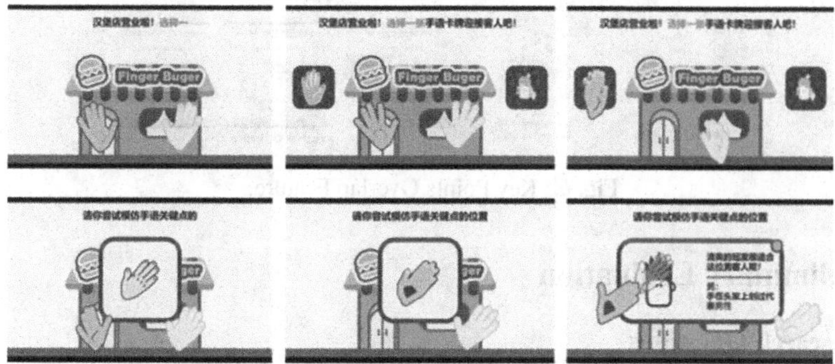

Fig. 4. Screenshots of structured learning steps while the game is running.

Fig. 5. Sign language library after the first round of the game.

3.3 Technical Solution and Key Features

The game was developed using the Unity engine. We used a Key Points Overlap Feature (KPOF) based on the MediaPipe Unity plugi to implement natural interaction rather than train the CSL recognition model because (1) training models require a large number of datasets; and (2) the recognition speed and accuracy of complex sign gestures are relatively lower than expected for a game. We implemented KPOF as a core feature of our game (see Fig. 6). The plugin calls and turns on the camera of the running device during the game play, it captures real-time hand images and retrieves the landmarks information of each hand, storing 21 key points (see Fig. 6). We mapped the landmark position information in Unity to create a dynamic hand model that is displayed on the game screen in real-time (see Fig. 6).

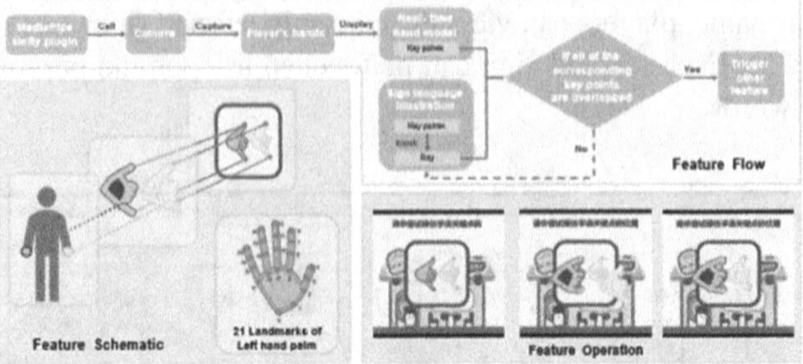

Fig. 6. Key Points Overlap Feature.

4 Preliminary Evaluation

4.1 Research Questions

We conducted a preliminary experiment to explore whether Natural Interaction (NI) provides a better learning outcomes and game experiences compared to the traditional Mouse-Click Interaction (MCI). We chose the within-subject design because the personal characteristics (e.g., prior experience with natural interaction, spatial abilities) may influence the results. Two design versions of the Finger Burger game were selected as the research instruments. We posed the two research questions (RQ):

- **RQ1**: What are the learning gains in sign language and deaf social etiquette in the serious game with natural interaction and with the mouse-click interaction respectively?
- **RQ2**: What are the game experiences in the two conditions?

4.2 Participants

We recruited 12 participants from a university in Beijing, China, through social media platforms. The participants aged 20 to 25 (with an average age of 22.6) had diverse majors. Among them, the majority were female ($n = 9$) while 25% were male ($n = 3$). Academic levels varied, with 25% being graduate students ($n = 3$) and 75% undergraduates ($n = 9$). None of the participants had prior knowledge of CSL and deaf social etiquette to be taught in the game. All participants reported normal hearing. In terms of game habits, 66.7% played sensory games for less than 8 h in the last year ($n = 8$) and 33.3% reported almost never playing ($n = 4$). Almost half ($n = 5$) reported a good spatial imagination level, and the rest ($n = 7$) reported an average level. For hand motor skills, 25% ($n = 3$) reported good, 58% ($n = 7$) reported average, and 16.7% ($n = 2$) reported poor. The study was approved by our university ethical board. We obtained all the written consents from the participants.

4.3 Procedure

We introduced the research project at the beginning of the experiment, informing that a test of sign language learning would be conducted at the end of the experiment. Participants then filled out a personal ability assessment questionnaire to collect their prior knowledge and learning capabilities on sign language and deaf social etiquette. During the experiment, each participant experienced two interaction modes of Finger Burger and the order was counterbalanced. Each participant, accompanied by two facilitators, played with two versions of the games for approximately 30 min in a quiet room. To avoid overlearning effects, participants learned different signs in each condition (learned 9 in the first condition and 6 in the second condition), for a lot of 15 sign languages. Participants were not forced but encouraged to explore the five hidden cards for deaf social etiquette, which were same in the two conditions. A facilitator observed the participants' behaviors during the experiment, while the other facilitator guided the participants and provided necessary assistance as needed. After completing each version, participants were required to fill out a questionnaire about the game experience and answer questions related to signs and deaf social etiquette learned in the version. Each participant received a compensation of CNY15.

4.4 Data Collection and Analysis

We used a self-developed questionnaire to collect participants' personal characteristics related to learning and game experience, including questions about spatial imagination and hand motor ability as well as their prior knowledge on CSL and deaf social etiquette (Appendix 1). During the experiment, two researchers took semi-structured observational notes about participants' behaviors (which were not reported in this study due to the scope of the current research). The entire process was also videotaped. At the end of each condition, we collected participants' accuracy on CSL recognition and making, deaf social etiquette recall accuracy, game experience questionnaire scores. We randomly selected six sign words that the participant had learnt from this condition. The participant needed to answer the meanings of the three random signs displayed on cards (CSL recognition) while making the rest three signs based on their meanings (CSL gesture-making), for a total of 12 CSL tests (6 on CSL recognition tests and 6 gesture-making tests) for the two conditions. Participants also needed complete a multiple-choice question regarding the deaf social etiquette learned from this condition. Game experience data was collected through the In-game GEQ (Game Experience Questionnaire–Core Module) (Appendix 2) [17]. The questionnaire contains 14 questions with 5-point Likert that measure the player's game experience across seven dimensions: Immersion, Flow, Competence, Positive and Negative Affect, Tension, and Challenge.

To answer RQ1, we employed Wilcoxon signed-rank test to assess participants' raw scores on CSL and the social etiquette question between pretest and posttest, as the data violated normality. We further conducted statistical[3] and descriptive analysis (mean $\pm$ SD) to compare the learning gains the between the MCI and NI conditions. We further used descriptive analysis to compare the accuracy percentages of the CSL recognition and gesture-making tests with high-level difficulty between the two conditions. To address RQ2, we analyzed the in-GEQ questionnaire using the descriptive analysis (mean $\pm$ SD and mediation). For both RQ1 and RQ2, we supplemented with parts of the qualitative

[3] We conducted the Wilcoxon signed-rank test to analyze the CSL raw scores and the Mann-Whitney U Test to compare the social etiquette scores based on the data types.

results we observed. The data was analyzed using thematic analysis method by three researchers.

5 Results

5.1 RQ1: Learning Gains in Deaf Culture

The results showed that participants made statistically significant learning gains in deaf culture from pretest to posttest (Table 1). All participants ($n = 12$) demonstrated significant improvement in learning CSL from pretest to posttest, with a median increase of 9.00 out of 12.00, $z = 3.074$, $p < 0.050$. Five participants showed improvements in deaf social etiquette from pretest to posttest, while seven remained the same. The median score increased significantly by 1, from 0 to 1, $z = 2.236$, $p < 0.050$.

We also conducted statistical analysis to compare the pre-post learning gains between the MCI and NI conditions but found no significant differences (Table 2). The descriptive analysis showed that the mean value of CSL was slightly higher in MCI (4.54 ± 1.21) than in the NI condition (4.25 ± 1.39). The learning gain in deaf social etiquette was slightly lower in MCI (0.17 ± 0.41) than in the NI condition (0.67 ± 0.52). However, these differences between the two conditions were not statistically different ($p > 0.05$).

Table 1. Participants' deaf culture learning gains from pretest to posttest.

Variables	Raw scores in pretest (Med)	Raw scores in posttest (Med)	Differences from pretest to posttest	z	p
CSL	0.00	9.00	9.00	3.074	0.002
Social etiquette	0.00	1.00	1.00	2.236	0.025

Table 2. Participants' deaf culture learning gains between the MCI and NI conditions.

Variable	MCI (Mean ± SD)	NI (Mean ± SD)	MCI (Med)	NI (Med)	p
CSL	4.54 ± 1.21	4.25 ± 1.39	4.75	4.50	0.654
Social etiquette	0.17 ± 0.41	0.67 ± 0.52	0.00	1.00	0.180

To further investigate the potential influence of MCI and NI on various difficulty-level of learning tasks, we classified all the learned sign words into three levels of difficulty: *easy*, *medium*, and *hard*. The difficulty of recognition tasks was classified based on the presence of pictorial elements and daily actions in the sign actions. The difficulty of gesture-making tasks was classified based on factors such as changes in angle and position and the combination of two hands. The results showed that each condition had an equal number of the hard tasks ($n = 27$). Interestingly, we found that for the most challenging recognition tasks, the accuracy percentage in the MCI condition (0.55) was

Table 3. Participants' learning gains on CSL recognition and gesture-making tasks with high-level difficulty between the MCI and NI conditions.

Conditions	Task categories	Hard tasks in total	Accurate tasks in total	Accuracy percentages
MCI	Recognition tasks	20	11	0.55
	Gesture-making tasks	7	2	0.29
	A total of CSL tasks	27	13	0.48
NI	Recognition tasks	15	6	0.4
	Gesture-making tasks	12	6	0.5
	A total of CSL tasks	27	12	0.44

slightly higher than that in the NI condition (0.4). However, for the most challenging gesture-making tasks, the accuracy percentage in the NI condition (0.5) was significantly higher than that in the MCI condition (0.29) (Table 3).

We asked participants how they felt about learning sign language with gesture interaction. Three participants responded that the gesture interaction was beneficial for recognizing the angles and spatial positions (front and back) of the hands. However, nearly half ($n = 5$) found figure matching challenging, as it required significant effort to match key points, detracting from their ability to focus on learning content. P8 specifically mentioned, "*The difficulties in the gesture matching tasks affected my memorization*".

5.2 RQ2: Game Experiences

We conducted descriptive and thematic analyses of the In-game GEQ. Compared to the MCI, the NI enhanced participants' feelings of immersion, flow, positive affect, and challenge (Table 4). The results suggested that the NI made a deeper impression on participants and stimulated their interest in continuing to play. One-third of the participants ($n = 4$) expressed their surprise and enjoyment of learning through gesture recognition. Hand involvement appeared to bring a higher level of sensory engagement and achievement. However, it also required more cognitive effort to complete the challenges, with three participants expressing "*It was too hard*" during the experience. On the contrary, the MCI provided participants a stronger sense of control and skillfulness. Regarding the feelings of irritation and frustration, both versions were similar. However, due to the small sample size and narrow scoring intervals, the differences between the two versions were minor and not statistically different.

Table 4. Participants' gaming experiences in MCI and NI conditions.

Variable	MCI (Mean ± SD, Med)		NI (Mean ± SD, Med)	
Immersion	3.08 ± 0.71	3.00	3.17 ± 0.82	3.00
Flow	2.91 ± 0.71	3.00	3.13 ± 0.90	3.00
Competence	3.17 ± 0.87	3.00	3.17 ± 0.82	3.00
Positive affect	3.00 ± 0.72	3.00	3.20 ± 0.72	3.00
Negative affect	1.16 ± 1.13	1.00	1.00 ± 1.25	0.00
Tension	1.33 ± 1.31	1.00	1.33 ± 1.27	1.00
Challenge	2.38 ± 1.21	2.50	2.88 ± 1.16	3.00

6 Discussion and Limitations

Our results showed that our games could significantly improve participants' learning of deaf culture, whenever through NI or MCI. This suggests that serious games incorporating situated learning, animations, and narratives have the potential to enhance users' proficiency in CSL and deaf social etiquette. This can be explained by the situated learning theory, which posits that complex practices are acquired more effectively in environments with clear and supportive social context [18]. This may partially explain why participants in the NI condition performed better in answering social etiquette question compared to that in the MCI condition. For this multiple-choice task, participants only got the score as long as they correctly answered all the five correct options. Although we observed that participants in both conditions tended to spend less attention learning social etiquette compared to learning CSL, it appeared that they could correctly recall all the knowledge points (complex information) with NI compared to with MCI. The results also demonstrated that the traditional MCI design outperformed the NI design in learning CSL. We infer that it may be because most participants were more familiar with traditional interaction, allowing them to focus on their attention and cognition on the learning content. Interestingly, for complex tasks, traditional interaction better supported recognition tasks, while natural interaction offered advantages for gesture-making tasks. This suggests that hands-on and embodied participation is particularly effective for learning complex sign actions.

It is noteworthy that participants in the NI condition had an overall better game experience compared to those in the MCI condition, regardless of whether they were novices or experienced users of natural user interfaces. In fact, the two games shared the same design of narratives, animations, game mechanics (tasks, feedback, points), and user interface layout, differing only in the interaction. The varied questionnaire results suggest the influence of interaction design on the overall game experience. Specifically, NI may enhance immersion, flow, positive affect, tension, and challenge in the game experience compared MCI. In our case, participants in the NI condition had to accurately imitate the hand gestures and match figure points to proceed, resulting in a high level of physical participation (from two-handed action to full-body movement). This mode of interaction led participants to spend almost twice as much time playing compared to the other condition, while consistently rating the overall game experience higher. This suggests that NI can effectively engage users in the game experience, which aligns with previous research, although that research did not specifically focus on educational games [16].

Natural user interfaces may present a learning curve for both novice and experienced users, particularly those with little prior experience. Despite the tutorial at the beginning of the game, several participants still experienced occasional confusion with their interaction gestures and positioning movements, and they were not as relaxed as they were in the MCI condition. We found that this may be attributed to the requirement of performing both hand gestures (manipulations) and body movements (motion) simultaneously, whereas users usually only need to perform one type of behaviours [19]. And the tasks posed challenges for individuals who self-reported relatively poor spatial imagination or fine motor skills. The results suggested that (1) designers should exercise caution when designing interaction that involve both gestures and body movements in NI; and (2) real-time guidance is essential, especially when guiding users in performing both locomotion and fine motor behaviours.

As for the preliminary evaluation, we acknowledged the small sample size for quantitative evaluation, so we supplemented with qualitative findings for explaining the results. Moreover, we utilized KPOF instead of training a gesture recognition model, which may have led participants to focus more on overlaying key points rather than learning CSL. Lastly, the chosen context was a restaurant, which offers limited communication scenarios for deaf individuals. We recognize the importance of expanding learning materials for different contexts through co-design.

7 Conclusions and Future Work

We present the design and a preliminary evaluation of a serious game that utilizes natural interaction, situated learning, animation, and narratives to teach Chinese sign language and deaf social etiquette to both deaf and non-deaf individuals. A within-subject pilot study was conducted with 12 non-deaf young adults to experience our game with two interaction versions: the natural interaction and mouse-clicked interaction versions. The study showed that participants' deaf culture knowledge increased statistically significantly after playing with our games. Natural interactions were more effective in supporting learning complex social etiquette and sign actions. Participants also gained a greater sense of engagement and achievement through natural interaction. Our work contributes to the design knowledge of Chinese sign language learning and provides further support for the use of natural interaction as a digital enhancement in sign language learning to improve students' learning effectiveness and experience. Future directions include improving the system design (e.g., strengthening the gamification) and conducting large-scaled experiments with diverse groups of population, such as individuals of different ages and those with hearing impairments.

Acknowledgments. We thanked all the volunteers who participated in our study. This work was funded by the National Social Science Fund of China under grant [22BG137] and the Beijing Nova Program (Z211100002121160).

Disclosure of Interests. We have no competing interests to declare.

Appendix 1. Questionnaire on Participants' Demographic Information

Ability	Question	Choice Options
Sensing gaming experiences	Have you ever played motion-sensing games?	A. Almost never B. Rarely, less than 8 h in the last year C. Often, more than 8 h in the last year
Spatial imagination	How do you rate your spatial imagination ability? (Can you visualize spatial positional relationships?)	A. Poor B. Average C. Good
Hand motor skills	How do your rate your hand motor skills? (Ability to perform complex movements with hand precision)	A. Poor B. Average C. Good
Prior CSL learning experiences	Have you ever learned or studied sign language?	A. No, I have never learned about it B. Yes, I have some knowledge of sign language C. Yes, I have studied sign language and can use it a little bit
Deaf social etiquette	If you were about to go out to dinner with a deaf friend, which of the following behaviors would you consider appropriate? (A multiple- choice question)	A. Carry a shoulder bag instead of a handbag when you go out B. Remove the vase from the dining table when having a meal C. Sit on the opposite side of the person who is deaf instead of beside him/her during meals D. Keep eye contact with the other person and pay attention to his/her facial expressions during the meal E. If you have trouble communicating, draw on a piece of paper to make your meaning clear F. Attract the other person's attention by raising your hand or tapping their shoulder

Appendix 2. The In-Game GEQ (Game Experience Questionnaire – Core Module)

not at all 0 < >	slightly 1 < >	Moderately 2 < >	fairly 3 < >	extremely 4 < >

1. I was interested in the game's story	8. I felt irritable
2. I felt successful	9. I felt skillful
3. I felt bored	10. I felt completely absorbed
4. I found it impressive	11. I felt content
5. I forgot everything around me	12. I felt challenged
6. I felt frustrated	13. I had to put a lot of effort into it
7. I found it tiresome	14. I felt good

Note. Competence: Items 2 and 9. Sensory and Imaginative Immersion: Items 1 and 4. Flow: Items 5 and 10. Tension: Items 6 and 8. Challenge: Items 12 and 13. Negative affect: Items 3 and 7. Positive affect: Items 11 and 14

References

1. Padden, C.: The deaf community and the culture of deaf people. In: Baker, C., Pattison, R. (eds.), Sign language and the deaf community. Silver Spring: National Association of the Deaf (1980)
2. Quinto-Pozos, D.: Teaching American Sign Language to hearing adult learners. Annu. Rev. Appl. Linguist. **31**, 137–158 (2011). https://doi.org/10.1017/S0267190511000195
3. Herzig, M., Allen, T.E.: Deaf children's engagement with American sign language-English bilingual storybook apps. J. Deaf Stud. Deaf Educ. **28**(1), 53–67 (2022). https://doi.org/10.1093/deafed/enac032
4. Novaliendry, D., Budayawan, K., Auvi, R., Fajri, B.R., Huda, Y.: Design of sign language learning media based on virtual reality. Int. J. Online Biomed. Eng. (iJOE) **19**(16), 111–126 (2023). https://doi.org/10.3991/ijoe.v19i16.44671
5. Pontes, H.P., Furlan, D.J., B., Pinheiro, P. R.: An educational game to teach numbers in Brazilian Sign Language while having fun. Comput. Hum. Behav. **107**, 105825 (2020). https://doi.org/10.1016/j.chb.2018.12.003
6. Ullah, F., AbuAli, N.A., Ullah, A., Ullah, R., Siddiqui, U.A., Siddiqui, A.A.: Fusion-based body-worn IOT sensor platform for gesture recognition of autism spectrum disorder children. Sensors **23**(3), 1672 (2023). https://doi.org/10.3390/s23031672
7. Joy, J., Balakrishnan, K., Sreeraj, M.: SignQuiz: a Quiz based tool for learning fingerspelled signs in Indian Sign Language using ASLR. IEEE Access **7**, 28363–28371 (2019). https://doi.org/10.1109/ACCESS.2019.2901863
8. Mehra, V., Pandey, D.: Assistive technology-based solution for hearing impairment using smartphones. Int. J. Softw. Innovation (IJSI) **10**(1), 1–17 (2022). https://doi.org/10.4018/IJSI.292024
9. Valli, A.: The design of natural interaction. Multimed. Tools Appl. **38**(3), 295–305 (2008). https://doi.org/10.1007/s11042-007-0190-z

10. Köse, H., Uluer, P., Akalın, N., Yorgancı, R., Özkul, A., Ince, G.: The effect of embodiment in sign language tutoring with assistive humanoid robots. Int. J. Soc. Robot. **7**(4), 537–548 (2015). https://doi.org/10.1007/s12369-015-0311-1
11. Hyeon-Jun, K., Baek, S.-W.: Application of wearable gloves for assisted learning of sign language using artificial neural networks. Processes **11**(4), 1065 (2023). https://doi.org/10.3390/pr11041065
12. Rho, E., Chan, K., Varoy, E.J., Giacaman, N.: An experiential learning approach to learning manual communication through a virtual reality environment. IEEE Trans. Learn. Technol. **13**(3), 477–490 (2020). https://doi.org/10.1109/TLT.2020.2988523
13. Morett, L.M.: Lending a hand to signed language acquisition: enactment and iconicity enhance sign recall in hearing adult American Sign language learners. J. Cogn. Psychol. **27**(3), 251–276 (2015). https://doi.org/10.1080/20445911.2014.999684
14. Bangaru, S.S., Wang, C., Zhou, X., Jeon, H.W., Li, Y.: Gesture recognition–based smart training assistant system for construction worker earplug-wearing training. J. Constr. Eng. Manag. **146**(12), 04020144 (2020). https://doi.org/10.1061/(ASCE)CO.1943-7862.0001941
15. Mcgonigal, J.: Reality Is Broken (2011). http://bcsciences.com/subjects/humor-and-entertainment/puzzles-and-games/video-and-electronic-games/B008GAXAM6.html. Accessed 17 Dec 2023
16. Economou, D., Russi, M., Doumanis, I., Mentzelopoulos, M., Bouki, V., Ferguson, J.: Using serious games for learning British Sign Language combining video, enhanced interactivity, and VR technology. JUCS **26**(8), 996–1016 (2020).https://doi.org/10.3897/jucs.2020.053
17. IJsselsteijn, W.A., de Kort, Y.A.W., Poels, K.: The Game Experience Questionnaire. Eindhoven: Technische Universiteit Eindhoven (2013)
18. Gaffney, A.L.H., Kercsmar, S.E.: Students' affective learning in a technologically mediated writing and speaking course: a situated learning perspective. J. Bus. Tech. Commun. **30**(3), 322–351 (2016). https://doi.org/10.1177/1050651916636371
19. Shiratuddin, M.F., Wong, K.W.: Game design considerations when using non-touch based natural user interface. In: Pan, Z., Cheok, A.D., Müller, W., Chang, M., Zhang, M. (eds.) Transactions on Edutainment VIII. LNCS, vol. 7220, pp. 35–45. Springer, Heidelberg (2012). https://doi.org/10.1007/978-3-642-31439-1_4

A Nonlinear Mapping-Based Virtual Touchpad for One-Handed Smartphone Operation

Ryuzo Nakamura and Hiroshi Hosobe(✉)

Faculty of Computer and Information Sciences, Hosei University, Tokyo, Japan
hosobe@acm.org

Abstract. Smartphones with 6-inch or larger screens have become popular. However, such large-screen smartphones are difficult to operate with one hand. Widely used techniques for assisting the user in one-handed operation, such as iPhone's Reachability and Android's one-handed mode, reduce the display areas of screens, which degrades the benefits of large-screen smartphones. In this paper, we propose a virtual touchpad for a large-screen smartphone that uses nonlinear mapping to enable the user to manipulate distant areas as well as to accurately manipulate close areas. We conducted a preliminary experiment to compare eight instances of the proposed virtual touchpad with different mappings and conditions in a target selection task. In addition, we performed experiments to compare the three best instances of the virtual touchpad with conventional normal touchscreen operation and also to evaluate it in web browsing. The results show that the proposed virtual touchpad could reduce the target selection time and largely reduce the strain on the thumb.

Keywords: Smartphone · One-handed operation · Virtual touchpad

1 Introduction

Smartphones with 6-inch or larger screens have become popular. For example, in series of smartphones such as iPhone, Galaxy, and Xperia, models with 6-inch or larger screens are mainstream. Although such large-screen smartphones have the advantage of being able to display a large amount of information, they also have the disadvantage of being difficult to operate with one hand. Therefore, it is hard to comfortably operate a smartphone in situations where one-handed operation is required, such as when carrying a bag with one hand or holding a strap in a train. Widely used techniques for assisting the user in one-handed operation, such as iPhone's Reachability and Android's one-handed mode, reduce the display areas of screens, which degrades the benefits of large-screen smartphones.

In this paper, we propose a virtual touchpad for a large-screen smartphone that uses nonlinear mapping to enable the user to manipulate distant areas as well as to accurately manipulate close areas. The virtual touchpad is displayed in a semi-transparent manner on the dominant-hand side at the bottom of the

M. Kurosu and A. Hashizume (Eds.): HCII 2024, LNCS 14688, pp. 67–78, 2024.
https://doi.org/10.1007/978-3-031-60449-2_5

screen. The user moves a cursor on the screen by sliding the thumb on the virtual touchpad and determines the cursor position by releasing the thumb. We conducted a preliminary experiment to compare eight instances of the proposed virtual touchpad with different mappings and conditions in a target selection task. In addition, we performed experiments to compare the three best instances of the virtual touchpad with conventional normal touchscreen operation and also to evaluate it in web browsing. The results show that the proposed virtual touchpad could reduce the target selection time and largely reduce the strain on the thumb.

The rest of this paper is organized as follows. Section 2 describes previous work related to our method. Section 3 proposes our method, and Sect. 4 gives its implementation. Sections 5, 6, and 7 present the results of the experiments, and Sect. 8 discusses the results. Finally, Sect. 9 provides conclusions and future work.

2 Related Work

Chang et al. [1] divided one-handed pointing techniques for touchscreens into three categories, namely, screen transform, proxy region, and cursor. First, screen transform techniques improve the reachability of targets by transforming the screen space. The widely used iPhone's Reachability and Android's one-handed mode fall into this category. AppLens [6] is another screen transform technique that uses tabular fisheye to simultaneously show multiple applications in different levels of details. Next, proxy region techniques introduce a proxy space for the screen. This category includes ThumbSpace [4,5], which works like an absolute-position touchpad, and TapTap [11], which uses two tapping operations to enable the second tap on a magnified view produced by the first tap. Finally, cursor techniques adopt a pseudo-fingertip like a remote cursor. MagStick [11] uses a cursor that moves in the opposite direction to the thumb movement. Also, researchers have proposed many other techniques in this category including Extensible Cursor [7], BezelSpace and CornerSpace [12], TiltCursor [1], ExtendedThumb [8], Force Cursor and Event Forward Cursor [2], and the hover-based reachability technique [3].

Lai and Hwang [9] experimentally compared three virtual pointing techniques for thumb-based cursor control on smartphones, namely, a virtual touchpad, a virtual joystick, and a virtual direction key. As a result, the virtual touchpad obtained the shortest mean target selection time and received the highest user satisfaction ratings in three out of four categories. However, its mean error rate was nearly 0.6% higher than that of the virtual direction key. As a result, it received a lower rating than the virtual direction key in the accuracy category of user satisfaction.

Poupyrev et al. [10] proposed an interaction technique called Go-Go for manipulating distant objects in a virtual reality space. It is based on the metaphor of being able to freely change the length of a virtual arm, which allows the arm to nonlinearly extend and reach distant objects in the virtual space. If the user operates within a range shorter than a certain distance, the virtual arm moves in the same way as the real arm. However, once a certain distance is exceeded, the virtual arm will extend significantly according to a nonlinear mapping. This makes it possible to seamlessly and directly manipulate objects both near and far.

3 Proposed Method

We propose a virtual touchpad for a large-screen smartphone that uses nonlinear mapping to enable the user to manipulate distant areas as well as to accurately manipulate close areas. Adopting the basic idea behind Go-Go [10], our proposed virtual touchpad uses nonlinear mapping to move a cursor on a smartphone screen. We aim at reducing the error rate compared to the conventional virtual touchpad using linear mapping, which was used in Lai and Hwang's experiment [9]. From the viewpoint of Chang et al.'s categorization [1], our virtual touchpad can be regarded as a cursor technique with emphasis on the use of nonlinear mappings for moving the cursor.

As shown in Fig. 1(a), a semi-transparent virtual touchpad is displayed on the dominant-hand side at the bottom of the screen. The user can move a cursor on the screen by sliding the thumb on the touchpad and determine the cursor position by releasing the thumb, which allows the user to manipulate the entire screen only with the thumb. When the user releases the thumb from the touchpad, a touch event occurs at the cursor position. However, when the user releases the thumb outside the touchpad, no touch event occurs. If the user wants to select an area within the touchpad, normal tapping causes a tap event at the tapped position.

Unlike conventional virtual touchpads, the distance of the cursor movement relative to the distance of the thumb movement follows nonlinear mapping. We consider two specific nonlinear mappings A and B as shown in Fig. 2. Mapping A computes cursor movement distance $f_{\mathrm{A}}(d)$ from a thumb movement distance d with the following formula:

$$f_{\mathrm{A}}(d) = \begin{cases} d & \text{if } d \leq D \\ d + k(d-D) & \text{otherwise,} \end{cases}$$

where D is the distance at which the cursor starts faster movement than the thumb, and k is a certain coefficient between 0 and 1. This is obtained by applying the same formula as Go-Go to our virtual touchpad. Figure 2(a) shows mapping A. Intuitively, the cursor movement is equal to the thumb movement until it reaches D, but it increasingly becomes larger once it exceeds D.

Mapping B computes cursor movement distance $f_{\mathrm{B}}(d)$ with the following formula:

$$f_{\mathrm{B}}(d) = \begin{cases} d & \text{if } d \leq D_1 \\ d + k(d-D_1) & \text{if } D_1 < d \leq (D_1+D_2)/2 \\ d - k(d-D_2) + a & \text{if } (D_1+D_2)/2 < d \leq D_2 \\ d + a & \text{otherwise,} \end{cases}$$

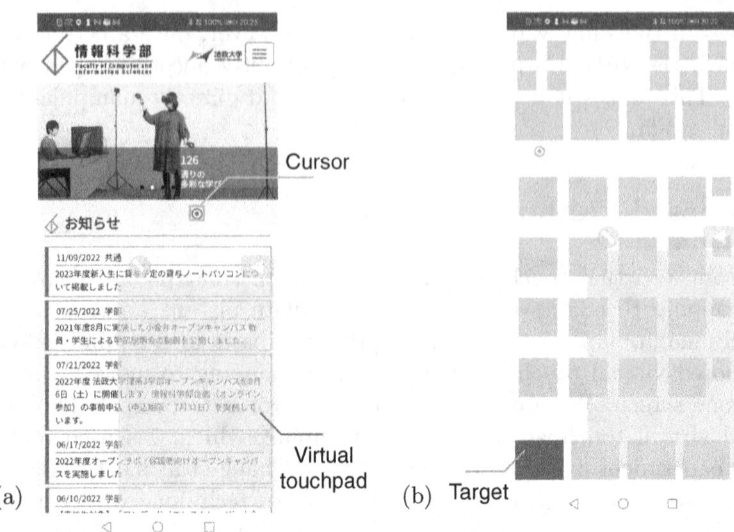

Fig. 1. (a) The proposed virtual touchpad and (b) the application used in the comparative experiment.

where D_1 is the distance at which the cursor starts faster movement than the thumb, D_2 is the distance at which the cursor finishes the faster movement, k is a certain coefficient between 0 and 1, and a is a constant. The constant a is determined in such a way that the quadratic function between D_1 and the midpoint of D_1 and D_2 and the quadratic function between D_2 and the midpoint of D_1 and D_2 have a tangent line at the midpoint of D_1 and D_2, which satisfies the following formula:

$$a = k\left(2\left(\frac{D_1 + D_2}{2}\right)^2 - 2D_1\left(\frac{D_1 + D_2}{2}\right) - 2D_2\left(\frac{D_1 + D_2}{2}\right) + D_1^2 + D_2^2\right).$$

Figure 2(b) shows mapping B. It is similar to mapping A in that, when D_1 is exceeded, the distance of the cursor movement becomes longer than the distance of the thumb movement. However, beyond the midpoint between D_1 and D_2, the distance of the cursor movement gradually approaches the distance of the thumb movement, and once it exceeds D_2, it becomes equal to the distance of the thumb movement again. The coefficient k is larger than that of mapping A, and the rate of increase in the distance of the cursor movement relative to the distance of the thumb movement is larger.

In our experiments on the proposed virtual touchpad, we consider an additional parameter called cursor reset. When the cursor reset is enabled, the cursor is forced to move back to the default position at the time of the thumb's release from the virtual touchpad.

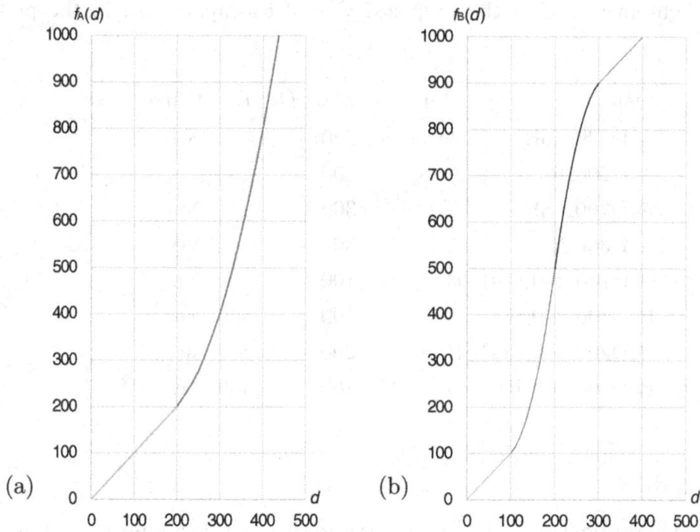

Fig. 2. Nonlinear mappings (a) A and (b) B for the proposed virtual touchpad.

4 Implementation

We implemented the proposed virtual touchpad and the applications used in our experiments in Java on Android Studio. The implemented virtual touchpad operates within these applications. We used Android's WebView to enable the web browsing in these applications. We first developed eight instances of the virtual touchpad and the application for the preliminary experiment that we present in Sect. 5. In addition, we implemented three instances of the virtual touchpad and the applications for the comparative and the user evaluation experiment that we present in Sects. 6 and 7 respectively. We also implemented conventional normal touchscreen operation for comparison. In these applications, the virtual touchpad is displayed at the bottom right of the screen.

5 Preliminary Experiment

We conducted a preliminary experiment to explore appropriate parameters for the distances at which the cursor using one of the two nonlinear mappings starts and finishes faster movement and also to investigate the need to reset the cursor position when the thumb is released. In this experiment, we used eight instances of our virtual touchpad with two patterns of parameters for each of the two nonlinear mappings and with or without the cursor reset as shown in Table 1. To distinguish these instances of the virtual touchpad, we use labels such as A_D200_noR, which indicates that the corresponding instance uses mapping A with $D = 200$ and no cursor reset.

Table 1. Eight instances of the proposed virtual touchpad used in the preliminary experiment.

Instance	Mapping	D or D_1	D_2	Cursor reset
A_D200_noR	A	200	-	No
A_D200_R	A	200	-	Yes
A_D300_noR	A	300	-	No
A_D300_R	A	300	-	Yes
B_D100-300_noR	B	100	300	No
B_D100-300_R	B	100	300	Yes
B_D200-400_noR	B	200	400	No
B_D200-400_R	B	200	400	Yes

5.1 Procedure

We recruited eight participants (six males and two females) who were right-handed and 21.8 years old on average. We used a smartphone HUAWEI P30 lite with a 6.2-inch screen in the experiment. We asked the participants to use the eight instances of the virtual touchpad to select 24 targets displayed evenly on the screen twice each (a total of 48 times) in a specified order. This order was made random and different for each instance of the virtual touchpad to avoid its influence on the selection time. We measured selection times and error rates, and conducted a questionnaire to obtain user evaluations in a five-point Likert scale on four items, i.e., accuracy, simplicity, less strain on the thumb, and overall satisfaction.

5.2 Results

The mean selection times, the mean error rates, and the mean points of the user evaluation are shown in Figs. 3(a), 3(b), and 3(c). The mean selection times were less than 1210 ms for all the instances of our virtual touchpad with cursor reset, and were more than 1300 ms for all the instances with no cursor reset. Similar to the mean selection times, the mean error rates with cursor reset were often lower than those with no cursor reset. In particular, the instances of our virtual touchpad using mapping B and no cursor reset resulted in error rates of over 9%. In most of the items of the user evaluation, the instances with cursor reset obtained higher points than those with no cursor reset. Also, concerning the distance at which the cursor starts faster movement, the instances using 200 for mapping A and the instances using 100 for mapping B obtained better results on the whole.

6 Comparative Experiment

Next, we conducted a comparative experiment to evaluate our proposed method by comparing it with normal touchscreen operation. In this experiment, we used three instances of our virtual touchpad, A_D200_noR, A_D200_R, and B_D100-300_R, which had showed good results in the preliminary experiment.

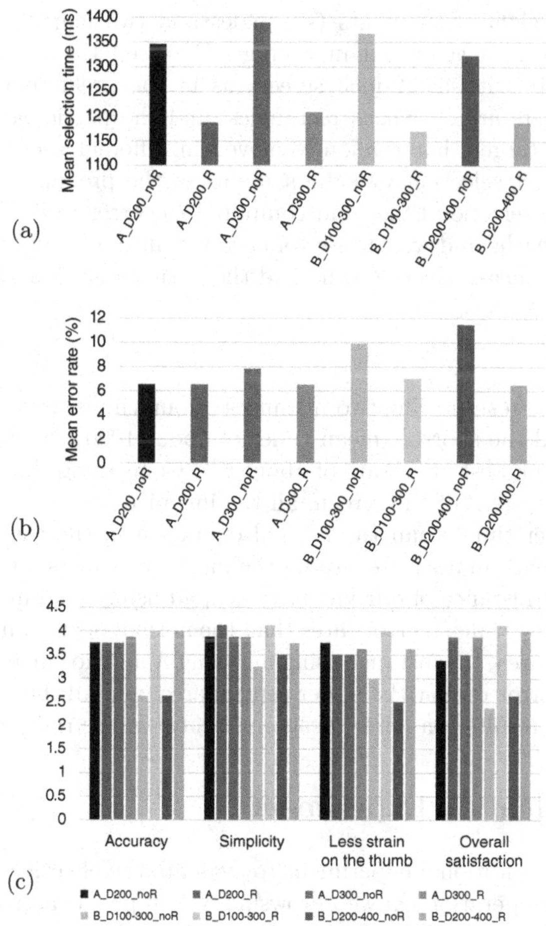

Fig. 3. Results of the preliminary experiment: (a) the mean selection times, (b) the mean error rates, and (c) the mean points of the user evaluation.

6.1 Procedure

For this experiment, we developed an application shown in Fig. 1(b). Although 24 targets were displayed evenly in the preliminary experiment, targets to be selected are not necessarily evenly positioned on the screens of ordinary applications. Many current touch-based user interfaces use areas near the corners and edges of screens [12]. For example, smartphone applications for X (formerly known as Twitter), Instagram, and LINE commonly place multiple small interfaces at the top corners of screens and also put interfaces for screen changes horizontally at the top or bottom of the screens. Also, applications for Instagram and YouTube have a small interface on the right edge of the center of the screens.

We recruited eight participants (six males and two females) who were all right-handed and 22.0 years old in average. We used the same smartphone, HUAWEI P30 lite with a 6.2-inch screen, as in the preliminary experiment. In Fig. 1(b), targets are shown as rectangles, and the participants were asked to select the red target that randomly moved in different areas of the screen. The order of target selection was the same as in the preliminary experiment. We measured the selection times and computed the error rates. In addition, to examine the strengths and weaknesses of each instance of the virtual touchpad, we calculated the mean selection time and the mean error rate for each target.

6.2 Results

Figure 4 shows the results. The two instances of our virtual touchpad with cursor reset obtained the shortest mean times of about 1090 ms while the normal operation had the lowest error rate of about 6%. Concerning the mean selection times for different areas of the screen, all the instances of our virtual touchpad resulted in shorter times than the normal operation in the top left, the right central, and the bottom area. Regarding the mean error rates for different areas of the screen, the instance of our virtual touchpad using mapping B and cursor reset resulted in lower mean error rates than the normal operation in the top left and the top right area, the instance using mapping A and no cursor reset resulted in a lower mean error rate at the upper central area, and all the instances of our virtual touchpad resulted in lower mean error rates at the right central area.

7 User Evaluation Experiment

We conducted an additional experiment to evaluate the effectiveness of our virtual touchpad for operations in web browsing, which people actually perform in daily life. We compared the same three instances of the virtual touchpad with normal touchscreen operation as in the comparative experiment.

7.1 Procedure

We used Android's WebView to display websites inside the application for this experiment. The participants and the used smartphone were the same as in the comparative experiment. The actual screen is shown in Fig. 1(a). We asked the participants to surf the Internet by using the three instances of the virtual touchpad as well as the normal operation. After five minutes of using each technique, we asked them to evaluate it in a five-point Likert scale on the four items, accuracy, simplicity, less strain on the thumb, and overall satisfaction.

7.2 Results

Figure 5 shows the results of the user evaluation. Concerning accuracy, the normal operation, which was familiar to the participants, obtained the highest point

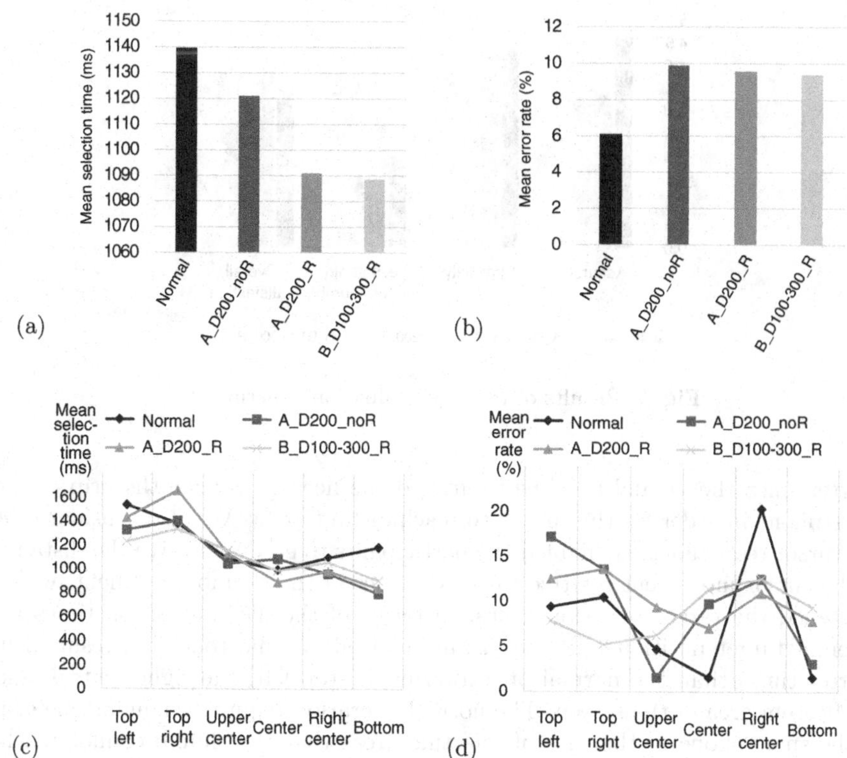

Fig. 4. Results of the comparative experiment: (a) the mean selection times and (b) the mean error rates for the entire areas, and (c) the mean selection times and (d) the mean error rates for different areas.

of over 4.5. However, all the instances of our virtual touchpad resulted in 4 or higher points in terms of less strain on the thumb, which was higher than the normal operation. Regarding overall satisfaction, the instance of our virtual touchpad using mapping B and cursor reset obtained the highest point of 4.2.

8 Discussion

This section discusses the results of the comparative and the user evaluation experiment.

8.1 On the Comparative Experiment

As a result of the comparative experiment, all the instances of our virtual touchpad obtained shorter mean selection times than normal touchscreen operation. In particular, the instances using cursor reset resulted in about 50 ms shorter times than the normal operation. We consider that the selection times became

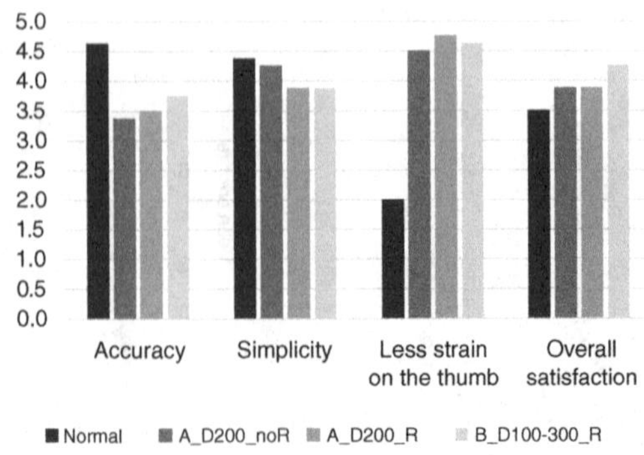

Fig. 5. Results of the user evaluation experiment.

shorter since the virtual touchpad removed the need to change the grip of the smartphone in order for the thumb to reach distant areas. We also consider that the cursor reset function enabled the participants to easily perceive the distance of the cursor movement relative to the distance of the thumb movement, which shortened the target selection times. In terms of the mean selection times for different target positions, all the instances of our virtual touchpad resulted in shorter times than the normal operation in the top left, the right central, and the bottom area of the screen. The normal operation requires changing the grip of the smartphone in the case of selecting areas that the thumb cannot reach. Therefore, we consider that the normal operation resulted in longer times than the virtual touchpad in the case of selecting the edges of the screen.

Concerning the mean error rates, all the virtual touchpad resulted in 9 to 10% while the normal operation achieved about 6%. This is because the normal operation of directly touching the screen made it less likely that the participants would select wrong targets. However, since the instance of our virtual touchpad using mapping B and cursor reset made the cursor behave in the same way as the thumb, it obtained lower mean error rates than the normal operation which often required changing the grip of the smartphone. In addition, since the instance of the virtual touchpad using mapping A and no cursor reset often placed the cursor in the upper area of the screen, it achieved lower error rates than the normal operation in the upper central area of the screen. We consider that the reason why the normal operation resulted in the highest mean error rate in the right central area of the screen was that changing the grip of the smartphone made the target positions hidden by the hand.

8.2 On the User Evaluation Experiment

As a result of the user evaluation experiment, many participants thought that the normal operation was superior in accuracy. However, in terms of less strain on the thumb, the normal operation, which required changing the grip of the smartphone resulted in a low point of 2 while all the instances of the virtual touchpad achieved high points of over 4. In terms of overall satisfaction, the instance of the virtual touchpad using mapping B and cursor reset obtained the highest point of over 4. Many participants found it easy to use because the cursor behaved in the same way as the thumb when they moved it to around the corners of the screen where small targets were placed. Therefore, we consider that it was more highly evaluated than the other two instances of the virtual touchpad that used mapping A.

9 Conclusions and Future Work

In this paper, we proposed a virtual touchpad that used nonlinear mapping to assist one-handed operation of a large-screen smartphone. The results of the experiment on its comparison with normal touchscreen operation indicated that our virtual touchpad had shortened the mean target selection times. Also, our user evaluation experiment showed that it largely reduced strain on the thumb. However, the normal operation obtained better results than all the instances of our virtual touchpad. Among the three instances of the virtual touchpad used in the comparative and the user evaluation experiment, the instance using mapping B and cursor reset achieved the best results.

Our future work includes reducing the error rates of the virtual touchpad. A promising approach will be to design an intelligent virtual touchpad that detects user-selectable targets to automatically attract the cursor when it becomes close to small targets as was done by BezelSpace and CornerSpace [12]. Another future direction is to conduct an experiment by using a smartphone with a larger screen, which might produce different results than the experiments that we conducted in this paper. Another direction is to consider the sizes of users' hands since the difficulty of one-handed smartphone operation may differ depending on the sizes of the hands, which will more clarify the effectiveness of the virtual touchpad for some group of users.

Acknowledgment. This work was partly supported by JSPS KAKENHI Grant Number JP21K11836.

References

1. Chang, Y., L'Yi, S., Koh, K., Seo, J.: Understanding users' touch behavior on large mobile touch-screens and assisted targeting by tilting gesture. In: Proceedings of ACM CHI, pp. 1499–1508 (2015)
2. Hakka, K., Isomoto, T., Shizuki, B.: One-handed interaction technique for single-touch gesture input on large smartphones. In: Proceedings of ACM SUI, pp. 21:1–2 (2019)
3. Ikeda, R., Hakka, K., Shizuki, B.: Hover-based reachability technique for executing single-touch gesture on smartphone. In: Proceedings of AsianCHI, pp. 9–15. ACM (2021)

4. Karlson, A.K., Bederson, B.B.: ThumbSpace: generalized one-handed input for touchscreen-based mobile devices. In: Baranauskas, C., Palanque, P., Abascal, J., Barbosa, S.D.J. (eds.) INTERACT 2007. LNCS, vol. 4662, pp. 324–338. Springer, Heidelberg (2007). https://doi.org/10.1007/978-3-540-74796-3_30
5. Karlson, A.K., Bederson, B.B.: One-handed touchscreen input for legacy applications. In: Proceedings of ACM CHI, pp. 1399–1408 (2008)
6. Karlson, A.K., Bederson, B.B., SanGiovanni, J.: AppLens and LaunchTile: two designs for one-handed thumb use on small devices. In: Proceedings of ACM CHI, pp. 201–210 (2005)
7. Kim, S., Yu, J., Lee, G.: Interaction techniques for unreachable objects on the touchscreen. In: Proceedings of OzCHI, pp. 295–298. ACM (2012)
8. Lai, J., Zhang, D.: ExtendedThumb: a target acquisition approach for one-handed interaction with touch-screen mobile phones. IEEE Trans. Hum. Mach. Syst. **45**(3) (2015)
9. Lai, Y.R., Philip Hwang, T.K.: Virtual touchpad for cursor control of touchscreen thumb operation in the mobile context. In: Marcus, A. (ed.) DUXU 2015. LNCS, vol. 9187, pp. 563–574. Springer, Cham (2015). https://doi.org/10.1007/978-3-319-20898-5_54
10. Poupyrev, I., Billinghurst, M., Weghorst, S., Ichikawa, T.: The Go-Go interaction technique: non-linear mapping for direct manipulation in VR. In: Proceedings of ACM UIST, pp. 79–80 (1996)
11. Roudaut, A., Huot, S., Lecolinet, E.: TapTap and MagStick: improving one-handed target acquisition on small touch-screens. In: Proceedings of AVI, pp. 146–153. ACM (2008)
12. Yu, N.H., Huang, D.Y., Hsu, J.J., Hung, Y.P.: Rapid selection of hard-to-access targets by thumb on mobile touch-screens. In: Proceedings of MobileHCI, pp. 400–403. ACM (2013)

Simple Wearable Vibration Device for Music Appreciation

Miyu Namba(✉) and Yumi Wakita

Osaka Institute of Technology, Osaka, Japan
m1m23r29@st.oit.ac.jp, yumi.wakita@oit.ac.jp

Abstract. To enjoy the same musical sounds as live performances at home, we are developing a music sound reproduction system with the wearable vibration device that can be worn easily as a means of experiencing live sounds. The unique features of our vibration device are extracting the rhythm of the drum section and reproduce vibrations synchronized with the rhythm, and designing the device so that it can be worn at only one place on the body and still provide a realism sense. In this paper, we report on the superiority of the above two features compared to conventional specifications using a music playback system with a vibration device under development. In addition, the effect on the realism sense when gradually decaying vibration is applied as a vibration specification will be discussed.

Keywords: Vibration device for music appreciation · Rhythm of drum section · Simple device · Realism sense

1 Introduction

The COVID-19 pandemic has increased the number of people who want to experience the same sound quality as that of a live performance at home. Because it is difficult to play loud music through speakers in the limited space of a home, headphones and earphones that can reproduce a high realism sense have become increasingly popular. However, many people feel that they cannot sufficiently replicate the realism of a live concert venue. Specifically, consumers have been complaining that headphones and earphones cannot reproduce the sense of presence provided by an entire venue echoing with the rhythm. The perception of the actual loudness experience does not solely depend on hearing. For music with a clear rhythm, people are particularly stimulated by the sense of touch (vibration), which is the most important sense in perceiving sound other than hearing. Therefore, we would like to pursue the possibility of supplementing the realism sense by utilizing vibration devices.

Several music reproduction systems have been proposed to achieve a sense of presence effect using vibration devices along with sound reproduction. Ref. [1] reported that the realism sense can be increased by integrating tactile information with a multi-speaker presence reproduction technique. They reported that this increased the realism sense by adding tactile and kinesthetic information that matched what was seen or heard. However, this system is cumbersome to install at home because it uses a considerable

M. Kurosu and A. Hashizume (Eds.): HCII 2024, LNCS 14688, pp. 79–88, 2024.
https://doi.org/10.1007/978-3-031-60449-2_6

number of multi-speakers (up to 24 channels) and actuators installed on the floor of the viewing area to reproduce vibrations synchronized with the bass sound. Music reproduction methods that complement the realistic sense with tactile information have also been proposed, such as "Body Sonic," a chair-type vibration device [2] that extends the sensation of listening to music, and wearable vibration devices [3] that attach vibration devices to multiple positions on the neck, chest, and back of the human body. The results of using these vibration devices have confirmed that the realistic sense could be enhanced by vibration stimuli in accordance with the music and low frequency range. However, when enjoying music at home, people often listen to music while doing other tasks in an environment where they can move their arms and legs relatively freely, such as searching for information on a smartphone or reading a book. Devices that cannot be moved freely or take time to put on would be considered inconvenient for a comfortable stay in one's room.

With the same purpose as ours, a simple system with vibration devices attached to two locations on the torso and neck has been proposed, confirming the improved realism effect [4]. However, this system comprised a device with vibration devices attached to two locations on the body, which we believe would be an issue owing to the lack of freedom when wearing the device. We propose a device that is attached to a single location on the human body to ensure ease of use and freedom of movement.

2 Simple Vibration Device for Music Appreciation

2.1 Vibration Timing

First, sound source separation was performed on the music piece using "Spleeter [5]," which is a tool available on GitHub that can isolate vocal, drum, and bass sounds from a mixed signal of multiple instruments using deep learning. Subsequently, the isolated drum sound is passed through a low-pass filter (LPF), with a cutoff frequency of 500 Hz, to extract only the bass drum sound. The rhythm of the bass drum was expressed by vibration during the time period when the extracted bass drum volume was above a threshold value and stopped the vibration during the time period when the volume was below the threshold value.

Figure 1 shows the original sound source waveform (upper row) and sound power (lower row) before sound source separation; Fig. 2 shows the waveform and sound power of the drum part sound source after sound source separation and LPF processing.

The horizontal and vertical axes in each figure indicate time(sec.) and sound power level(dB).

2.2 Mounting Position of the Vibration Device

Some studies exploring the body regions that are sensitive to vibration have been reported in the past. For example, the intensities of vibrations perceived in different parts of the body differ, with the xiphoid process and ribs being more sensitive than the shoulders and scapula [6]. Other studies have reported that the chest was the most sensitive to vibration transmission in the human body [7]. Considering the ease of wearing the

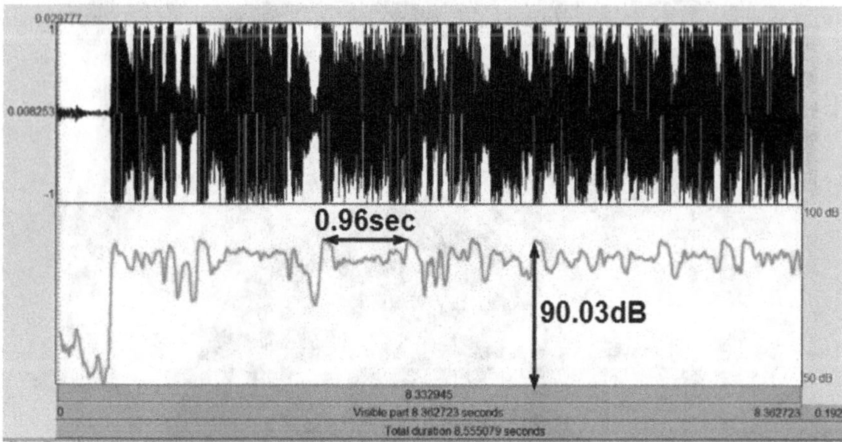

Fig. 1. Original sound source waveform (upper row) and sound power (lower row) before sound source separation.

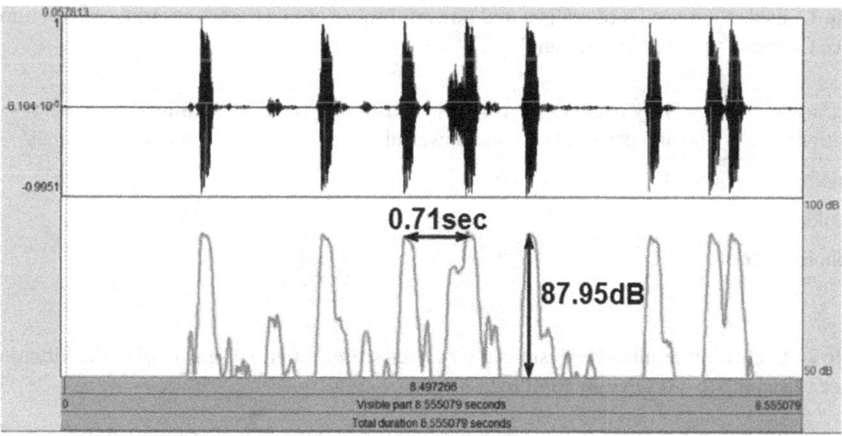

Fig. 2. Extracted drum waveform (upper row) and sound power (lower row) via sound source separation and LPF process.

device, we selected the xiphoid process of the body and shoulder as candidates for the wearing position and compared the realistic sense when listening to music with the device worn at each position (Fig. 3).

We selected two songs ("BOY by Treasure", "ALONE by My First Story") with relatively clear bass drum rhythms. We observed the differences between in music sensation with respect to the device wearing location, namely, on the shoulder and attached to the xiphoid process. The participants also listened to the music without the vibration device and evaluated the realism and power of the music under these three conditions using a 5-point rating scale. The evaluation results collected from nine participants are reported in Tables 1, 2 and 3.

Fig. 3. Experimental setup of the vibration device when it is attached to the shoulder and xiphoid process.

Table 1. Evaluation results of realism and powerful sense of musicwhen wearing the vibration device (listening to "BOY by Treasure").

Wearing Position	Very realistic and powerful	Slightly realistic and powerful	Neither	Slightly weak	Very weak
None	0	0	2	4	3
Shoulder	2	4	1	2	0
Xiphoid process	5	2	1	1	0

Table 2. Evaluation results of realism and powerful sense of musicwhen wearing the vibration device (listening to "ALONE by My First Story").

Wearing position	Very realistic and powerful	Slightly realistic and powerful	Neither	Slightly weak	Very weak
None	0	2	4	1	2
Shoulder	3	2	2	2	0
Xiphoid process	4	4	0	1	0

2.3 Effects of Expressing the Rhythm with Vibration Devices on Sense of Realism

We assume that an important condition for achieving a sense of presence is that the vibration device being synchronized with the rhythm of the drums. To confirm the validity of this assumption, we conducted a listening experiment assessing whether the sense of presence is felt more when the intensity of vibration is adjusted to match only the loudness of the musical sound or when the vibration device is synchronized with the

Table 3. Results for the vibration location that felt the most realistic for each song

	Sholder is very good	Sholder is good	Neither	Xiphoid process is good	Xiphoid process is very good
BOY	3	1	0	3	2
ALONE	1	0	0	2	6

rhythm of the drums. The listeners wore the vibration device on their xiphoid process. The song "Haegeum" was selected from the album D-DAY, which has a 128 BPM.

The following three vibration specifications, A to C, were used to compare which vibration provided the most realistic sensation.

A: Vibration in accordance with the rhythm of the bass drum.

B: Vibration in accordance with the volume of the sound.

C: Sound source only (no vibration).

Nine listeners were asked to listen to the music in all three specifications A–C and rate which they felt the most realistic and which they preferred using a 5-point rating scale. Scheffe's pairwise comparison method was used to clarify the superiority of each specification (Fig. 4).

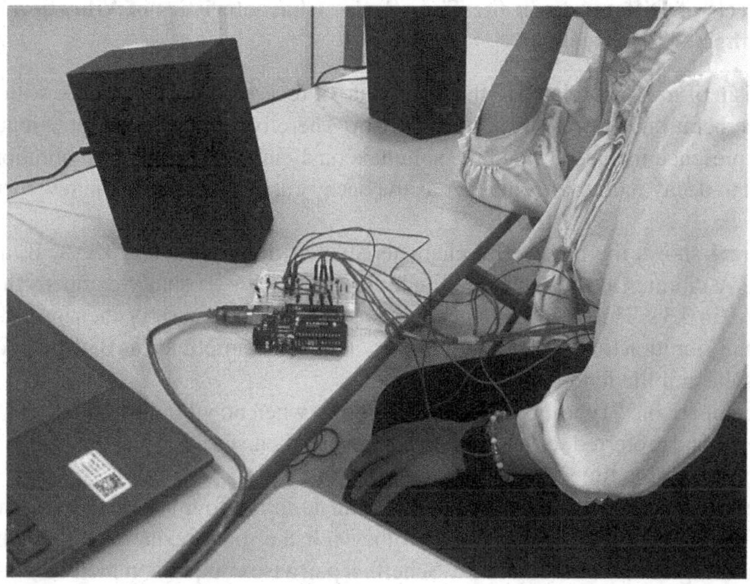

Fig. 4. Experimental setup when the vibration device was attached to the xiphoid process.

The results shown in Figs. 5 and 6 depict that the proposed method of providing vibration in sync with the rhythm of the drum is perceived more realistic by the participants than the conventional method of varying the intensity of the vibration with respect to the loudness of the sound. Furthermore, an overwhelming majority of participants

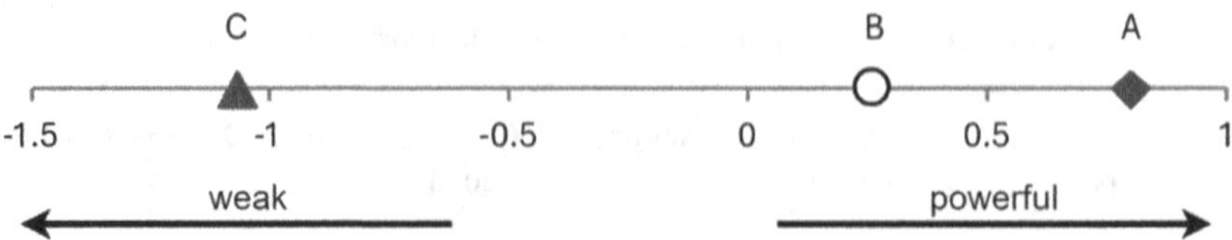

Fig. 5. Evaluation result regarding the degree of realism, comparing the 3 vibration specifications using Scheffe's pairwise comparison method.

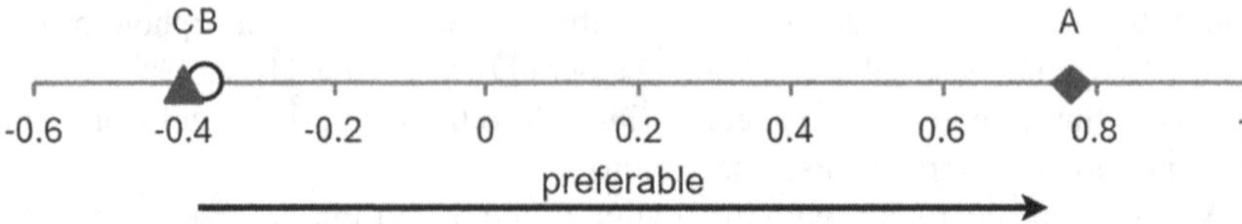

Fig. 6. Evaluation result regarding the preference degree, comparing the 3 vibration specifications using Scheffe's pairwise comparison method.

preferred the former method. The conventional method was perceived as realistic in some cases but was not preferred by many listeners.

2.4 Effects of Differences in the Time-Series Characteristics of Vibration on the Sense of Realism

The realism of music is related to the magnitude of reverberation, and music with moderate reverberation is necessary to feel realism. Therefore, we assessed how much the sense of presence increased when the simultaneously utilized exogenous vibration was specified to decay in the same manner as the decay curve observed in the reverberation sound.

Figure 7 shows the time series characteristics of the vibration types A, B, and C. The type-A vibrates at the same amplitude for 0.3 s, then gradually dampens the amplitude to 0 in 0.3 s. The type-B vibrates at the same amplitude for 0.6 s, then immediately reduces the vibration to 0. The type-C vibrates at the same amplitude as B, then gradually dampens the amplitude to 0 in 0.3 s.

For comparison, "Type-E" was added to signify when no vibration device was worn, and realistic and preferred sensation were compared when vibration was controlled based on the four vibration time series characteristics.

Nine listeners were asked to listen to the music in the four specifications, namely, types of A, B, C, and E, and rate which they felt the most realistic and which they preferred using a 5-point rating scale. Scheffe's pairwise comparison method was used to assess the performance of each specification.

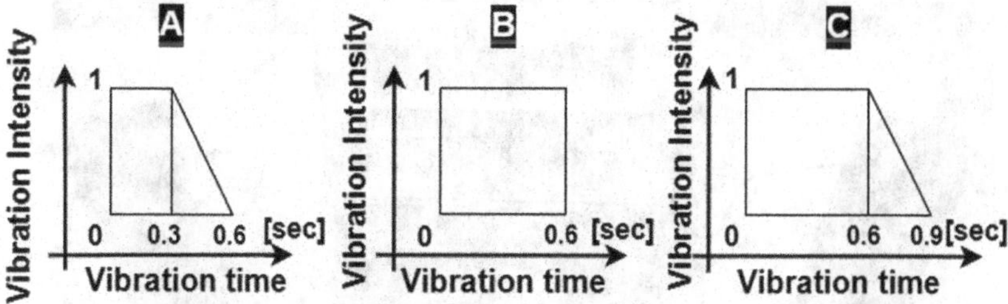

Fig. 7. Time series characteristics of the three vibration types.

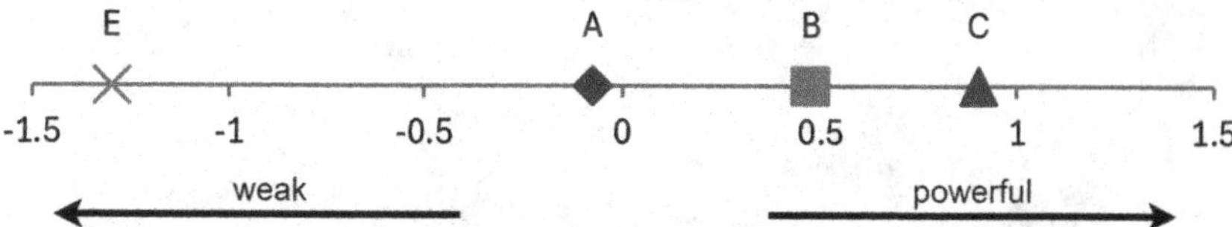

Fig. 8. Evaluation result regarding the realism and powerful degree, comparing the 4 vibration specifications using Scheffe's pairwise comparison method.

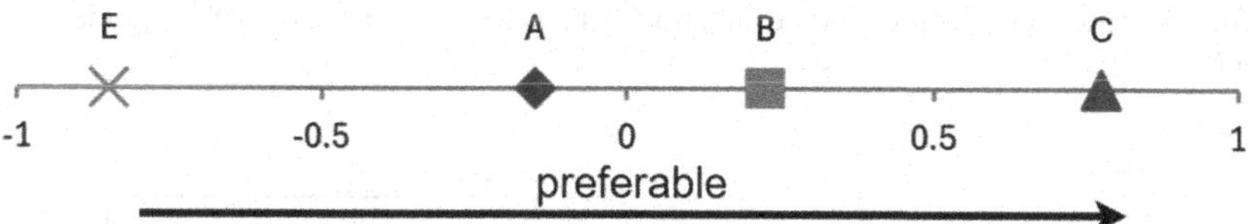

Fig. 9. Evaluation result regarding the preference degree, comparing the 4 vibration specifications using Scheffe's pairwise comparison method.

Figures 8 and 9 show the evaluation results: Comparing the four vibration characteristics, the scores for both realism and preference were the best when C was implemented. The results were improved when a damping was applied after the peak vibration compared to when the vibration ceased after 0.6 s. However, this experiment alone may indicate that the longer the vibration duration is, the more realistic and pleasing it is. To confirm the superiority of damped vibration, it is necessary to compare the results with those of longer vibration duration, which will be investigated in the future.

3 Development of Musical Sound Reproduction System with the Vibration Device

Figure 10 shows the outline of the music sound reproduction system with the vibration device at the current development stage; Fig. 11 shows the operation process of the system up to the reproduction of musical sounds. The system under development uses a PC to extract drum rhythms and generates vibration signals from the extracted rhythms. When the playback button is pressed, the sound source is played from the speaker and the vibrator vibrates in response.

Fig. 10. Musical sound reproduction evaluation system with the vibration device (under development),

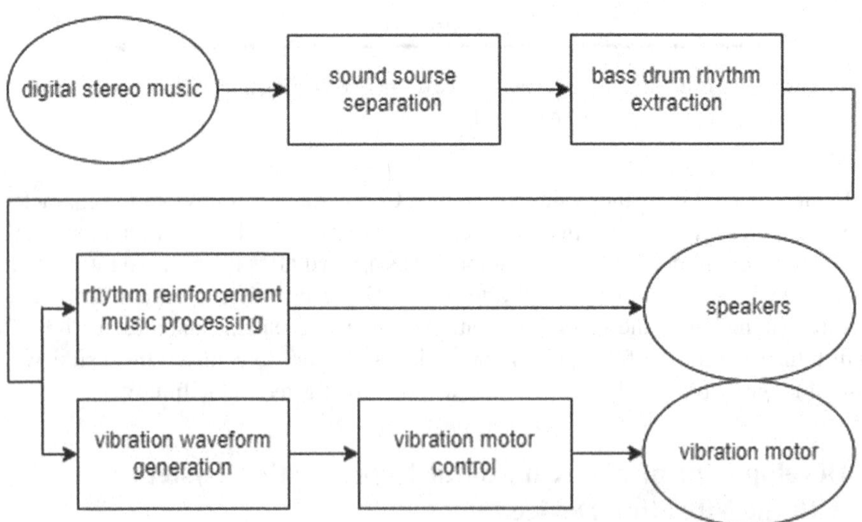

Fig. 11. Process of musical sound reproduction with the vibration device.

4 Conclusion

In this study, we focused on the sense of touch, which is crucial in perceiving sound, and developed a vibration device to mimic the realism of a live performance, which cannot be reproduced by headphones or speakers alone. The user wears the vibration device and listens to music while being provided with an exogenous vibration stimulus. Assuming that the device would be used in the user's room at home, it should be small and simple enough to be worn easily. Even if the device is simple and compact, it is necessary to devise the device and vibration specifications so that the listener can feel a sense of immersion.

Therefore, we experimentally confirmed the effects of the following two aspects: (1) The vibration should be synchronized with the drum rhythm so that it can reinforce the rhythm, (2) The vibration should be generated with respect to a certain specification such that the amplitude to would decay after a certain vibration duration to reproduce the vibrations received at a live concert venue. To further simplify the wearing of the device, we used a specification in which the vibration device is attached to only one location and identified the location where a sense of immersion can be obtained even when the device is attached to only one location.

A sound source separation software and low-pass filter were used to ensure that the drum sound could be isolated from the music; subsequently, the rhythm of the drum sound was extracted by determining the magnitude of the waveform obtained. Comparing the case where the music was vibrated synchronized with the extracted drum sound to the case where only the loudest part of the music was vibrated, as in the conventional method, it was found that the former yielded a more realistic sensation. Moreover, it was confirmed that among the body parts a realistic sense was felt the most when the vibrating device was attached to the xiphoid process.

To obtain more realistic vibrations, we proposed a vibration specification in which the amplitude decays over time. Experimental results showed that vibrations with gradually decreasing amplitude were perceived as more realistic compared to vibrations with suddenly decreasing amplitude after a certain period of time. However, this may not be solely because of damped vibration but could also be caused by the longer vibration duration. This is because the longer the vibration is, the more realistic it tends to feel. This point needs to be investigated further in the future using various songs.

References

1. Woszczyk, W., et al.: Shake, rattle and roll: getting immersed in multisensory, interactive music via broadband networks. J. Audio Eng. Soc. **53**, 4 (2005)
2. About the Body Listening Concert and Body Sonic. https://jpn.pioneer/ja/corp/sustainability/karadadekikou/about/(2023). Accessed 14 Feb 2024
3. Hashizume, S., Sakamoto, S., Suzuki, K., Ochiai, Y.: LIVEJACKET: Wearable Music Experience Device with Multiple Speakers. In: Streitz, N., Konomi, S. (eds.) DAPI 2018. LNCS, vol. 10921, pp. 359–371. Springer, Cham (2018). https://doi.org/10.1007/978-3-319-91125-0_30

4. Yonezawa, T., Yanagi, S., Yoshida, N., Ishikawa, Y.: Accelerating the physical experience of immersive and penetrating music using vibration-motor array in a wearable belt set. In: 15th International Conference on Entertainment Computing (ICEC), Wien, Austria, pp. 173–186 (2016)
5. GitHub homepage. https://github.com/deezer/spleeter/wiki/2.-Getting-started#using-5stems-model. Accessed 14 Feb 2024
6. Hirai, N., Igarashi, H.: Study of sensitivity and propagation of bass sound vibration on human torso. In: Special Issue of Japanese Society for the Science of Design 62nd, pp. 70–71 (2015)
7. Yamada, S., Watanabe, T., Kosaka, T.: Sensory organs of low frequency noise. J. INCE Jpn. **7**(5), 282–284 (1983)

Perception-Driven Design Approach: Towards Interaction Design for Simulating and Evoking Tactile Properties via Digital Interfaces

Marina Ricci, Alessandra Scarcelli, Piera Losciale, and Annalisa Di Roma(✉)

Department of Architecture, Construction and Design, Polytechnic University of Bari, Bari, Italy
annalisa.diroma@poliba.it

Abstract. Nowadays, digital and virtual user experiences lack of multisensory feedback necessary to assess product and material properties. Scientific literature related to haptic interface technology to address this issue is still limited and mostly employs a simulation-type approach. Yet, there are a few studies using and combining sensory modalities, such as visual and auditory stimuli. On the one hand, this research provides a literature framework with respect to interaction with digital and virtual materials, analyzing relevant case studies and providing guidelines for designing the interaction. On the other hand, we conceptualize a cross-modal approach, i.e., Perception-Driven Design, by exploiting two human senses - vision and hearing - in order to provide HCI researchers and interaction designers a novel approach not only to "simulate" but also "evoke" the actual tactile feedback related to the material properties. These interfaces would allow users to interact with displayed material subjected to deformation based on the gesture the user performs and producing visual feedback. Additionally, audio feedback could be recorded or synthetized in real-time, by exploiting simulated sounds of real materials or evocative sounds, in combination to the visual material deformation. The research objective is to develop a design approach for future researchers in the field of interaction, useful for designing digital and virtual interfaces valuable in all fields that highly rely on tactile perception as their pillar (e. g., fashion, furniture, automotive).

Keywords: Touch · Cross-Modality · Perception · Interaction Design · Materials Experience

1 Introduction

The lack of multisensory feedback necessary to assess product and material properties in digital user experiences is a relevant and open problem in the field of HCI [1–3]. Indeed, human perception of objects is a function of both their appearance and the sounds they make [4]. For example, when listening to an audio clip of objects interacting with each other, people can extract rich information about their texture, smoothness, and number of objects [5]. Furthermore, although visual information provides cues for some of these questions, others can only be assessed with sound.

M. Kurosu and A. Hashizume (Eds.): HCII 2024, LNCS 14688, pp. 89–101, 2024.
https://doi.org/10.1007/978-3-031-60449-2_7

In the existing literature, most of the approaches used to convey the tactile sensations of materials are of the "simulative" type [6]. The simulative dimension specifically concerns the transmission of the tactile properties of materials from a *sensory* perspective, simulating the real ones through an illusion [7]. However, materials tactile experience is not only a sensory experience but also an affective one [8].

Thus, starting from the knowledge about different models of human perception, cognition, and action - Interacting Cognitive Subsystems [9] and Bayesian Multimodal Cue Integration [10] - and pseudo-haptics theories [11], this research develops a Perception-Driven Design (PDD) approach. This cross-modal approach integrates two human senses (i.e., vision and hearing), in order to design interfaces with the aim of conveying material tactile properties.

Indeed, the sensory and affective responses associated with touching an object can have a profound impact on human perception [12–14]. Therefore, our goal is to explore the affective experience of materials not only with a simulative-type approach but by proposing also "evocative" experiences. Evocation, as opposed to simulation, which is based on purely sensory and psychophysical stimuli, is very much related to the emotional interpretation of cues, mediated by our experience and memory. By exploiting this approach, users can touch the displayed material while the digital image has a deformation according to the mechanical property of the material, depending on the gesture applied and generating visual feedback. Additionally, audio feedback is synthetized in real-time to simulate or evoke specific properties.

The remaining paper is structured in four sections. The first describes the state-of the-art about material tactile perception, focusing on existing literature and classifying relevant case studies by analysing them. The second describes the methods behind our approach. The third presents the discussion about our methodology, by focusing on the implementation of both visual and auditory feedback. Lastly, we report our conclusions.

2 Related Works

The sense of touch represents an essential part of our daily lives. As humans, we rely on touch to explore and interact with the world around us, enabling us to gather information, make judgments, and form emotional connections [15]. Information from the haptic system is linked to the sensory, motor, and cognitive mechanics of the nervous system, which connects the brain to the hand [16]. The motor skills of the hand in the form of "exploratory procedures," also called movement patterns, are used to extract object-specific properties, such as surface texture or hardness [17].

Indeed, when evaluating materials and products, users use multiple senses, including not only touch, but also vision, hearing and even smell, as indicated by Fiore [18]. Although the perception of materials incorporates several sensory modalities, visual and tactile sensations are predominantly influential. That is, users "view" and "feel" materials, as stated by Burns et al. [19].

Enriching touchscreens with haptic content belong to the "surface haptics" domain [20]. However, although haptic interface technology has advanced tremendously over the past decades, at this moment it cannot accurately simulate the haptic experience of material yet.

In this paper, we report a series of relevant case studies, selected from the literature, related to material experience and interactions with different types of materials (e. g., fabrics, skin, pets, etc.). We analysed the case studies with respect to several categories, useful for developing our approach. The categories we formulated are, in the following order (Table 1):

- **Interaction metaphor**, i.e., cognitive models for interaction that can profoundly influence the design of interfaces to data spaces, such as animated cursor or projected virtual hand.
- **Texture** indicates the material support that users had to interact with, in order to perceive its tactile properties, such as 2D images, virtual textures and pre-recorded videos.
- **Tool** refers to the interaction medium between the user and interface, such as the finger (for hand-held displays) and the mouse cursor (for the desktop displays).
- **Gestures** includes the exploratory procedures users must adopt to interact with the interface and perceive the properties.
- **Properties** refers to the tactile properties that are conveyed through the interface.
- **Display** includes the different types of displays where users can experience the interfaces, such as desktop displays, hand-held displays, and head-mounted displays.

After a preliminary analysis, we observed that most of the studies exploit only visual feedback for simulating tactile properties. Also, all the studies are of a simulative type rather than evocative. Argelaguet et al. [21] developed "elastic images", where interaction occurs with a mouse, by clicking on the elastic image that deforms locally by giving a sensation of stiffness, according to the elastic properties of the texture in the image (Fig. 1). The elasticity sensation is generated by a procedural image deformation algorithm which modifies the image simulating the properties of the texture basing on the Hooke's law, depending on the pressure exerted by the user through the button of the mouse. When the user releases the mouse button, the image returns in its original state. The deformation of the image is generated by a displacement of the pixels towards the mouse cursor creating a small animation at pixel level. To reinforce the user pressure, the cursor varies its size in proportion to the time pressure, recreating a metaphor of the touching gesture, combined to a changing of colour of the cursor. The strength is that the realism of the texture rendering, and deformation applied is high, since it consists of real textiles being deformed during a real hand-fabric interaction. The weakness is that the desktop-based interaction could reduce the freedom of hand interaction with the elastic images.

Punpongsanon et al. (2015) [22] introduced SoftAR, an innovative spatial augmented reality (AR) method founded on a pseudo-haptic mechanism (Fig. 2). This mechanism visually alters the perceived softness experienced by a user interacting with a soft physical object. Softness adjustment enables users to modify the softness parameter of a physical object, while softness transfer enables users to substitute the softness parameter of a physical object. Also, they implemented a prototype system to demonstrate potential applications and evaluated how accurately the system can manipulate a user's perception of softness for each user scenario.

Orzechowski (2016) [23] designed iShoogle, a fabric simulation system with a multi-gesture touchscreen and sound capabilities to faithfully replicate fabric characteristics,

Table 1. Case studies categorisation with respect to interaction design.

authors, year	project	interaction metaphor	texture	tool	gestures	properties	display
Argelaguet et al. (2013)	Elastic Images I	Animated cursor of a pointing hand	2D image	cursor	Push	local elasticity	desktop displays
Punponsanon et al. (2015)	SoftAR	two projection visual effects: surface deformation and body appearance effects	real objects under projections	finger	Push	softness	spatial augmented reality
Orzechowski et al. (2016)	iShoogle	real gestures of real life instead of a metaphor	pre-recorded video	finger	stroke, turn, scrunch, hug, pinch	crispness, hardness, softness, texture, flexibility, furryness, roughness, smoothness	Iphone, Ipad
Fleureau et al. (2016)	Elastic images II	circular shadow under the user's finger according to the contact area and rubbing motions	pictures of real fabrics	finger	stroke, push, rub	friction	tablet
Geometrieva (2016)	I Love Fur	animation that moves the texture	cartoon style fur	finger	stroke	furryness	Iphone, Ipad
Costes et al. (2019)	Touchy	symbolic cursor under the user's finger through changes in its shape and motion	virtual texture	finger	push, stick and slide, displace, size, and encase	hardness, friction, fine roughness, macro roughness	tablet
Sato et al. (2020)	Projected Virtual Hand Interface	projected virtual hand by moving the right real hand on the panel	virtual texture	virtual hand	stroke, push	unevenness, slipperiness, softness	touch panel (and projector)
Connie (2021)	Interactive Soft Tissue simulation	medical tool interaction with a fragment of skin fragment responsive to touching and cutting	virtual skin	medical tool	stick, (2) scalpel	stickiness	desktop displays

eliminating the necessity of physically interacting with fabrics (Fig. 3). This fabric simulator employs on-screen gestures inspired by natural fabric movements, such as crunching, to govern pre-recorded videos and fabric deformation sounds, simulating actions like crunching. iShoogle effectively conveys the impression of directly manipulating both the displayed fabric and associated videos, providing a comprehensive fabric representation experience.

Fleaureau et al. [24] developed an application exploiting texture-haptic rendering system based on visual and audio pseudo-haptic feedback (Fig. 4). It consists of an interactive interface on a tactile screen that rendered a material image deforming to user's touches of pressure and rubbing. This method improves the typology of elastic images proposed firstly by Argelaguet [21] that was limited to punctual pressure contact with a mouse device. Differently by Argelaguet [21], the texture image is not considered as a 2D deformable object by a 3D grid where each node is associated with one pixel of the image. During sliding or rubbing interactions, this grid is continuously updated. In order to create shadows to increase the realism of the simulation, a light source has been included. The strength is that rendered texture are realistic because real material images were employed. The pressure is distributed on the whole contact surface according to the contact area with the finger and rubbing motions. Also, the intensity of friction sound depends on the speed of the finger. Sometimes, also the deformation does not seem realistic, especially for not elastic materials. In addition, the region next to the contact area, has not a realistic control of shadows and deformation shape.

Another relevant case study is "I love fur" is an iOS game where it is possible to pet different kinds of cartoonish pets that happen to have different furs and sensibilities, designed in 2016 by Nina Geometrieva (Fig. 5). The interesting aspect of this application is the perceived sensation that these cartoonish textures cause in those who stroke them. In fact, the developers' goal is to produce positive emotions in the user who interacts with these "digital animals" with their fingers.

Costes et al. [25] designed Touchy, an application based on an interactive interface for touchscreen devices (Fig. 6). Touchy exploits an interaction method that expresses a variety of haptic features through the alteration of the motion or the shape of a cursor co-localized with the user's finger. By changing, the cursor tries to evoke various haptic properties. The properties in analysis are hardness, friction, fine roughness, and macro roughness. The roughness is conveyed through vibration, the stiffness by stretches, dilatation and compression of the cursor immediately under the user's finger. The cursor is a white circle two times larger than a finger.

Fig. 1. Elastic Images I

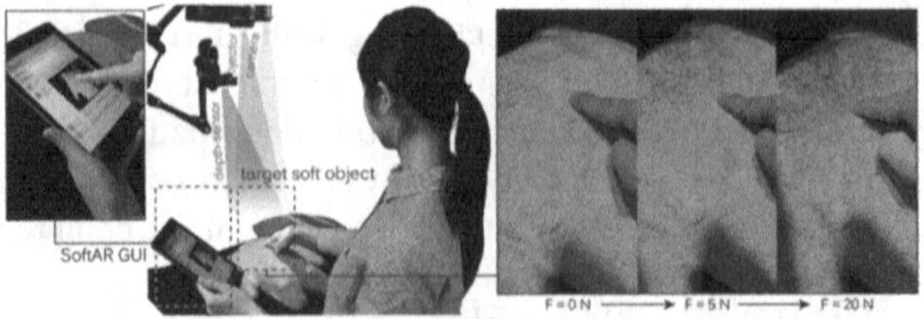

Fig. 2. SoftAR

Fig. 3. iShoogle

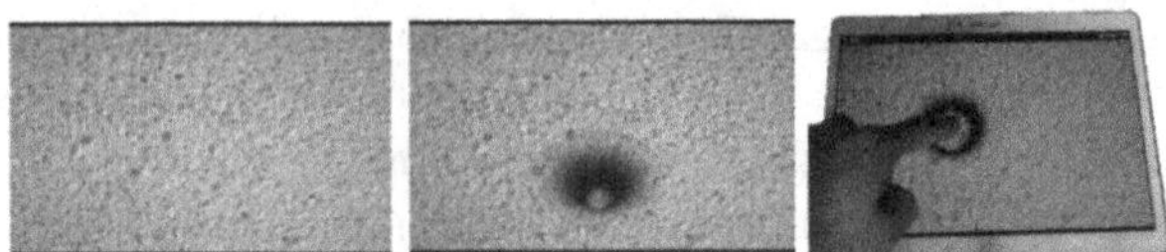

Fig. 4. Elastic Images II

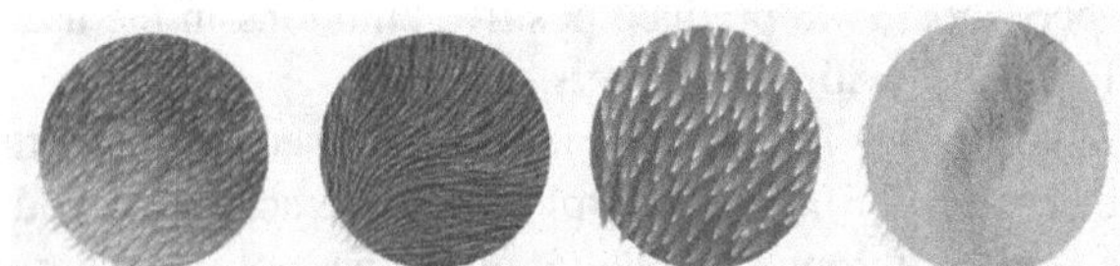

Fig. 5. I Love Fur

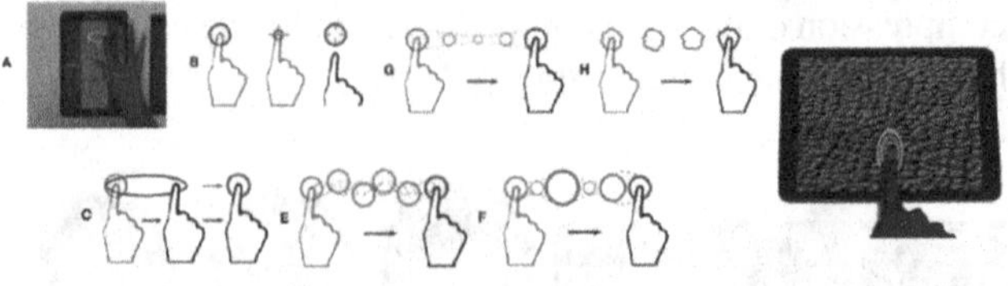

Fig. 6. Touchy

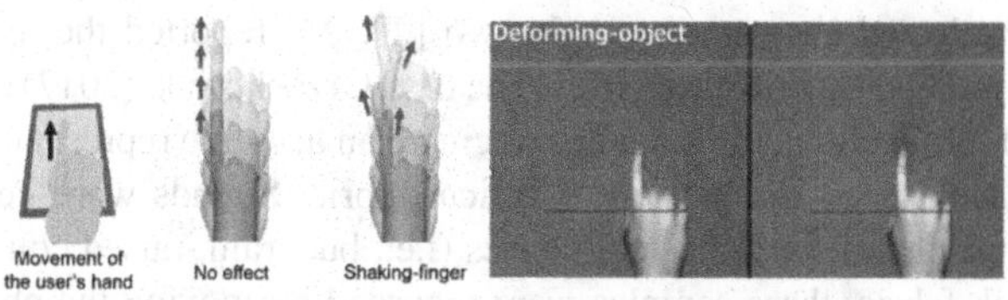

Fig. 7. Projected Virtual Hand

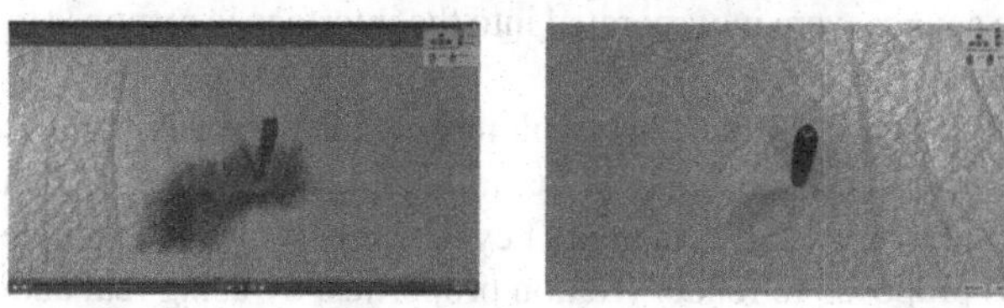

Fig. 8. Soft Human Skin

For the softness/hardness property is used the time of pressure of the finger with the cursor shrinking during the touch to a value depending on the time pressure; the friction is characterized by "stick" effect through which the cursor is stretched with a one extremity fixed and the other deformed and by the "slide" effect, that simulate fluid friction, the cursor accelerates proportionally to the finger speed and decelerates depending on the viscosity force. For the roughness, the vibration is activated with different amplitude and frequencies depending on the friction and the finger speed. The strength is that the material property to convey is set by parameters that control the cursor shape and motion, while it is not necessary modifying the texture in the background. As a weakness, the visual feedback related to material properties shown is not applied directly on the texture and this may convey lower realism.

Sato et al. 2020 [26] designed a novel approach for body augmentation, by using a projected virtual hand interface without the need to wear a device (Fig. 7). Although users can manipulate a projected virtual hand as if it were their own hand and can interact with distant objects through it, they cannot feel the sensation of touch when the projected virtual hand is overlaid on a real object. They designed three types of visual effects that produce unevenness, slipperiness, and softness.

The last case study is the project developed by Aunie Connie as part of a Master's Degree thesis in Computer Science of Video Games at Jagiellonian University in Krakow. The project concerns the simulation of an interaction with a touch- and cut-sensitive soft tissue fragment for medical purposes (Fig. 8), where the soft tissue is human skin. The field of application is medical surgery, and it is particularly useful for training in these tasks in virtual environments.

The literature showed that most of the existing studies involve only vision to communicate tactile properties. Yet, the literature has shown that audio stimuli may also modify the perception of texture. For instance, Kim et al. show that the intensity of the sound changes the perception of roughness with or without haptic feedback [27]. Even with actual materials such as abrasive papers, sound modifies the perceived roughness [28].

Among our selected case studies, only two [23, 24] reported the use of auditory feedback to communicate tactile properties. The first, Orzechowski (2017) [23] presented a sound-enabled fabric simulator that aims to create an accurate representation of fabric qualities without the need to touch the physical fabric. Sounds were generated from Mp3 sound recordings of four physical fabrics (i.e., buckram, raised cotton, latex, and ripstop). For each fabric, three samples were recorded by moving the physical fabrics in front of a microphone (without contact with the fabric) and three types of sounds for each fabric, scratching, crunching, and rustling. Then the recordings were edited in Audacity and the sounds were incorporated into the interface in response to user actions, like visual feedback.

Also, Fleaureau et al. (2016) [24] exploited audio feedback synthesized in real-time to simulate friction, by using real audio samples to create synthetized friction sound synchronized to user's movements. They developed a novel example-based audio synthesis process proposed to render friction properties, by using real audio samples to create a friction sound synchronized to the user's exploratory movement and consistent with the actual texture and rubbing speed. As a weakness, the sound feedback used to reproduce the friction sound makes the interaction less realistic, because the content captured during sound recording for the synthetization was not adapted to render the complexity of the friction sound of each of the material rendered.

The literature survey shows that studies using and combining sensory modalities such as visual and auditory stimuli are still few and do not present a standardized approach. Therefore, considering this gap, we authored a design approach for developing digital/virtual interfaces aimed at communicating the tactile properties of materials by exploiting the senses of vision and hearing.

3 Perception-Driven Design Approach

Most approaches used to convey tactile sensations in the literature, are of the "simulative" type [6, 29]. Instead, in this paper we present an approach that designers can deploy at their convenience depending on whether they want to simulate or evoke the tactile properties of matter.

Our approach (Fig. 9) is based on the foundation's synthesis framework based on ICS and BMI model designed by Push and Lécuyer [30], which represents the foundation model of pseudo-haptics. The framework aims to provide a useful approach for both HCI researchers and designers, consisting of a series of steps:

- **Multimodal raw data.** The user's experience starts with observation of their surroundings and themselves. Multimodal "raw data" from vision, hearing, and body state are processed next, based on whether the objective is to simulate or evoke properties.
- **Sensory combination and integration.** In this phase, an initial fusion, i.e., "sensory combination," takes place. The brain attempts to align the multimodal raw data spatially to obtain consistent coordinates for the final "sensory integration" stage.
- **Intention/Memory.** "Intention" has another strong influence on multisensory processing and emphasizes certain modalities and attributes. "Memory," on the other

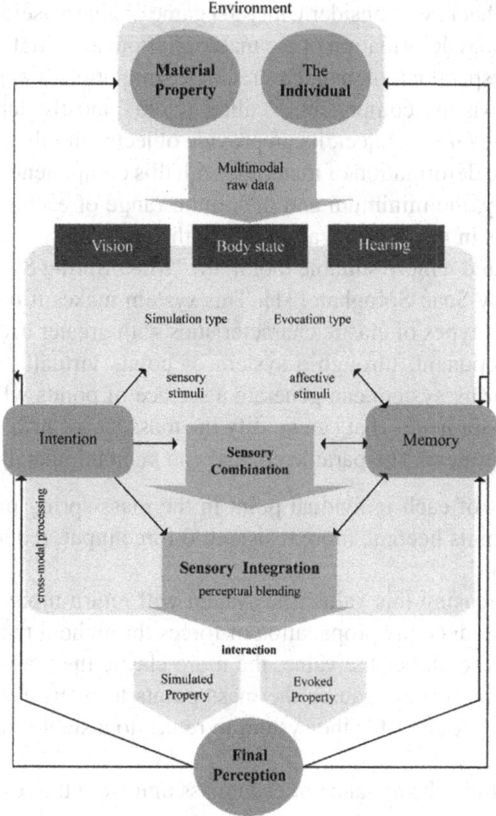

Fig. 9. PDD approach framework

hand, represents our prior knowledge that contributes to perceiving a stimulus (simulated or evoked), in a specific way.

- **Final perception.** The brain calculates the most likely perception from the following three main elements: incoming multimodal data, user memory, and intention. Illusory perception is thus the result of successful multisensory integration, whether it is simulated or evoked.

The main outcome of the proposed approach is the design of digital/virtual interactive interfaces, that can simulate/evoke the tactile properties of materials. By developing these interfaces, users could touch the displayed material, while the computer-generated image is deformed according to the mechanical property of the material and generating visual and auditory feedback to convey tactile properties.

4 Discussion

After a selection and analysis of relevant case studies, we develop the framework of a PDD approach, also hypothesizing how to implement visual and auditory feedback for the design of interfaces.

As for visual feedback, we consider Unity 3D game engine a useful tool, working for real-time interaction and deformation of the material. From an initial research phase, we found that there is no specific tool to make a realistic simulation of material deformation on Unity. The only existing component is called "cloth," mostly deployed for fabrics, and when added to the Game Object, it can provide objects with the physical properties of cloth. However, the deformation of materials with this component is not very realistic and, most importantly, the minimum and maximum range of each parameter does not show high differences in the customization of "cloth" properties.

Therefore, we found a more suitable tool in the "Mass Spring System," a free Unity resource developed by Sean Soraghan [31]. This system makes it possible to simulate a surface with various types of elastic characteristics with greater accuracy and realism than the "cloth" component, through a system of points virtually interconnected by springs. The mass spring system can generate a surface of points whose deformability is varied by a set of parameters that can modify the mass spring grid through the "Mass Spring System" component. The parameters that can be manipulated are:

- **Mass:** is the mass of each individual point in the mass-spring model. As its value increases, mass points become more resistant to force input, reducing their velocity during deformation.
- **Damping:** by increasing this value, the system will return more quickly to a more "stable" state and reduce the propagation of forces throughout the grid.
- **Spring stiffness:** the higher the value, the more elastic the mass spring system. In fact, an increase in stiffness causes the mass points to bounce with greater speed, decreasing the time it takes for the system to return to a stable state. It ranges from 0.1 to 200.
- **Spring length** defines the distance of each mass unit from the rest state.

There is also a feature in the "Mass Spring System" that allows mouse and touch input events to be transferred to the pressure applied to the mass-spring grid. This makes the mass-spring plane directly interactive and allows different gestures to be simulated. This functionality is handled by the "CanvasTouchManager" script. It reads which type of gesture is applied through a visual output of the plane deformation in response, communicating with the other scripts.

Beyond vision, we considered also how to implement auditory feedback. As we observed from the case studies, the only two with auditory feedback [23, 24] are concerned with simulating tactile properties, by recording real sounds and editing the mp3 on the Audacity software. On the other hand, if instead of simulating a property we think about evoking it, we should consider evocative sounds. When referring to "evocative sounds", we refer to sounds that do not simulate reality, but are abstract and can evoke specific sensations, memories, or even tactile properties in relation to perceptual rules. Evocative sounds could create a stronger affective response by activating the unconscious ability to connect abstract and congruent perceptions. Evocative sounds should be able to convey familiar feelings with tools far from simulation but that, overall, can generate a new system of digital/virtual material perception.

Kohler, a renowned psychologist, and representative of Gestalt theory [32] was the first one demonstrating this perceptual ability. In particular, he performed a psychological experiment in which people were asked to associate abstract words with visual forms.

This experiment aimed to show whether there was an unconscious association between visual and auditory channels even if abstract elements were used, due to a form of synaesthesia. The words were “Maluma” (in further research became “Bouba”) and “Takeke” (which became “Kiki”). The result was that the human brain tends to attribute abstract meanings to shapes and sounds consistently. In fact, the word “Takeke” was associated with pointed figures and “Maluma” with rounded figures.

According to the concept of evocative sounds, we consider implementing the audio component not with simple recordings of real sounds. In fact, by doing so, the output would not have been fully interactive since the sounds triggered by each gesture would have come from pre-recorded recordings and would not have been adaptable. We consider synthesis as the right method to generate audio content synchronized with applied gestures, by exploiting tools such as Pure Data, useful for real-time audio synthesis and processing [33].

5 Conclusion

After our exploration into the realm of digital and virtual user experiences, we have discovered a significant gap in multisensory feedback, particularly in the perception and evaluation of product and material properties. The existing scientific literature on haptic interface technology that addresses this aspect is limited and often relies on simulative approaches. Nonetheless, few selected studies have investigated the integration of sensory modalities, such as visual and auditory stimuli.

The contribution is twofold. First, we present a comprehensive overview of the literature examining interactions with digital and virtual materials, offering a detailed analysis of relevant case studies, and providing practical guidelines for designing interactive experiences. Second, we introduce an original design concept - Perception-Driven Design - a cross-modal approach that leverages vision and hearing not only to simulate but also to evoke haptic feedback associated with material properties. Our proposed approach focuses on the design of interactive digital and virtual interfaces, emphasizing the design of visual and auditory feedback.

These interfaces are designed to interact with displayed materials so that the user can perceive haptic properties through corresponding visual feedback. In addition, real-time audio feedback can be recorded or synthesized to simulate or evoke haptic properties, using authentic material sounds or evocative sounds from alternative contexts, synchronized with the visual deformation of the material. In addition, based on previous literature, we have suggested the tools and software that could be used to design these interfaces, both simulative and evocative.

The research objective is to establish a solid design framework, that can guide future researchers in the domain of HCI and interaction design. This approach has the potential to be pivotal in the design of digital and virtual interfaces that can be used in several domains that rely heavily on haptic perception. The approach opens new avenues for immersive and sensorially rich user experiences, pushing the boundaries of traditional simulation into the digital realm.

As future work, we aim to conduct psychophysical experiments to validate the approach, evaluating whether PDD approach can effectively convey tactile properties of materials, such as softness and roughness.

References

1. Wijntjes, M.W.A., Xiao, B., Volcic, R.: Visual communication of how fabrics feel. J. Vis. **19**, 4 (2019). https://doi.org/10.1167/19.2.4
2. Xue, J., Petreca, B.B., Dawes, C., Obrist, M.: FabTouch: a tool to enable communication and design of tactile and affective fabric experiences. In: Conference on Human Factors in Computing Systems - Proceedings (2023). https://doi.org/10.1145/3544548.3581288
3. Li, P., Guo, X., Wu, C., Spence, C.: How multisensory perception promotes purchase intent in the context of clothing e-customisation. Front. Psychol. **13**, 1039875 (2022). https://doi.org/10.3389/FPSYG.2022.1039875/BIBTEX
4. Zhang, Z., Wu, J., Li, Q., Huang, Z., Tenenbaum, J.B., Freeman, W.T.: Inverting audio-visual simulation for shape and material perception. In: Proceedings of the IEEE Conference on Computer Vision and Pattern Recognition Workshops, pp. 2536–2538 (2018)
5. Kunkler-Peck, A.J., Turvey, M.T.: Hearing shape. J. Exp. Psychol. Hum. Percept. Perform. **26**, 279–294 (2000)
6. Xue, Z., Zeng, X., Koehl, L., Shen, L.: Interpretation of fabric tactile perceptions through visual features for textile products. J. Sens. Stud. **31**, 143–162 (2016). https://doi.org/10.1111/JOSS.12201
7. Sakamoto, M., Watanabe, J.: Exploring tactile perceptual dimensions using materials associated with sensory vocabulary. Front. Psychol. **8**, 250102 (2017). https://doi.org/10.3389/FPSYG.2017.00569/BIBTEX
8. Xue, J., Petreca, B.B., Dawes, C., Obrist, M.: FabTouch: a tool to enable communication and design of tactile and affective fabric experiences. In: Proceedings of the 2023 CHI Conference on Human Factors in Computing Systems, pp. 1–16 (2023). https://doi.org/10.1145/3544548.3581288
9. Barnard, P.J.: Interacting cognitive subsystems: a psycholinguistic approach to short-term memory. Prog. Psychol. Lang. **2**, 197–258 (1985)
10. Ernst, M.O.: A Bayesian view on multimodal cue integration. In: Knoblich, G., Thornton, I.M., Grosjean, M., Shiffrar, M. (eds.) Human Body Perception from the Inside Out: Advances in Visual Cognition, pp. 105–131. Oxford University Press (2006)
11. Pusch, A., Lécuyer, A.: Pseudo-haptics: from the theoretical foundations to practical system design guidelines. In: Proceedings of the 13th International Conference on Multimodal Interfaces, pp. 57–64 (2011)
12. Masaaki, Y.: Dimensions of tactual impressions. Jpn. Psychol. Res. **10**, 123–137 (1968)
13. Petreca, B., Bianchi-Berthouze, N., Baurley, S., Watkins, P., Atkinson, D.: An embodiment perspective of affective touch behaviour in experiencing digital textiles. In: 2013 Humaine Association Conference on Affective Computing and Intelligent Interaction, pp. 770–775 (2013). https://doi.org/10.1109/ACII.2013.143
14. Essick, G.K., James, A., McGlone, F.P.: Psychophysical assessment of the affective components of non-painful touch. NeuroReport **10**, 2083–2087 (1999). https://doi.org/10.1097/00001756-199907130-00017
15. Mattens, F.: The sense of touch: from tactility to tactual probing. Australas. J. Philos. **95**, 688–701 (2016). https://doi.org/10.1080/00048402.2016.1263870
16. Rodrigues, T., Silva, S.C., Duarte, P.: The value of textual haptic information in online clothing shopping. J. Fash. Mark. Manag. **21**, 88–102 (2017). https://doi.org/10.1108/JFMM-02-2016-0018/FULL/PDF
17. Klatzky, R.L., Lederman, S.J.: Stages of manual exploration in haptic object identification. Percept. Psychophys. **52**, 661–670 (1992). https://doi.org/10.3758/BF03211702/METRICS
18. Fiore, A.M.: Multisensory integration of visual, tactile, and olfactory aesthetic cues of appearance. Cloth. Text. Res. J. **11**, 45–52 (1993). https://doi.org/10.1177/0887302X9301100207

19. Burns, L.D., Chandler, J., Brown, D.M., Cameron, B., Dallas, M.J.: Sensory interaction and descriptions of fabric hand. Percept. Mot. Skills **81**, 120–122 (1995). https://doi.org/10.2466/PMS.1995.81.1.120
20. Chubb, E.C., Colgate, J.E., Peshkin, M.A.: ShiverPaD: a glass haptic surface that produces shear force on a bare finger. IEEE Trans. Haptics **3**, 189–198 (2010). https://doi.org/10.1109/TOH.2010.7
21. Argelaguet, F., Jauregui, D.A.G., Marchal, M., LeCuyer, A.: Elastic images: perceiving local elasticity of images through a novel pseudo-haptic deformation effect. ACM Trans. Appl. Percept. **10**, 1–14 (2013). https://doi.org/10.1145/2501599
22. Punpongsanon, P., Iwai, D., Sato, K.: SoftAR: visually manipulating haptic softness perception in spatial augmented reality. IEEE Trans. Vis. Comput. Graph. **21**, 1279–1288 (2015). https://doi.org/10.1109/TVCG.2015.2459792
23. Orzechowski, P.M.: iShoogle-Touching and Feeling Fabrics on a Touchscreen (2017)
24. Fleureau, J., Lefevre, Y., Danieau, F., Guillotel, P., Costes, A.: Texture rendering on a tactile surface using extended elastic images and example-based audio cues. LNCS **9774**, 350–359 (2016). https://doi.org/10.1007/978-3-319-42321-0_32/COVER
25. Costes, A., Argelaguet, F., Danieau, F., Guillotel, P., Lécuyer, A.: Touchy: a visual approach for simulating haptic effects on touchscreens. Front. ICT **6**, 1 (2019). https://doi.org/10.3389/FICT.2019.00001/BIBTEX
26. Sato, Y., Hiraki, T., Tanabe, N., Matsukura, H., Iwai, D., Sato, K.: Modifying texture perception with pseudo-haptic feedback for a projected virtual hand interface. IEEE Access **8**, 120473–120488 (2020). https://doi.org/10.1109/ACCESS.2020.3006440
27. Kim, S.C., Kyung, K.U., Kwon, D.S.: The effect of sound on haptic perception. In: Proceedings of the Second Joint EuroHaptics Conference and Symposium on Haptic Interfaces for Virtual Environment and Teleoperator Systems, World Haptics 2007, pp. 354–360 (2007). https://doi.org/10.1109/WHC.2007.110
28. Suzuki, Y., Gyoba, J.: Effects of sounds on tactile roughness depend on the congruency between modalities. In: Third Joint EuroHaptics conference and Symposium on Haptic Interfaces for Virtual Environment and Teleoperator Systems (World Haptics 2009), pp. 150–153 (2009). https://doi.org/10.1109/WHC.2009.4810857
29. Jang, S.Y., Ha, J.: The influence of tactile information on the human evaluation of tactile properties. Fashion Text. **8**, 1–14 (2021). https://doi.org/10.1186/S40691-020-00242-5
30. Pusch, A., Lécuyer, A.: Pseudo-haptics: From the theoretical foundations to practical system design guidelines. In: Proceedings of the 2011 ACM International Conference on Multimodal Interaction (ICMI 2011), pp. 57–64 (2011). https://doi.org/10.1145/2070481.2070494
31. Soraghan, S.: Mass Spring System. Unity Asset Store (2017). https://Assetstore.Unity.Com/Packages/Tools/Physics/Mass-Spring-System-81451
32. Kohler, W.: Gestalt psychology, an introduction to new concepts in modern psychology. Liveright (1947)
33. Tähtinen, E.: Use of Procedural Audio in Unity (2021). http://www.theseus.fi/handle/10024/499390

Haptic Perception Research and Facility Design for Virtual Spaces

Haoran Shi and Honghai Li(✉)

Beijing Information Science and Technology University, Beijing 100192, China
Lihonghai@bistu.edu.cn

Abstract. The goal of this study is to develop a smart device that can be used to enhance virtual space perception to improve the haptic perception experience of the user's space in virtual training, entertainment, and other scenarios. Haptic feedback is one of the key elements to enhance the experience of virtual space perception. At present, virtual reality technology has been able to accomplish a considerable degree of ultra visual virtual field experience, such as simulating terrain, constructing haptic proxies with airbags to refine the virtual scene, but lack of research on longitudinal spatial haptics, passive opening of fixed haptic devices cannot meet the sensory needs of switching between different virtual spaces. In this study, the introduction of props of haptic proxies in the virtual space helps to enhance the virtual sensory experience of users. Through experiments and preliminary validation of user perception indicators, four design strategies for haptic proxies props in purely visual virtual contexts are proposed. Based on the design strategies, this paper designs an intelligent device for constructing an immersive virtual reality system, which assists users to interactively surrogate vision through haptic perception in virtual reality, and to more realistically feel the obstruction experience and spatial sense in virtual space. The device is installed on both sides of the experience space by two groups of forty 50 cm × 40 cm rectangular panels in total to meet the need for different sizes of obstructions in different scenarios, where each rectangular block can be actuated up to five depth levels (one depth actuation level for every 10 cm). Each panel is driven by a motorized actuator and moves the panel to the target displacement. The motors are powered by a power supply, driven by a motor driver, and controlled by an Arduino Uno that receives commands via serial communication from a host PC running a custom Unity application written in c#. The facilities and methods of this research have a wide range of application scenarios, which can provide a more realistic sense of experience for the design and development of virtual systems for spatial training classes with strict requirements for spatial perception; optimize the display effect and evaluation of virtual display of indoor decoration and home furnishing options; Enhance the spatial experience of virtual gaming categories, providing multi-dimensional haptic stimulation for immersive games such as virtual escape rooms. Provide multidimensional haptic and sensory stimulation. Future research can use the developed smart devices to further optimize the sensory feedback of visual-haptic synchronization in virtual space.

Keywords: Augmented Virtualization · Haptic proxies · Confined space · Intelligent haptic proxies device

M. Kurosu and A. Hashizume (Eds.): HCII 2024, LNCS 14688, pp. 102–123, 2024.
https://doi.org/10.1007/978-3-031-60449-2_8

1 Introduction

The rise and development of the Metaverse concept has allowed virtual space to begin to become the vehicle for a new form of human society. With the launch of Apple Vision Pro, digital content can be integrated into the real world and controlled through the most natural and intuitive input methods such as eyes, hands, and voice, bringing users a new 3D interactive experience. Multisensory connectivity extends the sensory dimension, makes sensory interaction more natural and effective, and provides users with rich forms of sensory feedback in virtual space [1].

Traditional virtual spaces bring beauty and attraction with vivid visual impact, and head-mounted displays enable users to simply explore virtual worlds. Confined spaces, which are difficult to assess due to complex attributes, are often simulated using virtual scene restoration for perception and training to achieve safe and cost-effective goals. For typical scenarios in confined spaces such as ships [2], pipelines [3], airplane cabins [4], and automobile cabins [5], the construction or simulation of virtual spaces has been widely adopted to allow workers to simulate and evaluate the experience of performing tasks in actual confined spaces in a virtual environment.

However, current virtual reality systems for confined spaces only provide visual and auditory experiences, presenting a virtual space without haptic sensations from a distance. When the user's hand penetrates the virtual object, the sense of presence disappears, and the judgment of the size and spatial distance of the confined space will be biased, resulting in a poor sensory experience. Through the synchronous dynamic assistance of the physical device, combined with virtual visual feedback, it can effectively improve the users perception and judgment of objects, materials, environment, etc. in the virtual environment, and enhance the sense of reality and participation. Researchers have attempted a variety of "solutions". For example, haptic gloves integrate multi-haptic information to assist in perceiving dynamic changes in virtual objects [6], and physical props are deployed to provide omnidirectional haptic feedback [7]. Therefore, combining physical devices to enhance the virtual space experience is important to create a more comprehensive and realistic virtual reality sensory stimulation.

Haptic proxies are one of the ways to augment the virtual. At present, there are many types of virtual reality haptic proxies to provide a considerable degree of ultra visual haptic virtual field experience, such as simulating terrains with different stiffnesses [8], constructing proxy objects with airbags [9], and artificially synchronizing physical props manipulation to achieve physical representations of virtual objects for sensory touch [10]. However, there is less research on haptic devices for confined space, and the passively opened fixed touch assistive devices cannot meet the sensory needs of different virtual spaces, and the existing virtual reality assistive haptic devices can only be transformed by manual operation. The creation of dynamically transformable physical devices assists in enhancing the user's experience of haptic stimulation in confined spaces and promotes the development of virtual reality in areas such as training. Therefore, the study of intelligent haptic proxy for augmented virtualization in confined spaces is of great significance for virtual training systems with spatial perceptual rigor.

The purpose of this study is to investigate the impact of smart devices using haptic proxies on the user experience of virtual confined spaces. Through the design of intelligent haptic proxy and virtual space prototypes, the findings related to the enhancement of virtual confined space user experience by haptic proxies are verified. Based on the theory of virtual augmented technology and the interaction of haptic proxies, the design strategy of intelligent devices is constructed to categorize different forms of haptic proxies. The clarity, three-dimensionality and richness of the virtual experience are achieved through sensory synergistic stimulation, which provides a more realistic sense of experience for the virtual system of spatial training class, and at the same time optimizes the virtual display effect and evaluation of the program.

2 Related Work

2.1 Confined Spaces

As defined by the American National Standards Institute (ANSI), a confined space is described as an enclosed area that is of sufficient morphological size and configuration to allow entry by personnel and is characterized by the following features: the primary use is not for personnel; access is restricted; and there is a potential or definite hazard. Typical confined space scenarios include waste wells, cellars, ship's holds, and pipes.

Confined space now has a broader connotation and extension, and common types of confined spaces include, but are not limited to, the following: (1) storage tanks; (2) pipelines; (3) containers; (4) pits, tunnels; (5) shafts and similar structures, sewage channels, and sewers; (6) cellars; (7) ship compartments; and (8) access holes; (9) ships, caves, mines, underground passages, and other dark confined spaces [11].

Facing the environmental complexity and task specificity of some typical confined spaces, researchers and scholars in various fields have carried out relevant applied research through virtual reality technology (Table 1), which usually conducts perception and training simulation in the way of virtual scenario reduction construction, aiming to improve the efficiency of task completion in confined spaces and ensure the safety of personnel.

Through the above studies, it can be found that the researchers mainly focus on the application of virtual confined space in three aspects: the restoration and operation of the working environment, the overhauling and training of the equipment in the space, and the virtual emergency escape training. In addition, M. Lvov [18] and others believe that the use of virtual and augmented reality devices ensures the realization of the process of formation of skills and abilities and pedagogical requirements.

However, current virtual reality systems for confined spaces are more focused on satisfying the visual experience, and due to the lack of haptic capabilities, the judgment and manipulation of attributes that characterize the confined space may be inaccurate, thus affecting the quality and level of experience and assessment. Therefore, being able to touch objects in virtual reality becomes crucial to make the experience more engaging and natural.

2.2 Augmented Virtualization

Lee et al. [19] defined immersive technology as a technology that blurs the boundaries between the physical and virtual worlds, creates a sense of immersion and enhances

Table 1. Research of haptically enhanced virtual devices with different modalities.

	Researchers	Content of the study
1	Zhang et al. [12]	Establishing a 3D ship model, forming a virtual ship scene, and realizing the interactive operation of cabin devices based on Unity3D, so that the user can have an experience similar to the actual ship's working environment, which improves the effect of education and training
2	Dunwen Liu et al. [13]	Using three-dimensional software to build a tunnel fire emergency rescue training system (Fig. 1a), to realize a highly immersive virtual environment for tunnel rescue personnel, management personnel for fire emergency training, improve the enthusiasm of personnel to participate in drills, reduce the cost of drills
3	Hong Yang et al. [14]	A mine fire emergency training system was designed using VR technology to realize the interaction between the trainees and the virtual scene of mine fire through the headset equipment. The experiment proves that the user experience and training effect of the mine fire emergency training system in VR scenario are better
4	Yanbing Ren [15]	With the help of VR to simulate the visual effects of different underground street interface materials, to explore the relationship between interface materials, scale sense and spatial perception, and to explore the feasibility and methods of interface material design to improve the psychological environment of underground streets
5	Jiali Zhang et al. [16]	Construct three-dimensional virtual train model, realize the train maintenance scene roaming, train equipment fault repair and other functions of training, real and intuitive simulation of train equipment running status and fault conditions, improve training efficiency and operational accuracy
6	Tao Rui et al. [17]	A ship scenario fire training system (Fig. 1b) is designed to build a three-dimensional model of fixed water fire extinguishing system and firefighters' equipment, simulate the operation of the equipment from a first-person perspective and with a virtual crew, and improve the efficiency and level of ship fire training

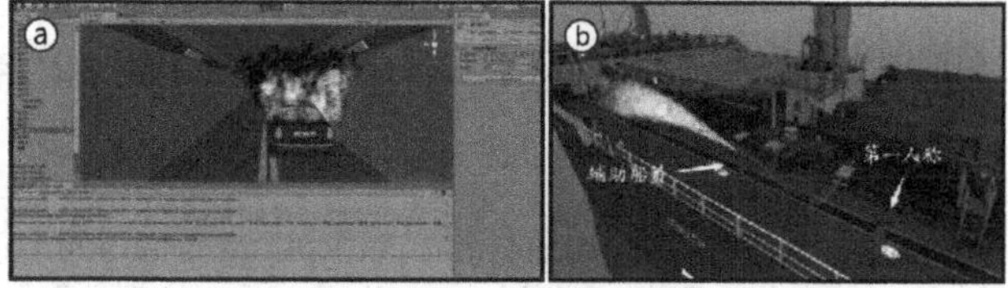

Fig. 1. Relevant applications of confined space virtual reality scenarios: (a) Construction of the tunnel fire emergency rescue scenario (Drawn by Dunwen Liu). (b) Module of the fixed water fire suppression system (Drawn by Tao Rui).

the realism of the virtual experience, and describes VR, AR, and MR technologies as a whole. Milgram and Kishino [20] proposed the concept of "Reality-virtual continuum" in 1994, as shown in Fig. 2. The concept of "reality-virtual continuum" is shown in Fig. 2. Real and virtual environments are two poles of a continuum, between which is classified as mixed reality (XR). In mixed reality systems, a further distinction is made between Augmented Reality and Augmented Virtual. Where Augmented Virtual (AV) refers to the addition of features from the real environment to the virtual environment, so as to perceive and interact with the virtual elements realistically, and the perceived stimuli are mainly purely virtual.

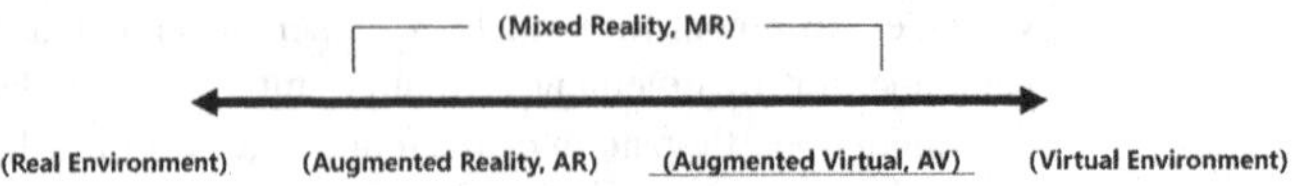

Fig. 2. The reality-virtuality continuum (Milgram & Kishino, 1994).

Seokhee Jeon and Seungmoon Choi [21] added the haptic dimension to the concept of "reality-virtual continuum" proposed by Milgram & Kishino, and extended it to "composite visual-haptic-reality-virtual continuum". "A new taxonomy of haptic-mixed reality is established", as shown in Fig. 3. The entire "visual-haptic continuum" is divided into nine categories based on the criteria of "virtual degree of touch" and "virtual degree of vision". This categorization aims to provide a more accurate framework and guidance for the research and design of haptic augmented reality systems.

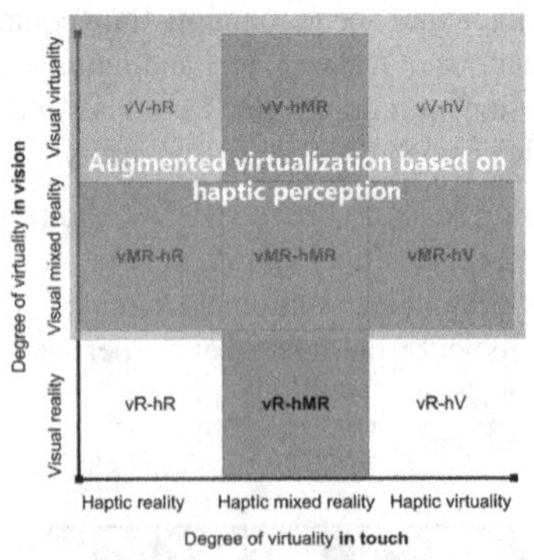

Fig. 3. Composite Visual-Haptic-Reality-Virtual Continuum (Seokhee Jeon & Seungmoon Choi, 2009).

For both continuums, it can be found that haptic perception-based augmented virtualization covers the six categories of the pink-blue gradient region in Fig. 3, i.e., the haptic portion associated with "visual mixed reality" and "visual virtualization". Although the literature [21] suggests that the center cross-shaded region is a region of mixed reality, "vV-hR" and "vV-hV", whether assisting real touch or providing virtual touch, enhance the haptic sensation to some extent. Some extent enhances the haptic sensory experience, so this paper categorizes them as augmented virtual based on haptic perception.

Since the concept of ultimate display was introduced in 1965, researchers have sought to better communicate the physicality of virtual worlds and reality. Scholars have constructed research and applications on haptic-augmented virtual installations in different modalities and technologies (Table 2), aiming to provide a more realistic haptic experience with the help of advanced technologies.

Table 2. Classification of haptic augmented virtual devices and research.

Haptic Augmented Virtual Appliances category	Related concepts and features	Content of the study
vV-hR Visual Virtual-Haptic Reality	Haptic restoration or simulation of item positions using real physical items or simple props for haptic enhancement of virtual scenes	G. Mullen et al. [22] explored the impact of users' use of physical props on time perception in virtual reality, creating a one-to-one model of a hazmat lab to provide tangible interactions with realistic physical props reductions of virtual items
vMR-hR Visual Mixed Reality - Haptic Reality	Providing a more interesting and rich visual experience rather than restoring a more realistic sense of touch, the physical entity serves more as a visual vehicle for manipulation	Yuki et al. [23] proposed a tangible projection mapping that enhances the dynamic appearance by projecting onto objects in the hands of the user
vV-hMR Visual Virtual - Haptic Mixed Reality	The use of synthetic visual stimuli effectively enhances the representation of visual virtual content to the user	Naoki et al. [24] realized the linkage between the user's hand and the hand in the virtual space through optical capture, and when the hand in the virtual space touches the surface of the virtual object, the controller sends a signal to the haptic device to provide resistance and realize haptic sensing
vMR-hMR Visual Mixed Reality - Haptic Mixed Reality	It also utilizes a variety of sensors to capture real signals from the human body and convert them into haptic information	Touch&Fold collapsible haptic actuators [25] provide haptic feedback to mixed reality environments through presses on finger pads, including haptic contact (pressure) and texture sense (vibration)

(*continued*)

Table 2. (*continued*)

Haptic Augmented Virtual Appliances category	Related concepts and features	Content of the study
vV-hV Visual Virtual - Haptic Reality	Typically used in interactive virtual simulators where both visual and haptic sensory information is virtual	Covaciu F et al. [26] developed an intelligent robotic system simulator to monitor the status in real time by transmitting ankle information through sensors worn by the subject, and guided stroke patients in ankle rehabilitation with a dummy apple picking task
vMR-hV Visual Mixed Reality - Haptic Virtual	Explore how augmented devices provide feedback to the user's sense of sight and touch	Xavier de Tinguy et al. [27] considered a wearable device that dynamically changes the perceived stiffness of a tangible object based on what happens in the AR scene when a virtual object is superimposed on a tangible object in an AR environment

These augmented virtual devices and props visually create a more immersive and realistic virtual environment mainly by combining real signals and virtual information. In terms of haptics, whether assisted by real physical tools, creating simple geometric forms of props, or conveying information through vibration, the aim is to provide more compatible natural and realistic haptic feedback in the virtual scene to enhance the user's perceptual experience in the virtual environment.

Augmented virtual haptic devices can be categorized primarily as graspable, wearable, and touchable from an interaction perspective, and are realized primarily through four technologies: kinesthetic devices, skin deformation devices, vibration, and haptic surface design [28]. In addition, augmented virtual devices often require synergistic perception of the physical and virtual environments. This synergistic perception is often realized in three main ways: sensors, code communication, and motion capture. Sensors sense environmental information, perform intelligent signal processing and interpret measurement information ranging from simple haptic positions to complex surface properties (e.g., roughness, stiffness and temperature) [29]. This information can accurately simulate the user's movement, posture and haptic interaction with virtual objects in the virtual environment through synchronized communication. Code communication synchronization is mainly through the serial communication protocol, which is usually used to connect the Unity 3D engine to the Arduino microcontroller. The serial connection is established by connecting the Arduino microcontroller to the computer through a USB port, sending sensor data to the application to adapt the perception and changes in the environment [30]. Motion capture can be based on forms such as markers or monoculars that digitize human movement to digitize performances and is mainly used for analysis and content creation [31, 32].

It can be seen that direct control and passive interaction are the two main ways of augmented virtual realization of perception, and gradually develop in the direction of deformable, in order to maximize the adaptation of more scene use. Information transfer and synergy are crucial in this process. Synchronization of data enables more precise operations and feedback. This trend is driving the development of augmented virtual device technology toward greater realism, interactivity, and malleability.

2.3 Haptic Proxies

Haptic proxies are physical props that are used as virtual object proxies during interaction with virtual environments (VEs). These props are similar to virtual props in terms of relevant haptic properties (e.g., shape, weight, or texture) and provide passive haptic feedback by definition. Haptic proxies provide an inexpensive, convenient, and compelling way to support touch in virtual reality. The benefits of using haptic proxies can be attributed to the fact that users can interact with physical objects to produce realistic perceptions and that physical objects do not need to simulate characteristics such as texture, hardness, weight, shape, and size.

Nilsson et al. [33] categorized technologies for VR haptic proxies into four main categories based on when the technology is deployed (offline or real-time) and the reality that is being manipulated (physical or virtual reality), with examples of their related studies shown in Table 3.

Although the above categorization clearly delineates haptic proxies applications, current research on haptic proxies focuses more on solving the lack of haptic perception in a specific scenario, and few research on haptic proxies strategies for the lack of haptic senses in a certain type of virtual space. As virtual environments continue to become more complex, this requires a haptic proxies that can have different properties for multi-scene assistance. This suggests the need for further strategy exploration to better match the virtual space experience in a scene.

3 Device Design Strategies for Enhancing Virtual Space Perception

3.1 Experiments and User Studies

To validate our approach, we conducted a user study for the localization adjustment strategy and collected metrics on perceived realism, difficulty, engagement, and fun. We asked each participant to explore the experience of walking in a narrow virtual container with cube obstacles on both sides in two contexts: one context with the use of haptic proxies props and the other without. Participants rated both experiences using a Likert scale. Our main hypothesis was that the use of haptic proxies props in virtual spaces under a localization-based adjustment strategy would help enhance the user's virtual sensory experience.

The experiment used foam board to build a physical solid model of the virtual space scene (Fig. 4) for a controlled experiment on virtual space perception through the Wizard of Oz method. The experiment required participants to walk back and forth with

Table 3. Classification of VR haptic proxy technologies and case studies.

VR haptic proxies technology category	Related concepts and features	Case Studies
Offline virtual strategies	Deploying offline technologies by means of substitutional reality and assisted VE generation to simulate the haptics of a virtual object or map the position of a virtual object before the VR program is run	Sra et al. [34] captured an indoor scene in 3D, detecting obstacles such as furniture and walls, by pairing the detected objects with virtual objects in order to utilize the physical properties of the real world for a haptic experience
Offline physical strategies	Similarity or localization co-matching of global shapes of virtual objects by means of reconfigurable props and construction sets	Seungwoo Je [35] and others constructed Elevate, a dynamically walkable pin-array floor, on which users can experience changes in shape and also details of the underlying terrain
		Wooje Chang et al. [8] built the PreloadStep platform, which applies different preloading forces to different sections based on springs between compression plates, allowing the user to perceive the stiffness of the virtual terrain and realize the illusion of walking on different terrains
Real-time virtual strategies	Manipulating audiovisual representations of VEs and virtual bodies with virtual property distortion and virtual remapping to enhance haptic perception	Seungwoo Je et al. [36] constructed Aero-plane, a handheld controller based on force-feedback technology, which enables weight movement by means of micro-jet propellers to help perceive and correctly recognize the real feeling of holding objects in virtual space

(continued)

Table 3. (*continued*)

VR haptic proxies technology category	Related concepts and features	Case Studies
Real-time physical strategies	Improving the scalability of passive haptic proxies during touch by means of property-changing proxies and physical realignment	Cheng et al. [10] proposed the TurkDeck system, which realizes multi-sensory virtual reality experiences that rely on human manipulation by rearranging and reconfiguring haptic proxies by non-virtual reality users
		Shan-Yuan Teng et al. [9] constructed a novel aerodynamic interface for TilePoP consisting of stacked 2D arrays of cubic airbags providing full-body interactive proxy objects

or without the use of touch devices by haptic proxies in two contexts. Upon completion of the two contexts, participants were required to rate the realism, difficulty, engagement, and fun of the task on a seven-point scale. A total of eight healthy participants (five women and three men), who tried out the virtual scenario through an Oculus head-mounted display, used their hands to interact with the haptic proxies.

The results of the responses of the participants are shown in Fig. 5. It was found that in the presence of haptic proxies, the participants rated the realism, difficulty, engagement, and fun of the task higher. This data suggest that immersive virtual sensory experiences can be enhanced by haptic proxies in virtual space elevations.

After collecting user perceptual evaluation scores, we conducted in-depth interviews with some users who were interested in the study (Table 4) to delve into the detailed details of haptic proxies schedulable props, characteristics of modular haptic proxies, dynamic synchronization methods, etc., so as to provide a more specific and in-depth research direction for the development of the subsequent design strategies.

3.2 Design Strategies Based on the "Technology Deployment Time - Scenario Openness" Taxonomy

In the case of fully visual virtualization, based on the concept of haptic-reality-virtual continuum, this paper extends the haptic proxies taxonomy. Inspired by the haptic proxy taxonomy proposed by Nilsson et al., we propose a taxonomy of haptic proxies in the case of purely visual virtualization, which classifies haptic proxies into four new categories based on two dimensions, namely, the time of deployment of the technology and the openness of the scenario, and constructs four corresponding design strategies accordingly (Fig. 6).

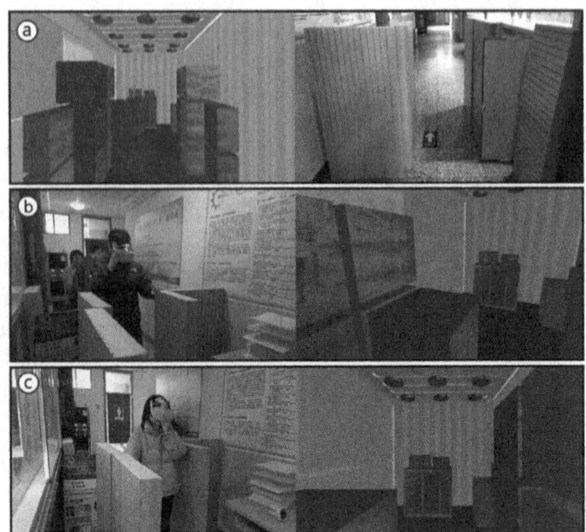

Fig. 4. a) A narrow virtual container virtual scene with cube obstacles on both sides with corresponding haptic proxies built using foam board. b) The user touching the props on a flat surface. c) User touching the side of the prop.

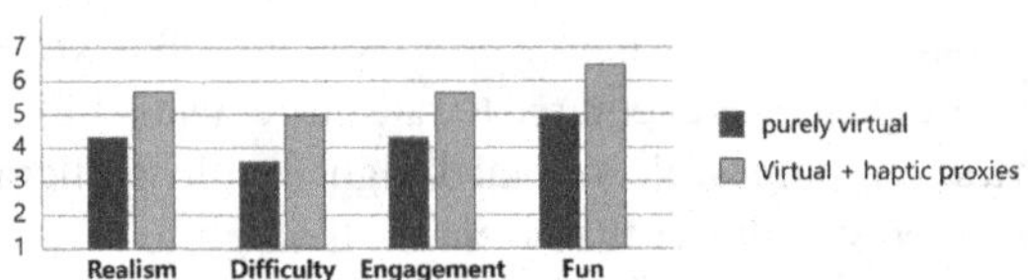

Fig. 5. Results of the user evaluation.

First, differentiate technologies based on the scene openness of the virtual space experience: Are they fixed scene experiences or are they explored in open-ended scenes? Second, the technologies are differentiated based on the deployment time of haptic proxies transformations: Are they deployed offline before the user is exposed to the VE or are they synchronized in real time to match the virtual scene? Based on this, the haptic proxies devices are categorized. In the following, these four strategies will be described in detail, providing case studies related to previous work belonging to each strategy, and attempting to summarize the form of haptic proxies suitable for each category in order to provide haptic proxies design strategies for different scenarios virtual spaces.

Strategy 1: Positioning Adjustment. The concept of positional adjustment is used for offline post-adjustment in static virtual scenes. Matching the position of virtual objects in the scene is achieved by analogizing their physical forms and providing corresponding haptic feedback. Cheng et al. [37] defined sparse haptic proxies, with geometries consisting of sparse primitives, to redirect the user's hand movements to the matched proxy parts, simulating the detailed geometry of the scene. Through user gaze and hand movement analysis, the user's intention to interact in the virtual space is predicted, and the position of the user's hand is redirected to a location matching the agent. This haptic proxies approach can effectively correlate the geometries in the virtual environment. Alternatively, multiple protruding standards can be designed and distributed at different locations to provide passive haptic localization feedback. Nagao et al. [38] represented the edges of staircase in a virtual environment by placing tiny protrusions under the user's feet. Combined with visual stimulation from a head-mounted display, the interaction between vision and haptics is stimulated to change the user's perception of the shape of the floor and experience different types of virtual stairs. The use of an optimized right-angle triangle cross-section shape enhances the user's perception of the presence of the stairs as well as walking up and down, providing greater creative freedom for VR applications.

Table 4. Content of user interviews.

	Interview Questions	Influencing factors
Question 1	How do you think the virtual space experience feels with the addition of haptic proxies?	1) The virtual experience with the addition of haptic proxies is more realistic and the spatial perception is more three-dimensional 2) To some extent, haptic proxies improve the vividness of the virtual scene
Question 2	If there are dispatchable props that can be used for haptic perception in virtual space, what characteristics do you think their props should have?	1) Dispatchable props surface can experience different touch changes (soft, rough, smooth) 2) The device should be safe, with no sharp edges on the mechanism 3) Dispatchable props have a certain adjustable range of activities to avoid the possibility of being wrapped by the haptic device brought about by the feeling of oppression 4) For confined space haptic device is best designed with an adjustable range of activities, easy to adapt to the scene, to avoid panic because the user can not see the device moving
Question 3	What kind of virtual experience do you think you would like to have with unit-replaceable haptic proxies?	1) Provides additional push, pull or squeeze sensations to enhance the haptic experience in virtual environments 2) Combine with small devices such as smart gloves or work with wearable haptic garments for different parts of the body to make haptic perception more comprehensive

(*continued*)

Table 4. (*continued*)

	Interview Questions	Influencing factors
Question 4	Could you please briefly suggest some expectations for a dynamic synchronization approach for modular haptic proxies?	1) Dynamic Synchronized Timing can provide haptic feedback for users focused on viewing a certain portion of the content based on the automatic synchronization of the headset for that portion 2) Synchronization can be initiated by the user's manual operation in the virtual scene of the headset to change, or through the device automatically senses the position of the character to achieve 3) The high degree of synchronization requires stable technical support, and the specific way depends mainly on the needs of the virtual scene and the user's ease of operation

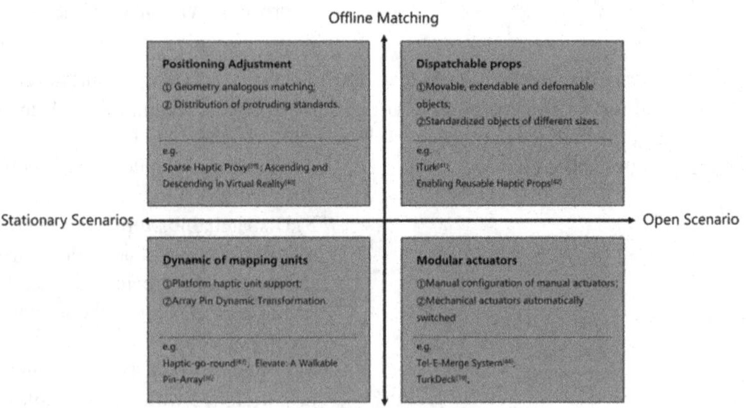

Fig. 6. Design strategy based on the "technology deployment time-scene openness" taxonomy for purely visual virtualization.

The localization adjustment strategy makes the haptic proxies fit the virtual environment more closely, which not only improves the realism of the haptic sensation and the three-dimensionality of the spatial perception, but also enhances the vividness of the virtual scene. By optimizing the shape and distribution of the haptic stimuli, we are able to provide a more natural and detailed haptic experience when the user interacts with the virtual environment. This provides a more immersive user experience for the design of virtual reality applications.

The shortcoming of localization tuning is that haptic proxies matching using simple physical form analogs may limit the accuracy of correspondence with actual scenes. In addition, a simple device design may trigger different perceptual differences among different users, which may affect the generalizability and acceptability of the method.

Strategy 2: Dispatchable Props. In open scenarios, haptic perception of objects in virtual environments is usually simulated by manually moving dispatchable props. One approach is to use a variety of movable, extensible, and deformable objects to replace the various shapes of virtual objects. Cheng et al. [39] proposed the iTurk system, which modifies the use of props based on the operation of the virtual world. Collapsible props allow users to reconfigure them into a variety of objects, such as suitcases, fuse cabinets, and railings. Suspended, long-pendulum props can not only represent inanimate objects, but also redirect energy and hit the user, thus enhancing the virtual reality experience. Another approach is to select standardized objects of different sizes to be used as haptic aids. Focusing on the application of haptic props to the perceptual matching problem, Auda et al. [40] developed three displacement functions to control the position of the user's virtual hand in a feature-rich virtual reality environment, thus giving the user the illusion that the virtual object is of a different size than the physical object.

To better fit the needs of the scenario, haptic differences can be introduced on the surfaces of the dispatchable props, such as adjusting the perceived material touch (soft, rough, smooth). When considering haptic proxies, it is important to ensure that mechanical devices do not have sharp edges to maintain safety. The adjustable range of motion of the disposable props should be adjustable so that the experience can be self-adjusted to avoid the oppressive feeling of being held hostage by the haptic device.

However, such dispatchable props are only capable of performing haptic proxies on virtual objects with a more defined morphology in the virtual scene, and thus cannot achieve haptic perception of the entire scene.

Strategy 3: Dynamic of Mapping Units. Unit dynamic mapping is the synchronization of the morphology of individual haptic proxies with the smallest individual haptic proxies as a unit when switching virtual scenes. Curved surrounds are more able to tactilely match a scene in three dimensions, while rectangular planes are able to satisfy the quest for detail in a particular scene's elevation. For example, Huang et al. [7] achieved providing haptic feedback to any direction of a virtual reality experience through a haptic-go-round surrounding platform. The go-around platform deploys interchangeable plug-and-play prop cartridges and devices; by inserting a prop cartridge into a haptically rotating adjacent slot, the haptic wheel recognizes the RFID tags on the cartridge and automatically rotates the correct haptic device to the correct orientation based on the virtual scenario to match what the user is about to touch. In addition to synchronizing the matching of different props in the platform by allowing them to be synchronized in the virtual scene, the transformation of the same form of array of pinned props can also provide dynamic haptic perception to the virtual scene. In the landscape application, staircase, and golf scene based on Elevate pinned haptic proxies developed by Seungwoo Je et al. [35], users are allowed to feel ground drop and different terrain textures in different contexts in VR with their feet. The designer can select the dynamic/static nature of the environment and control the refresh rate of the floor to help the user have an uninterrupted and seamless experience on the terrain.

The dynamic mapping of units has the advantage of allowing both point-to-point haptic mapping of different contents and the possibility of combining them to bring about a greater dimensionality of sensory experience. In this way, users can have a more nuanced haptic experience, such as providing additional push, pull, or squeeze sensations to fulfill their heightened haptic expectations. The use of this strategy in conjunction with wearable haptic garments can further create a more integrated haptic experience and make perception in virtual scenarios more realistic.

Although the unit dynamic mapping approach has some advantages, it still has some shortcomings. First of all, although the curved surround and rectangular flat platform as haptic unit support methods have their own advantages, they may not be able to meet the needs of complex environments in some scenarios. Second, how to ensure a smooth user experience during the point-to-point haptic mapping transformation requires in-depth research and continuous improvement.

Strategy 4: Modular Actuators. Modular actuators automate the morphing of haptic proxies by synchronizing or sensing virtual scenes in advance. There are two main implementations of this approach: one is a manual configuration based on visual position, and the other is a mechanical auto transformation using sensors and powered actuators. For example, the TurkDeck system developed by Cheng et al. [10] allows for the creation of arbitrarily large virtual worlds in a limited space using limited physical props. Users touch or manipulate objects in the virtual world while simultaneously touching or manipulating the corresponding physical props. The system allows a group of people to act as "human actuators" and create physical representations in real time through visual commands. The study showed that the participants rated TurkDeck's realism and immersion higher than the traditional prop-free baseline condition. On the other hand, Suzuki et al. [41] developed a modular inflatable actuator as a building block to prototyping room-scale shape-changing interfaces capable of rapidly constructing different geometries. Although the building block is not explicitly stated to synchronize haptic matching of open-ended scenes, in the application scenario exploration the scholars mention that the actuator concept can be used for large-scale haptic perception of automotive shapes in virtual and augmented reality, as well as exploring the pick and place approach for deployable pop-up structures. This modular actuator approach shows greater flexibility and freedom in achieving haptic matching of virtual scenes.

The dynamic synchronization time of the modular actuators allows for triggered transformations during different scene transitions, or when the user is focused on viewing a specific portion of the content, and the haptic proxies providing that portion of the content are automatically synchronized based on the content panels in the headset. This process may require highly synchronized technical support. The haptic proxies triggering method can be determined by the user's operation in the virtual scene of the headset, or it can be realized by the device sensors automatically sensing the position of the person. The dynamic synchronization strategy provides technical support for the realization of smarter and more interactive haptic proxies.

Potential shortcomings of modular actuators are that auto-changeover introduces sensors and power units, which may face cost issues, and without superior technical support there may be device delays or inconsistent haptics.

In summary, each of the four haptic proxies has its own focus. The haptic proxies under the modular actuator strategy are the most effective in terms of implementation, as they can be automatically adjusted without human intervention and reduce the exploration and deployment time. The disposable props strategy is the next most effective, providing a variety of interactive experiences through different types of individual haptic objects. In terms of cost, localization is less expensive and requires only simple physical analogies and does not involve complex technology. The modular actuator is more expensive to implement as it requires different sensors and synchronization techniques that require higher accuracy.

4 ArrayWalls Device Design Practice

4.1 Design Scheme of ArrayWalls Device Suitable for Confined Spaces

ArrayWalls is a facade haptic feedback device that simulates the positional properties of obstructions in a virtual confined space (Fig. 7). The device uses 2 sets × 20 wooden boards and motorized actuators for dynamic physical haptic simulation of obstacles in a virtual scene. The device is divided into four parts: wooden boards, motorized actuators, fixed brackets, and hardware equipment.

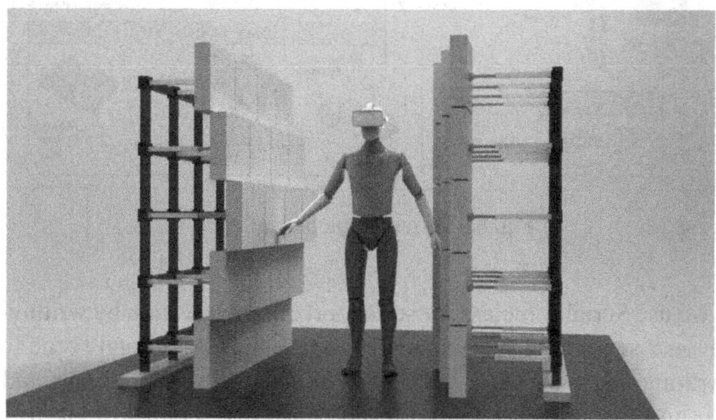

Fig. 7. Design concept.

The first part is a wooden board contacted by the user, located in the interaction area of the virtual space, which simulates the obstacles in the virtual scene and helps the user to perceive the boundary of the virtual environment and the location of the obstacles. The second part includes 2 groups × 20 motorized actuators, which realize the position expansion and contraction change through the driving force and drive the plank to pan horizontally. This design can more fully simulate various obstacle forms and positions in virtual confined space. The third part is the fixed bracket, which is used to stabilize and fix the position of the motorized actuators. The fourth part of the hardware equipment includes 2 sets × 5 Arduino Uno hardware, 2 motor drivers and 2 power supplies. Each

Arduino Uno controls the corresponding motorized actuator and receives virtual scene displacement change commands via serial communication. Two motor drivers are used for the actuator movement and two power supplies provide power support to ensure the normal operation of the whole hardware device.

4.2 Implementation Technology

The implementation of the ArrayWalls technical system is shown in Fig. 8. The overall dimensions of the device are 200 cm (L) × 225 cm (H), and each panel measures 50 cm × 40 cm, which produces 5 levels of horizontal displacement totaling 50 cm (10 cm displacement per level). Each panel is driven by a motorized actuator with motors powered by a power supply, driven by a motor driver, and controlled by an Arduino Uno, which receives commands from the Unity main PC via serial communication and is run by a custom application written in C#.

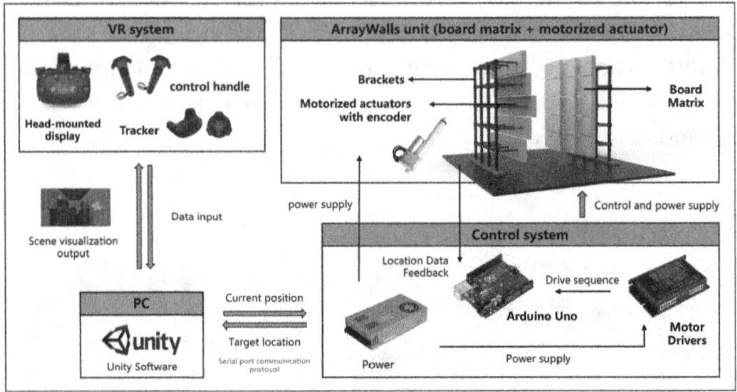

Fig. 8. System implementation.

In Unity, we use SerialPort class for serial port communication by writing C# scripts to encapsulate and send the displacement information of the virtual scene to Arduino, and on the Arduino side, we write a program to listen to the serial port and parse the received data, and then execute the corresponding displacement logic to realize the communication between Unity and Arduino, so that the displacement information of the virtual scene can be transmitted to Arduino in real time, thus controlling the electric actuator to drive the wooden board to perform the corresponding displacement movement and matching the haptic feedback with the obstacles in virtual space. The displacement transformation in the virtual scene can be transmitted to Arduino in real time, so as to control the electric actuator to drive the wooden board to carry out the corresponding displacement movement, and synchronize with the obstacles in the virtual space to match the haptic feedback.

The device is equipped with a VR system which consists of a VR headset, a tracker, and a control handle. The tracker is used to calibrate and detect the position of the user.

The synchronized transformation process of the device consists of three main states (Fig. 9). In the initial stage, the relative displacement of the device panels is set to

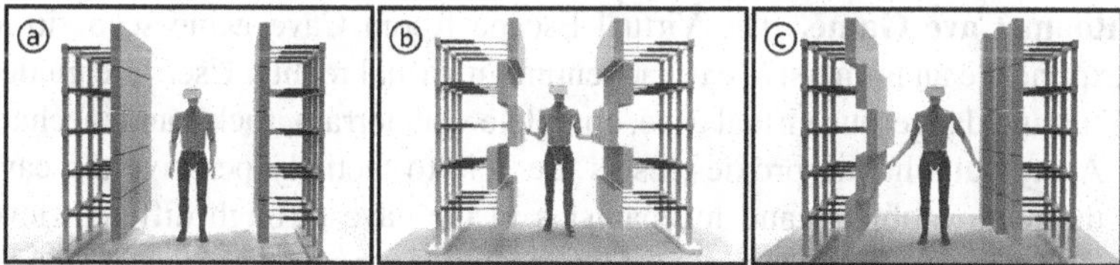

Fig. 9. Device state diagram: (a) State 1: Initial position. (b) State 2: Position change. (c) State 3: Update in position.

zero. The user selects the virtual scene through the VR headset and the device adjusts the position of each panel. During this process, Unity on the PC generates the virtual scene and communicates with Arduino Uno through the serial port to pass the position of obstacles in the scene. Arduino Uno parses the instruction and passes the target displacement to the motor driver. The motor follows the instruction and controls the movement of the electric actuator to realize the panel position adjustment. In the position update phase, the user switches the virtual scene, and based on the current position, the device drives the panel through the motorized actuator to make position matching changes again according to the displacement command received by the Arduino Uno.

4.3 Applications

Cabin Emergency Escape Training. The Virtual Cabin application allows users to build equipment, pipes, and other maneuvers and obstacles in cabin corridors in a virtual reality environment. The application offers a variety of equipment and obstacle configurations, and the ArrayWalls haptic proxies are level-driven to match cabin equipment of different sizes and shapes. Users work in the cabin through a virtual reality experience with deep haptic perception of confined space. Users can dynamically design new cabin situations and instantly adjust the shape of the haptic proxies to perceive the results of new scene configurations (Fig. 10).

Fig. 10. Installation of VR cabin aisle and facade haptic proxies.

Escape Room Cave Game. The Virtual Escape Room Cave game scenario allows users to experience an immersive cave adventure in virtual reality. Users are guided into a mysterious and dangerous virtual cave, complete with terrain, rocks, and mechanisms. Through ArrayWalls haptic proxies, users are able to tactilely perceive the cave and simulate the natural objects and mechanisms in the cave through different levels of actuation. A full range of sensory interactions provide immersive escape challenges and adventure experiences that inspire richer immersion.

5 Discussion and Future Work

In this paper, we discuss in detail the classification of classes of haptic proxies, systematically describe the haptic proxy design strategies in a scenario based on the range of the virtual scene and the deployment time of the haptic proxy transformations, and briefly analyze their impact on the user. It is worth noting that the various types of haptic proxy strategies are not mutually exclusive, and real-time techniques can be augmented or extended based on their offline counterparts. By employing hybrid strategies, it helps to render a more comprehensive haptic perception and create a broader matching experience between virtual and real objects. Second, the current categorization dimension focuses on the virtual scene scope and the deployment time of haptic proxies transformations, and subsequent research can further differentiate the techniques by haptic feedback approach, i.e., whether the haptic proxies device is actively explored by the user to perceive haptics or whether the device passively provides haptic sensations. This issue could be studied in depth as a focus of subsequent research.

This study developed ArrayWalls, a facade haptic feedback device designed to build immersive virtual reality systems.The device is capable of simulating the positional characteristics of obstructions in a virtual confined space, assisting users in interacting with visual surrogates in virtual reality through haptic perception, and enabling users to more realistically perceive the experience of obstructions and spatial sensations in a virtual space. However, the device is still in the conceptual stage, and future work will focus on development, fabrication, extensive testing and strategy validation. Meanwhile, we will look into testing a more rapid synchronization transformations system mechanism to reduce synchronization delays.

The research results have the potential for a wide range of applications in several scenarios. It can be used to design virtual training systems with stringent spatial perception requirements, such as fire escape and hazardous gas leak survival. Secondly, it can provide a more realistic sensory experience, reduce costs and increase efficiency in optimizing interior decoration and home selection schemes. In addition, for virtual immersive gaming experiences (e.g. virtual escape rooms), multi-dimensional tactile and sensory stimulation is provided. Future research could utilize the ArrayWalls device to further enhance visual-haptic synchronized sensory feedback in virtual spaces.

6 Conclusion

Haptic feedback is one of the key factors in improving the perceptual experience of virtual space. Despite the progress of virtual reality technology in hyper visual virtual immersive experience, there is still insufficient research on longitudinal spatial haptics.

This study argues that the introduction of haptic proxies can help enhance the virtual sensory experience. Through experimental validation, this study proposes a taxonomy of haptic proxies in a purely visual virtual context, based on the deployment time of the technology and the openness of the scene, and details the corresponding design strategy. It is worth noting that the haptic proxies strategies are not mutually exclusive, and future research may consider hybrid strategies to render a more comprehensive haptic perception. In this study, a facade haptic feedback device for ArrayWalls was designed to enhance the haptic experience of virtual reality. The device simulates the positional properties of obstructions in a virtual confined space to assist users in interacting with visual surrogates in virtual reality through haptic perception. However, the device is still in the conceptual stage, and future work will focus on development, fabrication, testing, and strategy validation, while exploring more rapid synchronized institutions.

Acknowledgments. This work was supported by R&D Program of Beijing Municipal Education Commission (SZ202211232025), "A Study of Emerging Groups and Design Strategies for Cultural Consumption in Beijing from the Perspective of Meaning Innovation".

References

1. Zhang, F.J., Dai, G.Z., Peng, X.L.: A review of human-computer interaction in virtual reality. Sci. China: Inf. Sci. **46**(12), 1711–1736 (2016)
2. Theodoropoulos, A., Kougioumtzoglou, G., Lepouras, G.: A virtual ship evacuation serious game: assessment of data and passenger training. In: Kiili, K., Antti, K., de Rosa, F., Dindar, M., Kickmeier-Rust, M., Bellotti, F. (eds.) Games and Learning Alliance. GALA 2022. LNCS, vol. 13647, pp. 212–222. Springer, Cham (2022)
3. Liang, Z., Zhou, K., Gao, K.: Development of virtual reality serious game for underground rock-related hazards safety training. IEEE Access **7**, 118639–118649 (2019). IEEE
4. Ricci, G., De Crescenzio, F., Santhosh, S., Magosso, E., Ursino, M.: Relationship between electroencephalographic data and comfort perception captured in a virtual reality design environment of an aircraft cabin. Sci. Rep. **12**(1), 10938 (2022)
5. Silvera, G., Biswas, A., Admoni, H.: DReye VR: democratizing virtual reality driving simulation for behavioural & interaction research. In: 2022 17th ACM/IEEE International Conference on Human-Robot Interaction (HRI) IEEE, pp. 639–643 (2022)
6. Qi, J., Gao, F., Sun, G., Yeo, J.C., Lim, C.T.: HaptGlove—untethered pneumatic glove for multimode haptic feedback in reality-virtuality continuum. Adv. Sci. **10**(25), 2301044 (2023)
7. Huang, H.Y., Ning, C.W., Wang, P.Y., Cheng, J.H., Cheng, L.P.: Haptic-go-round: a surrounding platform for encounter-type haptics in virtual reality experiences. In: Proceedings of the 2020 CHI Conference on Human Factors in Computing Systems, pp. 1–10 (2020)
8. Chang, W., Je, S., Pahud, M., Sinclair, M., Bianchi, A.: Rendering perceived terrain stiffness in VR via preload variation against body-weight. IEEE Trans. Haptics **16**(4), 616–621 (2023)
9. Teng, S.Y., et al.: Tilepop: tile-type pop-up prop for virtual reality. In: Proceedings of the 32nd Annual ACM Symposium on User Interface Software and Technology, pp. 639–649 (2019)
10. Cheng, L., et al.: Turkdeck: physical virtual reality based on people. In: Proceedings of the 28th Annual ACM Symposium on User Interface Software & Technology, pp. 417–426 (2015)
11. Yue, M.X., Xia, X.Y.: Types and characteristics of confined space accidents and application of new medical emergency rescue techniques. Chin. J. Injury Repair (Electron. Edn.) **8**(03), 238–240 (2013)

12. Zhang, Q., Chang, N., Shang, K.: Design and exploration of virtual marine ship engine room system based on Unity3D platform. J. Intell. Fuzzy Syst. **38**(2), 1241–1247 (2020)
13. Liu, D.W., Jia, H.Y., Jian, Y.H., Qiu, F.K., Yan, H.: Construction and research of tunnel fire emergency training system based on virtual reality technology. China Safety Prod. Sci. Technol. **15**(02), 131–137 (2019)
14. Hong, Y., Zhou, K.P., Liang, Z.P., Hu, Y.M.: Development of emergency training system for non-coal mine fire based on VR technology. Gold Sci. Technol. **27**(04), 629–636 (2019)
15. Ren., Y.B.: Research on interface design and scale perception of underground streets based on virtual reality. China University of Mining and Technology (2020)
16. Zhang, J.L., Lang, C.L.: Simulation research of subway train fault repair based on VR equipment. Railroad Comput. Appl. **27**(09), 21–24 (2018)
17. Tao, R., Zhu, Y.H., Ren, H.X., Guo, L.: Ship firefighting training system based on virtual reality technology. J. Shanghai Maritime Univ. **38**(01), 74–78+94 (2017)
18. Lvov, M.S., Popova, H.V.: Simulation technologies of virtual reality usage in the training of future ship navigators (2019)
19. Lee, H.G., Chung, S., Lee, W.H.: Presence in virtual golf simulators: the effects of presence on perceived enjoyment, perceived value, and behavioral intention. New Media Soc. **15**(6), 930–946 (2013)
20. Milgram, P., Kishino, F.: A taxonomy of mixed reality visual displays. IEICE Trans. Inf. Syst. **77**(12), 1321–1329 (1994)
21. Jeon, J., Choi, S.: Haptic augmented reality: taxonomy and an example of stiffness modulation. Presence **18**(5), 387–408 (2009)
22. Mullen, G., Davidenko, N.: Time compression in virtual reality. Timing Time Percept. **9**(4), 377–392 (2021)
23. Morikubo, Y., Lorenzo, E.S., Miyazaki, D., Hashimoto, N.: Tangible projection mapping: Dynamic appearance augmenting of objects in hands. In: SIGGRAPH Asia 2018 Emerging Technologies, pp. 1–2 (2018)
24. Asakawa, N., Wada, H., Shimomura, Y., Takasugi, K.: Development of VR tactile educational tool for visually impaired children: adaptation of optical motion capture as a tracker. Sens. Mater. **32**(11), 3617 (2020)
25. Teng, S.Y., Li, P., Nith, R., Fonseca, J., Lopes, P.: Touch&Fold: a foldable haptic actuator for rendering touch in mixed reality. In: Proceedings of the 2021 CHI Conference on Human Factors in Computing Systems, pp. 1–14 (2021)
26. Covaciu, F., Pisla, A., Iordan, A.E.: Development of a virtual reality simulator for an intelligent robotic system used in ankle rehabilitation. Sensors **21**(4), 1537 (2021)
27. De Tinguy, X., Pacchierotti, C., Marchal, M., Lécuyer, A.: Enhancing the stiffness perception of tangible objects in mixed reality using wearable haptics. In: 2018 IEEE Conference on Virtual Reality and 3D User Interfaces (VR), pp. 81–90. IEEE (2018)
28. Culbertson, H., Schorr, S.B., Okamura, A.M.: Haptics: the present and future of artificial touch sensation. Annu. Rev. Control Robot. Autonom. Syst. **1**, 385–409 (2018)
29. Zou, L., Ge, C., Wang, Z.J., Cretu, E., Li, X.: Novel tactile sensor technology and smart tactile sensing systems: a review. Sensors **17**(11), 2653 (2017)
30. Kučera, E., Haffner, O., Kozák, Š.: Connection between 3D engine unity and microcontroller arduino: a virtual smart house. In: 2018 Cybernetics & Informatics (K&I), pp. 1–8. IEEE (2018)
31. Chatzitofis, A., Zarpalas, D., Daras, P., Kollias, S.: DeMoCap: low-cost marker-based motion capture. Int. J. Comput. Vision **129**(12), 3338–3366 (2021)
32. Shimada, S., Golyanik, V., Xu, W., Theobalt, C.: Physcap: physically plausible monocular 3d motion capture in real time. ACM Trans. Graph. **39**(6), 1–16 (2020)
33. Nilsson, N.C., Zenner, A., Simeone, A.L.: Propping up virtual reality with haptic proxies. IEEE Comput. Graph. Appl. **41**(5), 104–112 (2021)

34. Sra, M., Garrido-Jurado, S., Schmandt, C., Maes, P.: Procedurally generated virtual reality from 3D reconstructed physical space. In: Proceedings of the 22nd ACM Conference on Virtual Reality Software and Technology, pp. 191–200 (2016)
35. Je, S., et al.: Elevate: a walkable pin-array for large shape-changing terrains. In: Proceedings of the 2021 CHI Conference on Human Factors in Computing Systems, pp. 1–11 (2021)
36. Je, S., et al.: Aero-plane: a handheld force-feedback device that renders weight motion illusion on a virtual 2d plane. In: Proceedings of the 32nd Annual ACM Symposium on User Interface Software and Technology, pp. 763–775 (2019)
37. Cheng, L.P., Ofek, E., Holz, C., Benko, H., Wilson, A.D.: Sparse haptic proxy: touch feedback in virtual environments using a general passive prop. In: Proceedings of the 2017 CHI Conference on Human Factors in Computing Systems, pp. 3718–3728 (2017)
38. Nagao, R., Matsumoto, K., Narumi, T., Tanikawa, T., Hirose, M.: Ascending and descending in virtual reality: simple and safe system using passive haptics. IEEE Trans. Visual Comput. Graph. **24**(4), 1584–1593 (2018)
39. Cheng, L.P., Chang, L., Marwecki, S., Baudisch, P.: iturk: turning passive haptics into active haptics by making users reconfigure props in virtual reality. In: Proceedings of the 2018 CHI Conference on Human Factors in Computing Systems, pp. 1–10 (2018)
40. Auda, J., Gruenefeld, U., Schneegass, S.: Enabling reusable haptic props for virtual reality by hand displacement. Proc. Mensch Comput. **2021**, 412–417 (2021)
41. Suzuki, R., Nakayama, R., Liu, D., Kakehi, Y., Gross, M.D., Leithinger, D.: LiftTiles: constructive building blocks for prototyping room-scale shape-changing interfaces. In: Proceedings of the Fourteenth International Conference on Tangible, Embedded, and Embodied Interaction, pp. 143–151 (2020)

Research on Auditory Guided Speech Experience Design Based on Traffic Light Scenarios in Urban Public Transport Spaces

Yu Wang[1,2,3](✉), Jie Wu[3](✉), and Xinping Sun[3]

[1] Shanghai Institute of Visual Arts, Shanghai, China
asterwangyu@126.com
[2] Digital Media Art, Key Laboratory of Sichuan Province, Sichuan Conservatory of Music, Chengdu 610021, China
[3] College of Design and Innovation, Tongji University, Shanghai, China
jiewu@tongji.edu.cn

Abstract. This study focuses on the design of auditory-guided speech experience in a typical urban traffic public space scenario of traffic lights, paying special attention to the three core design elements of voice gender, speech rate, and prompt word length. Through a well-designed experimental listening and data analysis process, we explored how these elements affect pedestrians' perceptions of two key experience dimensions: alertness and friendliness. The results show that the appropriate gender of the announcement voice, the reasonable speed of speech, and the appropriate length of the alert words can significantly increase the acceptance and satisfaction of pedestrians with the auditory guidance voice, which in turn can enhance their sense of safety and efficiency in the traffic environment. These findings provide strong theoretical support and practical guidance for further optimising the design of auditory guide speech in urban public transport spaces. The results of this research are of great value in promoting the design innovation and service enhancement of urban public transport spaces.

Keywords: Auditory Guided Speech · Urban Public Transport Spaces · Experience Design · Traffic Light

1 Introduction

With the continuous advancement of urbanisation and the continuous growth of traffic flow, the safety and efficiency of urban public transport space is becoming increasingly prominent. Traffic lights, as the core facilities of traffic signal control, play a pivotal role in traffic management. However, traditional traffic light visual signals may not be able to effectively convey traffic information to pedestrians in certain contexts (e.g., nighttime, bad weather, visual impairment, etc.), thus increasing traffic risks. Therefore, exploring an auxiliary guidance method that can make up for the insufficiency of visual signals and enhance the safety of pedestrians crossing the road has become an important issue in the field of smart city traffic design.

M. Kurosu and A. Hashizume (Eds.): HCII 2024, LNCS 14688, pp. 124–137, 2024.
https://doi.org/10.1007/978-3-031-60449-2_9

Auditory guided speech, as an auxiliary means of traffic information transmission, has received widespread attention in recent years and has entered the vision of researchers and designers. Auditory guided speech can effectively make up for the lack of visual signals by transmitting traffic information through sound signals, and enhance the sense of traffic safety and efficiency of pedestrians. However, the current design of auditory guidance voice in urban public transport space often lacks specificity and user experience considerations, and cannot effectively meet the diverse needs of pedestrians. Therefore, it is of great significance to carry out research on auditory guidance voice experience design based on traffic light scenarios in urban public transport space to improve the humanised service level of urban transport and promote the construction of smart cities.

This study aims to explore the design of auditory guided speech experience based on traffic light scenarios in urban public transport spaces. Specifically, the study will focus on the following aspects: firstly, analysing the current situation and existing problems of auditory guide speech design in existing traffic light scenarios; secondly, exploring pedestrians' needs and preferences for auditory guide speech through experimental audiometry and semi-structured interviews with users; and lastly, combining design theories and practices to put forward a targeted design solution for auditory guide speech.

Through this research, we expect to enrich and improve the design theory of urban public transport space, and enhance the crossing experience and traffic safety of pedestrians in traffic light scenarios. Meanwhile, the research results will also provide useful reference and guidance for practical applications in related fields.

2 Background

As an important means of traffic management, the development of traffic light systems in urban public transport spaces has gone through a process from simplicity to complexity, and from singularity to diversity. Initially, traffic light systems mainly rely on visual signals to convey traffic information, such as "stop on red, go on green". However, with the increasing complexity and diversity of urban traffic, simple visual signals can no longer meet the needs of all traffic participants. For example, visually impaired people, distracted pedestrians and drivers may not be able to accurately or timely access the information conveyed by visual signals, thus increasing the risk of traffic accidents.

In order to make up for the lack of visual signals, many cities have begun to introduce auditory guided speech in traffic light systems. Auditory-guided speech can convey traffic information directly through sound, without requiring traffic participants to make visual judgement and identification, and therefore has higher universality and accessibility. At the same time, auditory guidance voice can also be updated in real time according to changes in traffic conditions, providing traffic participants with more accurate and timely traffic information.

In this context, researchers have begun to explore more systematic and intelligent auditory guided speech design [1, 2]. Early related researches mainly focused on traffic guidance for visually impaired people, helping them to identify traffic signals and judge traffic conditions through sound signals [3, 4]. With the deepening of the research, the application scope of auditory guided speech is gradually expanded, not only covering the visually impaired people, but also beginning to pay attention to the traffic guidance needs of the elderly group, children and other special groups [5–8].

However, the design of auditory guidance speech is not an easy task. In practice, auditory guidance speech in many urban traffic light scenarios has problems such as unclear sound quality, too fast or too slow speech speed, and inappropriate speech length, which not only affect the effectiveness of auditory guidance speech, but also may have a negative impact on the listening experience of traffic participants. Therefore, how to design an effective and friendly auditory guidance speech for traffic lights has become an urgent problem.

Gender, speech rate and speech length are three important considerations in the design of auditory-guided speech. The choice of gender may affect the accessibility and authority of the voice, for example, female voices are often perceived as softer and kinder, while male voices are more assertive and powerful. The speed of speech has a direct impact on the clarity and intelligibility of the auditory-guided speech, as too fast a speech rate may result in the listener not being able to accurately understand the cue content, while too slow a speech rate may cause impatience in the listener. The setting of voice length needs to be reasonably adjusted according to the traffic condition and the size of the information, too long voice prompts may take up too much traffic time, while too short voice prompts may not be able to adequately convey traffic information.

At present, there are relatively few studies on the design of auditory-guided speech experience in traffic light scenarios, and they mainly focus on the implementation and optimisation of speech technology, with insufficient attention paid to the feelings and needs of different groups of people. At the level of auditory-guided speech design, there are still many issues worth exploring. Future research trends may include the following aspects: (1) deepening the understanding of user perception and preference, revealing the differences and needs of different user groups in auditory-guided speech perception through more refined user research; (2) how to combine the application scenarios and functions of auditory-guided speech with intelligent traffic systems and navigation systems to provide more comprehensive and intelligent traffic information services; (3) Strengthen interdisciplinary cooperation, drawing on theories and methods from psychology, linguistics, acoustics and other fields to improve the scientific and effective design of auditory-guided speech; (4) Focus on sustainable development and universal design principles to ensure that auditory-guided speech systems can work well in different traffic environments and cultural contexts.

The design of auditory guidance voice experience based on traffic light scenarios in urban public transport spaces is a complex problem involving multiple disciplines and factors. In this paper, we will start from the perspective of design science, and through in-depth experiments, we will measure and analyse the feelings and needs of different groups of people for auditory guidance speech in traffic light scenes, and explore the influence of factors such as the gender of the announcing voice, the speed of speech and the length of the voice on the alertness and friendliness of the auditory guidance speech, so as to provide a more comprehensive and humanistic guidance for the design of auditory guidance speech in traffic light scenes.

3 Subjective Evaluation Experiment

3.1 Purpose of the Experiment

The purpose of this experiment is to investigate the impact of design elements of auditory guidance speech on pedestrian experience in traffic light scenarios in urban public transport spaces. Through empirical research, we expect to provide useful references and suggestions for the design of auditory guided speech at traffic lights in order to improve pedestrians' crossing experience and traffic safety.

3.2 Experimental Sample

In our in-depth study of auditory guided speech experience design in traffic light scenarios in urban public transport spaces, we paid special attention to a number of representative cities in China, including Beijing, Shanghai, Guangzhou, Hangzhou, Chengdu and Wuhan. These cities not only have unique transport cultures, but also show certain regionalities and differences in auditory guidance speech at traffic lights.

In order to construct a comprehensive and contrasting sample library of auditory guidance speech, we carefully collected 24 auditory guidance voices from these urban traffic light scenarios. Each cue is considered as an independent data point that harbours a city-specific traffic information announcement style. However, direct experiments using these raw audios may introduce too many interfering factors, such as background noise, sound quality differences, etc., which can potentially affect the experimental results.

Therefore, we performed a careful clustering screening of these auditory guided speech. We refer to the international standard 'ISO9921:2003 Ergonomics Assessment of speech communication' [9] for the physicality parameters of speech announcements, and the screening criteria are based on three core elements: announcement voice gender, cue word length and speech rate. These three elements largely determine the basic characteristics of auditory-guided speech and the listener's intuition. After a rigorous selection process, we finally selected six red light auditory guidance voices with significant differences in voice gender, cue length and speech rate. These cues not only represent the styles of different cities, but also reflect the broadcasting effect under different design ideas.

However, during the preparation phase of the experiment, we found some problems with the underlying noise in the recorded audio. These bottom noises might interfere with the experimental participants' perception of the auditory guidance speech itself, thus affecting the accuracy of the experimental results. To solve this problem, we decided to recreate the six red light auditory guided speech.

The re-creation process makes full use of modern speech synthesis techniques. We synthesised a voice dry sound similar to the original recorded audio of the prompted voice in the red light scene using professional speech synthesis tools. The advantage of this is that we can retain the basic characteristics of the original audio while effectively removing the bottom noise and other unnecessary distractions. In addition, in order to more realistically simulate the acoustic environment of the actual road junction, we superimposed the environmental sound of the road junction and the sound cue audio of the fast pulse sound pattern in the red light scenario on the six reworked speech dry sound frequencies, and the fast pulse cue audio was spliced after the auditory guidance audio, with the beginning of the fast pulse cue sound spaced at an interval of 0.041 s from the end of the auditory guidance tone, and the beginning of the environmental sound spliced at an interval of 0.041 s from the end of the auditory guidance tone, and the beginning of the environmental sound spliced at the end of the auditory guidance tone. The beginning of the fast pulse cue was spaced 0.041 s from the end of the auditory guidance tone, and the beginning of the ambient sound was spaced 0.384 s from the beginning of the auditory guidance tone; after the fast pulse cue was finished, the ambient sound lasted no less than 3.6 s before it was finished, and the length of the fast pulse cue was 4.545 s. This not only controlled the experimental variables, but also reproduced the participants' auditory experience in the real scene as much as possible.

Eventually, we obtained a set of high-quality, representative auditory guided speech audios of red light scenarios as samples for listening. These samples varied in speech rate, announcement sound and cue word length to fully examine the impact of these design elements on the pedestrian experience. The specific parameters of the six samples are shown in Figs. 1 and 2.

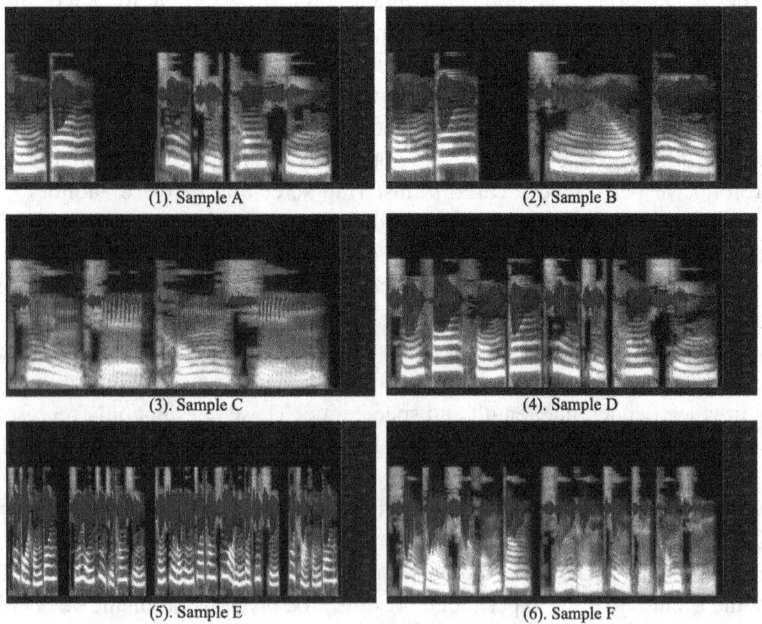

Fig. 1. Waveform and spectral composite diagram of 6 auditory guided speech dry sounds

No.	Guided Speech word (red light scene)	Announcing gender	Speech length (sec)	Speed of speech
A	Chinese: 红灯，（间隔0.378s）禁止通行。 English Translation: Red light, (0.378s interval) No passage allowed.	female voice	1.992 s	medium
B	Chinese: 红灯，（间隔0.202s）请留步。 English Translation: Red light, (interval of 0.202 seconds) Please stay.	female voice	1.457 s	slow
C	Chinese: 禁止通行。 English Translation: No passage allowed.	male voice	0.928 s	medium
D	Chinese: 前方红灯,（无间隔）禁止通行。 English Translation: Red light ahead, (no interval) no passing.	female voice	1.978 s	fast
E	Chinese: 现在红灯，行人禁止通行，城市文明交通需要您的支持，不闯红灯。 English Translation: Now the red light, pedestrians are prohibited, the city civilised traffic needs your support, do not run the red light.	female voice	6.816 s	medium
F	Chinese: 现在是红灯，行人禁止通行。 English Translation: The light is now red and pedestrians are prohibited.	male voice	2.458 s	fast

Fig. 2. Six red light guided speech detailed parameters

3.3 Experimental Process

In order to deeply explore the actual effect and user experience of auditory guided speech in traffic light scenarios in urban public transport spaces, this study adopts a refined online auditory testing method. The test relies on a professional online audio evaluation tool [10, 11], aiming to collect participants' intuitive feelings and preferences for different auditory guided speech samples.

The experiment was conducted in a quiet indoor environment to ensure that participants were able to focus on the audiometric task without external distractions. Each participant was seated in a comfortable seat and wore headphones to receive auditory-guided speech samples. Prior to the start of the experiment, the person in charge of the experiment briefed the participants on the purpose and procedure of the experiment to ensure that they understood the requirements of the task, and a preparatory test was conducted to ensure that the volume of the headphones was appropriate and that the participants were able to hear the auditory-guided speech clearly. Participants then followed the required steps on the online test page. At the end of the experiment, the person in charge of the experiment conducted a short semi-structured interview with the participants to collect additional feelings and suggestions about the auditory guided speech sample. The interviews were audio-recorded for subsequent analysis.

During the course of the experiment, the person in charge of the experiment needs to pay close attention to the participants' responses and performance to ensure that they are able to understand the requirements of the task and complete the grading conscientiously. If participants ask questions or are confused at any time, the person in charge of the experiment should answer and clarify immediately.

During the course of the experiment, we paid particular attention to two sets of core evaluative indicators: degree of WARNING and degree of FRIENDLINESS. Participants were asked to rate these two aspects in detail for each set of auditory-guided speech samples. The scoring process took the form of a continuous linear scale to ensure that participants were able to accurately and fluently express their feelings about each sound sample. The wariness scale varied continuously from 'lowest' to 'highest', while the friendliness scale similarly covered the range from 'least friendly' to 'most friendly'. The friendliness scale also covers the full range from 'least friendly' to 'most friendly'.

In order to enhance the rigour of the experiment and the accuracy of the results, all auditory-guided voice samples were carefully designed and processed. First, all voice samples were rigorously categorised into two different level grades, a design that aimed to encourage participants to capture subtle differences between samples more acutely in their comparisons. Second, the ordering of the samples as well as the ordering of the effect treatments of the samples within the categories were randomised to eliminate any possible order effects on the experimental results.

In addition, the experiment was conducted entirely based on an online platform. Participants were provided with high-quality open headphones for the test to ensure the clarity and fidelity of the audio transmission. Prior to the start of the test, they were instructed to adjust the volume to a personally comfortable listening level and to keep the volume constant throughout the test, thus ensuring that all participants were assessed under the same listening conditions. Figure 3 shows an example test page from the experiment.

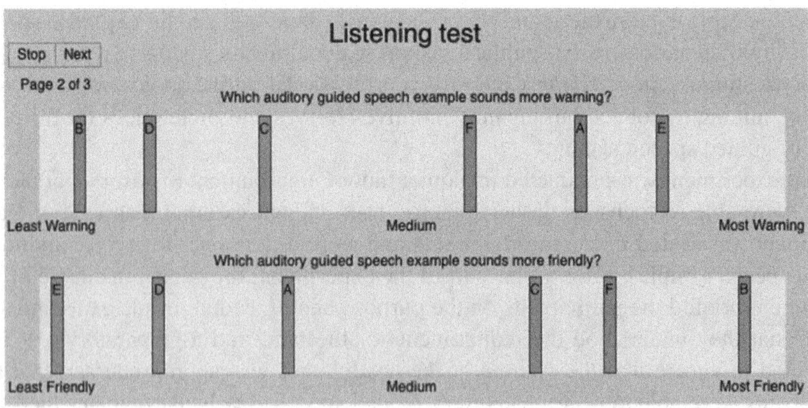

Fig. 3. Screen shot of the listening test interface, constructed with the Web Audio Evaluation Tool

3.4 Participant Information

A total of 34 participants took part in this experiment. These participants came from a variety of ages and occupational backgrounds to ensure diversity and representativeness of the results. Below are the details of the participants:

- Age distribution: 18–25 years old (12 people), 26–35 years old (10 people), 36–45 years old (8 people), 46 years old and above (4 people).

- Gender: male (18), female (16).
- Occupational background: students (10), office workers (12), teachers (4), retirees (4), others (4).

All participants had normal hearing and comprehension skills and had not participated in similar experiments before.

3.5 Experimental Data Collection and Processing

At the end of the experiment, the person in charge of the experiment collects test data and recorded interviews from all participants. These data will be collated and analysed to explore the impact of auditory guided speech design elements on the pedestrian experience. The data processing work relies on two major software tools, Python and Excel. We performed Shapiro-Wilk tests and Box-whisker Plot analyses on the data using Python. We performed a T-Test using Excel to further explore the differences and connections between the data. Through these analyses, we hope to produce quantitative results on whether there is an association between the speed of speech, the gender of the announcing voice, and the length of the cue words on the perceived level of alertness and friendliness for pedestrians. In addition, we will provide qualitative interpretations and discussions of these quantitative results in the context of the rich details from the interviews to provide a more comprehensive understanding of the important role of auditory-guided speech design in the pedestrian experience.

4 Results

According to the Shapiro-Wilk test, the p-value of the Shapiro-Wilk test for each group of data is greater than 0.05, so we can assume that the data all conform to normal distribution, and the specific results can be seen in Fig. 4.

	A	B	C	D	E	F
Friendliness	0.9489	0.9383	0.9380	0.9404	0.9405	0.9694
Warning	0.9379	0.9393	0.9438	0.9408	0.9387	0.9476
*Shapiro-Wilk W value, where p value for each test >0.05						

Fig. 4. Shapiro-Wilk Test for Friendliness and Warning Samples

Because the sample data in each group meets the requirement of normal distribution, we subsequently continued to use the paired one-sided T-test for comparing whether there is a significant monotonic difference between the two groups of sample data, and the specific results of Level of Friendliness and Level of Warning can be seen in Table 1 and Table 2. In addition, we continued to use the Box-whisker Plot to more visually compare the results of each sample between Level of Friendliness and Level of Warning, Fig. 5 shows overall Level of Friendliness across all examples whilst Fig. 6 shows Level of Warning.

Table 1. T-test of Level of Friendliness. Processor Type: o = p > 0.05, * = p < 0.05, ** = p < 0.01, *** = p < 0.001

	A	B	C	D	E	F
A	-	o	***	*	***	o
B	o	-	*	***	***	*
C	***	*	-	***	***	***
D	*	***	***	-	***	o
E	***	***	***	***	-	***
F	o	*	***	o	***	-

Table 2. T-test of Level of Warning. Processor Type: o = p > 0.05, * = p < 0.05, ** = p < 0.01, *** = p < 0.001

	A	B	C	D	E	F
A	-	*	o	*	**	***
B	*	-	o	**	***	***
C	o	o	-	*	***	***
D	*	**	*	-	o	*
E	**	***	***	o	-	o
F	***	***	***	*	o	-

The core of this study is to investigate empirically how the design elements of auditory guided speech in red light scenarios in urban public transport spaces affect the psychological experience of pedestrians. To this end, we conducted the 'Auditory Guided Speech at Red Lights Experiment' and semi-structured interviews with 34 participants. The results of the experiment are discussed in detail below, taking into account the specific experiences of the participants.

The results of the experimental data show that there is no significant difference in friendliness between Sample A and Sample B, which is mainly a difference in the speed of speech, but there is some difference in the alertness given. Also, by observing the results of Boxplot, it can be seen that faster speed of speech enhances participants' alertness. In addition, during the interviews, most of the participants stated that they were able to understand the content of the auditory-guided speech at both faster and slower speech rates, and therefore, they did not feel a significant difference in friendliness. However, they did feel a sense of urgency when the rate of speech was increased, and this sense of urgency led to increased attention and thus increased alertness.

In terms of the gender of the auditory-guided voice announcements, Sample A and Sample C, which are mainly gender-differentiated, have a high confidence significant difference in friendliness, while there is no significant difference in alertness. However, Sample D and Sample F, which also had different male and female voices, the same speed

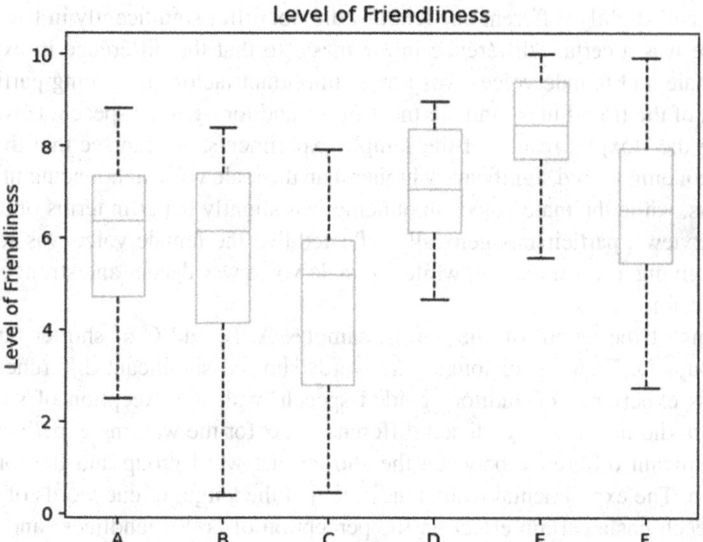

Fig. 5. Boxplot of the Friendliness rating of every processed sample

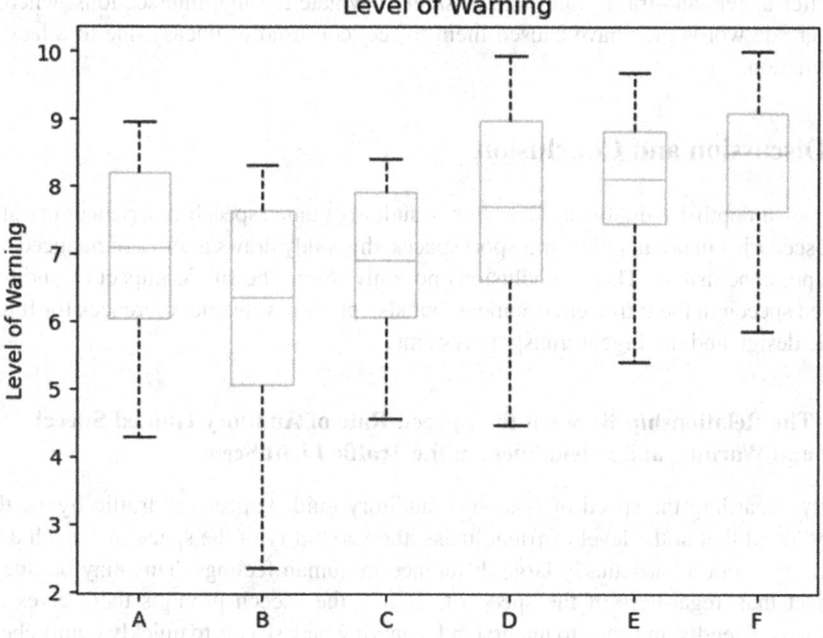

Fig. 6. Boxplot of the Level of Warning rating of every processed sample

of speech, and slightly different cue lengths, did not differ significantly in friendliness, while there was a certain difference in alertness, so that the difference in experience between male and female voices was not an important factor influencing participants' perception of the friendliness and alertness of the auditory-guided speech. However, by comparing the Boxplot results of the sample experiments, we can see that the female voice announcing scored significantly higher than the male voice announcing in terms of friendliness, while the male voice announcing was slightly better in terms of alertness. In the interviews, participants generally reflected that the female voice was softer and friendlier, giving a warm feeling, while the male voice was deeper and stronger, giving a serious feeling.

In terms of the length of cue words, samples A, B, and C of shorter cue words versus groups D, E, and F of longer cue words showed significant differences in the friendliness experience of auditory-guided speech, with the exception of samples A and F which did not show significant differences. As for the warning experience, there was a significant difference between the shorter cue word group and the longer cue word group. The experimental results indicate that the length of cue words of auditory guided speech has a certain effect on the perception of both friendliness and warning experience. Specifically, against the Boxplot results, the longer cue words scored higher on the friendliness experience and also increased alertness to some extent. In interviews, participants indicated that longer cue words provided more information, enabling them to better understand traffic rules and to safely navigate through intersections, whereas shorter cue words may have caused them to feel confused or uneasy due to a lack of information.

5 Discussion and Conclusion

After an in-depth discussion on the design of auditory guided speech experiences in traffic light scenarios in urban public transport spaces, this study draws a series of nuanced and in-depth conclusions. These conclusions not only reveal the subtle impact of auditory guided speech in the traffic environment, but also provide valuable references for future traffic design and intelligent transport systems.

5.1 The Relationship Between the Speech Rate of Auditory Guided Speech and Warning and Friendliness in the Traffic Light Scene

Firstly, regarding the speed of speech of auditory guided speech at traffic lights, this study found that at the level of friendliness, the variability of the speed of speech does not bring about a particularly large difference in human feelings. This may be due to the fact that, regardless of the speed of speech, the speech prompts themselves are somewhat friendly and easy to understand, enabling pedestrians to quickly comprehend their meaning. However, when the speed of speech gradually increased, an interesting phenomenon emerged: people's alertness began to increase. This seems to indicate that the faster speed of speech somehow activates people's attention mechanism, making them more focused on the current traffic environment. The faster the speed of speech, the more alert people became. This may be because faster speech conveys a sense of urgency, prompting people to react more quickly. However, it is worth noting that this increase in alertness is not very significant, suggesting that there are limitations to the effect of speech rate on alertness. This may be due to the fact that human beings have limited ability to perceive and process the speed of speech, and when the speed of speech is too fast, people may not be able to accurately understand the content of the speech prompts, which leads to a decrease in alertness.

Therefore, when designing a red light voice prompting system, it is necessary to weigh the relationship between speech rate and alertness and friendliness. Too fast a speech rate may impair the friendliness of the voice prompts and make the pedestrians feel nervous or uneasy; while too slow a speech rate may not be able to attract enough attention of the pedestrians and reduce their alertness. Therefore, choosing a moderate speech rate, which can ensure the friendliness of the voice prompts and effectively improve the alertness of pedestrians, is the key to the success of the design.

5.2 Relationship Between the Gender of the Announcing Voice of Auditory Guided Speech and Warning and Friendliness in the Traffic Light Scenario

Secondly, this study explored the effect of the announcement voice of auditory guided speech on alertness and friendliness. The results showed that the friendliness of the voice prompts was significantly better when the auditory-guided voice announcement voice was a female voice. This may be due to the fact that female voices are usually softer, friendlier, and more acceptable and enjoyable. In contrast, the auditory-guided voice announcements with male voices were slightly less friendly, but they showed some advantages in terms of alerting.

This may be due to the fact that male voices are usually deeper, more powerful and more likely to draw attention and alertness. However, it is worth noting that although the alertness of female voice announcements is slightly weaker than that of male voice announcements, this difference is not particularly significant. This suggests that both male and female voice announcements can effectively convey traffic signal information and remind pedestrians to pay attention to safety under appropriate design and application.

This finding is important for designing auditory guided voice prompting systems for traffic light scenarios. When choosing the auditory guidance voice announcement sound, it can be flexibly adjusted according to the actual needs and scene characteristics. For example, a female voice can be selected for scenes that emphasise friendliness and affinity (e.g. near schools, park entrances, etc.), while a male voice can be selected for scenes that emphasise warning and urgency (e.g. motorway entrances, large-scale traffic hubs, etc.). By reasonably matching the announcement voices of different genders, it can better meet the needs of different scenarios and improve the practicality and effectiveness of voice prompts.

5.3 Relationship Between the Length of Cue Words of Auditory Guided Speech and Warning and Friendliness in Traffic Light Scenarios

Finally, this study investigated the effect of the length of cue words of auditory guided speech on alertness and friendliness in red light scenarios. The results indicate that the longer the cue word the better the friendliness, which may be due to the fact that longer cue words can provide more detailed and comprehensive information to help pedestrians better understand and comply with traffic rules. Longer auditory-guided speech cues provide pedestrians with more contextual information, specific instructions, or additional safety warnings, thus enhancing their knowledge and understanding of the traffic environment. This detailed messaging makes pedestrians feel more cared for and attended to, which in turn increases their friendliness ratings of the auditory guidance voice.

Meanwhile, this study also found that the longer the auditory-guided speech cue words were the more alert, but the enhancement effect was relatively limited. This may be due to the fact that longer cue words increase the complexity and cognitive load of the message to some extent, requiring pedestrians to devote more attention to processing and understanding the information. This additional cognitive effort may motivate pedestrians to be alerted and make them more cautious and attentive in dealing with the traffic environment. However, it is worth noting that an increase in cue length may also lead to information overload or distraction for pedestrians, thus reducing their alertness. Therefore, when designing auditory guided speech systems for traffic light scenarios, the length of cue words needs to be set reasonably according to the actual situation and the characteristics of the target audience.

In summary, this study provides useful insights and suggestions for the design of auditory guided speech experience in traffic light scenarios in urban public transport spaces by thoroughly exploring the effects of speech rate, announcement sound and prompt word length on alertness and friendliness in traffic light scenarios. The future design of traffic signal system should pay more attention to the user experience and human needs, and improve the alertness and friendliness of traffic signal system by optimising the design elements of auditory guidance voice, so as to create a safer, more convenient and more comfortable urban traffic environment. At the same time, with the continuous development of technology and the popularisation of intelligent transport systems, the design of auditory-guided speech systems in traffic light scenarios will also face new challenges and opportunities. Future research can further explore how to optimise the design and implementation process of auditory-guided speech using advanced technological means (e.g., natural language processing, artificial intelligence, etc.) to improve its practicability and intelligence level.

Acknowledgements. This work was supported by grants from Digital Media Art, Key Laboratory of Sichuan Province, Sichuan Conservatory of Music, Chengdu, China, 610021. (Project No. 23DMAKL04) and Shanghai Education Science Research Project of Shanghai Municipal Education Commission (Project No. C2024202).

References

1. Cohen, M.H., Giangola, J.P., Balogh, J.: Voice User Interface Design. Addison-Wesley Professional (2004)
2. Meck, A.-M., Precht, L.: How to design the perfect prompt: a linguistic approach to prompt design in automotive voice assistants–an exploratory study. In: 13th International Conference on Automotive User Interfaces and Interactive Vehicular Applications (2021)

3. Helal, A., Moore, S.E., Ramachandran, B.: Drishti: an integrated navigation system for visually impaired and disabled. In: Proceedings Fifth International Symposium on Wearable Computers. IEEE (2001)
4. Swami, P.S., Futane, P.: Traffic light detection system for low vision or visually impaired person through voice. In: 2018 Fourth International Conference on Computing Communication Control and Automation (ICCUBEA). IEEE (2018)
5. Mittal, S., et al.: Hardware Based Traffic System for Visually Impaired Persons with Voice Guidance
6. Tang, L.: Design of portable intelligent traffic light alarm system for the blind. In: Qian, Z., Jabbar, M., Li, X. (eds.) Proceeding of 2021 International Conference on Wireless Communications, Networking and Applications, WCNA 2021. LNEE. Springer, Singapore (2022). https://doi.org/10.1007/978-981-19-2456-9_26
7. Mascetti, S., Ahmetovic, D., Gerino, A., Bernareggi, C., Busso, M., Rizzi, A.: Robust traffic lights detection on mobile devices for pedestrians with visual impairment. Comput. Vis. Image Underst. **148**, 123–135 (2016)
8. Ziman, R.: Factors Affecting Seniors' Perceptions of Voice User Interfaces (2017)
9. ISO 9921:2003:Ergonomics–Assessment of speech communication. British Standards Institution, London, UK (2003)
10. Jillings, N., et al.: Web audio evaluation tool: a browser-based listening test environment. In: Sound and Music Computing (2015)
11. Jillings, N., et al.: Web audio evaluation tool: a framework for subjective assessment of audio. In: Proceedings of the 2nd Web Audio Conference (2016)

Music-Touch: De-tactile Interactive Music Controller Design

Yu Wang[1,2,3](✉), Jie Wu[3], Xinping Sun[3], and Hanfu He[3,4](✉)

[1] Shanghai Institute of Visual Arts, Shanghai, China
asterwangyu@126.com
[2] Digital Media Art, Key Laboratory of Sichuan Province, Sichuan Conservatory of Music, Chengdu 610021, China
[3] College of Design and Innovation of Tongji University, Shanghai, China
[4] School of Humanities, Shanghai University of Finance and Economics, Shanghai, China
myside1919@163.com

Abstract. In recent years, as human-computer interaction (HCI) technology continues to evolve, it has become increasingly integrated with digital musical instruments, further extending the traditional notion of the instrument as an extension of the musician's body. In this study, we explored this area of innovation and successfully designed a light-sensitive interactive music controller called "Music-Touch", which is characterised by its de-tactile interaction. In order to gain a deeper understanding of the interaction patterns between players and the controller, we invited 12 professional musicians to learn and play Music-Touch. Through systematic testing and semi-structured interviews with these performers, we carefully analysed the subtle relationship between the design of the Music-Touch controller and their performance techniques, and explored the profound impact of the design on their performance styles and interactive music-making. Based on this, we have constructed an efficient and practical design model for interactive music controllers, aiming to bring a richer performance experience and musical inspiration to a wide range of performers.

Keywords: Digital Music Instrument · Human Interaction · Instrument Design · Performance Technique

1 Introduction

Philosopher Marshall McLuhan developed the concept of "The extensions of man." [1] He argued that the influence of the media on society stems primarily from its character, rather than the content it conveys. Over time, this concept has been expanded. Especially in the field of music performance, the idea of the instrument as an extension of the musician's body has been practised and innovated. From the perspective of human-computer interaction (HCI) in music, musical instruments can only be truly effective in the hands of the performer [2]. As a result, the expression of traditional musical instruments is constantly being expanded and reshaped.

M. Kurosu and A. Hashizume (Eds.): HCII 2024, LNCS 14688, pp. 138–156, 2024.
https://doi.org/10.1007/978-3-031-60449-2_10

As computer technology matures and sensor technology advances, the field of live performance of interactive music has been transformed. More and more composers are choosing to become personally involved in the design and manufacture of interactive music controllers (i.e., digital instruments), rather than relying solely on established traditional acoustic instruments. This trend has greatly facilitated the integration of HCI technologies with traditional musical instruments, giving rise to a wide variety of iterative interactive music controllers. For example, Essl's New Physical Instrument Design Framework [3] and Lauren's augmented instrument "Hybrid Piano" [4] are representative of this trend. However, in the journey of exploring interactive music controllers, it has become a challenge for researchers to break the limitations of traditional musical instruments and create controllers that are more integrated with the players. At the same time, how the design of interactive music controllers affects performance techniques and interactive music composition is also a question that many scholars continue to ponder during the exploration process. These issues are not only related to the innovation of technology, but also affect the future development direction of music art.

In this study, we designed an innovative de-tactile optical interactive music controller called "Music-Touch" and invited 12 players with different musical backgrounds to learn and play it. Through systematic testing and semi-structured interviews with these players, we explored the interaction patterns between the players and the Music-Touch, as well as the intrinsic relationship between the controller design and performance techniques. At the same time, we also discuss how the controller design itself influences the players' performance style and interactive music-making process. Based on these studies, we successfully constructed an efficient and practical model for designing interactive music controllers, which significantly enhances the players' performance experience and music creation experience. Our research results not only provide valuable references and guidance for the design of human-computer interaction interfaces for interactive music controllers, but also provide new ideas and directions for future music technology innovations.

2 Background

2.1 Interactive Music

Interactive music is a special form of music, which refers to the music generated in real time by the computer. With the development of music science and technology, the concept of interactive music is also being extended, and the object of interaction is not only limited to human and human or human and computer, but also the music automatically generated by computer programme in real time can be called interactive music. The degree of real-time control of the computer by the performer during the live performance is an important factor in defining whether a piece of music is interactive music or not [5]. Through different ways of human-computer interaction, computers can play different roles in the process of music creation. "The computer can be given the role of instrument, player, conductor or composer. These roles can both co-exist at the same time and in can change in real time." [6] At the same time, performers can take on different roles depending on the needs of the musical piece, either concentrating on operating the computer during the composition and performance of the piece or on manipulating interactive music controllers or other digital instruments, regardless of the computer's feedback on their performance. Composer Rowe Robert sees interactive music as a system in which performance behaviour changes in real time in response to musical input [7]. As long as there is interaction and feedback between the computer and the performer, interactive music can be built.

In an interactive music system, the performer's movements are captured in real time by microphones, controllers, or various types of sensors, and the captured performance information is transmitted to a computer system. The computer analyses the performer's movements and maps them into data, which is used to control the content of the computer's feedback. The feedback from the computer can be as varied as changing the timbre of the sound, altering the melody, or providing multisensory feedback. These feedbacks are usually in real time.

2.2 Interactive Music Controller

Interactive music controllers, also known as interactive instruments and digital instruments, are an important part of interactive music presentation. In the performance of interactive music, the controller captures the movement of the performer and maps the movement information into parameters that control the music, ultimately generating sound or music in real time. Performers playing interactive music controllers are more concerned with creating new forms of performance and generating interactions and feedbacks with the computer, rather than just generating new sounds. In recent years, research on interactive music controllers has not only been limited to exploring the hardware of the controllers themselves, but also to expanding the ways in which they can be played, and mapping the information between the computer and the performer's movements and the ways in which they can be presented.

As music technology has evolved, interactive music controllers have been updated, iterated and developed. The ubiquity of electronic sensors, the creation of the MIDI protocol, and the development of music visual programming software such as Maxmsp have lowered the barriers for scholars to investigate interactive music controllers; visual music programming interfaces such as Max allow for the construction of complex music programs for generating and controlling sensor-driven music or sounds. New research on interactive music controllers is spreading around the world, with independent artists and arts organizations, and university research organizations actively promoting research on interactive music controllers, but the practicality of interactive music controllers and the maturity of their applications still deserves attention and advancement.

The development of music technology has brought innovative sounds to composers and explored the possibilities of new forms of musical performance. The use of interactive music controllers is not only at the forefront of music technology but also crucial to the creation of new performance forms. The exploration of interactive music controllers is multidisciplinary, spanning the fields of human-computer interaction, music, psychology, and performing arts. The creation of each new music controller technology is a revolution in music creation and performance.

3 Design of Music-Touch, An Interactive Music Controller

"We want to create a complete piece of interactive music, not just an instrument or controller." [8] is one of the principles of interactive music controller design proposed by Perry Cook. Thus the ultimate goal of interactive music controller design lies in the creation of interactive music rather than just the implementation and iteration of the technology.

The design of an interactive music controller consists of 2 important components. These are the design of the performance technique and the design of the performance information mapping strategy. These 2 components define the effects of the gestural movements of the performance and the expression of the sound or other musical control parameters of the piece, which are not necessarily single-sensory, but can be audio-visual and multi-sensory. The design of the performance technique is what gestural movements are used to play the interactive music controllers. Excellent performance techniques and movements can make the performance of the work enjoyable and guide the audience to understand the meaning of the work more easily. The design of performance information mapping strategy refers to the process of converting the performance information captured by the interactive music controller into sound or other music control parameters.

The composition of an interactive music controller consists of a few main parts which are the controller body, the information mapping system and the feedback system. The body of the controller is used to capture the player's movements, and the hardware in this section consists of sensors, actuators, and the controller's form factor. The mapping system is the system that converts the performance parameters captured by the controller at the physical interface into music control or sound synthesis parameters. The feedback system can provide the player with feedback from the auditory channels of sound, music or other sensory channels.

3.1 Construction of the Design Pattern

The design of the interactive music controller Music-Touch consists of two parts. The first is the design of the control and feedback process between the player and the instrument. The second is the design of the effects presented by the audio-visual channel components, focusing mainly on the auditory channel, i.e. the design of the sound feedback system of Music-Touch.

The Music-Touch design model is based on plucked instruments, but our design does not aim to restore the traditional plucked instrument playing method, but to explore a new de-tactile interactive music playing mode, to expand new playing techniques and experiences, to establish a de-tactile interactive music controller design framework and to realise it. Music-Touch's playing mode can be understood as the process of converting human hand movements into sound through optical sensors. The Music-Touch performance mode can be understood as the process of converting human hand movements into sound through optical sensors, which focuses on how to capture human hand gestures and how to convert them into sound. We use laser sensors to capture the player's movements to achieve de-tactileisation. Figure 1 illustrates the flow of the Music-Touch human-computer interaction mode of the interactive music controller.

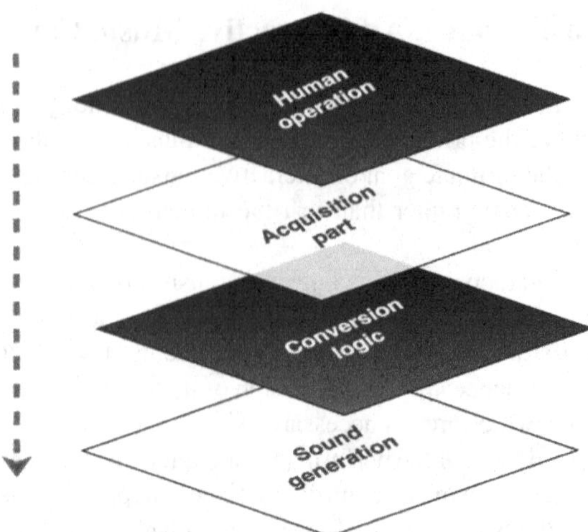

Fig. 1. Flow of Music-Touch's Human-Computer Interaction Mode

Music-Touch uses 21 pairs of pairs of laser sensors to simulate the "strings" of a traditional musical instrument. The interaction process between the player and the interactive music controller is as follows: the player triggers the light strings through gestures of different playing techniques, and the laser sensors capture and transmit the information of the player's gestures. Due to the characteristics of the laser, the player's gestures are no longer limited to the sense of touch, and his or her playing techniques are no longer limited to those of traditional plucked instruments. Special techniques such as slides and ornaments are realised with the Pitch Bend, the transposition of the Music-Touch is realised with a dip-switch that integrates a transposition programme, and the feedback process of the Music-Touch consists of translating the player's actions into acoustic or visual information.

Music-Touch converts the signal from the player's touch laser into a sound signal. In this case, the transformed information from the laser sensor is shown in Fig. 2:

We design the corresponding program to achieve the conversion of the performance information through the MIDI protocol, i.e. the Musical Instrument Digital Interface Protocol, which is a standardised technology. The standard MIDI protocol can achieve the transmission of 1 note information within 1ms, and the sequencing software on the upper end can implement the polyphony algorithm. We can directly communicate with the computer through a Microcontroller Unit (MCU) that supports the MIDI protocol, and ultimately connect to the sound system to produce sound (Fig. 3).

In this study, we designed the corresponding program to achieve the effective transformation of performance information by using the MIDI protocol (i.e., Musical Instrument Digital Interface Protocol.) The MIDI protocol, as a standardised technology, is capable of transmitting a note message within 1 ms to ensure the real-time and accuracy of the music data. At the same time, the sequencing software on the upper end supports polyphony algorithms, providing us with richer music creation and editing functions. Through the communication between the Microcontroller Unit (MCU), which supports

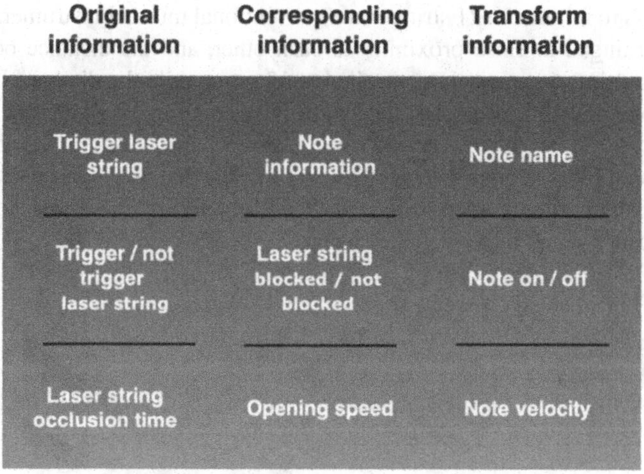

Original information	Corresponding information	Transform information
Trigger laser string	Note information	Note name
Trigger / not trigger laser string	Laser string blocked / not blocked	Note on / off
Laser string occlusion time	Opening speed	Note velocity

Fig. 2. Conversion information for laser sensors

the MIDI protocol, and the computer, we are able to transmit and process music data smoothly. Ultimately, by connecting to a sound system, we can transform these digital signals into pleasing musical sounds (as shown in Fig. 3).

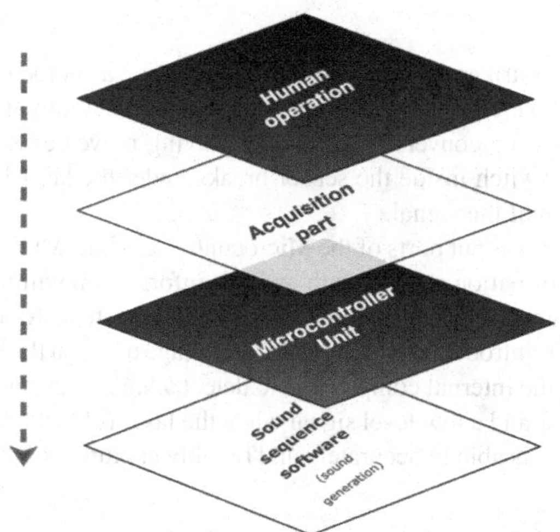

Fig. 3. Information flow for Music-Touch

3.2 Implementation of Information Collection End for Light Touch

In this study, we innovatively employ pairs of laser sensors as an alternative to traditional strings. Specifically, we constructed a laser array by carefully arranging 21 pairs of pairs of laser sensors to mimic the 21 strings on a conventional musical instrument. The laser sensors are arranged in close proximity to each other, and the distance between two adjacent laser strings is precisely controlled at 15 mm, while the distance between the ends of each pair of laser sensors, i.e., the length of the resulting laser strings, is uniformly set at 20 cm.

The M5 small laser counter sensor (Fig. 4) was chosen as the laser string, and its output is an NPN normally open switch. A "load" consisting of two resistors converts the switch closure signal into a voltage change.

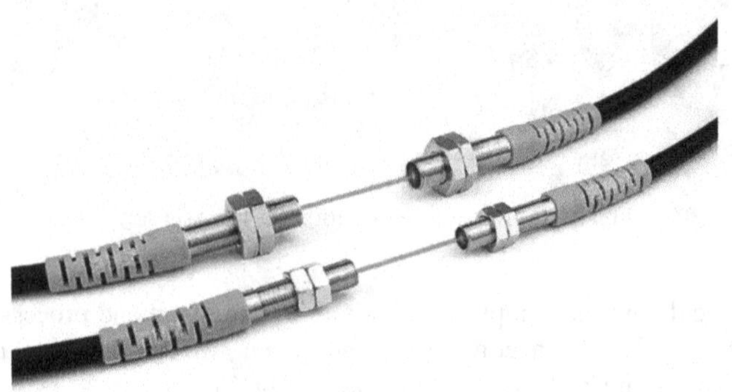

Fig. 4. M5 laser sensor

When a laser beam strikes the receiving end of the sensor, a photoelectric effect occurs inside the sensor, which efficiently converts the optical signal into an electrical signal. This process achieves the conversion of human playing movements into recognisable electrical signals. A switch inside the sensor breaks under the laser light, ensuring the accurate transmission of the signal.

Since the input and output ports of the Microcontroller Unit (MCU) can only receive analogue change information or level high and low information within a specific range, switching signals cannot be directly captured by the MCU system. To solve this problem, an additional circuit is introduced which performs voltage division through two resistors. This design enables the internal components to detect a high level signal when the laser is fired into the sensor and a low level signal when the laser is blocked. This mechanism ensures that the MCU is able to accurately and reliably capture the playing information from the sensor.

3.3 Implementation of Music-Touch Information Transformation

We design the corresponding programme based on the MIDI protocol to implement the message conversion. After analysing, the relevant MIDI protocol message part of Music-Touch (Fig. 5) is shown:

When playing, the capture terminal sends the corresponding frame data shown in Fig. 5 to the host computer, which receives, reads and generates the corresponding sound information.

Frame type	ID information	Number of data frames	Data Frame 1	Data Frame 2
Note on	0X9X	2	Note name	Opening speed (Velocity)
Note off	0X8X	2	Note name	Closing speed (Velocity)
Pitch Bend data	0XEX	2	Data-low	Data-high

Fig. 5. Related MIDI protocol information

In order to achieve convenient pitch switching, Music-Touch is specially equipped with a 12-digit dial switch module. In this module, each dial code corresponds to an independent dial switch, which allows the tone setting to be flexibly programmed and adjusted according to specific needs. The Microcontroller Unit of the acquisition system can read the status information of these 12 dials in real time, so as to accurately judge the current tone.

In Music-Touch, we have integrated the Pitch Bend module directly into the optical sensors for more direct control of pitch bends, based on the relationship between the voltage output of a sliding resistor and the pitch bend data. Through the analogue-to-digital conversion port of the Microcontroller Unit (MCU), we can read the voltage change information in real time and convert it into the corresponding pitch bend data. This process can be clearly understood and realised through the circuit diagram shown in Fig. 6, which ensures that Music-Touch excels in pitch-bending performance.

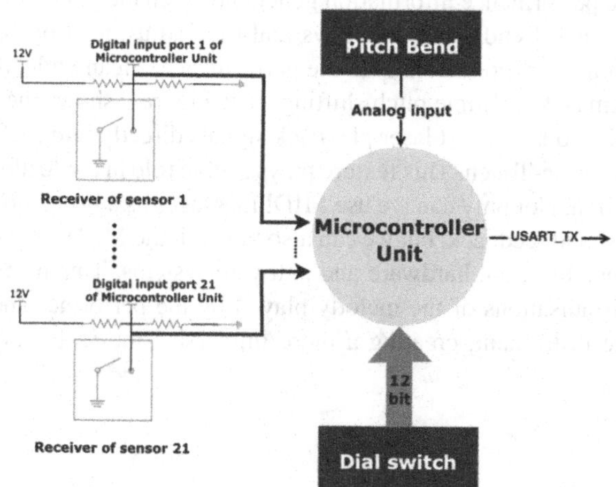

Fig. 6. Circuit schematic for Music-Touch

We developed specialised functions to correlate the note strength data with the plucking speed (i.e. the length of time that the laser string is obscured). Based on the actual playing experience and the feedback characteristics exhibited by the laser string, we initially constructed a correspondence rule between the two (see Fig. 7 for details). It is worth noting that this function is expected to be further optimised and refined as the HCI tests conducted at the acquisition side continue to deepen and iterate. In addition, it should be noted that the unit of time that the laser string is obscured is in milliseconds.

Time when the light string is blocked	Corresponding velocity according to MIDI protocol
0~150	127~110
150~250	110~80
250~350	80~65
350~400	65~35
400~1000	35~20
400~1000	20~0
More than 1000	0

Fig. 7. Correspondence between velocity and plucking speed

The programming idea of Music-Touch is shown in (Fig. 8):

After rigorous testing, we verified that Music-Touch can effectively transmit to the host computer the performance information generated when the player touches the laser string array. The Pitch Bend function allows real-time adjustment of the sound bending effect, adding more expressiveness to the performance. Meanwhile, the 12-position transpose switch makes real-time pitch shifting easy. Figure 9 shows the finished product, which is designed to convert laser playback signals directly into MIDI messages, a feature unique to Music-Touch. This feature plays a huge role in the feedback of human-computer interaction. Not only can we use MIDI messages as a bridge to various sound libraries for rich sound feedback, but we can also transmit the MIDI messages generated by the performance to visual hardware and software systems. This means that we can design unique visualisations of the melody played by the performer and the different techniques of the instrument, creating a more immersive musical experience for the audience.

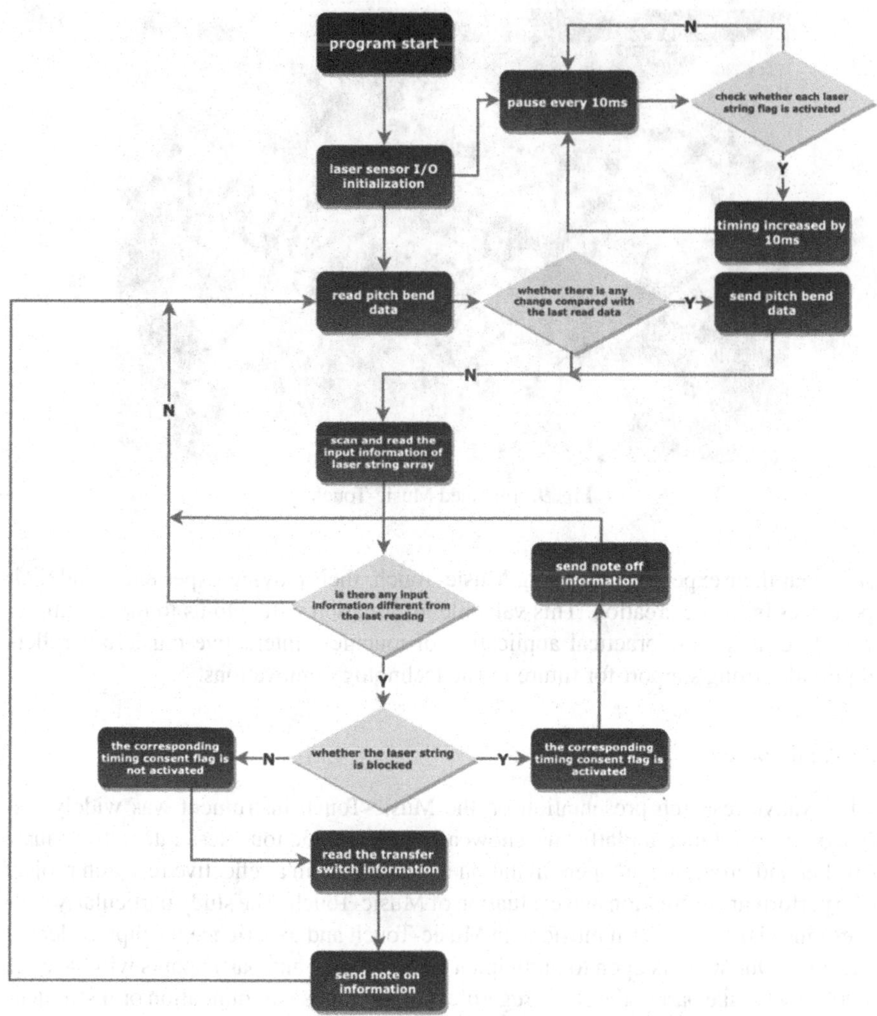

Fig. 8. Programming ideas diagram of Music-Touch

4 The Study

4.1 Study Design Overview

We conducted an exploratory study to investigate the profound impact that touchless interactive music controllers can have on a player's playing style, technique, and musicality. To this end, we invited a number of experienced musicians to participate in the study and to learn how to play music using our interactive music controller, Music-Touch. During the performance, participants were encouraged to use their imagination and play the Music-Touch freely without any limitations, while their performance was carefully observed and recorded for subsequent analysis. After the performance, the participants will be interviewed by us in a semi-structured manner. Through the interviews, we learnt

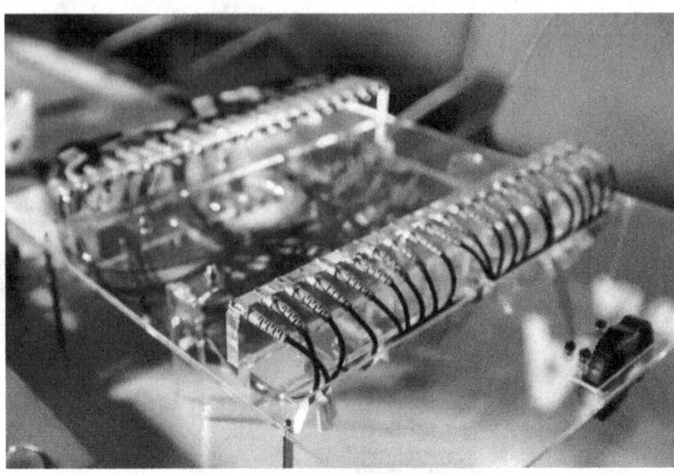

Fig. 9. Finished Music-Touch

more about their experience of using Music-Touch, their playing experience, and their experiences in music creation. This valuable information will help us to more comprehensively evaluate the practical application of touchless interactive music controllers and provide strong support for future music technology innovations.

4.2 Participants

An innovative research presentation on the Music-Touch instrument was widely distributed via social media platforms, showcasing the unique touchless interactive music controller and providing an open invitation to participate in a reflective research project on the performance, creation and evaluation of Music-Touch. The study particularly welcomes musicians to perform music with Music-Touch and experience its unprecedented interaction. Our study is open to participant backgrounds, and participants will have the opportunity to take part in the study regardless of their musical foundation or instrumental learning experience. This initiative aims to more fully explore the applicability and impact of Music-Touch on people from different backgrounds.

After screening, we invited a total of 12 participants to join this study, including 7 females and 5 males. These participants had a wide variety of instrumental learning experiences, not limited to plucked instruments, and all had some background in music learning. Their age range was between 16 and 40 years old, and their height ranged from 160 to 180 cm. All participants had normal finger dexterity and did not have any self-identified conditions that might affect their instrumental performance. This participant profile helped us to gain a deeper understanding of the actual performance and application potential of Music-Touch in different populations.

4.3 Study Sessions

Each participant will take part in Music-Touch performance teaching sessions at a frequency of twice a week, with each session lasting approximately two hours, for a cycle of three weeks. During this time, each participant will have the opportunity to practice playing independently with Music-Touch. They will be asked to demonstrate their understanding and experience of this innovative instrument by completing an interactive musical piece played on the Music-Touch according to given compositional instructions. During the course of the study, participants were encouraged to freely explore and innovate the playing techniques of the touchless interactive music controller Music-Touch without any constraints. Each of their performances was meticulously observed and recorded for subsequent analysis. In addition, a semi-structured interview was conducted with each participant after each session to collect their feedback and feelings. It is worth mentioning that this study had passed the rigorous review and approval of the ethics committee of the researcher's university prior to its commencement, which ensured the compliance of the study and the protection of participants' rights and interests. The entire course process, including presentations, interviews, recordings, and the management of the individual module projects, was personally handled by the first author of this study, thus ensuring the consistency and accuracy of the research information.

Firstly, the researchers grandly introduced Music-Touch, a unique interactive music controller, to the participants and elaborated on the precautions to be taken during its use. They emphasised that this instrument had been carefully designed to ensure that it was safe to use without any danger. After the participants had carefully observed and fully understood the Music-Touch, they confirmed their willingness to participate and solemnly signed a consent form.

The researchers then began to explain in detail the names of the tones represented by each of the laser-sensitive strings on the Music-Touch, as well as the relationships between the scales and pitches of the 21 laser-sensitive strings. They also showed the participants how to play with the Music-Touch. As Music-Touch is a de-tactile interactive music control interface, playing relies on precise interaction between the fingers and the laser-sensitive strings. In order to help the participants better grasp the playing technique, the researchers conducted a series of demonstrative demonstrations, the main gestures of which are shown in Fig. 10. These gestures not only demonstrated the unique playing style of Music-Touch, but also provided participants with valuable practical guidance.

1. Tap a single laser string with a single finger; each tap of the string produces a single clear, distinct monophonic sound.
2. Rapidly sweep the single laser beam back and forth a very short distance with a single finger to produce a dense monophonic sound effect, at this time, you can also rotate the Pitch Bend at the same time in order to produce a monophonic sound effect of glissando (rapid rise or fall in pitch).
3. Slowly pluck a single laser string with one finger while rotating the Pitch Bend on the left side of the Music-Touch interface with the other hand to create a monophonic glissando acoustic effect, the glissando range can be set according to the Music-Touch system's dip switches, ranging from 0 to 3 full tones.
4. Use several fingers to take turns touching a single light string, forming a single tone with a certain frequency rotation sound effect.

5. Use a single finger to slide back and forth between several laser light strings to form the acoustic effect of monophonic scales flowing back and forth, in which the speed of the finger sliding back and forth will also bring about different acoustic effects of monophonic syllables flowing back and forth.
6. Sweeping several laser light strings back and forth with several fingers at the same time in a very short distance to produce the sound effect of dense polyphonic sound clusters.
7. Use a single or several fingers to pluck several laser light strings at short intervals, and at the same time rotate the Pitch Bend on the left side of the Music-Touch system to form a polyphonic glissando sound group that emits sound successively.
8. Based on the plasticity of the laser sensor strings, it is possible to submerge several laser strings with smoke under low light conditions to form several laser optical fibres that randomly emit sound effects with different strengths.
9. Alternate fluctuation of laser light strings back and forth with both hands to produce the sound effect of intertwined scales.

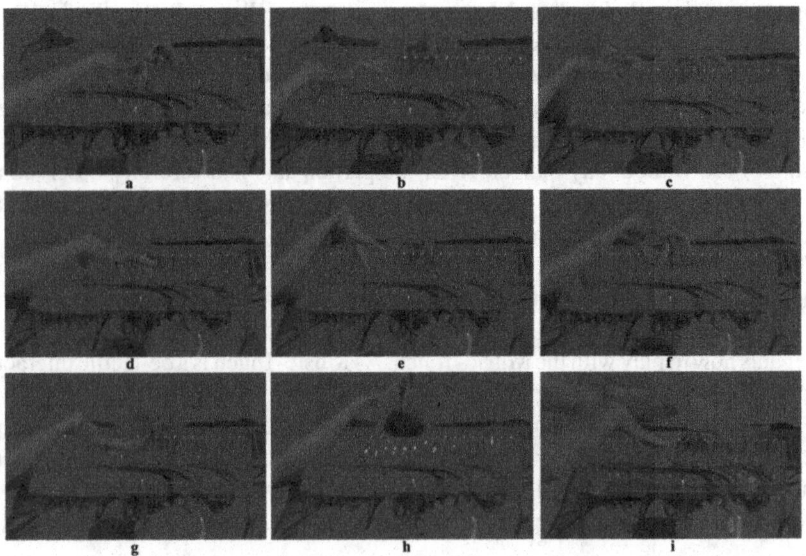

Fig. 10. Demonstration of gestures

Taking full advantage of the touchless nature of Music-Touch, an interactive music controller, and the plasticity of the laser, the researchers creatively devised unique performance techniques and provided participants with detailed demonstrations of their gestures. The laser beam is the core of the performance message, encompassing both pitch and velocity, providing the performer with plenty of room for expression, while the Pitch Bend function plays a key role in creating a glissando effect during the performance, adding a smooth and expressive element to the music. The Smoke mode is based on the plasticity of the laser, creating a fragmented particle acoustic effect through the interaction of the smoke with the laser light strings. The interaction between the smoke and the laser strings creates a fragmented particle acoustic effect, whereby each "scattered" single tone creates an acoustic effect of varying intensity in the smoke-filled environment, adding a mysterious and fascinating atmosphere to the performance. The dip-switch unit provides players with a convenient means of transposing the tone, allowing them to adjust the tone as required, bringing greater flexibility to their performance. Based on these unique features of the Music-Touch, players who have learnt to master the gestures can give full play to their imagination to further explore and innovate the Music-Touch's performance methods, and ultimately create unique and interactive musical works.

During each session, we set aside 10 min of free time for each participant to explore and familiarise themselves with the Music-Touch's unique playing style. During this 10-min period, participants can operate the Music-Touch as they wish and experience its unique musicality. Afterwards, each participant was given 40 min to conceptualise and sketch their own performance. This process is not only an in-depth exploration of interactive music-making, but also a practical application of the Music-Touch's tonal range and its laser-sensitive string characteristics. Participants will combine these elements to craft the dynamic registers, musical tempo, melodic direction, and timbral choices of the interactive music piece, thus giving it a unique personality and life. During this period, the researcher will ask detailed questions and take notes on the participants' experience of playing music with Music-Touch, in order to gain a more comprehensive understanding of their feelings and thoughts during the creative process. In the final stage of the course, during the last session, participants will have the opportunity to make a complete recording of the interactive music piece they have created using Music-Touch. This session is not only a demonstration of their creative achievements, but also a full recognition of their musical talent and innovative spirit.

4.4 Data Collection and Analysis

Each time a participant played with the Music-Touch, the entire process was meticulously recorded for subsequent analysis. The researchers also ensured that the semi-structured interviews with the participants were recorded in an exhaustive manner. These interviews were initially transcribed using the advanced ai transcription tool "suishenglu" and then carefully proofread manually to ensure the accuracy of the text.

For the collected interview data, the researchers adopted a rigorous thematic analysis method [9] for in-depth analysis. Through careful study of the original interview data, we systematically summarised the profound impact of the de-tactile interactive music controller Music-Touch on performance techniques, interactive music innovation and performance perception. In addition, we summarise the innovations of the de-tactile interface in terms of interactive music creation and digital instrument performance forms, and explore the feasibility of its further development. This study not only provides us with valuable practical experience, but also points out the direction for the future development of interactive music controllers.

5 Results and Discussion

5.1 Innovations in Playing Techniques

As participants became more familiar with Music-Touch over the course of the six study sessions, they added new gestures and performance techniques without any performance constraints. The gestures used to play Music-Touch included those demonstrated to the participants by the researcher (Figs. 11 and 12) as well as those innovated by the participants themselves.

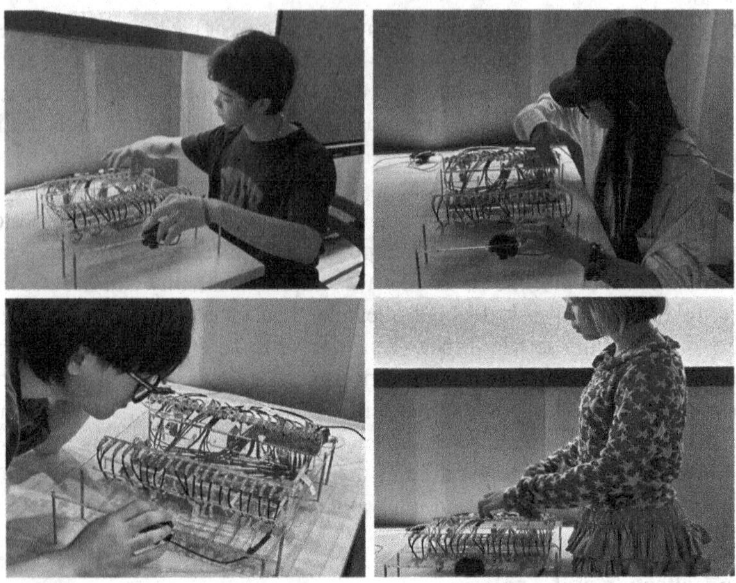

Fig. 11. Participants try to play Music-Touch alone

Nine participants (P1, P2, P4, P5, P6, P7, P8, P9, P11) created new playing techniques. Some of these new playing gestures were created to finely control the Music-Touch to produce new acoustic effects. For example, P2 used a single finger to rapidly sweep two strings back and forth while simultaneously rotating the Pitch Bend back and forth, commenting that with this technique he could create the acoustic effect of a dense cluster of polyphonic tones with rapid pitch rises and falls. P6 even experimented with playing with his entire head obscuring the light strings, which he thought would better express the emotional attitude of the interactive music he was composing and also create polyphonic tones. He thought that this would better express the emotional attitude of the interactive music he was creating, and also create the acoustic effect of an instantaneous columnar response of the polyphonic tone cluster.

P2 said, "Since I can't feel the tactile sensation of touching the light strings, I feel very free when I play, and I'm not limited by the tactile sensation of the specific 'strings', so I can use all kinds of finger movements to interact with the light strings as much as I want, which is something I've never had before when I learnt to play a plucked

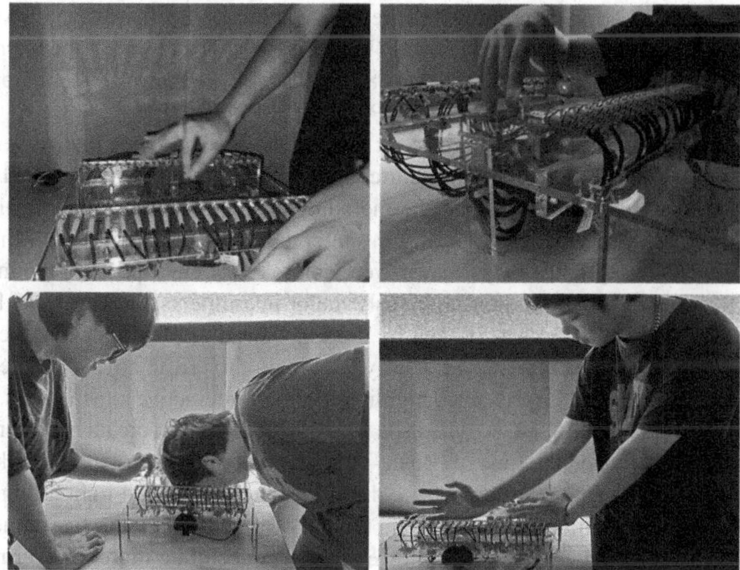

Fig. 12. Participants innovate new playing techniques

instrument." P5 said that in the past he had to spend a lot of time practising the basic playing techniques of his instrument, which he often found very boring, but with the Music-Touch, a de-tactile interactive music controller, he was free from this limitation. P6 thought that when he played with the Music-Touch, the same acoustic effect was no longer limited to a specific gesture, and after learning the basic demonstration, he could use various finger movements to interact with the light strings. After learning and exploring the basic demonstrative gestures, he was able to find several different gestures to produce the same sound effect, which gave him great freedom to play and inspired him to create interactive music. He could no longer limit himself to playing techniques to create melodies and sound effects. The de-tactile interface allows him to feel that his body has been 'extended' by the instrument, as if the Music-Touch is part of his body, his own limb to create music.

P7 said that the smoke played with a point-like dispersion of sound effects that he had never experienced before, and that the diffuse nature of the smoke gave him great creative surprises. He was able to use this method of playing to create a sound effect similar to the colourful percussion of "Tone Vertical". Since Music-Touch uses a sampling library, he can choose different libraries to create different dotted sound effects, and P9 feels that this new way of playing with smoke has expanded his body, and he feels as if he has more than one pair of hands to play the instrument. The diffuse acoustic effects of the smoke instruments have inspired him to create ambient interactive music.

5.2 Innovations in Composing Interactive Music

In terms of composing interactive music, five of the 12 participants created pieces without fixed beats (P1, P4, P6, P7, P9), and four created pieces with fixed beats (P2, P3, P5, P10), which were performed in their entirety. Three participants created pieces that switched back and forth between fixed and free beats (P8, P11, P12). The tempo of the interactive music they created ranged from 75 BPM (P8) to 170 BPM (P12), with the majority of pieces ranging from 85 BPM to 120 BPM (P2, P3, P5, P8, P10, P11).

Each participant was asked to create an interactive musical piece that represented their own musical style. In the semi-structured interviews, 2 participants (P8, P11) indicated that they reflexively associated the melodies of their previously learnt plucked instruments in the process of composing the interactive musical works, and thus the interactive musical melodies they created were similar in some aspects to the musical forms of the music played on their previously major instruments. However, the homogeneity of the musical form was broken by the innovation of playing techniques, and occasionally there were some innovative ways of playing to create novel sound effects, which became occasional surprises and highlights in their interactive music works. P10's major instrument is percussion, so when she used Music-Touch to create her interactive music work, she adjusted the tone of Music-Touch to that of a percussion drum kit and tried to create the rhythmic pattern of the drum kit by clapping the light strings with her hands. She said, "Although there was no touch, the percussion tones that came back from the non-tactile control interface allowed her to concentrate more on hearing and feeling the percussion tones in the process of creating the interactive music, rather than having to focus part of her attention on the percussive action of playing the percussion itself as she would have had to do. P12, a wind instrument player, believes that when he tries to create interactive music works with Music-Touch, the focus of his music creation has shifted from the timbral characteristics of the instrument itself to the technical innovations of the instrument, which often bring him new inspirations for composing music.

5.3 Discussion

Designing performance movements has profound implications for the creation and performance of interactive music. In traditional acoustic or electroacoustic instrument performance, a strong bond is established between the player and the instrument. In order to become proficient on their instrument and perform classical repertoire, players need to learn a variety of established performance techniques in depth and practice them to achieve proficiency. However, for the creator of the music (the composer), their relationship with their instrument may not be so strong. Even if a composer does not play a certain instrument, they can still create a piece of music based on the playing characteristics of that instrument through the theory of compositional techniques. In the case of the interactive music controller Music-Touch, the situation is different. Due to the de-tactile design of the Music-Touch interface, the playing technique is no longer limited to a set pattern, but is constantly being reinvented with the participation of different players. This makes the players themselves creators and composers of interactive music. They create interactive music by designing unique movements, a process that not only reflects their individuality, but also injects new vigour into the development of interactive music. Therefore, the process of designing performance movements is closely related to the process of creating interactive music, and the two are complementary to each other.

Through in-depth analyses of the participants' semi-structured interviews, we discovered an interesting phenomenon: when confronted with a new type of interactive instrument, many players will tend to play it directly and intuitively, rather than first learning its playing techniques. This intuitive playing process often gives rise to innovative playing methods that may develop naturally without much thought. From the listener's point of view, the specific movements of the performer and their amplitude not only form part of the performance, but also help the listener in some way to understand the interactive music being composed. Well-designed movements visualise some elements of the interactive music, allowing the listener to experience the music not only aurally, but also visually, enhancing the perception of the music. This combination of audio and visual enhances the intelligibility of interactive music for the listener, making it easier to understand and appreciate. In the context of today's rapid technological development, the software and hardware of digital musical instruments are constantly being updated, and new ways of playing and techniques are emerging. This makes it difficult for interactive music creators to find a standardised performance principle to adapt to the performance of various digital instruments. While haptics, one of the key senses in interactive digital instrument performance, plays an important role in designing performance techniques, it also has some limitations. A de-tactile digital instrument interface provides a solution to this problem. It breaks down the tactile sensory constraints on the performance interface, providing players with a broader space for thinking and physical extensibility. By removing the tactile constraints, players are better able to become one with the instrument, seeing it as part of their body and an extension of their limbs. This more boundless interaction between human and instrument brings infinite possibilities for the innovation of performance movement, which in turn promotes the continuous innovation and development of interactive music.

6 Conclusion

In this longitudinal exploratory study, we invited musicians to perform using the Music-Touch, a de-tactile interactive music controller. It was found that this de-tactile, light-sensitive control interface had a significant impact on the players' ability to create and perform interactive music. Traditionally, players have tended to rely on the tactile sensation of their fingers to play their instruments, which has resulted in the need to allocate some of their attention to the playing action itself during performance. However, the de-tactile interactive music controller interface allows the performer to focus more on the feedback end of the controller and concentrate more on the sound or music generated by the interactive music controller. At the same time, by removing the limitations of haptics, the players gained more freedom in their bodies. They were no longer bound by the sense of touch and could innovate their playing techniques more freely. We observed a significant increase in the amplitude of the playing movements of some of the performers, which made the performative aspect of the interactive music more prominent and enhanced the audience's understanding of the interactive music. In addition, we found that participants gained a new awareness of their bodies while playing with Music-Touch. They felt that their bodies were expanded, as if the interactive music controller itself became part of their limbs. This sense of bodily extension not only made the performers feel more flexible and powerful, but also enriched their inspiration to create interactive music, positively impacting the compositional process. However, we are also aware of certain limitations of this study. Since each player is a unique individual, repeating the same study with different players may yield different results. Therefore, in future studies, we will continue to explore more possibilities of de-tactile interactive music controllers and consider more individual difference factors.

We delve into the modes of interaction between the performer and the touchless interactive music controller, and analyse the strong links between the design of interactive music controllers and performance techniques. We focus on how the design of the controller itself affects the way the player plays and the process of creating interactive music. Through this series of studies, we successfully constructed an efficient and practical design model for interactive music controllers. This model not only significantly improves the players' performance experience, but also brings more inspiration and possibilities for their music creation. In addition, our research results also provide valuable reference and guidance for the design of human-computer interfaces for interactive music controllers, which will help promote the further development of this field.

Acknowledgements. This work was supported by grants from Shanghai Education Science Research Project of Shanghai Municipal Education Commission (Project No. C2024202) and Digital Media Art, Key Laboratory of Sichuan Province, Sichuan Conservatory of Music, Chengdu, China, 610021. (Project No. 23DMAKL04) and Chenguang Project of Shanghai Municipal Education Commission and Shanghai Education Development Foundation. (Project No. 19CGB06).

References

1. McLuhan, M.: Understanding Media: The Extensions of Man. McGraw-Hill, New York (1964)
2. Cascone, K.: The aesthetics of failure: "post-digital" tendencies in contemporary computer music. Comput. Music. J. **24**(4), 12–18 (2000)
3. Essl, G., O'modhrain, S.: An inactive approach to the design of new tangible musical instruments. Organised Sound **11**(3), 285–296 (2006)
4. Hayes, L.: Haptic augmentation of the hybrid piano. Contemp. Music. Rev. **32**(5), 499–509 (2013)
5. Fiebrink, R.A.: Real-time human interaction with supervised learning algorithms for music composition and performance. Princeton University (2011)
6. Lippe, C.: Real-time interaction among composers, performers, and computer systems. Inf. Process. Soc. Japan SIG Notes **2002**(123), 1–6 (2002)
7. Rowe, R.: The aesthetics of interactive music systems. Contemp. Music. Rev. **18**(3), 83–87 (1999)
8. Cook, P.: 2001: principles for designing computer music controllers. In: A NIME Reader: Fifteen Years of New Interfaces for Musical Expression, pp. 1–13 (2017)
9. DeCuir-Gunby, J.T., Marshall, P.L., McCulloch, A.W.: Developing and using a codebook for the analysis of interview data: an example from a professional development research project. Field Meth. **23**(2), 136–155 (2011)

Eye-Gaze-Based Intention Recognition for Selection Task by Using SVM-RF

Shuai Wang[1], Hongwei Niu[1,2], Wanni Wei[1], Xiaonan Yang[1,2,3(✉)], Shuoyang Zhang[1], and Mingyu Ai[1,2,3]

[1] Industrial and Systems Engineering Laboratory, School of Mechanical Engineering, Beijing Institute of Technology, Beijing, China
yangxn@bit.edu.cn

[2] Yangtze Delta Region Academy, Beijing Institute of Technology, Jiaxing, China

[3] Key Laboratory of Industry Knowledge and Data Fusion Technology and Application Ministry of Industry and Information Technology, Beijing Institute of Technology, Beijing, China

Abstract. This paper focuses on the problem of intention recognition in eye-gaze-based interaction. The user's intention could be divided into two types: selection and non-selection. In this study, a within-group experimental design was designed to complete the target letter selection task through eye-gaze-based interaction. Python is used to develop an experimental software for better flexibility in recording data. The SVM-RF model has been built and compared with other algorithms such as SVM, RF, etc. The importance weight of different eye movement behavior features on the accuracy of intention recognition has been analyzed by comparing the accuracy of the model through the permutation feature importance method. The results indicated that the SVM-RF model had a prediction accuracy of 94.3%, which can effectively predict the user's selection intention and provides reference value for the future development of eye-gaze-based interaction technology.

Keywords: eye-gaze-based interaction · intention recognition · selection task · SVM · RF

1 Introduction

Eye-gaze-based interaction is notable for its intuitive and natural characteristics, greatly enhancing the convenience and productivity of human-computer interaction. Additionally, its non-intrusive and non-contact nature confers unique benefits in specific scenarios. Consequently, eye-gaze-based interaction holds significant research value and vast untapped potential as a vital mode of interaction.

In the process of interaction, identifying and understanding user intentions play a crucial role. Intention recognition serves as a core technology for eye-gaze-based interactions by analyzing eye movement data to predict intended actions accurately while reducing user workload through providing shortcuts or facilitating interactions. The Midas Touch Problem (MTP) arises from inaccuracies in intention recognition during eye-gaze-based interactions [1]. To address this issue effectively, employing fixation

M. Kurosu and A. Hashizume (Eds.): HCII 2024, LNCS 14688, pp. 157–168, 2024.
https://doi.org/10.1007/978-3-031-60449-2_11

duration as a mechanism for target selection represents a classical yet widely adopted approach for intention recognition [2]. Additionally, eye-gaze-based interactions can be realized through behaviors such as blink and saccade. Fixation duration or dwell time is an indicator of a user's intent to select an object by eye-gaze alone [3–7]. However, this time threshold can negatively impact the user experience. Another common approach to avoid the MTP is to use a physical trigger as a confirmation mechanism, such as a hand controller or keyboard [8–10]. In such cases, it also makes sense to identify the interaction intention to simplify the physical button operation or to give more information as visual feedback based on the recognition result. However, constructing rules from a computer's perspective undermines the goal of achieving naturalistic interactions while potentially causing visual fatigue to occur more rapidly. To achieve more naturalistic eye-gaze-based interactions without compromising usability or inducing visual fatigue prematurely, there is an increasing trend towards utilizing machine learning techniques to analyze eye movement data for user intentions accurately [11–15]. Fixation count, fixation duration, saccade velocity, and pupil diameter are commonly employed as training data for eye movement analysis in order to reduce the learning cost associated with user interactions while preserving their inherent naturality [14]. This approach presents an ideal means of achieving eye-gaze-based interaction. However, its effectiveness is heavily influenced by the quality of eye movement data and data processing methods. Low accuracy and limited generalization ability remain significant challenges within this domain, necessitating further research to enhance the practical applicability of eye-gaze-based interaction.

This paper focuses on the problem of intention recognition in eye-gaze-based interaction. To simplify the study's complexity, we categorized the user's intentions into two types: selection and non-selection. The task interface is presented as a twenty-square grid with random letters assigned to each position. To minimize data acquisition quality impact, we utilized Tobii Pro Spectrum to acquire raw data on eye movement due to its high detection frame rate and ability to reduce head movement interference during experiments. A within-group experimental design was employed to accomplish the target letter selection task through eye-gaze-based interaction. Feedback regarding participants' gaze point locations throughout the experiment was provided [16]. We determined that various characteristics of fixation and saccade, such as the fixation count, the average fixation duration, the saccade count, and the dwell time, play a crucial role in the employed model. Furthermore, the SVM-RF algorithm exhibited a prediction accuracy of 94.3%, indicating its efficacy in predicting users' selection intentions.

2 Method

2.1 Participants

This experiment recruited a total of 23 college students as participants. One of the subjects was discarded due to irregularities found in their data. The age of the participants is between 18 and 30 years old, with uncorrected or corrected visual acuity of at least 1.0, no eye diseases, no contact lenses, contact lenses or false eyelashes. Participants are also required to ensure sufficient sleep before the experiment, avoid staying up late, excessive eye use, and use their right hand for dexterity. To gain a comprehensive understanding of the participants, they are also required to provide objective information such as their age, gender, and the duration of their sleep from the previous night. This information will help the researchers gain a deeper understanding of the subjects' backgrounds and their potential impact on the experiment's results. The conduct of this experiment required approval from the ethics committee. Before the experiment, each participant must complete an informed consent form and received a certain amount of reward after the experiment.

2.2 Apparatus

The experimental stimuli were presented on a 24-in. monitor with a resolution of 1920 × 1080, the background color was black, and the target object of the experiment was a random Microsoft YaHei UI 72-sized yellow English letter presented in the center of a 150 px × 150 px yellow square border. 20 interaction objects consisted of 20 uppercase English letters selected randomly without repetition were distributed in any position of a 4 × 5 layout structure, with a horizontal spacing of 195 px and a vertical spacing of 96 px between two neighboring square borders (as shown in Fig. 1).

To minimize data acquisition quality impact, we utilized Tobii Pro Spectrum to acquire raw data on eye movement due to its high detection frame rate and ability to reduce head movement interference during experiments. To ensure the seamless execution of the experiment procedure and the capture of vital data, the experiment software was crafted utilizing Python and PySide6, which is a Python binding for the QT framework. The software was structured with four distinct functional modules: procedure display, eye tracking, behavior detection, and data recording.

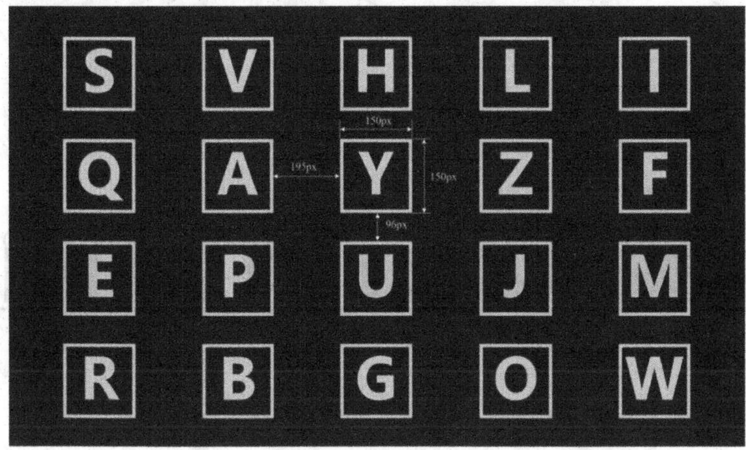

Fig. 1. The selection task interface (Color figure online)

2.3 Experiment Procedure

The experiment encompassed two sections: a pre-experimental phase and a formal experimental phase. The pre-experimental phase was designed primarily to familiarize the participants with the experimental protocol. To ensure consistency in participants' familiarity level, we established an 80% selection accuracy rate as the criterion for advancement. Once participants met this criterion, they were permitted to proceed to the formal experiment. Otherwise, they were required to continue with the pre-experimental phase (as shown in Fig. 2).

Based on the results of the pre-experimental phase, which aimed to minimize the impact of visual fatigue on selection tasks, we determined the maximum duration of trials per round. Following each round, participants were granted a five-minute rest period before resuming subsequent rounds until they experienced visual fatigue and were unable to continue. Participants were instructed to accomplish the task by selecting target letters, and their selection intentions were recorded through mouse clicks (as illustrated in Fig. 3).

To enhance the participants' eye-gaze-based interaction experience, the experiment offered two types of interactive visual feedback. One was visual marker feedback, which provided real-time feedback on the participants' gaze position in the form of a circular marker. The other was selection feedback, which indicated that the border of the target letter to be selected would turn blue, indicating selection, when the participant pressed the mouse to record their intention to select it.

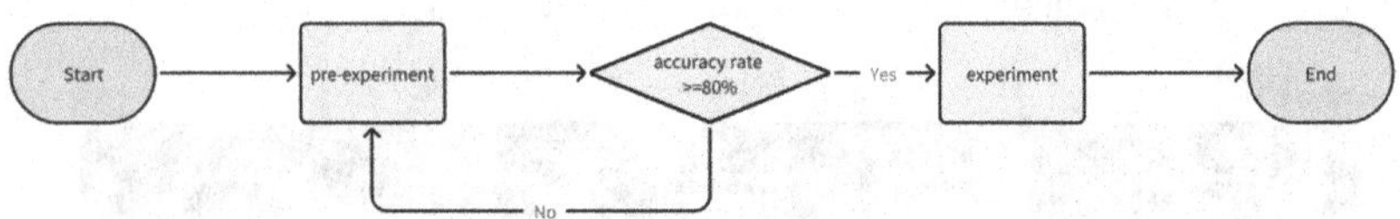

Fig. 2. Experiment procedure

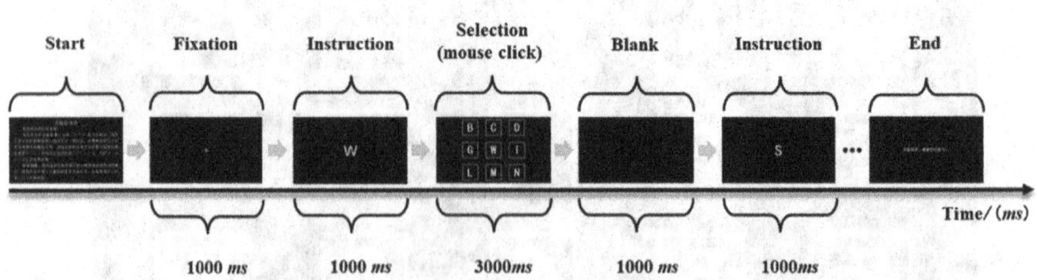

Fig. 3. Trial procedure

2.4 Data Processing

Behaviors. Prior to feature extraction, it is imperative to conduct eye movement behavior detection, as it serves as the foundation for calculating diverse eye movement behavior features. Consequently, eye movement behavior detection holds a pivotal position in data analysis. In our study, the I-VT algorithm was employed to detect fixation and saccade behaviors. For blink detection, we relied on the eye openness data captured by the Tobii Pro Spectrum. By analyzing this data, we derived judgment thresholds, such as blink openness range and blink duration. Subsequently, we implemented the blink detection algorithm. Table 1 presents the parameter range for the eye movement behavior detection algorithm.

Table 1. Parameters for eye movement behavior detection algorithm

Behavior	Parameter	Value
Fixation	Maximum Velocity	20°/s
	Minimum Duration	50 ms
Saccade	Minimum Velocity	80°/s
	Minimum Duration	25 ms
Blink	Eye Openness	3.5–5
	Blink Duration	67–300 ms

Features. Upon synthesizing the existing research, four key categories of eye movement patterns were identified: fixation, saccade, blink, and pupil dilation. These features are comprehensively enumerated in Table 2. Of particular note, dwell time quantifies the duration of gaze within the Area of Interest (AOI), potentially encompassing both fixations and saccades. This metric serves as a proxy for the level of interest in the AOI. The first fixation interval, on the other hand, measures the time elapsed from the initial entry into the AOI to the occurrence of the first fixation. This metric reflects the strength of the selection intention. Location interval denotes the time from the commencement of a trial until the initial entry into the AOI, indicating the proficiency in visually searching for the AOI. The first fixation total interval is computed as the sum of the first fixation interval and the location interval.

Dataset. Initially, it is crucial to utilize statistical analysis techniques to discern the distinctive patterns of eye movements that exhibit a robust predictive capability for decision-making intentions within the original data. This dataset comprises text labels, which are represented as tuples consisting of eye movement characteristics and corresponding user intention labels. The dataset is structured as $D = \left\{\left(f_{fc}^{i}, f_{afd}^{i}, f_{ffd}^{i}, f_{dt}^{i}, \ldots\right), y_i\right\}, i = 1, 2, 3, \ldots, N$. Where N represents the number of data, f_{fc}^{i} represents the fixation count, f_{afd}^{i} represents the average fixation duration, f_{ffd}^{i} represents the first fixation duration, f_{dt}^{i} represents the dwell time, y_i represents the label of eye-gaze-based selection intention. When the eye movement data collected by the eye tracker aligns with the current object and the designated target, it is designated as intentional eye movement data, labeled as 1. Conversely, if the eye movement characteristics captured by the eye tracker do not correspond to the target object, it is deemed non-intentional eye movement data, labeled as 0.

Table 2. Features derived from fixation, saccade, blink, pupil responses

Types	Features
Fixation Related	Fixation Count Average Fixation Duration First Fixation Duration Dwell Time First Fixation Interval Location Interval First Fixation Total Interval
Saccade Related	Saccade Count Average Saccade Duration
Blink Related	Blink Count Average Blink Duration
Pupil Related	Average Pupil Diameter Average Pupil Diameter Change Rate Average Pupil Diameter Maximum Difference

Classifiers. Utilizing the features outlined in preceding sections, we constructed models capable of automatically categorizing observations into positive (indicating selection intention) or negative outcomes. We integrated the Support Vector Machine (SVM) with the Random Forest (RF) algorithm, denoted as SVM-RF or SR, and evaluated its performance alongside other algorithms including SVM, RF, eXtreme Gradient Boosting (XGBoost), and Logistic Regression (LR). RF and XGBoost algorithms represent ensemble learning techniques, where the former employs bagging integration strategy while the latter utilizes boosting. Similar to RF, the SR algorithm leverages ensemble learning principles, combining the strengths of SVM and RF algorithms while compromising some training speed. To obtain the final model output, we employed soft voting, which combines the probability values derived from each individual model. All aforementioned algorithms were implemented using Scikit-learn, a popular open-source machine learning library in Python. To ensure optimal performance, we conducted parameter tuning to identify the best set of parameters for each classifier, utilizing the F_1-Score as the evaluation metric.

Metrics. Accuracy refers to the proportion of correct predictions in all predictions, which is the quantitative ratio between the correct predicted value of the model and the total predicted value. The calculation formula is given as follows:

$$Accuracy = \frac{TP + TN}{TP + FP + FN + TN}$$

Precision refers to the ratio between the number of correctly predicted values and the total predicted value of the model in samples with positive predicted values. The calculation formula is given as follows:

$$Precision = \frac{TP}{TP + FP}$$

Recall refers to the ratio between the correct predicted value of the model and the total predicted value in samples with positive real values. The calculation formula is given as follows:

$$Recall = \frac{TP}{TP + FN}$$

Precision and Recall are contradictory metrics. Generally speaking, when Precision is high, the Recall value tends to be low. When Precision is low, Recall is often high. When the classification confidence is high, Precision is high. When the classification confidence is low, Recall is high. In order to comprehensively consider these two metrics, F-measure was proposed (weighted harmonic mean of Precision and Recall). The formula for calculating the F_1-Score is given as follows:

$$F_1 = \frac{2 \times (Precision \times Recall)}{Precision + Recall}$$

AUC value refers to the probability that a classifier outputs a positive sample and a negative sample randomly, and the probability value that the positive sample is higher than the probability value that the classifier outputs a positive negative sample, reflecting the classifier's ability to sort the samples. The calculation method of AUC takes into account the classification ability for both positive and negative cases, and can still make reasonable evaluations of the classifier even in cases of imbalanced samples. Its value is the area under the ROC curve. Assuming that the ROC curve is formed by sequentially connecting points with coordinates $(x_1, y_1), (x_2, y_2), (x_3, y_3), \ldots, (x_m, y_m)$, then AUC can be estimated as:

$$AUC = \frac{1}{2}\sum_{i=1}^{m-1}(x_{i+1} - x_i)(y_i + y_{i+1})$$

3 Results

3.1 Feature Selection

Correlation Analysis. In the realm of data analysis, understanding the distribution of features and their relationship to one another is crucial for drawing meaningful insights. The data distribution of the features was first analysed to test that the features do not conform to a normal distribution. The spearman correlation coefficient was employed to correlate the features and obtained a feature heat map, which is shown as Fig. 4.

The analysis revealed that the correlation coefficient between average fixation duration and first fixation duration was 0.97, indicating a strong positive correlation. Since both measures related to fixation duration, it is reasonable to assume that they capture similar information. Therefore, to avoid redundancy, the first fixation duration was discarded. Similarly, the correlation coefficient between location interval and first fixation total interval is 1, indicating a perfect positive correlation. This suggests that the two intervals are identical and, therefore, the first fixation total interval was discarded. Furthermore, average saccade duration and average blink duration were also discarded due to their high correlation with other features.

On the other hand, fixation count, dwell time, average fixation duration, and saccade count exhibited relatively high correlation with the label. These features were found to characterise the strength of the intention to select. They provide valuable insights into the cognitive processes underlying visual attention and selection.

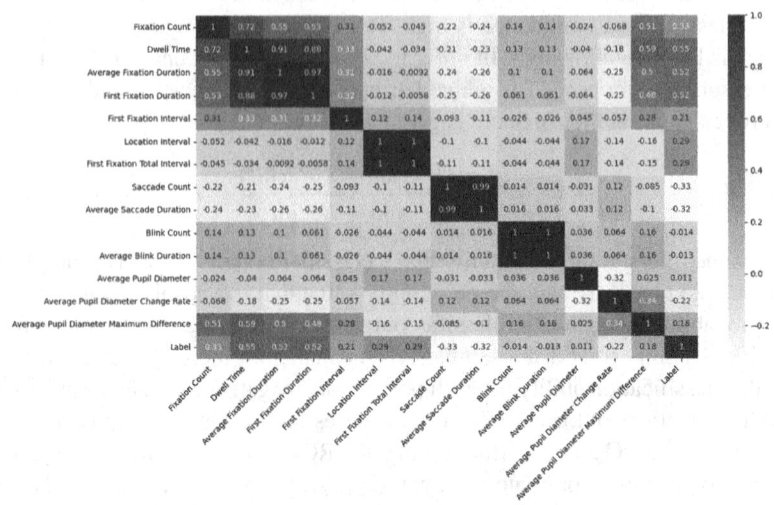

Fig. 4. Feature heat map

Feature Importance. After an initial screening of the features, the permutation feature importance methodology was employed to assess the importance of each individual feature. This method quantifies the importance of a feature by measuring the extent to which random perturbations to its values impact the overall performance of the model. To ensure a more objective evaluation, 20 distinct random shuffling orders were utilized, accounting for the stochastic nature of permutations. Accuracy was chosen as the metric to measure model performance.

The results of our analysis are presented in Fig. 5, which illustrates the impact of randomly altering the order of each feature on the accuracy of each model. The order of features for each model in the bar chart is the same as the order listed in the legend. The vertical axis represents the change in model accuracy before and after each disruption, providing a clear indication of the sensitivity of the model to perturbations in specific features. The analysis reveals that certain features stand out as more important for different models. Fixation count, dwell time, average fixation duration, first fixation interval, location interval, and saccade count are relatively more significant for SVM and SR compared to other features. Conversely, for RF and XGBoost, average fixation duration, dwell time, location interval, and saccade count are significantly more important than fixation count and first fixation interval. For LR, only average fixation duration and fixation count stand out as the most critical features.

These findings highlight the importance of considering the specific characteristics and sensitivities of different machine learning models when analyzing the significance of individual features. By understanding the unique requirements of each model, we can develop more targeted and effective feature selection strategies to improve model performance and accuracy.

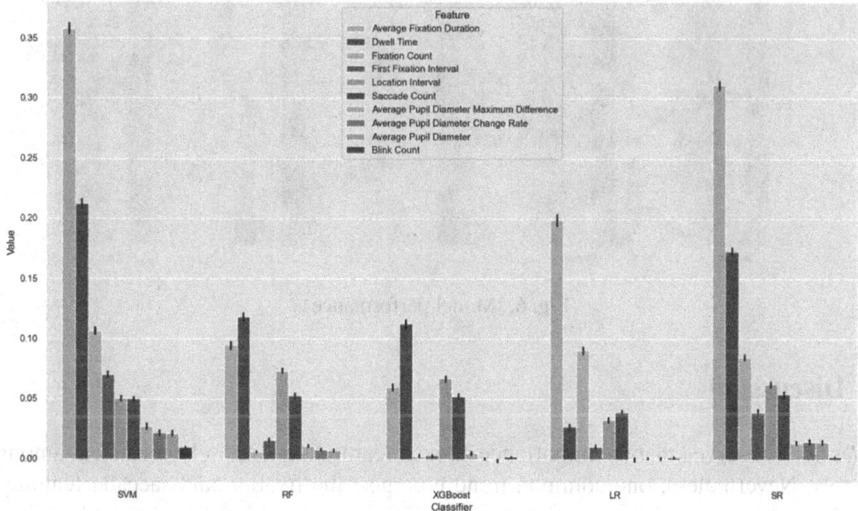

Fig. 5. Permutation feature importance

3.2 Model Performance

After tuning the parameters of each model, we obtained the corresponding performance metrics, which are presented in Fig. 6. A thorough comparison among the models reveals that the SR algorithm exhibits the most outstanding overall performance. Following closely behind is the RF algorithm, while SVM and XGBoost lag slightly behind. The least effective model is the LR algorithm. However, it's worth noting that the performance difference between SR, RF, and SVM algorithms is not particularly significant when viewed from a comprehensive perspective.

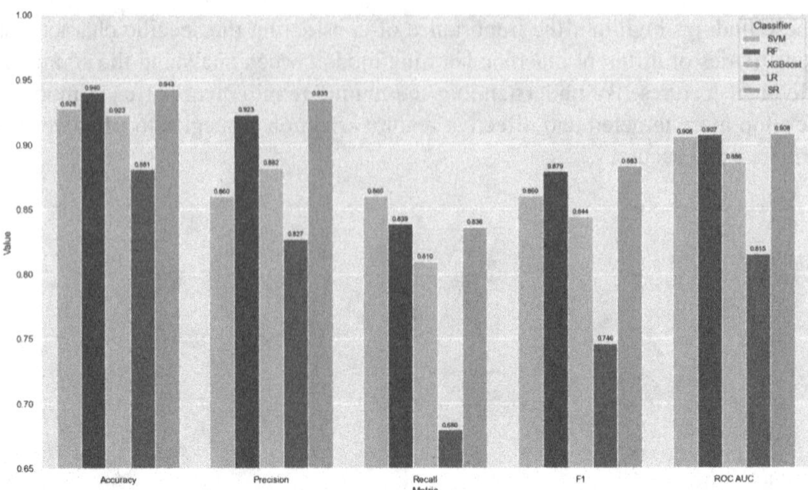

Fig. 6. Model performance

4 Discussion

It has been observed that the importance of each feature is not entirely consistent among models. Nevertheless, one common trend emerges: the fixation and saccade features, which capture the basic movement patterns of the eye, are crucial for model building. Fixation represents the stationary state of the eye, reflecting the processing of visual information, while saccade represents the rapid movement of the eye, indicating the transfer of attention. On the other hand, blink and pupil-related features seem to play a lesser role in almost all models. This might be due to the fact that these features are more sensitive to environmental factors and individual differences, making them less reliable for intention recognition.

Given the importance of fixation and saccade features, it becomes imperative to develop an accurate eye movement detection algorithm. This involves continuously adjusting and optimizing the thresholds of fixation and saccade detection algorithms. By fine-tuning these thresholds, we can enhance the algorithm's sensitivity and specificity, leading to more precise eye movement tracking.

Furthermore, it is worth mentioning that the performance of intention recognition models heavily relies on the quality of eye movement data. Therefore, it is essential to ensure that the data is collected under controlled conditions, using reliable eye tracking devices. Additionally, preprocessing techniques such as noise reduction and outlier removal can further enhance the quality of eye movement data, improving the accuracy of intention recognition models.

In conclusion, eye movement analysis plays a pivotal role in intention recognition. By understanding the importance of various eye movement features and optimizing eye movement detection algorithms, we can construct high-performance intention recognition models that meet the performance requirements. Future research can explore the integration of additional eye movement features to enhance the accuracy and reliability of intention recognition systems.

5 Conclusion

We conducted experiment to investigate eye-gaze-based interactions and employed various machine learning algorithms to model and analyze the collected eye movement data. Our findings suggest that the features associated with fixation and saccade play a crucial role across all models employed, including fixation count, average fixation duration, saccade count and dwell time. Therefore, we propose to optimize the algorithms used to detect eye movement behavior. This optimization is expected to enhance data quality and boost the accuracy of recognizing interaction intention, ultimately leading to more natural and efficient eye-gaze-based interactions. Additionally, the SVM-RF model exhibits a prediction accuracy of 94.3%, demonstrating its capability to accurately predict the user's selection intentions. This provides valuable insights and serves as a reference for the continued advancement of eye-gaze-based interaction technology.

Acknowledgement. The authors would like to thank the Foundation Strengthening Project (2022-JCJQ-JJ-0858).

References

1. Duchowski, A.T.: Gaze-based interaction: a 30 year retrospective. Comput. Graph. **73**, 59–69 (2018)
2. Mutasim, A.K., Batmaz, A.U., Stuerzlinger, W.: Pinch, click, or dwell: comparing different selection techniques for eye-gaze-based pointing in virtual reality. In: ACM Symposium on Eye Tracking Research and Applications, in ETRA 2021 Short Papers, pp. 1–7. Association for Computing Machinery, New York, NY, USA, May 2021
3. Isomoto, T., Yamanaka, S., Shizuki, B.: Dwell selection with Ml-based intent prediction using only gaze data. Proc. ACM Interact. Mob. Wearable Ubiquitous Technol. **6**, 1–21 (2022)
4. Isomoto, T., Ando, T., Shizuki, B., Takahashi, S.: Dwell time reduction technique using Fitts' law for gaze-based target acquisition. In: Proceedings of the 2018 ACM Symposium on Eye Tracking Research & Applications, in ETRA 2018, pp. 1–7. Association for Computing Machinery, New York, NY, USA (2018)
5. Pi, J., Koljonen, P.A., Hu, Y., Shi, B.E.: Dynamic Bayesian adjustment of dwell time for faster eye typing. IEEE Trans. Neural Syst. Rehabil. Eng. **28**, 2315–2324 (2020)
6. Mott, M.E., Williams, S., Wobbrock, J.O., Morris, M.R.: Improving dwell-based gaze typing with dynamic, cascading dwell times. In: Proceedings of the 2017 CHI Conference on Human Factors in Computing Systems, in CHI 2017, pp. 2558–2570. Association for Computing Machinery, New York, NY, USA (2017)
7. Chen, Z., Shi, B.E.: Using variable dwell time to accelerate gaze-based web browsing with two-step selection. Int. J. Hum.-Comput. Interact. **35**, 240–255 (2019)
8. Deng, C.-L., Tian, C.-Y., Kuai, S.-G.: A combination of eye-gaze and head-gaze interactions improves efficiency and user experience in an object positioning task in virtual environments. Appl. Ergon. **103**, 103785 (2022)

9. Parisay, M., Poullis, C., Kersten-Oertel, M.: EyeTAP: introducing a multimodal gaze-based technique using voice inputs with a comparative analysis of selection techniques. Int. J. Hum. Comput. Stud. **154**, 102676 (2021)
10. Rozado, D., Niu, J., Lochner, M.: Fast human-computer interaction by combining gaze pointing and face gestures. ACM Trans. Access. Comput. **10**, 1–18 (2017)
11. Çığ, Ç., Metin Sezgin, T.: Gaze-based prediction of pen-based virtual interaction tasks. Int. J. Hum.-Comput. Stud. **73**, 91–106 (2015)
12. Murata, A., Doi, T., Kageyama, K., Karwowski, W.: Development of an eye-gaze input system with high speed and accuracy through target prediction based on homing eye movements. IEEE Access **9**, 22688–22697 (2021)
13. Chen, X.-L., Hou, W.-J.: Gaze-based interaction intention recognition in virtual reality. Electronics **11**, 1647 (2022)
14. Jang, Y.-M., Mallipeddi, R., Lee, S., Kwak, H.-W., Lee, M.: Human intention recognition based on eyeball movement pattern and pupil size variation. Neurocomputing **128**, 421–432 (2014)
15. Lee, S.W., Kim, H., Yi, T., Hyun, K.H.: BIGaze: an eye-gaze action-guided Bayesian information gain framework for information exploration. Adv. Eng. Inf. **58**, 102159 (2023)
16. Zhang, X., Feng, W., Zha, H.: Effects of different visual feedback forms on eye cursor's stabilities. In: Rau, P.L.P. (ed.) Internationalization, Design and Global Development. LNCS, vol. 6775, pp. 273–282. Springer, Heidelberg (2011). https://doi.org/10.1007/978-3-642-21660-2_31

A Relative Pitch Based Approach to Non-verbal Vocal Interaction as a Continuous and One-Dimensional Controller

Samuel Williams(✉) and Denis Gračanin

Virginia Tech, Blacksburg, VA 24060, USA
{shwilliams,gracanin}@vt.edu

Abstract. Non-verbal vocal interaction (NVVI) allows for non-speech vocal inputs to be used to control applications. Prior work in the niche field has explored a variety of modalities of NVVI such as whistling, humming, blowing, and tongue clicking. Different techniques, including pitch gestures, continuous, and discrete control have been explored. In this work, we analyze results from a large-scale study exploring a pitch-based NVVI modality that uses a relative pitch interaction technique to offer a continuous mode of one-dimensional control. A user study is outlined and was performed via Amazon Mechanical Turk for recruitment and study access, and a modularized study website where participants controlled an HTML slider with the NVVI technique by humming and whistling. Additionally, participants performed similar tasks using the computer mouse as a baseline. In total, 72 participants' results are considered for analysis. Results show that the pitch based NVVI technique used in this study does not follow Fitts' Law, participants did not perform as well with the NVVI technique as they did with the computer mouse, and that participants experienced a significantly higher task workload using the NVVI technique than with the computer mouse.

Keywords: Human-centered computing · Human computer interaction (HCI) · Auditory feedback · Natural User Interfaces · Interaction techniques · Non-verbal Vocal Interaction (NVVI)

1 Introduction

Natural user interfaces, including verbal vocal interactions like speech processing, are ubiquitous and commonly used in both industry and academic settings. However, speech processing is limited by language requirements. Non-verbal vocal interaction (NVVI) provides further opportunities for people to use their vocals as an input modality. Despite the many possibilities of NVVI input modalities, such as whistling, humming, and tongue clicking, the field is niche and literature is few and far between.

Pitch is a notable exception, as a variety of pitch based NVVI techniques have been explored in prior work. However, interaction techniques differ in modalities

M. Kurosu and A. Hashizume (Eds.): HCII 2024, LNCS 14688, pp. 169–186, 2024.
https://doi.org/10.1007/978-3-031-60449-2_12

of input, underlying algorithms, and many of the interaction designs involve *pitch gestures* that translate into discrete commands. Additionally, prior work focused primarily on specific applications, such as accessibility (i.e., mouse clicking [10, 21] and keyboards [11,17]) and game-like inputs [6,19], and not on high level interaction design principles.

NVVI offers a wide variety of possible interaction schemes. Examples of NVVI include using human acoustics, such as whistling, humming, and clicking, as interaction techniques. Certain characteristics of these types of acoustics, such as volume, pitch, formant information (harmonic resonances produced during speech [8]), and spectral information from vowel sounds, can be detected, analyzed, and converted to numeric input. The bounds of NVVI extend to the range and variety of possible sounds humans can produce, sans speech.

Some fields NVVI can benefit include accessibility, as they can serve as inputs for physically/motor impaired individuals. For example, a person could control the dimness of their lighting with the pitch of their voice instead of physically adjusting a slider. Language barriers present in speech processing also limit the audience and functionality of speech processing tools.

The variety of possible NVVI types can provide continuous user-generated control inputs, like pitch, not possible with speech processing, in addition to discrete inputs/actions. Some example inputs include humming, whistling, clicking of the tongue, and blowing, among others. NVVI can also serve as an effective alternative/orthogonal mode of interaction, working on top of other modes of interaction.

For example, NVVI could be used in eXtended Reality (XR) environments to allow extended capabilities instead of just the buttons and axes provided by controllers. Compared with other controller schemes in mixed reality, such as any controller scheme that relies on point-to-point interactions involving distance like raycasting, a human acoustic controller scheme does not involve distance and therefore the precision or accuracy of any parameter modulation should theoretically not be effected by distance.

In this work, voiced-based natural user interfaces are explored, referred to as non-verbal vocal interaction (NVVI.) We first explored NVVI techniques from three aspects - human vocal modalities and characteristics, vocal characteristic detection and estimation algorithms, and state of the art NVVI techniques. Then, we chose to narrow our scope to focus on a pitch based NVVI technique to control a one-dimensional continous value.

We designed a large scale study to conduct an analysis with significantly more participants and data than most of the examined prior work. In the study, users were tasked with controlling an HTML slider with the NVVI technique via the pitch of their whistling or humming. Performance and feedback were also compared with the computer mouse to complete the same tasks. The following four research questions were proposed.

1. Does pitch-based NVVI follow Fitts' Law?
2. How does a pitch-based NVVI technique compare with a computer mouse?

2 Related Works

In 3D environments like virtual reality, non-traditional 3D user interfaces and interaction techniques allow users immersed in virtual environments to have the ability to provide more types of interaction. For example, Sardana et al. found that three-dimensional coordinated-multiple views interaction techniques is more efficient than two-dimensional interfaces [14].

Multi-modal techniques allow users to leverage multiple input modalities as a controller, which can be highly useful for abstract applications. For example, Handosa et al. suggest that multi-modal interactions are preferable to uni-modal interactions for controlling Smart Homes [5].

NVVI systems may be useful for providing controls during hands-busy situations and serve as a useful design for people with physical disabilities [6,9]. The two primary forms of NVVI described in the reviewed literature fit into 2 categories: triggered and continuous input. Additionally, some of the examined work used vocal gestures, short melodic or rhythmic patterns to trigger commands [12]. An example of a pitch based vocal gesture, or pitch gesture, is depicted in Fig. 1.

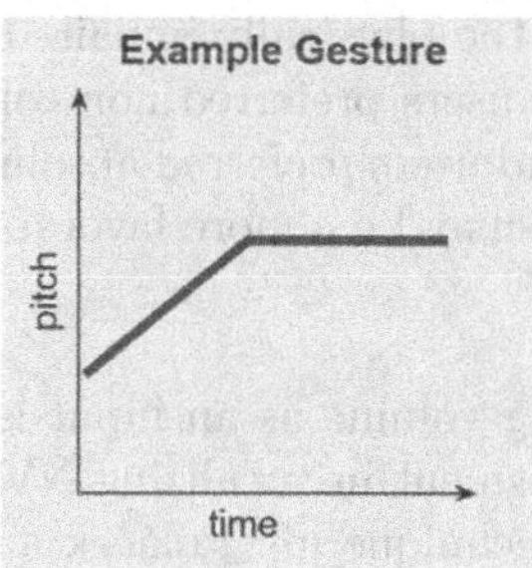

Fig. 1. An example pitch gesture, where the pitch is modulated upwards for a time and then held constant for a time.

Triggered Input. One study used blowing as an input to trigger clicking [21]. User input was captured and processed to determine if they were blowing, and if they were, a mouse click was triggered. The Vocal Joystick NVVI system processes a discrete *k* sound to trigger a mouse click [10].

Continuous Input. Pitch is a common mode of continuous NVVI input [6,7,11, 12,16,17,19]. Many of the systems use pitch as the basis for a vocal gesture-based interaction system, explained in the next section. However, properties of pitch alone can be used as an interaction technique [6,7]. Formant information can also be used as input to an NVVI system, as demonstrated by Harada et al. [2]. Their technique analyzed the user-produced formants pertaining to a set of vowels, and mapped them to a two-dimensional grid to be used like a joystick. Whistling and humming appear to be the most used forms of pitch input.

Vocal Gestures. Vocal gestures are short melodic or rhythmic patterns to trigger commands [12]. For example, if a user starts by humming a pitch at frequency f_0 and slides it up to a new pitch f_1, and the NVVI system has a mapping from this gesture to a command, the corresponding command will execute (if it is recognized properly). Gestures were used in several of the examined publications [11–13, 17, 19].

2.1 Discussion

User performance with NVVI compared with traditional techniques varied from study to study, and there does not appear to be any conclusive quantitative assessment of the effectiveness of NVVI in general compared to other interaction techniques. This is largely due to the variety and limited quantity of available work.

Users may prefer alternatives to NVVI systems [13], but some users still think favorably of NVVI in terms of interest and enjoyment [6, 7]. A major limitation of pitch and gesture-based NVVI systems appears to be skill and physical ability to produce the required frequencies [2, 12]. For example, fatigue is a common response to the use of NVVI systems. However, NVVI appears to be a strong alternative of interaction for the physically impaired [11, 17].

Poláček et al. found that users preferred non-complicated gestures, such as flat tones [12]. They also found users preferred absolute pitch gestures to relative pitch gestures. NVVI control may be a more favorable control style than speech commands [19].

Design Considerations. Using volume as an input is a considerable interaction technique, but user embarrassment in vocalizing NVVI input may play a factor in their comfort using this technique [6]. Poláček and Míkovec note that pitch gestures are a cultural and language independent mode of vocal interaction [13].

The ACF appears to be a common implementation for pitch detection and control as a continuous input [6, 12, 19]. Zielasko et al. used machine learning techniques to more accurately determine if a user was blowing [21]. Multiple algorithms may be used for better resolution depending on the frequency range [7].

2.2 Limitations

In the reviewed studies, the main limitation was the limited number of accessible publications found on existing NVVI systems. However, another two major limitations were the number of authors and the size of studies. Regarding the former, for example, Sporka was included as an author to 8 of the 14 included studies of NVVI systems [9–12, 16–19], while Poláček was included as an author in 4 [11–13, 17]. This supports the claim that the area of NVVI is a niche field of research. Only 3 studies were conducted with more than 20 participants [12, 13, 21], while 4 studies had 10 or less participants [2, 10, 17, 19].

Another limitation was the variety of projects and prototypes used these studies, including video games [6,7], keyboard alternatives [11,17], to controlling radio cars [19], among others. In conjunction with the limited quantity of literature and relatively small sample sizes, it is difficult to accurately synthesize corroborating information from the results of the variety of studies performed.

3 Approach

The NVVI interaction technique we chose to explore is a relative pitch-based NVVI technique [20] that converts user audio data into two components: a *pitch* and *confidence score*. The estimated pitch and confidence score calculated by the NVVI technique serve as inputs to an application, presented in (Fig. 2).

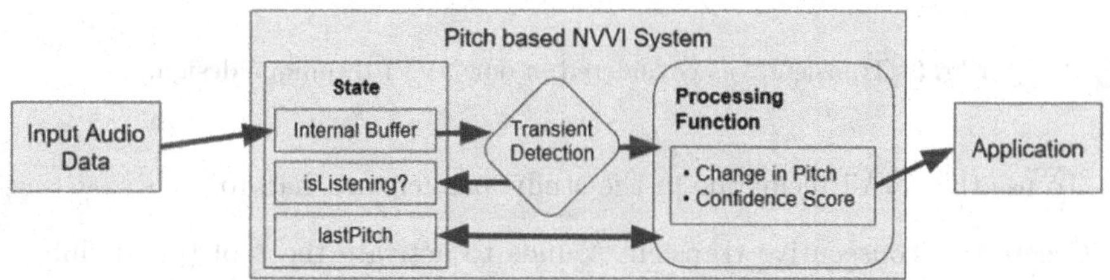

Fig. 2. Non-verbal Vocal Interaction (NVVI) framework.

The pitch detection algorithm used was the auto-correlation function (ACF, [15]) since it is a robust algorithm that is premised on correlating a unique periodic signal with itself. The confidence score is used in the technique to provide an idea of when the user is producing an intentional pitch or not. In our implementation, we used a normalized root mean square (RMS) volume to indicate confidence on a scale from 0 (not confident) to 1 (very confident.)

A logical issue arises when the tool is used in noisy environments, especially in environments where there are frequencies with strong presence in the background. Additionally, pitch is present in speech, so we decided that there should be a way to activate the technique only when the user intends to use it. Thus, the technique also provides *selection*, a capability to determine when the tool should be active or inactive, controlled via *transient detection*.

The particular pitch interaction technique used in the technique is a relative pitch technique. This technique involves identifying a relative change in the pitch of the user's voice to be used as a functionally continuous input to an application. In summary:

1. The user's voice is sent as audio data into the pitch based NVVI system.
2. The fundamental pitch produced by the user is estimated.
3. This pitch is compared to the previously identified pitch.
4. The difference between these two pitches is sent as an output.

The fundamental pitch of the user's voice is estimated in real time using the ACF pitch estimation algorithm. To activate/deactivate the NVVI technique, we implemented *selection* to be triggered when a user produces two quick transients (short, bursts of audio) such as clapping, knocking, or clicking one's tongue. An example of a transient in an audio signal is depicted in Fig. 3.

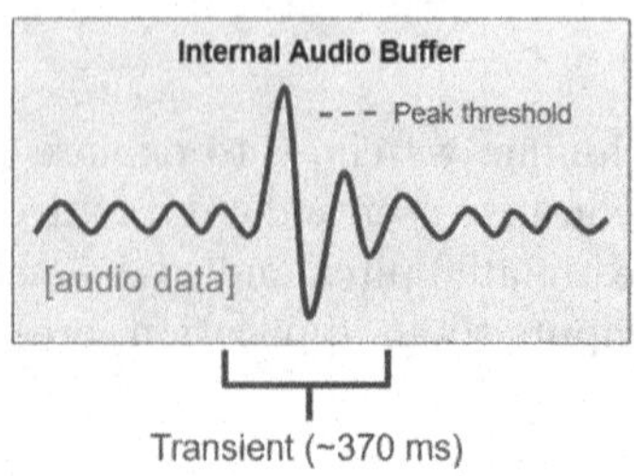

Fig. 3. Transients, as considered in our NVVI technique design.

To use the NVVI technique in the study, participants had to:

1. Create two consecutive transient sounds to activate the tool (put it into a listening state.)
2. Create a pitch by humming or whistling
3. Once the confidence of the frequency created exceeds the threshold, a *session* is created and the initial pitch is stored.
4. Modulate pitch up or down, clearly enough to maintain confidence, to allow for relative control of some parameter during use.
5. Stop producing pitch once parameter level is set appropriately, ending the session.
6. Create two consecutive transient sounds to deactivate tool.

4 User Study

A large-scale study was performed to assess our implementation of a relative pitch-based NVVI technique tasking users to control a continuous, one dimensional input. The parameter decided to be controlled by the pitch based NVVI technique was an HTML slider's knob position. Figure 4 provides an example usage of the technique to complete tasks in this study. The study was conducted via Amazon Mechanical Turk [1], and hosted on a Github Pages website [4]. Participants were rewarded $1 US$. The Institutional Review Board at our University approved the study.

The study was conducted in a modular format. Participants completed a series of readings on NVVI and our technique, performed tasks in *phases*, and completed *questionnaires*. A *phase* contains an introduction of what is assessed in the phase, the phase tasks that assess the user using the NVVI technique,

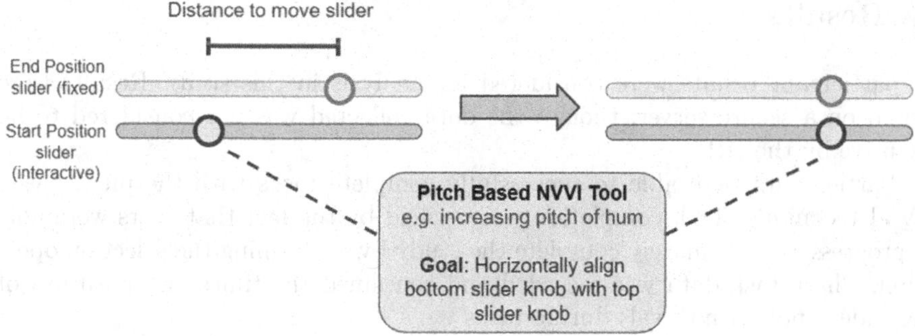

Fig. 4. A high level overview of tasks for participants to complete. Participants should use the pitch based NVVI technique to move the bottom slider's knob position to horizontally align with the top slider's knob position.

a NASA TLX task workload questionnaire, and a follow-up qualitative survey. Phase tasks are comprised of a number of *rounds* of *tasks*. A round is a collection of tasks that works with one customized instance of a pitch based NVVI technique. Participants completed three phases.

The first phase is an introductory phase where users practice using the technique with humming and whistling (the latter is done only if participants indicate they can whistle.) The second phase comprehensively assesses participants with their choice of modality (whistling or humming.) The third phase serves as a baseline where participants control the slider with their computer mouse.

Several questionnaires are administered throughout the study. The first is a demographic questionnaire, asking participants for basic information. There are also follow-up questions to every phase that allow participants to provide more context and expression of their experience using the tool.

After each phase assessment, a NASA TLX is administered to gauge the task workload for using the tool during the phase. The NASA TLX contains seven response options for participants regarding their experience with the NVVI technique from "Very Low" to "Very High." The questions administered are:

1. How mentally demanding was the task?
2. How physically demanding was the task?
3. How hurried or rushed was the pace of the task?
4. How successful were you in accomplishing what you were asked to do?
5. How hard did you have to work to accomplish your level of performance?
6. How insecure, discouraged, irritated, stressed, and annoyed were you?

In total, three or four TLXs are administered, depending on if the user can whistle and completes the second part of the first phase or not.

At the end of the study, a SUS questionnaire was administered. The goal of the SUS survey is to collect a "quick and dirty" understanding of the usability of a tool [3]. In this case, the goal of the SUS is to gain an understanding of the usability of the NVVI technique developed and used throughout this study.

5 Results

72 participant results were considered for analysis in this study. Results were stored on a secure server, though the data collected was not considered to be sensitive by the IRB.

Participants were able to successfully complete tasks with the pitch based NVVI technique. Task completion was verified by the fact that users were able to progress and ultimately complete the study by performing the selection operation. Phase task data was recorded and contained the times and positions of the slider knob at intervals during tasks.

However, upon closer examination of data, it was noticeable that some participants did not try to complete some tasks. Though there could be a variety of reasons why participants may not have tried to complete some tasks, two primary cases are considered. The first is when the user really did not try or want to complete a task for some reason. The second is that the participant may have perceived the starting and ending position of the slider knob to be close enough to the indicated position to skip the task.

To get a better understanding of results, a classification system was devised, as described in [20], to allow researchers to categorize and brush different tasks.

Tasks were assorted into 3 groups of 2 categories as depicted in Fig. 5. The classifications appear to be complete (partitions,) as no task was given an undefined category. The groups are divided into the three categories of not attempted, attempted and failure, and attempted and success. The metrics used for categorization were local variance, global variance, and the accuracy.

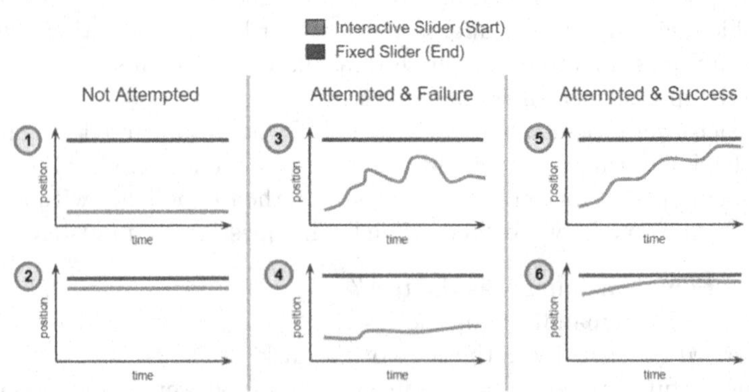

Fig. 5. The classifications of task performances.

The first of the three groups contains categories 1 and 2, essentially the two previous forms of task performances. **Category 1** contains tasks that were not attempted and likely not because participants thought it was close enough. The metrics identifying these tasks are a low global variance and inaccuracy. **Category 2** contains tasks that were not attempted likely because participants thought the slider knob was close enough to the end value. He metrics identifying these tasks are a low global variance and accuracy.

The second group contains tasks that were attempted but unsuccessful. Both categories in this group were inaccurate. **Category 3** contains tasks with a high local and high global variance, while **Category 4** contains tasks that had high local and low global variance.

The third group contains tasks that were attempted and successful, meaning both categories in this group were accurate. **Category 5** contains tasks with a high local and high global variance, while **Category 6** contains tasks that had high local and low global variance.

Tasks from phase 2, the comprehensive assessment phase, were analyzed. In total, 1,440 tasks were considered. The distribution of task classifications is depicted in Fig. 6.

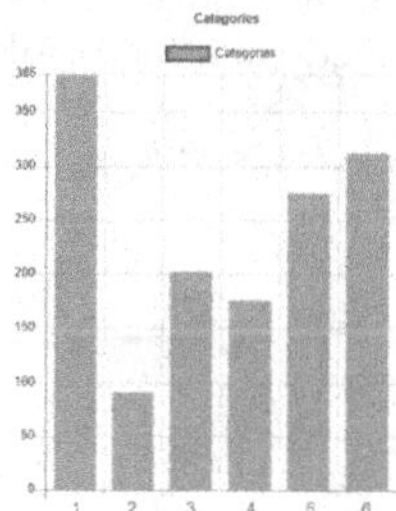

Fig. 6. Classifications of tasks in phase 2.

Successful tasks were those in Categories 5 and 6. In total, 475 tasks were not attempted, 378 tasks were attempted but unsuccessful, and 587 tasks were attempted and successful. Therefore, the total attempted success rate of all tasks was 60.82%.

5.1 NVVI Usage

Figure 7 provides all successfully completed tasks (in categories 5 and 6.) Fig. 8 provides a graph representing the average path taken in successful completing tasks. The domain of tasks used in the construction of this graph are successful tasks (from categories 5 and 6.) The graph was made by normalizing all task data from these categories in both the time and position axes, and then using linear interpolation to plot an average graph with 1000 sample points.

Many individual task data points were examined. In this section, a selection of individual task graphs are presented.

Figure 9a shows an instance of a phenomenon of what we refer to as "vocal scrolling." As shown in the figure, the position of the slider in similarly sized increments until the desired position is reached. The exact number of tasks exhibiting this phenomenon was not recorded.

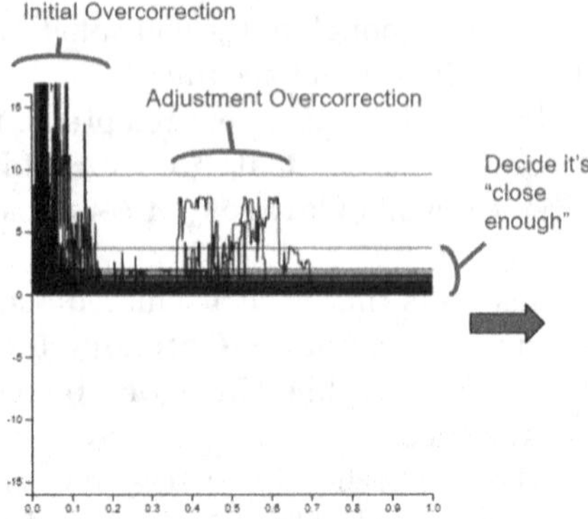

Fig. 7. Graphs containing all phase task paths in categories 5 and 6 (attempted and successful,) where each phase was normalized on the time axis by the total time taken and on the distance axis by the distance between the starting and ending positions. Additionally, the distance axis is scaled by a factor of 16.

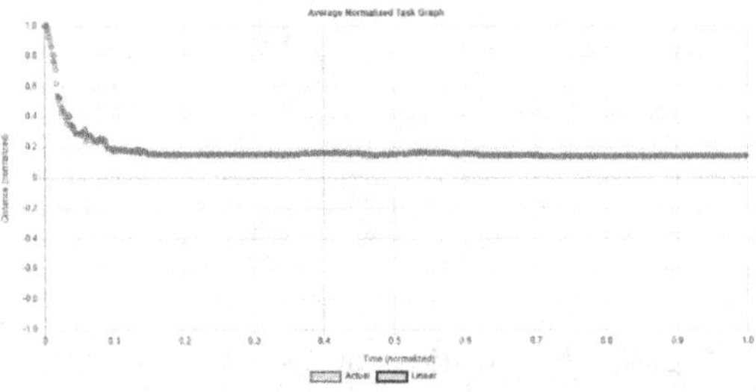

Fig. 8. A graph representing the average path taken during a phase task, where each phase was normalized on the time axis by the total time taken and on the distance axis by the distance between the starting and ending positions.

Figure 9b shows an instance of a participant overshooting using the tool. When trying to move the slider knob to the correct end position, they move it past this position to a distance almost equal to the initial distance from the start and end values.

Figure 9c shows an instance of a participant severely overshooting using the tool. When trying to move the slider knob to the correct end position, they move it past this position to a distance almost equal to six times the initial distance from the start and end values.

Fitts' Law. Figure 10a contains a plot depicting a relationship between the time taken to complete tasks and the logarithm of the distance from the start to end position of the slider knob. The top 7.5% of times were removed as a part of cleaning. A linear relationship would indicate an observance of Fitts' Law. However, the r^2 value of a linear regression model of this graph is 0.0093, which is not large enough to presume a linear relationship.

Figure 10b contains a plot depicting a relationship between the time taken to complete tasks and the distance from the start to end position of the slider knob. The top 7.5% of times were removed as a part of cleaning. A linear relationship would indicate a linear relationship between the time a task takes and the distance traveled by the slider. However, the r^2 value of a linear regression model of this graph is 0.0376, which is not large enough to presume a linear relationship.

r^2 is higher in this latter linear regression model than the former, which may indicate a stronger linear relationship between distance and time than a logarithmic one as defined in Fitts' Law.

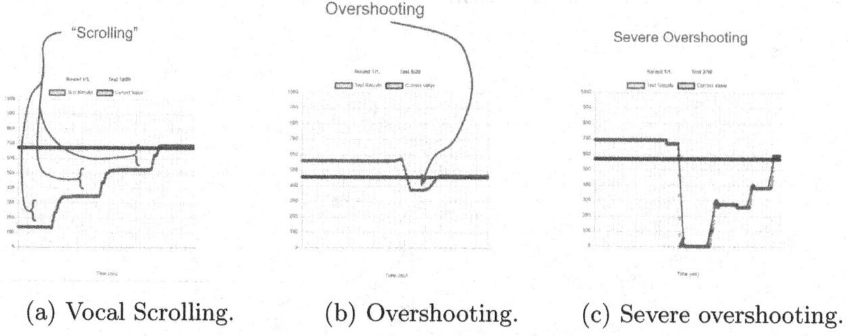

(a) Vocal Scrolling. (b) Overshooting. (c) Severe overshooting.

Fig. 9. Common phenomena occurring during tasks.

5.2 NVVI vs the Computer Mouse

Performance. In the study, participants were tasked with using the pitch based NVVI technique and a baseline using a computer mouse. In the second phase, participates chose the modality of their choice (whistling or humming) to use for a comprehensive assessment with the NVVI technique, and in the third phase participants were tasked with using the mouse. The average times taken to complete the tasks that were in categories 5 or 6 were recorded per participant.

Figure 11 shows a box plot comparing the performance between the use of the pitch based NVVI technique and the computer mouse, as described above. The number of participants considered varied between the two categories, as some participants did not complete any tasks in categories 5 or 6. ANOVA analysis revealed a significant difference of performance between the NVVI technique and the computer mouse ($p = 1.51 \times 10^{-9}$), in favor of the computer mouse.

Task Workload. After completing phase 3, where participants controlled a slider with a computer mouse, participants completed a NASA TLX. An ANOVA analysis was performed comparing the average and normalized NASA TLX scores of phase 2, a comprehensive assessment with the pitch based NVVI technique

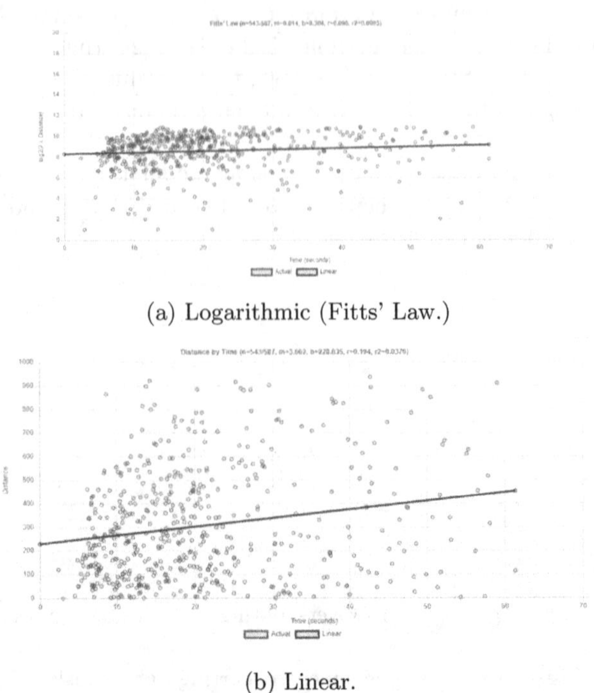

(a) Logarithmic (Fitts' Law.)

(b) Linear.

Fig. 10. Graphs plotting the relationship between the time taken to complete tasks and the distance between starting and ending positions.

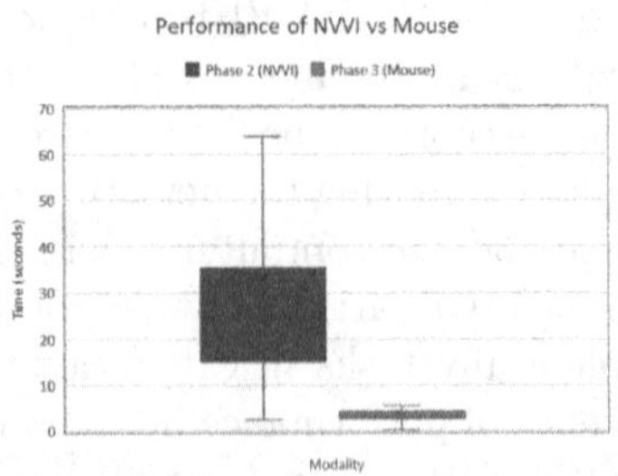

Fig. 11. A boxplot comparing the time taken between using the NVVI technique to complete tasks vs using a computer mouse.

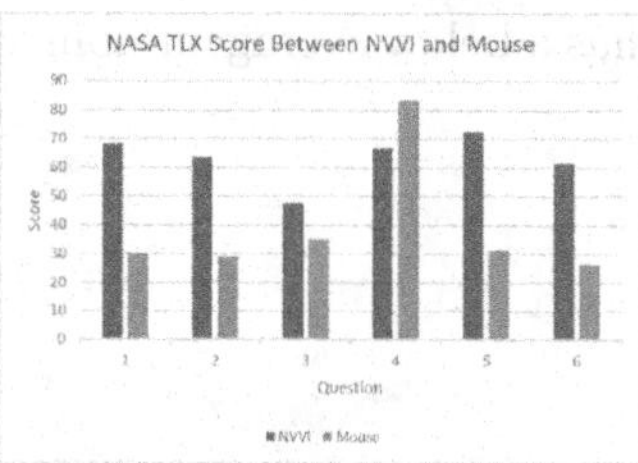

(a) NASA TLX scores by question of using the NVVI technique and the computer mouse.

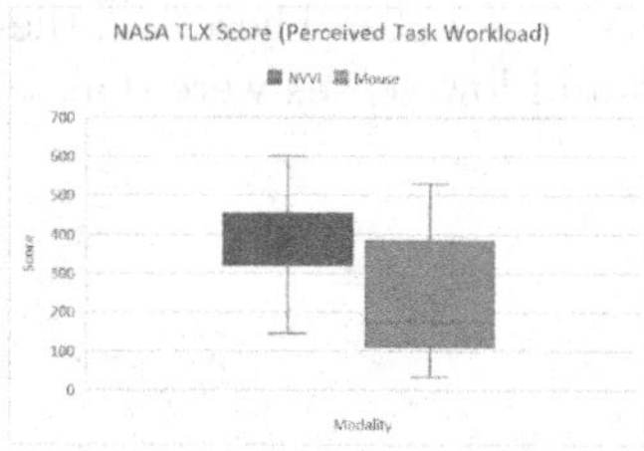

(b) Total task workload index between the NVVI technique vs. computer mouse.

Fig. 12. Box plots comparing NVVI performance with the computer mouse.

controlled with either whistling or humming, and phase 3, a baseline assessing performance with the computer mouse for each question. Figure 12a contains a bar chart comparing the scores between the two interaction modalities. The values are provided in Table 1. As depicted, the NASA TLX scores between the pitch based NVVI technique and the mouse are noticeably different for each question in favor of the mouse, but closer for questions 3 and 4.

A further analysis was performed to compare the normalized and summed score (total perceived task load index) of the TLX questionnaire between using the NVVI technique in phase 2 and the computer mouse in phase 3. Figure 12b shows a box plot of this comparison. An ANOVA revealed a significant difference ($p = 1.3 \times 10^{-8}$) of perceived task load index between using the NVVI technique and using the computer mouse (the use of the computer mouse being the lesser).

5.3 System Usability

After completing a comprehensive assessment with the NVVI technique in phase 2 and a baseline test with a computer mouse in phase 3, participants completed a system usability scale (SUS) questionnaire to provide a "quick and dirty" usability evaluation of the pitch based NVVI technique. A score above 68 indicates above average usability.

Figure 13 contains a box plot with the recorded SUS scores. The scores were normalized into the range of [0, 100]. The median score is approximately the

Table 1. A table containing the average scores for each NASA TLX question for using the NVVI technique and the computer mouse.

	Q1	Q2	Q3	Q4	Q5	Q6
NVVI	68.3	63.4	47.6	66.6	72.5	61.6
Mouse	30.2	29.2	35	83.6	31.3	26.4

average score of 48.31. Therefore, the system has a below average usability score. The high and low scores were 0 and 100.

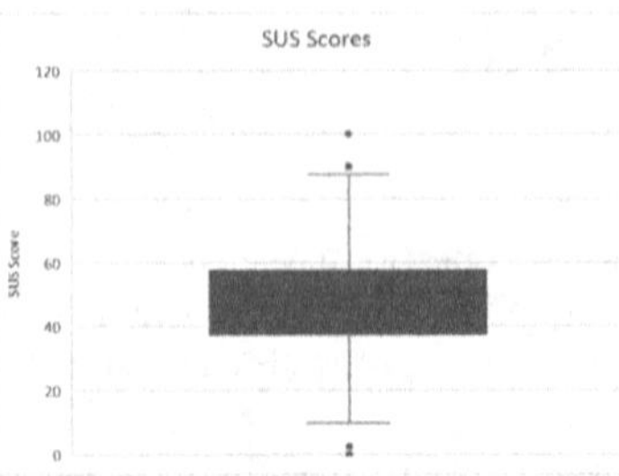

Fig. 13. A box plot of the System Usability Scale (SUS) questionnaire scores for the pitch based NVVI prototype used in the study.

6 Discussion

Participants were able to successfully complete tasks by using the described pitch based NVVI technique to control the sliders. The successfully attempted completion rate of 60.82% indicates moderate but less than ideal performance. However, limitations of the study design, including the asynchronous and unsupervised conduction of the study, may contribute to this number.

Task completion is an important metric in understanding user performance with the tool. Categories 5 and 6 were used for the analyses because they indicated succesfully completed tasks. Additionally, most of the analyses were performed with phase 2 because participants had undergone some training with the tool in phase 1. However, only 60.82% of attempted tasks were successful in these two categories for phase 2.

The pitch based NVVI technique received an average SUS score of 48.31, a below average usability score. Below average usability is supported by a 60.82% overall task attempted success rate during the comprehensive assessment.

6.1 Usage Phenomena

As described in the results section, Fitts' Law did not appear to be observed. Additionally, time taken to complete tasks and distance to move the slider did not appear to be linearly correlated. It appears that the described relative pitch based NVVI technique does not appear to observe traditional interaction patterns, such as Fitts' Law.

However, *vocal scrolling* was a phenomenon observed in phase task results. This appears to be a logical approach to adjusting the slider knob with pitch, as it involves increasing or decreasing the pitch of either whistling or humming multiple times. This is likely because the end position is too far away to adjust pitch in one increment. This design pattern should be considered when developing a pitch based NVVI system. This phenomenon alludes to a trade off made between precision and distance travelled. For this study, the amount of distance the slider knob makes per pitch adjustment (a weight) was an informally experimentally tuned value. If this value is large, this phenomenon would be less frequent, but it would likely come at the cost of precision (as informally supported via experimentation.)

Overshooting was also observed using the tool. The initial peaks present in Fig. 7 indicate a significant overshooting using the tool, as some paths are clipped that are over 16 times the initial distance. Figure 9c contains an example of severe overshooting. Severe overshooting is also noticeable in Fig. 7, as the noticeable heights of the paths range up to 6 times the initial distance at around the 40–70% time markers (as the time scale is normalized.) In other words, overshooting appears to occur during the middle of the time using the pitch based NVVI technique.

6.2 NVVI vs the Computer Mouse

To understand how user performance varied using the pitch based NVVI technique as compared with a computer mouse, a within subjects comparative analysis was performed. An ANOVA was administered to validate the null hypothesis that performance with a computer mouse and the pitch-based NVVI technique would not significantly differ. As mentioned in the Sect. 5.2, a significant difference was found between the average times of using a computer mouse and the NVVI technique. Therefore, we conclude that participants performed significantly better with the computer mouse than the pitch based NVVI technique for completing the tasks assigned in this study.

6.3 User Feedback

The following participant feedback from the study is also presented in [20]. As described in Sect. 3, *selection* was implemented to allow users to select when or when not to use the tool, since it could inadvertently be controlled during speech or any strong, noticeable frequency presence. Unfortunately, this was not initially understood clearly by participants. One participant said *"The humming part was easy. I got a little tripped up on the two succinct noises to turn it on and off but that may have been a mic issue."* Another participant said *"... The tool did not move at all at first but only because I forgot to clap twice. Once I got the hang of that it became easier..."*

Participants were asked to identify a pitch control strategy they used to complete phase tasks. Many users reported controlling the slider in small increments, or steps of pitch, to modulate the slider's position, a phenomenon we coined as "vocal scrolling" depicted in Fig. 9a. These techniques were similar for both humming and whistling.

However, some participants reported using large increments, and some described switching from large to small increments or vice versa. Participants did seem to agree that they felt they had more control with larger increments. One participant said *"I tried to move it in one Swift motion that found that task to be rather daunting so I ended up moving it mostly in small steps."* Another said *"Depending on the distance I had to move the slider I would start much lower or higher,"* indicating that the participant hadmentally and physically prepared to move the slider knob a longer distance by expanding the frequency range of their voice.

Some participants reported fatigue or discomfort during and after interaction. For example, one participant said *"...you need to really focus and get some serious air in your lungs ..."*, indicating that the NVVI technique required lots of air. Another participant said *"...now I have a sore throat and it wouldn't work at all it was horrible,"* another said *"Wish I chose humming. I'm lightheaded with a headache now from whistling so much continuously."* and a third said *"My palms sting from producing the loud claps. Ouch!"* This feedback alludes that NVVI can be physically and mentally demanding and potentially uncomfortable or even painful for extended use.

7 Conclusion

This work explores the usability of a pitch based NVVI system using a relative pitch based NVVI technique. The NVVI technique described in this work allows participants to control a slider with their voice by whistling and humming. In summary, the algorithm estimates the fundamental frequency of the users voice and provides a one-dimensional continuous control input based on the deviation of the current pitch from an initial pitch. The initial pitch is determined by a calculation that measures the confidence of if a pitch is being produced.

The relative pitch based NVVI technique did not appear to observe Fitts' Law, and the time taken to move the slider did not appear to be linearly correlated. However, the phenomenon of *vocal scrolling* was observed, where participants moved the position of the slider with the pitch of their voice in similarly-sized increments, similar to scrolling with a mouse. Overshooting was also found to be prevalent in task results.

Participants were found to perform significantly better with the computer mouse than with NVVI for completing the phase tasks. The perceived task workload experienced was significantly higher for the NVVI technique than using the computer mouse. Participant feedback supported this claim, and also indicated fatigue and in some cases pain experienced after using the NVVI technique.

Future work should explore pitch based NVVI systems in certain contexts where NVVI can be leveraged over traditional input modalities, including action at a distance and extended/virtual reality. We believe NVVI can be a viable alternative and orthogonal controller scheme for such applications. Vocal scrolling should also be explored in more detail.

Disclosure of Interests. The authors have no competing interests to declare that are relevant to the content of this article.

References

1. Amazon.com: Amazon mechanical turk. https://www.mturk.com/. Accessed 28 Nov 2023
2. Bilmes, J.A., et al.: The vocal joystick: a voice-based human-computer interface for individuals with motor impairments. In: Proceedings of the Conference on Human Language Technology and Empirical Methods in Natural Language Processing, HLT 2005, pp. 995–1002. Association for Computational Linguistics, USA (2005). https://doi.org/10.3115/1220575.1220700
3. Brooke, J.: SUS-a quick and dirty usability scale. Usability Eval. Ind. **189**, 4–7 (1996)
4. GitHub: Github pages (2023). https://pages.github.com/. Accessed 27 Nov 2023
5. Handosa, M., Dasgupta, A., Manuel, M., Gračanin, D.: Rethinking user interaction with smart environments—a comparative study of four interaction modalities. In: Streitz, N., Konomi, S. (eds.) HCII 2020. LNCS, vol. 12203, pp. 39–57. Springer, Cham (2020). https://doi.org/10.1007/978-3-030-50344-4_4
6. Hedeshy, R., Kumar, C., Lauer, M., Staab, S.: All birds must fly: the experience of multimodal hands-free gaming with gaze and nonverbal voice synchronization. In: Proceedings of the 2022 International Conference on Multimodal Interaction, ICMI 2022, pp. 278–287. ACM, New York (2022). https://doi.org/10.1145/3536221.3556593
7. Heerema, J., Parker, J.R.: Music as a game controller. In: 2013 IEEE International Games Innovation Conference (IGIC), pp. 72–76, September 2013. https://doi.org/10.1109/IGIC.2013.6659147
8. Kent, R.: Vocal tract acoustics. J. Voice **7**(2), 97–117 (1993). https://doi.org/10.1016/S0892-1997(05)80339-X, the Voice Foundation's 22nd Annual Symposium
9. Kurniawan, S.H., Sporka, A.J.: Vocal interaction. In: CHI '08 Extended Abstracts on Human Factors in Computing Systems, pp. 2407—2410. ACM, New York (2008). https://doi.org/10.1145/1358628.1358695
10. Mahmud, M., Sporka, A.J., Kurniawan, S.H., Slavík, P.: A comparative longitudinal study of non-verbal mouse pointer. In: Baranauskas, C., Palanque, P., Abascal, J., Barbosa, S.D.J. (eds.) INTERACT 2007. LNCS, vol. 4663, pp. 489–502. Springer, Heidelberg (2007). https://doi.org/10.1007/978-3-540-74800-7_44
11. Polacek, O., Mikovec, Z., Sporka, A.J., Slavik, P.: Humsher: a predictive keyboard operated by humming. In: Proceedings of the 13th International ACM SIGACCESS Conference on Computers and Accessibility, ASSETS 2011, pp. 75–82. ACM, New York (2011). https://doi.org/10.1145/2049536.2049552
12. Polacek, O., Sporka, A.J., Slavik, P.: A comparative study of pitch-based gestures in nonverbal vocal interaction. IEEE Trans. Syst. Man Cybern. - Part A Syst. Hum. **42**(6), 1567–1571 (2012). https://doi.org/10.1109/TSMCA.2012.2201937
13. Poláček, O., Míkovec, Z.: Hands free mouse: comparative study on mouse clicks controlled by humming. In: CHI '10 Extended Abstracts on Human Factors in Computing Systems, pp. 3769–3774. ACM, New York (2010). https://doi.org/10.1145/1753846.1754053
14. Sardana, D., Kahu, S.Y., Gračanin, D., Matković, K.: Multi-modal data exploration in a mixed reality environment using coordinated multiple views. In: Yamamoto, S., Mori, H. (eds.) HCII 2021. LNCS, vol. 12765, pp. 337–356. Springer, Cham (2021). https://doi.org/10.1007/978-3-030-78321-1_26
15. Sondhi, M.: New methods of pitch extraction. IEEE Trans. Audio Electroacoust. **16**(2), 262–266 (1968). https://doi.org/10.1109/TAU.1968.1161986

16. Sporka, A.J.: Pitch in non-verbal vocal input. SIGACCESS Access. Comput. **94**, 9–16 (2009). https://doi.org/10.1145/1595061.1595063
17. Sporka, A.J., Felzer, T., Kurniawan, S.H., Poláček, O., Haiduk, P., MacKenzie, I.S.: CHANTI: predictive text entry using non-verbal vocal input. In: Proceedings of the SIGCHI Conference on Human Factors in Computing Systems, CHI 2011, pp. 2463–2472. ACM, New York (2011). https://doi.org/10.1145/1978942.1979302
18. Sporka, A.J., Harada, S., Kurniawan, S.H.: Striking a c[h]Ord: vocal interaction in assistive technologies, games, and more. In: CHI '07 Extended Abstracts on Human Factors in Computing Systems, CHI EA 2007, pp. 2869–2872. ACM, New York (2007). https://doi.org/10.1145/1240866.1241098
19. Sporka, A.J., Slavík, P.: Vocal control of a radio-controlled car. SIGACCESS Access. Comput. (91), 3–8 (2008). https://doi.org/10.1145/1394427.1394428
20. Williams, S., Gračanin, D.: An approach to pitch based implementation of non-verbal vocal interaction (NVVI). In: Proceedings of the 2023 IEEE Conference on Virtual Reality and 3D User Interfaces Abstracts and Workshops (VRW) (2024), to appear
21. Zielasko, D., Neha, N., Weyers, B., Kuhlen, T.W.: BlowClick 2.0: a trigger based on non-verbal vocal input. In: Proceedings of the 2017 IEEE Virtual Reality Conference, pp. 319–320, March 2017. https://doi.org/10.1109/VR.2017.7892305

Research on Gesture Interaction Game Effects Based on the Representation and Feedback Theory

Danni Wu[1], Zhuohao Wu[1(✉)], Hailing Li[1], Sibo Yang[1], and Mohammad Shidujaman[2]

[1] School of Animation and Digital Arts, Communication University of China, Beijing, China
HiMrHOW@gmail.com

[2] Department of Computer Science and Engineering, Independent University, Dhaka, Bangladesh

Abstract. This study addresses the limitations of gesture interaction technology in game visual effects design, adopting an innovative approach that integrates specific design theories into this domain. Through an in-depth analysis of case studies on the application of the Representation and Feedback Theory in game visual effects, this research has successfully developed a set of methods to evaluate the practicality of this theory. The study used both qualitative and quantitative analysis to assess the impact of representation and feedback within specific games. The results showed that visual effects designed based on the Representation and Feedback Theory significantly improved the overall gaming experience. This research not only provides a theoretical foundation for the design of gesture interactive game effects but also offers valuable guidance for their practical application.

Keywords: Game Effects Design · Visual Effects · Gesture-based Interaction

1 Introduction

1.1 Concepts and Artistic Styles of Game Effects

Game effects in video games refer to spectacular special enhancements added to scenes and characters, impacting various environments, scenarios, and objects with a wide array of characteristics [1]. These effects are typically divided into three major categories: environmental effects, character effects, and interface effects, which collectively form the overall artistic impression of the game's visual effects [2]. The visual style of game effects is usually determined by visual concept designers. Under the current technological conditions, there are three main artistic styles in game visual effects [3].

1. Pixel Art Style: This style is a form of visual effects art based on pixels, commonly used to mimic the graphics of early computers and video game consoles. Its defining characteristic involves dividing images into small pixel blocks to achieve a pixelated appearance. This style is widely employed in various independent games and retro-styled works. It has the ability to evoke nostalgic feelings and create unique visual aesthetics.

M. Kurosu and A. Hashizume (Eds.): HCII 2024, LNCS 14688, pp. 187–202, 2024.
https://doi.org/10.1007/978-3-031-60449-2_13

2. Cartoon Rendering Style: This style, commonly used in games and animations, is characterized by its emulation of hand-drawn cartoons. It often employs bright colors, black outlines, and simplified shapes to achieve this effect. Suitable for light-hearted, humorous games and children's animations, it excels at creating endearing and eye-catching characters and scenes.
3. 3D Realistic Style: This style aims to simulate the real world as accurately as possible. It demands high levels of graphic detail and complex lighting effects to create a lifelike virtual environment. Commonly seen in high-end games and cinematic productions, it provides a stunning visual experience. Technically, the 3D realistic style involves the use of high-resolution textures, life-like physics simulations, and sophisticated rendering techniques.

1.2 Limitations of Gesture Interaction Technology in Game Effect Design

In the design of game effects, the application of gesture interaction technology not only opens up new ways of interaction but also brings a series of challenges. The following is an analysis of these challenges and the proposed solutions.

User Fatigue: Prolonged use of gestures for game interaction can lead to user arm fatigue, limiting the complexity and depth of effect design, thereby affecting the game's challenge and attractiveness. Combining other forms of interaction, such as voice commands or touch input, can reduce reliance on gestures and thus decrease user fatigue. Also, designing more natural and effortless gesture recognition mechanisms, as well as providing ample game rest prompts, are effective ways to alleviate user fatigue.

User Learning Curve: New users may require time to learn how to effectively use air gestures for interaction. Overly complex gesture operations and visual effects might lead to player frustration, reducing the overall appeal of the game. Gesture interaction schemes derived from event archetypes can reduce the learning time for users [4]. At the same time, intuitive and easy-to-understand gesture commands and visual effects can lessen the learning burden on users.

Interaction Environment Limitations: Environmental restrictions of gesture interaction, such as lighting conditions and space size, may limit the implementation environment for effect design and the possibilities for innovation by game designers. Developing more sensitive sensor technology that can work stably under different environmental conditions is key to overcoming this challenge. Moreover, designing an adaptive interaction system that can adjust interaction modes based on current environmental conditions can effectively enhance the flexibility and usability of game effect design.

Insufficient Accuracy and Responsiveness: If gesture recognition is inaccurate or slow, the triggering of game effects by players might be delayed or erroneous, leading to a disrupted gaming experience and reducing player immersion and satisfaction. Improving gesture recognition algorithms and enhancing sensor performance are key to increasing accuracy and response speed. By adopting advanced machine learning techniques, such as deep learning, the system's accuracy in recognizing complex gestures can be significantly improved. Additionally, optimizing the game engine and interaction feedback mechanisms to ensure high responsiveness even under high load is an effective way to address this issue.

2 Case Study of Gesture Interaction Game Effects

2.1 Representation and Feedback

Representation signifies symbolism [5], with its developmental history spanning multiple fields such as philosophy, art theory, and cultural studies. Post-structuralism thinker Stuart Hall, in the 20th century, critically reevaluated the concept of representation in his works, viewing it as an essential tool in cultural studies and social contexts. In the field of design, representation typically refers to the process of using visual means like graphics, symbols, images, and text to showcase and communicate design ideas, concepts, information, and emotions. These representational tools play a crucial role in design; they not only assist designers in conceptualizing and developing their ideas but also enable these ideas to be understood and evaluated by others. Feedback Theory was initially proposed by the renowned cognitive psychologist Donald Norman in his work *The Design of Everyday Things* [6]. This theory emphasizes the need for timely and clear user operation responses in design to enhance the intelligibility and effectiveness of interactions.

In the field of visual effects, Representation Theory focuses on the explicit expression between effects and control logic as well as their outcome presentation. This approach aims to facilitate users' intuitive understanding and efficient operation, thereby reducing the learning curve for users. Conversely, Feedback Theory emphasizes that effects should provide immediate and clear responses to user interactions, with the objective of enhancing the intelligibility and effectiveness of the interaction process.

2.2 Visual Effects Analysis of Drakheir

Drakheir is a bare-handed interactive virtual reality fantasy adventure game. The game allows users to control various magical elements, such as fire, electricity, and ice, through gestures. The visual effects design of the game aligns with users' prior knowledge. For instance, to cast a fireball spell, users point their index finger upwards, and the flames at their fingertip in the virtual space resemble the burning of a candle in reality. When the fireball collides with other objects, the explosion effect mimics real-world ammunition explosions. This design not only enhances the immersion of the game but also improves the intuitiveness of the user experience (see Fig. 1).

In the context of the game, when users wish to unleash special abilities, they are required to perform specific gestures for charging and forming seals. During the process of making these gestures, users will see their fingers emit light in various colors, which serves as feedback on the accuracy of their seal formation. Upon successful completion of the seal, users will observe a ring of light appearing between their fingers, accompanied by a glowing hand model effect emerging from the ring (see Fig. 2). Within the game's architecture, the visual effects are meticulously engineered to avoid obstruction of the user's visual field and operational maneuvers, ensuring a harmonious integration with the user's physical actions and vocal commands, thereby fostering a cohesive and intuitive interactive milieu. The game introduces an innovative cursor, manifested as an ocular pattern on the player's palms, strategically directing focus towards hand movements and concurrently amplifying manual expressiveness without compromising visual clarity.

These feedback mechanisms are strategically implemented to bolster user recall and enhance overall satisfaction.

Drakheir creates a visual environment that is both realistic and stylized, featuring rich colors and outstanding effects. The visual effects respond swiftly and are in harmony with character movements and environmental changes, maintaining consistency in operation logic. The effects in the game follow physical rules, such as the burning of fireballs, the freezing of frost, and the conductivity of lightning. Overall, the visual effects in *Drakheir* under the theory of representation and feedback are of a high standard, providing users with a satisfying and enjoyable gaming experience.

Fig. 1. The visual effects of the fire ability in *Drakheir*. Image sourced from the internet.

Fig. 2. The visual effects of charging and forming seals through specific gestures. Image sourced from the internet.

2.3 Visual Effects Analysis of *Job Simulator*

Job Simulator is a cartoon-style life simulation game that uses controllers for gesture interaction, utilizing virtual reality technology to immerse users in various work scenarios. It simulates the visual effects of real objects and movements. For instance, when users grab and eat fruits or donuts in the game, they observe splash effects of juice and food particles (see Fig. 3). Moreover, for objects floating in the scene, jet-style effects are added at the bottom, providing a sense of force support, which aligns with the theory of representation. When users touch and interact with specific items, these objects change color, offering guidance and reducing cognitive load. However, there are some shortcomings in the game's visual effects. For example, when users wash their hands, the faucet displays water flow effects, but there is no change in the hands upon contact with the water, leading to confusion about whether the hand washing step is completed. This inconsistency with reality violates the theory of feedback (see Fig. 4).

In summary, the visual effects in *Job Simulator* perform well in terms of representation and feedback, but there is still room for optimization.

Fig. 3. The visual effect of crumbs splattering when grabbing and consuming food. Image sourced from the internet.

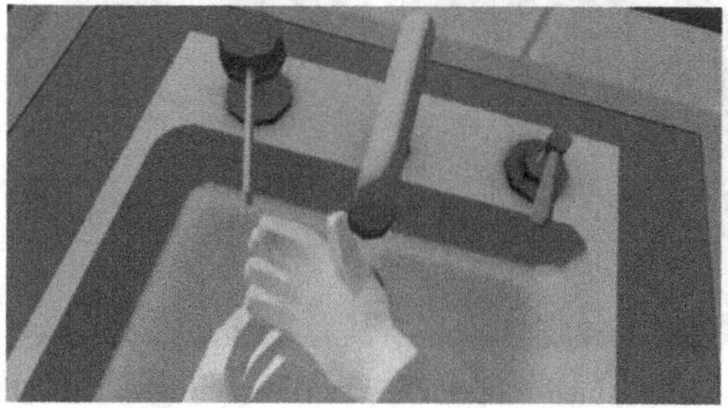

Fig. 4. The visual effect of water flow during hand washing does not affect the appearance of the palms. Image sourced from the internet.

2.4 Visual Effects Analysis of *Waltz of the Wizard*

Waltz of the Wizard, as a virtual reality magic simulation game, employs realistic-style rendering, with its visual effects aligning with users' intuitive cognition of physical effects. It uses controllers for gesture interaction, enhancing the immersive experience by allowing players to perform magic through intuitive hand movements. For instance, during potion brewing, the game simulates the phenomena of ripples and boiling on the water surface, as well as the corresponding changes in hand color with the potion's color, adhering to the Representation Theory (see Fig. 5). The palm interaction and rune generation design when returning to the main scene also provide detailed visual cues (see Fig. 6). However, the memorization and mastery of magical combinations, complex visual effects, and multitasking might increase the cognitive load on users. Moreover, the overuse of lighting and particle effects can lead to visual fatigue, particularly in dark labyrinth scenes. Therefore, despite its innovation in visual effects, the game still needs optimization in its feedback mechanism.

Fig. 5. Visual effects of boiling liquid in the cauldron during potion brewing. Image sourced from the internet.

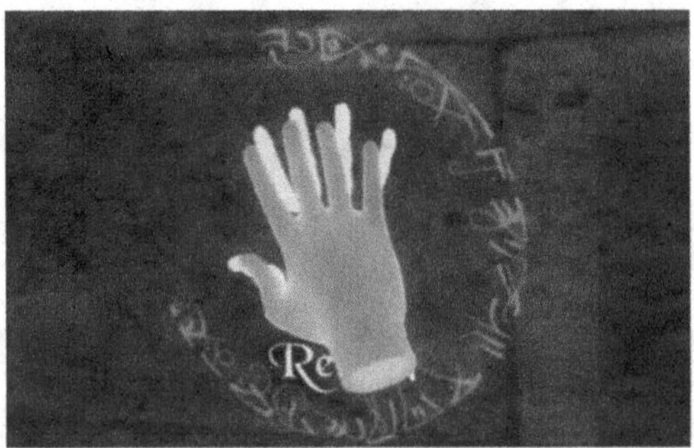

Fig. 6. Visual effect of text gradually appearing when interacting with a wall. Image sourced from the internet.

3 Design Concept of Gesture Effects Based on the Representation and Feedback Theory

3.1 Design Example

This design example is based on the theory of representation and feedback, focusing on gesture-based game effects, and aims to cater to the needs of professionals and students who are prone to hand fatigue. The core objective of the game is to facilitate hand exercises through the actions of tightening and stretching the fingers. In terms of game control design, we emphasize simplicity as a key element. In the game, each hand independently controls a jellyfish character, with the palm's orientation determining the movement direction and the frequency of finger movements controlling the speed. When a line is formed between the two jellyfish, it inflicts damage on enemies.

The design of the game's visual effects applies the theory of representation and feedback:

1. Characters are distinguished by vivid dynamic effect materials to enhance recognition, aligning with the Representation Theory (see Fig. 7).
2. The line between characters uses lightning linear dynamic effects, congruent with the visual effects of jellyfish venom, adhering to the Representation Theory (see Fig. 8).
3. The school of fish in the scene employs fountain particle effects, with motion trajectories following curves, mirroring the movement patterns of fish in real life, in line with the representation theory.
4. The trailing particle effect during movement is designed to beautify and indicate motion paths, reducing cognitive load, in accordance with the feedback theory.
5. Hand status is reflected through changes in the characters' colors and forms, minimizing the cognitive burden on the user, consistent with the feedback theory.
6. The particle effects when enemies are injured indicate their current state, in line with the feedback theory, and the dissolution effect upon death resembles real-life disintegration effects, adhering to the representation theory.

These design strategies are intended to follow the theory of representation and feedback, providing an enhanced gaming experience during hand training sessions.

Fig. 7. Overall visual style in visual effects practice, by Danni Wu, 2023

Fig. 8. Dynamic textures and motion visual effects of game characters, by Danni Wu, 2023

3.2 Gesture Effects Design Process

The main process of this special effects design is divided into three stages: the overall environmental effects design, the individual character effects design, and the design of interaction effects between the character and other elements in the scene (see Fig. 9).

In the overall environment effects design stage, the task involves stylized rendering of the scene, transforming the 3D environment into a 2D animated style. Initially, this involves using the scene's depth map to obtain offset values in four main directions, which are then used to derive contour lines. By subtracting the offset depth maps from the original depth map and summing these results, contour lines are obtained. Next, by replacing the scene depth with scene normal, structural contours are similarly generated. After obtaining the contour and structural outlines, bi-tonal shadows are created. This process starts with extracting shadows from the image, then using *if* nodes to differentiate between shadow and light areas, creating a black-and-white scheme. Introducing an additional nested *if* node adds intermediate shades. The final step involves multiplying color vectors with grayscale values to color within the contour lines [7]. This transformation plays a crucial role in reducing visual fatigue during gameplay and enhancing the visual appeal.

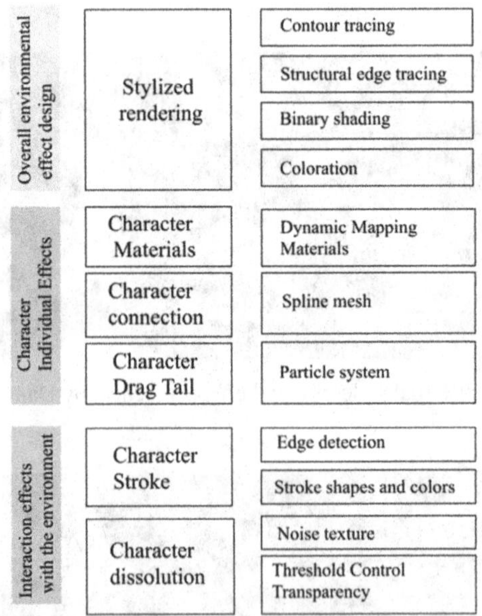

Fig. 9. Gesture effects design process framework, by Danni Wu, 2023

4 Experiment Assessment

4.1 Experiment Design

This experiment aims to apply the theory of representation and feedback in evaluating visual effects for usability testing in games. In the initial phase, we precisely defined multiple sub-dimensions of representation and feedback, and developed a series of guided and open-ended questions to facilitate in-depth user feedback.

The study targeted professionals and students prone to hand fatigue. During the experimental process, participants sequentially experienced *Drakheir*, *Job Simulator*, *Waltz of the Wizard*, and a game practice designed by the authors, with their intuitive reactions to the effects and comfort in operation being recorded. After the experiment, participants were asked to list their five most and least favorite details of the game effects for each game, and to score the game effects and the overall game experience.

In the data collection phase, we organized the user feedback on the details of the effects. During the data categorization and statistical phase, the effect details mentioned in user feedback were classified into representation, feedback, and other categories, and the frequency of effect details in each category was tallied. Finally, in the data analysis phase, we assessed the impact of the Representation and Feedback Theory on user experience through qualitative analysis of users' descriptions and feelings, and quantitative analysis of the statistical results.

4.2 Effectiveness Assessment

When conducting experiments on the Representation and Feedback Theory for game visual effects, the quantification of user experience can be implemented based on multiple specific dimensions. Collecting quantitative data through these dimensions allows for a comprehensive and objective assessment of the performance of game visual effects in terms of representation and feedback, providing a scientific basis for further optimization of the effects. Among these dimensions, visual cognition is an evaluative dimension of the Representation, while visual comfort and satisfaction are important indicators for measuring the Feedback. This division of dimensions helps to more precisely understand and improve the impact of game visual effects on user experience (Table 1).

4.3 User Game Experience Analysis

This study employed observational methods to conduct a game experience analysis on three users of varying ages, professions, and gaming experiences, preliminarily evaluating the performance of four games in terms of representation and feedback.

The first participant, a 24-year-old student with limited gaming experience, found the operation of gesture interactions somewhat unfamiliar. During the experience of *Drakheir*, despite undergoing a half-hour tutorial, the participant still forgot some of the relatively complex gestures during actual gameplay, leading to confusion over inadvertently triggered game effects. However, in *Job Simulator* and *Waltz of the Wizard*, the gesture interactions and game effects were more naturally integrated into daily activities, thus facilitating smoother operation. In the game developed by the author, with

Table 1. Visual effects evaluation dimension scale.

No.	Theory	Sub-Dimension	Description
1	Representation	Expectation	Evaluates if the effects align with players' prior knowledge and expectations
2	Representation	Memory	Assesses the effectiveness of memorizing visual information of game effects, including repetition and forgetfulness
3	Representation	Distinction	Determines if different attributes and functions of game effects are clearly distinguishable, avoiding confusion and misunderstanding
4	Representation	Learning Curve	Analyzes the time required for users to adapt to new effects
5	Feedback	Eye Fatigue	Observes if users experience eye fatigue, such as dryness, soreness, or blurring, while viewing game effects
6	Feedback	Visual Disturbance	Assesses if there are visual disturbances, like flickering, jitter, or double images, while viewing game effects
7	Feedback	Responsiveness and Smoothness	Evaluates if the rendering of game effects is smooth and responses are quick, checking for any lag
8	Feedback	Physical Discomfort	Determines if users feel dizzy, including symptoms like dizziness, nausea, or vomiting, when viewing game effects

its more straightforward gesture and effect design, the participant found it easy to get started. Nevertheless, due to the frequent need for hand movements and the prolonged and dense visual effects, hand fatigue and a reluctance to continue gameplay occurred after a certain duration. This indicates that game effect design must consider complexity and duration comprehensively to avoid user confusion and fatigue.

The second participant, a 22-year-old student with extensive VR gaming experience, was able to quickly familiarize themselves with the aforementioned games. In *Drakheir*, the participant efficiently utilized magic of various attributes and had corresponding expectations for each type of effect, such as flames and whirlwinds. However, while playing *Job Simulator*, the participant became impatient with overly mundane interactions, accelerating the pace and frequency of interactions, which led to effects being triggered simultaneously or abruptly interrupted to trigger another effect, along with clipping bugs, reducing the immersive experience of the game. In *Waltz of the Wizard*, the ability of different colored hands to produce varying effects sparked the participant's exploratory interest, leading to extensive gesture interaction, such as doodling across the entire screen or tossing items into the sky, occasionally causing visual inconsistencies due to proximity. This highlights the importance of not only creating impressive visual effects, but also choosing visuals that are familiar and coherent to the player's perception. Additionally, imposing interaction constraints can help avoid visual inconsistencies and improve inclusivity.

The third participant, a 28-year-old programmer with moderate gaming experience, exhibited a strong aversion to the three VR-required games due to susceptibility to motion sickness, opting to only experience the game designed by the author. However, rapid camera movements in response to hand motions and overly rich and saturated effect colors induced discomfort in the user. This suggests that game effect design should not only consider the style and color of effects but also the saturation and speed of movement to provide comfortable feedback.

4.4 Data Analysis

This study attracted 16 voluntary participants, yielding 149 opinions on game effects, including 75 positive and 74 negative viewpoints. These opinions were categorized by dimensions based on the aforementioned theory of effect assessment, resulting in a positive dimension analysis table and a negative dimension analysis table. Notably, during the classification by dimensions, some opinions aligned with the Representation and Feedback Theory. For example, an opinion like "The color is comfortable, and I like it" would be considered for the extent to which it matches and categorized under either Representation or Feedback. If an opinion did not clearly match either category, it was categorized as Other (Fig. 10).

According to the data, among the 75 positive opinions, 49 opinions were classified under Representation, accounting for 65.3% of the total opinions; 9 opinions were classified under Feedback, constituting 12% of the total; and 17 opinions were categorized as Other, making up 22.7% of the total opinions. Notably, in the viewpoints of users who gave the highest ratings, the combined opinions on the Representation and Feedback Theory accounted for 80% of all opinions, whereas in the viewpoints of users with the lowest ratings, the combined opinions on these theories constituted 60% of all opinions (Tables 2 and 3).

In a detailed analysis of the negative opinions, among the 74 negative viewpoints, 46 were explicitly identified as aligning with Representation Theory, accounting for 62.2% of the total. Another 20 opinions were defined as fitting Feedback Theory, making up 27.0% of the total. The remaining 8 opinions were categorized as Other, representing 10.8% of the total. This trend of increased attention to the Representation and Feedback Theory in negative opinions is noteworthy.

Positive opinions often focused on aesthetic value and emotional experience, suggesting that users pay more attention to these aspects when evaluating positively. In contrast, negative opinions were more concentrated on the Representation and Feedback Theory, indicating their foundational role in visual effect design. When users are

Table 2. Summary of positive views.

No.	Experimental Game Name	Opinion 1	Opinion 2	Opinion 3	Opinion 4	Opinion 5	Effect Score	Total Score
1	Drakheir	Other	Other	Representation	Representation	Feedback	4.6	4
2	Drakheir	Representation	Feedback	Representation	Other	Representation	4.5	5
3	Drakheir	Representation	Representation	Representation	Feedback	Representation	4	3
4	Drakheir	Other	Representation	Representation	Representation	Other	4	3.8
5	Job Simulator	Other	Feedback	Other	Representation	/	3	4.4
6	Job Simulator	Representation	Representation	Representation	Feedback	/	4.5	4
7	Job Simulator	Other	Representation	Representation	Representation	Other	3	2
8	Job Simulator	Feedback	Representation	Representation	Other	Representation	3.5	4.5
9	Waltz of the Wizard	Representation	Other	Representation	Representation	/	3.5	4.2
10	Waltz of the Wizard	Representation	Representation	Other	/	/	3	3.5
11	Waltz of the Wizard	Representation	Representation	Representation	Representation	Representation	3.5	3.8
12	Waltz of the Wizard	Other	Representation	Representation	Representation	Other	3.8	3.9
13	Design Example	Representation	Representation	Other	Representation	Representation	2.9	4.1
14	Design Example	Representation	Representation	Representation	Representation	Feedback	4	4.5
15	Design Example	Feedback	Representation	Other	Feedback	Representation	3.5	4.2
16	Design Example	Representation	Other	Representation	Representation	Representation	4.1	4.3

dissatisfied with visual effects, developers can review and trace improvements starting from these two theories to enhance the design and increase user satisfaction.

Particularly in negative opinions, the number of comments about Feedback significantly increased, highlighting its importance. Feedback, a relatively implicit dimension in game visual effects design, is often overlooked in positive evaluations but plays an indispensable role in the gaming experience. The absence of feedback in game effects tends to surface in negative user opinions, similar to the "Must-Be Quality" in the Kano model, where its absence leads to dissatisfaction. In contrast, Representation Theory is more akin to an "Expected Quality." As the quality of effects improves, adherence to Representation Theory tends to increase user satisfaction, thus drawing more attention.

Overall, 95 opinions were classified as Representation, accounting for 63.7% of the total; 29 as Feedback, making up 19.5%; and 25 as Other, constituting 16.8%. The combined the Representation and Feedback Theory accounted for 83.2% of the total, indicating their significant impact on user experience in game visual effects design.

No.	nickname	Positive Opinion 1	Positive Opinion 2	Positive Opinion 3	Positive Opinion 4	Positive Opinion 5	Reverse viewpoint 1	Reverse viewpoint 2	Reverse viewpoint 3	Reverse viewpoint 4	Reverse viewpoint 5	Visual effects rating	Overall Rating
1	Xirvan	The color combination has a dreamy and mysterious feeling under the sea Other	The dynamic scenery outside the window gives people a sense of imagination Other	The aquatic plants and jellyfish have a rich variety of animal and plant species Representation	The lightning between jellyfish is very sci-fi Representation	The approaching of fish gives people a 3D immersive experience Feedback	The three-dimensional sense of fish is not strong Representation	The scenery outside the window is not rich enough with only light spots Representation	Jellyfish don't even move Representation	The camera is shaking too much and not stable enough Feedback	The handle of the water grass carriage can add a sense of floating and shaking Representation	4.6	4
2	Cu	I really like the color scheme Representation	I really like the connection and dynamics of the pink and blue jellyfish, and I can feel their strength from far and near Feedback	The swimming of a school of fish is very realistic, and the fish's body still twists in a wavy shape when swimming, much like the kind seen in an aquarium Representation	The scenery on the far left outside the car at the beginning of the video is also very beautiful. It is very broad and has a sense of extension Other	The car window effect is really well done! The effect of double glass and light is exactly the same as what I saw in the subway Representation	The movement of the camera is a bit sluggish and not very smooth (I don't know if you want to simulate the shaking of a train) Feedback	The seaweed and pink jellyfish in the lower left corner have a relatively small range of movements, which appear stiff and abrupt compared to the dynamic contrast of other objects Representation	The advertising board and blue-green light blocks on the train are somewhat monotonous, and some graffiti illustrations can be added to enrich the visual experience. Representation	/	/	4.2	4.6
3	Yuyu	I like fish rushing towards the camera, feeling like I'm in the environment instead of looking at a fish tank Representation	It can be felt that the carriage has changed according to the environment and has become a part of the environment Representation	A little perspective, the depth of the scene feels very good, and there seems to be some content that doesn't look very flat Representation	The color of the scene is good, very dreamy Feedback	I like the special effects of car windows. It feels like I'm dreaming, in a space that doesn't exist in reality. Representation	There are a lot of parallel fish, and fish with faster movement speed can swing larger, which can produce some bubbles Representation	The yellow water grass grows directly on the seat, which is a bit abrupt and can spread from below Representation	The protagonist jellyfish feels like they are on a flat surface, somewhat disconnected from the three-dimensional scene Representation	Will the surrounding colors compete with the main character, making a distinction between brightness and purity. Feedback	/	4	3
4	Xiaofeng	The subway construction site is very attractive, and the color	The school of fish swimming back and forth adds	The jellyfish material looks good, and the tail effect is also	Jellyfish, as interactive objects, have high color saturation	The material of the car windows is very beautiful	Lack of bubble effects, not very underwater	The water grass is too straight and lacks animation	The connection effect between jellyfish is	The jellyfish in the upper left corner is motionless, which is too	Except for jellyfish, the water grass like object on the chair in	4	3.8

Fig. 10. Experimental questionnaire statistical tables (Part), by Danni Wu with volunteers, 2023

This underscores the importance and universality of these theories. Notably, users first consider whether effects are similar to those in games they've played before, their commonality, and whether they align with their preferences. They also consider whether effects are consistent with real-world physical phenomena or symbols and whether they can be reasonably explained, reflecting the influence of Representation Theory.

To delve deeper into how the Representation and Feedback Theory affect the overall game experience through visual effects, users rated the performance of the effects and the overall game, creating a scatter plot with effect performance on the x-axis and overall game rating on the y-axis (see Fig. 11). The plot clearly shows a corresponding increase in overall game ratings with higher effect ratings, indicating a positive correlation between visual effects and the overall game experience.

Moreover, as visual effect ratings improve, the proportion of positive opinions about Feedback increases, while negative opinions about Representation also rise. This shows that feedback remains crucial in pursuing an enhanced gaming experience, not only when it is lacking. After addressing feedback-related issues, continuous optimization of effects based on Representation Theory is necessary, as it's an ongoing process with ever-increasing user expectations. Relentless optimization of these effects can elevate user satisfaction with the effects, thereby enhancing the overall gaming experience.

4.5 Experiment Summary

This experiment aimed to investigate the impact of the Representation and Feedback Theory on user experience in game visual effect design. The results show that these theories significantly enhance the gaming experience.

Table 3. Summary of negative views.

No	Experimental Game Name	Opinion 1	Opinion 2	Opinion 3	Opinion 4	Opinion 5	Effect Score	Total Score
1	Drakheir	Representation	Representation	Representation	Feedback	Representation	4.6	4
2	Drakheir	Feedback	Representation	Representation	/	/	4.2	5
3	Drakheir	Representation	Representation	Representation	Feedback	/	4	3
4	Drakheir	Representation	Representation	Representation	Representation	Representation	4	3.8
5	Job Simulator	Feedback	Representation	Representation	Representation	Feedback	3	4.4
6	Job Simulator	Representation	Representation	Other	/	/	4.5	4
7	Job Simulator	Representation	Feedback	Representation	Feedback	Feedback	3	2
8	Job Simulator	Representation	Representation	Representation	Representation	Other	3.5	4.5
9	Waltz of the Wizard	Representation	Other	Feedback	Other	Feedback	3.5	4.2
10	Waltz of the Wizard	Feedback	Representation	Feedback	Representation	/	3	3.5
11	Waltz of the Wizard	Representation	Feedback	Representation	Representation	Feedback	3.5	3.8
12	Waltz of the Wizard	Representation	Feedback	Representation	Other	Representation	3.8	3.9
13	Design Example	Feedback	Feedback	Representation	Representation	Representation	2.9	4.1
14	Design Example	Representation	Representation	Representation	Representation	Representation	4	4.5
15	Design Example	Other	Representation	Feedback	Feedback	Representation	3.5	4.2
16	Design Example	Representation	Other	Representation	Feedback	Other	4.1	4.3

Firstly, through the classification and analysis of users' positive and negative opinions, it was found that positive evaluations often focus more on aesthetic value and emotional experience, whereas negative evaluations concentrate more on the Representation and Feedback Theory. This indicates that representation and feedback are fundamental elements in game visual effect design, significantly influencing user experience.

Secondly, the Representation Theory in user experience is analogous to the "Expected Quality" in the KANO model, where user satisfaction increases with the quality of effects that adhere to this theory. On the other hand, Feedback Theory resembles the "Must-Be Quality" in the KANO model. It often goes unmentioned by users, but its absence leads to dissatisfaction, underscoring its indispensable role in the gaming experience.

Based on these findings, the following suggestions for future game effect design are proposed:

Emphasize the Representation Theory: Developers should focus on effect designs that align with the Representation Theory, considering the similarity of effects to those

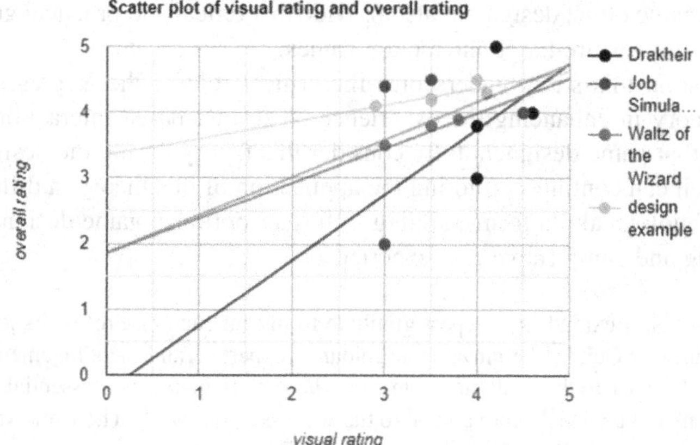

Fig. 11. Scatter plot of visual rating and overall rating, by Danni Wu, 2023

in games previously played by users, commonalities, and meeting users' preferences. By meeting users' expectations of representation, satisfaction can be increased.

Value the Feedback Theory: Feedback is equally crucial in game effect design. Developers must ensure the feedback quality of effects to avoid user dissatisfaction. Even if feedback is not explicitly mentioned by users, its absence can lead to dissatisfaction.

Continuously Optimize Effects: Optimizing effects is an ongoing process. Developers should continuously invest effort in improving effects based on the Representation and Feedback Theory to enhance user satisfaction with the effects, thereby enhancing the overall gaming experience.

Consider Effects in Relation to the Overall Experience: Analyzing the correlation between visual effect ratings and overall game ratings provides a more comprehensive understanding of the relationship between effects and the overall experience. Developers can use this analysis to adjust effect designs to improve the overall game experience.

In summary, the Representation and Feedback Theory play a crucial role in game visual effect design. Developers should fully consider these theories when designing and optimizing effects to enhance user experience and the overall quality of the game.

5 Conclusion

This study delves deeply into the application of the Representation and Feedback Theory in designing visual effects for gesture-based interaction games, examining their impact on user experience. Initially, it revisits the historical development of game effects styles and hand interactions. This is followed by a detailed analysis and case studies on the application of this theory in game visual effects. Through these case studies, the research demonstrates the theory's practical application in actual game effect design.

Experiments were conducted to thoroughly assess the designed gesture effects using both qualitative and quantitative methods. The results indicate that integrating the Representation and Feedback Theory into visual effect design significantly enhances user interaction and game satisfaction. These findings not only confirm the importance of this theory in game effect design but also provide theoretical and practical guidance for developing future gesture-based interaction games.

In conclusion, this study underscores the critical role of the Representation and Feedback Theory in enhancing the experience of gesture-based interaction games. It recommends that game designers fully consider this theory during the design process. Future research can continue exploring the application of this theory in different game types and technological platforms, aiming to further optimize game design and create more engaging and comfortable user experiences.

Acknowledgments. I extend my deepest gratitude to my instructors, Professors Zhuohao Wu, Min Fan, and Yunpeng Cui, for their invaluable guidance, expertise, and encouragement throughout this research. I also wish to thank all the volunteers whose participation was essential to this study. Their enthusiasm and feedback were crucial to the success of our work. The work was funded by National Social Science and Arts Foundation (22BG137).

References

1. He, S.: Study on the elements of game special effects design. Comput. Knowl. Technol. **18**(23), 89–91 (2022)
2. Wei, Z.: Study on 3D game special effects design and artistic style. Popular Lit. Art **06**, 71 (2019)
3. Shi, H.: From games to art: on the artistic language and visual style of independent games. Decoration **04**, 38–41 (2017). https://doi.org/10.16272/j.cnki.cn11-1392/j.2017.04.010
4. Chao, Y.: Natural Interaction Design and Application Derived from Event Archetypes. Hunan University (2014)
5. Hall, S., (ed.): Representation: Cultural Representations and Signifying Practices. Commercial Press (2003). Xu, L., Lu, X. (trans.)
6. Norman, D.A.: The Design of Everyday Things. Basic Books (2002)
7. Lele, F.: Essential Introduction to Unity Shaders, p. 393. People's Posts and Telecommunications Publishing House, June 2016

A Character Input Method for Smart Glasses that Allows You to Enter One Character in One Step with One Thumb

Takahiro Yamada(✉), Toshimitsu Tanaka, and Yuji Sagawa

Meijo University, Shiogamaguchi 1-501, Tenpaku-ku, Nagoya, Japan
223441701@ccmailg.meijo-u.ac.jp

Abstract. At HCII2023, we announced a method to input one character in two steps. The user holds the smartphone and operates it with their thumb. The first step is to select a group of five letters by rotating your thumb at the carpometacarpal joint (the joint at the base of your thumb) and sliding the tip of your thumb across the screen. The second step is to select one letter within that group by tapping or flicking.

In this research, that second step is replaced the method to select a letter by bending your thumb. The user rotates the thumb like the same as the previous method. When a letter group containing the letter that you want to enter appears on the input guidance window, start bending your thumb to select that group. Then bend your thumb until you see that letter in the guidance window. When it appears, move your thumb off the screen and input. This allows you to enter one character in one operation.

Character input can be done by rotating the thumb and bending and straightening the thumb, both of which are easy movements. There is no longer a time loss between group selection and letter selection that existed in the previous method. Therefore, character input speed has improved. In experiments with beginners, the speed increased by up to 20% after entering around 250 characters. A Mann-Whitney U test confirmed that there was a significant difference.

Keywords: Character input · One-hand operation · Touch typing · One step operation · Smart glasses · Mobile

1 Introduction

Head-mounted displays (HMDs) are used in virtual reality, 3D computer games, the Metaverse, and more. Smart glasses are see-through HMDs that allow you to see a virtual image superimposed on the real scene. In particular, XREAL Air 2 and ASUS Air Vision M1 have the same shape as regular glasses, so you can wear them around town without feeling awkward. So, you can use those smart glasses as a mobile display for your laptop or smartphone when you're out and about.

Although you can see both virtual and real images through smart glasses, it is not a good idea to perform input operations on a smartphone screen and view the results

M. Kurosu and A. Hashizume (Eds.): HCII 2024, LNCS 14688, pp. 203–214, 2024.
https://doi.org/10.1007/978-3-031-60449-2_14

on smart glasses. The distance from the eyes to the virtual screen is set to 2.5 to 5.0 m for normal smart glasses, but the distance between the smartphone held in the hand and the eyes is less than 0.5 m. Therefore, our vision system cannot focus on both distances at the same time. As a result, you have to adjust your focus every time you move your perspective between your smartphone and the virtual screen. This causes eye fatigue.

Most of the applications on computers and smartphones can be operated by pointing and keyboard input. Pointing involves moving and clicking the cursor displayed on the screen with your mouse or touchpad. This operation does not require you to see your fingers. Smartphones are operated by touching the screen with a finger, but this can also be replaced with pointer operations using a mouse. Many smartphones come with a preinstalled software keyboard in the phone layout or QWERTY layout. Phone keyboards have fewer keys than QWERTY keyboards, but they still have about 20 keys. Software keyboards require visual aids to select keys because you cannot locate keys by touching them with your fingers. Therefore, several input methods that do not require the user to look at their hands were developed as character input methods to replace the software keyboard.

In HCII2023, we presented a method to input one character in two steps [1]. This method divides the characters into 10 groups of 5 characters each. The first step is to hold your smartphone and rotate your thumb on the screen to select a group of letters. The second step is to tap or flick in any of the four directions to select one character within that group.

The method proposed in this study replaces the second step with a thumb flexion motion. And it connects that motion to the first step without removing the thumb from the screen. This allows you to enter one character with a one-step stroke gesture. No more moving your thumbs off the screen and back when typing. It is easy to rotate your thumb with its carpometacarpal joint or bend your thumb with its interphalangeal joint, even while holding your smartphone. Therefore, you can expect an improvement in input speed.

2 Related Researches

Many techniques have been developed for entering text without using a keyboard. Speech recognition [2–4] is a typical technology. Recently, recognition rates have been improved by utilizing AI technology. However, in a noisy environment, false recognition cannot be ignored. A significant drawback of voice input is that the speaker's voice is audible to those around them, so the privacy of the speaker is not protected. Another drawback is that it takes a lot of time and effort to fix typos using voice commands alone. Also, it cannot be used in places where silence is required.

Many methods have been developed for users to select characters from the on-screen keyboard by making finger, hand, or arm gestures [5–7]. These methods require motion capture devices such as game controllers, motion sensors, and depth cameras to detect hand position and arm orientation. Therefore, to use those methods outdoors, you will need to carry such devices. Additionally, the on-screen keyboard takes up a lot of screen space. The input speed is slow in the method of pointing to the characters one by one on the keyboard displayed on the screen. The input speed of the method of hitting a 3D keyboard with a stick in virtual space [8, 9] is relatively fast, but it requires long training to master.

Gesture-based methods can also be used in mobile environments. However, you will need to carry motion sensing devices such as data gloves [10], finger rings with motion sensors [11, 12], depth cameras for motion capture, and game controllers with accelerometer and gyro sensors. Also, in a crowded place, the method of drawing letters in the air [11] cannot be used because the arm will hit nearby people.

Projection-type keyboards have been developed that project key patterns onto the back of the hand or arm [13, 14]. However, just like when you type using a software keyboard on a smartphone, you need to visually check the position of your fingertips to select the key. These methods require the user to see both the nearby hand and the far virtual screen. Therefore, problems caused by eye focus adjustment are inevitable.

Methods have been developed to detect the position of the thumb by attaching touch sensors [15, 16] or micro touch panels [17] to the fingers. With these, one-handed eyes-free character input is possible. These sensors and panels can get in the way, come off, or break when the user is trying to grasp something with their hands. However, it is not practical to attach and detach sensors and panels every time you input characters.

There are devices that input characters by sensing vibrations when you tap with your finger. Tap Strap 2 [18] is a device with five rings connected by a string. Each ring detects the vibration of the inserted finger. Fingers in tapping can also be detected by the TapXR [19] worn on the wrist. Memorizing the finger combinations assigned to each letter allows you to type letters quickly without visual aids, but it takes a lot of practice. These devices require a hard plate that vibrates your finger when you tap on it, so you'll need to find one or carry one if you plan on using it outdoors.

There is also a method of selecting a character by the direction or rotation of the wrist [20–22]. However, it is difficult to input many characters with these methods, because the methods make your wrists tired. It also takes time to learn, as you have to memorize the wrist movement patterns assigned to each letter.

Character input methods for smart glasses used outdoors are required to have the following characteristics: (1) use a portable input device, (2) one-handed operation, and (3) no need to visually confirm the position. The first condition is essential for carrying the device. The second condition is necessary to keep the other hand free. This hand can be used, for example, to hold a bag, grab a strap, hold an umbrella, or open a door. The third is necessary to avoid the focus adjustment problem caused by alternating looking at the hand and the virtual screen, which strains the human visual system.

The method we presented at HCII2022 [25] satisfies these characteristics. The input device is a smartphone, and the screen is covered with a thin plate with holes. By tracing the edge of the hole, the user can make the correct stroke without visual aids. However, if you cover the screen, you will no longer be able to use it as a normal smartphone. It might be possible to make the cover removable, but it would be a pain to put it on and take it off every time you type.

Therefore, we developed a method that does not use a cover and presented in HCII2023 [1]. The details of this method will be explained in Sect. 3. With this method, each character is entered in two steps. The first action is to rotate your thumb, and the second action is a tap or flick. Each letter is typed with two finger strokes, which increases the distance you have to move your fingers. This increases input time. The second step, the flick, is performed by rotating, bending, and extending the thumb. Because it is performed using two joints at the same time, the movement may go in the wrong direction or the path may be curved.

In this study, we replace the second step of the previous method with a thumb flexion motion. It is a simple one-joint operation. It is connected to the first step at just before removing the finger from the screen. These changes enable character input using one-step gestures. This method is explained in Sect. 4.

3 Previous Method

As shown in the left table of Fig. 1, Japanese hiragana characters are divided into 10 groups of 5 characters each. All Japanese people learn this table in elementary school. So, we chose this table to group the letters. Alphanumeric characters are also divided into five-character groups so that they can be selected using the same procedure. The order is alphabetical. The numbers are divided into the first half (1–5) and the second half (6–10). It is also possible to use key bindings of the phone keyboard, but few Japanese people memorize that layout, so we didn't choose that.

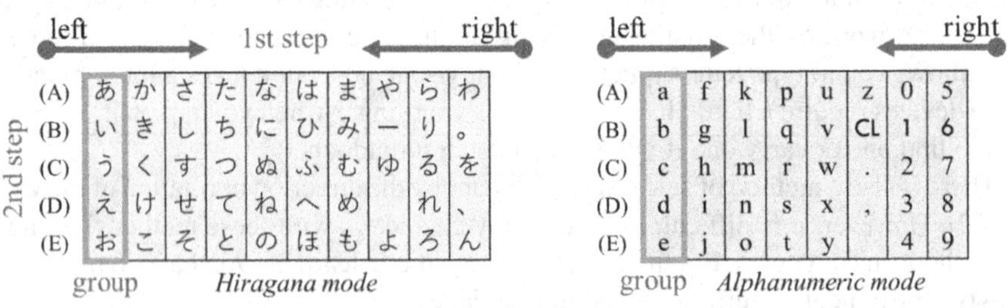

Fig. 1. Definition of letter groups containing 5 characters each.

In the previous method, one character is selected in two steps. When holding a smartphone with one hand, the place where the tip of the thumb can reach when the base of the thumb (the carpometacarpal joint) is rotated is the easiest to touch. The red arc in Fig. 2(a) shows the path of the thumb when turned. So, we decided to select a letter group with that thumb rotation. Touch the left side of the screen with your thumb and move it clockwise. There are no position restrictions as long as the touch is to the left of the centerline. When the distance traveled exceeds a certain length, the first group will appear on the screen. "あ" is displayed in hiragana mode, and "a" is displayed in alphanumeric mode.

After that, every time you move your thumb a certain distance, the display switches to the group on the right in Fig. 1. Moving your thumb back to the left also moves the displayed group back. The displayed group can be selected by lifting your finger from the screen. This operation can also be initiated from the right side. In this case, moving the thumb to the left displays the character groups in reverse order, starting with the last group.

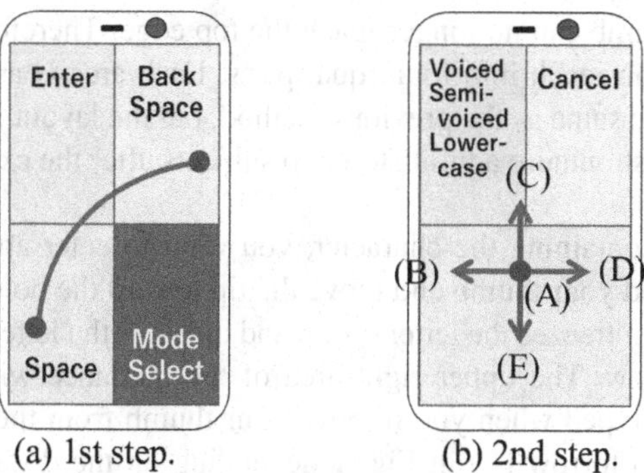

Fig. 2. Character input procedure in the two-step method of previous research.

In the first step, the touch screen is divided vertically and horizontally into four regions, as shown in Fig. 2(a). Space, backspace, and enter are assigned to the lower-left, upper-right, and upper-left areas, respectively. To the lower-right area, we assigned a function to switch between alphanumeric characters and hiragana. These functions are selected by tap. Although these regions and the thumb rotation trajectory overlap, they can be separated by the distance traveled by the fingertip. If the distance from the first touch location exceeds the threshold, the system considers the action to be a group selection. Otherwise, it is considered a tap to a function.

In the second step, you select one of five letters in the letter group. This operation follows to the flick keyboard. The flick keyboard is the most common text input method, at least on Japanese smartphones. Specifically, the first letter in a group can be selected by tapping. The second step splits the touch screen into a top and bottom part. The bottom part is used for this tapping. The second through fifth letters of the group can be selected by flicking left, up, right, or down respectively.

4 Proposed Method

In order to speed up character input, the previous 2-step input has been improved to 1-step input. The new method, similar to the previous method, specifies a letter group and selects one letter within that group. The grouping of letters is the same as the previous method shown in Fig. 1.

Group selection is done by rotating the thumb at the carpometacarpal joint and sliding its tip from left to right or vice versa. If you touch the left side of the screen with your thumb, moving the tip of your thumb a certain distance to the right will highlight the first group of letters. After that, every time you move your thumb to the right a certain distance, the highlight moves to the next group. The currently selected group name is displayed in a large size on the input guidance window. In Fig. 3(a), "は" is displayed in the upper right area. It will also be highlighted in red in the bottom right indicator.

The proposed method divides the screen into four regions, similar to the previous method. However, the horizontal border has been moved down. As smartphone screens have gotten larger, if you hold the smartphone by touching its lower corner to the center of your palm, your thumb can no longer reach the top edge. Therefore, we divided the area that the thumb can reach into four equal parts. Each area is assigned a function. The functionality is the same as the previous method, but the layout was changed based on the results of a questionnaire administered to subjects after the experiment using the previous method.

When the group containing the character, you want to enter appears on the input guidance window, bend your thumb and move the tip toward the bottom right as shown in Fig. 3(b). This action freezes the letter group and displays the letters within the group in the guidance window. The upper right area of the guidance window displays the character that will be typed when you remove your thumb from the screen. The letter changes from row (A) to row (E) in Fig. 1 depending on the distance traveled. This letter is also highlighted in red in the lower right indicator. When the guidance window displays the character you want to input, you remove your thumb from the screen to fix it. This operation allows you to input a single voiceless hiragana character.

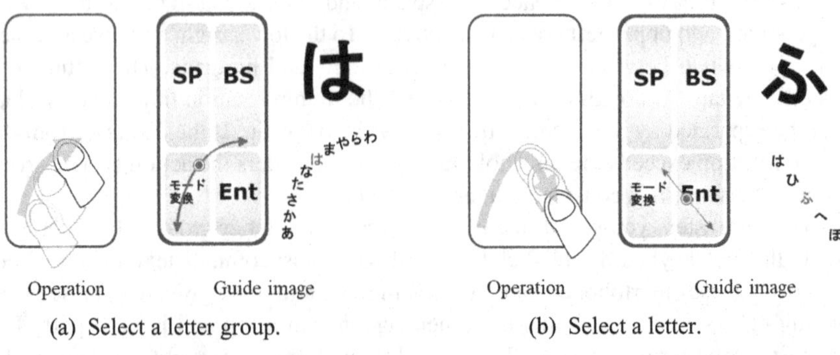

Fig. 3. Character input procedure in the one-step method of this research.

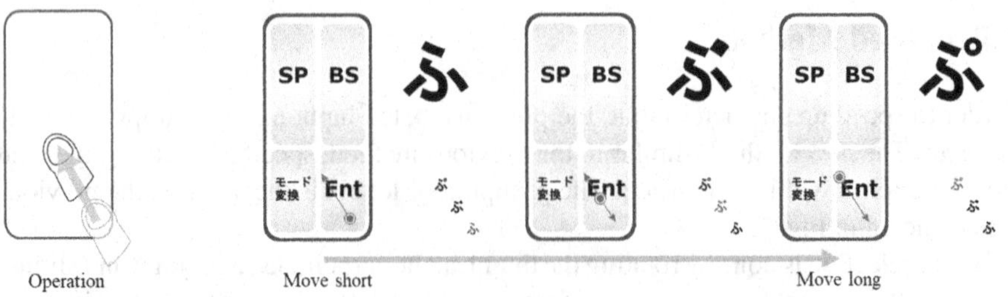

Fig. 4. Steps to replace the last character typed with the related voiced, semi-voiced, or lowercase letter.

Each voiced, semi-voiced, and lowercase letter is converted from its associated voiceless letter. As shown in the left-most image in Fig. 4, touching the bottom right corner of the screen with your thumb and moving it to the top left replaces the last character you typed. If it can be converted into two characters, select one by the distance your fingertip moves. The second image from the left in Fig. 4 shows an example of the guidance window that has just started this conversion operation. In this example, the voiceless sound character "は" is displayed. If you move your thumb towards the upper left, it will change to a voiced sound character "ば". Moving further changes it to a semi-voiced sound character "ぱ". This operation is ignored for characters that cannot be converted. In alphanumeric mode, the operation in Fig. 3 selects lowercase letters of the alphabet. Then converted to capital letters by the operation in Fig. 4 if necessary.

The new method allows you to select single characters in consecutive motions. This eliminates the need to take your finger off the touch panel in the middle of entering a character and then touch it again. Rotating and bending the thumb can each be mainly accomplished with a single-joint motion, which is easier than the two-joint motion required for a four-way flick. These can be expected to shorten input time.

5 Experiments and Results for Beginners

5.1 Procedure of Experiment

The input system was developed using Android Studio on a PC with Windows 10 OS. Its programming language is Java. The system works on smartphones. Use a smartphone SONY XPERIA 10 III running Android 11 as an input device. Connect to the PC monitor with a USB Type-C to HDMI cable. Mirror the smartphone screen to the monitor using Display Port Alternate Mode. Therefore, the display delay can be ignored.

This experiment was conducted by seven university students (three men and four women) in their 20 s. Before this experiment, the subjects received a 10-min lecture on the operating procedure for character input, the meaning of the input guide display, the experimental procedure, and precautions. Subjects were then asked to type the characters as accurately as possible. The subjects sat in a chair in a natural posture, facing the monitor as shown in Fig. 5. All subjects were right-handed, so they grabbed the smartphone with their right hand. They operated the system by placing their hand under the table to hide their hands from view.

Subjects enter 5 hiragana words in one task. In the experiment, they repeated this task 10 times with a 3-min break in between. Each task begins when the subject's thumb touches the input device. A single task word written in hiragana is displayed on the right side of the monitor. The characters entered by the subject are displayed directly below them. On the left side, the input guidance will appear. After entering all the characters of the task word, tap the bottom right area to input Enter. Then the next word is displayed. Enter is accepted even if some of the input characters do not match the task word. Enter 5 words to complete one task.

The task words were selected from the word list of the Balanced Corpus of Contemporary Written Japanese (BCCWJ) [23] of the National Institute for Japanese Language and Linguistics. From each of the 4, 5, and 6-letter nouns in hiragana notation, 100 words were extracted in order of frequency, excluding numbers and quantifiers. Then words which are the same in Hiragana notation but different in Kanji notation were merged. The frequency of the merged word is the sum of the frequency of the original words. Finally, the top 50 words in frequency from each of the 4, 5, and 6-letter words were selected. Those 150 words were combined into one list. In the experiment, 5 words are randomly selected from the list for each task.

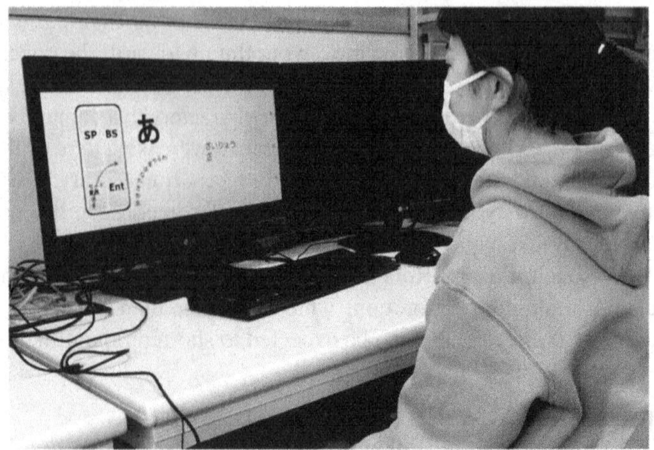

Fig. 5. Subject's posture and screen display during the experiment.

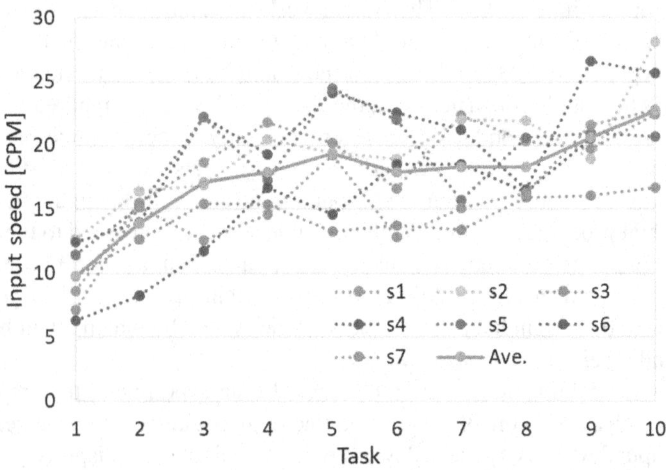

Fig. 6. Input speed for each of the seven subjects using the proposed one-step method.

The thin lines in Fig. 6 show the changes in input speed for each of the seven subjects. In the proposed method, the user needs to change the finger movement from rotation to bending while the name of the group containing the target character is displayed in the guidance window. If users change the direction of their finger movements after carefully checking the display, input becomes slow. On the other hand, if users quickly change it, they are more likely to incorrectly select the next/previous group. This reduces the input speed. Users need to learn the timing of the change. Some people can learn easily while others take a long time. Therefore, the speed of input varies depending on the subject. The average number of characters entered per task is only 25, so input speed largely varies according to the number of wrong inputs.

The thick line in Fig. 6 is the average value for all subjects. In Fig. 7, it is compared to the average input speed of the previous method presented at HCII 2023 [1], which is the average of six subjects. From the fourth task onwards, the proposed method is 10 to 20% faster than the previous method.

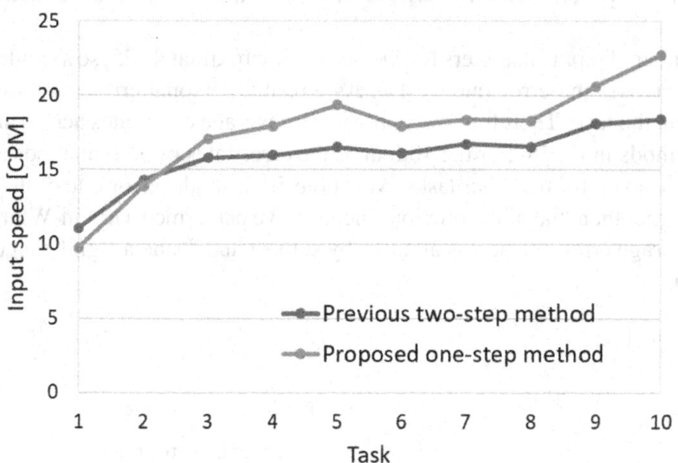

Fig. 7. Comparison of the average input speed for the two methods.

Table 1. Input speed of each test subject in the 10th task.

Proposed one-step method							
Subject	s1	s2	s3	s4	s5	s6	s7
Input speed [CPM]	22.4	28.1	16.7	25.7	20.7	22.8	22.8
Previous two-step method							
Subject	A	B	C	D	E	F	
Input speed [CPM]	20.6	14.2	18.5	17.5	19.0	20.5	

The input speed on the 10th task for both methods is shown in Table 1. A Mann-Whitney U test was performed on these values and the P value was 0.022. Therefore, it can be said that the proposed method is definitely faster than the previous method.

Figure 8 shows the average error rate for both methods. The error rate *Err* is calculated using the following formula:

$$Err = \frac{n_{incorrect} + n_{cancel}}{n_{task}}$$

Here, $n_{incorrect}$ is the sum of the number of characters in the input words that differ from the task words and the number of characters deleted by the subject using the backspace (BS) key. n_{cancel} is the number of letter groups that were incorrectly selected but canceled by the subject selecting the letter. In the previous method, if you realize before starting the second step that the letter group selected in the first step is incorrect, you can cancel the selection and return to the first step. In this case, no incorrect characters will be entered, but additional action will be required. Therefore, this counts as an input error. In the one-step method, a character is always input each time you lift your thumb, so n_{cancel} of the proposed method is always 0. n_{task} is the sum of the characters of task words.

The number of input characters for each task is approximately 25, so a single incorrect character increases the error rate by 4%. As a result, personal error rates vary greatly depending on the task. Therefore, we compare the average error rates across all subjects for both methods in Fig. 8. For the 10th task, the error rates of both methods are almost the same. However, for the other tasks except the 5th task, the error rate of the proposed method is higher than that of the previous method. We performed a Mann-Whitney U test using the average error rate across all tasks by subject and found a significant difference (p = 0.023).

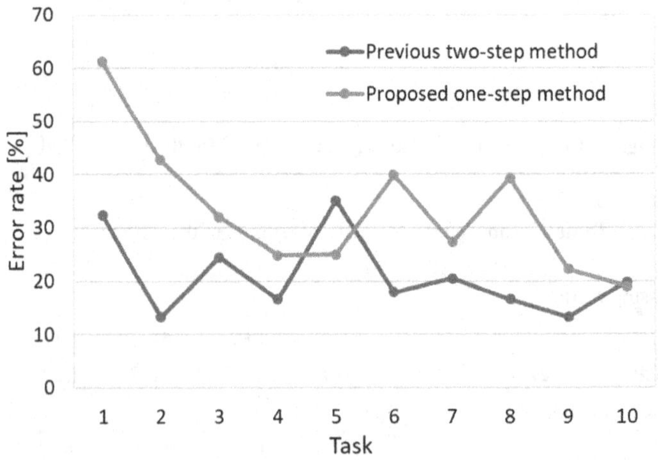

Fig. 8. Comparison of the average error rates of the two methods.

With the one-step method, when you bend your finger to move from group selection to character selection, you may unintentionally move to the previous or next group. If you move your thumb quickly when changing direction from rotation to bending, the trajectory of its tip will follow a small curve. Changes in movement direction are determined by comparing the current movement vector with the previous movement vector. Therefore, if the trajectory curve is relatively gentle, there is a possibility that it may be mistakenly recognized as continuing rotation. This misjudgment can be reduced by setting a small angle threshold for determining motion switching. However, if the threshold value is too small, there will be many erroneous judgments in which the process erroneously shifts to character selection when selecting a group.

The length of the movement vector also needs to be adjusted. In both rotation and flexion, small positional fluctuations are added to the trajectory of the thumb tip. Therefore, if the length of the movement vector is short, i.e. if the vector is calculated from a short motion, then its direction is less reliable. On the other hand, if the vector is calculated after a relatively long movement, the judgment will be delayed and the input time may become longer.

6 Conclusion

We developed a one-step character input method for smart glasses. Each character is stored in a table with 10 rows and 5 columns. To input a character, you grasp a smartphone and touch your thumb on the left side of its screen. Then you rotate your thumb right with its carpometacarpal joint. When the guidance window displays the name of the character group containing the character you want to enter, bend your thumb toward the bottom right. When the guidance window displays that character, you remove your thumb from the screen to input it.

Compared to the previous two-step method, our experiment with beginners showed a 20% faster input speed on the 10th task. A Mann-Whitney U test confirmed that there was a significant difference. However, the error rate increased.

Some errors occurred when the finger movement changed from rotation to bending. In this case, the next letter group is incorrectly selected. Furthermore, an error occurred where the operation moved to letter selection even though it was not intended. The cause of these errors is thought to be the conditions and judgment thresholds when switching from group selection to character selection. We are planning to narrow down the conditions and thresholds by examining the records of the movement path of the fingertip of subjects and examining the direction and speed of movement. It is expected that the optimal threshold will change as you get used to the input method. So, we plan to make an interface program that allows the user to change the values.

References

1. Yamada, T., et al.: One-handed character input method without screen cover for smart glasses that does not require visual confirmation of fingertip position. In: Kurosu, M., Hashizume, A. (eds.) HCII 2023. Part I. LNCS, vol. 14011, pp. 603–614 (2023). https://doi.org/10.1007/978-3-031-35596-7_39
2. Alexa Voice Service Overview (v20160207). https://developer.amazon.com/en-US/docs/alexa/alexa-voice-service/api-overview.html. Accessed 14 Jan 2024
3. Use Siri on all your Apple devices. https://support.apple.com/en-us/HT204389. Accessed 14 Jan 2024
4. Google Assistant is better than Alexa or Siri. https://www.cnbc.com/2019/06/19/google-assistant-beats-alexa-and-siri-at-recognizing-medications.html. Accessed 14 Jan 2024
5. Grubert, J., et al. : Text entry in immersive head-mounted display-based virtual reality using standard keyboards. In: 25th IEEE Conference on Virtual Reality and 3D User Interfaces, VR 2018 - Proceedings, pp.159–166 (2018)
6. Boletsis, C., Kongsvik, S.: Text input in virtual reality: a preliminary evaluation of the drum-like VR keyboard. Technologies **7**(2), 31:1–31:10 (2019)

7. Yu, C., et al.: Tap, dwell or gesture? Exploring head-based text entry techniques for HMDS. In: Proceedings of the 2017 CHI Conference on Human Factors in Computing Systems, pp. 4479–4488 (2017)
8. Boletsis, C., Kongsvik, S.: Text input in virtual reality a preliminary evaluation of the drum-like VR keyboard. Technologies **7**(2), 31 (2019). https://doi.org/10.3390/technologies7020031
9. Adhikary, J., Vertanen, K.: Typing on midair virtual keyboards: exploring visual designs and interaction styles proc. Interact **2021**, 132–151 (2021)
10. Fujitsu Develops Glove-Style Wearable Device. http://www.fujitsu.com/global/about/resources/news/press-releases/2014/0218-01.html. Accessed 14 Jan 2024
11. Fujitsu Laboratories Develops Ring-Type Wearable Device Capable of Text Input by Fingertip. https://www.fujitsu.com/global/about/resources/news/press-releases/2015/0113-01.html. Accessed 14 Jan 2024
12. Ring Zero. https://www.techinasia.com/ring-zero-new-start-japanese-wearable, https://www.g-mark.org/award/describe/42290?locale=en. Accessed 14 Jan 2024
13. Haier Asu Smartwatch. https://www.digitaltrends.com/smartwatch-reviews/haier-asu-review/. Accessed 14 Jan 2024
14. NEC develops ARmKeypad Air, a contact-free virtual keyboard for a user's arm. https://www.nec.com/en/press/201607/global_20160713_01.html. Accessed 14 Jan 2024
15. Wong, P., Zhu, K., Fu, H.: FingerT9: leveraging thumb- to-finger interaction for same-side-hand text entry on smartwatches. In: Proceedings CHI 2018, Paper No. 178 (2017)
16. Whitmier, E., et al.: DigiTouch: reconfigurable thumb-to-finger input and text entry on head-mounted displays. Proc. ACM IMWUT **1**(3) (2017). Article 133
17. Xu, Z., et al.: TipText: eyes-free text entry on a fingertip keyboard. In: Proceedings of the 32nd ACM Symposium on User Interface Software and Technology, pp. 883–899 (2019)
18. Tap Strap 2. https://www.wired.com/review/tap-strap-2/. Accessed 14 Jan 2024
19. TapXR. https://www.forbes.com/sites/charliefink/2021/10/12/tapxr-bracelet-enables-typing-without-a-keyboard/?sh=612e2b662d7f. Accessed 14 Jan 2024
20. Sun, K., et al.: Float: one-handed and touch-free target selection on smartwatches. In: Proceedings CHI 2017, pp. 692–704 (2017)
21. Gong, J., Yang, X., Irani, P.: WristWhirl: one-handed continuous smartwatch input using wrist gesture. In: Proceedings UIST 2016, pp. 861–872 (2016)
22. Gong, J., et al.: WrisText: one-handed text entry on smartwatch using wrist gestures. In: Proceedings CHI 2018 (2018). Paper No. 181
23. The word list of the Balanced Corpus of Contemporary Written Japanese of the National Institute for Japanese Language and Linguistics. https://ccd.ninjal.ac.jp/bccwj/en/freq-list.html. Accessed 14 Jan 2024
24. Soukoreff, W., MacKenzie, S.: Metrics for text entry research: an evaluation of MSD and KSPC, and a new unified error metric. In: Proceedings of ACM CHI 2003, pp. 113–120 (2003)
25. Tanaka, T., et al.: One-handed character input method for smart glasses that does not require visual confirmation of fingertip position. In: Kurosu, M. (ed.) HCII 2022 Part II. LNCS, vol. 13303, pp.165–179. Springer, Cham (2022). https://doi.org/10.1007/978-3-031-05409-9_13

Preliminary Study on Flick-Based Text Input on HMD's Front

Taisei Yamaguchi(✉), Yoshiki Nishikawa, and Buntarou Shizuki

University of Tsukuba, 1-1-1 Tennodai, Tsukuba, Ibaraki 305-8573, Japan
{yamaguchi,nishikawa,shizuki}@iplab.cs.tsukuba.ac.jp

Abstract. In virtual reality (VR), users use text input in various situations, including text chat, email, and search. For text input in VR, various methods have been developed. In this work, we designed a text input method, which we call FaceFlick, which uses the front of the HMD to provide tactile feedback for flick input in VR. We conducted a preliminary user study to compare the input speed and accuracy of FaceFlick with an existing flick input method in VR. The results showed that FaceFlick surpassed the baseline in terms of input speed and NASA-TLX score.

Keywords: Text entry · Virtual reality · VR input · Back-of-device interaction · Flick input · Japanese input · KANA input

1 Introduction

In virtual reality (VR), users use text input in various situations, including text chat, email, and search. For text input in VR, various methods have been developed. There are methods that use handheld controllers [24], in which the user taps on virtual keyboard keys with the controllers or points at the key with a ray from the controller [1,21]. In recent years, advances in hand-tracking technology have led to methods that allow the user to input text by tracking the user's hand movements. For example, input methods using gestures [5,20,22], and input methods emulating actual QWERTY input [7,18] and flick input [8,15] have been proposed. These input methods display a virtual keyboard in VR, and the user manipulates it directly with the tracked hand.

However, there are problems with using a virtual keyboard [6]. Unlike physical keyboards, virtual keyboards do not provide tactile feedback when keys are touched; this can affect text input speed, accuracy, and ease of use. This problem can become particularly notable with flick input, which is a widely used Japanese text input method (Fig. 1), due to the specific procedures involved in this method. In flick input, a consonant is selected by touching one of the consonant keys; then, a character is entered either by releasing a finger or by swiping in a specific direction to select one of the vowel variations (Fig. 2). Flick input using physical surfaces allows the user to transit smoothly from touch to swipe,

M. Kurosu and A. Hashizume (Eds.): HCII 2024, LNCS 14688, pp. 215–227, 2024.
https://doi.org/10.1007/978-3-031-60449-2_15

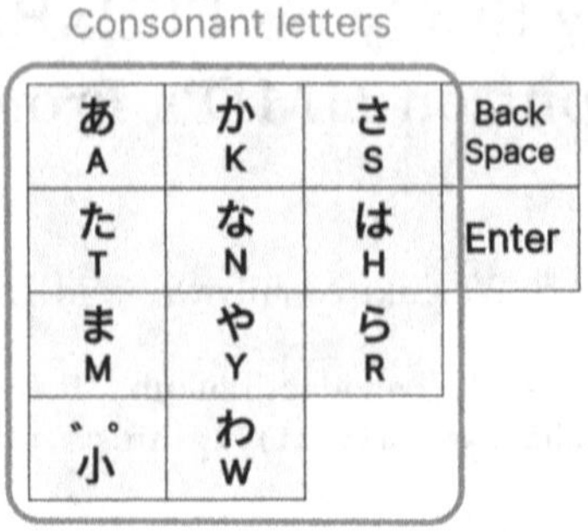

Fig. 1. The flick keyboard designed for Japanese text input.

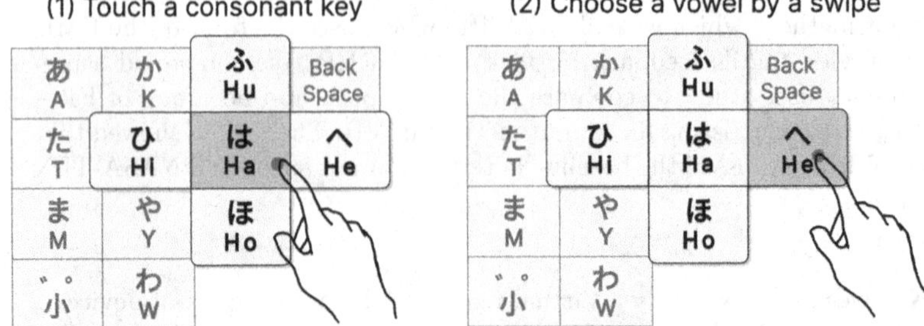

Fig. 2. Flick input procedure.

as the user can sense the touch of the keys without the need to confirm the key contact through visual feedback. However, unlike physical keyboards, flick input in VR using a virtual keyboard requires the user to first confirm the key contact with visual feedback before transitioning to swipe, which may hinder a smooth transition [8,15]. Therefore, it is important to incorporate tactile feedback into flick input in VR using a virtual keyboard. Previous studies have explored the significance of incorporating tactile feedback or using physical surfaces for flick input in VR [14,18]; however, the benefit remains unclear due to the inaccuracy in hand tracking caused by the overlap of hands.

To address this problem, we focused on an input method that uses the front surface of a head-mounted display (HMD) as the physical surface for the virtual keyboard [10,17]. Based on this, we designed our text input method, which we call FaceFlick, which uses the front of the HMD to provide tactile feedback for flick input in VR (hereafter, VR flick input). In addition, we conducted a user study to compare the input speed, accuracy, usability, and task workload of FaceFlick with an existing VR flick input method as a baseline.

The contributions of our work are the following two unique pieces of knowledge in designing the text input system:

- Presenting a flick input method in VR using a physical touch surface, unaffected by the performance of hand tracking.
- Demonstrating that the flick input method using the front of the HMD has significantly higher CPM and NASA-TLX scores than conventional flick input methods in VR.

2 Related Work

This section describes VR flick input methods related to FaceFlick, including those using virtual flick keyboards in mid-air, those using physical touch surfaces, and those using devices attached to the HMD.

2.1 VR Flick Input Methods Using Virtual Keyboard in Mid-Air

Many VR flick input methods use a virtual keyboard in mid-air for input.

Kita et al. [15] presented a flick input method in VR using a virtual flick keyboard and compared its performance of character input with an input method using a virtual QWERTY keyboard. In this study, text input using the virtual QWERTY keyboard was superior to VR flick input in terms of input speed and accuracy. However, according to a questionnaire survey, many participants wanted to use VR flick input for text input in VR. It was also stated that these performances may have been influenced by the lack of visual and auditory feedback during input.

Fukunaka et al. [8] presented a virtual flick keyboard that provides visual feedback to indicate that the user touches the keys in VR flick input. Comparative experiments showed that in terms of text input speed, the method was at least as fast as the method using a QWERTY keyboard and controller in VR; however, the average number of incorrect inputs was approximately 4.6 times higher.

Ozawa et al. [19] proposed a method in which key selection in VR flick input was performed by pinch gestures instead of touch. In this method, the user could perceive the timing of key selection through pinch gestures. However, since there was no sensation of touching the keys, the user had to rely solely on visual feedback to confirm a successful selection of the intended key.

In contrast to these methods, in FaceFlick, since the user interacts with a physical touch surface, they can sense the contact of the keys and swipe their finger over the physical surface without the need to confirm visual feedback.

2.2 VR Flick Input Methods Using Physical Surfaces

Some VR flick input methods use physical surfaces.

Kawaguchi et al. [14] and Ogitani et al. [18] presented a method in which a virtual flick keyboard displayed on the palm of the non-dominant hand was operated by the index finger of the dominant hand. The input speed and accuracy of this method were lower than those of VR flick input methods using a virtual flick keyboard due to misrecognition caused by the overlap of the dominant and non-dominant hands.

Kiyohara et al. [16] proposed a VR flick input method using a touch device equipped with the non-dominant hand. This method had lower input speed and accuracy than the VR flick input method due to misalignment between the virtual flick keyboard displayed in VR and the touch device used for input, as well as the misalignment between the fingertips in reality and in VR.

These methods have poor text input performance, which can be attributed to the misrecognition of hand-tracking or the misalignment of fingertips. In addition, the touch device needs to be equipped with the hand. FaceFlick does not require the user to equip the device because the touch surface is on the front of the HMD, and text can be input using only one hand. In addition, it is not affected by the performance of hand-tracking because it does not use hand-tracking.

2.3 VR Flick Input Methods Using Input Devices Attached to an HMD

There are input methods using input devices attached to HMDs, which are employed for purposes beyond just text entry. Gugenheimer et al. [10] and Lee et al. [17] presented an input method using a touch device attached to the front of the HMD. These studies investigated the display position and input characteristics of the touch device attached to an HMD for the input method using the front of the HMD. Hutama et al. [13] showed a text input method in which the user uses a physical QWERTY keyboard that is split and equipped to both sides of an HMD. Grossman et al. [9] showed a text input method using a smart-glass temple as a touch surface for text input.

In these methods, the user's hand is not tracked; therefore, the user relies on proprioceptive sense and tactile sensation when touching the keyboard to type. Similarly, in FaceFlick, the user touches the touch device attached to the front of the HMD according to their proprioceptive sense. The purpose of this study is to explore the effectiveness of character input using flick input on the front of the HMD, which has not been explored in previous studies.

3 FaceFlick: VR Flick Input Method Using the Front of the HMD

We designed FaceFlick, which is a Japanese kana text input system in VR, based on the input method using the front of the HMD. To implement FaceFlick, we attached a smartphone to the HMD as a touch device, while we envision that a touch position detection mechanism will be incorporated directly into the front of the HMD in the future.

3.1 Procedure of Text Input

In FaceFlick, the user performs flick input using a touch device attached to the front of the HMD (Fig. 3). A touch input capability on the front of the HMD allows the user to directly interact with the virtual keyboard. The user can perform flick input by touching the front of the HMD as if touching the virtual keyboard displayed in the VR from behind (Fig. 3a). The virtual keyboard is always displayed in the center of the user's field of view (Fig. 3b), which is placed in the corresponding area on the front of the HMD. This displayed position reduces the discrepancy between the input as perceived by the user and the displayed position, making it easier for the user to touch or flick to the intended position. To touch to the intended position or to swipe to the intended direction.

In the current implementation of FaceFlick, the user's fingers cannot be displayed in the VR because the flick input is performed at the front of the HMD, which is outside the range of the tracking sensor. However, due to the user's proprioception, the user has a good estimate of the user's hand and finger positions in their bodies.

Furthermore, when the user touches the front of the HMD, the selected key and the touched position on the virtual keyboard are highlighted with a red pointer, as shown in Fig. 3c. This design allows the user to input text while receiving visual feedback in addition to tactile feedback.

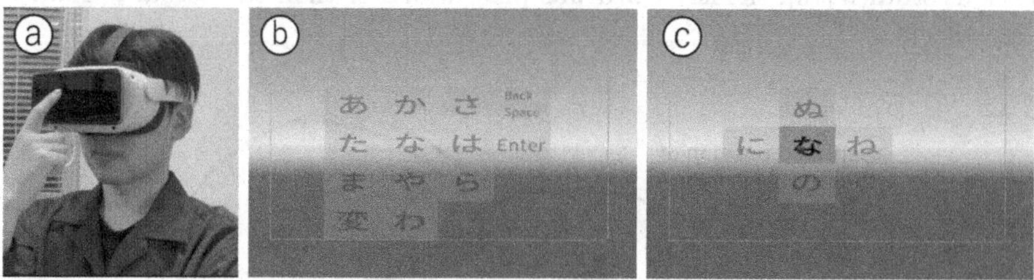

Fig. 3. View of the input of FaceFlick. a) FaceFlick used by a user. b) Keyboard when the user does not touch the device. c) Keyboard when the user touches a consonant key.

3.2 Key Layout on Touch Device

Figure 4 shows the key layout on the touch device for FaceFlick. We placed 10 consonant keys and a modifier key on the touch screen and additionally provided a backspace and an enter key alongside them. The area of each key is defined based on a lattice of five vertical and six horizontal divisions of the touch device area, as shown in Fig. 4. The top row is the space required to input the characters assigned to the upward swipes, i.e., "う(U)," "く(Ku)," and "す(Su)." The size of the virtual keyboard is the same as that of the screen of the touch device.

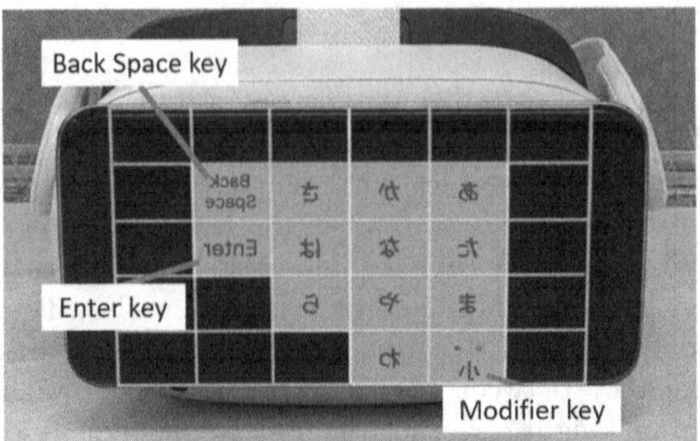

Fig. 4. The key layout on the touch device. When viewed from the outside, the layout of the flick keyboard on the touch device is left and right reversed.

3.3 Displayed Position of the Virtual Keyboard in VR

In FaceFlick, the virtual keyboard is displayed at a distance of 25 cm from the user's eyes, as shown in Fig. 5. When the virtual keyboard is displayed at the position where the actual touch device is attached (about 10 cm away from the user's eyes), the user tends to feel pressure and eye fatigue due to the proximity of the virtual keyboard. Therefore, based on the Oculus guidelines [23] and previous studies [10], the keyboard was placed farther than the actual to reduce these effects.

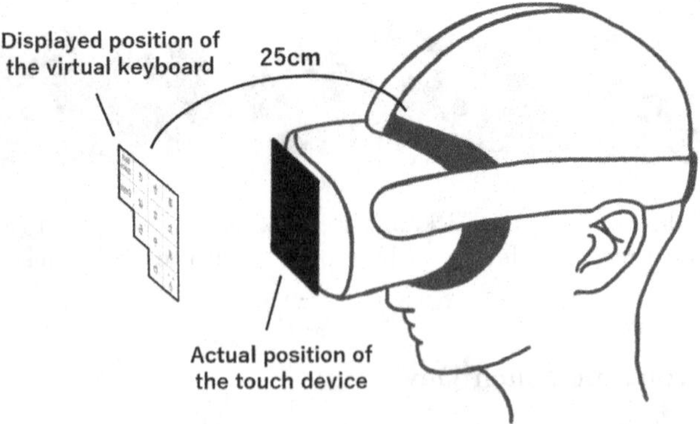

Fig. 5. The displayed position of the virtual keyboard in VR and the actual position of the touch device.

4 Preliminary User Study

We conducted a preliminary user study to compare the input speed and accuracy of FaceFlick (Fig. 6) with an existing VR flick input method [8] (Fig. 7).

Fig. 6. The text box and keyboard position in FaceFlick. The input location is in front of the HMD.

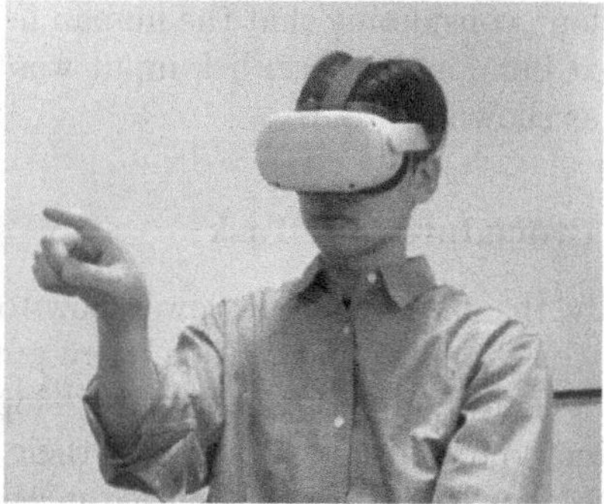

Fig. 7. The text box and keyboard position in the existing VR flick input method. The input location is in the air in front of the user.

Additionally, we assessed the usability of FaceFlick by collecting scores of SUS [3] and NASA-TLX [11]. The reason for choosing the VR flick input method [8] as the baseline is its similarities with FaceFlick in terms of the input method being analogous to actual flick input operations and being a one-handed text input method.

4.1 Participants

Eight participants (seven males and one female, seven right-handed and one ambidextrous, aged 21–24), ranging from undergraduate to graduate students, took part in the user study as volunteers. All participants were fluent in both speaking and writing Japanese. To investigate the participants' frequency of use and experiences with flick input and VR, we used a 5-point Likert scale, ranging from 5 (strongly agree) to 1 (strongly disagree). For flick input, six participants scored 5, one scored 4, and one scored 2. Similarly, for VR ratings, one participant scored 4, two scored 3, one scored 2, and four scored 1.

4.2 Apparatus and Environments

For FaceFlick, we used an HMD with a touch device attached to its front. The HMD used was Meta Quest 2, and the touch device attached to its front was a Galaxy S7 edge. In contrast, for the baseline, we used Meta Quest 2 without any attachments. The weight of the devices for each method was 820.6 g for FaceFlick and 650.5 g for the baseline.

In the baseline, the text box displaying the task text and inputted characters and keyboard were arranged vertically relative to the floor, as shown in Fig. 7. However, in text input for FaceFlick, the keyboard was always displayed at the center of the field of view, making it difficult to shift focus if the text box is positioned directly in front, as it would overlap with the keyboard's position. Therefore, considering that the human field of view is broader at the bottom [4], the text box for the FaceFlick input was placed at the lower part of the field of view, as shown in Fig. 6.

4.3 Procedure and Task

Initially, the participants reviewed how to operate Meta Quest 2, which was necessary for the user study. Then, they put on different HMDs for each method, sat in a chair, and performed the text input tasks. During this, the participants were instructed to input text with their right hand and to follow the postures depicted in Fig. 6 or Fig. 7 for each method. They were also instructed to transcribe phrases as quickly and accurately as possible and to correct errors they noticed through backspacing.

For each method, we conducted two practice sessions followed by one task session, totaling three sessions. In the practice sessions, the participants entered 35 sentences in the first round and 25 in the second; the task session also required entering 25 sentences. These task sentences consisted of short phrases, each distinct from the others, with an average length of 6.92 characters (SD = 1.62 characters). The participants took a break of over 10 min between each session. After completing all sessions, the participants responded to a questionnaire about the text input method used in that task, which included SUS, NASA-TLX, and a free description section. The total time required for the user study was within two hours.

Furthermore, to counterbalance the potential order effects, half of the participants performed the input methods in the order of FaceFlick first, followed by the baseline, while the other half did it in the reverse order.

4.4 Result

The results of input speed and error rates for each method obtained from the user study (Fig. 8), as well as the SUS and NASA-TLX scores, gathered from the questionnaires (Fig. 9), were presented along with the results of statistical analysis. A significance threshold of $p = 0.05$ was used for all statistical analyses.

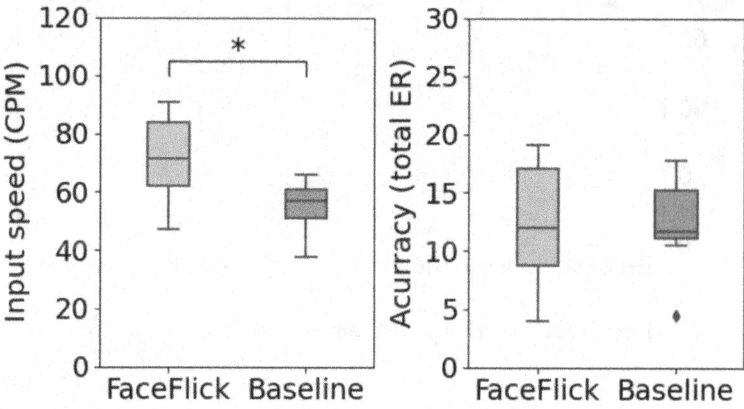

Fig. 8. Each method's input speed and accuracy.

Input Speed. Characters per minute (CPM) was computed by dividing the number of transcribed characters by the time it takes to transcribe the text. The average input speed for FaceFlick was 71.46 CPM (SD = 15.55 CPM), higher than the baseline of 54.48 CPM (SD = 9.67 CPM). Since the results of a Shapiro-Wilk normality test found that the data were normally distributed for both methods, with FaceFlick ($p = 0.744 > 0.05$, $W = 0.953$) and the baseline ($p = 0.278 > 0.05$, $W = 0.898$), we tested differences in input speeds using a paired t-test. We observed a significant difference between the input speed of FaceFlick and that of the baseline ($p = 0.0053 < 0.05$, $d = 1.41$). The above results revealed that the input speed of FaceFlick was significantly better than that of the baseline.

Accuracy. The error rates for each method were computed as total error rate (total ER) [2]. The Total ER for FaceFlick was 12.36% (SD = 5.24%), while that of the baseline was 12.30% (SD = 4.08%). Since a Shapiro-Wilk normality test found that the data were normally distributed for both methods, with FaceFlick ($p = 0.730 > 0.05$, $W = 0.952$) and the baseline ($p = 0.499 > 0.05$, $W = 0.928$), we tested differences in the total ER using a paired t-test. We did not observe a significant difference between the total ER of FaceFlick and that of the baseline ($p = 0.975 > 0.05$, $d = 0.011$).

Usability. We computed SUS scores to evaluate the usability of each method. FaceFlick's SUS score was 76.25 (SD = 11.57), while that of the baseline was

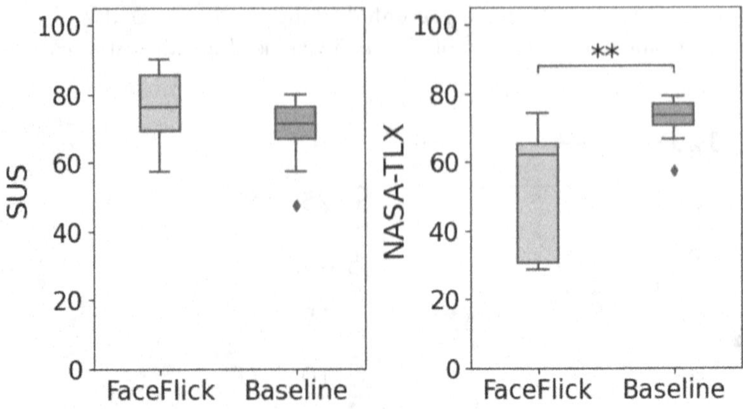

Fig. 9. Each method's SUS and NASA-TLX scores.

69.06 (SD = 11.25). Since the results of the Shapiro-Wilk normality test found normal distribution for both FaceFlick ($p = 0.407 > 0.05$, $W = 0.917$) and the baseline ($p = 0.156 > 0.05, W = 0.871$), we tested differences in the SUS score using a paired t-test. The result indicated no significant usability difference between FaceFlick and the baseline ($p = 0.267 > 0.05$).

We computed NASA-TLX scores to evaluate the task load for each method. The NASA-TLX score for FaceFlick was 52.42 (SD = 19.23), lower than the baseline's 72.04 (SD = 7.11). The results of the Shapiro-Wilk normality test indicated a non-normal distribution for FaceFlick ($p = 0.027 < 0.05$, $W = 0.797$) and a normal distribution for the baseline ($p = 0.173 > 0.05$, $W = 0.876$). Given the non-normal distribution for FaceFlick, we tested the differences in task load using a Wilcoxon signed-rank test. The test revealed a significant reduction in task load for FaceFlick compared to the baseline ($p = 0.023 < 0.05$).

5 Discussion

In this section, we discuss the reasons behind the performance of FaceFlick in comparison to the baseline, based on the results of the user study.

In terms of input speed, FaceFlick facilitated faster text input compared to the baseline. This can be largely attributed to the participants' familiarity with flick input. In the questionnaire before the user study, seven out of eight participants answered that their experience and frequency of use of flick input was 4 or 5 (hereafter, expert users), and all their input speeds using FaceFlick were higher than the baseline. The remaining one user answered that their experience and frequency of use of flick input was 2 and showed higher input speed in baseline than FaceFlick. Notably, despite FaceFlick requiring flick input from the opposite side as if manipulating the keyboard from behind, there was no confusion among the participants.

In terms of accuracy, although FaceFlick had a slightly higher error rate, the difference was not significant. In the baseline, while the user could see their hands, there was no tactile feedback. It was difficult for the user to understand if they were touching the keys, leading to input errors. In contrast, FaceFlick, which did not display the user's hands and relied solely on proprioception, made it difficult to touch the intended keys. However, among the expert users, 5 out of 7 recorded lower error rates with FaceFlick than with the baseline, suggesting that familiarity with the input method could mitigate the error rates.

The SUS scores showed no significant difference between FaceFlick and the baseline. This is attributed to the fact that because FaceFlick does not allow the user to see their hand, making it difficult to touch the intended key, and the baseline does not provide tactile feedback, making it difficult for the user to understand if they were touching the keys.

NASA-TLX score showed a significant advantage for FaceFlick, indicating a lower task load than the baseline. Feedback from the free description section of the questionnaire suggested that this result was due to reduced arm strain during the text input. The baseline method required the users to extend and swing their arms forward largely, imposing considerable physical fatigue. In contrast, FaceFlick's input location, the front of the HMD and closer to the body's center, likely resulted in less arm strain. However, since the virtual keyboard's position and size of the baseline could influence its performance, further refinement of these variables would be necessary to evaluate FaceFlick's performance.

6 Limitation

User Fatigue During Text Input. Although FaceFlick reduced arm fatigue compared to the baseline by not requiring the user to keep their arms out in front of them or move their entire arm, actions such as touching the front of the HMD also imposed a strain on the arms [12]. In addition, the weight of the entire HMD increased due to the attachment of the touch device to the front of the HMD. To reduce user fatigue, a lighter touch device that is attached to the front of the HMD would be considered better.

Key Layout. The key layout of FaceFlick used in this user study is a simple grid of key areas on the touch device and does not take into account the characteristics of flick input using the front of the HMD. Although the characteristics of touch on the front of the HMD have been studied previously [10,17], the characteristics of the flick input key layout were not investigated in terms of key size and key spacing. Therefore, we should investigate key layouts suitable for flick input using the front of the HMD, and using such key layouts will improve the text input performance of FaceFlick.

7 Conclusion

In this research, we demonstrated FaceFlick, a VR flick input method using the front of an HMD. As a preliminary user study, we compared the text input performance of FaceFlick with that of the baseline. The results showed that FaceFlick surpassed the baseline in terms of input speed and NASA-TLX score. In the future, we plan to test keyboard layouts suitable for flick input using the front of an HMD.

References

1. An open-source keyboard to make your own - normal. https://www.normalvr.com/blog/an-open-source-keyboard-to-make-your-own/. Accessed 02 Feb 2024
2. Arif, A.S., Stuerzlinger, W.: Analysis of text entry performance metrics. In: 2009 IEEE Toronto International Conference Science and Technology for Humanity, pp. 100–105. IEEE (2009)
3. Brooke, J.: SUS: A Quick and Dirty Usability Scale. Usability Evaluation in Industry, pp. 189–194 (1996)
4. Deering, M.F.: The limits of human vision. In: 2nd International Immersive Projection Technology Workshop, vol. 2, pp. 1–6 (1998)
5. Fashimpaur, J., Kin, K., Longest, M.: PinchType: text entry for virtual and augmented reality using comfortable thumb to fingertip pinches. In: Extended Abstracts of the 2020 CHI Conference on Human Factors in Computing Systems, CHI EA 2020, pp. 1–7. Association for Computing Machinery, New York (2020)
6. Freeman, E., Brewster, S., Lantz, V.: Tactile feedback for above-device gesture interfaces: adding touch to touchless interactions. In: Proceedings of the 16th International Conference on Multimodal Interaction, ICMI 2014, pp. 419–426. Association for Computing Machinery, New York (2014)
7. Frutos-Pascual, M., Gale, C., Harrison, J.M., Creed, C., Williams, I.: Character input in augmented reality: an evaluation of keyboard position and interaction visualisation for head-mounted displays. In: Ardito, C., Lanzilotti, R., Malizia, A., Petrie, H., Piccinno, A., Desolda, G., Inkpen, K. (eds.) INTERACT 2021. LNCS, vol. 12932, pp. 480–501. Springer, Cham (2021). https://doi.org/10.1007/978-3-030-85623-6_29
8. Fukunaka, I., XIE, H., Miyata, K.: Development of Flick Input Interface in Virtual Reality. IPSJ SIG Technical Report 2019-HCI-182(3), pp. 1–8 (2019). (in Japanese)
9. Grossman, T., Chen, X.A., Fitzmaurice, G.: Typing on glasses: adapting text entry to smart eyewear. In: Proceedings of the 17th International Conference on Human-Computer Interaction with Mobile Devices and Services, MobileHCI 2015, pp. 144–152. Association for Computing Machinery, New York (2015)
10. Gugenheimer, J., Dobbelstein, D., Winkler, C., Haas, G., Rukzio, E.: FaceTouch: enabling touch interaction in display fixed UIS for mobile virtual reality. In: Proceedings of the 29th Annual Symposium on User Interface Software and Technology, UIST 2016, pp. 49–60. Association for Computing Machinery, New York (2016)
11. Hart, S.G., Staveland, L.E.: Development of NASA-TLX (Task Load Index): results of empirical and theoretical research. Adv. Psychol. **52**, 139–183 (1988)
12. Hincapié-Ramos, J.D., Guo, X., Moghadasian, P., Irani, P.: Consumed endurance: a metric to quantify arm fatigue of mid-air interactions. In: Proceedings of the SIGCHI Conference on Human Factors in Computing Systems, CHI 2014, pp. 1063–1072. Association for Computing Machinery, New York (2014)

13. Hutama, W., Harashima, H., Ishikawa, H., Manabe, H.: HMK: head-mounted-keyboard for text input in virtual or augmented reality. In: Adjunct Proceedings of the 34th Annual ACM Symposium on User Interface Software and Technology, UIST 2021 Adjunct, pp. 115–117. Association for Computing Machinery, New York (2021)
14. Kawaguchi, K., Isomoto, T., Shizuki, B., Takahashi, S.: Flick-based japanese text entry method on palm for virtual reality. In: Proceedings of the Human Interface Symposium 2019, pp. 676–682 (2019). (in Japanese)
15. Kita, S., Ogura, K., Bahadur, B.B., Takata, T.: Investigation of Text Entry Methods in VR Using LeapMotion. IPSJ SIG Technical Report 2019-HCI-181(21), pp. 1–7 (2019). (in Japanese)
16. Kiyohara, R., Sawada, A., Noro, M.: Tactile flick text entry method in virtual reality. In: Proceedings of the 39th JSSST Annual Conference, 27-L (2022). (in Japanese)
17. Lee, J., Kim, B., Suh, B., Koh, E.: Exploring the front touch interface for virtual reality headsets. In: Proceedings of the 2016 CHI Conference Extended Abstracts on Human Factors in Computing Systems, CHI EA 2016, pp. 2585–2591. Association for Computing Machinery, New York (2016)
18. Ogitani, T., Arahori, Y., Shinyama, Y., Gondow, K.: Space saving text input method for head mounted display with virtual 12-key keyboard. In: 2018 IEEE 32nd International Conference on Advanced Information Networking and Applications (AINA), pp. 342–349 (2018)
19. Ozawa, S., Umezawa, T., Osawa, N.: Mid-air text entry method using pinch motion. In: Forum on Information Technology 2015, vol. 14, pp. 389–390 (2015), (in Japanese)
20. Rahim, M.A., Shin, J., Islam, M.R.: Gestural flick input-based non-touch interface for character input. Vis. Comput. **36**(8), 1559–1572 (2020)
21. Speicher, M., Feit, A.M., Ziegler, P., Krüger, A.: Selection-based text entry in virtual reality. In: Proceedings of the 2018 CHI Conference on Human Factors in Computing Systems, CHI 2018, pp. 1–13. Association for Computing Machinery, New York (2018)
22. Wang, C.Y., Chu, W.C., Chiu, P.T., Hsiu, M.C., Chiang, Y.H., Chen, M.Y.: PalmType: using palms as keyboards for smart glasses. In: Proceedings of the 17th International Conference on Human-Computer Interaction with Mobile Devices and Services, MobileHCI 2015, pp. 153–160. Association for Computing Machinery, New York (2015)
23. Yao, R., Heath, T., Davies, A., Forsyth, T., Mitchell, N., Hoberman, P.: Oculus VR Best Practices Guide. Oculus VR 4 (2014)
24. Yu, D., Fan, K., Zhang, H., Monteiro, D., Xu, W., Liang, H.N.: PizzaText: text entry for virtual reality systems using dual thumbsticks. IEEE Trans. Visual Comput. Graphics **24**(11), 2927–2935 (2018)

Research on Eye Tracking Process Optimization Based on Combined Kalman Filtering

Shuoyang Zhang[1], Hongwei Niu[1,2,3], Jia Hao[1,2,3](✉), Liya Yao[1], Yuekang Wang[1], and Xiaonan Yang[1,2,3]

[1] School of Mechanical Engineering, Beijing Institute of Technology, Beijing 100081, China
haojia632@bit.edu.cn

[2] Yangtze Delta Region Academy, Beijing Institute of Technology, Jiaxing 314019, China

[3] Key Laboratory of Industry Knowledge and Data Fusion Technology and Application, Ministry of Industry and Information Technology, Beijing Institute of Technology, Beijing 100081, China

Abstract. The application of eye tracking is becoming increasingly widespread and significant in daily life. However, due to physiological and technological limitations, eye tracking often contains noise and inaccuracies, which poses a challenge to its efficient use. This study aims to enhance the accuracy and precision of eye tracking, thereby improving the performance of human-computer interaction systems. We explore the application effects of various algorithms on eye-tracking data processing, including the Simple Moving Average, Weighted Moving Average, Exponential Weighted Moving Average, Kalman Filter Algorithm, and Combined Kalman Filter Algorithm. The advantages and disadvantages of these five algorithms are analyzed using eye-tracking data evaluation metrics focused on accuracy and precision. The findings of this study have practical application value in fields requiring high-precision eye movement data.

Keywords: Eye Tracking · Accuracy · Precision · Kalman Filter Algorithm

1 Introduction

Eye tracking is a process that measures where the eyes are focused and how they move. Eye tracking technology monitors the direction of users' real-time gaze and is widely used in various fields such as intelligent interactive devices, psychological research, and medical devices. For instance, integrating intelligent human-computer interaction devices with Internet of Things (IoT) technology enables the controlling of a range of smart devices, including smart TVs and other smart home appliances.

During the eye tracking process, several factors can be the cause of tracking imprecision, impacting the accuracy and stability of human-computer interaction. Physiological characteristics, such as the shape and size of the eyes and head movement along with other factors, will affect the effectiveness and precision of eye tracking. The data collected often contains noise, potential anomalies, and missing values. Additionally, the presence of microsaccades and drifts in eye movements significantly affects tracking

M. Kurosu and A. Hashizume (Eds.): HCII 2024, LNCS 14688, pp. 228–239, 2024.
https://doi.org/10.1007/978-3-031-60449-2_16

accuracy. Hence, accurate and efficient real-time processing of raw eye movement data is essential for achieving accurate eye tracking localization.

Several researchers have employed calibration and correction techniques to enhance the accuracy of eye tracking localization. Constantino et al. [1] achieved dynamic automatic drift correction by using visible gaze targets and accuracy standards. Oleg Spakov et al. [2] dynamically expanded targets based on the relative changes in the gaze point locations to achieve online calibration correction of eye trackers. This technique significantly improved selection accuracy. Harezlak et al. [3] analyzed methods to simplify calibration steps and processes, proposing that a well-arranged layout of calibration points could reduce the number of points needed, thereby shortening the calibration process without compromising the level of precision.

Some scholars have introduced filtering and smoothing methods to enhance the accuracy of eye tracking localization. Holmqvist et al. [4, 5] studied the accuracy and precision of eye trackers, finding relatively small precision differences among subjects on each eye tracker, while the distribution of RMS precision varied by up to two orders of magnitude between different eye trackers. They also found high levels of accuracy similarity among eye trackers. Van der Stigchel et al. [6] conducted experiments using head restraints and discovered that data recorded with restricted head movement had better quality. Larsson et al. [7] introduced a new method based on various filtering and noise reduction techniques that can detect saccades and post-saccadic oscillations during smooth pursuit. Bottos et al. [8] proposed a novel sliding Kalman filter to detect the direction of a reader's gaze. This method improved the estimation accuracy of the X coordinate while maintaining follow sensitivity and smoothness.

Some researchers have considered the relative motion of the head and the screen to improve the precision of eye tracking localization. Hermens [9] researched eye tracking and concluded that in some cases, minor head movements could cause slight eye saccades during eye tracking. Spakov et al. [10] attempted to actively use head movements to adjust inaccuracies in gaze estimation. Mejia-Romero et al. [11] proposed using a Wiener filter to denoise the eye tracking signal, and the results indicated that this method effectively eliminated noise during the eye tracking process. Chu et al. [12] proposed a system combining multicore tracking with Kalman filtering, using the Kalman filter's prediction as the initial position for multicore tracking, effectively addressing the issue of information loss due to occlusion affecting eye tracking localization. This paper organizes the references from important dimensions into a table as shown in Table 1.

Therefore, calibration and filtering algorithms for eye tracking are crucial in the real-time processing of eye movement data and ensuring the stability and accuracy of eye tracking. In terms of calibration for eye tracking, this paper considers the resolution differences of calibration displays and the possibility of variation in each user's eye structure and gaze behavior. Thus, it proposes an adaptive multipoint calibration method. Aiming at the stability and smoothing of eye tracking, this paper introduces a combined weighted moving average algorithm with Kalman filtering, leveraging the advantages of both techniques.

Table 1. Evaluation of the existing literature.

References	Method	Application effect
Constantino [1]	Different types of experimental stimulation	Dynamic correction
Oleg Špakov [2]	Dynamically expand the gaze point target	Improve selection accuracy
Harezlak [3]	Simplify the calibration steps	Improve the layout of calibration points
Holmqvist [4, 5]	Contrast experiment	Differences in the accuracy of eye trackers
Van der Stigchel [6]	Restrict head movement	Better data quality
Larsson [7]	Saccade and oscillation detection algorithm	More accurate detection and classification
Bottos [8]	Slip-Kalman filter	Accurate tracking of eye gaze
Hermens [9]	Microsaccade automatic detection algorithm	Improve accuracy
Spakov [10]	Compared various real-time filters	FIR filter with Gaussian kernel shows excellent performance
Mejia-Romero [11]	Wiener filter	Eliminates noise efficiently
Chu [12]	Combined multiple kernels tracking and Kalman filtering	Solved the loss of information

The rest of this paper is organized as follows: Section 2 outlines the methods used in this paper and how to improve and optimize the Kalman filter. Section 3 outlines the participants, equipment, and experimental procedures. Section 4 analyzes the experimental data. Finally, Sect. 5 concludes the paper.

2 Method

2.1 Calibration

To ensure the accurate functioning of eye tracking, each user must complete a specific calibration for the eye tracker. This involves staring at a set of holographic targets, a process that maps the eye positions measured by the eye tracker to the actual physical gaze locations, thereby ensuring accurate eye tracking [13]. In response to the occasional need for multiple calibrations due to suboptimal calibration results, this paper proposes to establish a calibration error threshold to limit the calibration inaccuracies and ensure the effectiveness of calibration. The specific eye movement calibration process is shown in Fig. 1. Firstly, the layout and size of the calibration target points are automatically adjusted according to the resolution of the calibration screen. In the calibration process, if the calibration results at certain locations do not meet the predefined error threshold, a local 5-point recalibration is conducted for those areas. The results of these local 5-point recalibrations are combined to improve the calibration at these specific points, thereby enhancing the overall calibration effect and the accuracy of eye tracking.

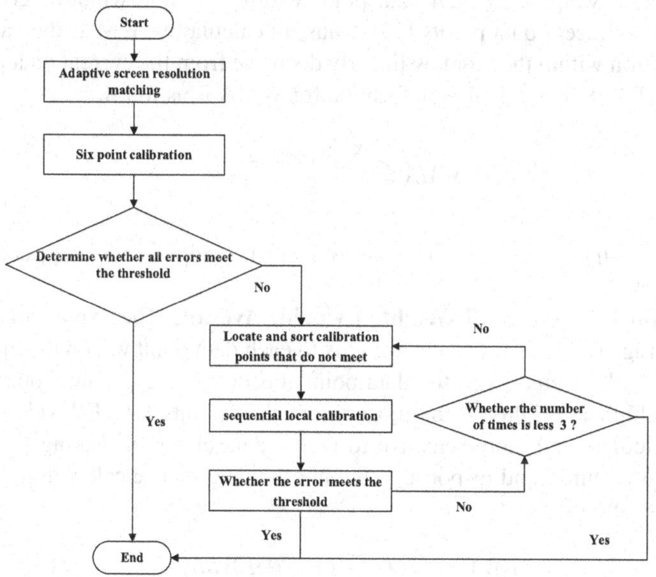

Fig. 1. Eye tracking calibration process

The selection of the calibration error threshold can be adjusted according to the actual conditions of the experiment. In this study, to retain better calibration scenarios and exclude extremely poor ones, the error threshold was set relatively leniently at 1.5°.

2.2 Algorithms for Eye Tracking Process

There is a lot of noise and microsaccade in eye movement data. Therefore, in the process of real-time data processing, the filtering algorithm should be used to process the eye movement data to eliminate the influence of noise and microsaccade. Therefore, this section compares the effects of four classical filtering algorithms and a combination algorithm of Weighted Moving Average and Kalman filter on eye movement data processing.

Algorithm 1: Simple Moving Average. The principle of the Simple Moving Average (SMA) involves setting a fixed-size window and calculating the average value of all data within this window as the output for that window [14]. Subsequently, the window slides forward by a fixed step, and the process of calculating the new average is repeated until all data in the sequence has been processed. The SMA is straightforward to implement and suitable for general smoothing requirements, but it is not sensitive to sudden changes in the data. The calculation formula is as follows:

$$SMA = \frac{1}{N}\sum\nolimits_{i=t-N+1}^{t} x_i \tag{1}$$

N is the size of the time window, x_i represents the value of each data point, and t is the current time point.

Algorithm 2: Weighted Moving Average. Weighted Moving Average (WMA) assigns different weights to each data point within the time window, giving higher weights to more recent data points [15]. Thus, in calculating WMA, the values of the filtering function within the window linearly decrease from the current data point to the data point at T − 1. The calculation formula for WMA is as follows:

$$WMA = \frac{\sum_{i-1}^{N} w_i x_{t-i+1}}{\sum_{i-1}^{N} w_i} \tag{2}$$

N represents the size of the time window, w_i is the weight, and x_{t-i+1} is the value of each data point.

Algorithm 3: Exponential Weighted Moving Average. The Exponential Weighted Moving Average (EWMA) allocates weights to each data point within the time window that exponentially decreases as the data points become more distant from the current time, giving higher weights to the most recent data points [16] EWMA is relatively simple to calculate and more sensitive to recent data changes, making it suitable for scenarios that require rapid response to the latest changes. The calculation formula for EWMA is as follows:

$$EWMA_t = \alpha x_t + (1 - \alpha) EWMA_{t-1} \tag{3}$$

α is the smoothing factor, x_t is the current data point, and $EWMA_{t-1}$ is the EWMA value of the previous moment.

Algorithm 4: Kalman Filter. Due to the irregular movements of saccades and microsaccades in eye tracking, which can be approximated as Gaussian white noise, they are well suited for processing with Kalman filtering. Therefore, to improve the accuracy of eye movement component discrimination and data processing, it is necessary to filter the eye movement data.

Kalman filtering is an algorithm that uses linear system state equations to optimally estimate system states based on system input-output observational data. Kalman filtering minimizes the error between predicted states and actual measurements [17] It is highly flexible, capable of handling noisy data, and applicable to complex systems requiring real-time updates and predictions. The state equation and observation equation of Kalman filtering are as follows.

$$x_t = Ax_{t-1} + Bu_t + w_t \tag{4}$$

x_t represents the current state value, x_{t-1} is the value of the last moment, A is the state transition matrix, B is the control matrix and w_t represents the process noise.

$$z_t = Hx_t + v_t \tag{5}$$

z_t is the observed value, v_t is the observation noise.

Kalman filtering uses the optimal result of the previous moment to predict the current value (prior estimate); it then uses the observation value to correct the current value to obtain the optimal estimation result. Therefore, it mainly divides into prediction and update parts.

Predict. Predict the state of the current moment by the previous state quantity and distribution.

Prior estimate:

$$\hat{x}_t^- = F\hat{x}_{t-1}^- + Bu_{t-1} + W_t \tag{6}$$

$\hat{x}_t^-$ symbolizes the state prediction at t time, F is the state transition matrix, u_{t-1} is the control input vector at time t – 1, B is the control matrix, $W_t \sim N(0, Q)$ represents the process noise.

Prediction error covariance matrix:

$$P_t^- = FP_{t-1}F^T + Q \tag{7}$$

P_t^- is the covariance of the prior estimate, and Q is the process noise.

Update. Update the parameters such as state quantity and covariance at the current moment by using the observed values and the predicted values.

Kalman gain:

$$K_t = P_t^- H^T (HP_t^- H^T + R_t)^{-1} \tag{8}$$

P_t^- is the covariance of the predicted value currently, R_t is the variance of the observation noise. The Kalman Gain acts as a sort of weight.

State estimation update:

$$\hat{x}_t = \hat{x}_t^- + K_t(z_t - H\hat{x}_t^-) \tag{9}$$

$\hat{x}_t$ is the output at the current time and represents the optimal estimation value, z_t is the measurement value at t time.

Error covariance update:

$$P_t = (I - K_t H)P_t^- \tag{10}$$

P_t is the covariance of the optimal estimate currently.

Algorithm 5. Combined Kalman Filtering Algorithm. Upon comprehensive analysis, it is found that both the Weighted Moving Average filtering algorithm and the Kalman filtering algorithm are effective, but each has its shortcomings. Thus, combining the advantages of the WMA filtering algorithm and the Kalman filtering algorithm can improve the Kalman filtering algorithm.

Use the WMA algorithm for preliminary smoothing of the raw data, determining the appropriate window size and weights to reduce random noise. The weights are assigned using a Gaussian distribution function, and the time window is set to 5 so that values closer to the current moment have a higher weight and those farther away have a lower weight.

Establish a state-space model for the system state transition and observation model, input the data processed by the WMA filtering algorithm into the Kalman filter as observation variable, adjust the process noise and observation noise covariance parameters of the Kalman filter, and analyze the output of the Kalman filter to achieve better smoothness and accuracy. In this process, it is mainly to adjust the variance Q of process noise and the variance R of observation noise, so that the eye movement data can not only ensure better sensitivity and accuracy, but also obtain higher precision. The structural diagram of the Combined Kalman filtering algorithm is shown in Fig. 2.

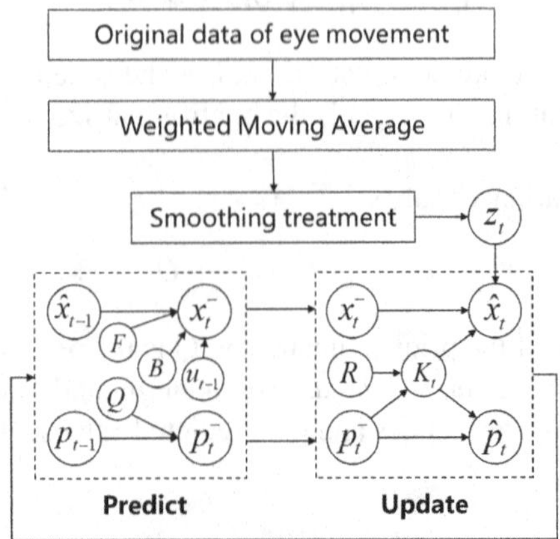

Fig. 2. Structure diagram of Combined Kalman filter algorithm

3 Experiment

3.1 Participants

The total number of participants in this study was 15, comprising 12 males and 3 females. The age range of the participants was primarily between 20 and 30 years. The experiment required all participants to be physical health, with a normal mental state and good eyesight. Participants with glasses were required to have a corrected visual acuity within the normal range and to be free of any eye diseases. Criteria for participation included having unaided or corrected vision above 1.0, and no use of contact lenses, cosmetic lenses, or false eyelashes. Participants with severe perceptual or motor disorders, cognitive impairments, or other similar conditions were excluded. Additionally, participants were asked to ensure adequate sleep the night before the experiment, avoid staying up late or overusing their eyes, and were able to provide personal information such as age and gender. Furthermore, this experiment received approval from the ethics committee, and the participants were informed in advance about the research conducted in this paper.

3.2 Experimental Environment

The experimental equipment used was the Tobii Pro Spectrum eye tracker, a video-based desktop pupil-corneal reflection eye tracker capable of sampling frequency of 150 Hz. The Tobii Pro Spectrum is based on a 3D eye model, supporting smooth angle adjustments to accommodate subjects of varying heights. Its binocular tracking sensors capture 1200 eye images per second, accurately and stably measuring gaze data and the position of the eyes in three-dimensional space, providing precise pupil diameter data. The screen resolution is 1920 × 1080 pixels, with a refresh rate of 60 Hz. The experimental stimulus is shown in Fig. 3. The experimental scene and equipment are illustrated in Fig. 4.

Fig. 3. The experimental stimuli were presented and subjects were asked to focus on a yellow central point.

Fig. 4. An eye tracker is located below the display, and a participant looks at the yellow target center point. The distance between the computer screen and the user is about 60 cm.

3.3 Experiment Procedure

An eye tracking experiment was designed and conducted, comprising five distinct steps, each involving the same eye movement localization task. These five steps were executed under the conditions of the original scenario, moving average algorithm, weighted filtering, Kalman filtering algorithm, and Combined Kalman filtering algorithm respectively.

Prior to the start of the experiment, the experimenter explained the tasks to the participants and had them sign informed consent forms. During the experiment, participants were allowed to move their heads slightly. The raw data were collected from multiple participants' eye tracking, as well as data processed using the moving average algorithm, weighted filtering algorithm, Kalman filtering algorithm, and the Combined Kalman filtering algorithm. By conducting comparative experiments and preprocessing the data, further data analysis and validation were performed to assess the precision of the eye tracking and to explore filtering algorithms that make the eye tracking interaction process more accurate and stable.

4 Results and Discussion

Eye tracker records eye movements by monitoring gaze points (the current position on the screen where the subject is looking at any given moment), thereby collecting a time series of gaze points during the eye tracking process. Thus, the quality of filtering effects can be assessed by analyzing the collected gaze point time series data. The main evaluation metrics for eye tracking are accuracy and precision. Accuracy is defined as the average error between the actual position of the gaze and the position recorded by the eye tracker. Precision refers to the degree of dispersion when the eye tracker continuously records the same gaze point. A reliable and high-performing eye tracking system should exhibit high accuracy and precision.

4.1 Accuracy Analysis

In the experiment, subjects were asked to look at a series of targets in a fixed position on the screen. Then the deviation between the eye gaze position recorded by the eye tracker and the actual position of the fixed target is compared. Accuracy can be measured by calculating the average deviation between these positions. The average deviation is represented by the average absolute error and angular error. The calculation formula and results are as follows.

$$MAE = \frac{1}{n}\sum_{i=1}^{n}\sqrt{(P_{ix} - T_{ix})^2 + (P_{iy} - T_{iy})^2} \tag{11}$$

(p_{ix}, p_{iy}) is the recorded gaze point coordinate at time i in the sequence, (T_{ix}, T_{iy}) is the actual target point coordinate at time i, and n is the total number of sample points (Table 2).

Table 2. Accuracy result

Method	Angle error	Pixel error
Raw data	1.58°	60.00 px
SMA	1.68°	63.77 px
WMA	1.58°	60.00 px
EWMA	1.61°	60.80 px
Kalman filter	1.59°	60.13 px
Combined Kalman filter	1.54°	58.58 px

It is evident that the improvement in accuracy using filtering algorithms is limited and in some cases, the results may even be slightly decreased. This is attributed to the fact that filtering algorithms, while smoothing the data, also reduce the sensitivity of the eye tracking data. The Combined Kalman Filtering algorithm proposed in this article, which integrates the Weighted Moving Average with the Kalman Filter, achieved an accuracy of 1.54°, an improvement of 0.04° compared to the original data.

4.2 Precision Analysis

Precision describes the consistency and stability of data in repeated measurements under the same gaze conditions. Precision focuses on the proximity of the measurements of eye tracker, expressed by the root mean square sample-to-sample deviation. The root mean square sample-to-sample deviation is a measure of the change between continuous data points. The calculation formula and results are as follows.

$$RMS - S2S = \sqrt{\frac{1}{n-1}\sum_{i=1}^{n-1}((x_{i+1} - x_i)^2 + (y_{i+1} - y_i)^2)} \tag{12}$$

(x_i, y_i) and (x_{i+1}, y_{i+1}) are the coordinates of two consecutive sample points in the sequence respectively, and n is the total number of sample points (Table 3).

Table 3. Precision result

Method	Angle error	Pixel error
raw data	0.77°	29.10 px
SMA	0.30°	11.42 px
WMA	0.36°	13.77 px
EWMA	0.52°	19.78 px
Kalman filter	0.31°	11.99 px
Combined Kalman filter	0.26°	10.00 px

The application of filtering algorithms can significantly improve the precision of eye movement data. SMA, WMA, Kalman filtering and Combined Kalman filtering have achieved good results, of which Combined Kalman filtering performed the best, improving the precision of eye movement data to 0.26°.

5 Conclusion

A multi-point calibration method is proposed in this paper. This method dynamically adjusts the positions of calibration points, sets error thresholds, and specifically recalibrates local areas that do not meet the threshold. According to the characteristics of noise and microsaccades in eye movement data, several filtering algorithms suitable for processing the data with these characteristics are introduced in this paper. The eye movement comparison experiment was conducted, during which the accuracy and precision of eye movement tracking were compared in six scenarios: raw data, SMA, WMA, EWMA, Kalman filter algorithm and Combined Kalman filtering algorithm. We found that there is no difference in accuracy in these six cases, indicating that the filtering algorithm has little effect on improving the accuracy of eye movement data. However, these algorithms have improved the precision of eye movement data to varying degrees, indicating that algorithms can effectively improve the precision of eye tracking. Additionally, the Combined filtering algorithm proposed in this paper can improve the precision of eye movement data, reaching 0.26°, which is the highest in these six conditions. In conclusion, the Combined filtering algorithms can effectively improve the precision of eye tracking, significantly enhancing the practical application of eye tracking.

Acknowledgments. The authors would like to thank the Foundation Strengthening Project (2022-JCJQ-JJ-0858).

References

1. Constantino, J.N., et al.: Infant viewing of social scenes is under genetic control and is atypical in autism. Nature **547**(7663), 340–344 (2017)
2. Špakov, O., Miniotas, D.: Gaze-based selection of standard-size menu items. In: Proceedings of the 7th International Conference on Multimodal Interfaces (ICMI 2005), pp. 124–128. Association for Computing Machinery, New York, NY, USA (2005)
3. Harezlak, K., Kasprowski, P., Stasch, M.: Towards accurate eye tracker calibration – methods and procedures [J/OL]. Procedia Comput. Sci. **35**, 1073–1081 (2014). https://doi.org/10.1016/j.procs.2014.08.194
4. Holmqvist, K., Andersson, R.: Eye tracking: a comprehensive guide to methods, paradigms and measures. Lund Eye-Tracking Research Institute, Lund (2017)
5. Holmqvist, K., Blignaut, P.: Small eye movements cannot be reliably measured by video-based P-CR eyetrackers. Behav. Res. Methods **52**, 2098–2121 (2020). https://doi.org/10.3758/s13428-020-01363-x
6. Van der Stigchel, S., Hessels, R.S., van Elst, J.C., Kemner, C.: The disengagement of visual attention in the gap paradigm across adolescence. Exp. Brain Res. **235**(12), 3585–3592 (2017). https://doi.org/10.1007/s00221-017-5085-2
7. Larsson, L., Nyström, M., Stridh, M.: Detection of saccades and postsaccadic oscillations in the presence of smooth pursuit. IEEE Trans. Biomed. Eng. **60**(9), 2484–2493 (2013). https://doi.org/10.1109/TBME.2013.2258918
8. Bottos, S., Balasingam, B.: A novel slip-Kalman filter to track the progression of reading through eye-gaze measurements. In: 2019 IEEE Global Conference on Signal and Information Processing (GlobalSIP). IEEE (2019)
9. Hermens, F.: Dummy eye measurements of microsaccades: testing the influence of system noise and head movements on microsaccade detection in a popular video-based eye tracker. J. Eye Mov. Res. **8**(1), 1–17 (2015). https://doi.org/10.16910/jemr.8.1.1
10. Spakov, O.: Comparison of eye movement filters used in HCI. In: Proceedings of the Symposium on Eye Tracking Research and Applications, pp. 281–284 (2012)
11. Mejia-Romero, S., Eduardo Lugo, J., Bernardin, D., Faubert, J.: An effective filtering process for the noise suppression in eye movement signals. In: Ray, K., Roy, K.C., Toshniwal, S.K., Sharma, H., Bandyopadhyay, A. (eds.) Proceedings of International Conference on Data Science and Applications. LNNS, vol. 148, pp. 33–46. Springer, Singapore (2021). https://doi.org/10.1007/978-981-15-7561-7_2
12. Chu, C.-T., Hwang, J.-N., Wang, S.-Z., Chen, Y.-Y.: Human tracking by adaptive Kalman filtering and multiple kernels tracking with projected gradients. In: 2011 Fifth ACM/IEEE International Conference on Distributed Smart Cameras, Ghent, Belgium, pp. 1–6 (2011). https://doi.org/10.1109/ICDSC.2011.6042939
13. Chris, E., Syed, Z.M., Marshall, F.T., et al.: Exploring the trade-off between accuracy and observational latency in action recognition. Int. J. Comput. Vis. **101**(3) (2013)
14. Hansun, S.: A new approach of moving average method in time series analysis. In: 2013 Conference on New Media Studies (CoNMedia), Tangerang, Indonesia, pp. 1–4 (2013)
15. Zhuang, Y., Chen, L., Wang, X.S., Lian, J.: A weighted moving average-based approach for cleaning sensor data. In: 27th International Conference on Distributed Computing Systems (ICDCS 2007), p. 38, Toronto, ON, Canada (2007)

16. Holt, C.C.: Forecasting seasonals and trends by exponentially weighted moving averages. Int. J. Forecast. **20**(1), 5–10 (2004). ISSN 0169-2070
17. Toivanen, M.: An advanced Kalman filter for gaze tracking signal. Biomed. Signal Process. Control **25**, 150–158 (2016)

Mid-Air Hand Gesture Design Tool for Interaction Designers

Lei Zhang[1(✉)] and Madhawa Perera[1,2]

[1] Australian National University, Canberra, Australia
{lei.zhang,madhawa.perera}@anu.edu.au, madhawa.perera@csiro.au
[2] Commonwealth Scientific and Industrial Research Organisation, Canberra, Australia

Abstract. Mid-air hand gesture interfaces have proliferated with the increased use of immersive computing technologies. Yet, hand gesture interaction design is often overlooked, resulting in a lack of interaction design guidelines and best practices, poor user experiences (UX), and a lack of consistency across these interfaces. Hence, the involvement of interaction designers for better hand gesture designs has become important. Hence, aiming to aid designers, we introduce a novel hand gesture design tool that enables designers to intuitively prototype 3D hand gestures for gesture-controlled interfaces. This tool allows designing mid-air hand gestures using free hands, reducing the learning curve of tool-specific mechanisms and 3D modeling skills, overcoming the challenges associated with custom gesture creation for interaction designers. We have made this tool open-source for collaborative community use. As hand gesture recognition research advances, along with its applications, with this work, we further highlight the importance of facilitating interaction designers with tools for enhancing the adoption, UX, and usability of hand gesture-controlled interfaces.

Keywords: Hand Gesture Design · Deign Tools · Interaction Design

1 Introduction

Interaction design (IxD) is a comprehensive discipline that explores the ways to foster symbiosis between users and machines/products, looking to enhance user experiences (UX) [15]. Within the field of IxD, the study of natural user interaction, such as human hand gestures, has been a focal point for Human-Computer Interaction (HCI) researchers for decades. The recent proliferation in consumer level immersive technologies and concepts such as the Internet of Things (IoT) has propelled the prominence of hand gesture interactions. As users increasingly engage with 3D environments, the significance of understanding and refining gesture-based interactions has become prevalent.

In a typical hand gesture interaction design process, as shown in Fig. 1, the first step involves identifying system affordances, possibly during requirement

M. Kurosu and A. Hashizume (Eds.): HCII 2024, LNCS 14688, pp. 240–258, 2024.
https://doi.org/10.1007/978-3-031-60449-2_17

gathering or the early system design stage. Subsequently, interaction designers review literature to identify similar use cases and conduct a Gesture Elicitation Studies (GESs) [22,23] to understand user-preferred gesture interactions. GESs can be time-consuming during its analysis phase, depending on the sample size. After analyzing the gesture agreement with the help of a GES and conducting a literature review, interaction designers can identify user-preferred gestures. They can then determine the most suitable hand gestures for the identified system affordances, taking into account agreement rates and considering factors such as memorability, ergonomics, and the feasibility of gestures. During this process, designers may have to converge several best gestures due to a similar agreement rates in the GES or other factors and design the final and most suitable interaction for a specific affordance. Then these designed hand gesture interactions will be ready to use in the development phase for implementation.

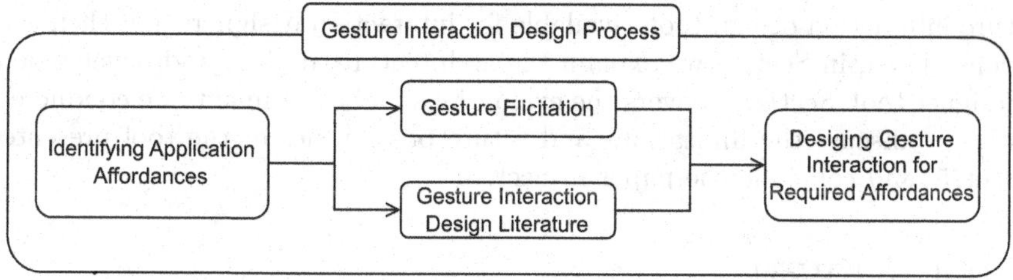

Fig. 1. Overview of gesture interaction design process.

This gesture design process shows that interaction designers needs the ability to design hand gesture interactions while ensure it can be effectively communicated to the development phase for utilization. While sketching is a common method, it is less useful and hard to convert in the development phase, particularly for gesture recognition algorithms that require more detailed input. On the other hand, designers could utilize 3D modeling or animation software, but it demands specific technical capabilities and could be time-consuming. Besides, video recording could require designers to capture a gesture from multiple views for communicating gesture properties effectively. Due to these reasons, we have observed that the hand gesture interaction designing phase is often overlooked in the gesture controlled application development process. There's plethora of research in gesture recognition and hand tracking yet there's lack of adaptation of these design process and techniques. For instance, many head-mounted displays (HMDs) have the ability to track hands in the current context, but the number of applications fully support or even utilize hand gesture interactions is low, because the lack of design guidelines around hand interaction design. Therefore, having easy-to-use and dedicated tools for designing hand gesture interactions is important for interaction designers. Such tools enable designers to swiftly and effectively develop hand interactions, facilitating seamless communication within the development stage in a more practical manner.

There are attempts in the state-of-the-art that propose frameworks and tools for this purpose, which we discuss in Sect. 2 along with their limitations. A common challenge in these frameworks and tools is that they carry a steep learning curve and have several limits on design freedom; for example, designers have to limit the scope of a hand interaction design to primitives defined in the design tool. In this work, we present a tool that use pre-trained machine learning models to assist hand gesture interaction designers in developing hand interaction designs using their free hands, with a minimum learning curve. It provides the functionality to present the design in a useful format for gesture recognition in development stages. We have open-sourced the code repository for researchers and designers to attempt and further develop, and provide feedback via GitHub[1]. We hope this work will encourage the incorporation of the interaction design phase into the system/application development process, ensuring a more positive user experience.

The rest of the paper is structured as follows: In Sect. 2, we discuss the current gesture interaction design tools available for interaction designers and their limitations. Then, in Sect. 3, we explain the architecture, design, and development of designer tool. Section 4 covers the evaluations and experiments we conducted. Lastly, we discuss the limitations and future possibilities of the tool presented in Sect. 5, and conclude the paper in Sect. 6.

2 Related Work

HCI researchers identified the need for intuitive interaction design tools that are easy to use and that help designers focus on creativity, user needs, and design thinking. The use of informal, sketch-based design tools [10] and declarative scripts [6] are commonly used techniques in the literature that align with the work practices of interaction designers. Researchers have attempted to apply these techniques to the gesture interaction design process, yet most of these tools mainly focus on touch-oriented gesture designs [11,12]. For example, Lu et al. [11] introduced the "Gesture Script interface," a tool that allows to create a gesture recognizer by providing examples of desired gestures, yet the tool focuses only on 2D pen-based gestures. Following a similar methodology, Mo et al. [14] proposed 'Gesture Knitter' for mid-air gesture design aiming at mixed reality (MR) applications. However, the work by Mo et al. [14] paid comprehensive attention to utilizing 2D declarative scripts and easing data overhead in the gesture recognition task over prioritizing ease of use for interaction designers. Furthermore, Mo et al.'s [14] work defines a gesture based on primitive poses and movements [19], a approach that may restrict the creative freedom of a designer. Complex gestures, often challenging to represent using primitive poses, could involve unique postures that cannot be constructed using these predefined primitives. However, due to the high complexity and agility of the human body and human motion trajectories, primitives are often used as a set of generic

[1] https://github.com/immersive-envs/designer-hands.

basic elements of human body motions [8,17]. With an appropriate and sufficient set of primitives, complicated motions and human joint movements can be represented using combinations of these elements. This concept of using motion primitives has been used for various motion analysis purposes and applications like analysing motion difference under Transcranial Current Stimulation [24] and developing natural-looking motion system for humanoid robots [7]. Thus, we argue that the design freedom, at least using free mid-air poses without restricting to primitive poses from defined motion primitives combinations, is an improvement for Mo et al.'s [14] framework.

Figueiredo et al. [5] propose a domain-specific language (DSL) for easily building gesture recognizers and demonstrate its usage in domains such as physical therapy, tai-chi, and ballet. Yet, knowledge of DSL has become a necessity to utilize this method. Also, there are several attempts in the literature that use aids from externals such as mobile devices [16], Bluetooth bracelets [1], and ring-shaped wearable device - GestuRING [21]. However, the use of external equipment could be invasive when designing natural mid-air hand gestures, and most often, there's instability in fingertip tracking. Furthermore, while scripting-based tools have a lower learning curve compared to learning 3D modelling and platform-specific development skills, they could be less intuitive than designing a gesture using our own hands. Using our own hands requires zero or minimal learning and allows designers to empathize and experience the best gestures that come from elicitation studies by themselves, adjusting the required ergonomics if needed. Thus, authoring gesture design using bare hands remains an area that still has potential for improvement in interaction design research, especially when compared to the extensive research in the field of gesture recognition. Henceforth, as gesture recognition research continues to evolve, it is crucial for interaction designers to actively participate in the process of designing these interactions, the necessity of easy-to-use gesture interaction design tools facilitates the adaptation of gesture interactions for novel application interfaces.

3 Proposed Gesture Interaction Design Tool

3.1 Terminology

Our tool incorporates several established concepts from the literature on hand gesture interaction design. We consider a *pose* represent a specific and distinctive shape of the hand involving the wrist, palm, and fingers and a *movement* involves a change in wrist's spatial position or rotation. A *hand gesture* (or sometimes referred to as *gesture* in this paper) in our tool's context can take various forms: it could be a *pose/s*, a *sequence of poses*; a *sequence of poses and/or movements*, or a *movement/s* regardless of the pose. Therefore, within to our tool's context, a gesture could be a *single pose*, *single movement*, *sequence of poses or movements* or a *sequence of combination of poses and movements*. Furthermore, we categorize gestures as either *simple* or *complex* based on the following criteria. If we refer to the term "*complex gesture*," it indicates a gesture that contains more than one *pose* and *movement.* If we use the term "*simple gesture*," it implies that the gesture is either a *pose* or a *movement.*

3.2 Overview

One of the main goal of our tool is to allow designers to use their hands to design and create required gesture interaction designs for applications. With our tool, designers can create a simple gesture directly, designing a complex gesture requires the designers to decompose it into a proper sequence of poses and movements (simple gestures) first. To facilitate the creation of gestures using bare hands, our tool utilizes computer vision-based hand tracking, allowing designers to use a RGB camera for designing hand gestures. Therefore, the only required hardware is a computer with a Windows 10/11 operating system and an RGB camera.

As discussed in Sect. 2, current hand gesture design tools or representation mechanisms use textual representations [14], resembling block programming languages, abstract numerical representations [3], or animated sketches [13]. Yet, some of these representations don't provide tool support for designers and employ a set of primitive poses as atomic blocks, which designers have to use when designing custom gestures. This could limit the freedom of creating custom poses. Also, these approaches introduce a tool-specific learning curve, as designers must comprehend the tool-specific representations. Our tool addresses this constraints by allowing designers to use natural and free hand gestures when designing or modifying gestures as required.

3.3 Design Tool Architecture

Figure 2 shows the high-level pipeline of the design tool. Firstly, designers' hand poses and movements will be captured and sent to the backend, where we use two leading hand tracking machine learning models, namely IntagHand [9] and Mediapipe Hand [25]. We selected these two machine learning models because of IntagHand's hand reconstruction accuracy and Mediapipe Hand's high prediction quality with real-time processing capability. Hand data is captured in its original form, and the models are used to identify the 3D coordinates of each landmark on the hands (either right, left, or both). Thus, our tool removes the necessity to use primitive poses. The hand pose information is preserved in as landmarks and 3D hand meshes, and the hand gesture designs resemble the gestures presented by designers in reality.

Our design tool consists of four operational functionalities: 1) hand pose recording; 2) spatial hand movement recording; 3) hand gesture design normalization; and 4) design presentation. Furthermore, it provides real-time visualization of the hand skeleton even before the gesture design's recording process begins. This allows designers to observe how the model tracks their hands. After a designer starts recording, each captured pose undergoes 3D reconstruction and is visualized in near real time. This feature enables designers to promptly correct

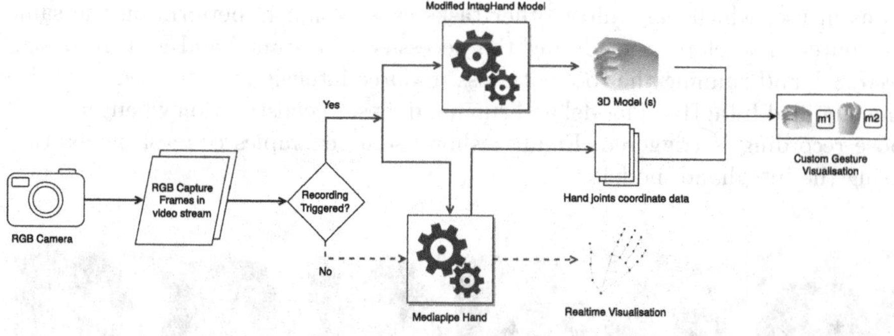

Fig. 2. High-level architecture of our gesture interaction design tool.

any inaccuracies in the construction of poses during the design process. Furthermore, the inclusion of two independent recording functionalities, one for poses and another for movements, provides designers with full flexibility in designing and recording hand poses and spatial hand movements in any sequence they desire. The recorded sequence of poses and movements is also visualized real time to the designer with the capability to undo and redo poses and movements, allows a designer to edit before saving the design if they think the model's prediction doesn't resemble the intended pose or movement.

1) Hand Pose Recording: As shown in Fig. 2, the design tool uses both IntagHand and Mediapipe models in the hand pose recording process. They have applied the same hand mesh topology of the MANO [18] hand model for each hand, and each contains 778 vertices. The IntagHand is a state-of-the-art two-hand mesh reconstruction model powered by the Transformer attention block and Graphic Convolutional layer. It takes a single RGB image as the model input and provides hand mesh vertices. We modified the original image overlay of the hand reconstruction output of the Intaghand into '.obj' 3D hand pose mesh generation. The '.obj' format is one of the most widely used 3D mesh model formats supported by popular 3D editors like Blender [2] and real time engines like Unity [20].

However, the IntagHand consists of three constructed layers in its structure, while each layer consists of two Graphical Convolutional Neural (GCN) cells and four small transformer cells. The complicated network structure has resulted in the computational complexity being high, and the prediction results would not be available realtime. When our output-modified Intaghand model is used for the hand pose 3D reconstruction, we observe average processing time for reconstructing a single 3D hand pose model from the RGB camera's frame is around 122.2 milliseconds. As no more than 8 frames of hand poses could be reconstructed to 3D '.obj' models in a second. This created a noticeable lag. Besides, our modified IntagHand model, which reconstructs the pose, still occupies a significant amount of system computational resources. This greatly impacts other applications in use, which may affect other tasks that designers perform on the same computer. Therefore, considering the necessity of instant hand gesture design feedback and running the tool with less resource intensity, we decided to utilize the modified IntagHand model and run hand mesh reconstruction when the hand pose recording is triggered. Figure 3 shows some examples of mesh generation using the Integhand model.

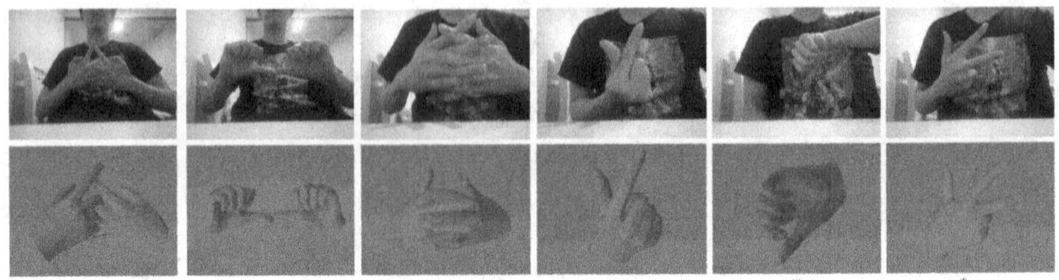

Fig. 3. Sample pose generated using our tool. This illustrates the possibility of complex poses created using both hands even with occlusions.

For gathering the hand pose landmarks data and providing real-time feedback, we used the Mediapipe Hand model. It is computational efficient while maintaining a great level of accuracy. The Mediapipe Hand takes a frame of hand(s) as input and generates a set of 21 joints 3D coordinates for each hand. The predicted 3D hand joints coordinates which relative to the camera frame (camera as the coordinate origin), are extracted from the Mediapipe Hand API. For the Mediapipe Hand configurations, we have set the maximum number of hands to detect to be 2 to avoid other people walking into the camera frame and affecting the designer's hand gesture designing process. We set the model complexity to 1, which utilize the full model for the optimal detecting accuracy. Also, it did not create any impact on the output frames per second. In addition, the Mediapipe Hand API's hand joints 3D coordinates grid is used to display the hand pose predicted by the Mediapipe Hand from the RGB camera frames in real time. Within the hand joints 3D coordinates grid, each group of the biological bone linking joints are linked by lines, and left or right hands are sketched in different line colours (orange indicates left hand, blue indicates right hand). Thus, designers could easily distinguish their hand poses current recognized by the tool and are committed to getting the exact hand pose design as they see and save (Fig. 8).

2) Spatial Hand Movement Recording: Our tool covers both static and dynamic gestures; hence, it is necessary to support movement tracking. However, hand spatial movement recording is a challenging task, as spatial movements involve directions, speeds, and patterns. Thus, most state-of-the-art tools and frameworks use primitive movements. To determine spatial movements in 3D spaces, it is required to have a fixed 3D coordinate system with a globally fixed origin point as a reference.

The Mediapipe Hand model [25] that we use for predicting hand joint coordinates uses the RGB camera's position as origin. If the camera's position is adjusted, the hand joint coordinates predicted by the Mediapipe Hand model will change accordingly due to the hands' position relative to the camera frame alternates, so does the 3D coordinate system. Beside, hand pose design recordings are predicted based on the relative positions of the hand joints, making them robust to changes in camera transforms. Thus, when recording hand movements, the coordinates may vary depending on the designers' setups, resulting in changes to the coordinate origins.

Therefore, following the state-of-the-art, our design tool also incorporates eight primitive movements (Fig. 4) that designers can use when creating new gestures. For the most optimal spatial movement recording, designers are required to use the open hand pose (Fig. 6) when defining a movement for three seconds.

Primitive movement identification involves two steps: identifying the type of hand movement (either rotational or positional) and predicting the primitive movement label out of the eight displayed in Fig. 4)

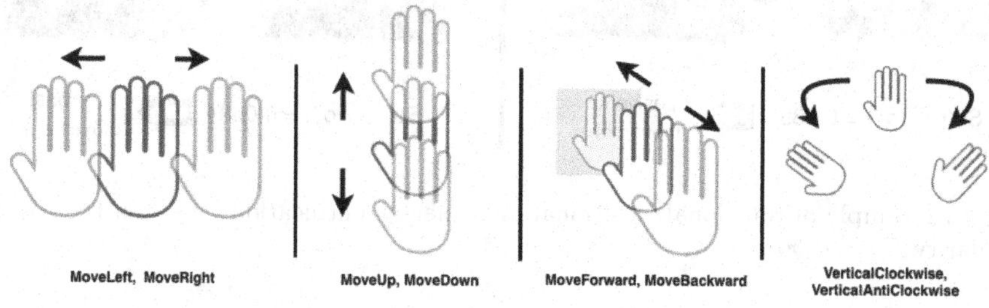

Fig. 4. Primitive movements are used in our tool to aid in custom gesture design.

For identifying the type of hand movement performed by the designer during the three-second recording period, we use a 3D vector (named $\boldsymbol{rot}$ vector) from the hand wrist joint coordinate to the index finger knuckle coordinate as shown in Fig. 5). We assume that the $\boldsymbol{rot}$ vector will only change in hand rotations and the positional movements such as moving up, left, and forward will not change $\boldsymbol{rot}$ vector. However, designers may slightly rotate their right hand inevitably during the movement recordings, even in performing positional movements. Thus, in our calculations which uses cosine similarity we have assigned 0.9 as the threshold to distinguish whether designers are performing a rotation movement while maintaining a tolerance for usability (Fig. 6). $\boldsymbol{rot}$ vector will be fetched and computed at the beginning and at the end of the recording, and cosine similarity is used to measure the degree of rotation between the two vectors. When cosine similarity between $\boldsymbol{rot}$ and $\boldsymbol{rot'}$ is lower than 0.9, the bone connects the wrist joint and the index finger knuckle has a rotation at the wrist during the movement recording. Thus, the movement being performed is likely to be a rotational movement.

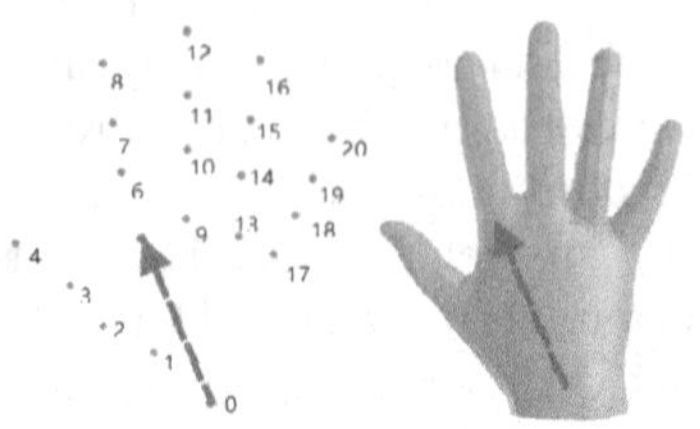

Fig. 5. An illustration of the ***rot*** vector.

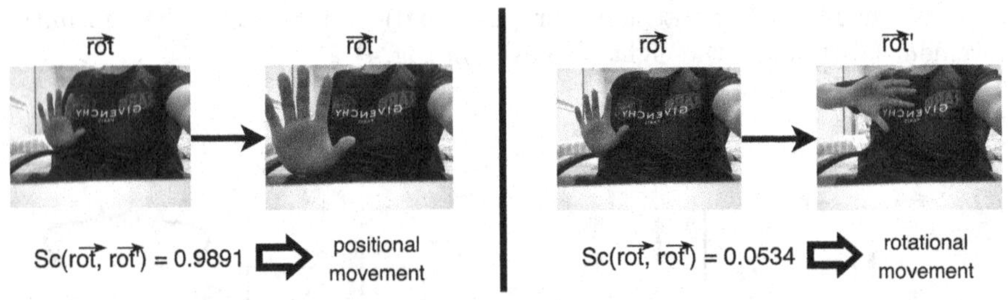

Fig. 6. Example of rotational/positional movement identification based on the cosine similarity $S_C(\boldsymbol{rot}, \boldsymbol{rot'})$.

For primitive movement label prediction, our design tool utilize index finger knuckle joints coordinates to predict the exact direction of rotation. As the predicted index finger knuckle joint coordinates move left horizontally relative to the frame compared to the coordinates at the beginning, the rotational movement is labelled as *VerticalAntiClockwise*. In contrast, when they move right horizontally, the rotational movement is labelled as *VerticalClockwise*, as the index knuckle joint is performing a clockwise rotational movement from the designer's perspective

If the identified hand movement is a positional hand movement, it could be: *MoveRight*; *MoveLeft*; *MoveUp*; *MoveDown*; *Forward*; *MoveBackward*. The design tool extracts the magnitude of movement in horizontal (Δx), vertical (Δy), and depth (Δz) (as shown in Fig. 7) from the three seconds hand wrist joint's 3D coordinates. Then, the most probable primitive movement's direction is selected as the direction with the most significant magnitude of movement.

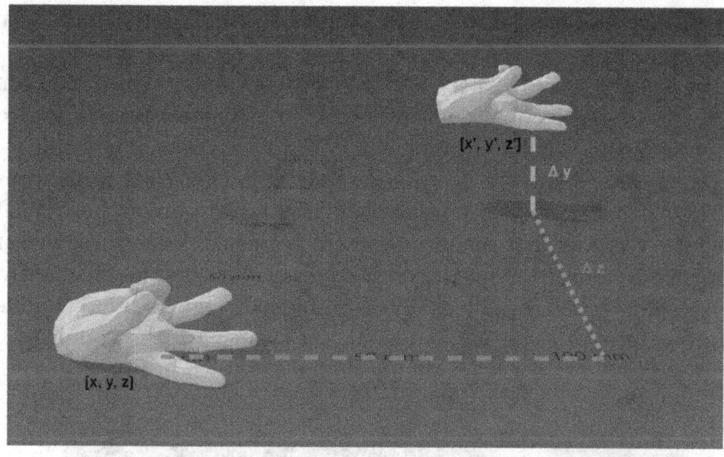

Fig. 7. Magnitude of movement in horizontal (Δx), vertical (Δy), and depth (Δz) graph description.

3) Normalization: The third functionality, hand gesture design normalization, is optional and initiates once the designer is satisfied with the designed gesture and decides to save it. Since we use MediaPipe Hands, the pose data recorded utilizes 21 hand landmarks to transform data and represent a pose. However, different hand gesture recognition algorithms may use different landmarks to represent the hand, as observed in application development for VR (e.g., Meta Quest) and AR (e.g., Hololens 2) HMDs. Thus, the purpose of hand gesture design data normalization is to offer a more generalized numerical presentation of the hand gesture designs, potentially serving as a shared template for hand gesture designs across various platforms, enabling the reusability of the designer's hand gesture design. We further use these normalized representations to compare gesture design outputs from this design tool.

To normalize the numerical hand pose recording, our approach involves using vector representations instead of fixed coordinate points. We have designed a normalization process that transforms the 3D coordinates of 21 hand joints from each hand into a set comprising 20 *Bone Vectors* $\boldsymbol{BV}$ (see Fig. 11). Each *Bone Vector* represents the displacement information in three dimensions between a joint and its linking joint, conveying both magnitude and direction. By using this set of $\boldsymbol{BV}$, we transition from absolute to relative position information, eliminating ambiguity arising from differences in the origins of hand pose recording coordinate systems. This transformation enables direct verification and discernability testing for various hand gesture designs from different setups.

4) Gesture Design Presentation: Designer hand consist with an easy-to-use graphical user interface (GUI). The GUI is built with ElectronJS [4], an open-source software framework designed for desktop applications with web development technologies. It has cross-platform potential which could benefit future to make this design tool compatible with other operating systems and platforms (e.g. Linux, macOS).

The GUI's purpose is to provide an interface to aforementioned functionalities and to provide design feedback in one place, requiring no prior knowledge for using this design tool. The GUI (as shown in Fig. 8) consists of multiple features, including the hand joints 3D coordinates prediction in a 3D grid, frames per second (FPS) counter, RGB camera playback, last recorded pose's 3D hand model, and the recorded poses and movement sequence. With these features, we aim to support designers to visually check their gesture designs frequently, allow designers to apply any real time changes, and help designers build confidence in their designs. Once a design is completed, they can view the complete gesture using our dedicated web-based designer viewer as shown in Fig. 9

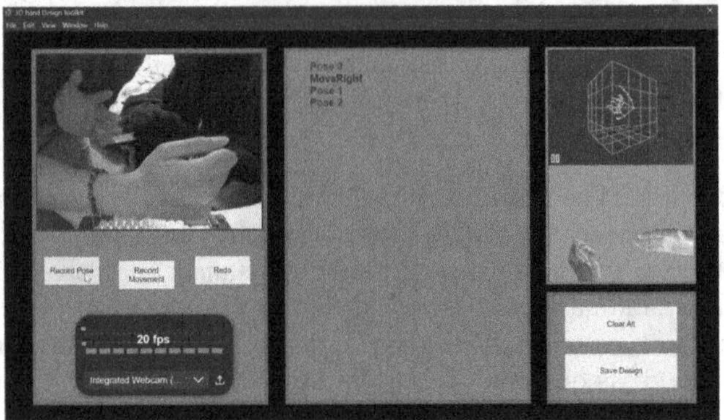

(a) This is an instance of the GUI showing a designer creating a gesture for using a bow and arrow.

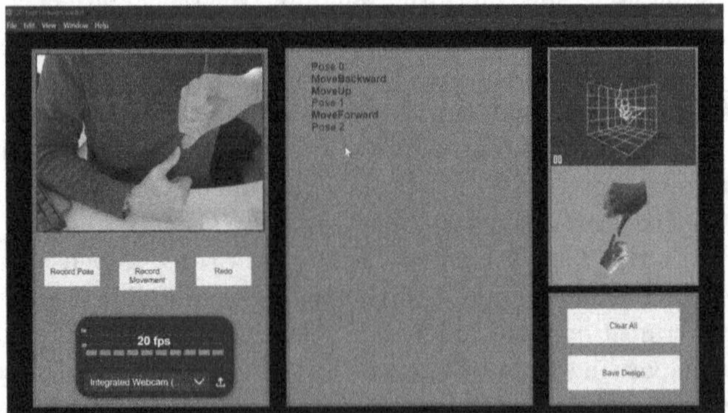

(b) Another instance of the GUI where a designer creates an abstract gesture.

Fig. 8. Graphical user interface of our hand gesture interaction design tool.

We have added three seconds of preparation time for the hand pose recordings after pressing 'Record Pose' or 'Record Movement' buttons on the GUI. Most of the time, designers may work independently, and they will need both hands to perform dual hand pose recordings and designs. The three-second preparation time (configurable) allows the designers to casually trigger the pose recording functionality and make sure they are always ready to pose whether it is a single-hand or dual-hand pose design. In addition, the predicted joints' 3D coordinate grid and previous hand pose model windows allow mouse manipulations. Designers could zoom in or out and turn to any view according to their wish, giving a complete look to the hand gesture designs. The 'Save Design' button generates an intuitive and human-readable gesture output structure, encapsulating all hand pose and movement recordings. This includes numerical hand gesture design output in JSON format, which comes in two versions: normalized and unnormalized, as well as the RGB captures and the corresponding 3D reconstructed OBJ meshes of all the poses. A sample data output can be viewed here[2].

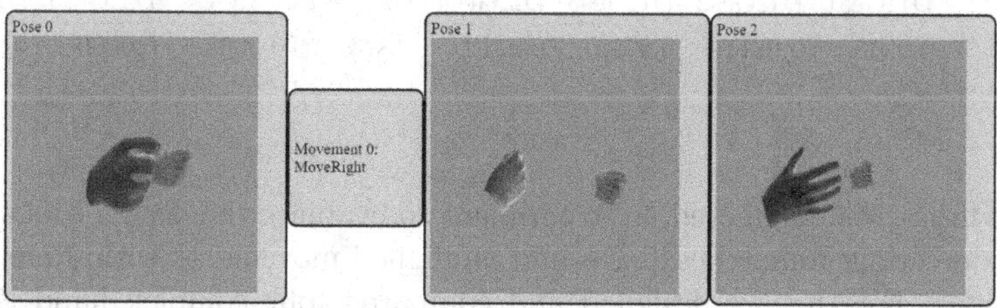

(a) Design Viewer - bow and arrow gesture.

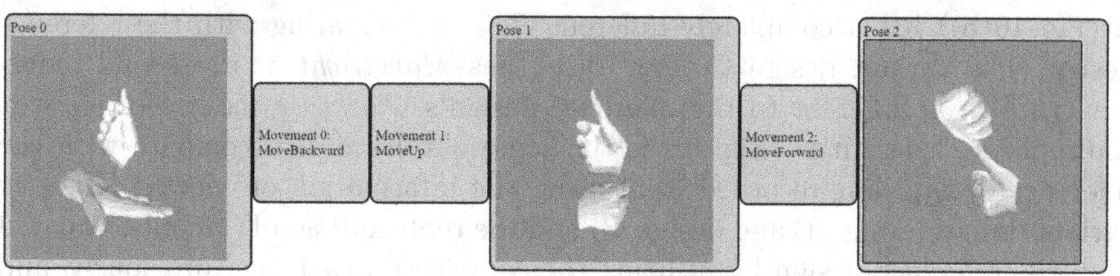

(b) Design Viewer - abstract demo gesture.

Fig. 9. Web-based hand gesture design viewer.

4 Design Outputs Verification

In order to verify the gesture design output from the tool, we engaged two interaction designers. They were told to independently think of 4 gesture designs.

[2] https://github.com/immersive-envs/designer-hands/tree/master/sample-gesture-design.

Then, they utilized our tool to create these gestures individually. Neither of them know what are the 4 gesture other designer is going to design. After creating the hand gesture designs, outputs were exchanged with each other. Then each designer looked at the output from the other designer and attempted to recreate other designers' gesture designs. Then all the gesture design outputs were collected. The objective was to assess whether the gesture designs created by one designer using our tool is comprehensible to another human designer.

To conduct the comparison, we employed a similarity comparison tool that we developed, as explained in Sect. 4.1. Table 1 shows the similarity score comparison results for each gesture. The similarity scores of the gesture designs by the two distinct designers consistently exceed 85%. Therefore, this preliminary evaluation result indicates that the hand gesture designs created by our tool effectively communicate gestures in human-understandable formats, thus useful in the gesture design phase of applications.

Table 1. Designers gesture verification.

Gesture	D1_Ges1	D1_Ges2	D1_Ges3	D1_Ges4	D2_Ges1	D2_Ges2	D2_Ges3	D2_Ges4
Similarity **Score**	0.9243	0.9711	0.9775	0.9112	0.8732	0.9663	0.9060	0.9358

In addition, we conducted an experiment to evaluate the design tool's capability in detecting unmatched poses and unaligned movements within hand gesture designs. For this we designed and compared four complex hand gesture designs, with one reference design, two variant designs, and a design replica of reference design (Fig. 10). As the gesture viewer shows, the first variant design B (Fig. 10(b)) has a completely different *Pose 2* comparing with the reference design. The variant design C (Fig. 10(d)) has *MoveRight* as its second movement, which is different to the reference design's *Clockwise* movement. Lastly, the replicated design D (Fig. 10) is the same gesture design compare with the reference design, but recorded from using the information on viewer. The two variant design (design B and design C) and the replica design D are all compared with the reference design by utilizing the comparison tool used previously, and the results are showed (Table 2).

As evident from the results presented, the design tool effectively identifies unmatched hand poses in the variant design B, yielding a low similarity score of 0.4159 on the *Pose 2*. Simultaneously, it successfully detects the unmatched hand movement in the variant design C, indicating the index position where the deviation occurs. Finally, the replica of the reference design shows a high similarity score of 0.9347, with no unaligned movement detected.

4.1 Gesture Design Comparison

In order to verify that the normalized hand gesture output provided by our tool correctly represents a gesture, we developed a discernability test. This can

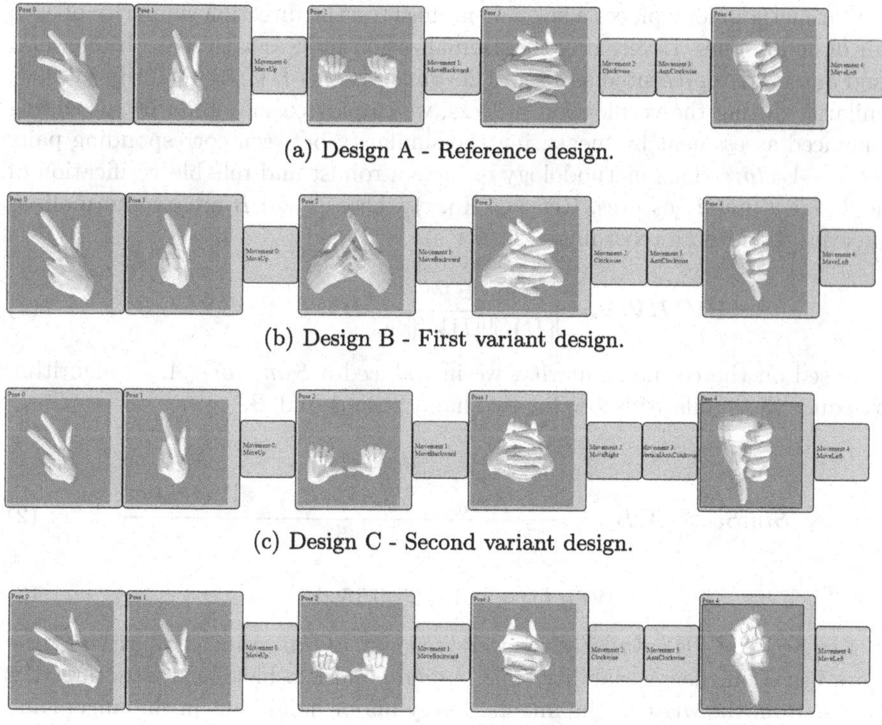

(a) Design A - Reference design.

(b) Design B - First variant design.

(c) Design C - Second variant design.

(d) Design D - Replication of reference design.

Fig. 10. The design viewer instances of four gesture designs used to evaluate unmatched detection.

examine two normalized designed outputs from our tool. For instance, if we create the same gesture twice using our tool, this method will help us determine alignment of pose and movement involved the gesture.

Table 2. Pose and Movement variation detection.

Experiment	Design B	Design C	Design D
Similarity Score	0.4159	Movement unmatched	0.9347
Detected error	Pose 2	Movement 2	NaN

Normalized output provide from our tool contains 20 Bone Vectors (***BV***) for each hand. Although this normalization addresses coordinate system variations, comparing ***BV*** directly is hindered by potential hand scale differences. To overcome this challenge, we introduce an additional mechanism, designed to minimize the impact of hand size variations during the hand pose comparison process.

Our methodology places a special emphasis on the direction similarity of each pair of hand bones. Leveraging the normalization process within our framework, hand bones are represented as a set of 20 *Bone Vectors* $\boldsymbol{BV}$. To quantify rotation similarity during the verification process, we employ cosine similarity, providing a nuanced assessment by measuring the similarity between corresponding pairs of *Bone Vectors*. This methodology ensures a robust and reliable verification of the designed hand gestures. Refer to Eq. 1) where A and B are two normalized numerical hand pose recordings (20 $\boldsymbol{BV}$s).

$$S_C(\boldsymbol{BV}, \boldsymbol{BV'}) := \frac{\boldsymbol{BV} \cdot \boldsymbol{BV'}}{\|\boldsymbol{BV}\|\|\boldsymbol{BV'}\|}, \quad \boldsymbol{BV} \in A \quad \boldsymbol{BV'} \in B \tag{1}$$

Based on the cosine similarity, we introduced a $SimScore(A, B)$ algorithm to deduce the similarity score for two hand pose A and B.

$$SimScore(A, B) = \frac{\sum_{f=1}^{5}(\sum_{c=1}^{4} S_C(A_{f,c}, B_{f,c}) * Weight[c])}{5} \tag{2}$$

$$Weight = [0.5, 0.25, 0.15, 0.1] \tag{3}$$

$SimScore(A, B)$ calculates the weighted sum of the cosine similarity of hand bones based on their variability. The human hand is a biological structure that extends from the wrist to the fingers. Every major hand joint in the fingers and palm can trace back to the wrist joint. More distal hand joints' movements are more constrained by the joints closer to the wrist where they extended from. Among 21 hand joints used in hand tracking topology, the wrist joint(0) has the largest biological rotation flexibility so capable to rotate all five metacarpal bones $(0-1, 0-5, 0-9, 0-13, 0-17)$. Moreover, thumb carpometacarpal joint and four fingers' knuckle joints control the rotation of proximal phalanges $(1-2, 5-6, 9-10, 13-14, 17-18)$, which affect the thumb metacarpophalangeal and the other four proximal interphalangeal joints. Besides, the thumb carpometacarpal joint and four fingers' metacarpophalangeal joints are affected by the five metacarpal bones $(0-1,\ 0-5,\ 0-9,\ 0-13,\ 0-17)$, the rotations of the proximal phalanges $(1-2, 5-6, 9-10, 13-14, 17-18)$ depend on the latter which controlled by the hand wrist joint.

Based on this dependence relations and joint flexibility, we classified the 20 *Bone Vectors* into 4 classes based on their individual flexibility and their distance to the wrist. Each class of the *Bone Vectors* has their designated contribution weights $(0.5, 0.25, 0.15, 0.1)$ which will be assigned when calculating the hand pose recording similarity in $SimScore$ (Fig. 11). The numerical hand pose recording similarity value could reflect and be responsive to the major hand pose difference and robust to the noise or minor reproducing variance.

When comparing two hand gesture designs, their hand poses will be compared accordingly with the $SimScore(A, B)$ algorithm. Each pair of corresponding normalized hand pose returns a similarity score, and the final hand poses similarity score of the designs is from taking the average of all hand pose similarity scores

(Table 1). For hand movements, all movements are checked based on their primitive hand movement label alignment in the designs. A mismatch in either the order or exact movement label will result in an unmatched movement.

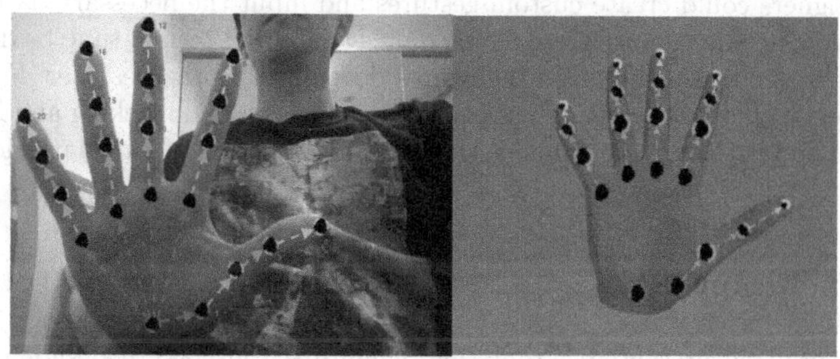

Fig. 11. Classes of *Bone Vectors*, with each corresponding weight.

5 Discussion and Future Work

Our tool simplifies the process of gesture interaction design by enabling designers to use their free hands when creating custom hand gestures, and makes those gesture designs useful in development stages. Our tool provides reusable and human-readable representations for custom gestures. In this section, we discuss the identified future research and development opportunities for this tool's design. We have made our tool's source code open to the community for further enhancement and contributions. We assume this will encourage interaction designers to get more involved in developing gesture-controlled interfaces.

In our tool, we provide complete freedom for creating poses by overcoming the necessity to use tool- or framework-defined primitive gestures to develop custom gestures. This offers more opportunities for designers to be creative and reflect results found from GESs. However, as we discussed before, we currently use primitive movements similar to the state-of-the-art. Hence, a potential future improvement would be to remove the constraint of designers having to use the given primitive movements when developing custom gestures. With the improvements of deep learning used for hand gesture tracking, we think there's potential research opportunity in this area.

Our tool currently runs only on the Windows operating system. Therefore, a potential future engineering improvement would be to support different platforms or to make it a cross-platform tool, allowing designers to use other operating systems or even carry out hand gesture designing using VR or AR HMDs.

In terms of user experience, we identified that providing more natural user input, such as voice control for our tool's GUI, would make the process of designing hand gestures much more enjoyable. Instead of having to perform button presses on the GUI, the tool can be further improved to respond to designers' voice commands, such as start recording a gesture, redo pose, redo movement, save the gesture, etc.

Finally, there's potential to integrate a gesture recognition pipeline into this tool. Designers could create custom gestures and input the necessary data from GESs, allowing the tool to prepare the dataset required to fine-tune or develop a models to recognize the custom gestures developed by the designer. Furthermore, there's an opportunity to use concepts such as spatial tracking and Neural Radiance Fields (NeRF) to enhance the 3D reconstruction of hands provided by our tool.

6 Conclusion

In this work, we presented a tool that facilitates the gesture design process for interaction designers without requiring tool-specific learning or other technical knowledge, such as 3D modeling. Our objective is to encourage greater involvement of interaction designers in the development of the proliferating hand gesture-controlled interfaces especially with advances in the Metaverse. We discuss the state-of-the-art and highlight how this tool introduces a novel experience by allowing designers to create custom gesture designs using just their hands. The architecture and development of the tool are explained, and we have made the tool open-source, inviting the community to use and contribute to further improvements. Finally, we discuss several existing limitations and potential opportunities to explore. We hope this work will encourage interaction designers to play a more active role in the gesture-controlled interface design process, thereby enhancing user experience and usability.

References

1. Ashbrook, D., Starner, T.: Magic: A motion gesture design tool. In: Proceedings of the SIGCHI Conference on Human Factors in Computing Systems, CHI 2010, pp. 2159–2168. Association for Computing Machinery, New York (2010). https://doi.org/10.1145/1753326.1753653
2. Blender Foundation, B.: Blender - a 3d modelling and rendering package (2018). http://www.blender.org
3. Choi, E., Kim, H., Chung, M.K.: A taxonomy and notation method for three-dimensional hand gestures. Int. J. Ind. Ergon. **44**(1), 171–188 (2014)
4. ElectronJS: Electronjs (2024). https://www.electronjs.org/
5. Figueiredo, L.S., Livshits, B., Molnar, D., Veanes, M.: Prepose: privacy, security, and reliability for gesture-based programming. In: 2016 IEEE Symposium on Security and Privacy (SP), pp. 122–137. IEEE (2016)
6. Hammond, T., Davis, R.: Ladder, a sketching language for user interface developers. Comput. Graph. **29**(4), 518–532 (2005). https://doi.org/10.1016/j.cag.2005.05.005. https://www.sciencedirect.com/science/article/pii/S0097849305000865

7. Hauser, K.K., Bretl, T., Harada, K., Latombe, J.: Using motion primitives in probabilistic sample-based planning for humanoid robots. In: Akella, S., Amato, N.M., Huang, W.H., Mishra, B. (eds.) Algorithmic Foundation of Robotics VII. Springer Tracts in Advanced Robotics, vol 47, pp. 507–522. Springer, Heidelberg (2006). https://doi.org/10.1007/978-3-540-68405-3_32
8. Kulić, D., Ott, C., Lee, D., Ishikawa, J., Nakamura, Y.: Incremental learning of full body motion primitives and their sequencing through human motion observation. Int. J. Robot. Res. **31**(3), 330–345 (2012)
9. Li, M., et al.: Interacting attention graph for single image two-hand reconstruction. In: IEEE/CVF Conference on Computer Vision and Pattern Recognition (CVPR), June 2022
10. Lin, J., Thomsen, M., Landay, J.A.: A visual language for sketching large and complex interactive designs. In: Proceedings of the SIGCHI Conference on Human Factors in Computing Systems, pp. 307–314 (2002)
11. Lü, H., Fogarty, J.A., Li, Y.: Gesture script: recognizing gestures and their structure using rendering scripts and interactively trained parts. In: Proceedings of the SIGCHI Conference on Human Factors in Computing Systems, pp. 1685–1694 (2014)
12. Lü, H., Li, Y.: Gesture coder: a tool for programming multi-touch gestures by demonstration. In: Proceedings of the SIGCHI Conference on Human Factors in Computing Systems, pp. 2875–2884 (2012)
13. McAweeney, E., Zhang, H., Nebeling, M.: User-driven design principles for gesture representations. In: Proceedings of the 2018 CHI Conference on Human Factors in Computing Systems, pp. 1–13 (2018)
14. Mo, G.B., Dudley, J.J., Kristensson, P.O.: Gesture knitter: a hand gesture design tool for head-mounted mixed reality applications. In: Proceedings of the 2021 CHI Conference on Human Factors in Computing Systems, pp. 1–13 (2021)
15. Moggridge, B., Atkinson, B.: Designing Interactions, vol. 17. MIT Press Cambridge (2007)
16. Parnami, A., Gupta, A., Reyes, G., Sadana, R., Li, Y., Abowd, G.D.: Mogeste: a mobile tool for in-situ motion gesture design. In: Proceedings of the 8th Indian Conference on Human Computer Interaction, IHCI 2016, pp. 35–43. Association for Computing Machinery, New York (2016). https://doi.org/10.1145/3014362.3014365
17. Reng, L., Moeslund, T.B., Granum, E.: Finding motion primitives in human body gestures. In: Gibet, S., Courty, N., Kamp, J.-F. (eds.) GW 2005. LNCS (LNAI), vol. 3881, pp. 133–144. Springer, Heidelberg (2006). https://doi.org/10.1007/11678816_16
18. Romero, J., Tzionas, D., Black, M.J.: Embodied hands: modeling and capturing hands and bodies together. ACM Trans. Graph. **36**(6), 245:1–245:17 (2017). https://doi.org/10.1145/3130800.3130883
19. Shon, S., Beh, J., Yang, C., Han, D.K., Ko, H.: Motion primitives for designing flexible gesture set in human-robot interface. In: 2011 11th International Conference on Control, Automation and Systems, pp. 1501–1504 (2011)
20. Unity Technologies, U.: Unity engine (2022). https://unity.com
21. Vatavu, R.D., Bilius, L.B.: Gesturing: A web-based tool for designing gesture input with rings, ring-like, and ring-ready devices. In: The 34th Annual ACM Symposium on User Interface Software and Technology, UIST 2021, pp. 710–723. Association for Computing Machinery, New York (2021). https://doi.org/10.1145/3472749.3474780

22. Wobbrock, J.O., Aung, H.H., Rothrock, B., Myers, B.A.: Maximizing the guessability of symbolic input. In: CHI'05 Extended Abstracts on Human Factors in Computing Systems, pp. 1869–1872 (2005)
23. Wobbrock, J.O., Morris, M.R., Wilson, A.D.: User-defined gestures for surface computing. In: Proceedings of the SIGCHI Conference on Human Factors in Computing Systems, pp. 1083–1092 (2009)
24. Xue, H., Herzog, R., Berger, T.M., Bäumer, T., Weissbach, A., Rueckert, E.: Using probabilistic movement primitives in analyzing human motion differences under transcranial current stimulation. Frontiers Robotics AI **8**, 721890 (2021). https://doi.org/10.3389/frobt.2021.721890
25. Zhang, F., Bazarevsky, V., Vakunov, A., Tkachenka, A., Sung, G., Chang, C., Grundmann, M.: Mediapipe hands: on-device real-time hand tracking. CoRR abs/2006.10214 (2020). https://arxiv.org/abs/2006.10214

HCI, AI, Creativity, Art and Culture

HCI for the Made in Italy Cultural Design

Vincenzo Paolo Bagnato(✉)

Polytechnic University of Bari, Via Orabona 4, Bari, Italy
vincenzopaolo.bagnato@poliba.it

Abstract. The article, in the form of an essay, presents a reflection on the relationship between HCI and Design applied to the Made in Italy contemporary productive system and represent a preliminary step in a wider research called 'Circular and Sustainable Made in Italy - Cultural value chain. From the local traditional production districts to a new country of origin effect' funded by the European Community and under development at the Polytechnic University of Bari (Italy) (The research is part of the program: MICS – Circular and Sustainable Made in Italy, Spoke 7 'New and consumer driven business models for resilient and circular Scs' P.5 Research Project 'Cultural value chains: From local traditional production districts to a new country of origin effect' (Coord. Annalisa Di Roma). Project funded by the European Union – NextGenerationEU – National Plan of Recovery and Resilience (PNRR) – Mission 4, Component 2, Investment 1.3, Call No. 341 (15th of March 2022) of the Ministry of University and Research. Protocol instance PE00000004, Decree granting of funding No. 1551 (11th of October 2022), CUP D93C22000920001.). The article is divided in three parts: in the first one it presents an analysis of the relationship between HCI and design; in the second part the reflection focuses on the Made in Italy productive system, analysing how HCI have contributed to change its paradigm; the third part comes to the design responsibility in updating its role within the scenario described in the previous parts. Lastly, in the conclusion the article tries to summarize the main methodological and operative aspects which can constitute starting points for further contributions on the subject.

Keywords: HCI · Made in Italy · Country of origin effect · Product design

1 Design for HCI vs HCI for Design

Human-Computer interaction represents nowadays a dimension that in contrast with its very first interpretations given by the design disciplines (architecture, urban planning, design, etc.) becomes a fundamental field of experimentation and challenge in order to improve both the design artefacts productive processes and the customers' requirements satisfaction. From being expression of a trans humanist thinking, the HCI is actually an approach which interestingly can contribute to maintain the human dimension of things respecting on one hand the relationship between tradition and innovation, on the other hand the social identity and memory of the cultural contexts [34].

M. Kurosu and A. Hashizume (Eds.): HCII 2024, LNCS 14688, pp. 261–271, 2024.
https://doi.org/10.1007/978-3-031-60449-2_18

After a period of big enthusiasm for the computer, which can be referred to the Sixties, during the Seventies and Eighties, although an interaction between man and computer was necessary even if just in terms of exchanging sequences of information and only for professional purposes, the interfaces were rudimental and not really helpful, as well as no importance was used to be given to the design dimension [17].

It's from the end of the Nineties that a certain reflection about the necessity to 'humanize' the computer through design solution started to be taken into account, now still for mere commercial purposes: the problem was to expand the market bringing the computers into the people's everyday life and design was selected as a means of facilitating conditions of aesthetic attractiveness and ease of use [12].

Actually, the participation of design in HCI research is passing from a condition of lack to a more collaborative, interdisciplinary and open dialogical framework, due on one hand to the humanization of interaction between man and machine, on the other hand to the rediscovery of a holistic approach both by designers and engineers, scientists and sociologists that leads to collaborative methods and actions which at the same time maintain each own disciplinary identity. The need for dialogue, deeper than was used to be at the beginning of the digital revolution to revolve around the mere concept of usability, has transformed designers from graphic and communication experts just able to let people more easily access to computer interfaces into fundamental actors in the process of creating innovative digital products and services [14].

This important change has occurred in the framework of a new sensibility for the social aspects and for the user experience in the design processes aimed at facilitating the HCI but also within the scope of a renewed responsibility in always innovating the user centred approaches, both in the new (commercial) product development and in the production of cultural knowledge. But it's also true that the vision and the common ground that the two areas (HCI community and the design thinking) share are not enough to ensure the achievement of concrete objectives in terms of user satisfaction: if the definition of methods aimed at increasing empathy between new interactive products and end-users/customers (such are bodystorming, experience prototyping, construction of virtual scenarios, etc.) has become undoubtedly fundamental for the improvement of HCI, the participation of designer in constructing real smart environment or interactive devices as well as in driving the product innovation processes, addressing and framing real problems doesn't happen so often and very occasionally it turns into real concrete opportunities [15].

As technology evolves and becomes more and more human-centred, its impact on productivity and on people's freedom to interact with products before and after their put-on market gets higher and higher: we only have to look at the latest contribution of the digital technology, from the VUI to the gesture-based interaction, from the AR and VR to the MR and XR, from the emotion and biometric sensing to the NLP advancements, from the touchless interfaces to the haptic feedback enhancements, from the multi-nodal interfaces to the BCI, with a language that has become easier and easier [20].

Furthermore, the digital conversion systems and management development of the manufacturing processes, made possible through the use of reverse engineering design, robotic systems for printing and digital archives, has led to the optimization of the time to market and to a better exploitation of materials, especially when reused or recycled.

In this scenario, the system of tools offered by a phenomenon that can now be considered as a constant revolution cannot be seen any more as a sort of pre-condition or as a boost to the social transformations but, on the contrary, as a necessary answer to the constantly new and always changing users' demands and requirements, as well as degrees of freedom for those craftsmen who want to improve their supply chain process.

Therefore, if HCI can offer unprecedented possibilities in terms of economic and social benefits in defining strategies of communication and dialogue with AI systems, IoT, UI, human interface and neuro-technologies, the design discipline is asked to define ethically balanced and human centred approaches to control and manage this interaction.

Within the specific aspects of HCI which can be translated into design ambits and/or research topics, it's possible to consider at least three main elements that they have in common and which the project is asked to focus on: physical aspects of things (ergonomics, comfortable interfaces, for all accessibility, etc.); psychological factors of people (cognitive processes, perceptions, attitudes, behaviours, etc.); social characteristics of groups (social rules, rituals, relationship between public and private dimension, etc.) [9]. These three categories of elements, with all their possible declinations, can be seen as plausible directions that HCI can take in helping the work of a designer, not only translatable on the morphological final configuration of the products but, on the contrary, mainly on the process (design as well as productive), this one made both of a rationally replicable part and of a creative heuristic dimension, and on the innovative elements as necessary outcomes, always extensible to the community, from a deep knowledge of the state of art [14].

2 HCI and Made in Italy Design

2.1 Elements for a New Made in Italy

In a condition of liquidity such as that of our contemporary age, uncertain instead of certain, temporary instead of definitive, flexible instead of solid [2], it's not easy, and perhaps it doesn't make reasonably much sense, to establish a universal definition of 'Made in Italy' (and not even if it coincides with that which came from the famous exposition 'Italy: the new domestic landscape' at MoMA of New York in 1972), at least for a couple of reasons: first of all because it's original meaning was defined *ex post*, that is only after having observed the results of a very complex process in which creativity, social sensibility, artisan know-how, industrial technologies built an unrepeatable historic conjuncture which produced design artifacts with a very high (aesthetical and ethical) quality level [16]; secondly, because it's evidently anachronistic to make reference to a national context intended as a closed territorial unit in a moment in which the match is played between the local context (sub-national dimension) and the global market (trans-national dimension).

What can today probably have an interest, beyond the speculations about the origin of this phenomenon, is considering the Made in Italy in terms of a more general idea of excellence, in which the objects always have not only a function but also a 'soul' [8], transferable to other cultural contexts, filtered through the actual contemporary social and economic situation; on the other hand, the importance of reaffirming the Made in Italy brand can be seen as the possibility to detect the cultural elements that it produced (also independently from the original socio-economic framework) anticipating the times and the forms through which it now flows into the idea of sustainability first and of 'country of origin effect' then [27].

Moreover, if it's true that the idea of Made in Italy coincides with that of a complex and heterogeneous industrial model made of an archipelago of local clusters with deep roots in artisan tradition, human capital and territorial culture able to produce always new high-quality objects starting from the ability to do things and the deep knowledge of materials and processes, always within a strong physical interaction and interpersonal relationships [3, 33], this complexity should be now divided into elements that, without claiming to be exhaustive, can be summarized as follow:

- Synthesis between art, tradition and material culture;
- Unicity in the product's character and identity;
- Strong relationship between row materials, transformation techniques and supply chain;
- Propensity for innovation in the mark of a historically sedimented know-how;
- Capacity of finding out solution using the latest technologies, always seen as a means and not as end;
- Confluence of the artisanal manufacturing production into high quality design objects through industrial productive processes;
- Social attention, communication and interaction with the final users' need and requirements, those intended both as individuals and as members of a cultural community;
- Production based on cooperation, intercultural dialogue and sharing;
- Aesthetical aspects based on semantic and semiotic elements.

2.2 HCI for Sustainable Consumption of Made in Italy

Sense and aesthetical sensibility, empathy and adaptive flexibility, humanistic mode, meticulousness and attention to details, thinkering, enjoyable modernity [1] are keywords related to the concept of Made in Italy that can help us to reach the specific dimension of sustainability of its brand: an *ante-litteram* social and environmental sustainability strongly connected to a cultural context, with a central role of design that becomes an active subject in managing innovation processes, communication systems, cultural meaning of the functional solutions.

Furthermore, this extended interpretative perspective of the concept of sustainability is a key to change our point of view on the actual idea of 'consumption' which tends to become a critical action done by the users/buyers that, without passively suffering choices 'from above', on one hand actively ask the company to demonstrate them their strategies in terms of environmental respect and resource-saving, on the other hand claim to 'communicate' with products that recognize their values and their identity instead of (only) that of the productive company [23].

Actually, the attitude with respect to the consumption has acquired at least three 'sustainable' declinations of meaning: consumption as communication, consumption as participation and consumption as experience [7].

As already underlined, this is certainly a form of sustainability, on one hand considered in its social aspects, on the other hand as a fundamental ingredient in the search for innovation: the increase in the number of actors involved, the extension to the intangible dimension of things and the open character of the manufacturing processes create the conditions for maintaining a constant updating independent from the companies' push and more and more related to the encounter of a large number of contributions at any level.

In the ambit of this new paradigm of the idea of sustainability, HCI becomes a main partner for design because the new information technologies and systems of interaction allow buyers and users to participate in the design decisions through individual experiences, collective interpretations and definition of new meanings, symbols and rituals: through the HCI is now possible to share knowledge and become active creators, co-designing and sometimes co-producing, starting the product development process from the bottom and not any more from above [25], but also living real experiences in specific real contexts or virtual spaces as sublimation of the sharing of cultural meanings and ethical values with the companies, in a socially and economically sustainable way. In other words, thanks to the HCI technologies, consumers have now tools to get out from individuality and build social relationship with companies and with other consumers, so that all the manufacturing system, in this case of the Made in Italy, cannot live any more on the old image of its brand, but it's now asked to redesign not only its productive framework but also its context of consumption to allow participation and definition of new significances.

2.3 HCI Between 'Made in' and Country of Origin Effect

The possibilities offered by the new relationship between HCI and Made in Italy, as well as the necessity now socially shared to build a condition of circular economy, brings us to overcome the concept of 'made in' and arrive at that of 'country of origin' [22]. The country-of-origin effect is the impact of the idea of quality associated to a specific cultural context on the users/buyers' purchasing processes. In the case of the Made in Italy products, the COOE can be considered as the trust people place on the objects whose design and production has been totally developed in Italy, because of the positive image they have of this country, with its abilities, experiences, knowledges and capacities [5, 7].

Being related to the buyers' perception and behavior (especially foreigners), downstream of the processes of market integration, standardization and trend for delocalization, the COOE is now taken into account by the companies through strategic systems of communication, interaction and participation, in order to re-build their identity.

Hence, the companies address the shopping experiences of their clients but, as we have said before, is not possible any more to consider the users/buyers as passive consumers, so becomes important for the companies to respect their consciousness and awareness about the cultural values of the products. But actually, the problem is that, due to the difficulty of a product to be designed, manufactured and assembled in one unique country, the COOE has become fragmented at least into three main constitutive elements: overall image of a country, image of a country and its products, images of products from a country [5]. It's here that the HCI can help to re-join together design, assembly, parts/components, manufacture and brand in a new COOE with an innovative meaning (may be regional or trans-national) and attribution of a cultural value.

The user experience is therefore fundamental in the dialogue between companies and buyers, but it must be intended not as something added to the ordinary object with the mere objective of selling a product, but, on the contrary, as an occasion made of specific spatiality, temporalities and rituals when companies and buyers can share a common ground of iconographic repertories, ethical values, bonds with tradition, socially eligible degrees of innovation, forms of customization [30].

The global scenario has changed and its dynamism turns it into a constantly evolving framework in which the enterprise Made in Italy is called to adapt its own specificities: this is a framework in which the Made in Italy design is trying to rediscover and reinventing itself aiming at building a new system of values in the framework of the so-called 'New Normal', starting from the valorization of the local production districts so to give a contribution in creating a new country of origin effect extendable at international level [21].

The companies are now asked to better explain their products, integrate sustainability within their strategy, strengthen customer service to be close to customers as consultants and assistants and finally start designing in a different way; content is fundamental for the future of the production in the local contexts: with which to communicate, inspire and bring the target audience closer by creating suggestions of living lifestyles through the product, as well as sustainability and circular economy are increasingly concrete resources and challenges for all the actors involved in the design process.

Today, communicating one's impact and the sustainability index by informing the consumer about the creation of green products, the use of natural and recycled materials or the circularity of products is a competitiveness factor for local companies and the attention to quality of life is an issue to be addressed through the HCI strategies to make people understand the new directions that more careful design and production is taking, rediscovering an approach that in our modernity has as a founder in the person of Adriano Olivetti which, ahead of his time, investigated the problem of HCI already between the Fifties and the beginning of the Sixties working with designers like Sottsass and Maldonado [29].

Therefore, local traditions and global futures represent a crucial dichotomy in the field of action of design in which HCI gives a new perspective in defining new ethical values able to follow the contemporary social senses and sensibilities of each local community according to the objectives defined by the New European Bauhaus initiative. The challenges of the global dimension of things cannot be tackled any more by deleting or restricting the local traditions and this is true both in the dimension of the production processes and in that of the consumer awareness. Sustainability, innovation and identity as never before are now parts of a more general 'cultural dimension' which can be considered as a bridge between different backgrounds and as a *fil rouge* connecting all the local contexts with their specific relationships between industrial design and manufacturing knowledge.

2.4 HCI and Made in Italy Towards a New Paradigm

In the mark of the Made in Italy there are many sectors working with HCI systems and platforms and/or digital design, such as, beyond the 'traditional' 4A (*Alimentari, Abbigliamento, Arredo, Automazione*): automotive, fashion, craftsmanship, furniture, graphics and communication, urban spaces, enhancement of cultural heritage, new digital technology, but this condition still needs to be implemented in those cases in which the companies belong to small local productive context with little chance of emerging in the global market, where the difference between success and failure is not dependent on the products' aesthetical aspects but rather on the strategies of innovation, sustainability and customization and on the offered user experience possibilities and usability.

Even if the approach to HCI started with the transition to the industry 4.0 with its four components (cyber-physical production system, internet of things, smart factory and internet of service), it's now that the Made in Italy is going to re-invent its identity trying to update its historical relationship between technology and craftsmanship, overcoming stereotypes and misrepresentations on behalf of its real social, economic and cultural characteristics, reconstructing the relationship between 'image' and 'information on it', taking advantage of the opportunities offered by the HCI [6].

While the European Union identifies the productive factor of the manufacturing sector as fundamental for the future sustainable economic development, in 2017 the Italian Government promoted and presented the Industry Plan 4.0 (*Piano Industria 4.0*) aimed at improving the digital innovation for the manufacturing sector (advanced craftsmanship), but the crisis has slowed down in approaching the new possibilities offered by the latest technologies of HCI.

Nevertheless, all the sectors are now showing signs of recovery both at productive and management level: this is leading to an important contribution to the construction of a new paradigm of Made in Italy, made of innovative supply chain, technology transfer, preservation of the artisanal dimension beside the acquisition of computer tools (hardware and software), clear traceability and authenticity of products, equilibrium between productive responsibility and necessity of quickly placing on market, new ethical relationship between specific user requirements and mass customization [19].

Regarding the stark imbalance in company size, which sometimes can be observed within the Made in Italy productive system, it should be considered that the fragmentation which characterizes it very often tends to becomes an opportunity to transform the signs of recognition into a system of socio-cultural distinctive values; when these values take on a certain strength, they are intercepted by the contemporary scenario that, after having accepted them, it translate them into possible directions to which address the design, productive and marketing strategies with a greater awareness. These directions can be: the interoperability between objects, machines and people; the virtualization as a function of the productive, economic, environmental and social sustainability; the modularity of adaptable and open product, services and processes; the decentralization as organizational form of the processes [11].

This awareness is furthermore confirmed by a large number of bachelor and master degree in many Italian universities (Milan, Naples, Rome, Turin, Trento, etc.), where the interest for the dialogue with HCI is testified by the institution of courses in the field of strategic and/or service design, design management, design engineering, digital design, interaction design, design of responsive web applications, etc., always focusing on skills based on the Made in Italy design.

In the professional world, and on a productive level, the new possibilities offered by the dialogue between software CAD/CAM and physical prototype systems via 3D printing, CNC machines and/or augmented reality, improves the potentialities of the products in terms of customization and non-standardization through the sharing of information and the participation in taking decisions, as well as it expands the freedom of movement of design already in the concept phase where many possible final product proposals can be created in a digital environment. This means that design and production build a new relationship which is very similar to that of a traditional craftsmanship activity: what happens, then, is that design and production are not sequential steps any more but they become synchronic and simultaneous activities, artisanal creativity and rational management of the processes are no longer in opposition, self-manufacturing is increasingly available [28].

3 The Design Responsibility: For a New Cultural Manufacturing

The new contours of the contemporary Made in Italy, its cultural value chain and the user engagement's new paradigms of the companies, as we have seen, are nowadays interested by a process of transformation in which a fundamental role is represented by the HCI strategies used by the product-service systems and by the new consumer-driven business models. The resilient and circular supply chain is now fully recognized as a necessary condition, as well as the fact that the ethical components of products and processes prevail over the aesthetic ones is not an option any more but a widely recognized fact. The way Italian design supply companies today address the public (visitors, buyers, customers, users, etc.) and the narrative forms, both physical and virtual, through which companies present, to an increasingly sensitive and attentive audience to environmental issues, not their products but their strategies related to sustainability, inclusion, respect for the environment and control of their products' life cycle, as well as the ways in which they pursue the objectives of product, process and social innovation, are all elements that the new design approach must consider in its background research. How customers, users and clients (internal, final and partners) attribute value and significance to the products? How companies manage the relationship between brand identity and (mass) customization? How companies declare and show their way of being inclusive, sustainable and innovative? Which is in general the relationship between cultural dimension and marketing? [13].

Although the level of awareness, as often pointed out, is higher than in the recent past both in the companies and in the consumers, what seems to be by no means certain is first of all the fact that the Made in Italy design with its many local cultures could build automatically a relationship with the global design landscape; secondly, that the entity of the social and emotional level of the communication, its natural modalities, as well as the dimension of time (the temporality of the experience) defines always a compatibility with the physical context, its social acceptance and its eco-sustainability [18]; thirdly, the fact that all the forces involved in the new product development process (designers, engineers, marketing experts, etc.) easily reach a balance between them without a cultural coordination [7]. This is the reason why the figure of the designer is still fundamental in its capacity to mediate between different knowledge, activate interdisciplinary contributions, give sense to innovation, improve the cultural dimension of the objects, humanize technology, promoting eco-efficient behaviors [22].

Furthermore, as well as we put the word 'new' beside the concept of Made in Italy and that of country of origin effect, the same should be done for the idea of 'authenticity': also in this case design can be a privileged actor in detecting and managing the forms of expression of all the possible new authenticities which can come out from any local context, productive territory, social community and innovative reality at different scale, with the aim of linking them together in a unique (even if diversified) cultural common ground within a new multiverse geography of productive systems able to improve, through good objects and services, the environment and the people's everyday life [26, 32].

Going more specifically, the power of HCI that the Made in Italy design is interested in belongs to its narrative power and the possibilities offered by the digital and/or virtual storytelling, whose impact is not measured on a generic final user but on a 'social capital' made of people belonging to a specific cultural context with strong and dynamic relationships between them, sharing a common system of ethical and aesthetical values, rituals and behaviors and open to the global world [4]. This aspect has a deep impact on the conception of the new products because changes on one hand the ways of consumption and the customer expectations, on the other hand the companies' approach to production which becomes more and more customized and personalized: this encounter produces a dimension called 'cultural manufacturing', that in the cases of territories characterized by strong cultural roots, such as Italy, it becomes a cultural experience closely linked to a specific physical and social context of use [10].

4 Conclusions

Even if the relationship between design and HCI can be investigated with uncertain scientific results due to the different outcomes that can be reached by different processes or analogous processes in different context, we can consider the relevance (more than validity) of the analysis and investigations as an acceptable objective of the applied methodology.

If Stefano Micelli, paraphrasing the work of Maholo Uchida, says that empathy is the key through which design can make the digital world acceptable, avoiding that technology reduce the role of the human dimension and, in the meanwhile, aiming at a new form of co-habitation between man and computer based on innovative aesthetics and new forms of interaction [24], trusting technology seems to be now a more easily accessible street: in the case of the made in Italy districts, this change of behaviour undoubtedly leads to a real and diffused cultural change, as well as to a concrete opportunity to raise and an increase in the competitiveness in the global market. Certainly, but not only that, because this perspective re-activates an artisanal dimension made of small productive archipelago, auto-production systems, etc., in those territories in which the big industry is physically too far away: economy, simplicity, clarity and beauty but also awareness, privacy, context, experience, synergy, emotions, participation, identity and cultural meaning are the main ingredients of the cultural framework of the new relationship between HCI, design and made in Italy brand. But the very big power of this new dialogue goes at least in four main directions:

- Possibility for products to be manufactured locally;
- Facility in preserving over time the cultural manufacturing know-how;
- Capacity of joining together the humanistic aspects of production with the technologic-scientific ones.
- Sensibility in combining virtuality and reality in the user's interaction and participation processes.

Furthermore, this new relationship facilitates the preservation of the artisanal know-how and its transmission to the future and at the same time allows companies to clearly detect and better control the operations that need and can be replicated [19], in specific ambits that without being exhaustive, can be summarized as follow:

- Graphic design for user's interaction;
- Robot for support to production;
- CAD/Cam systems for support to design;
- Development of time to market;
- Creation of digital archives and catalogues;
- Taxonomy/description of the artisanal manufacturing and serial industrial processes;
- Lifecycle management;
- Construction of abacuses of components, distinguishing the already existing ones to those of new production, with the aim of easily manage the eventual substitutions and the possibility to better customize each product.

As already happened in the past, also in this case the technological innovation flows into a radical social and economic innovation, thanks to the strong union between products (with its components of design, production and put on market), productive system, territories, natural environment and people, so that the digital transition has been able to help producing democratic and socially virtuous processes that have been returned to the creative dimension of the craftsmanship [31].

References

1. Amatulli, C., De Angelis, M., Costabile, M., Guido, G.: Sustainable Luxury Brands: Evidence from Research and Implications for Managers. Palgrave Macmillan, London (2017)
2. Bauman, Z.: Lyquid Modernity. Polity Press, Cambridge UK (2000)
3. Becattini, G.: Distretti industriali e made in Italy: le basi socioculturali del nostro sviluppo economico. Bollati Boringhieri, Turin (1998)
4. Bertola, P., Colombi, C.: Rebranding made in Italy: a design driven reading. Fash. Pract. **6**(2), 175–200 (2014)
5. Bertoli, G., Resciniti, R.: International Marketing and the Country-of-Origin Effect. The Global Impact of 'Made in Italy'. Edward Elgar, London (2013)
6. Bettiol, M.: Raccontare il made in Italy: un nuovo legame tra cultura e manifattura. Marsilio Editori, Venice (2015)
7. Bettiol, M., Micelli, S.: Design e creatività del made in Italy. Proposte per i distretti industriali, Mondadori, Milan (2005)
8. Branzi, A.: Mediterraneo profondo. In: Fagnoni, R., Gambaro, P., Vannicola, C. (eds.) Medesign_Forme del Mediterraneo, pp. 34–41. Alinea, Florence (2004)
9. Card, S.K., Monar, T.P., Newell, A.: The Psychology of Human Interaction. L. Erlbaum Associates, Michigan (1983)

10. Ceconello, M.A: Circular economy solutions and strategies for the furniture sector in the European union. DIID **78**, 108–117 (2022)
11. Celaschi, F., Di Lucchio, L., Imbesi, L.: Design e phigital production: progettare nell'era dell'industria 4.0. MD J. **4**, 6–11 (2017)
12. Crampton Smith, G.: Why it took so long. AIS Des. **4**(8), 16–28 (2016)
13. Dalla Mura, M.: Il design italiano oltre la crisi. Autarchia, austerità, autoproduzione: VII edizione del triennale design museum. AIS/Des. J./Storia e Ricerche **3** (6), 233–241 (2015)
14. Evenson, S., Forlizzi, J., Zimmerman, J.: Crafting a place for interaction design research in HCI. Des. Issues **3**(24), 19–29 (2008)
15. Fallman, D.: Design-oriented human-computer interaction. In: Proceedings of Conference on Human Factors in Computing Systems, pp. 225–232. ACM Press, Fort Lauderdale (2003)
16. Fortis, M.: Le due sfide del Made in Italy: globalizzazione e innovazione. Il Mulino, Bologna (2005)
17. Gamberini, L., Chittaro, L., Paternò, F.: Human-Computer Interaction. I fondamenti dell'interazione tra persone e tecnologie. Pearson, London (2012)
18. Giovannella, C.: L'uomo, la macchina e la comunicazione mediata: evoluzione di paradigmi e design per le esperienze nell'era organica dell'interazione. In: Barletta, G. (ed) Machinae. Tecniche arti saperi nel Novecento, pp. 471–490. B.A. Graphics, Bari (2008)
19. Goretti G., Cianfanelli, E., Terenzi, B., Tufarelli, M.: Advanced craftsmanship in furniture. The Tuscan sector between tradition and innovation 4.0. DIID **62**, 27–33 (2019)
20. Jacko, J.A.: Human-Computer Interaction Handbook, 3rd edn. CRC Press, Boca Raton (2012)
21. Lotti, G., Tosi, F., Follesa, S., Rinaldi, A.: Artigianato Design Innovazione. Le nuove prospettive del saper fare. DidaPRESS, Firenze (2015)
22. Lotti, G., Trivellin, E.: Una possibile strategia per il prodotto italiano. MD J. **4**, 60–73 (2017)
23. Micelli, S.: Le tre rivoluzioni del management digitale. Sinergie. Ital. J. Manag. **35**(103) (2017)
24. Micelli, S.: Made in Italy, la sfida di empatia e tecnologia. Il Sole 24 Ore, 12th of July 2018 (2018)
25. Micelli, S., Di Maria, E.: Distretti industriali e tecnologie di rete: progettare la convergenza. Franco Angeli, Turin (2000)
26. Norman, D.: The Design of Everyday Things. The MIT Press, Boston (2013)
27. Pellegrini, S.: Il Marketing del Made in Italy. Armando Editore, Rome (2016)
28. Ramoglu, M., Coskun, A.: Scientific craftsmanship: the changing role of product designer in the digital era. Des. J. **20**, S4497–S4508 (2017)
29. Riccini, R.: Un'impresa aperta al mondo. Conversazione con Tomás Maldonado. In: Bigatti, C., Vinti, C. (eds.) Comunicare l'impresa. Cultura e strategie dell'immagine nell'industria italiana (1945–1970), pp. 134–152. Guerini e Associati, Milan (2010)
30. Rinaldi, A.: la user experience dei prodotti made in Italy. In: Lotti, G., Tosi, F., Follesa, S., Rinaldi, A. (eds.) Artigianato Design Innovazione. Le nuove prospettive del saper fare, pp. 203–215. DidaPRESS, Firenze (2015)
31. Sbordone, M.A., Turrini, D.: Designed & Made in Italy. Invarianti, transizioni, nuove mappe valoriali. MD J. **9**, 6–19 (2020)
32. Scalera, G.: Unique & universal. MD J. **9**, 154–161 (2020)
33. Sennett, R.: The Craftsman. Yale University Press, New Haven (2008)
34. Vanderdonckt, J., Palanque, P., Winckler, M.: Handbook of Human Computer Interaction. Springer, Cham (2020). https://doi.org/10.1007/978-3-319-27648-9

An Image is Worth a Thousand Words: Colour and Artificial Intelligence, Beyond the Generative Chromatic Palettes

Cristina Caramelo Gomes[1,2(✉)]

[1] CITAD, Lusíada University of Lisbon, Rua da Junqueira, 188-198, 1349-001 Lisbon, Portugal
cris_caramelo@netcabo.pt

[2] CIAUD, Research Centre for Architecture, Urbanism and Design, Lisbon School of Architecture, Universidade de Lisboa, Lisbon, Portugal

Abstract. The progression of technology continues to shape our access to information, activities, and interactions within our physical and social environments. This radical transformation challenges traditional boundaries, as technology now extends beyond mechanical tasks to encompass intellectual pursuits previously exclusive to human cognition. Artificial intelligence, a pivotal technological innovation, has transitioned from merely supporting intellectual activities to actively engaging in creative endeavours, prompting various ethical and practical concerns.

Central to creative work, colour serves as a compelling attribute, captivating attention, conveying information, reflecting social and cultural contexts, defining aesthetic values, and expressing emotional nuances. Among its manifold dimensions, the aesthetic aspect frequently takes precedence, raising fundamental questions about the ultimate purpose of communication. As artificial intelligence endeavours to partake in artistic creation through generative imagery, a critical inquiry emerges: how does this technology comprehend and employ colour to convey ideas? This article seeks to address this question. Does artificial intelligence possess a nuanced understanding of colour's multifaceted dimensions, and does it leverage this comprehension in image generation? Alternatively, does it rely exclusively on pre-existing image datasets available on the internet? To unravel these queries, our investigation involved querying ChatGPT, a free version, which demonstrated that artificial intelligence can discern the various dimensions of colour. Additionally, utilizing the Stable Diffusion, free version, we generated images to visually elucidate the application of this knowledge. Our findings revealed that while the theoretical knowledge is discerning, the visual output disproportionately emphasizes aesthetic values, potentially overshadowing other dimensions of colour. This apparent discrepancy underscores the necessity for human intervention and collaboration to bridge this perceptible gap and fully leverage the symbiosis between technology and human creativity.

Keywords: Artificial Intelligence · AI tools · Colour · Creative Process · Human Interactions

M. Kurosu and A. Hashizume (Eds.): HCII 2024, LNCS 14688, pp. 272–291, 2024.
https://doi.org/10.1007/978-3-031-60449-2_19

1 Introduction

Colour constitutes a fundamental element that profoundly shapes the human experience of life. Universally acknowledged as a defining factor in character, function, symbolism, and aesthetics, the concept of colour plays a pivotal role in human understanding of the physical world. Beyond its aesthetic significance, colour's attributes exert a substantial impact on conveying messages and fostering interactions, both among individuals and within the broader context they inhabit.

In the conceptualization of graphic layouts, colour emerges as a potent communicative tool, influencing human perception, emotion, and behaviour. The composition's choice between a chromatic or monochrome expression, guided by the message's purpose, target audience, or the creator's preferences, reflects a deliberate aesthetic intent. The attention drawn by colour extends beyond its physical wavelength stimulus to include the rich references and symbolism associated with specific colours or chromatic compositions. Throughout the design process, the integration of colour theory and psychology facilitates a meaningful connection between the chosen colour palette and human perception and behaviour, guided by the creator's comprehension of the subject matter.

For digital creatives, technological advancements have revolutionized the graphic design process, offering diverse avenues for conceiving, and executing final layouts. While technology has traditionally been viewed as a tool devoid of intelligence, serving as a conduit for data input and human choices, the advent of artificial intelligence (AI) challenges this paradigm. AI's impact permeates various sectors of contemporary society, including the creative domain, prompting discussions and debates within intellectual circles. Despite varying opinions—some embracing AI's benefits and others resisting change based on entrenched views—AI's transformative influence on activities, interactions, and creative processes is undeniable.

Numerous research endeavours, employing diverse objectives and methodologies, alongside individual opinions expressed in scientific journals, media, and social networks, contribute to the ongoing discourse surrounding AI's role in creativity. However, personal biases and perspectives do not impede AI's integration into daily routines, affecting human performances and interactions across diverse contexts.

Within the creative realm, concerns regarding AI often centre on issues of intellectual property, such as the potential for replication and authorship, as well as the use of generated images in the propagation of misinformation. Despite these ethical concerns, the incorporation of AI into daily routines necessitates legislative frameworks to manage undesirable outcomes and human conduct. A crucial inquiry should focus on the impact of AI on human reasoning, the creative process, and interactions between individuals and technology, particularly considering the enticing prospect of cost reduction through AI implementation.

In creative domains, AI's potential lies in alleviating repetitive and time-consuming tasks, aiding in information search and analysis, and generating diverse solutions to support idea conceptualization and implementation. While AI excels in managing vast amounts of information within limited timeframes, human qualities such as creativity, originality, and empathy remain indispensable and, to some extent, resistant to full emulation by technology.

The use of AI in generating images and chromatic palettes hinges on the specificity of the prompt entered into the application, underscoring the importance of precise and judicious word choices. Whether the generated image serves as an experimental iteration or the final solution, it remains subject to improvement through subsequent technological applications.

As this new creative process unfolds, several questions come to the forefront:

a) What is the relationship between the words chosen (prompt) and the generated chromatic composition?
b) What is the relationship between the sequence of words chosen (prompt) and the generated chromatic composition?
c) What is the relationship between the chromatic composition generated and the theory and psychology of colour?
d) What is the relationship between the chromatic composition generated by AI and a chromatic composition made without this technology?

The aim of this article is to raise the discussion around the AI topic and demonstrate the contribution of AI in the appliance of colour in graphic layouts.

2 Artificial Intelligence

Artificial intelligence (AI) can be delineated as a field that intersects computer science and datasets, harnessing them to facilitate complex problem-solving processes (IBM, 2024). Definitions from authoritative sources such as Oxford Languages and Britannica characterize AI as "the theory and development of computer systems able to perform tasks that normally require human intelligence" and "the ability of a digital computer or computer-controlled robot to perform tasks commonly associated with intelligent beings," respectively (Oxford Reference and Britannica).

Artificial intelligence encompasses concepts like machine learning and deep learning, employing algorithms to construct expert systems capable of making projections or organizing information based on input data (Coursera, 2024). Despite the evolution of AI since the mid-20th century and the diverse interpretations of its achievements, the advent of user-friendly applications like OpenAI's ChatGPT marks a turning point. This facilitates and promotes the utilization of AI in intellectual activities such as reasoning, analysis, decision-making, and problem-solving (European Parliament, 2024).

The collaborative interaction between individuals and machines characterizes the essence of artificial intelligence. Platforms like ChatGPT play a pivotal role in this interaction, fostering brainstorming sessions that can lead to the creation of thematic images, colour schemes, and atmospheres. (Art Education & Leadership Academy, n.d.)

AI applications tailored for creative endeavours, including DALL-E, MidJourney, and Stable Diffusion, have garnered attention due to their continuous references in literature. DALL-E 3 is built on ChatGPT, establishing a robust relationship between the prompts entered in ChatGPT and the resulting image solutions. Redefining prompts significantly influences the generation of new images, illustrating the bidirectional relationship between written narratives and visual output.

These AI applications, functioning as text-to-image generators, simulate human artistic ability by analysing image datasets and associating keywords with styles and details.

The final image produced is responsive to the prompt, according to the analysis conducted during the process. (Yale Daily News, 2024).

The introduction of AI in creative domains, such as art, design, and architecture, accelerates time-consuming activities during the conceptual process. This shift raises pertinent questions regarding authorship, authenticity, ethics, standardization, and the evolving role of humans in this new creative paradigm (Hyseni, 2024). The challenges posed by AI parallel those encountered during the dissemination of Computer-Aided Design (CAD) systems in the late 20th century, with the difference lying in the expanded communication possibilities facilitated by internet development.

Ethical concerns associated with AI should be directed towards human behaviour rather than the technology itself. Issues such as plagiarism, data security, and the creation of misleading information existed before AI, and the responsibility lies with human users to uphold ethical standards (Caramelo Gomes, 2002).

The central issue revolves around the impact of AI on the creative process, collaborative work between humans and machines, and the future role of creatives. The emergence of AI challenges the traditional boundaries between human and machine intervention, necessitating a nuanced understanding of authorship in this evolving creative landscape.

The co-creation process between humans and machines presents an engaging opportunity (Fuzzy Math, n.d.). While creativity remains a distinct human attribute, AI serves as a valuable assistant in suggesting solutions without the burden of time-consuming and repetitive tasks. This collaboration can enhance creative performance, but it is imperative to attribute the responsibility of creativity to the human creator to preserve diversity in creative contexts. AI tools, though invaluable, cannot replicate human empathy, mood, and originality, crucial elements in the expressive nature of art. As AI continues to evolve, it will not undermine the future of creatives but rather foster new forms of collaboration and workflow management in the creative process.

3 Colour

Colour is an omnipresent element in the human environment, continuously influencing our experiences, be it by brightening or dimming our surroundings. It plays a pivotal role in evoking excitement or relaxation, irrespective of our location. The human perceptual system processes an extensive spectrum of visible colours throughout the day, significantly impacting our senses, emotional states, and behaviours. It is an intrinsic aspect of our psychological experience, shaping the way we think and act. (Mahnke, 1996).

Colour holds a fundamental place in visual perception, occurring within the brain's cerebral cortex, where the received visual information is comprehended. Visual perception involves both direct and indirect processes, where sensory input and cognitive interpretations, past experiences, and memory collectively contribute to our understanding of the environment. (Buether, 2014).

Colour vision encompasses the response of sensory receptors to specific wavelengths, while the perception of colour involves the ability to distinguish colours and the meanings and symbolisms associated with them (Noury, 2020). Beyond visual experiences, colour influences other senses such as touch, hearing, balance, taste, and movement. It can affect how we perceive sound, the texture of a surface, or even the flavour of food.

Moreover, colour has tangible effects on physiological responses, including heart rate, anxiety levels, and overall arousal (Ellwood, 2024).

The field of colour psychology delves into how colours impact human behaviours, acknowledging that individual, social, and cultural backgrounds influence colour interpretations. While these differences exist, there is a general acceptance that warm colours like yellow, orange, and red evoke emotions ranging from energy and happiness to anger and hostility, whereas cool colours such as purple, blue, and green induce feelings of peace, calmness, sadness, or indifference. Studies, like the one conducted by Jonauskaite, Mohr et al. (2020), affirm the universality of colour-emotion associations, emphasizing the influence of geographic, linguistic, and cultural proximity on these relationships. The study revealed consistent emotional associations with specific colours across diverse nations and languages.

The intricate relationship between colour and emotions evolves through environmental experiences and is intertwined with language, history, religion, and folklore. For instance, variations in colour associations, such as the significance of red or the mourning colour in Western and Eastern cultures, reflect the impact of linguistic and cultural differences.

Creatives leverage colour-emotion associations to attract attention and influence behaviours. Colour serves as a potent communication channel, capable of shaping mood, decisions, and behaviours. It carries meaning through metaphors, symbols, and cultural references, contributing to the interpretation of visual information. Despite the wealth of knowledge about colour and its influence on human perception, decisions, and behaviour, it is often haphazardly applied, succumbing to fashions, trends, and personal preferences without rational justification. (Caramelo Gomes, 2023).

As artificial intelligence becomes involved in content production, whether alphanumeric or graphic, the question arises: will AI predominantly rely on scientific knowledge or succumb to prevailing fashions and trends when it comes to explaining or applying colour? This bears significant implications for culture, symbolic references, and social interactions, emphasizing the need for thoughtful and informed applications of colour in AI-generated content.

4 Colour and AI

Understanding theoretical knowledge about colour should ideally be within the domain of expertise for creatives. However, persistently, colour is often applied based on trends, tendencies, and personal preferences, overlooking its dimensions and impact on individual perceptions, behaviours, and decisions. This bias is not only associated with AI but is a reality in the traditional creative process, which can, in turn, influence how AI utilizes this attribute.

In both AI and traditional creative processes, colour plays a crucial role in image and video identification, classification, pattern recognition, and predicting the content of analysed objects. In natural language processing, colour, with its inherent symbolisms and references, can aid in comprehending the emotions conveyed in textual content.

When associating colour with an image generated by AI, a well-crafted prompt is essential to communicate the objectives and target audience of the image. The question arises: What precautions are necessary to ensure that the generated image is responsive to the various dimensions of colour? Is the key to resolution primarily in the choice of words and their sequence in the prompt, or does it depend more on the patterns embedded in the image dataset on which artificial intelligence relies?

5 Methodology

To gain insights into how artificial intelligence approaches colour in both narrative and graphic terms, we employed GPT-3.5 Chat and Stable Diffusion, both in their free versions. The objective was to understand how the generated image communicates different colour dimensions depending on the given prompt.

In exploring colour and graphic layout with ChatGPT, the responses consistently highlight the crucial role of colour, transcending the specific context. ChatGPT emphasizes the importance of colour across the identified significant issues and underscores its performance as a tool to assist human creatives in enhancing their expertise rather than replacing them. The questions to underscore the significance of colour include (Table 1):

a) What is the relationship between AI and graphic layout colour?

The detailed responses provided by ChatGPT underscore the necessity for research into the intricate interconnections between two crucial domains: colour and artificial intelligence. This article aims to delve into how artificial intelligence interprets text, shaping the mood of generated images through colour. While the sequence of words and the narrative in the prompt theoretically hold significance in defining image content and attributes, it is acknowledged that the creation process is influenced by the patterns observed and analysed by artificial intelligence in generating results. As we explore the capacity of artificial intelligence to generate images, several questions emerge. In our pursuit of answers, we will pose queries to the ChatGPT and subsequently generate images using Stable Diffusion. The rationale behind selecting these applications lies in their accessibility through free versions.

The primary focus of this research is to unravel the nuances of how artificial intelligence comprehends text and shapes the mood of generated images based on colour. As we navigate through the questions posed to ChatGPT and analyse images created in Stable Diffusion, we aim to shed light on the intricate relationship between textual prompts, colour representation, and the influence of underlying image patterns in the AI-driven creative process.

To gain insights into the AI's interpretation of text and its impact on the mood of generated images, we will create images in Stable Diffusion to observe the manifestation of colour based on the prompts provided. The application offers free access, making it accessible for a preliminary exploration of the chosen research focus.

How does the sequence of words and the narrative in the prompt influence the mood and colour representation in the generated image? To what extent does the influence of image patterns, seen and analysed by artificial intelligence, contribute to the result? What are the implications of AI-generated images for creative processes, particularly in terms of colour choices and emotional impact?

By addressing these key questions, we aim to contribute to a deeper understanding of the intersection between artificial intelligence, text interpretation, and the role of colour

Table 1. Question: What is the relationship between AI and graphic layout colour?

Colour Palette Generation:	• AI algorithms can analyse images and suggest suitable colour palettes based on the content and mood of the design. This helps designers choose harmonious and visually appealing colour schemes
Image Recognition for Layout Suggestions:	• AI-powered image recognition can assist designers by identifying elements in an image and suggesting layout arrangements. This can streamline the design process and offer creative input
Personalized Design Recommendations:	• AI can analyse user preferences and behaviours to offer personalized design recommendations. This includes suggesting colours and layouts that are more likely to resonate with a specific target audience
Automatic Colour Correction:	• AI algorithms can be employed to automatically correct or enhance colours in images, ensuring consistency and coherence in graphic design
Dynamic Colour Adaptation:	• AI systems can be programmed to adapt colour schemes dynamically based on external factors, such as time of day, user interactions, or seasonal changes. This can be particularly useful in web design or applications where the visual appearance needs to adjust in real-time
Layout Optimization:	• AI-driven algorithms can optimize the layout of elements within a design for better visual balance and readability. This includes adjusting the size, position, and spacing of elements based on design principles
Generative Design:	• Generative design using AI allows for the creation of unique design variations. This can be applied to generate different layouts and colour combinations, providing designers with a range of options to choose from
Market Trend Analysis:	• AI can analyse current design trends by processing large amounts of visual data from various sources. This information can help designers stay current with popular colour schemes and layout styles

(continued)

Table 1. *(continued)*

Accessibility Considerations:	• AI tools can assist in ensuring that graphic layouts are accessible to a diverse audience by providing recommendations for colour combinations that meet accessibility standards
A/B Testing Optimization:	• AI can facilitate A/B testing of different colour schemes and layouts to determine which options perform better in terms of user engagement or other specified metrics

in image generation. This exploration has the potential to inform future developments in AI-assisted creative processes and foster a more nuanced approach to the utilization of colour in generated visual content (Tables 2, 3, 4 and 5).

The comprehensive insights offered by ChatGPT responses highlight valuable perspectives that align with existing literature on the topic. These responses are marked by their informativeness, coherence in addressing the subject matter, and a well-structured argument, covering an introduction, development, and conclusion. ChatGPT emerges as a significant tool for both enriching and challenging our understanding of various topics.

Artificial intelligence, especially tools like ChatGPT, excels in processing and delivering information in textual format. However, representing knowledge through images adds an extra layer of complexity. The prevailing belief is that AI efficiently handles large amounts of information quickly, while human creativity, originality, and empathy contribute to a deeper understanding of themes, contexts, and target audiences. The challenge lies in determining whether AI can effectively communicate or represent knowledge in a visually cohesive manner.

The experiment conducted in Stable Diffusion, utilizing the free version with concise and direct prompts, aimed to explore AI's capability to communicate information beyond aesthetic expression, particularly focusing on the associations between colour, cultural manifestations, colour theory, and human mood. Acknowledging the inherent limitations of free versions, the experience sought to gauge how well AI, under constrained conditions, could capture and convey the nuanced relationships between colour and cultural contexts.

The evaluation of ChatGPT responses underscores the tool's efficacy in conveying detailed information and engaging in coherent discussions. However, the experiment in Stable Diffusion raises intriguing questions about AI's ability to represent knowledge through images, especially in capturing the nuances of colour in cultural contexts. The interplay between textual and visual representation remains an area of exploration, and future advancements in AI may provide further insights into the potential of these technologies in conveying complex knowledge through both mediums.

To investigate how artificial intelligence relates colour and culture, specific prompts were provided to Stable Diffusion. These prompts were characterised by simple sentences aimed at exploring colour associations and emphasising chromatic expression more than the contextual environment or topic. The prompts are expressed in the legends of the generated images.

Table 2. Question: What is the relationship between the words chosen (prompt) and the generated chromatic composition?

The relationship between the words chosen in a prompt and the generated chromatic composition depends on the context and the specific instructions provided. When using AI to generate a chromatic composition based on a prompt, the AI system typically interprets the textual input and generates an output that aligns with the concepts, emotions, or visual descriptions conveyed in the prompt. Here's how the relationship works:	
Semantic Understanding:	• The AI system analyses the semantic meaning of the words in the prompt. It tries to understand the concepts, emotions, or themes conveyed by the language
Colour Association:	• Based on the semantic understanding, the AI associates colours with the elements mentioned in the prompt. For example, if the prompt includes words like "warm," "serene," or "fiery," the AI may generate a chromatic composition with warm tones like reds, oranges, and yellows
Visual Imagery:	• The AI may also consider visual imagery associated with the words in the prompt. If the prompt describes a scene or mood, the AI may attempt to translate those descriptions into a visual representation through the choice of colours
Training Data Influence:	• The AI's output is influenced by the data it has been trained on. If the model has learned associations between certain words and colours from its training data, it may incorporate those learned associations into the generated chromatic composition
Creative Interpretation:	• Depending on the level of creativity and generativity of the AI model, it may provide a unique and creative interpretation of the prompt. This could involve unexpected colour combinations or stylistic choices that align with the general theme of the prompt
It's important to note that while AI can generate chromatic compositions based on textual prompts, the results are generated patterns and associations rather than a direct understanding of visual aesthetics. The quality and relevance of the output depend on the capabilities of the AI model, the richness of its training data, and the specificity of the prompt provided. Additionally, human interpretation and refinement are often needed to ensure that the generated composition meets specific design or artistic requirements	

The response from Stable Diffusion, although constrained by the simplicity of the prompt and the limitations of the free version, provides visual interpretations of the traditional colour of a Chinese bride and the colour associated with mourning in Indian culture. It aims to capture the cultural nuances and associations linked to these specific colours.

The image interpretations generated by Stable Diffusion serve as visual representations of cultural colour associations. However, it's important to note that the AI's response is influenced by the data it has been trained on and the specific wording of the prompt. The interpretations should be considered as approximations based on the AI's understanding of common cultural colour practices rather than definitive representations.

Table 3. Question: What is the relationship between the sequence of words chosen (prompt) and the generated chromatic composition?

The relationship between the sequence of words chosen in a prompt and the generated chromatic composition is influenced by how the AI model processes and interprets the textual input. Here are some key points regarding this relationship:	
Sequential Understanding	• The AI model typically processes words in a sequential manner, considering the order in which they appear in the prompt. This sequential understanding helps the model grasp the evolving context and potential relationships between words
Contextual Analysis	• The sequence of words contributes to the contextual analysis performed by the AI. The model considers how each word influences the meaning of the others and the overall context of the prompt
Phrase and Sentence Structure	• Sentence and phrase structures, including grammar and syntax, play a role in guiding the AI's understanding of the prompt. The relationships between words within phrases and sentences contribute to the overall meaning
Dependency on Preceding Words	• Some AI models are designed to consider dependencies on preceding words. The choice of a particular word in the sequence may affect the interpretation and selection of subsequent words, influencing the final chromatic composition
Temporal and Emotional Flow	• The sequence of words can convey a temporal and emotional flow in the prompt. For instance, words at the beginning may set the mood, while those later in the sequence may introduce additional details or nuances. The AI attempts to capture and reflect this flow in the generated chromatic composition
Association Patterns	• The AI model may learn association patterns from its training data, where certain sequences of words are statistically associated with specific chromatic compositions. This learned knowledge can influence the model's output based on the prompt's word sequence
Creative Interpretation of Phrases	• Depending on the generative capabilities of the AI, it may creatively interpret phrases or combinations of words to generate unique and visually interesting chromatic compositions. The sequential arrangement can impact the creativity and coherence of the output

(continued)

Table 3. (*continued*)

<table>
<tr><td>Consideration of Adjacent Words</td><td>• The AI may consider not only the immediately preceding and succeeding words but also those in the broader context of adjacent phrases or clauses. This broader context helps in capturing the overall meaning and intent of the prompt</td></tr>
<tr><td colspan="2">The relationship between the sequence of words in a prompt and the generated chromatic composition is intricate, and the AI's ability to understand and respond to sequential input depends on the architecture and training of the specific model. While AI can generate creative outputs, it may still benefit from human interpretation and refinement to ensure that the resulting chromatic composition aligns with specific design goals or artistic intentions</td></tr>
</table>

The experiment sheds light on how artificial intelligence, even in limited settings, can provide visual interpretations of colour associations with cultural practices. However, the nuanced nature of cultural symbolism and variations may require more sophisticated AI models and detailed prompts for a more accurate representation. This exploration highlights the potential of AI in capturing cultural colour nuances and signifies an area for further research and development (Figs. 1).

The first images show a wedding dress with a Western style, although the surrounding background presents details of Chinese interior design.

The introduction of the word "tradition", in the Fig. 2, adds a new stylistic element, which can be associated with the emotional goodwill (symbolised by the red colour) towards the wedding dress.

What could be the reason for this result? Is it the immediate response of the AI model favouring Western models? Or could it be attributed to the westernization of Chinese culture?

Do the analysed images influence the result more than theoretical information about the associations of colour and culture? (Fig. 3).

A similar prompt oriented to Indian culture offered a wedding dress where the red colour dominates. Is it a reflection of the previous prompts? Or the recognition of colour and colour association?

A similar experiment was conducted addressing the subject of mourning and the associated colours in Western and Eastern cultures. The first result depicts a woman dressed in dark shades of grey, with an urban environment background, suggesting a Western context. The image related to the Indian context, however, is more representative of the poverty of the mourning woman, yet her clothes have colour even though India's mourning colour is white. Could this be a way to highlight a detail that identifies the geographic origin of the picture? Or it is just a reference to Indian culture but forgetting rituals associated with mourning? (Fig. 4).

The experiment sheds light on how artificial intelligence, even in limited settings, can provide visual interpretations of colour associations with cultural practices. However, the nuanced nature of cultural symbolism and variations may require more sophisticated AI models and detailed prompts for a more accurate representation. This exploration

Table 4. Question: What is the relationship between the chromatic composition generated and the theory and psychology of colour?

The relationship between the chromatic composition generated by AI and the theory and psychology of colour involves a connection between the visual elements produced by the AI and the principles and emotional responses associated with colours. Here are some aspects of this relationship:	
Colour Theory Principles	• The generated chromatic composition may align with established colour theory principles, such as the colour wheel, complementary colours, analogous colours, and triadic colour schemes. The AI may subconsciously follow these principles when selecting and combining colours
Emotional Impact	• The choice of colours in the chromatic composition can evoke specific emotional responses. This aligns with the psychology of colour, where certain colours are associated with specific emotions. For example, warm colours like red and orange might convey energy or passion, while cool colours like blue and green may evoke calmness or tranquillity
Cultural and Symbolic Associations	• The generated colours may carry cultural or symbolic associations. Different cultures attribute various meanings to colours, and the AI may inadvertently reflect these associations in the chromatic composition. Additionally, certain colours may have universal symbolism, influencing the overall perception of the composition
Contrast and Harmony	• The AI may consider principles of contrast and harmony when generating a chromatic composition. These principles, rooted in colour theory, involve balancing and juxtaposing colours to create visually appealing or dynamic designs
Aesthetic Preferences	• The output may reflect aesthetic preferences based on the psychology of individual or collective taste. Certain colour combinations may be preferred or perceived as more aesthetically pleasing, depending on cultural and personal factors
Colour Symbolism in Context	• The AI might consider the context of the prompt and generate colours that symbolize or represent specific concepts mentioned in the prompt. This relates to the symbolic interpretation of colours in the psychology of colour

(continued)

Table 4. (*continued*)

Accessibility Considerations	• The AI may be programmed to consider accessibility standards, ensuring that the chromatic composition is suitable for a broad audience. This includes considering colour contrast for readability and considering colour choices for users with visual impairments
Temporal and Trend Influences:	• The choice of colours may reflect temporal influences and design trends. The AI might be trained on data that captures current colour preferences and trends, influencing the chromatic composition to align with contemporary aesthetics
While AI can generate chromatic compositions based on input, it's important to note that the resulting colour choices may not always have a deep understanding of cultural nuances or specific emotional contexts. Interpretation and refinement by human designers are often necessary to ensure that the generated colours effectively convey the intended meaning and emotional impact in line with the theory and psychology of colour	

highlights the potential of AI in capturing cultural colour nuances and signifies an area for further research and development.

After the experience that relates colour with a cultural context, the following experience aims to understand the application of colour theory in an abstract composition.

Abstract compositions feature less saturated colours and a predominance of orange and blue tones. However, the image related to a chromatic composition for colour-blind people does not meet the requirements of the concept. The predominant colours are not safe, and furthermore, the colours used are poorly differentiated in terms of chroma and brightness (Figs. 5 and 6).

The experiment revealed the predominance of red, orange, and blue tints, while colours like purple, green, and yellow did not have significant representation. It was also observed that the word "colour" in the prompt was more effective than the expression "chromatic composition". The results demonstrated an understanding of warm and cold colours, but the same did not occur with concepts such as monochromatic (the interpretation was an achromatic image), and concepts such as complementary or analogous colours raised some questions. Furthermore, in an organized sequence of generated images, certain colours and hues predominated, as evidenced by the colour palettes and their respective identification in RGB (Fig. 7).

Another objective of the experiment was to understand how artificial intelligence communicates the identity of an object through colour and highlights it in relation to the background. Even in the image produced from the prompt "colour as an information vehicle for square shapes," it is possible to discern some shapes with different colours. Despite the predominance of red and blue colour tints, this image presents a higher percentage of green colour than the others before. However, when introducing the prompt "colour as an information vehicle between background and foreground," the result is not clear.

Table 5. Question: What is the relationship between the chromatic composition generated by AI and a chromatic composition made without this technology?

The relationship between a chromatic composition generated by AI and one created without technology involves differences in the creative process, intent, and the level of human input. Here are some key aspects of this relationship:	
Creative Process	• Chromatic compositions created with and without AI involve different creative processes. When using AI, the generation is often algorithmic, with the model making choices based on patterns learned from training data. In contrast, human-made compositions may involve a more intuitive, subjective, and experiential creative process
Algorithmic vs. Human Intuition	• AI-generated compositions rely on algorithms and statistical patterns learned from data. They lack the intuition, personal experiences, and subjective decision-making that human creators bring to their work. Human-made compositions often incorporate a deeper level of emotional and contextual understanding
Intent and Conceptualization	• Human-made compositions are usually driven by specific intent, conceptualization, and artistic vision. The artist has a conscious understanding of the meaning, message, or emotion they want to convey through the chosen colours. AI, on the other hand, may lack a deep understanding of the conceptualization behind the composition
Flexibility and Adaptability	• Humans can adapt their creative process dynamically, responding to personal inspiration, emotions, and real-time considerations. AI, while capable of generating compositions, may lack the same level of adaptability and flexibility in responding to nuanced or unforeseen factors
Subjectivity and Artistic Expression	• Human-made compositions often reflect the subjective and unique artistic expression of the creator. The artist's style, preferences, and individuality are embedded in the work. AI, while capable of mimicking certain styles, may lack the same level of subjective, personal touch
Contextual Understanding	• Humans bring contextual understanding, cultural awareness, and symbolic significance to their colour choices based on their experiences and knowledge. AI may generate colours based on statistical associations without a deep understanding of the contextual nuances

(*continued*)

Table 5. (*continued*)

Iterative Process and Refinement	• Human designers often engage in an iterative process, refining their compositions based on feedback, personal reflection, and evolving ideas. AI, while capable of generating outputs, may not actively engage in an iterative refinement process without human intervention
Emotional and Narrative Depth	• Human-made compositions may carry deeper emotional and narrative depth as they often draw from personal experiences, storytelling, and cultural references. AI-generated compositions may lack the same level of emotional depth and narrative storytelling
Real-time Adaptation	• Human creators can adapt their compositions in real-time, responding to immediate inspiration or changes in the creative direction. AI, once trained, operates within the constraints of its programming and training data
In summary, while AI can generate chromatic compositions efficiently and provide creative outputs, the relationship with compositions made without technology highlights the distinctions between algorithmic generation and the nuanced, subjective, and emotionally rich nature of human creativity. The most impactful and meaningful results often emerge when AI is used as a tool to augment human creativity, allowing for a harmonious blend of technology and artistic intuition	

Fig. 1. Stable Diffusion generated images with the prompts: China, wedding, bride, wedding dress and Chinese bride, wedding dress.

The final experiment aimed to understand how technology interprets the names of colours to attribute a mood to the generated image. How can artificial intelligence interpret written expressions such as "feeling blue," "green with envy," or "red with

Fig. 2. Stable Diffusion generated images with the prompts: China, traditional wedding, bride, wedding dress and Chinese bride, wedding dress, good luck, colour.

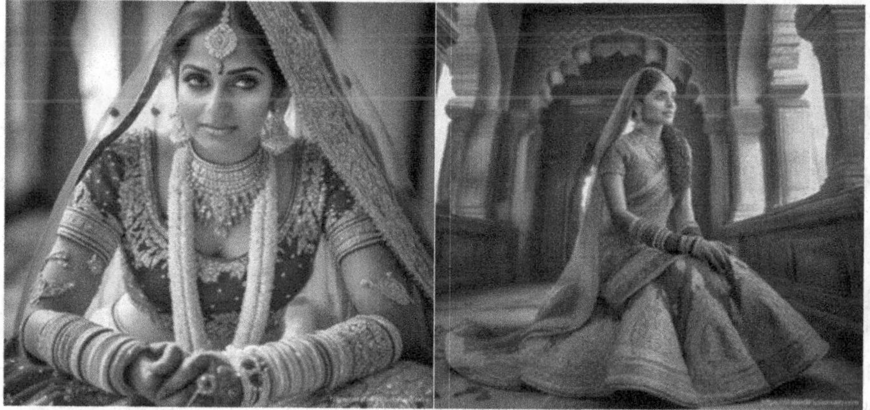

Fig. 3. Stable Diffusion generated images with the prompts: Indian bride, wedding dress and India, wedding, bride, wedding dress.

anger," and how does it translate them into a chromatic palette? The experiment includes two generated images, both with the same prompt but in different styles: abstract and photographic (Fig. 8 and 9).

The images primarily feature the blue colour as their main attribute. Despite depicting an apprehensive face, the colour blue emerges as the chromatic feature or identity of the image. While the intention was to attribute a certain mood to the character represented by the name of the colour, it was not necessary for the colour blue to dominate the image. In the example of the photograph-style image, the presence of blue and the insertion of nature as a background contradict the mood of the girl as well as the expected interpretation of the written expression.

Fig. 4. Stable Diffusion generated images with the prompts: mourning woman and India, mourning woman.

Fig. 5. Stable Diffusion generated images with the prompts: chromatic composition, complementary colours, Fibonacci sequence, organic forms | monochromatic composition, Fibonacci sequence, organic forms. Colour identification and respective RGB code.

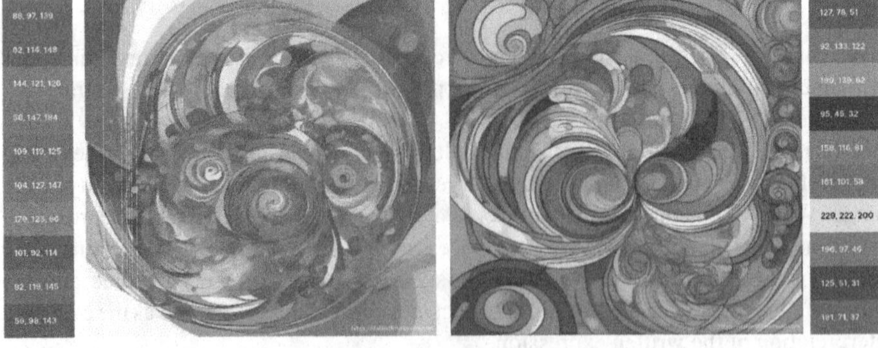

Fig. 6. Stable Diffusion generated images with the prompts: cold colours, Fibonacci sequence, organic forms and warm colours, Fibonacci sequence, organic forms. Colour identification and respective RGB code.

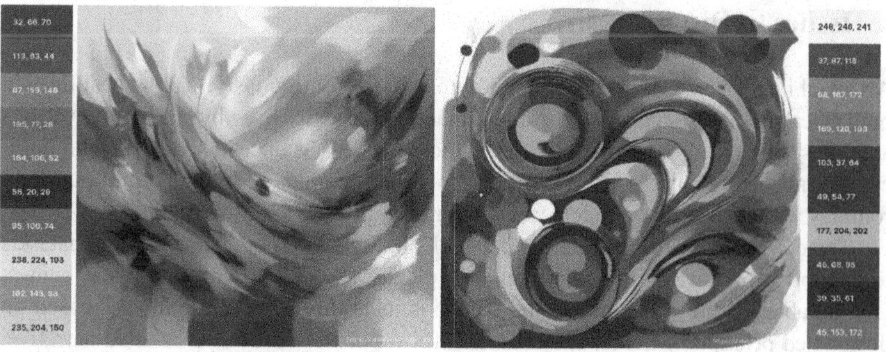

Fig. 7. Stable Diffusion generated images with the prompts: warm analogous colours | cold analogous colours. Colour identification and respective RGB code.

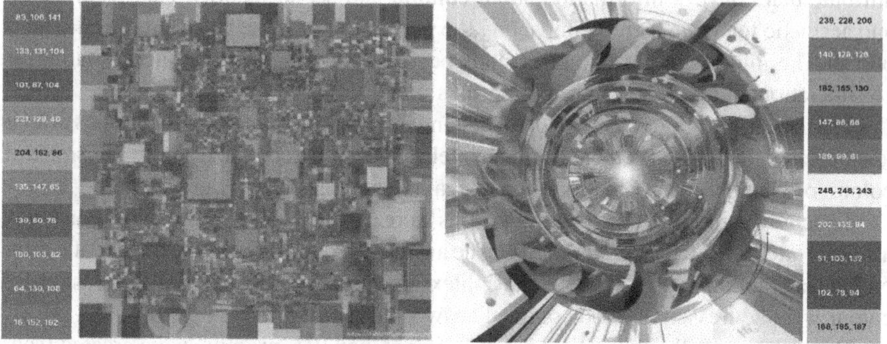

Fig. 8. Stable Diffusion generated images with the prompts: colour as information vehicle of square shapes | colour as information vehicle between background and foreground. Colour identification and respective RGB code.

Fig. 9. Stable Diffusion generated images with the prompt: teenager feeling blue, with abstract and photo styles.

6 Issues to Discuss

Artificial intelligence has become a ubiquitous term, continuously making headlines in both scientific and social contexts, and impacting our daily lives by facilitating various activities, often without our explicit awareness of its assistance. The latest technological advancements have been so profound that they seamlessly integrate into our daily routines without warning, underscoring their ubiquity and significance.

The concept of artificial intelligence seeks to merge computer science and datasets to support problem-solving in a manner typically associated with intelligent beings. One notable feature of artificial intelligence is its ability to generate images based on designated prompts, whether they consist of a set of keywords or a detailed narrative. These images are created using both graphical and alphanumeric information available on the internet.

Regardless of the context of the generated image, colour emerges as a significant attribute that conveys information about cultural and social identity, emotional states, and aesthetic features, thereby impacting the perception of those who observe and interpret it. The importance of colour extends beyond its aesthetic value, necessitating its consideration and recognition across various dimensions.

The objective of the article is to understand how artificial intelligence applies colour to generated images, whether artificial intelligence can recognize the dimensions of colour, or whether its application is once again a mere aesthetic exercise.

To achieve this objective, some questions were asked to ChatGPT to understand how artificial intelligence interprets colours. The answers given validated the impact of colour on the way human beings perceive the context in which they operate. All dimensions of colour were addressed in the theoretical answers given.

To complement the theoretical answers from ChatGPT, prompts were created (sentences intended to establish a relationship between colour and cultural context, colour theory, and human mood) to generate images in Stable Diffusion. Depending on the prompt, the images were then analysed.

However, the generated images did not address the subject of colour with the same assertiveness as the theoretical answers. This discrepancy can be attributed to the construction of the sentences, which were intentionally focused on colour rather than graphic composition, and the limitations of the free version of Stable Diffusion, which does not offer many options.

These two factors constitute the limitation of the experience, and further tests with more developed sentences and other options in terms of image generation would be necessary. However, despite the identified limitations, the results obtained justify continued research into how artificial intelligence applies colour to the images it generates—whether it can effectively communicate all its dimensions through colour or whether it primarily focuses on its aesthetic dimension.

Perhaps this is the gap that requires human creative intervention and justifies human and machine collaboration.

Acknowledgments. This work was support by FCT - Fundação para a Ciência e Tecnologia, I.P. by project reference UIDB/04026/2020 and DOI identifier 10.54499/UIDB/04026/2020 (https://doi.org/10.54499/UIDB/04026/2020) and the Strategic Project with the references UIDB704008/2020 and UIDP/04008/2020.

Disclosure of Interests. The author has no competing interests to declare that are relevant to the content of this article.

References

IBM, Artificial Intelligence. https://www.ibm.com/topics/artificial-intelligence. Accessed 7 Feb 2024

Oxford University Press, Artificial Intelligence. https://www.oxfordreference.com/display/10.1093/oi/authority.20110803095426960. Accessed 7 Feb 2024

Encyclopaedia Britannica, Artificial intelligence (AI). https://www.britannica.com/technology/artificial-intelligence. Accessed 7 Feb 2024

Coursera, What Is Artificial Intelligence? Definition, Uses, and Types. https://www.coursera.org/articles/what-is-artificial-intelligence. Accessed 7 Feb 2024

European Parliament, what is artificial intelligence and how is it used? https://www.europarl.europa.eu/topics/en/article/20200827STO85804/what-is-artificial-intelligence-and-how-is-it-used. Accessed 7 Feb 2024

Art Education & Leadership Academy, Artificial Intelligence: How AI is Changing Art. AELA School. https://aelaschool.com/en/art/artificial-intelligence-art-changes/#:~:text=AI%20has%20had%20a%20huge,authorship%20and%20authenticity%20in%20art. Accessed 7 Feb 2024

Yale Daily News, What AI Art Means for Society, According to Yale Experts. Yale Daily News. https://yaledailynews.com/blog/2023/01/23/what-ai-art-means-for-society-according-to-yale-experts/. Accessed 7 Feb 2024

Hyseni, V.: Artificial intelligence, ethics, and social responsibility. https://pecb.com/article/artificial-intelligence-ethics-and-social-responsibility. Accessed 7 Feb 2024

Gomes, C.: ETHIC and AESTHETIC: the homo-informatics paradigm. In: Rogerson, S., Alvarez, I., Lopes, A. (eds.) Proceedings of ETHICOMP 2002, pp. 781–797 (2002)

Fuzzy Math, Embracing AI in Design: How Designers and AI Can Collaborate. https://fuzzymath.com/blog/embracing-ai-in-design-how-designers-and-ai-can-collaborate/. Accessed 7 Feb 2024

Buether, A.: The function of colour – an introduction to colour theory and a definition of terms. Colour, München: DETAIL, pp. 7–20 (2014)

Noury, L.: Symbolique des couleurs – art, design and architecture. Les Editions du Palais (2020)

Ellwood, M.: How colours affect the way you think. https://www.bbc.com/future/article/20220713-the-hidden-meaning-of-your-favourite-colour. Accessed 7 Feb 2024

Jonauskaite, D., Mohr, C., et al.: Universal patterns in colour-emotion associations are further shaped by linguistic and geographic proximity. Psychol. Sci. **31**, 1245–1260 (2020)

Caramelo Gomes, C.: Colour? What Colour? A difficult understanding between urban environment' professionals and users. In: Karwowski, W., Ahram, T., Milicevic, M., Etinger, D., Zubrinic, K. (eds.) Human Systems Engineering and Design (IHSED 2023): Future Trends and Applications, pp. 178–186 (2023)

Mahnke, F.: Colour, Environment, and Human Response: An Interdisciplinary Understanding of Colour and Its Use as a Beneficial Element in the Design of the Architectural Environment. Wiley (1996)

Developing an Intermediate Framework for Enhancing Comic Creation Through Generative AI

Wenjuan Chen, Jingke Li, Congyun Tang, and Guoyu Sun(✉)

School of Animation and Digital Arts, Communication University of China, Beijing, China
gysun@cuc.edu.cn

Abstract. This paper endeavors to explore the challenges and opportunities arising in the collaborative creation of comics involving cartoonists and Generative Artificial Intelligence (GAI), specifically the AI Image Generator, such as stable diffusion. Presently, AI Image Generators heavily rely on text prompts and reference images. However, these elements lack direct alignment with the story scripts and sketches of cartoonists. Consequently, cartoonists are required to gain a substantial understanding of AI generation, leading to extensive communication between cartoonists and AI engineers. To comprehensively understand and analyze the current role of AI in comic creation, we conducted a focus group discussion involving both cartoonists and AI engineers. Subsequently, we provide detailed insights into the design of an upcoming comic generation workshop scheduled for the next two weeks. Expanding upon the aforementioned research, we suggest design elements for the intermediate layer that bridges comic creation and AI generation. To validate these design elements, the paper utilizes the AI comic "MBTI: i and e personalities" as a case study. Our conclusion underscores that establishing an intermediate layer between comic creation and AI generation, coupled with the effective design of corresponding elements, can significantly enhance the control and precision of AI comic image generation.

Keywords: Collaborative Creation · Generative AI · Intermediate Bridge · Interactive Design Elements · AI Image Generator

1 Introduction

The emergence of Generative Artificial Intelligence (GAI) has brought about a revolution in content creation, spanning various forms such as images, codes, music, text, and videos. Recent strides in text-to-image diffusion models, in particular, have substantially transformed our approach to image creation, often surpassing human capabilities in diverse aspects. These AI tools empower users to modify and enhance images with new elements based on provided prompts, streamlining image editing without the need for advanced skills or extensive knowledge. Moreover, Graphic Content AI can autonomously generate images tailored to specific requirements, facilitating the rapid creation of posters or logos in desired formats. The open-source release of Stable Diffusion has given rise to numerous derivative models, renowned for their reduced computational demands and ease of customization (Rombach et al., 2022).

M. Kurosu and A. Hashizume (Eds.): HCII 2024, LNCS 14688, pp. 292–306, 2024.
https://doi.org/10.1007/978-3-031-60449-2_20

Comic strips, boasting a rich history dating back to the late 19th century, have undergone significant evolution. The inaugural comics, exemplified by Richard F. Outcault's "The Yellow Kid" (1895), found publication in newspapers and magazines, eventually establishing themselves as integral components of popular culture. Despite the creative talents and ideas possessed by many cartoonists, the production of complete comics from stories and storyboards remains a time-consuming and labor-intensive process. This creative endeavor, which may extend over several hours for a comic read in mere seconds, involves successive stages such as storyboarding, drafting, line drawing, coloring, and post-production. Each step significantly influences the quality, impact, and style of the final work. The essence of a comic predominantly resides in storyboarding and drafting, constituting a substantial portion of the overall effort. However, the remaining portion often involves repetitive manual tasks, hindering production and imposing constraints on the industry.

In the era of Artificial General Intelligence (AGI), a pivotal question emerges: how can we leverage the strengths of cartoonists and harness the mass-production capabilities of AGI to establish an efficient workflow for comic generation? The primary AI Image Generator utilizes text-to-image methods, presenting a significant deviation from the initial stages of comic creation, namely storyboards and drafts, thereby posing a challenge for direct correspondence. Our research is focused on the development of an intermediate layer between cartoonists and AGI, aiming to enhance the efficiency of comic creation and infuse uniqueness into AI-generated comics. Key inquiries guiding our investigation include: 1) What is the impact of the degree of freedom granted by cartoonists to AI on image generation? 2) Apart from storyline, storyboards and drafts, what additional information can be provided to the AI generator to optimize the final output? 3) How can we deconstruct image of comics from an AI generation perspective?

Following two rounds of focus group discussions and a two-week workshop, we conducted continuous interviews with cartoonists and AI engineers, refining their collaborative processes. This iterative approach resulted in the establishment of a system where human cartoonists and AI tools synergistically amplify each other's strengths. The collaborative intermediate layer, along with its design elements, is depicted in Fig. 1. Through the process of collaborative research, we have explored new possibilities in comic creation with an open and inclusive approach. It includes both human-machine co-creation and cross-border collaboration between artists and engineers.

Our research contributes by: 1) Introducing parameters to regulate the degree of freedom in AI-generated comic sketches, providing cartoonists with the ability to intentionally strike a balance between the creativity of AI and the precision required in image generation. 2) Enabling additional information, such as reference images and grid-based image content, to be supplied to the AI image generator by cartoonists. This inclusion enhances the accuracy of AI-generated images. 3) We propose a separation between comic images and symbols in the creative process. AI is tasked with generating comic images, while cartoonists take charge of adding comic symbols in the final stages. This division of labor streamlines the workflow, allowing AI to focus on visual elements while cartoonists contribute unique symbols, enhancing the overall quality and creativity of the final comic.

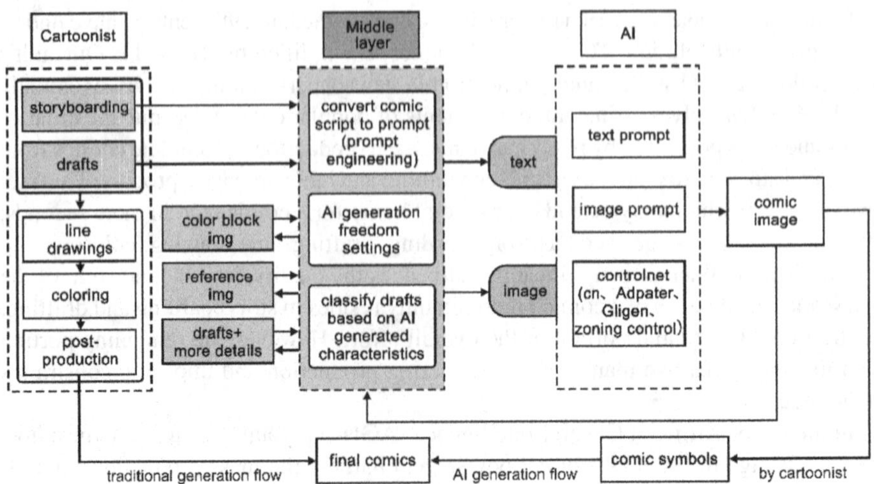

Fig. 1. AI comic generation workflow

2 Literature Review

The integration of Artificial Intelligence (AI) in the field of comic creation represents a burgeoning area of research and application, redefining the traditional processes and artistic expressions in comic art. This literature review examines the current state of AI comic generation, its evolution, technological advancements, and its implications for artists and the industry.

Throughout the history of the development of artificial intelligence technology, ChatGPT, along with other generative AI models such as DALL-E-2 and Codex, has brought about a revolution in artistic creation in fields such as graphic arts, poetry, and novels. Through the integration of research and creative practice in the arts, AI-related technologies are primarily applied in two main areas: understanding art using AI and generating AI art. Cetinic, E., & She, J. (2022) [1] reviewed two comprehensive areas of AI and visual art: AI used for art analysis and digital curation (using AI to understand art) and AI used for generating novel artworks (creating AI art). In the field of comic art, the application of AI technology has gradually shifted from understanding and recognizing comic content and storylines to generating comic panels from storyboards and character dialogues, as well as transforming sketches into finished comic illustrations.

Recent advancements in AI have led to the development of sophisticated models capable of generating comic strips and graphic narratives. Chen, J., et al. (2019) [2] focused on frame recognition in comic understanding and computation. They used NLP methods to analyze how AI understands the content of Japanese and English comics through sentiment analysis algorithms. Tsai, S. (2018) [3] explored the application of computer intelligence in comic storylines and character design, They developed an "intelligent comic character storyline dialogue recommendation system" that automatically generates corresponding comic dialogues based on comparing basic character dialogues with a "comic character personality database" according to the plot. Daiku, Y., et al.

(2018) [4] proposed a system for describing comic stories that analyzes narrative structures based on the genre of the comic story using CNN convolutional neural networks. Jin, Z., & Song, Z. (2023) [5] presented a new method for comic creation by combining ChatGPT and Stable Diffusion in practical application cases. They evaluated the generation effects of both text and images. With the use of AIGC, it is possible to generate comics with interesting storylines while preserving the artist's artistic style.

The collaboration between human artists and AI in comic creation is a focal point of recent research. AI can recognize and generate realistic images from sketches, playing a role in the comic creation process and assisting human artists in comic illustration. In Poongodi, M. (2023) [6], an unsupervised generative adversarial network is trained to generate comic images that are very similar to neighboring images from sketches. The study also identified some challenges, such as subpar performance when dealing with batch images and the difficulty of generating desired background images. Gao, R., & Jie, L. (2023) [7] and Golyadkin, M., & Makarov, I. (2023) [8] focused on comic coloring models based on the Pix2Pix infrastructure and adversarial generative networks, providing solutions for coloring black-and-white comics by human artists.

The impact of AI on the comic industry and artists has been profound. Bedi, K. (2023) [9] investigated AI comics as a positive medium for media creation and their application in design education. Artificial intelligence (AI), similar to traditional literacies like digital literacy, should be regarded as a new type of literacy skill to cope with this intelligent new era. By utilizing AI technology in creative activities related to comic books, a bridge can be built between the real and virtual worlds, while also fostering students' creative design thinking. AI-generated comics can reduce the production time and costs associated with traditional comics, making comic creation more accessible. However, the relationship between humans and machines in AI comic creation, the novelty of AI art, and issues related to copyright and ethics also need to be considered [1].

3 A Design Exploration of Intermediate Framework

In our research, we executed a series of qualitative studies to address our research questions, primarily employing two rounds of focus group discussions and a two-week workshop dedicated to AI comic creation.

Initially, a focus group was assembled, comprising three cartoonists, with the aim of gaining profound insights into the existing challenges within comic creation, the complexities associated with AI-generated comics, and potential points for AI intervention in the comic creation process. This comprehensive discussion extended over a total duration of four hours. The focus group also engaged in strategic deliberations for the subsequent AI comic generation workshop.

Subsequently, a two-week workshop was conducted where AI engineers generated AI comics based on the strategies developed in the preceding workshop. The primary emphasis was on addressing challenges encountered during the transition of sketches and storyboards from the traditional comic creation process to AI-based methods.

Finally, a follow-up round of focus group discussions took place, this time involving the initial three cartoonists and two AI engineers who actively participated in the workshop. The focal point of these discussions was to delve into the issues raised by both cartoonists and AI engineers during the workshop and collaboratively seek viable solutions.

3.1 First Round of Focus Group Discussion

Participants. The focus group comprised three cartoonists and two researchers, each exhibiting a distinct style of creation and varying familiarity with different AI generation technologies. One cartoonist, recognized for a strong personal style, was unfamiliar with AI technology and somewhat skeptical of its role in comics. The other two, primarily working in Japanese cartoon styles, had different levels of AI interaction; one had experimented with AI comic generation using Midjourney before the interview, while the other was acquainted with Stable Diffusion's AI capabilities but had not yet applied them in comic creation. The focus group discussion was conducted via Tencent Meeting.

Process. The focus group's interview primarily utilized questions and communication, addressing the following:

Question 1: Which part of the comic creation process best showcases human creativity? Which part is the most time-consuming?

Question 2: What are the current issues with AI-generated comics?

Question 3: How should the next workshop be designed?

Analysis and Results

Regarding Question 1. The cartoonists emphasized that storytelling is the primary function and purpose of modern comics. The challenge lies in how AI comics can harness generative capabilities while preserving the narrative's essential core. Comics, distinct from other two-dimensional art forms, involve a process akin to film directing, starting with storyboarding and progressing to redrawing the comic based on initial sketches. Storyboarding, a fundamental early-stage task, involves page allocation and framing within each page, linking contemporary and traditional comic styles closely.

A page of comics, though consumed in seconds, undergoes a creation cycle lasting nearly 16 h, encompassing storyboarding, drafting, line drawing, coloring, and post-production. While each step impacts the work's quality, effect, and style, the true essence of the work lies predominantly in the storyboarding and drafting phases, constituting only 30% of the total work. This underscores that a cartoonist's inspiration and enthusiasm are significantly harnessed during one-third of the working time, only to be gradually diminished by tedious manual labor in the remaining two-thirds. This 70% of manual labor impedes the production cycle, creating a productivity trap for creators, readers, and the comic market.

Cartoonists also noted that certain visual details in comic creation, such as complex architectural backgrounds, scene depictions, character costumes, and action details, are time-consuming but often overlooked by readers. This constraint inhibits cartoonists from dedicating ample time to capturing essential visual details, such as character expressions, composition, and narrative elements. Leveraging AI's generative capabilities while allowing cartoonists to focus on creativity seems a promising approach.

Regarding Question 2. Currently, AI-generated comics offer more possibilities for amateurs but fall short in professional comic production. The content produced by AI tends to be diffuse and random, lacking consistency in image content, style, and details required for professional comics.

Regarding Question 3. In our discussions, the next phase of the workshop will center on AI's intervention in comics. The initial creative stage will be entrusted to cartoonists, with AI's generative capabilities introduced in the mid-stage. The main focus will be on how AI engineers can utilize preliminary works (sketches and storyboard scripts) submitted by cartoonists to achieve consistency in comic style, detail handling, and narrative elements.

3.2 Two-Week AI Comic Generation Workshop

Participants. The workshop included two researchers, two AI engineers, and two cartoonists assisting in the process.

Process. During this phase, our primary focus was to observe how AI engineers generated comic visuals based on the cartoonists' storyboards. We closely monitored the quality of the generated images and the challenges encountered throughout the process. The assigned task for the two cartoonists involved designing a four-page comic titled "MBTI: i and e personalities". The cartoonists undertook responsibilities for character settings, script creation, and storyboarding. Subsequently, the AI engineers were tasked with generating visuals for the first page using their AI techniques. For key characters, the engineers employed a fine-tuned diffusion model named 'LoRA' to stabilize character imagery and train the overall style of the images (see Fig. 4).

In the process of collaborating on creating comics, we found that AI engineers use parameters such as prompts, fine-tuning diffusion models, images, and conditional controls to generate comic images. However, cartoonists primarily use sketches and scripts. There is a need for setting the degree of freedom in between and for comic artists to provide necessary assistance to guide AI comic creation. The following issues and discussions are all focused on this intermediate layer (Figs. 2 and 3).

Page One

(Morning, outside the house)
"It's too late! It's going to be late!" Hu Xiaodie rushed out of the house in a hurry, holding a bowl of rice noodles."Being late on the first day of school, that's too bad! It'll leave a bad impression on the new classmates, wuwu..." Hu Xiaodie felt very guilty because she overslept. She flashed tears in her eyes, ate rice noodles with all her might, and ran towards the school.
At the corner at the end of the road, a black figure suddenly appeared.

Page Two

"Oh no! It's going to crash!!!" Hu Xiaodie stopped immediately, but her body fell forward due to inertia. Plop! Hu Xiaodie fell down, and the bowl of rice noodles in her hand fell onto her head.
"I'm sorry, are you okay?" (Small text: Do you want some rice noodles?) Hu Xiaodie rubbed her eyes, and although she had a huge fall, she still subconsciously cared about others first.
Standing in front of her was a tall and powerful adult man, eyebrows arched into a very weird arc, an evil smile on his face, and disgusting cockroach-like tentacles on his head. (entp)
"Oh my God! I'm so sorry. Such a beautiful lady, she was injured because of me." The male struck a Broadway burlesque pose, pretending to be a gentleman by removing the rice noodles from Hu's head and attempting to help her up, but his pompous movements scared Hu Xiaodie away."I'm sorry! I have something urgent to do! Thank you!" Hu Xiaodie trembled and rushed to the school quickly.

Page Three

Hu Xiaodie sat nervously in her seat, surrounded by a lot of noise."What a shock, luckily I wasn't late. But all these unlucky things happened on the first day of school, the alarm clock broke, I met a weirdo on the road, andI don't know anyone in the class. .... Will high school life go smoothly after this? ... " Thinking about it, Hu Xiaodie was in a low mood again.Kucha! The classroom door was opened by a pair of strong hands, and the classroom instantly quieted downHu Xiaodie was stunned, she couldn't believe her eyes.Standing at the doorway was actually the weirdo she had met by chance on the road! Only to see this man walking idly up to the podium, the tentacles (close-up) on his head trembling in rhythm with his steps. The students showed shocked expressions, their eyes following the tentacles on his head as they moved.

Page Four

"From today, I'm your homeroom teacher! My name is..." in a flash, the man picked up the chalk on the lecture table as quick as a flash, his suit was blown up by a strong air current, and with the chalk in his hand, he wrote down a few big words on the blackboard - Guzhe Zhanglang,the whole process was completed in one go."Everyone here, let's get along together in the future!"Saying that, his mouth show ed his trademark evil smile.

Fig. 2. Character design and storyline of "MBTI: i and e personalities"

Fig. 3. Four-page comic storyboard of "MBTI: i and e personalities"

Fig. 4. (a) Character LoRA: i; (b) character LoRA: e

Analysis and Results (The AI Engineers). Following the workshop, the AI engineers reported encountering several challenges.

Issue 1- Difficulty with Comic Symbols. Engineers faced challenges processing comic symbols, such as traditional atmospheric lines, special effects lines, light and shadow lines, and comic frames in the sketches. Clarity was often needed before generation and replicating these symbols in the generated images posed difficulties.

Issue 2- Use of Sketches. The primary utility of sketches by AI engineers was for character poses and composition.

Issue 3- Understanding and Translating Scripts. A substantial gap existed between understanding the script created by cartoonists and converting it into AI generation prompts. Scripts, focused on storytelling, contrasted with AI image generation's emphasis on describing the current scene.

Issue 4- Handling Non-Standard Actions. Directly referencing sketches for unconventional actions, such as characters with items on their heads or exaggerated poses, presented challenges.

Issue 5- Complex Scenes. Engineers dedicated considerable time to researching generation methods, particularly for complex scenes involving intricate backgrounds, multiple characters, and unique interactions between characters and objects.

Analysis and Results (The Cartoonists). Upon reviewing the generated images, the cartoonists identified several issues.

Issue 1- Drafting Limitations. In the drafting phase, cartoonists tended to prioritize storyboarding, potentially neglecting detailed design within frames. The emphasis on completeness in sketching may lead AI engineers to overemphasize storyboards, restricting AI's creative freedom.

Issue 2- AI's Role in Integration. Cartoonist Jiawen expressed that AI seemed to play a role in integrating processes like finding reference images, extracting elements from these images, integrating references, and creating the desired background. This shift from the traditional direct involvement of cartoonists now involves assessing whether the outcome aligns with expectations.

3.3 Second Round of Focus Group Discussion

Participants. The discussion involved two researchers, two AI engineers, and four cartoonists.

Process. The focus of this round of discussion was to analyze and address the issues raised by the engineers and cartoonists in the previous phase.

Analysis and Results

Regarding Engineers' Issue 1. One cartoonist proposed a perspective on viewing comics as a blend of images and symbols, recognizing the risk of oversimplifying the medium. Images encompass all visible forms created by dots, lines, and shapes representing real-life or fantasy elements. In contrast, comic symbols, exclusive to the medium, include various elements like dialogue bubbles, speed lines, explosions, dots, and emotional lines. In the context of comic generation, it was suggested that AI could handle the creation of concrete images, leaving the addition of abstract comic symbols to the team at a later stage.

Regarding Issue 2 and the Cartoonist's Issue 1. Addressing the cartoonist's concerns about AI's creative freedom, a proposed solution involves allowing AI to generate images with high creative freedom based mainly on prompt text. For images intended to follow the sketch's composition but not strictly adhere to its content, the consideration of block color images, given Stable Diffusion's reliance on color blocks, was suggested. In cases where strict adherence to sketches is desired, further refinement of the sketches may be necessary.

Regarding Issue 3. to address discrepancies between AI engineers' understanding of scripts and cartoonists' intentions, it is recommended that cartoonists provide simple descriptions of scenes based on sketches. These descriptions can serve as a bridge between the script and prompts and later be transformed into direct prompts through prompt engineering research.

Regarding Issue 4. For the challenge of generating exaggerated expressions, behaviors, and actions in comic sketches, it was acknowledged that AI struggles with unconventional actions. A suggested approach is using a base image, where relevant images can be found online or constructed in Photoshop as a reference.

Regarding Issue 5. Considering AI's drawing characteristics, a proposed solution is to categorize generated images into different types, each with a corresponding workflow.

Leveraging tools like ComfyUI for setting up workflows can efficiently address problems, and strategies applied to similar image types in the future can be adapted based on this categorization.

4 Design Consideration

Drawing upon our five empirical results and insights derived from previous theoretical and empirical studies, we present three key design considerations for incorporating generative AI as an intermediate layer in comic generation. In essence, we posit that a fundamental reevaluation of the mid-term generation phase of comics, as seen through the lens of AI-generated images, is imperative for the seamless integration of AI into the comic creation process. It is apparent that cartoonists and AI engineers frequently approach problems from distinct perspectives, with engineers seeking more explicit instructions while cartoonists require clarity on the method of conveying corresponding instructions.

4.1 Degree of Freedom in Image Creation: Assessing the AI's Creative Autonomy in Early Comic Production

In our workshop, we observed that the conventional process of transitioning from sketches to refined drawings and subsequently to coloring may not be optimal for AI generation. AI demonstrates greater proficiency in creating comprehensive images directly from sketches. During the sketch phase, cartoonists typically employ simple, generalized lines to outline character positions, dynamics, postures, essential details, and emotions. While these sketches may be rough, they convey expressive elements. Subsequently, cartoonists refine their creations between the sketch and line art stages, adjusting the extent of this creative refinement based on the image's requirements.

Upon completing the overall sketch design, cartoonists can select specific annotations to denote the desired degree of freedom for AI generation. The settings for the intermediate layer's freedom degree can be tailored accordingly, enabling greater creative latitude for AI. For instance, sketches may only necessitate large color blocks and prompts for control. Alternatively, for more precise control by the cartoonist, the sketch can undergo slight refinement and be accompanied by detailed prompt words for generation.

4.2 Facilitating Enhanced Information Input for AI Image Generation

Our research contributes significantly by empowering cartoonists to provide supplementary information, including reference images and grid-based image content, to the AI image generator. This inclusive approach augments the precision of AI-generated images by furnishing essential context and guidance.

Comic storyboards, primarily crafted for storytelling, serve as the foundation for cartoonists. They interpret the storyboard comprehensively before translating it into sketches. Presently, our AI generation processes individual image frames, lacking a holistic perspective of the entire series. Challenges arise in generating images with incomplete objects that may unfold later in the story. To address this, cartoonists are encouraged to offer simple scene descriptions based on sketches, serving as a connective bridge between the script and prompts. These descriptions can subsequently undergo transformation into direct prompts through prompt engineering research.

In the iterative process involving reference images and hand-drawn sketches, followed by partial redrawing with AI, methods for obtaining object reference images encompass web searches and tools like MJ. Leveraging Photoshop, reference images seamlessly integrate into sketches or generated images, stabilizing object depiction. The sketching of objects, inclusive of color and form using tools like Photoshop or Procreate, precedes subsequent partial redrawing that introduces intricate details to hand-drawn objects. This process vividly demonstrates the effectiveness of human initiative in swiftly achieving desired outcomes.

Furthermore, AI, while proficient in understanding conventional actions, grapples with unconventional scenarios due to limited exposure during training. For example, comprehending a scene where a bowl is placed on someone's head poses a challenge for AI. The provision of reference images proves to be an effective means of aiding AI in generating such unconventional scenes.

4.3 Separation of Comic Images and Symbols

We propose a separation between comic images and symbols in the creative process. AI is tasked with generating comic images, while cartoonists take charge of adding comic symbols in the final stages. This division of labor streamlines the workflow, allowing AI to focus on visual elements while cartoonists contribute unique symbols, enhancing the overall quality and creativity of the final comic.

By decoupling the generation and addition of comic images and symbols, we have achieved optimization and improvement in the creative process. Entrusting the task of generating comic images to artificial intelligence has its benefits. It can automatically create characters, backgrounds, and actions based on input text or instructions. However, symbols play an equally important role in comics. Symbols are a core component of the comic language, encompassing emoticons, dynamic symbols, and specific comic elements. Cartoonists possess a unique understanding and creativity when it comes to symbols. They can carefully select and design symbols based on the plot, enhancing the expressiveness and appeal of the comics.

5 Result

In accordance with the design experiences derived from the AI comic image generation discussed earlier, the comic "MBTI: i and e People" was subjected to several strategic modifications. These included annotating the degree of AI's creative freedom, labeling the types of images, adjusting the script, and providing reference images. Below are the final visual outcomes generated by Stable Diffusion (Fig. 5).

Fig. 5. AI comic "MBTI: i and e personalities"

5.1 Setting AI's Degree of Freedom in Image Generation

The adjustment of the level of detail in storyboard images was intricately linked to the designated degree of freedom for AI. In instances with elevated creative freedom, storyboards were streamlined, often reduced to color blocks or predominantly constructed through prompt words.

For instance, the initial draft of the first page's background bestowed upon AI a high degree of freedom, in Fig. 6 below, allowing for flexibility in image generation. Devoid of a specific degree of freedom, AI would strictly adhere to the cartoonist's original setup. However, the cartoonist's conceptualization of background settings was more generalized, lacking intricate details. By granting a higher degree of freedom, AI engineers could generate building images primarily relying on keyword prompts. While this deviated from the original sketch, it perfectly aligned with the cartoonist's vision.

Illustratively, in Fig. 7 below, the cartoonist accentuated the characters' actions and accorded substantial creative freedom to the overall scene. Operating under these settings, the AI engineer produced the image on the right, impressively integrating a background that harmonized seamlessly with the characters. The outcome not only met but pleasantly exceeded the cartoonist's expectations. This exemplifies the successful collaboration wherein AI's creative autonomy, calibrated by the degree of freedom, complemented and enhanced the cartoonist's artistic intent. The level of detail in storyboard images was adjusted based on the assigned degree of freedom. For images with higher freedom, the storyboard was simplified to color blocks or mainly generated through prompt words.

5.2 Enhanced Information Input for Comic "MBTI: i and e People"

Within the AI comic "MBTI: i and e People", cartoonists play a pivotal role in bridging the conceptualization of scenes from the script to the AI prompts. They contribute simple scene descriptions derived from sketches, in Fig. 8 below, acting as a crucial connective link in the creative process. These scene descriptions provide a tangible and interpretable medium that aids in aligning the script's narrative intent with the nuances required for effective AI prompts.

Fig. 6. (a) Draft; (b) Low freedom setting; (c) High freedom setting

1.covered his chest with one hand and unfolded the other
2.presents a confident,self-assured,and extremely powerful demeanor
3.a narcissistic guy
4.the background is gorgeous and abstract (can include some exaggerated flowers, roses,glitter effects ...)

Fig. 7. (a) Color blocks; (b) Image content setting; (c) High freedom setting

As part of a seamless transformation process, these scene descriptions can undergo refinement and precision through prompt engineering research. This metamorphosis allows for the conversion of descriptive scene elements into direct and actionable prompts, facilitating a smoother integration of artistic vision and technological execution. This collaborative approach ensures a harmonious synergy between the creative insights of the cartoonists and the technical capabilities of AI in the dynamic realm of comic creation.

Besides adding descriptions to storyboard scripts, cartoonists can provide reference images for unconventional actions (e.g., non-standard character postures) or scene styles, aiding AI engineers in generation or using these images as control conditions.

For instance: Without reference images, perspective relationships are often strange, see Fig. 9. (a) Setting reference images provides better guidance for AI, see Fig. 9. (b).

5.3 Decoupling Comic Images and Symbols

In the realm of comic creation, cartoonists embellish AI-generated images with a myriad of comic symbols, including dialogue boxes, speed lines, and various effects such as twinkling lights, atmospheric dots, annotated text, and more. The addition of these symbols by the cartoonist takes approximately 10 min, showcasing not only the efficiency but also the overall effectiveness of human-generated symbols compared to those generated by AI.

The following illustration depicts the impact of AI-generated comic images alongside the augmentation introduced by the cartoonist, incorporating various comic symbols onto the image (Fig. 10).

Fig. 8. (a) Storyboard; (b) Color block and content setting

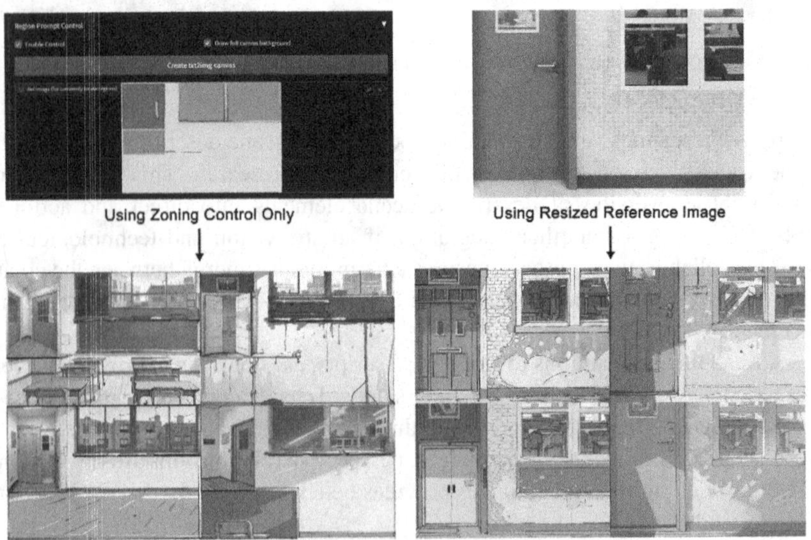

Fig. 9. (a) Without reference image; (b) With reference image

Fig. 10. (a) AI generated comic image (b) Incorporating comic symbols

6 Conclusion

This paper delves into the convergence of generative AI and comic creation, shedding light on the challenges and potentials inherent in this groundbreaking collaboration. Through empirical studies and workshops, our research has culminated in the identification of four pivotal design considerations for seamlessly integrating AI as an intermediate layer in comic generation.

The synergistic alliance between AI and cartoonists emerges as a transformative force, significantly elevating the comic creation process. By judiciously allocating degrees of creative freedom to AI and meticulously annotating sketches, AI becomes a valuable contributor to the early stages of comic creation. Moreover, the translation of comic scripts into AI-understandable prompts and the incorporation of reference images for complex scenes underscore the capacity of AI to support and amplify human creativity.

Looking forward, future research avenues beckon. Enhancing AI's comprehension of comic scripts and visual nuances is paramount, necessitating a nuanced understanding of context-specific elements in comic storytelling. The development of advanced AI models seamlessly integrating into the comic creation workflow, respecting artistic intent while providing creative enhancements, stands out as a crucial next step. The exploration of AI's role in narrative development within comics emerges as a promising frontier. Beyond image generation, envisioning AI's involvement in plot development, character creation, and dialogue construction pushes the boundaries of storytelling in comics.

In conclusion, the integration of generative AI into comic creation is a dynamic and evolving sphere, brimming with vast potential. As we navigate challenges and unveil possibilities, the future of comic art and storytelling emerges as both exciting and promising.

Acknowledgments. The authors like to thank all the comic artists (Wang Baile, Wei Jiawen,Yang Suyi) for their contribution in this paper. This work was supported by National Social Science Fund of China under grant [22BG137].

References

1. Cetinic, E., She, J.: Understanding and creating art with AI: Review and outlook. ACM Trans. Multimedia Comput. Commun. Appli. (TOMM), **18**(2), 1–22 (2022)
2. Chen, J., Iwasaki, R., Mori, N., Okada, M., Ueno, M.: Understanding multilingual four-scene comics with deep learning methods. In: 2019 International Conference on Document Analysis and Recognition Workshops (ICDARW), vol. 1, pp. 32–37. IEEE (September 2019).
3. Tsai, S.: Intelligent comic role plot dialogue recommendation system for comic script creation educational application. In: 2018 1st IEEE International Conference on Knowledge Innovation and Invention (ICKII), pp. 258–261. IEEE (July 2018)
4. Daiku, Y., Iwata, M., Augereau, O., Kise, K.: . Comics story representation system based on genre. In: 2018 13th IAPR International Workshop on Document Analysis Systems (DAS), pp. 257–262. IEEE (April 2018)
5. Jin, Z., Song, Z.: Generating coherent comic with rich story using ChatGPT and Stable Diffusion (2023). arxiv preprint arxiv:2305.11067
6. Poongodi, M., Buvaneswari, N., Bose, S., Maheswaran, N., Vijayalakshmi, S.: Secure translation from sketch to image using an unsupervised generative adversarial network with het for AI based images. In: 2023 International Conference on Research Methodologies in Knowledge Management, Artificial Intelligence and Telecommunication Engineering (RMKMATE), pp. 1–7. IEEE (November 2023)
7. Gao, R., Jie, L.: Complex manga coloring method based on improved Pix2Pix Model. In: 2023 International Conference on Machine Learning and Cybernetics (ICMLC), pp. 582–587. IEEE (July 2023)
8. Golyadkin, M., Makarov, I.: Robust manga page colorization via coloring latent space. IEEE Access (2023)
9. Bedi, K.: AI comics as art: scientific analysis of the multimedia content of AI comics in education. In: 2023 46th MIPRO ICT and Electronics Convention (MIPRO), pp. 750–753. IEEE (May 2023)

A Proposal of AI-Powered HCI System to Enhance Spatial Design Creativity: InSpace

Esra Nur Gündüz[1], Alper Karatoyun[1], Betül Uyan[1](✉), and Halil Erhan[2]

[1] Istanbul Technical University, Istanbul, Turkey
{gunduz21,karatoyun22,uyan16}@itu.edu.tr
[2] Simon Fraser University, Surrey, B.C, Canada
herhan@sfu.ca

Abstract. Creativity is a natural activity of the human mind. Tools, systems and environments can be facilitated to support creativity. This study proposes an InSpace system that inspires the creative process regarding text-based idea representations in the spatial design domain. In addition to customary idea visualization approaches such as mood boards and mind maps, the system is novel and developing through ongoing research regarding human-computer interactions (HCI) powered by artificial intelligence (AI). To propose a system allowing cognitive flexibility and establishing an incremental process in the early stages of the spatial design process, use-case-driven methods are adopted, and graphical user interface (GUI) mockups are produced via Figma. Participants from the spatial design domain test the system. It is evaluated through usability heuristics for user interface (UI) and comparative analysis based on the creativity support index (CSI). InSpace showed better performance in exploration, enjoyment and expressiveness factors of creativity support based on the CSI of participants. Based on these results, InSpace has the potential to support exploration and assist the iterative process in the early stages of spatial design.

Keywords: Creativity Support Environment · Design Thinking · Human-Computer Interaction Powered by Artificial Intelligence

1 Introduction

There needs to be more effectively conveying ambiguous concepts through a single environment in the creative thinking process. This gap requires the utilization of multiple environments that will facilitate the expression and emergence of innovative ideas. To address this requirement, creative users who are designers and design students in this study should employ environments that include diverse tools, such as textual and visual representations, to express and bring to light their thoughts simultaneously without favouring one over the other.

As an ordinary mental process, creative thinking can emerge through deliberate spontaneous and cognitive-emotional patterns [1]. It has an incremental and iterative pattern [2] and can be related to the intentional and cognitive pattern. Applied research

M. Kurosu and A. Hashizume (Eds.): HCII 2024, LNCS 14688, pp. 307–323, 2024.
https://doi.org/10.1007/978-3-031-60449-2_21

conducted [3] on creativity established Creativity Support Tools (CSTs) that highlight the possibility of enhancing human creativity. The deliberate and cognitive pattern of creative thinking occurs in the design domain that employs many computer-aided environments for innovative solutions. The nature of design creativity is described as the capacity to expand their thinking space, which is the designers' interpretations, particularly in the early, preliminary concept generation phases of design thinking [4]. She emphasizes the significance of linking former and latter ideas, going back and forth in thought, meaning convergent and divergent thinking, often aided by drafting via drawing and writing [5]. Drafting as ambiguous and complex (ill-structured) representations also impacts the creative solutions for design problems that are primarily ambiguous and complex, similar to the representations [6]. The indispensable role of representation systems in translating interpretations into tangible solutions throughout design thinking is underlined by research. These representation systems derive outputs called design artifacts (Fig. 1) that enhance creativity as incrementations of the iterative design thinking process [7].

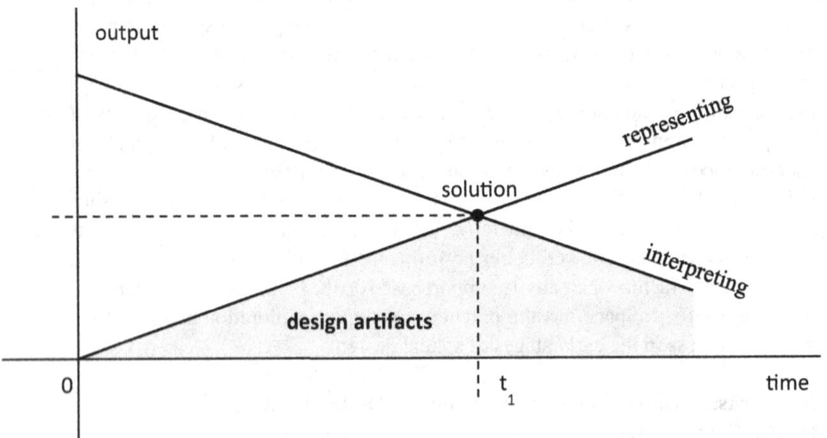

Fig. 1. Design artifacts being derived by representing and interpreting. (Figure by authors)

In this study, the framework of iterative spatial design thinking was established by proposing a representation system (Fig. 2) utilizing HCI and expanding CSTs from tools to a creativity support environment that includes diverse tools such as diagrams, text, images, and models for drafting.

The system was proposed using mixed methods and adopted an object-oriented approach [8]. Indexed knowledge of creativity and CSTs was an input for selective search on spatial design domain that guides the proposal of an HCI system powered by artificial intelligence (AI). There are some specific design support tools if the user would like to create a mind map or mood board for the design process, like Canva [9], Mural [10], and Miro [11]. Those are relatively popular tools for visualizing ideas with diagrams collaboratively. Prompt-based visual content generator tools like Dall-E[12] and Midjourney [13] are also used. However, these AI-supported tools primarily focused on singular image generations with alternatives. The designed support tool stands on

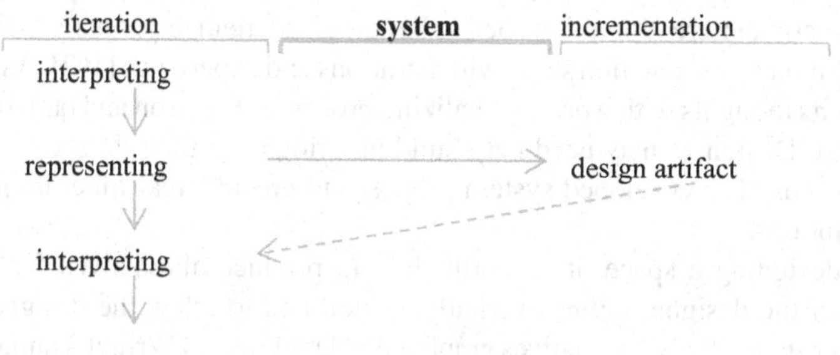

Fig. 2. Position of the proposed system in the iterative design thinking. (Figure by authors)

a synthesis between these existing features and combines their approaches in design processes. InSpace enhances users to work on spatial design domains with an interactive text-to-image order iterative design process for visualizing ideas.

The study provides a holistic approach to spatial design thinking, allowing human and AI collaboration [14] and HCI. Use case modelling [15] was used to define the requirements and functionality of the interactive system that would stimulate creativity. The system was presented as a prototype by creating graphical user interface (GUI) mock-ups to receive feedback from potential users. Collaboration arising from AI-powered HCI was anticipated to support the idea development phase. User experience with the prototype enabled the usability [16] and system testing. The user experience outcomes were revealed through survey questions of CSI established by [17] and discussed by referring to the theoretical and applied studies in the literature. As a result, enhancement in collaboration, enjoyment, exploration, expressiveness, immersion and results worth effort factors was detected.

The study's main goal is to develop a system used by the user (the designer) who designs spaces. A spatial designer can be a level designer, an architect, a decorator, a product designer or an artist who desires to design a game level, a spatial fantasy (or utopia), a film set, an advertisement or an animation. The proposed system creates spaces and atmospheric images from texts and scenarios. The user interface (UI) flow divides the process into three phases to create a simple user experience (UX) while offering the designer an exploratory and iterative process.

Verbal communication is one of our main senses and one of the most substantial ways of communication. Usually, people talk by themselves even while thinking. To describe what other senses detect or imagine, humans tag a descriptive name to define and express their thoughts or flow of events; it is basically how much we can express. While verbal expression has neural processes, the creative design process is built upon expressing verbal and other visual representations.

Designing a space is always challenging when embodying the idea and reflecting inner thoughts of it. The main goal of the designed system is to provide a platform for designers, illustrators, painters, scriptwriters, or curious minds without any specified domain who want to create a spatial design based on verbal descriptions.

Creative content creation might be challenging, as creative people should improve and educate their representation skills with iterations and experience [1, 2]. As the human mind forms its thoughts with words, visualizing processes based on and built upon verbal thinking first. Designers may need help building bridges on their design scenarios and visual equations. The developed system proposes to create a real-time bridge between these two notions.

While designing a space, it is worthwhile to produce alternatives for the spatial proposal that the designer defines verbally/written and to allow the designer to make changes after seeing these alternatives graphically. Drawings of Wright's unbuilt projects can be decoded by accessing graphs in space syntax methodology (Fig. 3). Schemes like space syntax orient a projection for a broad understanding of spatial configuration and social relationships in a particular narrative.

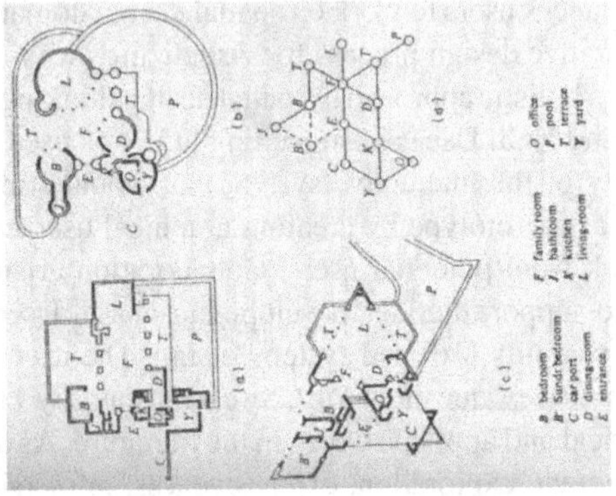

Fig. 3. Three houses by Wright: (a) Life House, 1938; (b) Ralph Jester House, 1938; (c) Vigo Sundt House, 1941; (d) access graph for the three projects. The dotted lines refer to the additional bedroom, B, in the Sundt House [18]

If a designer wants to create a space, since the creative process is based on iteration, each iteration takes effort and source. Ordering events and spaces can be challenging, especially at first; scenarios can be mixed up, and definitions may need to be more explicit. Drawing [19] and collage [20] are the main methods for architects to design imaginary spaces. The process of drawing and collage is sometimes unique and can be hardly iterated, insomuch that it is only meaningful to its designer.

Designers need to visualize their spatial ideas to communicate. In set design, Kubrick uses methods that combine drawing, writing and annotating to recreate a New York Street in the film set located in Hatton Garden, London (Fig. 4).

Designers of game levels use similar sketches to represent their spatial ideas (Fig. 5). As Totten mentions, they "need to understand how to link these spaces together in interesting and meaningful ways." [23].

While the sketches of film sets and game levels are explanatory, they lack exploration. From a technical perspective, molecule designs should have supported import and export among software, especially for game spaces. A spatial design tool feeds novel ideas and gets designers as users thinking outside the box.

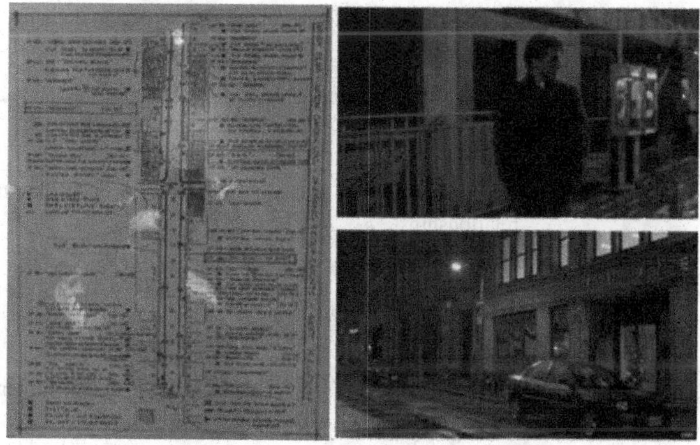

Fig. 4. Instructions by Kubrick. [21, 22]

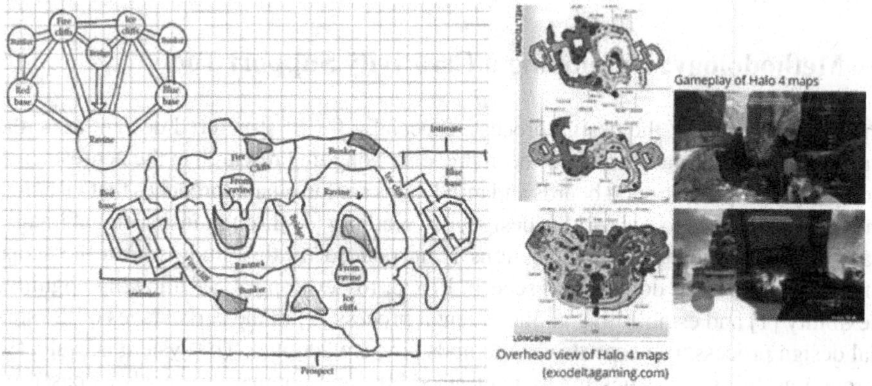

Fig. 5. Molecule design for a game level [23]

Examined scenarios from the spatial design domain, user goals, current methods and gaps that could improve via a creativity support tool (CST) to be designed are summarized in Table 1.

Consequently, multidisciplinary research in neuroscience, design cognition, interaction technologies and spatial design was conducted. The proposal of a novel system for design drafting by using diverse tools aims to investigate the full potential of enhancing creativity in the design domain. The research contributes not only to the field of spatial design but also to a broader understanding of human creativity and its facilitation through AI-powered HCI environments. This research is a foundation for further exploration and development in HCI and AI collaboration within the spatial design domain, benefiting practitioners, researchers, and stakeholders alike. The study is intended to reference other researchers and software developers in future studies as a preliminary study.

Table 1. Scenarios, goals, methods and gaps in the spatial design domain.

#	Scenario	User Goals	Methods	Gap
1	Imaginary Space	Creating genius loci	Drawing, Collage	Iteration
2	Spatial Configuration	Establish social relationships among spaces	Space Syntax	Collaboration
3	Film Set	Creating spaces based on scenarios and convincing	Instructive Sketches	Exploration
4	Gamespace	Link spaces in interesting and meaningful ways based on play scenarios	Molecule Design	Open Interchange

2 Methodology: Developing a Creativity Support Tool

In the early phase of the design process, especially for ill-structured design tasks, the impact of inspirational stimuli has been proven by ongoing research in the neuroscience domain [24]. Making mood boards and mind maps are familiar approaches that visualize the ideas. A system to support the designer's creativity [3] through inspirational images based on verbal ideas and explanations is introduced by this study within the scope of the spatial design domain. As seen in Fig. 6, to develop a CST allowing cognitive flexibility [1] and establishing an incremental process [2] in the early stages of the spatial design process, use-case-driven methods [15] are adopted. The system is evaluated through usability heuristics for user interface [16] and comparative analysis based on the Creativity Support Index (CSI) [17].

In addition to customary idea visualization approaches such as mood boards and mind maps, the system is novel and developing through ongoing research regarding human-computer interactions and artificial intelligence support. It is expected to improve the spatial design process by supporting exploration and assisting an iterative process in the early stages.

2.1 Scenarios and User Stories

User stories drive the development of the system and use cases from initial stages to required features. Different scenarios are examined to document the user stories and use cases (Table 1). The scenarios examined at the initial stages of the study are developed into user stories (Table 2) that help to define use cases from the perspective of the system's users.

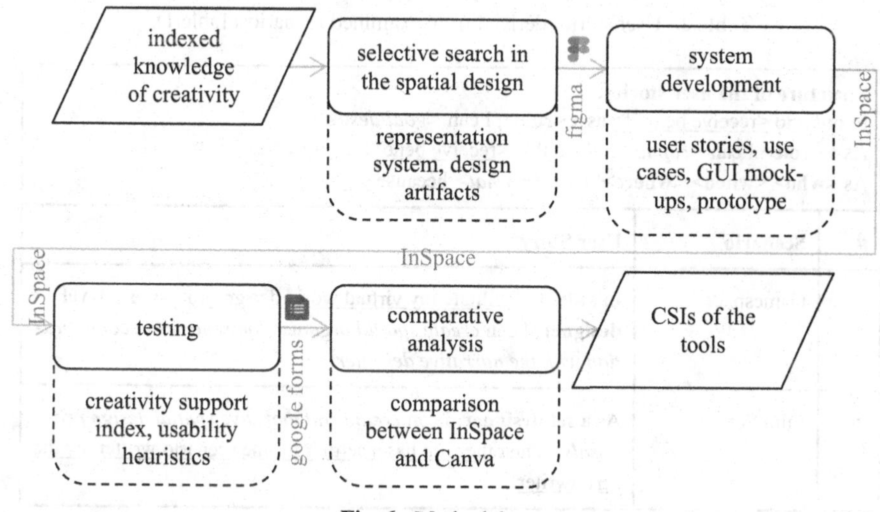

Fig. 6. Methodology.

2.2 Prototyping

To communicate their spatial design ideas visually, designers start by inputting a verbal description (a story, a narrative, a scenario, some keywords, etc.) to the system. Then, AI will review the text and highlight spatial concepts for the user. Users can interfere with the highlighted concepts. From highlighted spatial concepts, AI configures a spatial diagram that can be interfered with by the user. Then, the user can interact with a mood board and form an appearance proposed by the AI to illustrate the atmosphere of the narrated space by creating mood sections. Additionally, users can get involved in mood boards by randomizing images, editing colors and keywords, and forming appearances by using assets on placeholders. Users can export content generated at any phase to provide collaboration and open interchange. An overview of the system is explained in the use-case model (Fig. 7).

Input Story UI is developed to create an interface for the users to enter a verbally described idea about their spatial design (Fig. 8). Users can divide text into scenes for sequences which appear in different spaces. As in user stories #1, #2 and #3 in Table 2, the UI starts a spatial design proposal based on a narrative and collaboration between writer and designer.

Review Text UI includes highlighting the spatial concepts in the text by the AI. User involvement is also possible for highlighting additional concepts or removing some highlighted ones (Fig. 9). It responds to requirements of user stories #1, #2 and #3in Table 2.

Configure Space UI is defined for generating conceptual and spatial diagrams based on the text inputted by the user and reviewed by AI (Fig. 10). Users can edit the generated conceptual diagram, and AI will regenerate a spatial one accordingly. The user stories #3, #4 and #8 in Table 2 are parallel this use-case and interface.

Table 2. User stories derived from examined scenarios(Table 1).

Structure of the user stories.
In order to <receive benefit> as a **<role>**, I can <*goal/desire*>
As a **<role>** I can <*capability*>, so that <receive benefit>
As **<who> <when> <where>**, I want <*what*> because <why>

#	Scenario	User Story
1	Gamespace	In order to facilitate my virtual world design process as a **level designer**, I can *create spatial organization schemes in collaboration with the narrative designer.*
2	Film Set	As a **set designer**, I can *create collaborative spatial design proposals* so that the film has a setting for the scenario written by the scriptwriter.
3	Spatial Configuration	As an **architectural designer**, I can *generate alternative spatial organizations based on a scenario*, so that I realize programmatic ideas as spatial equivalents.
4	Imaginary Space	As a **spatial designer**, I can *link spaces in the narrative* so that the spatial proposal can convince the audience and create a memorable experience of the virtual world.
5	Imaginary Space	As an **interior designer**, I can *generate atmospheric images of imaginary spaces,* so that I work further on spatial properties.
6	Spatial Configuration	In order to visualize my spatial design proposals as a **level designer**, I can *use my spatial organization schemes as inputs and generate 3D/2,5D configurations.*
7	Spatial Configuration	In order to visualize my spatial design proposals as a **designer**, I can use *placeholders and adjust their parameters.*
8	Imaginary Space	As a **level designer**, I want to *create visuals to represent my narrated spaces* because communication among the design team becomes more effective when different representations are involved.
9	Imaginary Space	As a **level designer**, I want to *create visuals to represent my narrated spaces* because I want to iterate my conceptual design process before a detailed modeling process.

Create Moodboard UI is developed to create an interface for the users to generate exploratory visual material about their spatial design (Fig. 11). As in the user stories

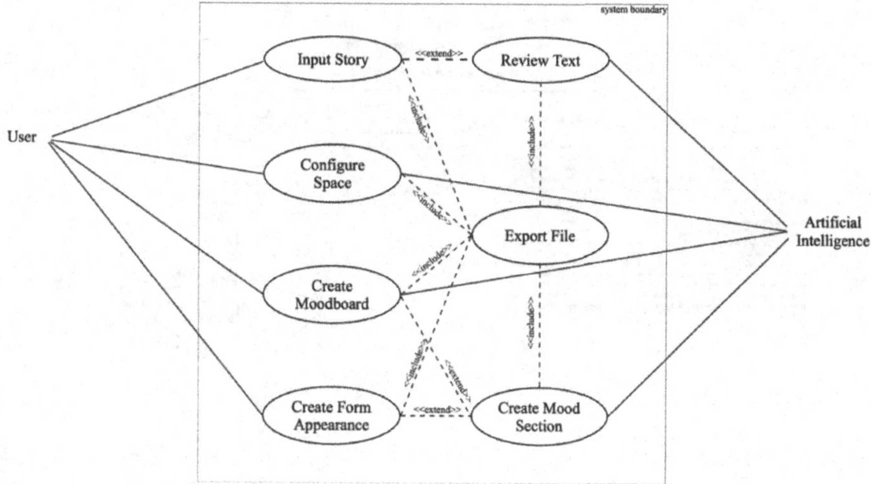

Fig. 7. Use-case model.

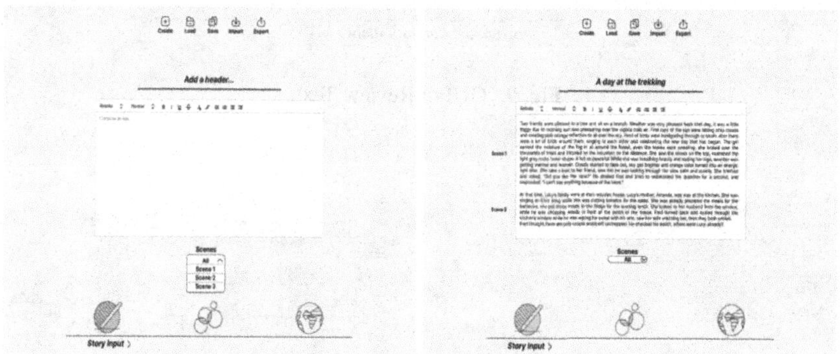

Fig. 8. Graphical User Interface (GUI) of Input Story.

#5, #8 and #9 in Table 2, the UI provides an AI-generated atmosphere for spatial design proposals based on a narrative. The users can interact with the mood board by changing the layout, randomizing the images, or editing colors and keywords. They can go back and forth at this stage and AI will regenerate the mood board accordingly.

Create Form Appearance UI includes generating an isometric view of the AI's spatial design proposal. User involvement is also possible for using placeholder assets (Fig. 12). It responds to user stories requirements of #6, #7, #8 and #9 in Table 2.

Create Mood Section UI is defined for re-generating mood boards whose layouts are organized according to the placeholders (Fig. 13). Users can edit the generated mood board and share it to discuss any spatial sequence. The user stories #4, #5 and #8 in Table 2 are parallel this use-case and interface.

Export UI is developed to create an interface for the users to share visual and textual material about their spatial design at any stage (Fig. 14). As in the user stories #8 and

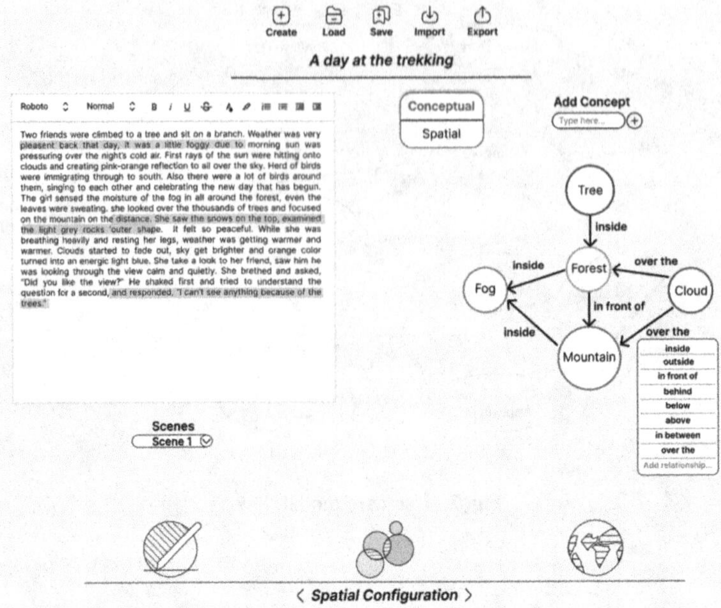

Fig. 9. GUI of Review Text.

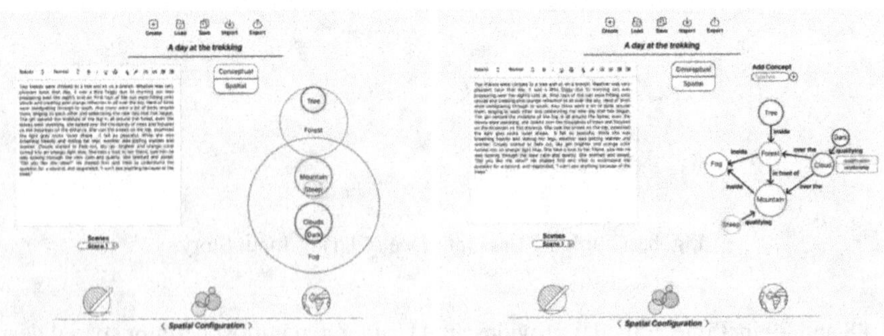

Fig. 10. GUI of Configure Space.

#9 in Table 2, it enables exporting content at different stages as the users go back and forth during the design process.

Creativity support tool design principles were used in the design of this system, whose potential users include product and graphic designers, architects, educators, students and others.

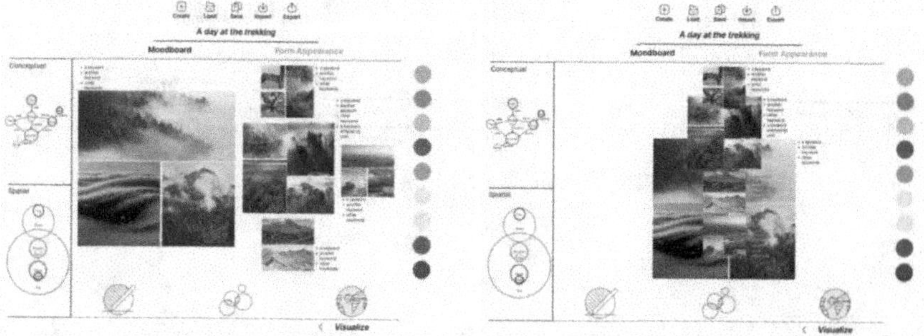

Fig. 11. GUI of Create Moodboard.

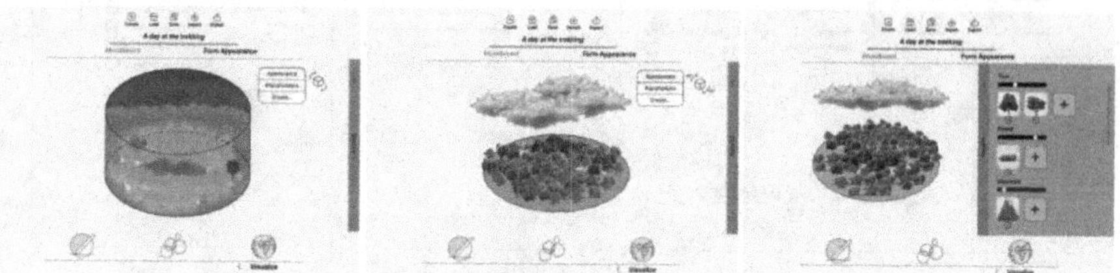

Fig. 12. GUI of Create Form Appearance.

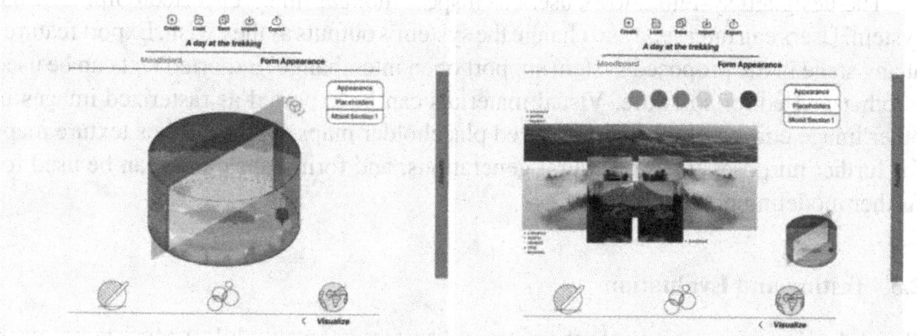

Fig. 13. GUI of Create Mood Section.

The designed system supports exploration via AI-supported text editing and alternative mood board generation features that support exploration. The user can come back and edit the concept map at any time, and the AI updates the mood board and appearance accordingly. The export and import tools of the proposed system in this study are very significant in working with other tools.

Visual and verbal representations are essential in this developed system for the spatial design, making it easy to iterate and compare output differences. The system assists in developing novel spatial design ideas for a specific design problem or further work. The inspirational outcomes of verbal ideas developed by the designed system can be used as a draft that contributes to the iterative and creative process of the designer.

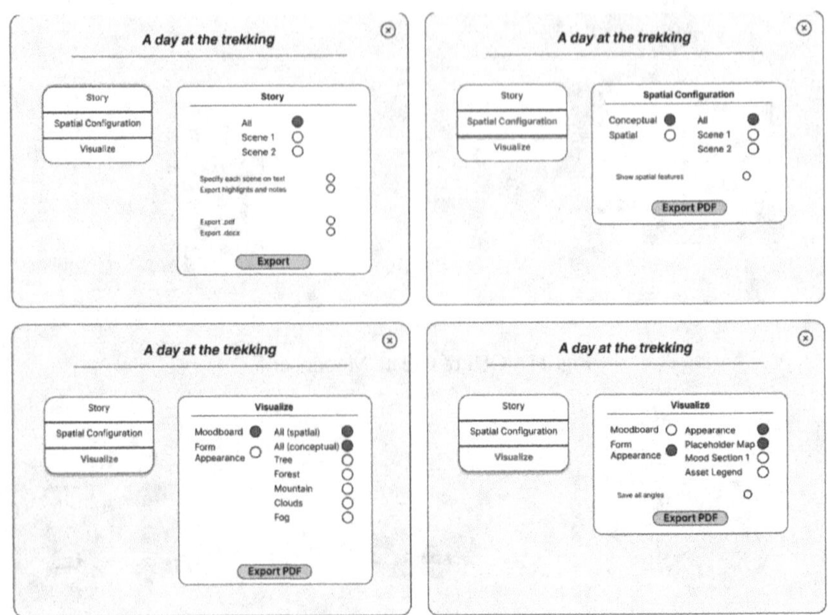

Fig. 14. GUI of Export.

The designed system allows users to inspect the real time-generated outputs of the system. Users can intervene and change the system's outputs as they wish. Export features at any stage in the proposed system support open interchange. Exported text can be used in other text editor software. Visual materials can be exported as rasterized images in other image editing platforms. Exported placeholder maps can be used as texture maps for further purposes like procedural generations, and form appearance can be used for further modeling processes.

2.3 Testing and Evaluation

Through this ongoing research, the proposed system adopts usability heuristics to evaluate itself right after prototyping. Each of the heuristics is explained in relation to UI design. The study also applies the CSI survey quantifying the creativity of CSTs to evaluate the proposed system. Two arguments for each creativity support factor have been asked to be rated out of ten by participants/potential users.

3 Results & Discussion

The system empowers spatial designers to push the boundaries of their creativity, enabling them to write and visualize their conceptual ideas at the early stages. In order to explore the proposed system, possible use cases for architectural designers, stage designers, and level designers as spatial designers were established (Table 3).

To evaluate the system, usability heuristics are applied. Furthermore, volunteer participants as potential users rated the arguments for two systems which are Canva and InSpace. Canva is a graphic design tool which has been widely used by designers to support their creativity [9]. InSpace is the developing system through this research to support users' creativity via generating inspirational images based on verbal ideas. Participants' ratings have been compared accordingly.

Table 3. Possible Workflows of Spatial Designers using InSpace

Spatial Designer	Possible Workflow of Spatial Designers using InSpace
Architectural Designer	Input Story → Review Text → Configure Space → Export → Discuss and improve for detailed architectural drawings
Stage Designer	Input Story → Review Text → Configure Space → Create Moodboard → Discuss atmospheric features with film production team
	Input Story → Review Text → Configure Space → Create Moodboard → Create Mood Section → Explore and discuss specific spatial sequences
Level Designer	Input Story → Review Text → Configure Space → Create Form Appearance → Export → Appearance for exploration before further modeling process // Placeholders for procedural generation

3.1 Usability of InSpace

First, visibility of system status is provided in the UI through the guiding icons at the bottom and highlights (Fig. 18). During the domain analysis, potential users were researched and ensured that the concepts and words in the system and the real world match. To illustrate, the system creates inspirational images as stimuli based on verbal ideas. To match the concept of inspirational images as stimuli, the word "visualize" is used in the UI. "Mood board" and "form appearance" are other familiar concepts from the real world that match the system. Then, instead of using verbal ideas as a concept, "story" is used for UI designed to explain verbal ideas. The system supports user control and freedom by going back and forth on the text-to-image process. For example, users can go back and edit text at any stage, and AI will update spatial configuration and visualization outputs, or they can edit spatial configuration, and AI will update story and visualization outputs simultaneously. Industry conventions of the digital idea visualization tools are mostly followed while developing the system. Mood board concepts consisting of images, colors, keywords and form appearance are examples of this track from an isometric perspective. However, the interactive features of the system between users and AI are novel. There is an internal consistency among these features. Error prevention has not been considered yet because the system development has recently completed its prototyping phase. However, going back to the experience of using the system partly responds to error prevention. To make users recognize rather than recall information while using the system, guiding icons are designed (Fig. 18). Short-written definitions in UI are provided to reduce information that needs to be remembered by users. The system provides personalization and customization to offer flexibility and efficiency of use. Users can decide on custom layouts for the visualization phase (mood boards and available assets) and create novel sequences to work on personally (mood sections). Aesthetic and minimalist design is regarded through the development of the UI. Nevertheless, it is an ongoing development and has not been completed yet. Thus, helpful error messages and solutions or presentation of documentation, if needed by users, are heuristics that cannot be evaluated for now (Fig. 15).

Fig. 15. Guiding icons and highlights.

3.2 Creativity Support Index of InSpace

Five participants as potential users who are architecture students (3), 3D environment artists (1) and filmmakers (1) rated the creativity support arguments for Canva and InSpace.

When the factors of enjoyment, exploration and expressiveness are considered, the result can be mentioned: The designed system (InSpace) is more enjoyable for users than an existing tool (Canva). The designed system is more supportive of exploring different ideas, options and outcomes than an existing one. The designed system is more available for being creative and expressive than an existing one. It needed to be emphasized that standard deviation values are a bit high in the evaluation (Table 4) because the number of participants is relatively low for this kind of qualitative method.

Table 4. Comparative Analysis Results based on CSI.

Tools	**Canva**	**InSpace**	**Canva**	**InSpace**	**Canva**	**InSpace**
Factors	**Enjoyment**		**Exploration**		**Expressiveness**	
Mean Values	16,4	**16,6**	15,8	**16,0**	14,4	**15,2**
Standard Dev	3,26	2,33	1,46	4,64	3,13	4,30
Factors	**Results Worth Effort**		**Immersion**		**Collaboration**	
Mean Values	17	**15**	14	**13,6**	16,2	**12,2**
Standard Dev	1,26	4,60	5,09	6,28	2,48	3,61

4 Discussion and Conclusion

Cognitive studies prove that inspirational stimuli are effective in creative design. Visual representation of verbal ideas is supportive and inspirational for exploring outputs, advancing the design process, and communicating among the design team. The proposed system inspiringly contributes to the creative process regarding text-to-image idea representations. It produces the spatial organization of the entered text and allows intervention by schematically showing it with atmospheric visual materials.

An AI-powered HCI system to enhance spatial design creativity was proposed in this study. Throughout the development of this system proposal, a domain analysis of spatial design was conducted. The analyzed information is combined in the development process. This combination was facilitated by user stories and use-case modelling. GUI mock-ups in Figma contributed to the prototyping of the system. The prototypes are tested by potential users who have agreed that InSpace shows a better performance in enjoyment, exploration and expression factors of creativity support.

While CST design principles are easy to follow in the development process and useful for improving and checking the system, user stories and use cases must be modified and adapted.

The system can be improved further in terms of its features and UI. It could provide a multi-user experience. The appearance view could have filters like daytime, temperature, and weather. Users could change the scene's mood. In the current design, the form appearance is a plane filled with 2D raster images; the existing goal is not more than to influence the user. For further improvement, the system could create a topography instead of a plane; users could add 3D assets instead of 2D images and export the map in a 3D file format like fbx or obj. The system could also generate images from AI tools, not just Google Images.

The developer team itself uses heuristics to evaluate their own system design. This can be expanded to UI experts doing the evaluation with heuristics at certain periods in the process. Also, the comparative analysis based on CSI can be expanded to a larger number of participants from alternative spatial design domains so that more precise results can be obtained at the further stages of development.

The proposed system outputs research carried out in an academic semester. It is currently in the prototype stage, limited to an eight-week development period. In addition, the technical skills of the researchers were also limited while prototyping the tool. Therefore, the designed features are animated with GUI mock-ups. Coding or technical development could not be involved. The process can span over time for future work with an expanded design team. Comprehensive evaluation methods suitable with the CSTs can be sustained to improve the designed system.

References

1. Dietrich, A.: The cognitive neuroscience of creativity. Psychon. Bull. Rev. **11**(6), 1011–1026 (2004). https://doi.org/10.3758/BF03196731
2. Simon, H.A.: Creativity in the arts and sciences. Kenyon Rev. **23**(2), 203–220 (2001)
3. Shneiderman, B., et al.: Creativity support tools: report from a u.s. national science foundation sponsored workshop. Inter. J. Hum.-Comput. Interact. **20**(2), 61–77 (2006). https://doi.org/10.1207/s15327590ijhc2002_1
4. Goldschmidt, G.: Disciplinary Knowledge and the Design Space. Edited by Naz Börekçi, Dalsu Koçyıldırım, Fatma Korkut, and Derek Jones. METU Department of Industrial Design (2019)
5. Goldschmidt, G.: Design Creativity. In: Linkography. The MIT Press (2014). https://doi.org/10.7551/mitpress/9455.003.0008
6. Goel, V.: Ill-Structured Representations "for Ill-Structured Problems (1992)
7. Sawyer, R.K.: The dialogue of creativity: teaching the creative process by animating student work as a collaborating creative agent. Cognition Instruction **40**(4), 459–487 (2022). https://doi.org/10.1080/07370008.2021.1958219
8. Larman, C.: Applying UML and Patterns: An Introduction to Object-Oriented Analysis and Design and Iterative Development, 3rd ed. Pearson (2004)
9. Canva Homepage. https://www.canva.com, (Accessed 25 Oct 2023)
10. Mural Homepage. https://www.mural.co, (Accessed 25 Oct 2023)
11. Miro Homepage. https://miro.com, (Accessed 25 Oct 2023)
12. Dall-E Homepage. https://openai.com/dall-e-2, (Accessed 25 Oct 2023)
13. Midjourney Homepage. https://www.midjourney.com, (Accessed 25 Oct 2023)
14. Shneiderman, B.: Human-centered artificial intelligence: three fresh ideas. AIS Trans. Hum.-Comput. Interact., 109–124 (2020). https://doi.org/10.17705/1thci.00131
15. Jacobson, I., Spence, I., Kerr, B.: Use-Case 2.0. Queue **14**(1), 94–123 (2016). https://doi.org/10.1145/2898442.2912151
16. Nielsen, J.: Enhancing the Explanatory Power of Usability Heuristics. ACM Press (1994). https://doi.org/10.1145/191666.191729
17. Cherry, E., Latulipe, C.: Quantifying the creativity support of digital tools through the creativity support index. ACM Trans. Comput.-Hum. Interact. **21**(4), 1–25 (2014). https://doi.org/10.1145/2617588
18. March, L., Steadman, P.: The Geometry of Environment, 1st ed. Routledge (2020)
19. Cook, P.: Drawing: The Motive Force of Architecture, 2nd ed. Wiley (2014)

20. Shields, J.: Collage and Architecture, 1st ed. Routledge (2013)
21. Kubrick, S., (Director). Eyes Wide Shut [Film]. Stanley Kubrick Productions (1999)
22. İstanbul Sinema Müzesi [Istanbul Cinema Museum]. Stanley Kubrick [Exhibition] (2022)
23. Totten, C.W.: An Architectural Approach to Level Design, 2nd edn. CRC Press (2019)
24. Goucher-Lambert, K., Cagan, J.: Crowdsourcing inspiration: using crowd generated inspirational stimuli to support designer ideation. Des. Stud. **61**, 1–29 (2019). https://doi.org/10.1016/j.destud.2019.01.001

A Study on Gamification Design of Intangible Cultural Heritage Based on ARCS Theory

Mingyu Han, Yi Ji(✉), Gengxin Lin, Leer Liang, and Shengyang Zhong

School of Art and Design, Guangdong University of Technology, District of Dongfeng East Road No. 729, Guangzhou, Yuexiu 510000, China
jiyi001@hotmail.com

Abstract. In the process of digitizing and preserving intangible cultural heritage (ICH), the exploration of innovative integration with various new media has become a hot topic in the industry. Games have gradually emerged as a new opportunity for the dissemination and learning of intangible heritage. This study, starting from the perspective of gamifying intangible heritage, explores the implementation path of gamified intangible heritage based on the game paradigm of Attention, Relevance, Confidence, and Satisfaction (ARCS). It aims to enhance the potential for the general public to actively engage with and explore intangible heritage, fostering interest and motivation. Using Cantonese Porcelain as a practical example, this research deeply integrates traditional cultural elements with gaming elements, providing new insights for the digital inheritance of intangible heritage and the dissemination of digital games.

Keywords: Traditional Culture · Intangible Cultural Heritage · Gamification of Intangible Heritage · Motivation Theory · Cantonese Porcelain

The revitalization and inheritance of intangible cultural heritage are key sources for cultural construction and the enhancement of cultural confidence. The integration of digital technology has opened up limitless possibilities and spaces for the display, dissemination, preservation, and reuse of ICH information. In recent years, the exploration and innovative integration of revitalizing ICH through gamified education and serious games have emerged as hot research trends in the industry. Gradually, gaming is becoming a new medium for the transmission and learning of traditional culture [1]. Internationally, the field of gamifying ICH has achieved varying degrees of success. However, there are still some issues in the field of ICH gamification, which can be summarized into two main aspects: firstly, there is a lack of sufficient gameplay elements, where gameplay is subordinated to the educational purposes. Games are often seen merely as educational tools, leading to a disconnect between ICH content and game mechanics. This is typically manifested through simplistic forms of content presentation such as quizzes and background introductions. Such designs tend to ignore the core needs of game users, such as entertainment, interactivity, and engagement, resulting in poor effectiveness in attracting and retaining user interest. This leads to insufficient gaming motivation and suboptimal outcomes. The second issue is the lack of balance between informativeness and entertainment value. Excessive focus on the entertaining game mechanics can lead

M. Kurosu and A. Hashizume (Eds.): HCII 2024, LNCS 14688, pp. 324–342, 2024.
https://doi.org/10.1007/978-3-031-60449-2_22

to a disconnect between game content and actual ICH, with games only superficially using visual representations or partial elements of ICH, failing to convey its deeper cultural meanings. Consequently, there is a prevalent issue in current gamified ICH products where educational and gaming elements are awkwardly combined. The crux of the problem lies in the misalignment between the intentions of game designers and the needs of game users, indicating a mismatch in motivations between the two parties.

In this context, the introduction of the ARCS Motivation Theory offers a fresh perspective and approach to ICH gamification. At the heart of ARCS theory is the enhancement of learning outcomes through the stimulation and sustenance of user motivation. Applying this theory to the gamification of ICH enables a deeper comprehension of user requirements. A framework, informed by ARCS theory, harmonizes the design and dissemination goals of ICH games. This leads to the development of games that not only adhere to cultural preservation and user experience but also facilitate innovative engagement with ICH. This methodology not only serves the functional aspects of gaming but also nurtures a renewed understanding and creativity in ICH, thus effectively bridging traditional heritage with contemporary digital platforms and fulfilling the the goal of ICH cultural inheritance.

1 Overview of ARCS Motivation Theory

In the realm of human-computer interaction, the emphasis on user motivation is increasingly pivotal. Key to enhancing engagement and satisfaction is addressing users' intrinsic needs. Motivation theories explore the generation, operation of motivation, and delve into the interplay between motivation, needs, behaviors and goals, centering on user requirements. Keller's Motivational-Achievement-Teaching (MAT) model, derived from extensive motivation research, analyzes the factors influencing an individual's effort, outcome, and performance, considering both personal and environmental influences from a macro perspective. This model evolved into the ARCS Motivation Theory, emphasizing the role of external design in fostering and sustaining internal motivation. The goal of the ARCS model is to guide designers to strategically modify external environments to positively impact learning motivation. The components of ARCS are:

Attention (A): Learners choose to focus on learning content based on their interests and willingness.

Relevance (R): Learning content aligns with learners' needs, cognitive levels, and connects with their life experiences and future development.

Confidence (C): Learners have a certain level of knowledge and basic understanding, which boosts their confidence in achieving learning objectives.

Satisfaction (S): Learners generate positive psychological cues as a result of meeting their own expectations during the learning process [3]. As in Fig. 1

Yang Kaicheng and colleagues have provided a detailed refinement of the ARCS model, concentrating on four aspects: learning materials, learning auxiliary support, learning tool support, and learning management. This refinement has led to the development of specific design principles and methodologies for online learning platforms. Their research underscores the critical role of teacher involvement in the effective, closed-loop application of the ARCS model [2]. Li Na's team applied the ARCS model's four elements to evaluate the motivational preferences of users in Chinese language learning

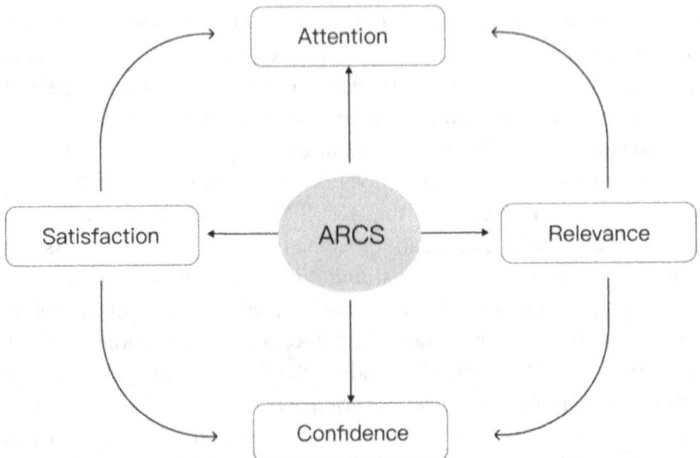

Fig. 1. ARCS theoretical model diagram

across various indicators. Their findings confirm that this approach effectively activates and sustains learning motivation. Building on these insights, they developed a visual interface design pattern for a Chinese language learning app tailored to Mongolian preschool children [4].

In recent years, the application of ARCS motivation theory has become increasingly prominent in instructional design and educational gaming [3]. The ARCS theory emphasizes the four motivational elements that influence learning motivation, which can transform external design into users' internal experiential learning motivation. In the digital era, gamification emerges as a pivotal tool for disseminating ICH, fostering its deep integration with innovation. The depth of cultural value dissemination in the gamification of intangible cultural heritage is determined by the level of game participation and cultural experience it provides to users. To align with user preferences and interests, the design of such games necessitates a thorough comprehension of user motivations.

Given the escalating significance of intangible cultural heritage (ICH) gamification and the prevalent adoption of online educational games, the pressing need to utilize digital games for effective popularization of ICH and deep interactive engagement of ICH with users is evident. Consequently, this article, by integrating theories related to user motivation and adopting a user motivation perspective, explores multi-dimensional aspects of user motivation. This approach aids designers in originating from a motivation-centric design philosophy, transforming game design into a format that aligns with user cognition and expectations. This process not only enhances the user experience but also facilitates the effective internalization and dissemination of intangible cultural heritage knowledge.

2 Analysis of the Current Status of Intangible Cultural Heritage Gamification Design

The gamified products of ICH are ideally suited to its knowledge system, given their educational, entertaining, and highly interactive characteristics. The purpose of ICH gamification is to revitalize ICH projects within mainstream culture through digital means, ensuring their relevance and vibrancy in contemporary times. Addressing this objective necessitates a reassessment of the core essence and motivational needs of culture.

The beauty of intangible cultural heritage is encapsulated in three aspects: the "tangible manifestations" - such as ceramics and paintings, which are concrete examples of material cultural heritage; the "exquisite artistry" - represented by the underlying craftsmanship and techniques; and the "philosophical essence" - embodied in the regional cultural wisdom and philosophical thoughts conveyed through these works. This integration fosters the ongoing development of traditional culture. Within the ICH knowledge system, there is a distinction between explicit knowledge (such as appearance, history, tools) and tacit knowledge (including craft processes and usage techniques). The latter, being the core of traditional craftsmanship, depends on experience and practice and requires comprehension through specific experiences, contexts, or specialized dissemination methods [5].

From the perspective of knowledge dissemination, the designer's motivation--to facilitate the learning and inheritance of intangible cultural heritage through gaming--can be categorized into three levels: interactive display for cultural immersion, interactive experiences of skill inheritance, and cultural participation and emotional resonance (Fig. 2).

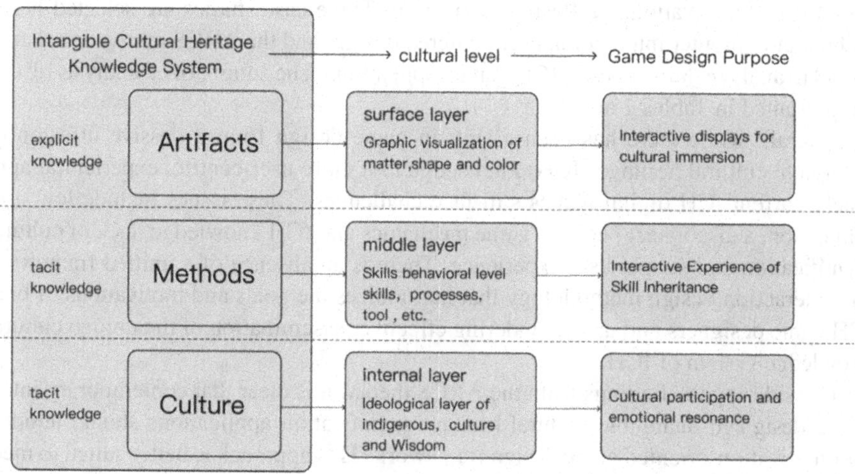

Fig. 2. Mapping relationship between ICH knowledge system and game design purpose

Interactive Display for Cultural Immersion: Such products recreate ICH imagery or production processes using animations or physical representations, complemented by exquisite visuals. Users engage in simple interactions to learn about the history, craft characteristics, and folk customs of the ICH. These games typically lack complex gameplay and have relatively simple level designs. They fail to satisfy users' motivation for confidence and satisfaction, and therefore cannot establish a long-term engagement mechanism.

Interactive Experiences of Skill Inheritance: In games where the acquisition of traditional skills and knowledge is central, such as in crafts, dance, or opera, the focus is on procedural learning. These games emphasize craftsmanship, processes, and related knowledge. For example, in "Carving Master," players engage in the woodcarving process, acquiring an experience of cutting and creating. The game incorporates material selection, production techniques, finished products, and related knowledge as its core content. It has garnered significant acclaim and sparked interest in traditional skills among many. The primary goal is to facilitate learners' acquisition of procedural knowledge in traditional arts through gaming.

Cultural Participation and Emotional Resonance: This aspect primarily focuses on understanding ethnic history and cultural norms, with the goal of enhancing cultural awareness, cultural identity, and cultural participation. Nielsen's theory about the third generation of educational games emphasizes a key point: knowledge transfer in game design should be context-dependent. This concept is based on the interactional unity between players, culture, and the game. Within this framework, games are not just entertainment tools but rather multi-dimensional learning environments where players' experiences, cultural backgrounds, and game elements merge to create a rich educational setting.

Drawing on domestic and international research on intangible cultural heritage ICH gamification and a survey of nearly 80 gamified ICH applications and platforms on mobile app stores, this study analyzes their strengths and weaknesses from the perspectives of user motivation and design motivation. Three case studies are selected based on human-computer interaction, user-centered design, and the ARCS motivation theory model to analyze three types of ICH game applications. The summarized analysis results are presented in Tables 1 and 2.

Overall, while there has been a shift in game design from a passive infusion of intangible cultural heritage (ICH) knowledge to a more user-centric, experiential approach, current ICH digital games still face challenges. These issues include low user immersion, a disconnect between game mechanics and ICH knowledge, lack of cultural identification and subpar user experience. There is an absence of a unified framework and interaction design methodology that harmonizes the goals and motivations of both ICH game designers and users, hindering effective dissemination of the unique cultural knowledge system of ICH.

Considering the findings from the ARCS theory, it is clear that contemporary interactive design in intangible cultural heritage gamification applications should adopt a user motivation-oriented game design framework. This approach is better suited to meet the current expectations of users for interactive experiences and cultural engagement in intangible cultural heritage games.

Table 1. Competitive Product Analysis of Gamified Intangible Cultural Heritage Applications

Design element	Objective function		
	Interactive displays for cultural immersionInteractive	Experience of skill Inheritance	Cultural participation and emotional resonanc
	Qing Dynasty Emperor's Clothing	Master sculptor	Nishan shaman
Attention	Visual Engagement: 3D models and collages capture attention, boosting exploration with interactive and vibrant visuals. Conflict Exploration: Exploring attire's history and craftsmanship piques curiosity for further discovery.	Visual Appeal: Outdated visuals don't engage users or highlight cultural heritage effectively. Monotony: A lack of innovation in teaching traditional skills may lead to short-lived user interest.	Environment Design: Engaging scenes and characters grab player attention. Atmosphere: Shaman-themed music and visuals keep players focused and curious about the culture
Relevance	Objective-Driven: A platform for exploring Qing Dynasty attire, tailored to interests in Chinese history and culture. Value: Provides detailed visuals and insights into Chinese history, culture, art, and design.	Practical Value: Emphasizing theory over practical use may lead users to find the content less applicable to their lives or interests.	Cultural Engagement: Aims to boost interest in shamanic culture, yet may feel irrelevant to players not drawn to or familiar with shamanism, distancing them from its themes.
Self-confidence	Content Depth: Delivers in-depth cultural and historical insights, which may be challenging for non-experts and impact their confidence. Without tailored learning options, users may experience frustration.	Stepwise Learning: Enhances confidence with structured steps and outcomes. Learner Adaptability: Offers levels for all skill sets, challenging and supporting every learner.	Gradual Learning and Accomplishment: The game guides players through shamanic culture with tasks and challenges, where a structured learning path boosts confidence.
Satisfaction	Interactive Feedback: The absence of interaction features may leave users feeling neglected, impacting their satisfaction. User Engagement: Focusing more on display than on active participation diminishes sustained interest and satisfaction.	Tangible Outcomes and Feedback: Allowing users to create visible works and receive positive feedback significantly boosts satisfaction.	Cultural Awareness and Respect: Immersive gameplay enables deep understanding of shamanic culture, fostering appreciation for cultural heritage and enhancing intrinsic satisfaction.

3 Intangible Cultural Heritage Game Design Model and Strategies Based on ARCS Theory

Building on the aforementioned analysis, the study suggests that it is essential to adopt a user motivation perspective in the interaction and experience design of gamified ICH applications, proposing a novel design framework. Based on the ARCS theory, an experiential model of user motivation in ICH games can be deduced, as illustrated in Fig. 4. This model depicts motivation as a closed-loop process within the game world, where users construct their cognitive structures through experiences, observations, and practices, driven fundamentally by user motivation.

Within the context of ICH game applications, user motivations can be encapsulated as the acquisition of knowledge, a sense of progress and achievement, long-term feedback, and aspects of entertainment and enjoyment [6]. These motivations can be further distilled into four key motivations: situational awareness motivation, immersive

Table 2. Cantonese Porcelain Knowledge System

explicit knowledge	**material layer**	**Theme**	Traditional themes featuring flowers, birds, fish, and insects; a blend of Eastern and Western elements in depictions of people, landscapes, and ships; unique badge patterns specific to custom-export porcelain; and contemporary themes with commemorative significance.
		Color	Dominated by rich reds, greens, and golds for decorative hues, complemented by purple, blue, and yellow palettes, and integrated with Western-style light, bright, and vivid "foreign colors," resulting in a palette that is vibrant and eye-catching.
		Pattern	Doufang pattern: Commonly used on dishes, bowls, plates, or at the shoulders and mouths of vases and pots; Jindi Patterns: A design used along the edges, which can be extensively and continuously applied in large square areas; Corner Interval Patterns: Suitable for the edges, feet, mouths, and shoulders of porcelain, serving to create a secondary interval and contrast with the main patterns; Organizational Patterns: Decorative designs that complement the main theme, with representative motifs including fans, flowers, lamps, vases, umbrellas, double fish, six-ears, etc.
		Form	The porcelain blanks of Cantonese Porcelain are transported from Jingdezhen, and commonly include forms such as vases, bowls, plates, cups, pots, basins, and jars.
tacit knowledge	**technological layer**	**Tools**	A special box for raw materials, a hammer and bowl for grinding powder, a spatula for picking up pigments, a pen, an inkwell and a brush wash tool; special tools include a circle-drawing pen and a pillow case for storage and padding.
		Crafts	Utilizing a color grinding mortar and bowl to prepare pigments, selecting a white porcelain blank, then commence with layout (using light ink lines to divide proportions). Based on the layout and draft, sketch the design, proceeding to fill in colors. The process includes edging (applying gold along the rims of plates, bowls, and similar items), and finally, the piece is placed in the kiln for firing.
	cultural layer	**History**	The Birth, Rise, Development and Prosperity of Cantonese Porcelain
		Cultural Values	Cantonese Porcelain embodies the spirit of the nation, the artisan's craftsmanship, and the spirit of collaboration; it serves as a vital vessel and historical cultural symbol of Sino-Western exchange. It reflects the prosperity of the Thirteen-hong of Canton port during the Qing Dynasty and its significant commercial and trade value.
		Cultural Implications	Cantonese Porcelain carries the distinctive features of Lingnan culture and also integrates Western cultural styles. It encompasses auspicious, celebratory, and blessing themes, as well as connotations of inclusivity and openness, representing a rich tapestry of cultural symbolism.

narrative motivation, interactive experience motivation, and exploratory practice motivation. Users are initially motivated by situational perception to capture their attention and promote perceptual retention. They then gain immersive narrative motivation by understanding clear game objectives through tasks and their relevance to learning goals. Subsequently, unstructured knowledge acquired through interactive experiences is synthesized into structured memory, fostering confidence motivation through interactive feedback. Finally, users consolidate learned knowledge and skills through active practice, internalizing ICH tacit knowledge into their cultural perception, thus activating satisfaction motivation by achieving a sense of accomplishment. Ultimately, this leads to cultural identification with ICH, achieving its digital dissemination and dynamic inheritance (Fig. 3).

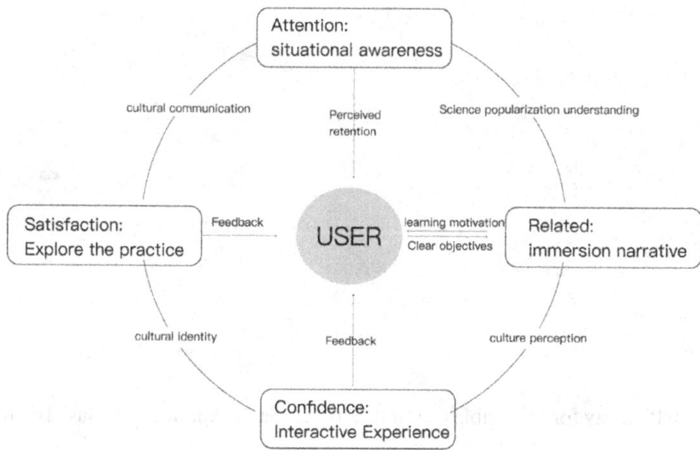

Fig. 3. Implementation Pathways for Intangible Cultural Heritage Game Motivation Based on Motivation Theory

Jesse Schell proposed the Four Keys to Fun game design framework, which looks at games from the perspective of game developers. According to this framework, digital games consist of four core dimensions: game mechanics, game narrative, game art, and technical implementation. These four dimensions collectively shape the gaming experience. Game mechanics refer to the rules, processes, and data that make up the core part of the game. They not only determine how players interact with the game but also guide the learning path. The game narrative, constituting the game's storyline and setting, impacts the content learned by players. It includes narrative frameworks and script settings, where the latter activates the visual aspects of characters, props, and internal spirit, serving as a vessel for player emotions and offering a sense of realism. The narrative framework, as the controller and guide of the process, helps players navigate the game world filled with details, characters, and conflicts, and leads them through various events within the game narrative. Game art involves the player's perception of the game's overall visual design, encompassing not only visual presentation but also conveying the deeper cultural meanings [7]. Technical implementation is the integration core of these elements, supporting the construction of the game. It pertains to the use of game design and development technology, though it falls outside the scope of this discussion.

Therefore, following the Four Keys to Fun game design framework and considering the purpose of digital ICH games, the levels of game design can be categorized into the following: Scenario Design Layer, Task Presentation Layer, Gameplay Mechanics Layer, Practice Feedback Layer. These not only constitute the dimensions of a digital game but also represent a cognitive framework for understanding the game's essence.

Based on this framework, this research establishes the relationship mapping between the ARCS motivation theory model and the educational game applications for ICH, as shown in Fig. 4. This mapping aims to elucidate the connection between user motivation and game implementation mechanisms, striving to create a gaming experience that is both engaging and educationally enriching.

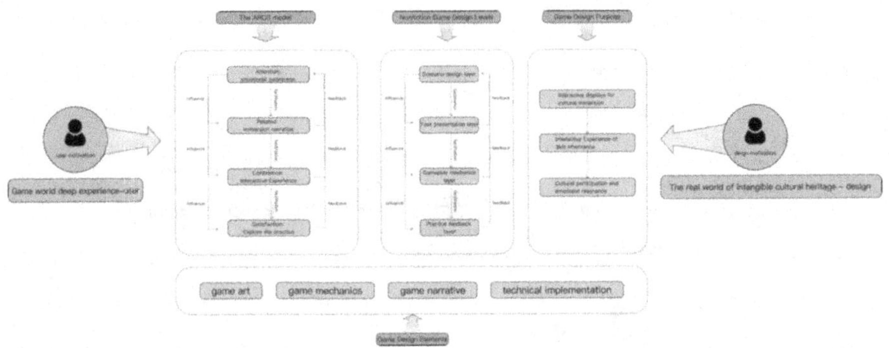

Fig. 4. Design Pathway for Intangible Cultural Heritage Game Applications Based on Motivation Theory

The following section will sequentially introduce the four levels of ICH game design as depicted in Fig. 4.

Scenario Design Layer: Situational Awareness Motivation Stimulation. This layer primarily focuses on attention motivation, encompassing the game's representational and narrative scenarios. It is crucial to capture user attention early in the game. The design of the representational scenario should include visually appealing elements, as attention in digital games is largely sensory-driven. To amplify sensory perception, the design must enrich aesthetic elements, such as traditional patterns and music, translating the visual symbols of the external material layer of ICH. This includes the visual symbols with explicit characteristics such as object modeling, color, ornamentation, and material. These elements are extracted, analyzed, deconstructed, and then redesigned to be integrated into the digital product's interface, including persistent basic module navigation icons, functional icon design, and text. They present the basic functional structure through static information with low interactivity. The design structures the game scenarios, time frames, and interactive actions, refining information elements that align with user operational feedback, such as process navigation and operation reminders [8]. In terms of auditory elements, spatial music predominates, including background music for different scenes. This aspect involves culturally interpreting the various operations in the ICH game and matching them with suitable atmospheric tunes, guiding users into the ICH context. In the narrative scenarios of the game, narrative-driven design is used to evoke empathy in learners, ensuring the game is sufficiently engaging to draw users in. This includes incorporating origin stories of the ICH as background narratives, prompting users to explore actively. Character portrayal in these stories creates emotional connections for the user, thus attracting attention. As the plot unfolds, users are guided to seek out the story's conclusion.

Task Presentation Layer: Immersive Narrative Motivation Elicitation. According to the ARCS motivation model, the task setting and narrative of the game should enhance the connection between the user and ICH, aiming for a more sustainable and multidimensional gaming experience. The content of ICH culture should be intricately and ingeniously integrated with level design, allowing users to pursue learning objectives subtly and effectively through game-driven tasks. In the game narrative, the roles played by gamers are integral to the game tasks, achieving a virtual "firsthand presence." By immersing themselves in the role they play in the game narrative, users become both external experiential subjects and internal in-game characters. This high degree of role-playing immersion leads users to wholeheartedly engage in the game world [8]. Game tasks must be integrally connected to the storyline, utilizing engaging and anticipatory story elements and tasks to establish a relationship between the player and the game narrative. This connection fosters user identification with both the game and ICH cultures. It cultivates an emotional experience on a psychological level in users, further establishing long-term bonds. This approach builds upon a close association and interactive foundation with ICH, deepening emotional connections. By engaging the immersive narrative motivation, the design draws users into ongoing participation and enhances their cultural experience within the game. This approach underscores the cultural connotations within the game, focusing the game's story on the expression of culture.

Gameplay Mechanism Layer: Interactive Experience Motivation Elicitation. Gameplay, essentially the game mechanics, focuses on maintaining user confidence to foster sustainable gaming motivation. It is critical to align these mechanics with the principles of ICH culture, ensuring that users find enjoyment and educational value without fatigue. The mechanics should be designed to be both challenging and achievable, building player confidence through progressive teaching and timely feedback. Gameplay design related to ICH craft processes and level challenge feedback mechanisms should encourage active user interaction. This involves adapting ICH processes into engaging and enjoyable gameplay, transforming ICH techniques into game mechanics, using ICH tools as key props, and modularizing the ICH knowledge system into interactive elements like knowledge-based quizzes. Players should receive immediate rewards upon achieving game objectives, and the game should also foster a sense of long-term accomplishment, such as collecting and preserving virtual cultural artifacts. Setting clear goals and providing positive feedback encourages players to make progress in learning ICH cultural knowledge and skills [9].

Practice Feedback Layer: Exploratory Practice Motivation Elicitation. By stimulating the exploratory practice motivation, this approach fosters a continuous sense of satisfaction in users, thereby enhancing user engagement. Given the unique nature of the ICH knowledge system, game mechanics involving practical components enable players to process and deepen their understanding of the acquired knowledge subjectively and experientially. Specifically, the mechanism of practical feedback in the game allows players to recreate and apply ICH knowledge, effectively transferring learning outcomes. This process internalizes more nuanced aspects of ICH tacit knowledge for learners, such as cultural significance, value, and innovation in traditional crafts. The game tasks are structured to encourage post-learning re-creation of ICH content, progressively increasing the complexity of tasks. Adjustments in difficulty and enhanced achievement feedback mechanisms are employed to boost the user's initiative in learning, creating a positive learning cycle. Moreover, through technology, players can share their achievements, such as social media integration, further amplifying their sense of fulfillment.

This design framework ensures that users experience different dimensions of the ARCS model at various stages of the game, as illustrated in Fig. 5.

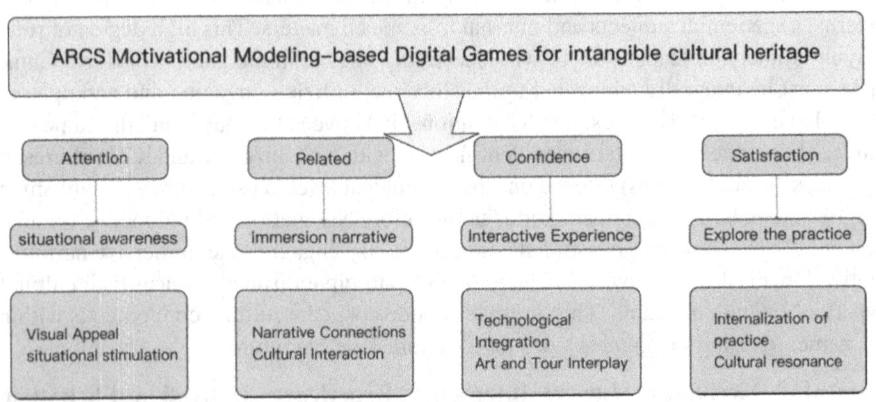

Fig. 5. Game Design Strategies for Intangible Cultural Heritage Digital Games Based on ARCS Motivation Theory

4 Gameification Design Practices Based on Motivation Theory: A Case Study of Cantonese Porcelain Cultural Games

4.1 Reconstruction of Gamified Practices in Cantonese Porcelain

Cantonese Porcelain, inscribed in 2008 as a national intangible cultural heritage, represents the glazed painting of the Lingnan region and serves as a vital cultural vessel. It is distinguished by its richness in painting techniques and themes, and the uniqueness of its colors, embodying a wealth of cultural connotations and heritage value. In recent years, the digital dissemination of Cantonese Porcelain has become a focal point of research [10]. Numerous scholars have gradually turned their attention to the study and preservation of Cantonese Porcelain. However, the research and application of gamified preservation and dissemination of Cantonese Porcelain culture, utilizing new media, are still relatively scarce. This article, guided by motivation theory and delving into the cultural essence of Cantonese Porcelain, aims to discern a balance in the motivations of both designers and users. This understanding will be applied to reconstruct the dynamic digital inheritance of Cantonese Porcelain through gamified practices. Using Cantonese Porcelain n games as a case study, this research initiates gamification design practices based on the principles of motivation theory and the integration of ICH knowledge.

Scenario Design Layer: Situational Awareness Motivation. In the VR game centered on Cantonese Porcelain, "Splendors of Painted Porcelain," situational design is utilized to create situational awareness and attention motivation for users. Initially, the game abstracts and deconstructs Cantonese Porcelain motifs like Doufang and Jindi. It extracts connotations from intuitive visual elements such as scene guidance icons, navigation bars, and pop-ups, aligning them with the abstract elements of Cantonese Porcelain to form ICH-themed scene patterns. For instance, the pattern of the Doufang in Cantonese Porcelain is used as a guide in dialogue boxes. The collected data on Cantonese Porcelain is organized and processed for information and graphics, and contextualized. Tools like 3D Max and Unity are employed to construct models and virtual realistic spaces, accompanied by music and sound effects consistent with the corresponding historical periods. This multi-sensory simulation, encompassing visual, auditory, and tactile elements, enhances the user's perceptual experience. The "real" environment of a Cantonese Porcelain workshop is recreated, immersing users visually and providing voice guidance and event-triggered sound effects.

Furthermore, engaging scenarios are designed to enhance the user's situational perception. In the first scene, players assume the role of a Cantonese Porcelain apprentice in the the thirteen-hong of Canton port scene. Here, interactions with an NPC, a Cantonese Porcelain craftsman - the player's master, guide them to undertake learning tasks. The attraction of representational information and the initial introduction to the scene capture the player's attention, effectively showcasing ICH culture and aligning with user motivation (Figs. 6 and 7).

Fig. 6. Translation of Guangcai porcelain visual elements

Task Presentation Layer: Immersive Narrative Motivation. In the task design phase, players take on the role of a Cantonese Porcelain apprentice tasked with the revival of Cantonese Porcelain craftsmanship. The game narrative and tasks immerse the user in

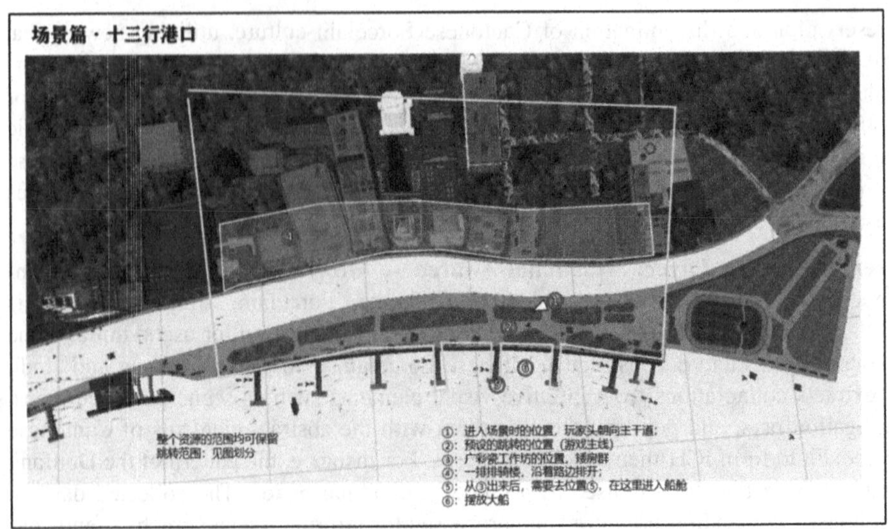

Fig. 7. Advance introduction of situational information

the role of an apprentice in a Cantonese Porcelain workshop, experiencing the process of crafting and exporting Cantonese Porcelain, and appreciating its historical and cultural significance as well as national sentiments. Participants, as apprentices, learn about the journey of Cantonese Porcelain and are tasked by a Cantonese Porcelain master after triggering his memories. They search for tools used in porcelain firing within the workshop setting and sequentially complete stages of selection, ingredient preparation, and firing. Finally, they are required to take the finished porcelain to the port warehouse and deliver it to foreign merchants.

Throughout these stages, knowledge about Cantonese Porcelain, including its techniques and tools, is presented in different scenes, narrated to the user. Stylized character guides facilitate this learning through interactive dialogues, answering questions and providing personalized guidance for both main and side tasks. The setup of tasks and narrative engages players in a state of immersion. This immersion, connected with the game world and player identity, satisfies the motivational need for an immersive narrative. As players invest time, mental effort, and emotion in the game, their understanding of traditional crafts like Cantonese Porcelain deepens. This not only fulfills their entertainment needs but also facilitates a meaningful exchange with the ICH (Fig. 8).

Gameplay Mechanics Layer: Interactive Experience Motivation. The design of game mechanics should balance task difficulty and reward-penalty feedback to help users facilitate understanding of both explicit and tacit knowledge in the traditional cultural knowledge graph. The equilibrium between skill and challenge is crucial for immersing users in the game and forms the basis for fulfilling the interactive experience motivation to boost confidence [11]. In "Splendors of Painted Porcelain," the knowledge system of Cantonese Porcelain is organized and conveyed, including both its explicit and tacit aspects. At the game's outset, players complete the firing of Cantonese Porcelainin a workshop. They must first search for firing tools, interacting with various elements in

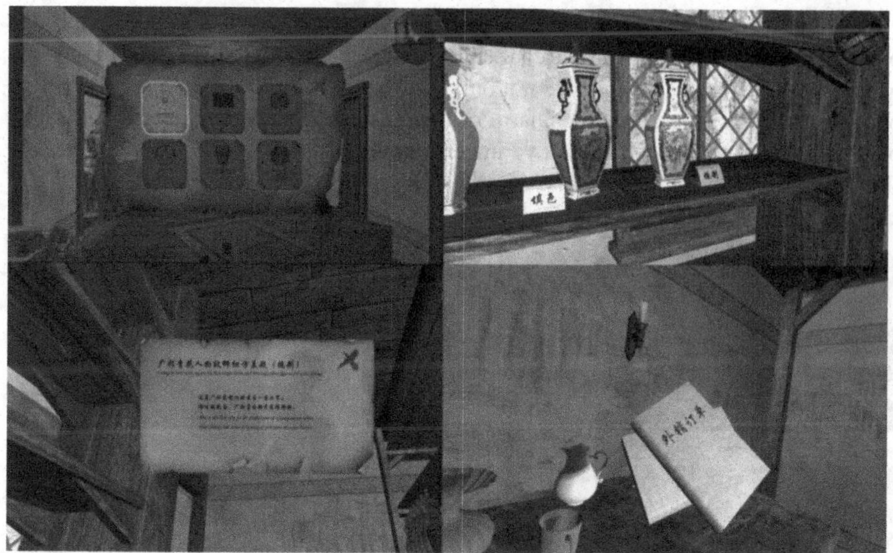

Fig. 8. Task information prompts

the environment, such as opening drawers, browsing books, or conversing with a master for clues. Upon finding the correct tools, detailed information about the tool's historical background, usage, and cultural significance is provided. If a wrong item is selected, animated feedback and auditory cues offer hints to prompt reconsideration, like, "Think about it – how could a hammer be used for detailed painting? Try finding a more suitable tool."

Subsequently, under the guidance of a Cantonese Porcelain master, players will assemble the correct pigments in a puzzle-like fashion. The workshop is set with white porcelain blanks, and players are tasked with selecting the appropriate shape and quality of porcelain blanks for Cantonese Porcelain firing. They then engage in different steps of layout, outlining, and coloring. Players can try the unique Cantonese Porcelain technique of "sealing with gold," a high-level skill requiring precise operation and a keen sense of color control. The entire process is simulated through virtual controllers, with audio effects and progress bars providing feedback. Once the painting is complete, players place their work in a virtual kiln for firing. They must use motion-sensitive controls to select the correct temperature for firing, mastering precise control of temperature and time. After completion, the Cantonese Porcelain master evaluates and scores the player's porcelain. Players can save and share their finished pieces. They can also sell or exchange them in the game's virtual market, adding interactive and social elements to the game.

Every step in the game is accompanied by detailed historical and cultural background information, allowing players to immerse themselves in the joy of creation while gaining an in-depth understanding of the cultural significance and artistic value of Cantonese Porcelain. Beyond the main storyline, players can explore a storeroom to view Cantonese Porcelain pieces and books related to the porcelain firing techniques displayed on shelves, with detailed descriptions available for famous Cantonese Porcelain pieces. Additionally, the game features various difficulty levels and tasks, such as replicating masterpieces or completing specific designs within a set time. These challenges are designed to improve players' skills while adding fun and challenge to the game. This interactive and immersive gaming experience enables players not only to master the craft of Cantonese Porcelain but also to deeply appreciate the charm of this ancient art. Throughout the gameplay, players gradually develop a cognitive understanding of the ICH and its practices [12] (Fig. 9).

Fig. 9. Design of Game Mechanisms

Practical Feedback Layer: Exploratory Practice Motivation. Stimulating exploratory practice motivation in users fosters a continuous sense of satisfaction, thereby enhancing user engagement. The unique nature of the ICH knowledge system, incorporated through game mechanics, allows players to experientially process the information acquired within the game, leading to a deeper level of understanding. Specifically, the mechanism of practical feedback enables players to recreate and transfer ICH knowledge within the game context. This process internalizes the subtler aspects of tacit ICH knowledge, deepening players' understanding of the cultural significance, value, and innovation inherent in traditional crafts. By sequentially linking game tasks, players engage in the re-creation of ICH content following their learning, progressively increasing the difficulty of game tasks. Adjusting challenges and enhancing achievement feedback mechanisms heighten users' initiative in learning, fostering a positive learning cycle.

In the final level, players need to present their completed porcelain pieces for selection by European merchants as part of the export porcelain trade. Guided by interactions with these merchants, players choose different bronzeware and stands to combine with their Cantonese Porcelain, creating items that appeal to European aesthetics and customs. Players can also craft multiple Cantonese Porcelain for sale. Once designed, their creations are displayed in the dockside market, where European merchants provide feedback and evaluation based on the style and creativity of the works. Players can showcase their creations in the game's virtual museum and share them with other players.

Throughout this process, players actively achieve goals using previously acquired knowledge, forming a positive feedback loop with repeated creation, fostering cultural identification. Completion of objectives provides feedback to the user. Gradually, players build a deeper understanding of Cantonese Porcelain's cultural characteristics, value concepts, and profound cultural meanings, encompassing more abstract dimensions. This learning process is not just an accumulation of knowledge but also an experience of enhancing self-efficacy and long-term motivational satisfaction through exploration and fulfillment in practice. During this process, users' cultural knowledge systems intertwine with the essence of intangible cultural heritage, forming a virtuous cycle of learning [13] (Fig. 10).

Fig. 10. Display of Re-creation Works

4.2 Advancing the Design Model of Intangible Cultural Heritage Games Rooted in Motivational Theory

This investigation adopts empirical methodologies to concentrate on the endeavors of student cohorts in gamifying the cultural essence of Cantonese Porcelain. In dedicated training modules, participants were immersed in the ARCS theory of motivation and its practical application within the realm of game design. This foundational theory guided them in crafting prototypes that encapsulate the rich heritage of Cantonese Porcelain. The process demanded from students not only the application of ARCS's four pivotal components—Attention, Relevance, Confidence, Satisfaction—but also a seamless synthesis of innovation with theoretical principles to digitally narrate the distinct allure of Cantonese Porcelain culture (Figs. 11 and 12).

Fig. 11. Students are making Cantonese Porcelain games

Following the design phase, the effectiveness of these endeavors was showcased through presentations that detailed the innovative thought process, theoretical integration, and demonstrations of the final game prototypes. Analysis of the design methodology and prototype demonstrations revealed a profound level of creative ingenuity and strategic thinking, underscoring the impact of ARCS motivational theory in facilitating gamified learning experiences. The student groups adeptly captured the attention of participants through their designs, tethered the learning objectives to the cultural significance of Cantonese Porcelain, bolstered user confidence with appropriately challenging tasks, and ultimately elevated user satisfaction through task completion and reward mechanisms. These findings suggest that the applicability and efficacy of a gaming design framework, grounded in ARCS theory, can be effectively ascertained without recourse to traditional user testing, through reflective observation of the design journey and prototype unveilings.

4.3 Future Directions

The empirical inquiry of this study illuminates the vast potential for applying a motivational theory-based game design framework within the educational gamification of Intangible Cultural Heritage (ICH). Future research avenues may explore the adaptability of this framework across diverse cultural landscapes and technological infrastructures, aiming to refine and personalize the learning experience design. Furthermore, the integration of burgeoning technologies such as Augmented Reality (AR), Virtual Reality (VR), and Artificial Intelligence (AI) with the ARCS theory emerges as a pivotal

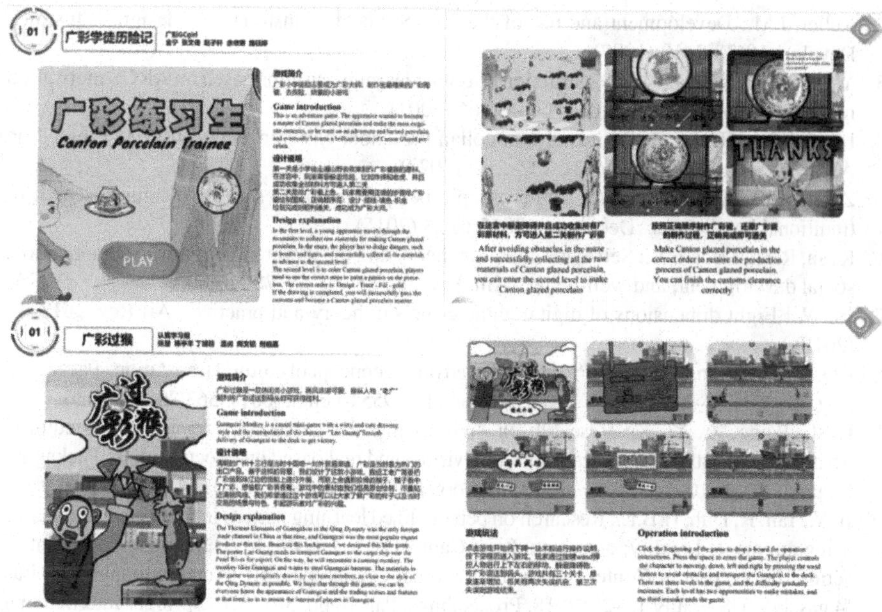

Fig. 12. Cantonese Porcelain Game Based on ARCS Theory's Game Design Model for ICH

research trajectory. This fusion promises to significantly enhance game interactivity and immersion, efficaciously invigorating user engagement and motivation in learning.

5 Conclusion

The exploration of the positive impact and novel value of games beyond entertainment has become a recent societal focus. As a multifaceted, interactive art form that integrates new technologies, interactive media, and emotional narratives, games have emerged as vivid carriers for practicing cultural confidence and awareness. However, the challenge lies in enhancing the gaming experience by deeply understanding user motivation, bridging the gap between designers and users, and integrating traditional cultural elements into games to offer more appealing gamified learning experiences to younger audiences. Current research in this area is somewhat lagging. Therefore, this study, grounded in motivation theory, proposes a framework and principles for the interactive design of digital intangible cultural heritage (ICH) games. This framework offers practical insights for creating digital ICH game interactions that enhance user autonomy in learning experiences, aiming to design games with more self-propagating and practical features, thereby improving independent learning experiences for users.

References

1. Mortara, M., Catalano, C.E., Bellotti, F., et al.: Learning cultural heritage by serious games. J. Cultural Heritage **15**(3), 318–325 (2014)

2. Keller, J.M.: Development and use of the ARCS model of instructional design. J. Instruct. Develop. **10**(3), 2–10 (1987)
3. Yang, K., Li, X., Fan, W.: Construction of online learning systems based on ARCS motivation model. E-Educ. Res. **2001**(06), 46–49+66 (2001)
4. Li, N., Han, H.: Visual design of mongolian preschool children's education APP based on ARCS. Packaging Eng. **44**(10), 202–212 (2023)
5. Zhang, D.: Tacit knowledge: a microscopic perspective on design innovation research of traditional handicrafts. Decoration **2015**(6), 3 (2015)
6. Ryan, R.M., Deci, E.L.: Self-determination theory and the facilitation of intrinsic motivation, social development, and well-being. Am. Psychol. **55**(1), 68–78 (2000)
7. He, W.: Eight dimensions of digital game criticism theory and practice. Art Rev. **2018**, 11 (2018)
8. Liu, X.: Traditional culture APP design based on the concept of cultural translation. Packaging Eng. **41**(02) 237–242 (2020). https://doi.org/10.19554/j.cnki.1001-3563.2020.02.036.
9. Li, J., Wang, Z., Yi, X.: Research on digital game design strategy for intangible cultural heritage: a case study of games combining virtual and real based on nuoculture. In: Packaging Eng. **44**(22), 1–10+16 (2023). https://doi.org/10.19554/j.cnki.1001-3563.2023.22.001.
10. Ji, Y., Tan, P., Duh, H.B.L.: Research on personalized learning pattern in traditional handicraft using augmented reality: a case study of Cantonese porcelain. In: Human-Computer Interaction. Interaction in Context: 20th International Conference, HCI International 2018, Las Vegas, NV, USA, July 15–20, 2018, Proceedings, Part II, pp. 304–316. Springer International Publishing (2018). https://doi.org/10.1007/978-3-319-91244-8_25
11. Wan, L., Zhao, M., Zhao, C.: From the perspective of experiential game learning model to the design of educational digital games. China Educ. Technol. **2006**(10), 5–8 (2006)
12. Zhong, S., Ji, Y., Dai, X., et al.: Research on Immersive Virtual Reality Display Design Mode of Cantonese Porcelain Based on Embodied Interaction. In: Human-Computer Interaction. Design and User Experience Case Studies: Thematic Area, HCI 2021, Held as Part of the 23rd HCI International Conference, HCII 2021, Virtual Event, July 24–29, 2021, Proceedings, Part III, pp. 198–213. Springer International Publishing. (2021). https://doi.org/10.1007/978-3-030-78468-3_14
13. Yan, B., Huang, Q., Yuan, C.: Research on digital design of intangible cultural heritage from the perspective of playfulness. Packaging Eng. **42**(22), 40–46 (2021). https://doi.org/10.19554/j.cnki.1001-3563.2021.22.007.

Research on Innovative Strategies of Museum Display Design to Improve User Experience

Jiaying Huang and Wenhua Li(✉)

Guangzhou Academy of Fine Arts, No. 168 Waihuan West Road, Panyu District, Guangzhou 510000, China
vivian.lee8686@gmail.com

Abstract. This research aims to explore innovative strategies in museum exhibition design to enhance user experience. Through a comprehensive analysis of the evolution of museum exhibition design and relevant theories of user experience, coupled with case studies, the study delves into the application of innovative strategies in exhibition design, including technological innovation, interactive design, cultural diversity design, and sustainable design.

In terms of technological innovation, the study focuses on the integration of new technologies in exhibition design practices. These technologies not only provide visitors with immersive experiences but also make exhibition content more vivid and captivating. In the realm of interactive design, the paper discusses how new technologies meet users' multidimensional needs, enhance interaction between visitors and museum exhibits, stimulate user engagement, and improve the overall exhibition experience. Concerning cultural diversity design, the research highlights cross-cultural collaborations between museums and other international or cultural institutions. In sustainable design, the study investigates museums' use of eco-friendly materials and sustainable development strategies to reduce environmental impact.The research findings reveal that these innovative strategies have varying degrees of impact on enhancing the attractiveness, engagement, and comprehensibility of museum exhibitions. Case studies further validate the effectiveness of these strategies in practical applications. The results provide practical recommendations for professionals in the field of museum exhibition design to optimize visitors' experiences and offer directions for future research.

Keywords: museum · exhibition design · user experience · innovative strategies

1 Introduction

1.1 Background

As people's living environments rapidly evolve and lifestyles change, the current state of museum exhibition design is in need of innovation, with room for improvement in both the realm of physical artifacts and exhibition design strategies. Diverging from the past, where "non-material entities" were included in the exhibition category, such as visual, tactile, and auditory elements, the category of physical artifacts is deeply

M. Kurosu and A. Hashizume (Eds.): HCII 2024, LNCS 14688, pp. 343–358, 2024.
https://doi.org/10.1007/978-3-031-60449-2_23

influenced by concepts like "ecological museums" and the "post-museum," incorporating specific scenarios and skills into its scope [1]. A plenty of emerging "non-material" exhibits continues to surface, but the concepts behind these new entities are not clearly defined, and their exhibition design methods are still in the process of exploration. Based on this, it becomes crucial to find a logical thread that can traverse the chaos and uncertainty between "material" and "non-material," guiding development consistently and enhancing the viewer's experience. Therefore, innovation in museum exhibition design strategies is imperative.

In this new context, museums must undergo a fresh reflection on their identity, acknowledging the inherent limitations of truth. Curators need to recognize that the perspectives they provide are observations or even subjective statements, not requiring absolute agreement from the audience but aiming to offer beneficial insights or stimulate reflective thinking [2]. Throughout the entire experience of interacting with exhibits, museums interpret their understanding of the exhibition to participants, and a logically structured, widely accepted exhibition design needs to depict the exhibits from the participants' five senses—vision, hearing, touch, smell, and taste [3]. Simultaneously, the use of new technological means is necessary to supplement the exhibition effects that traditional museums cannot achieve, extending the narrative of exhibition places for better communication.

In summary, museum exhibition design plays a crucial role in enhancing user experience. A well-designed exhibition can spark curiosity, enhance the learning experience for visitors, and transform the entire museum into a captivating place for cultural, historical, or scientific exploration."

1.2 Research Questions

A well-designed and captivating exhibition can guide visitors to better understand the exhibition content through layout, display, and interactive elements. Enhancing visitors' awareness of historical, cultural, or scientific themes is achieved by conveying information and storytelling. Exhibition design needs to ensure a structured exploration of exhibits, ensuring visitors can navigate according to themes or timelines, while avoiding information overload or missing important content. Excessive information and exhibits may leave visitors unsure of where to begin, making it challenging to focus. When using new technologies, complexities or difficulties in understanding may arise, causing visitor discomfort. Museums must ensure purposeful use of technology that enhances rather than disrupts the user experience. As Mies van der Rohe stated, "The form and communication of exhibition design are part of the viewer's appreciation of the exhibition, but its essence is the design of the medium, as a medium that satisfies the viewer's demands and presents the exhibits. This implies that exhibition design without the context of exhibit content is not universally meaningful [4]. " Museums need to strive to create an environment that is easily accessible and understandable for everyone.

Some traditional museum exhibitions lack interactive elements, resulting in a relatively passive visitor experience. To attract younger visitors and enhance engagement, museums may need to integrate more interactive elements. Visitors of different ages, cultural backgrounds, and interests have varied expectations and needs from museums. Museums must balance these diverse requirements to ensure all types of visitors have a satisfying experience. Additionally, cultural sensitivity needs to be considered in design to avoid misunderstandings or inappropriate reactions to exhibition content. It is essential to ensure that the design of the display and the presentation of the artifacts respect various cultural differences. In the digital age, museums need to adapt to the development of new technologies while maintaining traditional exhibition methods. Improving user experience is a comprehensive challenge, which requires museums to strike a balance in design, technological applications, cultural sensitivity, and sustainability to create an engaging, educational, diverse, and sustainable visiting experience.

1.3 Research Objectives

The research aims to understand the needs and expectations of visitors of museum, enabling the customization of exhibition designs based on visitors' interests and backgrounds. This, in turn, assists museums in optimizing the layout of exhibition spaces to enhance the overall spatial experience.

Through the investigation, we seek to explore innovative exhibition designs that augment visitors' engagement. This involves integrating interactive elements, employing new technologies, or adopting participatory display methods to encourage active participation from visitors. Museums are encouraged to make full use of technologies for enhancing the attractiveness and educational value of exhibitions, thereby advancing the application of cutting-edge technologies.

The research also delves into understanding the cultural backgrounds and sensitivities of audiences, aiding museums in creating more inclusive display designs. This understanding contributes to museums' sustainability by formulating sustainable exhibition design strategies, including considerations for material selection, display methods, and exhibition update frequencies, ensuring that the attractiveness of museum displays endures over the long term.

In summary, the purpose of researching innovative strategies for museum exhibition design is to better meet visitors' demands, enhance user experiences, promote technological advancements, and foster cultural sensitivity. The ultimate goal is to create more compelling and educational exhibition experiences.

2 Literature Review

2.1 Major Perspectives and Developments in Museum Exhibition Design in the Literature

Since the creation of the "Interactive Experience Model" by John H. Falk and Lynn Dierking in "*The Museum Experience*" in 1992 [5], research on museum experiences has become a prominent topic in the museum community. Pekarik and Andrew J emphasized from the perspective of emotional interaction that the museum experience is the curiosity and excitement triggered during the exhibition process, awakening hearts and minds [6]. Professor Jixiang Shi categorized museum experiences into entertainment, education, aesthetics, and escapism based on the multidimensionality of experiences, noting that experiences involving multiple senses are the most memorable [7]. Kotler described the museum experience as immediate, emphasizing that it involves the audience directly, allowing them to understand relevant information through sensory stimulation [8].

The previous research and literature on museum exhibition design have highlighted the following major points:

- **Static Displays**: Previous museum exhibition designs often focused on static displays, presenting exhibits through showcases, labels, and textual explanations. This traditional approach emphasized the objective presentation of items but had limitations in interactivity and engagement.
- **Expertise and Authority**: Earlier designs emphasized the museum's image as a knowledge authority and academic institution. Display layouts, labels, and explanatory texts prioritized conveying professional knowledge, highlighting the museum's scholarly nature.
- **Linear Storytelling**: Past exhibition designs typically employed linear storytelling, arranging exhibits in chronological or thematic order, guiding visitors along a predesigned path.
- The current perspectives include the following major aspects:
- **Interactivity and Engagement**: Modern museum exhibition design emphasizes the interactivity and engagement of the visitors. Designers strive to create more participatory experiences through technological means, allowing visitors to actively engage in the exhibition.
- **Narrative and Emotional Connection**: Contemporary designs focus on attracting audiences through narrative elements and emotional connections. Instead of just emphasizing the objective information of the objects on display, efforts are made to resonate with visitors through storytelling and emotions.
- **Diversified Educational Approaches**: Current museum exhibition design places more emphasis on diversified educational methods, including elements based on experiential learning, using multisensory experiences to help visitors better understand exhibits.
- **Customized Experiences**: Modern designs lean towards providing personalized and customized experiences. Through the use of smart technology, museums can tailor guides and exhibition content based on visitors' interests and specific needs.
- **Social Interaction**: Today's museum exhibition design places greater emphasis on social interaction, encouraging visitors to share their museum experiences and fostering communication among visitors.

It can be observed that traditional museum layouts focused on categorizing exhibits and chronological order, while modern museums increasingly emphasize interactivity, engagement, and experiential aspects. Spatial design needs to consider the flow of visitors to ensure that they can smoothly appreciate exhibits while providing a rich visual and sensory experience. Modern museum exhibition design places greater emphasis on audience participation and experience, incorporating more interactive technologies and emotional design elements to create a more attractive and personalized museum experience. This reflects an understanding of changing visitors' demands and the impact of technological development on museum exhibition methods.

2.2 Application of Different User Experience Models in the Museum Context

The application of various user experience models in the museum context aims to gain a deeper understanding of visitors' perceptions, engagement, and satisfaction within the museum environment. Here are some common user experience models that have been practically applied in museums:

a. **Service Blueprint Model.** The service blueprint model is used to visualize service processes and emphasizes the interaction between users and service providers. In museums, the service blueprint can help identify interactions between visitors and exhibits, staff, and other service points to optimize service processes. For example, identifying the interaction between guided tours, ticket purchases, and explanatory activities to enhance the overall experience.
b. **Customer Journey Mapping.** Customer journey mapping covers the entire user experience process [9], from entering the museum to leaving, for a comprehensive understanding of user interactions. Through customer journey mapping, museums can identify potential bottlenecks or highlights in the visitor experience. For instance, mapping paths between exhibition areas, interactive installations, and service points to determine areas of visitor interest and improve layout and information delivery.
c. **Five E Model.** The Five E model consists of "Engage," "Explore," "Explain," "Elaborate," and "Evaluate" stages [10]. This model emphasizes the process from visitor introduction to in-depth engagement, which provide a more comprehensive learning experience. In exhibition design, this model can be implemented by engaging interactive elements (Engage), in-depth artifact explanations (Explain), and participatory activities (Elaborate).
d. **Emotion Design Model.** The emotion design model focuses on the emotional and affective aspects of the user experience to create a more profound and resonant experience [11]. In museums, through the emotion design model, designers can focus on how to evoke emotional experiences through exhibition design, sound effects, and interactive elements. For example, adding music or sound effects to exhibition areas to enhance the emotional connection between visitors and exhibits.

These models are often used in conjunction in the museum design and operation process to comprehensively understand and improve the user experience. For example, museums may use service blueprints and customer journey mapping to identify issues in operational processes, and then enhance users' perception in exhibitions through the Five E model and emotion design model. Such integrated applications contribute to creating a more meaningful and satisfying museum experience.

2.3 Innovative Strategies in Museum Exhibition Design Mentioned in the Literature

The literature highlights several innovative strategies in the field of museum exhibition design, covering various aspects. Some crucial innovative strategies include: enhancing interactivity and engagement, digitizing displays, offering personalized guided tours, interdisciplinary exhibitions, integrating with social media, promoting sustainability and eco-friendly design, experimenting with exhibitions, and engaging with the community.

These innovative strategies reflect the ongoing trend in the field of museum exhibition design to enhance engagement, integrate digital technology, focus on sustainability, provide personalized services, and encourage social interaction. With the evolution of technology and changing visitors' expectations, these strategies will continue to evolve and bring about even more enriching and captivating museum experiences. These viewpoints and developments signify the continuous evolution of the museum exhibition design field, transitioning from traditional display methods to modern design concepts emphasizing interactivity, education, and sustainability. The research and literature play a guiding and inspiring role, providing designers with rich insights and practical experiences.

3 Innovative Strategies for Enhancing User Experience in Museum Exhibition Design

3.1 Technology Integration

Integrating new technologies into museum exhibition design to enhance visitor's experience and appeal involves various innovative strategies. Here are some ways to integrate new technologies:

Augmented Reality (AR) and Virtual Reality (VR). Utilize AR and VR technologies to provide immersive experiences for visitors, enabling them to interact with exhibits, explore virtual environments, or traverse through time. Offer AR guidance to help visitors gain deeper insights into exhibition content, such as displaying additional information or multimedia content through AR tags. For historical exhibitions, AR glasses or mobile apps can allow visitors to see virtual reconstructions of the buildings in the past period at the same location, providing insights into historical changes. The "Virtual Museum" project at the Nature and History Museum in the UK, utilizing VR technology, allows visitors to experience museum exhibitions at home or within the museum through wearable devices.

Interactive Technologies. Employ touchscreens, gesture recognition, and other technologies to design interactive exhibits, allowing visitors to actively engage and interact with exhibition content. Develop multi-user interactive experiences, encouraging collaboration and communication among visitors. For example, in a science museum, a large globe controlled by gestures enables visitors to freely rotate, zoom, and explore different aspects of the Earth.

Internet of Things (IoT) and Sensor Technology. Use sensors to collect visitors' behavior data for improving exhibit layout and enhancing personalized experiences. Combine IoT technology to create smart exhibits that interact with visitors, providing personalized information. In art museums, sensors are installed to track the time visitors spend, and lighting and exhibits are adjusted according to the data to improve visitors' comfort and attention.

Multimedia and Real-time Data. Multimedia projection, holographic imaging, and other technologies are employed to create visually engaging effects, making exhibits more attractive. Integrate real-time data, such as social media feedback and visitor hotspots, to provide dynamic and engaging experiences. For instance, in a natural history museum, dinosaur reconstructions are displayed using holograms and real-time weather data is integrated, allowing visitors to see simulated behaviors of dinosaurs in different weather conditions on the screen.

Artificial Intelligence (AI) and Machine Learning. Utilize AI to offer personalized exhibit recommendations based on visitors' interests and their previous visiting experiences. Their behaviors are analyzed through machine learning algorithms to improve exhibit layout and content presentation. In art museums, facial recognition technology and machine learning algorithms are used to recommend exhibits relevant to visitors' art preferences.

Wearable Devices and Mobile Applications. Develop mobile applications related to exhibitions, providing guided tours, interactive games, augmented reality browsing, etc. Integrate wearable devices like smart glasses to offer enhanced visual and informational layers. For museums near historical sites, provide a mobile app supporting real-time navigation and AR displays, allowing visitors to gain in-depth knowledge of the historical sites.

Digital Archives and Online Interaction. Digitize museum collections, create online platforms for visitors to access exhibits anytime, anywhere. Facilitate interaction and sharing among visitors through social media, blogs, online discussions, etc. For example, provide digital exhibition content, including high-resolution images, explanatory texts, and online discussion features on the museum's official website or app.

Sustainable Technology. Utilize sustainable technologies like energy-efficient lighting, smart temperature control systems, etc., to reduce the museum's environmental impact. Promote digital displays to decrease reliance on paper materials, enhancing sustainability.

The examples above show how museums enhance visitors' interaction, personalized perception, and in-depth understanding of exhibition content by integrating new technologies. The successful integration of innovative strategies requires a profound understanding of visitor needs, exhibition themes, and available technologies.

3.2 Narrative Design

Engaging narrative design is a common and effective approach in museum exhibition design. This design method helps stimulate visitors' interest, enhance their sense of involvement, and improve the learning experience. An engaging story or plot can capture visitors' attention as they enter the exhibition area, making them more willing to delve into the exhibition content. Through narrative and storytelling displays, visitors find it easier to establish emotional connections with exhibits. An engaging narrative can trigger visitors' emotions, making them feel involved and facilitating a deeper understanding of the exhibition's theme. Additionally, captivating storytelling helps establish the exhibition's theme and core information clearly. Visitors gradually grasp the meaning behind the exhibition through the plot, going beyond merely viewing exhibited items. Narrative designs can be interactive, allowing visitors to participate by making choices, solving problems, or engaging in interactive displays, thereby enhancing their involvement. This interactivity can be achieved through visitors' choices, problem-solving, or participation in interactive displays, increasing engagement.

Narrative designs can attract visitors to explore exhibition spaces progressively, prolonging their stay. Interesting storylines and captivating narratives are more likely to be remembered by visitors. By creating an attractive narrative, museums can increase the depth of visitor memory regarding the exhibited information. Engaging narrative designs focus not only on individual exhibits but also on creating a coherent experience for the entire exhibition. Visitors experience a complete storyline during their visit, improving their overall understanding of the exhibition's significance.

In summary, adopting engaging narrative design enhances the attractiveness, educational value, and interactivity of museum exhibition design, thus meeting visitor expectations and encouraging deeper engagement and experience.

3.3 Personalized Experience

Providing a personalized experience is a crucial task in museum exhibition design to cater to the diverse interests and demands of different visitors. Here are some strategies to assist museums in offering more targeted experiences through personalized content:

User Analysis and Data Collection. Utilize technological means such as mobile apps, smart devices, etc., to collect visitor behavior data, including dwell time, visiting paths, interaction information, etc. Conduct user surveys to understand visitors' interests, age groups, academic backgrounds, etc.

Personalized Guided Tours. Utilize mobile apps or guided devices to offer personalized exhibition tour routes based on users' interests and preferences. By setting up personalized guides, users can gain more in-depth knowledge about exhibits related to their interests.

Interactive Experience Design. Design interactive exhibits using technologies such as touchscreens, gesture recognition, etc., allowing visitors to interact with exhibits in a personalized manner. Provide personalized interactive games or tasks to stimulate visitors' interests and curiosity. For instance, set up touchscreen displays in the museum, allowing visitors to interactively explore exhibit information. The Museum of Modern Art (MoMA) in New York has touchscreen areas where visitors can delve into the stories behind artworks.

Some museums offer online or mobile applications that allow visitors to virtually tour exhibits outside the museum, providing an opportunity to preview exhibition content. This design can increase visitors' anticipation and interest, as seen in the "Museum of the World" online project by the British Museum.

Multisensory Experience. Employ audio, aroma, touch, and other multisensory elements to enhance visitors' perception of exhibition content. Donald A. Norman categorizes user experience into the visceral, behavioral, and reflective levels, corresponding to sensory, interactive, and emotional dimensions, respectively. Use sensory elements related to visitors' daily experiences to design exhibits that are easier to understand and resonate with. By introducing visual, auditory, tactile, olfactory, and gustatory elements, with attractive colors, lighting effects, sounds, aromas, etc., museums can stimulate visitors' perception and emotions. Specific implementations include audio guides, aroma machines, and allowing tactile interaction with exhibits, providing visitors with a richer sensory experience. The Los Angeles County Museum of Art garnered attention with its multisensory exhibit "Rain Room," creating a unique experience where visitors could walk in the rain without getting wet, thanks to sensors and technology.

Digital Content Presentation. Digitize museum collections and provide online platforms for users to access exhibits remotely. Utilize virtual reality (VR) or augmented reality (AR) technology to offer immersive experiences with digital exhibits.

Social Media Interaction. Encourage visitors to share their museum experiences through social media. Create interactive exhibits allowing real-time interaction via social media, such as taking photos in front of exhibits and sharing them.

Personalized Narration and Commentary. Provide audio guides or multilingual support, allowing visitors to understand exhibit content in their preferred language. Based on visitors' previous visit records, offer personalized exhibit commentary or in-depth information.

Participatory Experience. Design interactive stations within exhibits, allowing visitors to participate in content creation, such as message boards, digital walls, etc. Organizing themed events allows visitors to contribute to exhibit creation or selection.

Personalized Recommendation Systems. Use artificial intelligence (AI) and machine learning to analyze visitors' previous data, providing personalized exhibit recommendations. Integrate recommendation systems into museum apps, pushing exhibition information relevant to users' interests.

By comprehensively applying these strategies, museums can better meet the needs of different visitors, providing a more personalized and targeted exhibition experience. This helps improve engagement, interest, and satisfaction, making museums more appealing cultural experience venues.

3.4 Collaboration and Resource Sharing

Collaboration between museums and other institutions can optimize resource utilization, increase interactivity, and contribute to achieving cultural and educational goals. Consider collaborating with other museums or cultural institutions to share resources and experiences. This may involve jointly developing technological platforms, sharing exhibition content, or coordinating educational activities. Through collaboration, museums can get more support in situations where resources are limited. Here are common ways museums collaborate with other institutions:

Academic Collaboration Establish research collaborations with universities, research institutions, academic societies, and other scholarly organizations to jointly explore and conduct research projects on cultural, historical, or artistic subjects. This can include organizing academic lectures, workshops, research projects, etc.

Educational Institution Collaboration. Assist educational institutions in developing museum education programs, providing student visits, internships, teaching resources, etc. Collaborating with schools, training centers, etc., can offer interdisciplinary learning opportunities, allowing students to gain a comprehensive understanding of history, culture, and art. Modern museum exhibition design aims to balance education and entertainment. The design is intended to provide both educational and enjoyable experiences. Visitors need to gain knowledge during the exhibition while also having an enjoyable experience. Therefore, museums need to find a balance between education and entertainment to attract a broader audience.

Art and Cultural Group Collaboration. Collaborate with artists to co-host art exhibitions, literary events, concerts, etc. This helps connect the museum with the local art and cultural scene, providing visitors with diverse cultural experiences.

Business and Industry Collaboration. Leverage resources from businesses, industrial parks, chambers of commerce, etc., to support and sponsor museum projects. Collaboration may also include jointly organizing events like corporate culture exhibitions, industry forums, fostering communication between museums and the business sector.

Community and Non-Profit Organization Collaboration. Collaborate with the community to organize community engagement activities, social service projects, enhancing the museum's social responsibility. Collaboration with non-profit organizations can address shared societal issues such as environmental conservation, social justice, etc.

Tourism and Cultural Institution Collaboration. Engage in joint promotional activities, cultural tourism packages, etc., to attract more visitors. Museums can collaborate with local tourism agencies to collectively promote local culture and tourism development.

Digital Media and Technology Company Collaboration. Collaborate with digital media and technology companies to develop virtual tour applications, online exhibitions, digital exhibits, etc., enhancing the museum's digital capabilities and expanding the audience.

Government Collaboration. Collaborate with local governments, cultural departments, seeking resources, and financial support to jointly promote cultural development. Collaboration may also involve urban planning, making the museum a cultural landmark in the city.

Through collaboration with various institutions, museums can optimize resource utilization, expand influence, and increase the likelihood of sustainable development. This comprehensive collaboration helps drive cultural exchange, broaden the museum's social role, and create more mutually beneficial opportunities.

3.5 Cultural Diversity Design

In recent years, museum exhibition design has increasingly emphasized cultural diversity and reflection. Museums need to consider how to present viewpoints from different cultural backgrounds, avoid a singular perspective, and promote understanding and respect. Museums can engage in cross-cultural collaborations with other countries or cultural institutions to co-curate exhibitions, showcasing diverse cultures. For example, the Louvre Museum in Paris collaborated with the National Museum of China, co-hosting cultural exchange exhibitions that allow visitors to better understand both cultures.

To cater to visitors with different language backgrounds, museums can adopt multilingual commentary systems to ensure that all visitors comprehend exhibition content. For instance, the Berlin Museum Island uses multilingual commentary devices, providing commentary in English, French, Spanish, and other languages.

3.6 Sustainable Design

Sustainability has become a significant consideration in museum exhibition design—how to use eco-friendly materials, reduce energy consumption, and implement recyclability of materials post-exhibition. Utilizing eco-friendly materials involves using biodegradable or recyclable materials for constructing exhibit stands and display installations.

Implementing energy-efficient and eco-friendly design strategies considers energy-saving and environmental strategies in museum building and venue operation, such as adopting solar power generation, rainwater harvesting, and other technologies. The Sydney Science Museum is an example, incorporating various sustainable technologies, including renewable energy and energy-efficient equipment.

Through social media and digital platforms, museums can extend their influence through online exhibitions and virtual experiences while reducing some physical exhibition design and maintenance costs, minimizing material consumption.

These application examples of innovative strategies indicate that museum exhibition design continually pursues innovation to enhance visitor experiences and deepen appreciation and understanding of exhibitions.

4 Strategies for Addressing Limited Resources in Museum Exhibition Design

Addressing the challenges of limited resources in museum exhibition design involves a series of strategies encompassing technology, design, collaboration.

4.1 Modular and Upgradable Technology Integration

Implement modular technology integration, allowing different components to operate independently, facilitating gradual upgrades and replacements. Opt for open-source technologies to reduce costs and enhance maintainability. The American Museum of Natural History utilizes an open-source exhibition management system, customizable based on the museum's needs, featuring a modular design to adapt to various exhibition requirements.

4.2 Simplified Narrative Design

Adopt a simplified yet powerful narrative structure to enable visitors to easily understand and engage. Use interactive displays and storyboards to convey information in a simple yet captivating manner. The British Museum employs digital interactive panels in exhibitions, allowing visitors to click and explore the stories behind each artifact in a simple and profound narrative presentation.

4.3 Data-Driven Personalized Experience

Utilize visitor data and intelligent algorithms to provide personalized exhibition experiences. This includes customized audio guides, personalized virtual exhibitions, and recommendation systems. The Rijksmuseum's mobile app analyzes user browsing history and interests, offering personalized art recommendations and interactive experiences.

4.4 Collaboration and Resource Sharing

Establish partnerships with other museums, cultural institutions, and technology companies to share exhibition content, technology platforms, and resources, reducing costs. The European Museum Collaboration Organization (EMYA) is an alliance of multiple museums that share exhibitions, educational projects, and digital resources to enhance overall efficiency.

4.5 Digital Platforms and Social Media

Expand exhibition content to online spaces using digital platforms and social media, attracting more visitors. This includes virtual exhibitions, online lectures, and social media interactions. The Metropolitan Museum of Art collaborates with Google, providing a virtual museum tour feature, allowing global visitors to explore the museum's art online.

In addition, different museums need customized solutions based on their specific situations and goals. Small museums face unique challenges due to more limited resources.

4.6 Challenges and Solutions for Small Museums

Limited Budget Challenge. Tetley's Brewery Wharf, a small museum in Leeds, overcame budget constraints through creative exhibition design. They utilized old equipment and architectural structures to design an historically immersive exhibit, conveying the history of brewing through informative display boards and simple interactive elements.

Limited Space Challenge. Mini Bottle Gallery in Oslo, Norway, one of the world's smallest museums, focused on collecting various small bottles. Facing limited space, they implemented design elements like wall cabinets, miniature displays, and magnifying glasses, enabling visitors to closely appreciate each bottle in a unique and space-efficient exhibition environment.

Technology Equipment Cost Challenge. The Museum of Broken Relationships in Zagreb, Croatia, a small museum showcasing items related to past relationships, minimized technology costs by using simple display methods such as photos, handwritten letters, and short videos instead of investing heavily in expensive technical equipment.

Exhibit Protection Challenge. The Museum of Portable Sound in London, a unique small museum dedicated to sound collections, overcame exhibit protection costs by digitizing artifacts. Digital exhibits are experienced through visitors' personal headphones, with regular backups to ensure preservation.

Updating Exhibits Challenge. The Museum of the American Cocktail in New Orleans tackles the challenge of updating exhibits by collaborating with local cocktail industry professionals. They regularly rotate exhibits and stories, ensuring the museum's content remains fresh and engaging.

Education and Training Challenge. The Museum of Bad Art in Massachusetts, known for displaying poorly executed artworks, addresses budget constraints by recruiting enthusiastic volunteers, including students and art enthusiasts. The museum provides free training and practical opportunities, ensuring an adequate workforce for maintenance and development.

These cases illustrate that small museums can successfully overcome resource limitations through creative exhibition design, partnerships, community engagement, and volunteer support, delivering unique and enjoyable exhibition experiences. Starting from user cognition and emotions, exploring user needs throughout the entire experience, and employing a user-centric core philosophy in service design can improve the current inadequacies in museum services, maximizing the exhibition value while meeting personalized user needs.

5 Discussion

5.1 Practical Significance

Innovative strategies have multiple practical implications for museum exhibition design practice, including improved user experiences, cultural heritage promotion, and audience expansion. Introducing innovative strategies can transform traditional museum visitation, providing visitors with richer, more interactive, and immersive experiences. The application of digital displays, virtual reality, multimedia elements, and other technologies can spark visitors' interest, enhance the enjoyment of visits, and increase user satisfaction. The use of modern technological means facilitates a better presentation of cultural heritage, fostering its inheritance and preservation.

Digital displays offer more comprehensive and in-depth historical and artistic information, enabling visitors to better understand and appreciate cultural heritage. Digital exhibits attract a broader audience, particularly younger generations interested in new technologies. By utilizing digital learning resources, social media interaction, and other means, museums can expand their audience base, engaging more people in learning and appreciating culture and art.

The adoption of new technologies and design concepts allows museums to better adapt to societal trends and lead cultural innovation. Moreover, it contributes to enhancing the social influence of museums, making them integral to the cultural and creative industry. By continuously experimenting with and applying new exhibition design concepts and technologies, museums can take a leading position in the industry, providing new ideas and examples, driving the continuous development of the museum sector.

Innovative strategies make museums more educational by offering flexible and rich educational resources to schools and students through digital learning resources, online educational activities. This helps cultivate the learning interests and artistic literacy of the visitors. Innovative strategies enable museums to better cope with the challenges and opportunities of the digital age. Up-to-date designs such as digital displays, online interactions, and other progressive approaches meet the modern audience's demand for digital experiences, raising the overall digitalization level of museums.

In conclusion, the practical significance of innovative strategies in museum exhibition design lies in making museums more dynamic, attractive, and better fulfilling their cultural inheritance and educational missions. Simultaneously, it helps museums adapt to societal changes and technological advancements, elevating their status and influence in society.

5.2 Future Research Directions

Future research in innovative strategies for museum exhibition design continues to focus on the application of artificial intelligence (AI) and further explores the use of augmented reality (AR) and virtual reality (VR) technologies to provide more immersive and interactive exhibition experiences. Further research is needed on how to leverage AI technologies, including natural language processing and image recognition, to offer visitors more personalized and intelligent guidance services, recommending content based on their interests and feedback. Additionally, research on multisensory experience design is crucial, employing touch, smell, hearing, and other sensory modalities to provide a richer, three-dimensional sensory experience, enhancing audience perception of artifacts and exhibitions.

On another note, research into the sustainability of museum exhibition design, including material selection and energy utilization, is essential to minimize environmental impact and advocate for eco-friendlier museum operations. For designing museum exhibitions, sustainability and environmental conservation should be considered, incorporating renewable materials, energy-efficient devices, and green technologies. Emphasis should be placed on how museums can more closely relate to contemporary societal issues, presenting topics related to society, culture, technology, etc., through exhibition design to enhance the museum's sense of social responsibility. Promoting international cooperation in the field of museum exhibition design is crucial to facilitate knowledge and experience exchange among different museums. Moreover, interdisciplinary collaboration with other fields such as technology, design and sociology should be pursued to drive innovation.

These research directions will contribute to advancing innovation in the field of museum exhibition design, enhancing the attractiveness and influence of museums while meeting the diverse needs of audiences. In expanding this field, interdisciplinary collaboration and sharing of practical experiences will play a key role.

6 Conclusion

The contributions of innovative strategies to the field of museum exhibition design are diverse. They inject new ideas and elements into traditional exhibition design, propel museum development, enhance user experiences, and enable museums to better adapt to the demands of modern society. Encouraging museums to break free from traditional display models and experiment with more creative and unique designs, including open architectural designs, integration of multimedia elements, and multisensory experiences, creates entirely new visiting experiences for audiences.

The introduction of innovative strategies incorporating novel technologies and design concepts allows museums to attract a wider audience, including the younger generation interested in new technologies. This helps broaden the audience base of museums, engaging more people in learning and appreciating culture, history, and art. Through forms such as social media interaction and online communities, museums become platforms for social interaction and participation. Audiences can share viewpoints and exchange experiences through digital platforms, enhancing the interactivity between museums and visitors.

Museums need to better adapt to the challenges and opportunities of the digital age. Up-to-date designs such as digital displays, online interactions, and other progressive approaches meet the modern audience's demand for digital experiences, raising the overall digitalization level of museums and allowing them to better showcase and pass on cultural heritage. The progress of the entire museum industry is propelled through the introduction of new design concepts and technologies. Innovative practices in the museum industry not only stimulate competition but also provide opportunities for the industry to share new templates and experiences.

The application of new technologies can provide more in-depth historical and artistic information, aiding in better preserving and passing on culture. This makes museums more attractive and competitive, ultimately raising their status and influence in society. Through the introduction of new design concepts and technologies, museums transform into comprehensive entities for culture, education, and entertainment, attracting increased social attention.

In conclusion, innovative strategies bring new possibilities and opportunities to the field of museum exhibition design, driving a more comprehensive and diverse development of museums, better meeting the needs and expectations of audiences.

Acknowledgement. This article is for the 2022 Guangdong Province General Universities Youth Innovative Talent Project (Philosophy and Social Sciences) - Guangdong-Hong Kong-Macao Greater Bay Area Cultural and Creative Cross-media Design Research (No.: 2022WQNCX034), Guangzhou Academy of Fine Arts 2021 Guangzhou Academy of Fine Arts "Academic Improvement "Plan" scientific research project - Guangdong-Hong Kong-Macao Greater Bay Area intangible cultural heritage creative cross-media design and communication research (No. 21XSC52) phased results.

References

1. Degeng, L.: Liquid Museum. Culture and Art Publishing House, Beijing (2020)
2. Duan, J,-j.: Museum as an Educational Method. Southeast Cult. **283**(05), 183–189+191–192 (2021)
3. Harada, T., Hideyoshi, Y., Gressier-Soudan, E., et al.: Museum experience design based on multi-sensory transformation approach. In: 15th International Design Conference (2018)
4. Raju, P., Ahmed, V., Anumba, C.J.: Editorial: special issue on use of virtual world technology in architecture, engineering and construction. Itcon 2011(11)
5. Falk, J.H., Dierking, L.D.: The Museum Experience, p. 6. Routledge, New York (2016)

6. PEKARIK, ANDREW J. Studying Visitors and Making Museums Better[J]. Curator, 2004, 50(1): 34
7. Ji-xiang, S.H.I.: Audience research is a basic point of education research in museum: a new exploration of the definition of museum audience. Southeast Cult. **6**, 95–99 (2009)
8. Kotler, N.: Delivering experience; marketing the museum's full range of assets. Museum News **78**(3), 30 (1999)
9. Bernard, G., Andritsos, P.: A process mining based model for customer journey mapping. In: Forum and doctoral consortium papers presented at the 29th International Conference on Advanced Information Systems Engineering (CAiSE 2017). CEUR Workshop Proceedings, vol. 1848, pp. 49–56 (2017)
10. Albers, M. J.: Enhancing user experience with 5e models for multiple audiences. Terminology Science & Research Terminologie : Science Et Recherche 24, 4–12. Consulté à l'adresse (2023). https://journal-eaft-aet.net/index.php/tsr/article/view/5855
11. Ho, A.G., Michael, K.W., Siu, G.: Emotion design, emotional design, emotionalize design: a review on their relationships from a new perspective. Des. J. **15**(1), 9–32 (2012). https://doi.org/10.2752/175630612X13192035508462
12. Dal Falco, F., Vassos, S.: Museum experience design: a modern storytelling methodology. Des. J. **20**(sup1), S3975–S3983 (2017). https://doi.org/10.1080/14606925.2017.1352900
13. Hidayat, J.: Creating an Inclusive Museum with A Narrative Design Approach. In: 3rd International Conference on Creative Media, Design and Technology (REKA 2018), pp. 153–159. Atlantis Press (2018)
14. Norman, D.A.: Emotional Design: Why We Love (or Hate) Everyday Things. Basic Books, New York (2005)
15. Stogner, M.B.: The immersive cultural museum experience-creating context and story with new media technology. Inter. J. Inclusive Museum **3**(3), 117–130 (2010)

The Application of Miryoku Engineering to Artists' Books

Man-Wei Kao[1,2], Chia-Han Yang[1,2(✉)], and Hsi-Jen Chen[1,2(✉)]

[1] Institute of Creative Industries Design, National Cheng Kung University, Tainan city, Taiwan
PA6111040@gs.ncku.edu.tw, chyang@ncku.edu.tw, hsijen_chen@mail.ncku.edu.tw

[2] Industrial Design, National Cheng Kung University, Tainan city, Taiwan

Abstract. Artist's books take the form of a book as an artistic medium and utilize publishing as an artistic practice. Creators have complete control over the structure, content, paper, and printing of the entire book, making it a favored medium for its freedom and versatility. Artist's books have maintained a significant presence in the art world from the early 20th-century modern art movement to the present, and their portable and easily disseminated nature has rapidly garnered a community of enthusiasts. Books require active engagement, prompting readers to touch, open the cover, and explore their contents. Interactivity and a sense of participation are distinctive features of artist's books. These books are not merely passive reading materials but interactive artworks that engage the reader. This interactivity sparks the reader's creativity, placing them within the shared context of the artist's creation. The relationship between creator, book, and reader is inseparable. This study appreciates artists' books from the reader's perspective, utilizing the evaluation structure of attraction engineering and quantitative statistical analysis. Through the results of these analyses, an artist's book will be created to test the research hypotheses empirically. This book will embody the artist's creative vision, presenting unique insights into visual and sensory expression. The thesis aims to provide a substantive and practical perspective on the study of artists' books, emphasizing their inherent attractiveness and offering insights for future research. By combining theoretical exploration, we hope to comprehensively understand and highlight the unique value of artists' books.

Keywords: Artists' books · Miryoku Engineering · Attractiveness factors · Evaluation Grid Method

1 Introduction

1.1 Research Background

The art form known as artists' books resembles a book in appearance. Still, it grants creators a broad and unbridled range of control over their decoration methods, content, paper materials, printing, and more, resulting in a vast array of creations. The introduction of artists' books has invited readers into a new world, with related exhibitions and stores emerging to showcase the works and attract enthusiastic followers.

M. Kurosu and A. Hashizume (Eds.): HCII 2024, LNCS 14688, pp. 359–366, 2024.
https://doi.org/10.1007/978-3-031-60449-2_24

Initially emerging as a metaphorical space for curations in the 1960s, artists' books have evolved and transformed alongside art history, incorporating elements of Surrealism, Dadaism, post-modernism, and pop art. This ongoing development has resulted in a constantly shifting and evolving art form, which has gradually become an utterly individual expression, showcasing an artist's attempt, creativity, and cognition. Through evaluation, portability, copyability, and accessibility, artists' books have established three distinct and exceptional qualities, providing artists with a unique medium and greater creative latitude.

Artists' books are unique, book-like creations that are meticulously crafted by artists to achieve a specific aesthetic. These books are designed to be viewed as works of art in their own right. A variety of terms are used to describe this art form, such as Artistic Books, Book Art, Fine Press Books, Handmade Books, Art Books, Book Arts, and Limited Edition Books. Each term highlights different aspects of these books, such as the emphasis on books as art in Book Art or the use of high-quality materials in Fine Press Books. Limited Edition Books also accurately describes these books, as they are typically produced in limited quantities.

The term "Artists' books" gained popularity in the latter half of the 20th century. Clive Phillpot investigated why this particular term was used, given that there are no equivalents such as "artists' videos" or "artists' photography". However, there are two reasons why the term "artists' books" should be acknowledged. Firstly, it was necessary to distinguish between the traditional "art-of-the-book" practice and the commercial art book industry. Secondly, the term suggested that artist books were merely a hobby for artists who primarily focused on painting or sculpture. Nonetheless, this term may be misleading because artists' book production is not limited to artists. Musicians, poets, designers, philosophers, and others can all contribute to the creation of artists' books and be considered part of this category. While the term "artists' books" may not fully capture the essence of this art form, it is still useful for distinguishing between artists' books and other book-related works. This period marked the emergence of artists' books as an independent art form, with many artists viewing books as a new medium for their creative expression. Therefore, the use of this term may be attributed to its early adoption and widespread acceptance during this period, as well as the scholarly research and institutional attention devoted to artists' books.

Producing a work of artists' books involves careful consideration of layout, binding, printing, and materials. The artist's ideas are the driving force behind the creation, with no limits to the form it can take. Whether it's text, illustration, paper-cutting, or photography, the creator's vision can be conveyed. Communication is also an integral part of the process, with the viewer understanding the meaning behind the artists' books through their graphics, words, material, color, and even the artists' backgrounds. While every step in the book-making process requires ingenuity, it can also be inconvenient. The unique format, printing, and other details make these works of art difficult to produce in large quantities, with most artists' books limited to a few hundred copies. This limited nature makes collecting these works important and fosters a close relationship between creators and readers.

In 1977, Clive Phillpot took over as head of the Museum of Modern Art Library, where he began collecting and founding the artists' books collection. Soon after, these unique books were curated and promoted, and various bookstores and fairs began to emerge. Today, there are countless bookstores of all styles, but Printed Matter stands out as the world's leading non-profit organization dedicated to artists' books. Other bookstores, such as Whitechapel Gallery in London and POST in Tokyo, have their own unique targets and approaches. The goal is to bring these books to art museums and the public so that more people can appreciate this art form. Rather than simply displaying works, bookstores actively invite people in to experience the charm of artists' books, and creators can even meet and talk with customers. The first fair of artists' books was held in New York in 2005, attracting hundreds of publishers from around the world. As interest in artists' books grows, other fairs have emerged, such as the Seoul Art Book Fair and Tokyo Art Book Fair, showcasing the spirit and atmosphere of different countries.

1.2 The Application of Miryoku Engineering on Artists' Books

Compared with other works of art, artists' books are relatively cheap, portable, and reproducible. Many places can be used to show the personal charm of the creator in the same art form so as to attract readers to flip through it. Millions of records of artist books can be made, which gives artists a lot of freedom and unlimited imagination to play. The characteristics of the artist's books are numerous, and their charm is shown in different places with other senses. Because of the freedom to create, the idea of presenting or conveying each book is often beyond people's expectations, and through continuous appreciation of the work, we can expand our understanding of the artist's books. While reading through time, space, and dynamics, the viewer, the book, and the artist are left to discuss and stir up the excitement of the work.

It is not uncommon to come across the use of artists' books as a means of organizing the creative process and ideas into a cohesive ideology. Despite the rigorous nature of this art form, its meaning and the underlying reasons for choosing it can be easily comprehended by all. By delving into the works and the artists behind them, one can gain a deep understanding of this fascinating medium.

In addition, because of its vague scope and intertwined thoughts and development paths, many studies discuss its definition, role, and positioning so that everyone can slowly erase the hazy veil and better understand it.

Although many papers on artists' books approach the medium from the perspective of the artist, focusing on production and definition, the role of the viewer in the communication process is equally important. However, there has been less emphasis on the viewer's experience of this art form. This study seeks to bridge this gap by exploring the use of Miryoku Engineering, a design concept proposed by Masato Ujigaawa in 1911, to achieve a balance between artist and viewer. Specifically, we employ the Evaluation Grid Method in Miryoku Engineering, as developed by Junichiro Sanui and Masao Inui in 1985, to assess the perceptual connection between people and things and apply it to the field of artists' books. This research method is no longer limited to product development but can be used to explore the emotional communication between readers and creators that is central to the medium of artists' books. By using Miryoku Engineering to identify the elements that attract readers to these works, artists can better understand their audience and create works that strengthen communication between creator and viewer.

Hence, this research aims to delve into the key factors that make artists' books appealing. The reason for utilizing Miryoku Engineering in this study is because it is a well-established research methodology that focuses on attractiveness, appeal, and user experience. As artists' books are not just a form of reading material but also a work of art, it is crucial to place emphasis on user experience and interaction. Miryoku Engineering is particularly suited to this study as it highlights the factors that make readers enjoy artists' books. When it comes to artist books, the application of Miryoku Engineering can serve several purposes. Such as artists' books usually contain rich visual elements, such as artwork, illustrations, designs, etc. Miryoku Engineering can help to understand how these visual elements affect the readers' perceptual experience, including touch, visual enjoyment, etc. Miryoku Engineering provides a methodology for quantitative analysis and evaluation, which can quantify the degree of attraction and charm of the books and then compare the differences between books by different artists. This helps establish objective research methods and provides an empirical basis. Miryoku Engineering's methods are not only used for evaluation but can also guide design improvement. By understanding readers' feelings and expectations, artists and designers can specifically improve the appeal and interactivity of books. Also, Miryoku Engineering helps to gain a deeper understanding of the value of artists' books as works of art and explore their appeal to readers and the art community. This helps advance research and understanding in the field. The allure and charm of these books have a direct impact on the reader's emotions and engagement. Miryoku Engineering provides a comprehensive research framework that helps to understand the appeal, interactivity, and overall user experience of artist books. This approach helps to better integrate artist books into the context of design and research. A favorable impression of a particular book can lead to profound insights.

2 Research Design

2.1 Research Design

Miryoku Engineering. The concept of Miryoku Engineering was initially proposed by Japanese scholar Masato Ujigawa in 1911. He gathered several scholars to develop this research method and its purpose for research purposes. In 1998, the Japan Kansei Engineering Society was established, and Miryoku Engineering was incorporated into one of its branches. To capture the factors that make a product attractive, it is essential to understand how customers choose and their successful experiences while using it (Tomono, A, 2001). This research method believes charm is a subjective feeling composed of various factors, such as the product's appearance, function, sense of use, brand, emotion, etc. (Chen, C.-C., 2005). Miryoku Engineering aims to study these factors and determine how to create a product or space that will appeal to consumers. The process begins with product development and captures the alluring qualities through the intuitive senses of consumers. The theoretical basis of the study of Miryoku Engineering is mainly divided into three parts: fundamental theoretical doctrine, modeling, and design. The elements that need to be discussed for attractive products are listed in the table. Nowadays, due to changes in people's consumption patterns, related applications of Miryoku Engineering have expanded to various industries, such as tourism, festivals, and cultural and creative industries (Ma, M.-Y, 2010).

Evaluation Grid Method. The Evaluation Grid Method is a crucial research technique within the field of Miryoku Engineering, stemming from the realm of psychology. Its interview design is specifically crafted to capture an object's various factors of attractiveness. The EGM was first proposed by Junichiro Sanui and Masao Inui in 1985 and has since been utilized as a method to capture personal cognition and preferences, as well as their abstract and specific reasons. By listing and analyzing these factors, one can better understand the confusing, attractive, inducing, appealing, and emotional power of a product. This is achieved by asking respondents about the similarities and differences between two objects, selecting one based on their personal preferences, and then clarifying the reasoning behind their choice through supplementary questions. This process, which includes both abstract concepts and concrete elements, allows for the creation of a three-layer evaluation hierarchal map (Chen, Y.-F., & Ma, M.-Y., 2015).

2.2 Data Collection

Our plan is to conduct thorough interviews with 4–6 individuals utilizing the Evaluation Grid Method to gain insight into what makes an artist's book attractive. In the first part of the EGM process, visitors will be asked to share 3–5 artists' books that they personally enjoy and explain what they find appealing about them. This step serves as the median in EGM and allows us to analyze the abstract reasons behind their preferences. From there, we move to the upper level of EGM, where we conduct interviews to identify the specific features that contribute to these abstract reasons. By integrating these features, we can determine the attractiveness factors in EGM.

3 Results

Following the interview process outlined above, EGM conducted interviews with four readers. The resulting hierarchical maps were combined and integrated to form an overall map. The final map includes 4 high-level abstract emotions, 11 mid-level evaluation items, and 38 lower-level concrete features, which were further simplified and streamlined.

Upon analysis, it was discovered that the interviewees commonly expressed a sense of novelty and refreshment when discussing abstract emotions. The themes crafted by the creators often leave readers in awe. Approaching events or creations from a unique perspective can elicit a fresh and exciting response from readers. Furthermore, utilizing paper materials and binding techniques to convey concepts during the creative process is an innovative approach that can provide readers with a multi-sensory experience. This unexpected encounter can enhance readers' understanding of the work through experiential learning (Fig. 1).

Furthermore, the unique qualities of the artist's book, including its limited quantity, add to its allure. With a small number of copies in circulation, possessing this work fosters a deeply personal connection between the creator and reader, elevating its significance.

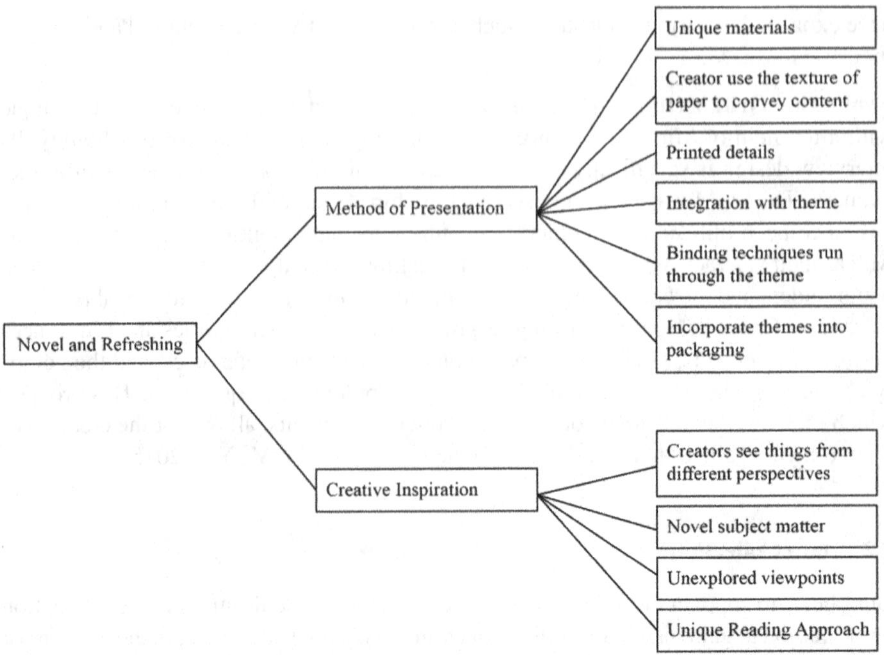

Fig. 1. Part of the Hierarchical Maps (Novel and Refreshing)

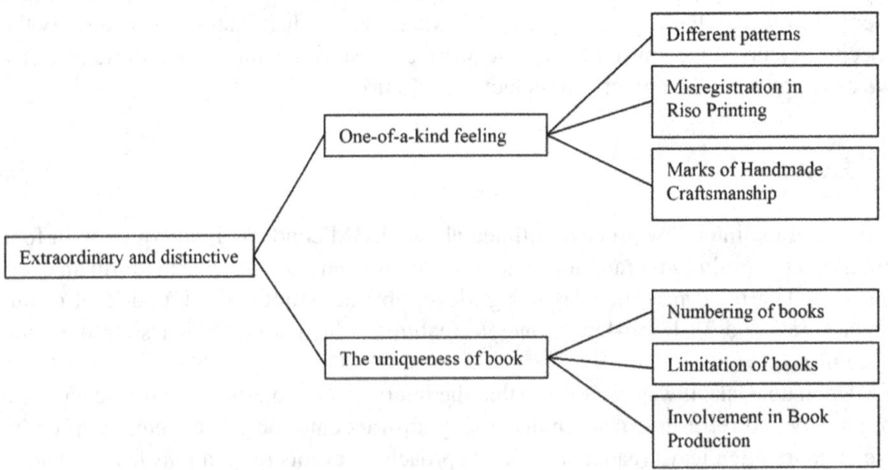

Fig. 2. Part of the Hierarchical Maps (Extraordinary and distinctive)

In fact, some artists' books are even numbered, further emphasizing their exclusivity. This feature instills a sense of pride in readers as they become one of the select few to own such a rare and coveted piece of art (Fig. 2).

While Clive Phillpot's definition of artists' books highlights the book's reproducibility, many interviewees often refer to the uniqueness of each book during interviews. This uniqueness is due to the uncertainty of the printing process, resulting in slight variations in the final output. Such variations enhance the reader's sense of ownership and participation in completing the work, ultimately fostering a deeper conversation between the reader and the creator.

4 Discussion

Based on the interviews, it's clear that readers appreciate a work more when they understand the author's intentions and techniques. They want to know who the author is, why they created the work, and what they're trying to express. This all adds to the overall experience of the work, and what readers love most is the unique perspective and ideas that the creator brings to the table. This can be eye-opening for readers, allowing them to see things in a new light. Additionally, the limited nature of artists' books is also a defining characteristic, making each one a special treasure for its owner to enjoy.

However, this study does not fully explore the appeal of artists' books. Miryoku Engineering is a field that examines consumers' perceptions of product attributes such as appearance, design, texture, emotional response, and more to gain a deeper understanding of how consumers feel about and respond to products. However, customers' views on products are highly subjective, and the range of products available is limitless. As a result, consumers' perceptions of charm vary greatly. The sample used in the study may not fully represent the entire consumer population, and certain Charisma preferences of specific ethnic groups or subgroups may have been overlooked, resulting in limited research findings.

Despite its limitations, Miryoku Engineering remains a valuable methodology. The proportion and number of mentions in the interviews serve as rankings for the attractiveness factors. Although the number of interviews conducted was limited, they still represent a portion of the readership. This study provides insight into the emotional and perceptual relationships between readers and artists' books and can inspire creators in their future endeavors.

5 Conclusion

Artists' books are crafted using various media, including paper, printing, and binding techniques. Through these methods, the creator conveys their message, while readers experience the work on a deeper level, influenced by factors such as the choice of paper. The selection of paper affects both the visual and tactile aspects of appreciating the work. Therefore, it is critical for the designer to carefully choose the appropriate paper material and printing method to convey the intended characteristics and message of the work.

Artists' books serve as a medium for communication between artists and readers. This research acknowledges the appeal of artist's books from the reader's point of view, facilitating an effortless dialogue between the two groups and providing creative inspiration and ideas for future artistic endeavors. This way, the readers can better appreciate and assimilate the content of the artist's books.

References

Bury, S.: Artists' books: the book as a work of art, 1963–1995. (No Title) (1995).

Chen, C.-C.: A study on the relationship between formative features and style evolution—taking circle chairs as an example. J. National Kaohsiung Normal Univ.: Natural Sci. Technol. **19**, 27–43 (2005)

Chen, Y.-F., Ma, M.-Y.: A Study on the Charm Factors of Coffee Shops in Old Houses in Tainan. Industrial Design, 133 (2015)

Chang, W.-H.: Not Even About Books: Publishing as (Art) Practice. (Master's thesis). Taipei National University of the Arts, Taiwan (2018). https://hdl.handle.net/11296/etkrk2

Chu, Y.-H.: Reading Notes: Book Phenomenon (2021)

Drucker, J.: The Century of Artists' Books. Granary Books (2004)

Elvin, K.: Materials & design. Mean. Mater. Sens. Prop. Manufact. Process. **30**(7), 2778–2784 (2009)

Hopkins, D.: Dada and Surrealism: A Very Short Introduction. Oxford University Press (2004). https://doi.org/10.1093/actrade/9780192802545.001.0001

Hildebrand-Schat, V.: The Exhibition Space: On the Hybridity of the Publication Between Execution and Extension of Spatiotemporal Concepts. In: Hildebrand-Schat, V., Bazarnik, K., Schulz, C.B. (eds.) Refresh the Book: On the Hybrid Nature of the Book in the Age of Electronic Publishing, pp. 273–287. BRILL (2021). https://doi.org/10.1163/9789004443556_013

Lai, W.-S.: The teaching art practice of artists' books at Yang-Ming Chiao Tung university. J. Modern Art, **42**, 78–119 (2021). https://www.tfam.museum/File/Journal/Content/47/20211223135749812315.pdf?ddlLang=zh-tw

Mohsen, R., Ahmed, S.: Using abstract color paintings expressing feelings to design textile prints showing emotional human factors of design and considering differences of color perception between humans. Int. J. Innov. Appl. Stud. **5**(1), 49 (2014)

National Museum of History Editorial Committee. (2007). Artists' Books: From Matisse to Contemporary Art = Le livre d'artiste: de Matisse a l'art contemporain (1st ed.). National Museum of History

Phillpot, C.: Books, bookworks, book objects, artists' books. Artforum **20**(9), 77–79 (1982)

Phillpot, C.: BOOKTREK. JRP/Ringier (2013)

Tomono, A.: Practical Attraction Engineering: An Approach to Creating Hit Products. Kaibundo (2001)

Tsai, Y.-Q.: Home Letters — The Paper Sensation of Memory. (Master's thesis). National Chiao Tung University, Taiwan (2017). https://hdl.handle.net/11296/8t23qs

Reynolds, M. Documents of Dada and Surrealism: Dada and Surrealist Journals in the Mary Reynolds Collection

Integrating Virtual and Real: A Holistic Framework for Mixed Reality Interactive Design in Museum Exhibitions

Jingyu Liu[1], Guoyu Sun[2](✉), and Mohammad Shidujaman[1,2]

[1] Communication University of China, No. 1 Dinfuzhuang East Street, Beijing, China
cucliujingyu@cuc.edu.cn, Shidujaman@iub.edu.bd

[2] Department of Computer Science and Engineering, Independent University Bangladesh, Dhaka, Bangladesh
gysun@cuc.edu.cn

Abstract. This paper proposes a framework for interaction design in museums that utilizes Mixed Reality (MR) technology. The framework combines virtual and real exhibition spaces to improve the connection between exhibit information and the user. The framework includes creating immersive environments with virtual-physical integration, designing for multi-temporal and spatial interactive narratives, and developing multimodal sensory interactions. This framework aims to bridge research gaps in the characteristics of mixed reality technology and museum interaction design, while strengthening the relationship between the exhibition space and its theme. These elements have already been examined individually. The 'Chuanmei Guiding' case study demonstrates the effectiveness of the proposed interaction design framework and the potential of MR technology to improve the interactivity and educational functions of museum exhibits.

Keywords: Mixed Reality · Museum Exhibition · Interaction Framework · Meta Quest Pro

1 Introduction

Museums are undergoing a crucial period of digital transformation. In today's society, museums are no longer just large cabinets of cultural heritage; they have also become important venues for information dissemination and cultural exchange. During this transformation, with the development of emerging media technologies, we have witnessed a fundamental change in the ways people acquire knowledge and experience culture. This change has prompted museum exhibition models to shift from traditional information displays to more interactive and immersive experience designs. The application of digital media initially focused on digital information assistance functions through public spaces or online mobile platforms [14,22], and later evolved to use smart devices for providing explanations and interactive information guides. To enhance visitors' experiences

M. Kurosu and A. Hashizume (Eds.): HCII 2024, LNCS 14688, pp. 367–387, 2024.
https://doi.org/10.1007/978-3-031-60449-2_25

further, museums have begun integrating social media and developing gamification interaction modes, such as treasure hunts, "Horuss," "Museum Conspiracy," or collecting souvenirs and photos [20], continuously exploring how to leverage media technology to strengthen visitors' experiences.

However, the digital transformation of museums still faces challenges. Museums, as educational venues that convey historical and cultural information and showcase individual and collective memories, are characterized by high information density, complex narrative spatiotemporal structures, and high interconnectivity [15], necessitating the provision of more comprehensive immersive experiences and deep information cognition for users. This raises higher requirements for the digital transformation of museums, demanding the construction of a dynamic, context-rich, multimodal interactive environment that integrates virtual and real elements. There has been considerable research focusing on the exploration of Virtual Reality (VR) and Mixed Reality (MR) technologies, which offer users novel immersive experiences, enabling them to fully appreciate the environment surrounding them [12,14,22].

Mixed Reality technology has the potential to meet the needs of museum exhibitions with its characteristics of integrating virtual and real environments, real-time interaction, and three-dimensional spatial perception. On one hand, these features compensate for the shortcomings of abstract concepts and the concrete representation of knowledge in the physical world, providing users with richer information channels for a deeper cognitive experience. On the other hand, museums have a high potential to project an entire MR scene that includes virtual locations, storytelling, characters, objects, and user interface (UI) [16], enhancing visitors' spatial perception within the exhibition through a seamless integration of physical and virtual spaces. This not only strengthens visitors' spatial awareness in exhibitions but also expands the flow of information between exhibition spaces, exhibits, and audiences. By presenting the spatial information of physical world exhibitions and two-dimensional information such as visiting paths in a richer format, it creates an immersive visiting environment that blends virtual and real elements [27,28], thereby redefining the traditional museum experience and increasing the efficiency of cultural information dissemination.

Despite the immense potential offered by Mixed Reality technology, effectively integrating MR technology into museum exhibitions remains a challenge. With the rapid development of MR technology platforms and the diversification of devices, traditional Graphical User Interfaces (GUI) and 3D User Interfaces (3DUI) in virtual reality cannot adapt to the interactive scenarios of integrating virtual and real worlds. MR applications require a systematic 3D spatial interface design paradigm that meticulously considers user behavior and experience in such environments. On the other hand, current research on MR applications primarily focuses on the construction of virtual object presentation scenes or its spatial user interaction (UI) [16], without sufficiently considering the construction and interaction experiences of scenes that are integrated with the physical environment and contextually related. Museum spaces, due to their complex spatial organization, require careful consideration not only of interaction points with individual objects but also of the complete visiting experience and spatial narrative design.

This study delves into the connections between exhibition spaces, exhibition information, and users in a museum environment that integrates virtual and real elements, and conducts a comprehensive analysis of museum user experience and interaction design principles for wearable MR devices. By considering both the exhibition requirements of museums and user needs, the study proposes an interactive design framework for innovative museum exhibits that integrates virtual and real elements. This framework includes strategies for constructing immersive environments that blend virtual and real elements, designing multi-temporal interactive narratives, and developing multimodal interaction designs. As a case study, this paper selected the Museum of Communication University of China as the experimental setting and developed an application using the Meta Quest Pro mixed reality platform, aiming to provide users with a novel and more immersive museum visit experience. Through practical application and user experience analysis, the effectiveness of the proposed interactive design framework was verified, and the current limitations and areas for improvement of the framework were further analyzed. Through such research and practice, this paper offers new perspectives and deep insights into the application of mixed reality technology in the fields of cultural heritage display and education.

2 Related Work

2.1 Interaction Design Theory in Museums

Over the last twenty years, advancements in digital technology have revolutionized the way people gain knowledge and engage with culture. Consequently, museum design has evolved to cater to the growing desire for natural interactive experiences. Museums that provide exceptional surroundings enable visitors to engage with exhibits and acquire knowledge through interactive experiences and the development of their own ideas and concepts [34]. M. Danks et al. [12] assert that augmenting interactivity and autonomy greatly enhances the visitor experience in contrast to information browsing on static screens. The ability for visitors to independently choose tour routes and schedules is essential. By providing transparent and unobtrusive ways of perceptual interaction, visitors are encouraged to actively investigate, allowing them to learn and understand through experiences and games. Daniel Wigdor et al. [33] propose that media tools have the potential to cause user attention fragmentation, while the concept of "Calm Technology" by Weiser et al. [32] aims to reduce cognitive load by minimizing technological distractions. Therefore, in the process of interactive design in museums, there is a consideration to move away from traditional command-line interfaces and the inherent interaction paradigms of graphical user interfaces. Instead, the focus is on simplifying interaction tasks and adding elements that are engaging, immersive, and inspiring, making the visitor's experience more captivating and insightful.

2.2 Natural User Interface Design in Museums

Many scholars have researched how to enhance user experience through the design principles of natural user interface (NUI). Wigdor et al. [33] first summarized the basic principles of NUI design in detail and adopted "conceptual metaphor" as the theoretical cornerstone of natural human-computer user interaction design. This approach emphasizes the use of graphical and linguistic metaphors to bridge the gap between the user's concrete physical mind model and abstract operations, thus realizing natural and intuitive human-computer interaction. Hernández et al. [18] build on this foundation by exploring the usability of two different modes of natural interaction, "metaphorical" and "natural", in a museum environment. In terms of implementation strategies, Cafaro et al. [10] introduces the concept of Human-Data Interaction (HDI), which sees data as an active element that can communicate directly with the user, allowing for interaction with the data in a variety of ways, such as tactile, visual, and auditory. This interaction is not limited to touching the screen, but also includes physical interaction with virtual objects using physical world experiences such as pose recognition, facial recognition, and line-of-sight tracking, which enhances the interaction between the user and the exhibit [26,31]. The Cleveland Museum of Art (USA) [1], they are an example of utilizing NUI design to enhance viewer interaction with exhibits through the ArtLens Gallery system (which includes interactive exhibits, interactive drawing rooms, giant touch screens, and apps to implement a range of innovative ways of interacting with the exhibits), these ways include "Posing (pose recognition)," "making faces (face recognition)," and "gaze tracker" interactions. The results of the study show that the accessibility and engagement of museums can be effectively enhanced through innovative natural user interface design to improve user experience [33].

2.3 Interaction Design in Mixed Reality

According to Milgram and Kishino et al. [23] the reality-virtual continuum reality-virtual continuum describes the span between real and virtual environments, augmented reality (AR) and augmented virtual (AV) are in between. AR is closer to the real world and AV is closer to the virtual environment. Whereas Mixed Reality covers the continuum from AR to AV and aims to blending real and virtual environments in different ways. Azuma et al. [7] define AR as complementing the real world with information rather than completely replacing it. Although there is no generally accepted collective term for these technologies, this study relies on the aforementioned theories and presents a proposal based on a concise definition of Mixed Reality technology, clearly distinguishing it from Augmented Reality (AR). That is, augmented reality enhances our perception and understanding of the real world by superimposing virtual information on it. Whereas mixed reality aims to provide a seamless mix of real and virtual environments, providing users with a sense of immersion and a dual superimposition of information from both the real and virtual worlds.

With the development of mixed reality technology, its application in museum exhibitions has been gradually recognized as having the potential to realize contextually integrated exhibition venues, based on the fact that the value of each collection is derived from the original context (contextual information) [30], which is usually associated with a specific environment consisting of a specific space and time period. The display of exhibits is a process of re-contextualization [22], which reveals the historical or cultural information inherent in the objects by fully restoring the historical context. The use of mixed reality technologies can provide a new way of presenting contextualized information by combining physical and digital elements, allowing visitors to interact with virtual information in an environment where physical and virtual spaces are superimposed.

Jacob et al. [19] proposed a real-world-based interaction design framework (reality-based interaction, RBI), the framework contains four elements of the real physical world, personal perception and motor skills, environmental perception and interaction skills, social perception and social skills, which provides theoretical support for the shift from real space to virtual-reality fusion space, in this background, many researchers have conducted applied research in museums. And with the technological progress to continuously improve the interaction experience design. In the early stage, Ephraim Schott et al. [28] aligned the physical and virtual spaces of museums through the joint use of AR and virtu reality(VR) technologies, and provided guided tours through virtual companions and path visualization maps. Applied research in museums continues to evolve as technology advances, from the early use of AR and VR technologies to the current proliferation of MR head-mounted display devices (e.g. Microsoft HoloLens [3], Quest 3 [2], and Vision Pro [4]), which have expanded the possibilities for interactive experiences. In 2021, the Muséum National d'Histoire Naturelle in Paris is launching "Revivre," [5] a mixed reality experience using Hololens that brings visitors face-to-face with now-extinct digital animals. Also, Hammady et al.'s [17]study on the design of a user guide system at the Egyptian Museum using HoloLens shows the potential of MR technology to improve the visitor experience. However, despite the great potential shown by MR technology in museum exhibitions, there are still shortcomings in integrating physical environments with contextual relationships with building a complete interactive experience. This is the focus of this paper and future research.

3 Framework for Mixed Reality Interactive Design in Museums

This study proposes that the optimal utilization of Mixed Reality technology's multisensory capabilities and integration of real and virtual elements develops when it is thoroughly integrated with the scene's semantic context. Thus, when creating exhibition content pertaining to museums, it is important to develop interactive experiences that connect the distinct attributes of MR technology with the expected experiential requirements of museum visitors. In order to achieve this objective, the study initially performs an examination of the exhibition prerequisites and the user experience demands of museums. By conducting an initial analysis of surveys, the research establishes precise design criteria for wearable MR exhibits. An interactive framework for museum MR design is suggested based on these specifications (Fig. 1).

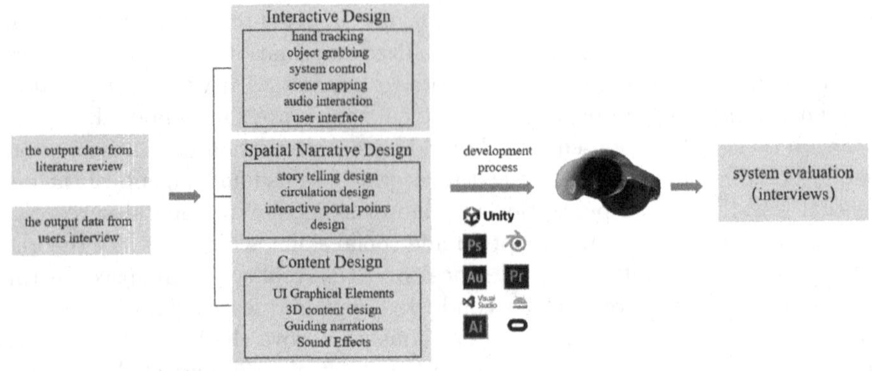

Fig. 1. System development process

3.1 User Expectations and Experiential Demands for Museums

From the outset, it should be noted that as digital technology advances, museums are expected to take on more tasks and meet higher expectations. This includes a shift towards prioritizing diverse, interactive, and experiential audience engagement. In the past, museums have functioned as institutions for the storage and conservation of objective records and communal memories, achieved through the preservation of things and specimens [29]. Nevertheless, studies conducted by Pekarik et al. [25], have proved that the conventional museum setting fails to completely satisfy the demands and desires of contemporary museumgoers [11]. Modern museums should serve as platforms that effectively convey significant information in engaging ways, appealing to visitors driven by a need for knowledge [24]. Due to the evolving social landscape and modes of communication, visitors' goals for learning have transitioned from "self-construction" of knowledge to a stronger inclination towards engaging in interactive experiences [13]. Due to the evolving social landscape and modes of communication, visitors' goals for learning have transitioned from "self-construction" of knowledge to a stronger inclination towards engaging in interactive experiences.

In their exploration of museum experience needs, Pekarik et al. [25] identified four basic types of experiences: object, cognitive, introspective, and social experiences (Table 1). To gain a deeper understanding of users' specific expectations for museum experiences, this study conducted interviews with 23 users,

Table 1. Enhanced Experiences with MR Technology when Viewing Museum Artifacts

Type of museum experience	The enhanced experiences with MR technology
Objective experience	The experience of directly touching the replicated virtual artifact, manipulating it, andexploring it in detail. The experience of viewing enlarged scale artifacts.
Cognitive experience	The experience of being quickly answered when asking questions about the artifact. The experience of learning abundant information through means such as text, images, and videos. The experience of knowing information about the artifact through games or animation. The experience of viewing the restored original appearance of a damaged artifactremnant.
Introspective experience	The experience of facing situations in historical time realized through 3D animation. The experience of talking with people from the past.
Social experiences	The experience of sharing the experience of an artifact with other viewers. The experience of expressing one's opinions or feelings and sharing with others abouteach artifact

Table 2. User Focus Research

Key Focus Elementsof visit visiting the museum	Number	Percentage of People
Exhibition Venue Size/Exhibition Capacity	8	34.8%
Exhibition Venue Cultural Atmosphere/Compelling Theme Narration	16	69.6%
Guided Services/Detail of Introduction Information/Reading Experience	14	60.9%
Route Experience	11	47.8%
Appreciation Experience of Exhibits/Exhibit Richness	15	65.2%
Presence of Influential/Popular Exhibits or Photo Spots	6	26.1%
Other (Clarity of Content/Presence of Interesting Cultural Products/Level of Crowding, etc.)	4	17.4%

analyzing their focal points and interaction experiences during museum visits. The interview results, organized in Table 2, reveal the following user concerns: the most significant concern was whether there was a sufficiently attractive cultural atmosphere and thematic narrative (69.5%), followed by the richness of the exhibits and the appreciation experience (65.2%), and information acquisition and reading experience (60.8%). Additionally, some people paid attention to the design of the exhibition route (47.8%) and the capacity of the exhibition (34.7%). Relatively fewer people were concerned about whether the exhibited content had a "web celebrity effect" (26.9%) and whether there were cultural and creative peripherals and foot traffic, etc. (17.3%). These data points clearly correspond to the experience types proposed by Doering and Pekarik: the three most significant concerns correspond to cognitive, introspective, and object experiences, respectively, which relate to scientifically rational and narrative-rich spatial experiences, rich exhibit perception experiences, and clear, low-load information acquisition.

3.2 Mixed Reality Interactive Design Framework for Museums

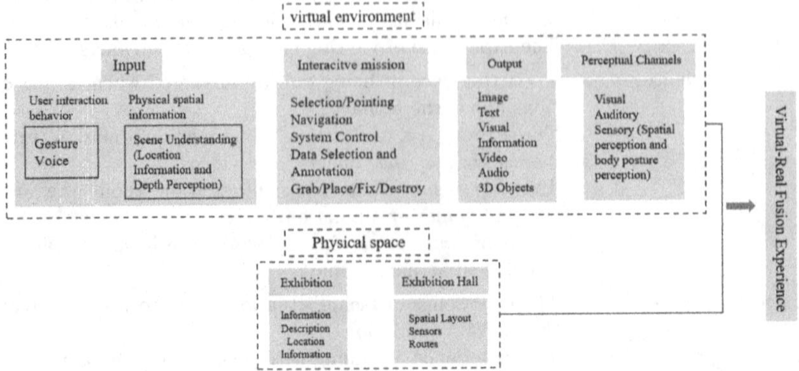

Fig. 2. Mixed Reality Interaction Design Framework for Museums

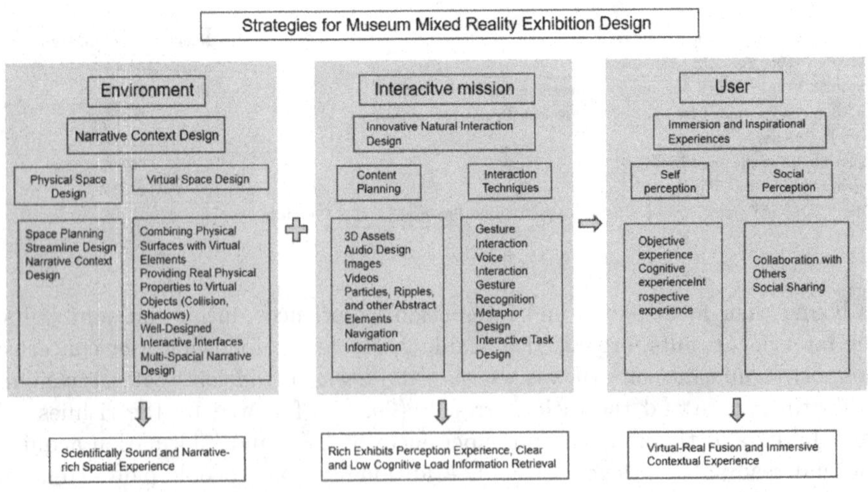

Fig. 3. Strategies for Museum Mixed Reality Exhibition Design

The key to a systematic approach to interaction design lies in the integrated consideration of research user tasks, existing interaction technologies, and user, environment, or system characteristics that may affect performance [9]. Mixed reality technology has three core features: virtual-reality fusion, real-time interaction and 3D registration [6,7], which bring a shift in the process of receiving information from passive to actively experiencing the information and context through interaction, enhancing interactivity and combining immersive perceptual experiences with the environment.

Mixed reality technology makes museums hybrid spaces combining physical and virtual. Banfi and Pontisso et al. [8] proposed six dimensions to be considered for museum spaces in mixed reality: the length of time for users to experience the interaction, the design of the type of immersion, the way of experiencing in mixed reality spaces, the design of the quality of the space and the depth of the experience, the application of new tools of learning and cognition and the The spatial and temporal narrative of the exhibition and the way visitors interact, which is in line with the theory of the elements of RBI theory proposed by Jacob et al. [19] has become the theoretical support for the design framework proposed in this study. Zhang FL. [13] further emphasized that museums should adopt the concept of natural interaction design with letter contextualization and multisensory to ensure that the interaction is multi-channel and parallel; the content is intelligent and non-precise; Interaction interfaces are intuitive and easy to use; and interaction environments are immersive and simulated. In this study, a Head-mounted hybrid display device (HMD) is used, which incorporates the characteristics of 3D interaction and multimodal interaction to provide a hybrid interactive interface for users. Among them, 3D interaction includes basic tasks such as navigation, selection and manipulation, and system control [7,9], while multimodal interaction introduces gestures, speech, text, and interactions that utilize multiple sensory channels such as vision, smell, and hearing in a coexisting manner [21]. Based on such a technical foundation, this paper first refines the interaction tasks and objects in the design in order to construct a comprehensive and efficient interaction design framework (Fig. 2).

Based on the above mixed reality interaction design elements and interaction design requirements applicable to museums, and centered on the six dimensions of user experience, immersive design, participation, spatial quality, learning tools, and exhibition narrative, the following strategies for museum mixed reality design (Fig. 3).

3.3 Strategies for Museum Mixed Reality Exhibition Design

In terms of specific implementation methods, the following interactive design Framework are proposed:

1. Create a Narrative Exhibition Space Integrating Virtual and Real Elements. The design of mixed reality museum interactive spaces can proceed from both physical and virtual dimensions. In physical space, it is necessary to make reasonable spatial planning and scenario design in line with the exhibition theme. In the virtual space, it is possible to overlay walls, open spaces, etc., with virtual portals and virtual objects, and provide real physical properties for virtual objects, such as shadows and collisions. Meanwhile, considering user experience and the occlusion relationship between virtual assets and actual space, it should be as clear and simple as possible to reduce cognitive load. Combining the characteristics of museums as carriers of memory, a

multi-temporal overlay of virtual and real design can be carried out to form a context-rich space integrating virtual and real elements.

2. Develop Innovative Natural Interaction Design. A key point of mixed reality-based museum exhibition interaction design is to enrich user interaction experience through 3D interactions and multimodal interactions, reducing cognitive load through natural interactions. On one hand, audio, images, videos, and 3D content oriented towards visual and auditory senses serve as multisensory design combined with exhibition content. On the other hand, fully integrating the characteristics of exhibits, interactive task design is performed. Interaction methods such as gestures, voice, and posture can be provided based on Head-Mounted Display (HMD) devices. Thus, enriching the exhibit perception experience and bringing users detailed and low-load information acquisition.
3. Create an Immersive Contextualized Visitor Experience. By combining users' anticipated needs for museums, through well-designed interactive experiences and spaces that integrate virtual and real scenarios, users' own perceptions can be stimulated to satisfy objective experiences, introspective experiences, and cognitive experiences. Meanwhile, with the development of social media, the need for collaborative and social sharing can also be incorporated into the design experience. With the aid of mixed reality technology, museums become places for historical context reenactment. Through reasonable narrative tours, interacting with both real and virtual integrated exhibits, users can gain a sense of presence in historical memory experiences, trigger emotional awakenings, and acquire scientifically and humanistically rich knowledge. Thus, forming an immersive contextualized mixed reality tour experience.

4 Implementation and Validation

4.1 Application Design Overview

The "Chuanmei Guiding" application employs the Meta Quest Pro to deploy a guiding MR system. This application is an MR experience interactive guiding system, based on the museum's visitor flow design, arranging interactive points, and providing interaction functions with 3D objects as well as voice-guided tours and interactive point guidance. Integrating natural interaction designs such as gesture recognition and voice interaction, it connects multiple senses and integrates interactive narratives throughout the entire museum visit process.

4.2 Design and Development

"Chuanmei Guiding" is developed with the Unity game engine and the Oculus Mixed Reality Toolkit. Some 3D objects are generated through mesh captures of museum spaces, while others are created with Blender. Image and video information are processed using Photoshop and Premiere, and audio data is managed with Adobe Audition. Finally, assets are integrated and imported into the Unity

Fig. 4. Overview and Floor Plan of the museum of Communication University of China

Fig. 5. Museum information display and guided Tours

scene. Local spatial anchors are utilized to store assets at their actual locations within the museum space. A custom manager script is used to activate or deactivate 3D objects and voice interaction features based on the narrative or interactive points that visitors are experiencing, thus facilitating auxiliary narratives and interactions within the museum space.

"Chuanmei Guiding" provides users with navigation functions. In terms of spatial design, the Media Museum of Communication University of China (CUC) has three exhibition areas and eight branch museums, with meandering internal corridors and unclear design of the moving lines. In this study, we chose one of the exhibition areas and determined the visiting line according to the theme and characteristics of the exhibition hall (Fig. 4). Users can use mixed reality devices to view maps or conduct spatial navigation at any time, giving them a high degree of freedom. In conjunction with the layout of each sub-branch, mixed reality interactive points are strategically placed in open and safe areas, creating a well-paced interactive experience. Visitors can activate the application by wearing mixed reality devices to access basic venue information and choose their preferred tour routes, allowing navigation between the sub-branches of the Communication Museum. In the context of immersive exhibition design, the spatial flow has been designed as a narrative route to explore the historical development trajectory of China's media industry, with users taking on the role of journal-

Fig. 6. Announcer interactive game

Fig. 7. Little treasure hunt game

ists for a storytelling experience. Leveraging spatial mapping capabilities, the "Chuanmei Guiding" application can display relevant text or video introductions in front of the corresponding exhibition areas or exhibits to assist visitors in understanding the content (Fig. 5).

The application has set up multiple interaction points, offering not only basic information display and explanations but also small games based on gesture interactions. For example, spot 1 displays a "BX 434 A" Philips radio, which was widely used in the 1950s and has become a carrier of historical memory. Users can look at the vacuum tube parts of the radio, assemble them and restore them to complete the process of using the radio, thus experiencing the communication history of that era. Based on the broadcasting theme, auditory and visual multimodal interactions can better display the history of communication (Fig. 6). Point 2 is designed as a treasure hunt game, requiring users to follow sounds to find clues for the story's development and locate the "First Screen of Huaxia" among many televisions (Fig. 7). When users approach the target exhibit, the screen within the virtual interface automatically lights up, overlaying the physical exhibit to create the effect of a television playing a documentary, narrating the history of the exhibit and its commemorative significance. In addition, video materials and 3D models are used to visually reproduce the original appearance of the exhibits and highlight key information to focus the audience's attention. By combining gamified interaction design, audiences engage in the game's role for interaction, naturally acquiring knowledge through the fun game plot while continuously exploring and thinking during the challenge, thereby deepening their memory of the knowledge. Finally, to meet the needs of social sharing, users can take photos and share them at any time during the interaction process.

4.3 User Test

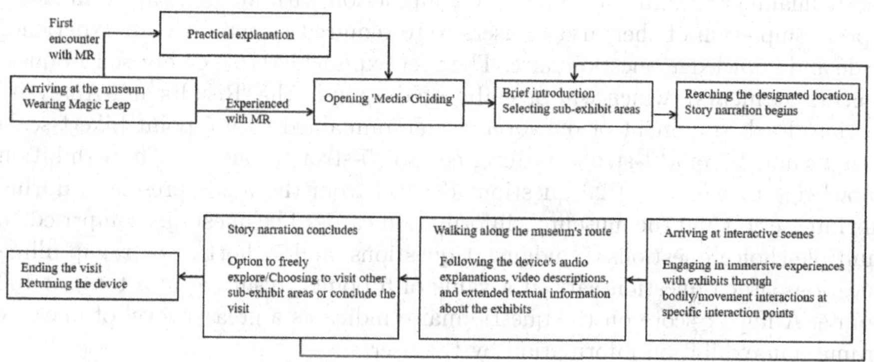

Fig. 8. Exploration game

In order to verify the feasibility of the theory and its application, this study conducted a multidimensional measurement of the user experience and learning effect of Chuanmei Guiding. In the validation experiment, taking into account the actual conditions of the site and the number of staff, we plan to use a pilot study, a mixed study (combining a scale survey and semi-structured interviews) as the research tool, and an inter-group comparison experiment as our experimental method. The user is shown in the Fig. 8 for the use of the Chuanmei Guiding application.

Based on the design goals and previous research, we identified user experience (satisfaction, interaction, personalization) and learning outcomes as the two main macro-indicators. Then, we developed more detailed statements or questions corresponding to each of the indicators in the user experience scale.

Table 3. Basic information of the experimental group

Group	Age Data Distribution	Mean	SD	male		numbe
Controlgroup	14∼16	29.1	12.1	9	Students (9), teachers (2), designers (1), company employee (4), worker (1), Freelancer (2), retired (1)	N=20
Experimental Group	13∼58	29.6	10.4	9	Students (8), teachers (2), Library Librarian (1), company staff (5), programmer (2), freelancers (1), Retirement (1)	N=20
Overall Situation	13∼66	29.4	11.2	8	Ditto	N=20

A group of 40 individuals was enlisted for the pilot project via research invitation and social media recruiting. In order to assure the accuracy and scientific validity of the experiment, respondents who lacked a comprehensive knowledge of the exhibition content were specifically chosen and categorized together (Table 3).

The control group utilizes the H5 iteration of "Chuanmei Guiding", wherein visitors are able to scan the QR code and access the HTML5(H5) page to peruse the visual data pertaining to the exhibits. The experimental group employed the "Chuanmei Guiding" technique in conjunction with Magic Leap technology. Upon completion of their usage, users were required to complete an experience scale and knowledge questionnaire. The user experience scale comprised 14 questions (statements), which will be elaborated upon in the "Results and Analysis" section. Each statement or question was accompanied by a 5-point Likert scale that spanned from "1-strongly disagree" to "5-strongly agree". The exhibition knowledge test paper of 20 questions derived from the items presented during the interaction and the museum's information cards. The questions comprised 10 multiple-choice questions, 5 judgment questions, and 5 short answer/gap filling questions. Each question carried a value of 5 points, resulting in a total of 100 points. A higher score on the questionnaire indicates a greater level of mastery of museum exhibition information by the user.

The Cronbach α for the user experience scale and questionnaire was determined to be 0.875/0.896 (>0.8) after conducting tests. This indicates that the study data is of good quality and reliability, allowing for additional analysis.

Initially, this paper used the T-test to investigate the differences in user experience, specifically personalization, between the groups and further utilized the effect size to study the magnitude of these differences. The results revealed significant disparities in the personalized aspect of user experience between the two interaction modalities: users in the experimental group using mixed reality applications scored significantly higher than those in the control group using standard H5.

The T-test was used to test the differences between the groups for user experience-satisfaction, interaction quality, and the results are shown in the table. In terms of satisfaction (Table 4) with the interaction method, the experimental group received higher and more significant user ratings than the control group ($t = 5.8$, $p = 0.000$), and about 30% of the users in the experimental group gave it a perfect score, which indicates to a certain extent that the interaction method of mixed reality is attractive. In the interviews, many users said that this interaction method was "novel" and "interesting" because it allowed the fusion of reality and reality, and the digital content was superimposed on the real objects. Additionally, we asked Question 4 to explore the comparative advantages of Mixed Reality systems, which was answered by 12 users and was recognized by more than a majority of users ($n = 10$).

In terms of interaction quality (Table 5), all of them received high scores from users. This suggests that our mixed reality application ensures the quality of interaction in terms of clarity, timeliness and comprehensibility of the system

Table 4. Satisfaction Analysis results of T test

Question	Group (mean values ± standard deviations)		t	p
	Experimental group (n = 20)	Control group (n = 20)		
Q1	4.40 ± 0.68	4.35 ± 0.67	0.23	0.82
Q2	3.90 ± 0.64	4.65 ± 0.49	−4.16	0.00**
Q3	4.15 ± 0.59	2.75 ± 0.91	5.78	0.00**
Q4	4.00 ± 0.60	null ± null	null	null

*P<0.05 **p <0.01(Results retained to two decimal places)
Questions:
Q1: I believe the time spent during the interaction process is reasonable.
Q2: I think the difficulty of the interactive tasks is appropriate.
Q3: I like this method of interacting with the exhibition.
Q4: Compared to VR and traditional touch screens (smartphones or interactive kiosks), I think this system has more advantages. (This question is only for those in the experimental group who have experience with VR and touch screens)

Table 5. Interaction Quality (Usability)Analysis results of T test

Question	Group (mean values ± standard deviations)		t	p
	Experimental group (n = 20)	Control group (n = 20)		
Q5	4.55±0.51	4.50±0.51	0.30	0.76
Q6	4.05±0.76	3.65±0.49	1.98	0.05*
Q7	4.60±0.50	4.70±0.47	-0.65	0.52

*P<0.05 **p <0.01(Results retained to two decimal places)
Questions:
Q5: I feel the system's feedback is clear and timely.
Q6: I feel the interaction is smooth and natural.
Q7: I find the system's instructions easy to understand.

feedback compared with the conventional H5. Especially in terms of smoothness and naturalness, the mixed reality application also shows better scores than the traditional H5 form, and presents a certain degree of significance, which indicates that the mixed reality application brings a more natural and genuine experience to the users in terms of interaction.

In the personalization test (Imagination, Immersion, Motivation), this paper used T-tests to investigate the differences between groups for the user experience personalization (Table 6), and went on to investigate the magnitude of the differences using Effect Size (Table 7), which showed that the two interactive experiences showed extremely significant differences in the personalization of the user experience: user ratings of the experimental group using the mixed-reality application were much higher than those of the control group using the regular H5 application. The experimental group using the Mixed Reality appli-

Table 6. Personalization (Imagination, Immersion, Positivity0) Analysis results of T test

Question	Group (mean values ± standard deviations)		t	p
	Experimental group (n = 20)	Control group (n = 20)		
Q8	3.95 ± 0.60	3.15 ± 0.75	3.7279	0.00**
Q9	3.90 ± 0.72	3.25 ± 0.79	2.7295	0.00**
Q10	3.90 ± 0.64	3.10 ± 0.79	3.5225	0.00**
Q11	3.65 ± 0.81	2.85 ± 0.88	2.9957	0.00**
Q12	3.15 ± 0.74	1.85 ± 0.59	6.1283	0.00**
Q13	3.70 ± 0.57	2.85 ± 0.88	3.6375	0.00**
Q14	3.75 ± 0.64	2.45 ± 0.83	5.5699	0.00**

* $p<0.05$ ** $p<0.01$ (Results are reported to two decimal places)
Questions:
Q8: Using this interactive system gave me a better experience with museum exhibits.
Q9: I think after this experience, my impression of the exhibits is more concrete and vivid.
Q10: I believe this experience has narrowed the distance between me and the exhibits, reducing the sense of unfamiliarity.
Q11: I think during the interaction, my attention was completely captured by the system.
Q12: I feel the gestures used in the interaction gave me a better sense of immersion.
Q13: I think this system can increase my interest.
Q14: I wish other exhibits would also use this system to facilitate my understanding of them.

Table 7. In-depth Analysis of Effect Size Indicators

Analysis Term	S2pooled	Cohen's d
Q8	0.4605	1.1789
Q9	0.5671	0.8631
Q10	0.5158	1.1139
Q11	0.7132	0.9473
Q12	0.4500	1.9379
Q13	0.5461	1.1503
Q14	0.5447	1.7614

Cohen's d value indicates that when the effect size is large, the distinguishing points for small, medium and large effect sizes are 0.20, 0.50 and 0.80, respectively cation scored significantly higher than the control group using the regular H5 application. The experimental group continues to show better scores.

Regarding imagination, the subjective accounts of participants in both the experimental and control groups exhibited a high level of coherence among their respective groups. A majority of the participants in the experimental group, over 80%, said that the interactive system enhanced their experience of the media museum exhibition, enriched their comprehension and perception of the media history materials, and fostered a sense of proximity to the display to varied extents. During the interviews, multiple participants expressed that "The modern media development exhibited in the museum is both arduous and stimulating." and "Seeing the struggles and efforts of the previous generation of scientists and technologists has created admiration in me."

Regarding immersion, despite our utilization of mixed reality instead of a fully encompassing virtual reality setting, the findings indicate that our technology still offers a more preferable immersive encounter for consumers. One positive aspect of the system was its ability to effectively direct users' attention towards the physical displays and their digital content through the use of multi-sensory guidance and a multimedia environment. The majority of users, exceeding 80%, reported experiencing a high level of concentration during the engagement. Conversely, a majority of the users reported feeling more engaged as a result of adopting gestures. Hence, the incorporation of gestures into the design proves to be efficient and enhances the users' contextual immersion and empathy. At the same time, many people have noted that integrating the exhibition objects with the physical surroundings can evoke a sense of freshness and fascination. Additionally, they have a greater sense of the exhibition's narrative flow. This highlights the import of seamlessly incorporating the virtual display objects with the physical location in the design.

The results indicate that the interactive mode offered by the technology enhances motivation for learning. Undoubtedly, this could be attributed to the users' initial lack of familiarity with the exhibition and its associated information. Nevertheless, based on our participant observations and subsequent interviews, we discovered that virtually all participants continued to actively engage with the interactions even after finishing the interactive tasks. This indicates that the motivation provided by the system to the users was enduring and not solely attributable to their initial lack of familiarity. A significant number of participants noted that museums had previously offered limited options for interacting with exhibitions. However, this time, they were able to engage with the exhibits through the use of mixed reality technology, which generated a profound feeling of enthusiasm and a notable sense of achievement.

In terms of learning outcomes, the study initially assessed the normality of participants' scores in museum knowledge, finding the data to be normally distributed (Table 8). Continuing with an independent samples T-test, the study compared the significant differences in learning scores between the two groups. The results indicated a disparity in learning outcomes on museum knowledge between the experimental and control groups. Specifically, the experimental

Table 8. T-test analysis results

Question	Group (mean values ± standard deviations)		t	p
	Experimental group (n = 20)	Control group (n = 20)		
Post-test score	71.50±8.90	62.00±11.85	2.87	0.00**

*P<0.05 **p <0.01 (Results retained to two decimal places)

group's average score (71.50) was notably higher than that of the control group (62.00), and the scores in the experimental group were more concentrated (SD experimental = 8.9 < SD control = 11.9). This suggests that most users utilizing mixed reality applications significantly outperformed those in the control group in terms of museum learning outcomes. The developed mixed reality application, incorporating multimodal interfaces such as visual, auditory, and tactile elements, along with integrating aspects of space, narrative, and experience, enhanced users' perception and understanding of abstract knowledge. Consequently, it facilitated a deeper comprehension and learning of museum knowledge among users.

5 Limitations and Future Work

This study explores the application of mixed reality technology in interactive design for museum exhibitions, aiming to provide an immersive interaction design framework. By implementing 'Chuanmei Guiding,' diverse exhibitions with a mix of virtual and real elements are created in a real environment. Considering cost and space constraints, the application prototype selected the relatively small-scale and moderately informative campus museum of the Communication University of China as the application scenario. Compared to large museums, this application scenario is relatively simple in terms of spatial layout, narrative design, and immersion-based information overlay. Therefore, for users, the complexity of receiving information is relatively low. Especially considering that museums are public spaces, the presence of multiple people in the environment can also affect the interactive experience. However, despite these limitations, this prototype still demonstrates that the interaction design framework proposed based on mixed reality interaction and museum exhibition requirements contributes to enhancing the user experience and knowledge acquisition. With the advancement of mixed reality technology and the standardization of interaction paradigms, more universally applicable mixed reality devices can use this framework to be applied in museums with larger volumes and complex scenarios, providing users with a better exhibition and learning experience.

6 Conclusions

Through the in-depth analysis conducted in this research, we have recognized that mixed reality technology can meet the needs of museums to provide immersive contextual exhibitions for users. In terms of environmental design, we emphasized the importance of effectively integrating physical and virtual spaces, including spatial planning, narrative context creation, and optimization of information presentation. In the area of interaction design, we proposed innovative and low-load natural, multimodal 3D interaction requirements to provide users with engaging interactive experiences. This, in turn, stimulates users' self-perception of objective experience, introspective experience, and cognitive experience, as well as social awareness for collaboration and social sharing. Thus, creating a mixed reality contextual touring experience.

Our case study, particularly the "Chuanmei Guiding" application at the Communication University of China Museum, has demonstrated the effectiveness of these Framework in bridging abstract concepts, enhancing information dissemination, and deepening cultural perception. Through this research, we have showcased how mixed reality technology can enhance the presentation and communication functions of museums while providing new perspectives and solutions for interactive design in current museum exhibitions.

While this research has provided valuable insights into the application of mixed reality in museum exhibitions, it still has limitations, particularly in terms of technical implementation and large-scale application. Future work will focus on addressing these challenges, further exploring the application of mixed reality technology in a broader museum environment, and how to more effectively integrate physical and virtual elements to create richer and more engaging museum experiences.

Acknowledgments. Fundamental Research Funds for the Central Universities(CUC23GZ006). Also we thank the Beijing Nova Program (Z211100002121160) for funding this project.

References

1. Artlens gallery. https://www.clevelandart.org/articles/artlens-gallery. Accessed 02 Nov 2024
2. Expand your world with meta quest 3. https://www.meta.com/quest/quest-3/. Accessed 02 Nov 2024
3. Interaction fundamentals - mixed reality. https://learn.microsoft.com/en-us/windows/mixed-reality/design/interaction-fundamentals. Accessed 02 Nov 2024
4. Introducing apple vision pro. apple newsroom. https://www.apple.com/newsroom/2023/06/introducing-apple-vision-pro/. Accessed 02 Nov 2024
5. Try the adventure!what if you created your own project in augmented reality? https://www.saolastudio.com/en-gb/votre-projet. Accessed 02 Nov 2024
6. Azuma, R., Baillot, Y., Behringer, R., Feiner, S., Julier, S., MacIntyre, B.: Recent advances in augmented reality. IEEE Comput. Graphics Appl. **21**(6), 34–47 (2001)
7. Azuma, R.T.: A survey of augmented reality. Presence: Teleoperators Virtual Environ. **6**(4), 355–385 (1997)
8. Banfi, F., Pontisso, M., Paolillo, F.R., Roascio, S., Spallino, C., Stanga, C.: Interactive and immersive digital representation for virtual museum: Vr and ar for semantic enrichment of museo nazionale romano, antiquarium di lucrezia romana and antiquarium di villa dei quintili. ISPRS Int. J. Geo Inf. **12**(2), 28 (2023)

9. Bowman, D.A., Kruijff, E., LaViola, J.J., Poupyrev, I.: An introduction to 3-d user interface design. Presence **10**(1), 96–108 (2001)
10. Cafaro, F.: Using embodied allegories to design gesture suites for human-data interaction. In: Proceedings of the 2012 ACM Conference on Ubiquitous Computing, pp. 560–563 (2012)
11. Choi, H.s., Kim, S.h.: A content service deployment plan for metaverse museum exhibitions—centering on the combination of beacons and HMDs. Int. J. Inf. Manage. **37**(1), 1519–1527 (2017)
12. Danks, M., Goodchild, M., Rodriguez-Echavarria, K., Arnold, D.B., Griffiths, R.: interactive storytelling and gaming environments for museums: the interactive storytelling exhibition project. In: Hui, K., Pan, Z., Chung, R.C., Wang, C.C.L., Jin, X., Göbel, S., Li, E.C.-L. (eds.) Edutainment 2007. LNCS, vol. 4469, pp. 104–115. Springer, Heidelberg (2007). https://doi.org/10.1007/978-3-540-73011-8_13
13. FL, Z.: A study on the natural Human-computer Interaction in Museum Exhibitions (Ph.D. dissertation). Ph.D. thesis, Zhejiang University (2021)
14. Goodman, C.: The future of museums: the post-pandemic transformation of experiences and expectations. In: Transitioning Media in a Post Covid World: Digital Transformation, Immersive Technologies, and Consumer Behavior, pp. 115–127. Springer (2022)
15. Graf, H., Keil, J., Pagano, A., Pescarin, S.: A contextualized educational museum experience connecting objects, places and themes through mobile virtual museums. In: 2015 Digital Heritage, vol. 1, pp. 337–340. IEEE (2015)
16. Hammady, R., Ma, M., Strathearn, C.: Ambient information visualisation and visitors' technology acceptance of mixed reality in museums. J. Comput. Cultural Heritage (JOCCH) **13**(2), 1–22 (2020)
17. Hammady, R., Ma, M., Strathern, C., Mohamad, M.: Design and development of a spatial mixed reality touring guide to the Egyptian museum. Multimed. Tools Appl. **79**, 3465–3494 (2020)
18. Hernández-Ibáñez, L.A., Barneche-Naya, V., Mihura-López, R.: Natural interaction and movement paradigms. a comparison of usability for a kinect enabled museum installation. In: Zaphiris, P., Ioannou, A. (eds.) LCT 2016. LNCS, vol. 9753, pp. 145–155. Springer, Cham (2016). https://doi.org/10.1007/978-3-319-39483-1_14
19. Jacob, R.J., et al.: Reality-based interaction: a framework for post-wimp interfaces. In: Proceedings of the SIGCHI Conference on Human Factors in Computing Systems, pp. 201–210 (2008)
20. Jeffery-Clay, K.R.: Constructivism in museums: how museums create meaningful learning environments. J. Museum Educ. **23**(1), 3–7 (1998)
21. Jin, H., Han, D., Chen, Y., et al.: A survey on human-computer interaction in mixed reality. J. Comput.-Aided Des. Comput. Graph. **28**(6), 869–880 (2016)
22. Martinez, M.M., Sears, E.L., Sieg, L.: Contextualizing museum collections at the smithsonian institution: the relevance of collections-based research in the twenty-first century (2022)
23. Milgram, P., Kishino, F.: A taxonomy of mixed reality visual displays. IEICE Trans. Inf. Syst. **77**(12), 1321–1329 (1994)
24. Packer, J., Ballantyne, R.: Motivational factors and the visitor experience: a comparison of three sites. Curator Museum J. **45**(3), 183–198 (2002)
25. Pekarik, A.J., Doering, Z.D., Karns, D.A.: Exploring satisfying experiences in museums. Curator Museum J. **42**(2), 152–173 (1999)
26. Price, S., Sakr, M., Jewitt, C.: Exploring whole-body interaction and design for museums. Interact. Comput. **28**(5), 569–583 (2016)

27. Ridel, B., Reuter, P., Laviole, J., Mellado, N., Couture, N., Granier, X.: The revealing flashlight: interactive spatial augmented reality for detail exploration of cultural heritage artifacts. J. Comput. Cultural Heritage (JOCCH) **7**(2), 1–18 (2014)
28. Schott, E., et al.: Unitexr: joint exploration of a real-world museum and its digital twin. In: Proceedings of the 29th ACM Symposium on Virtual Reality Software and Technology, pp. 1–10 (2023)
29. Seifi, M., Schauer, S., Fadzila Abd Rahman, H.: Experiencing the architectural evolution of a heritage museum in extended reality application. In: Proceedings of the 20th International Conference on Culture and Computer Science: Code and Materiality, pp. 1–7 (2023)
30. Thompson, C.: The role of the museum in interpretation: the problem of context. Int. J. Herit. Stud. **1**(1), 40–51 (1994)
31. Trajkova, M., Alhakamy, A., Cafaro, F., Mallappa, R., Kankara, S.R.: Move your body: engaging museum visitors with human-data interaction. In: Proceedings of the 2020 CHI Conference on Human Factors in Computing Systems, pp. 1–13 (2020)
32. Weiser, M., Brown, J.S.: Designing calm technology. PowerGrid J. **1**(1), 75–85 (1996)
33. Wigdor, D., Wixon, D.: Brave NUI world: designing natural user interfaces for touch and gesture. Elsevier (2011)
34. Zancanaro, M., Stock, O., Alfaro, I.: Using cinematic techniques in a multimedia museum guide (2003)

Human-Data Interaction Design for the Taxonomy Visualization of Made in Italy Upholstered Systems

Piera Losciale, Alessandra Scarcelli(✉), Marina Ricci, and Annalisa Di Roma

Department of Architecture, Construction and Design, Polytechnic University of Bari, Bari, Italy
alessandra.scarcelli@poliba.it

Abstract. The article proposes an innovative approach in the field of Human-Data Interaction (HDI) applied to an interactive data visualization concerning an original taxonomy of upholstered products Made in Italy. Based on an in-depth analysis of the diversity of components, materials and production systems involved, the authors develop a complex taxonomy, culturally referable to a classification of standards regulations, in order to effectively manage the data related to the complex reference supply chain. Following this classification, the need to overcome the limitations of the traditional static visualization of information through a form that reveals patterns and relationships that are not known or easily deduced from the data is highlighted The main objective is to develop an interactive and implementable data visualization system that facilitates the understanding and management of the complexity of information, merging methods and tools from the field of Human-Data Interaction with those of industrial product design. In particular, the design of the second phase of the human-data interaction of the interactive infographic is reported, i.e. the relations chosen for the efficient and needs-based communication of information by users.

Keywords: Made in Italy · Taxonomy of Upholstered System · Human-Data Interaction Design

1 Introduction

The article is part of the "Made in Italy Circolare e Sostenibile" macro-project financed under the PNRR, which intervenes in promoting innovation in the Made in Italy production chains, with particular reference to 2F Furniture and Fashion. Specifically, the project to which refers "Cultural value chains: From local traditional production districts to a new country of origin effect" deals with the research of circular and resilient innovation related to the upholstered furniture supply chain.

This study applies to complex industrial products such as upholstered furniture, which, because they are characterized by a wide diversity of components, materials and production chain systems, generate complex patterns of understanding and data

M. Kurosu and A. Hashizume (Eds.): HCII 2024, LNCS 14688, pp. 388–400, 2024.
https://doi.org/10.1007/978-3-031-60449-2_26

assumption. These therefore require, in the logic of analysis and project support, a complex classification system such as a taxonomy. This assumption, developed in previous studies (Losciale et al., 2024), also supports the need for management of this complex model. In the field of product there are, to the authors' knowledge, no studies carried out to frame the specific product-system. Despite being unusual and non-traditional, the approach from the research supports the real-world need for a model that is able to handle complex information specific to the system-product in question.

With the awareness that the research encroaches on the proper field of study of Human-Data Interaction (HDI), the boundaries of the research exploration that applies tools and methods from the world of industrial products ('hard industry' understood in association with manufacturing processes, components, materials) with the world that approaches data management via a digital human-data interaction system are denounced here.

The complex classifications of industrial systems originated in the 1980s from a typically Italian history and, supported by a vast literature, fell into the classification systems of standards (e.g. ISO or UNI), which bring product-systems back to the physical dimension linked to the recognition of materials, elements, components, systems and their validation. Therefore, on this cultural basis, which has characterized the history of Made in Italy (MII) and its complex industrial products, was based the intuition of operating an ordered classification of upholstered furniture, currently not found in the literature, through the attribution of nomenclature and characteristics to models.

The taxonomy provided for the detailed analysis of the individual characteristics of upholstered furniture following specific selection criteria and reference categories useful for both the orderly collation of data from multi-form literature and the subsequent reconstruction of product properties. This supports the vision of the distribution and creation of value, also defined on a cultural basis, in all the elements of the product that reflect the respective stages of the supply chain (Porter, 1998; Losciale et al., 2024) characterized in turn by multiple producers and players who, with their know-how, specific production processes and services, have distinguished the reference territorial context and constituted the MII phenomenon.

The large amount of data collected and catalogued, following the traditional structural logic of standards classifications, has nevertheless found it difficult to be used in information (Jacobson, 1998) as it has a very low degree of access to users, be they designers, producers or experts in the field, as well as no model to find relational connections. Therefore, classification can become a true design tool if it moves from a listing system to a relational one: not just decoding data, but revealing patterns and relationships that are not known or easily deduced (Meirelles, 2013).

The research aims to innovate the traditional way of product knowledge using static dissemination tools such as manuals, encyclopaedias and technical glossaries, standardized and normative classification systems, towards interactive tools within digital systems to control the links between classification categories. Indeed, despite the increasing ease of acquiring, collecting and sharing data, persists the need for robust methods and effective visual tools to analyze and explore contemporary complexity (Ciuccarelli and Mauri, 2016). The aim is to identify a user-accessible interactive infographic system to support the complexity of data management.

The field of application research thus involves an original and personal declination of Human-Data Interaction and adapts its principles for the design of interactions between users and the complex data system (Mortier et al., 2020), albeit structured at the beginning, in order to provide users with the right information, extrapolated from the data themselves, through the choice of relations.

Research brings together the field of Industrial Product Design with the field of HDI, at the intersection of 'Data Visualization', 'Human-Computer Interaction', for the design and development of innovative systems through which information is extracted and knowledge is supported. Methodologically, it is considered effective for understanding information, designing interaction in the process of data visualization from the user's perspective, optimizing solutions from their experience (Xu & Song, 2011). The principles used are therefore based on user-centricity, where the design of systems through which people can explore and interpret data must match their skills, desires and needs.

The first part of the contribution is concerned with pointing out the theoretical and methodological references to the state of the art in the field of Human-Data Interaction, highlighting the authors' original approach. The next section refers to the taxonomy and addresses the questions and motivations behind its construction, the criteria and methodology used. The third section deals with the description of the relationships between the categories in a human-data interaction. Conclusions and research perspectives complete the contribution with an example of the interactive infographic under development.

2 An Interpretation of Human-Data Interaction (HDI)

The current scenario characterized by the expansion of data production, collection and use has sparked a lively academic debate regarding Human-Data Interaction (Mortier et al., 2013; Elmqvist, 2011; Cafaro, 2012). This concept denotes the ability of individuals to interact with data through cognitive and operational processes in order to extract meaning, understand context and draw useful conclusions (Mortier et al., 2020), analogous to the way Human-Computer Interaction investigates the relationship between people and computers (Hornung et al., 2015). HDI manifests itself simultaneously as a phenomenon and as a field of research that investigates that phenomenon: the phenomenon under study concerns the production, collection, processing, utilization and narration of data, in the sense of the creation of narratives following the process of datafication in the form of an orderly, cohesive and disclosing exposition of facts; the field of research, on the other hand, focuses on the actions of individuals and how these are influenced by data, both at the level of interpretation of phenomena, opinions and beliefs, and consequent decision-making and behavior (Hornung et al., 2015).

The comprehension and analysis of massive datasets play a crucial role in the empowerment of everyone, making relevant and exciting the challenge of managing the complexity of the ecosystem in which data are generated, collected, modified and used (Hornung et al., 2015). Scientific research has attempted to explain the goals and frontiers of the area of Human-Data Interaction in recent years, however, being a multidisciplinary field that covers different contexts, the interpretations are also various. This academic discussion also reflects the increasing importance placed on the human ability to navigate through the complexity of data in the digital age (Ranieri, 2018).

Definitions of HDI differ according to disciplinary context and area of interest, but generally converge on elements such as bidirectional interactivity between users and data, accessibility to data and tools to manipulate it, and facilitation of data analysis and understanding (Victorelli et al., 2020). Human-data interaction, although originally one-directional, can be historically dated back to the act of transposing, reading, and communicating signs, complex symbols and other forms of expression with meaning. The emergence of bi-directional interactive systems has fully realized interaction as a reciprocal process, allowing users to access data in accordance with their specific needs.

The concept of Human-Data Interaction began to take form in the field of computer science in the 1990s, highlighting the growing need for users to obtain customized, contextualized and comprehensible summaries from large datasets (Kennedy et al., 1996). More recently, the interpretation of the concept of Human-Data Interaction ranges from the manipulation, analysis and meaning-making of huge, unstructured and complex datasets through human intervention, underlining the facilitating role of physical environments in reasoning and deduction processes (Elmqvist, 2011), to the problem of providing personalized and comprehensible data from large datasets, emphasizing how the use of technologies improves human-data interaction (Cafaro, 2012).

Thus, it can be deduced that generally, the data considered within the traditional HDI landscape are generated autonomously by devices, by the exchange between platforms or by the Internet itself and therefore have a spontaneous nature (e.g. big data). These data come from the active and passive interaction of humans with the data, in the complete absence of a classification or filtering system at the source, provided for in the ex-post phase. The originality of the research derives from a data system that is not spontaneous, but filtered by users, where the analysis and design of the architecture makes the set implementable only through humans deciding to add, remove or modify data. Mutating the methods that come from the field of product design, the research's primary field, with those of Human-Data Interaction, the approach envisages an analogue and traditional data input, coherent with the classification system, a technical and experiential data acquisition phase, where the human component plays the role of validation through comparison with a given reference system, and an interactive system management model.

If in the Human-Data Interaction complex projections are generated, this research instead investigates an interpretative model that generates simple information systems, attempting to borrow tools from the HDI sphere that are linked to the management of complex data, being aware that such data are much less articulate than the usual HDI data but nevertheless considered articulate when compared to the sphere of the system-product.

It was on the construction of the artificial data model, which collected filtered information from the world of technical nomenclature, technical performance, and materials, that the model of use, reading and construction of meaning was reasoned.

2.1 Original Research Methodology

The original methodology of the proposed research (Fig. 1) is based on different phases and intersects with previous studies (Losciale et al., 2024). In fact, after the construction of the taxonomy (having its own methodology shown in Sect. 3), the research involved the design of the relationships between the data to be shown (the subject of the present contribution) and the subsequent design of an interactive infographic (currently being designed and therefore the subject of a forthcoming scientific contribution).

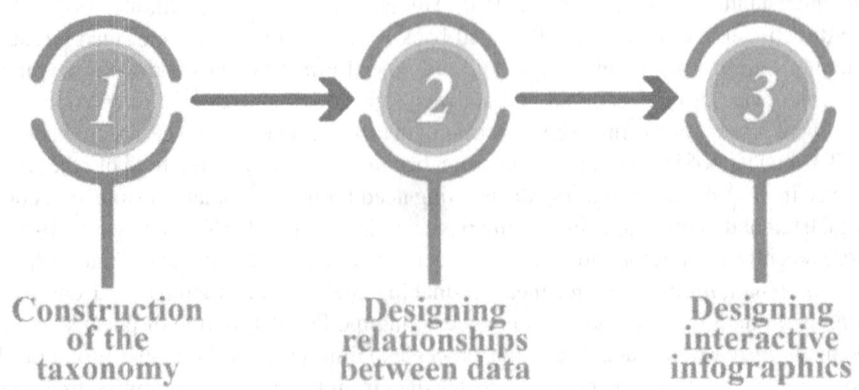

Fig. 1. Methodology used in the research

The design of information is based on the analysis and choice of possible relationships structured on the available data set through the use of original graphic and visual representations (paragraph 4). Interface design consists of developing accessible interactive infographics through the application of state-of-the-art techniques and tools: data visualization is based on a process of coding, with a specific language, and hierarchy-based mapping in order to create information structures (Cairo, 2016). In order to effectively communicate information, data visualization uses perceptual visual elements to process complex datasets or database information (Garrett, 2010), presented in terms of ergonomics and usability (Cabitza et al., 2016), with the aim of promoting readability, data comprehension process and analysis algorithms for people (Mortier et al., 2014). "Principles of design replicate principles of thought" describes the quality of effective translation of information and relationships between concepts into diagrammatic forms (Tufte, 1997), emphasizing the importance of clarity and accurate representation in the context of data visualization.

3 The Taxonomy of the Upholstered Product: Criteria, Categories and First Infographic Result

The evolution of furniture in the Italian upholstered furniture industry Made in Italy is widely documented in numerous texts on the history of design, highlighting the cultural value and promoting product knowledge in terms of both technical-material innovation and the aesthetic language of the finished product. However, the assignment of value to the entire supply chain requires an in-depth study aimed at recognizing the processes that support production at each stage of the final artefact, contextually identifying the role of all the supply chain actors that have historically collaborated in the consolidation of the MII phenomenon. The lack of a taxonomy for the upholstered product and the absence of a homogeneous literature of reference prompted the creation of an original model that brings together the complexity of both technical-formal and historical information.

The methodology for the construction of the original taxonomy of the Made in Italy upholstered product (Losciale et al., 2024) is briefly summarized in nine steps (Fig. 2).

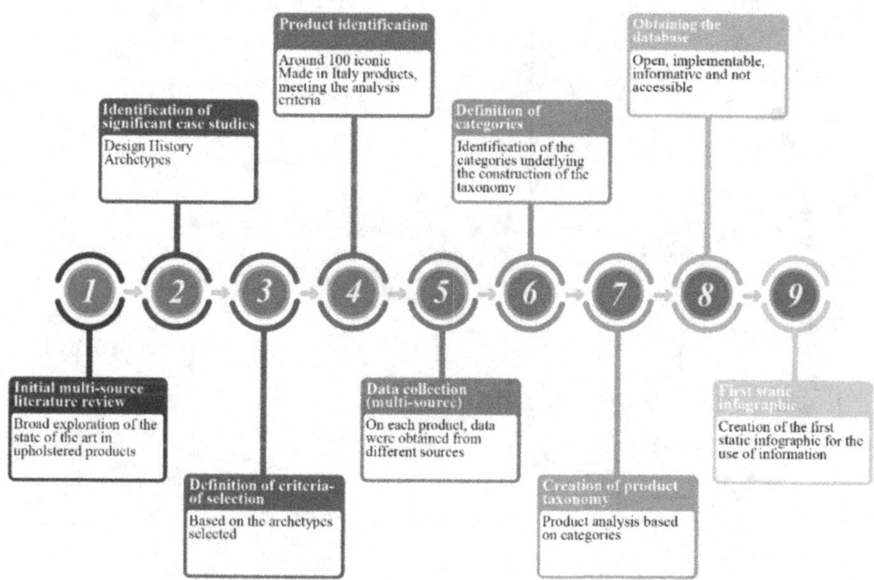

Fig. 2. Stages in the methodology for creating the taxonomy

An initial broad exploration of the state of the art concerning upholstered products made it possible to identify significant case studies useful for the definition of the two model selection criteria (historical-critical relevance and technological relevance). The subsequent selection and analysis of approximately 100 product-icons from multi-source literature defined the categories underlying the taxonomy, which concern model recognizability, technical-productive characteristics and formal innovation aspects. In particular, the recognizability of the model concerns the name of the product, the designer, the manufacturing company, and the year of production. The technical-formal characteristics are divided into structural system, holding system (armrests, seat, backrest) and set-up system. The aspects of formal innovation concern the shape and the aspects of functional innovation concern the mechanics of movement.

All the data of the taxonomy were collected in an open, implementable database consisting of information texts on the selected parameters. This database was imported into a first visual system which allowed the relationships between the data to be designed. (Fig. 3).

Figure 3 shows the visual system. In the center there are the macro-categories, in the upper part the data on technical, formal and functional aspects and in the lower part the products with specifications. The lines represent relationships.

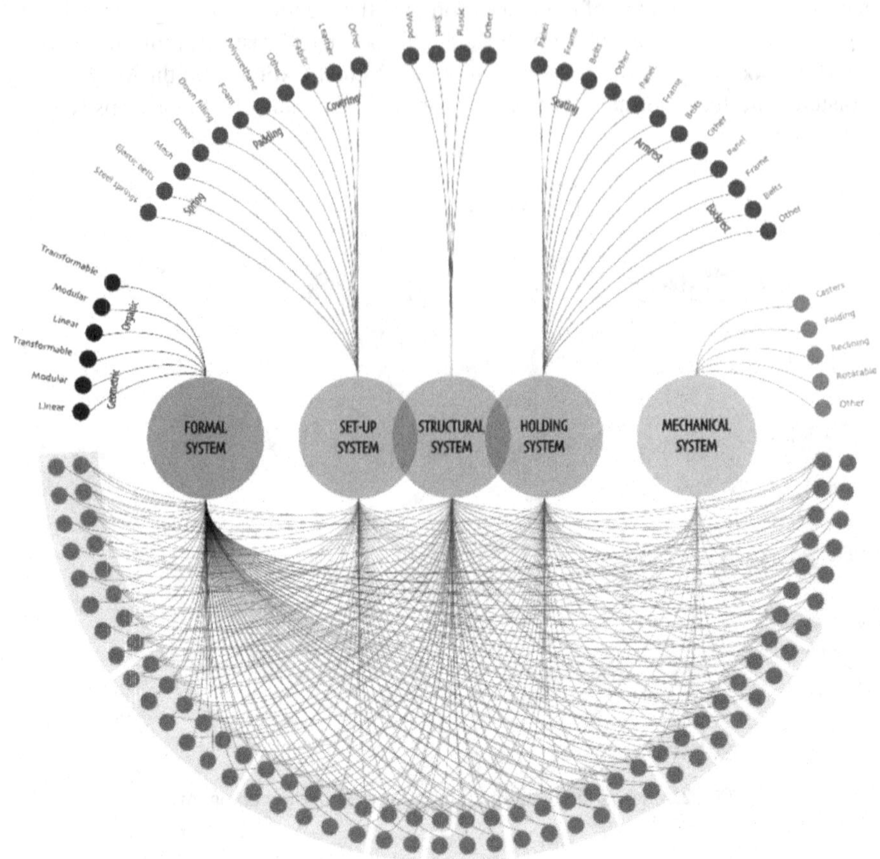

Fig. 3. First visual system

Although the arrangement of the data in the visual system was innovative compared to traditional manual knowledge access systems, it too showed limitations and constraints in visualization, such as the impossibility of comparing products due to the absence of interaction. It was possible to consult the relationships through a filter system, however, the navigation remained complex and not visually immediate for a complete user experience. Consequently, it was necessary to develop a digital and interactive data visualization, preceded by an initial phase of designing the relationships between the data, shown in the next section.

4 Designing the Human-Data Interaction of the Taxonomy: Relationships

The design of the human-data interaction, within the methodological process outlined above, is carried out in the second and third phases. Specifically, the second phase is reported here, i.e. the analysis of the relationships between the data, which can be implemented in the presence of further categorized data. Original graphic diagrams are used, in the absence of state-of-the-art tools, to describe the relationships, providing a clear visual representation that facilitates understanding. In particular, relationships are shown starting from the selected data (with double contour line) by grey arrows (a link not present indicates the absence of that category). The categories are marked by different colors only for ease of reading: the design of the final interactive infographic is not based on these chosen graphic signs.

The designed relationships can be divided into four types:

First type of relationship (Fig. 4)

Starting data: Product

Description: The selected product is described through the specifications of each category in the product.

Second type of relationship (Fig. 5)

Starting data: Macro-category (structural system, holding system, set-up system, form, mechanics)

Description: highlights the products associated with the macro-category, the specific sub-categories (e.g. structure system x, structure system y) within the macro-category, the company and the corresponding year.

Third type of relationship (Fig. 6)

Source data: Sub-category (e.g. armrest holding system x, spring set-up system x)

Description: Highlights the products that belong to that specific sub-category and all categories associated with the products.

Fourth type of relationship (Fig. 7)

Source data: Recognition category (e.g. year, company)

Description: highlights the products associated with the category and the specific categories associated with them.

The reported relationships show an example for each type and can be extended to other data that can be accumulated with the chosen data, with the exception of the first relationship, which only concerns products. Just to mention a few, the second relationship is also valid if the data chosen as the starting point is the set-up or holding system, just as the fourth relationship is also valid if the starting data is the manufacturing company. As the taxonomy is an open and implementable database, these proposed relationships are subject to implementation in the presence of further categories and data.

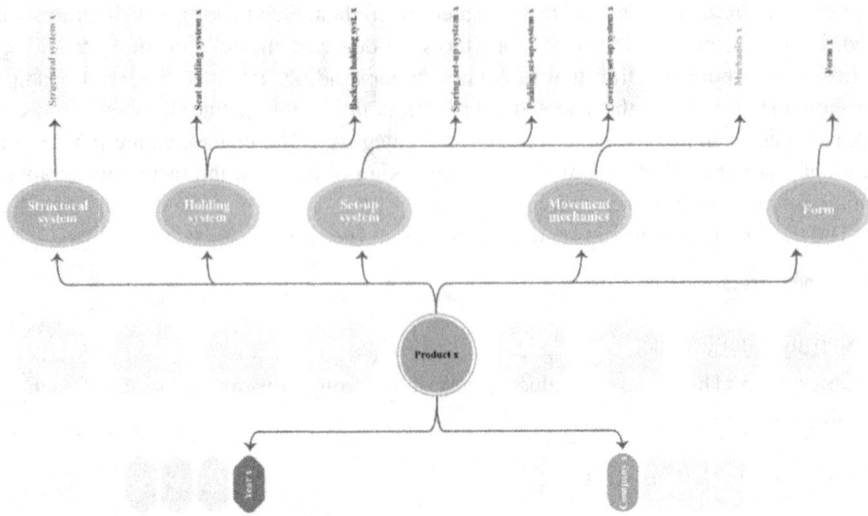

Fig. 4. First type of relationship

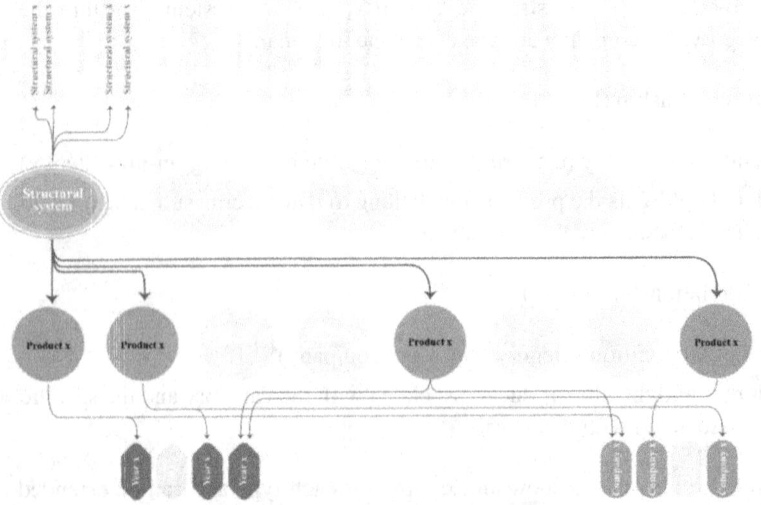

Fig. 5. Second type of relationship

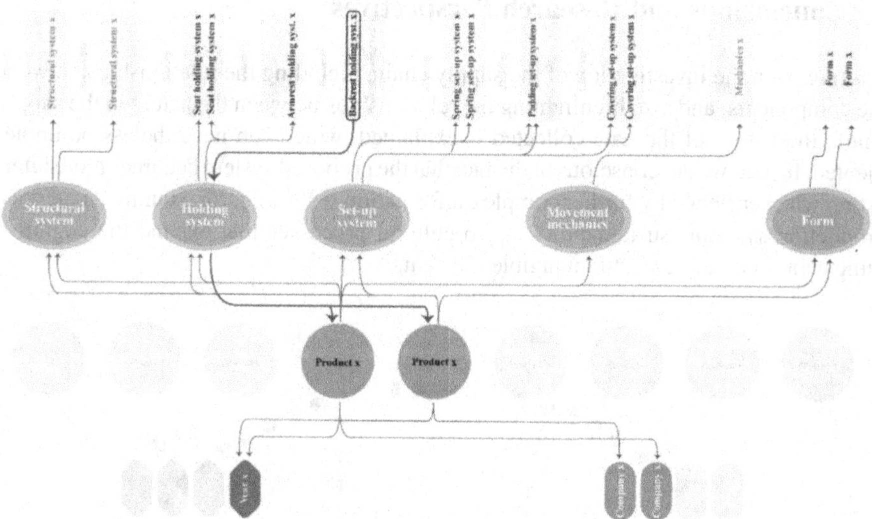

Fig. 6. Third type of relationship

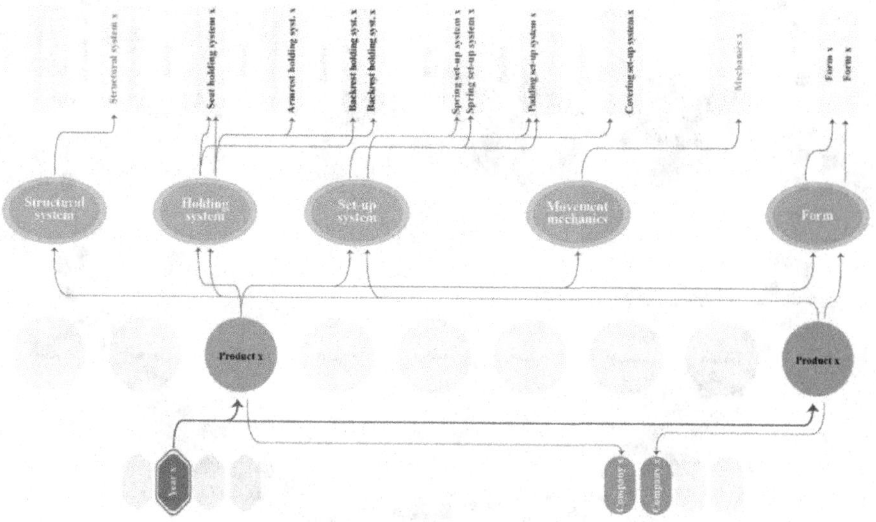

Fig. 7. Fourth type of relationship

5 Conclusions and Research Perspectives

Starting from the investigation of the supply chain, including the relationships between the components, and also highlighting the relationships between the actors in the supply chain, the nature of the data collected is explained, which can nevertheless be implemented. In fact, we are conscious of the fact that the proposed system becomes more interesting when enriched by further complex information regarding, for example, materials, production systems, sustainability, up to cultural processes that expand the cognitive dimension to intangible and intangible elements.

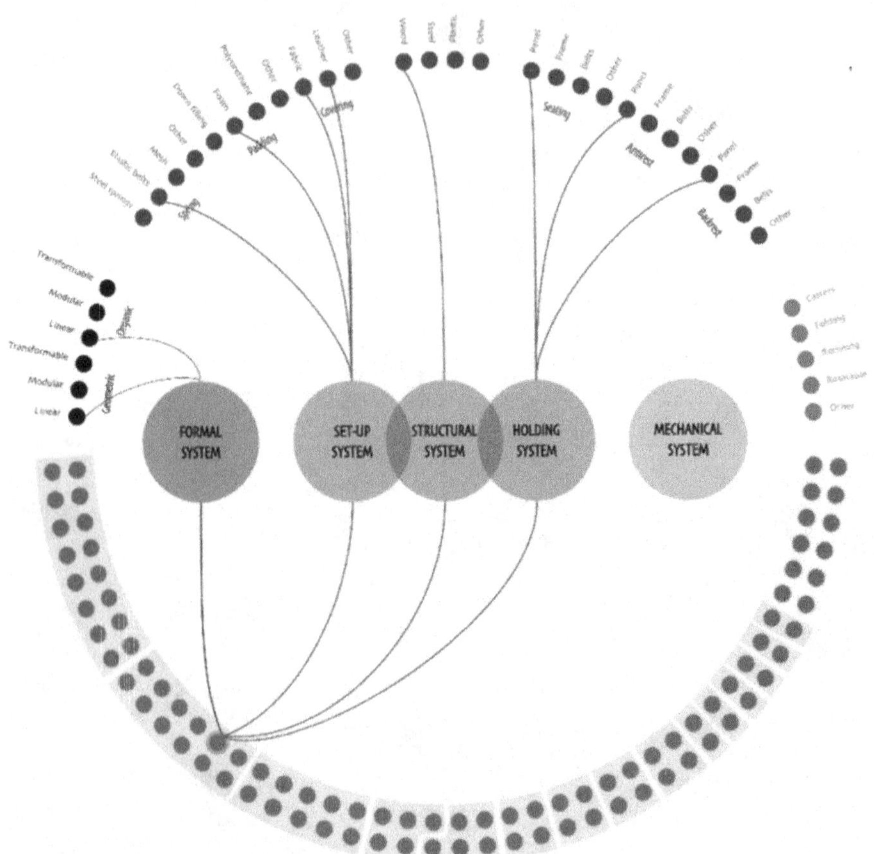

Fig. 8. Example first type of relationships: product (Fiorenza by Franco Albini)

Therefore, the research hopes to create an interactive information model that can be accessible and ergonomic, but also implementable to the aforementioned multiple information and complex relationships: in view of the changeability and fluidity of the contemporary landscape, a 'new complexity' must be addressed, characterized by emerging challenges in particular in the search for new, or innovative use of old, visualization tools (Manzini et al., 2006).

The following are the first hypotheses of the interactive data visualization, which is still at the design stage and not yet complete (Fig. 8; Fig. 9).

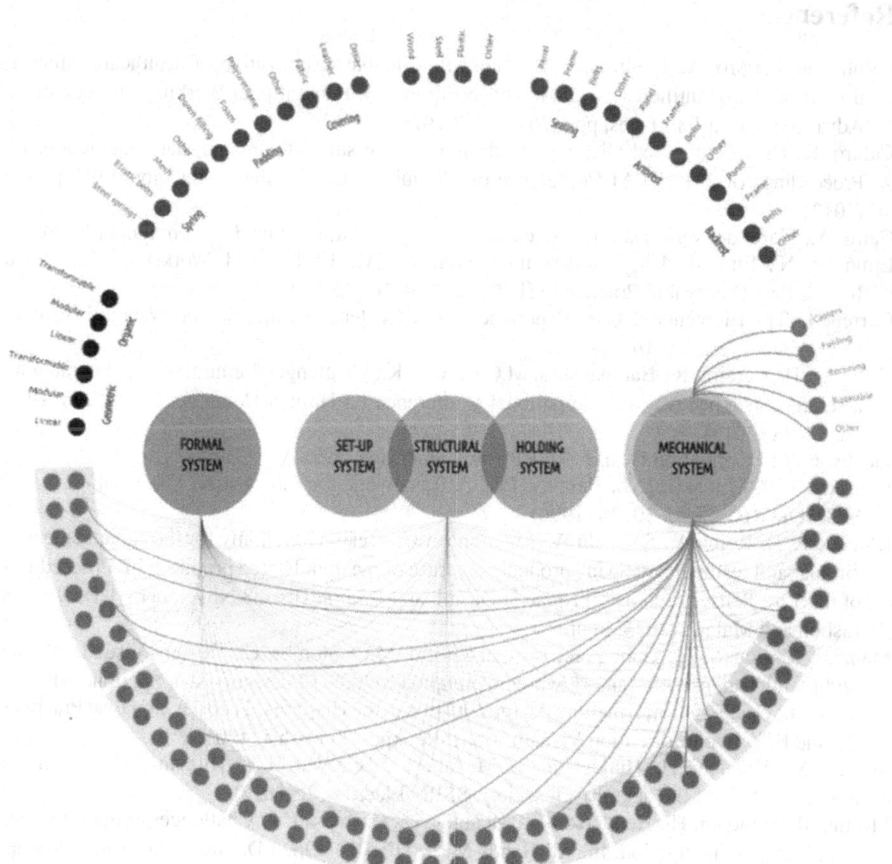

Fig. 9. Example second type of relationship: macro-category (movement mechanics)

It is believed that, even at an early stage, research has enriched, and may in the future do so in larger dimensions, the design space to support the knowledge of technical, production, historical and formal aspects, supporting design in the fruition of the complexity of information for circular and sustainable innovation in upholstered furniture.

Acknowledgments. Project financed by the European Union - NextGenerationEU – Piano Nazionale di Ripresa e Resilienza (PNRR) - Mission 4 Component 2 Investment 1.3 - Notice No. 341 of 03/15/2022 from the Ministry of University and Research. Protocol of the application PE00000004, decree granting the loan no. 1551 of 11/10/2022, CUP D93C22000920001, Made in

Italy Circular and Sustainable MICS. SPOKE 7 "New and consumer-driven business models for resilient and circular SCs" P.3 Research project "Cultural value chains: From local traditional production districts to a new country of origin effect" (coordinator Prof. Annalisa Di Roma) Wp1_ Sofa supply chain. Sustainable innovation (research group: Annalisa Di Roma, Piera Losciale, Anna Christiana Maiorano, Alessandra Scarcelli).

References

Cabitza, F., Locoro, A., Fogli, D., Giacomin, M.: Valuable visualization of healthcare information: from the quantified self data to conversations. In: International Working Conference on Advanced Visual Interfaces, pp. 376–380 (2016)

Cafaro, F.: Using embodied allegories to design gesture suites for human-data interaction. In: Proceedings of 2012 ACM Conference on Ubiquitous Computing - UbiComp 2012, p. 560 (2012)

Cairo, A.: L'arte del vero. Dati, grafici e mappe per la comunicazione. Pearson, Italia (2016)

Elmqvist, N.: Embodied human-data interaction. In: ACM CHI 2011 Workshop "Embodied Interaction: Theory and Practice in HCI", pp. 104–107 (2011)

Garrett, J.: The Elements of User Experience: User-Centered Design for the Web and Beyond. New Riders Press (2010)

Hornung, H., Pereira, R., Baranauskas, M.C.C., Liu, K.: Challenges for human-data interaction–a semiotic perspective. In: International Conference on Human-Computer Interaction, HCI, pp. 37–48 (2015)

Jacobson, R.: Information Design. MIT Press, Cambridge (1998)

Kennedy, J.B., Mitchell, K.J., Barclay, P.J.: A framework for information visualisation. ACM SIGMOD Rec. **25**(4), 30–34 (1996)

Losciale P., Di Roma A., Scarcelli A., Maiorano A.C.: Design taxonomy for the enhancement of circular and resilient "made in" products: the case of the upholstered products. In: Proceedings of the 12th Senses & Sensibility 2023. Design and Complexity. 28 November - 1 December, Lisbon and Malaga (2024, in press)

Manzini, E., Penati, A., Gabbatore, R., Quaggiotto, M., Colombi, C.: Design+Visualizzazione (2006). http://densitydesign.org/wp-content/uploads/2007/12/design-visualizzazione.pdf

Meirelles, I.: Design for Information: An Introduction to the Histories, Theories, and Best Practices Behind Effective Information Visualizations. Rockport Publishers (2013)

Mortier, M., Haddadi, H., Henderson, T., McAuley, D., Crowcroft, J.: Human-data interaction: the human face of the data-driven society. SSRN Electron. J. (2014)

Mortier, R., Haddadi, H., Henderson, T., Mcauley, D., Crowcroft, J.: Challenges & opportunities in human-data interaction. In: All Hands Meet. DE2013: Open Digital - The Fourth Annual Digital Economy All Hands Meeting, pp. 4–6 (2013)

Mortier, R., Haddadi, H., Henderson, T., McAuley, D., Crowcroft, J., Crabtree, A.: Human-data interaction. In: The Encyclopedia of Human-Computer Interaction (2nd). Interaction Design Foundation (2020)

Porter, M.: Clusters and the new economics of competition. Harvard Bus. Rev. **76**(6), 77–90 (1998)

Ranieri, M.: Oltre il "far di conto" nell'era digitale: la frontiera della data literacy. In: Teoria e pratica delle new media literacies (vol. 2). Aracné (2018)

Tufte, E.: Visual Explanations: Images and Quantities. Evidence and Narrative. Graphics Press, Cheshire (1997)

Victorelli, E.Z., Dos Reis, J.C., Hornung, H., Bolognesi Prado, A.: Understanding human-data interaction: literature review and recommendations for design author links open overlay panel. Int. J. Human Comput. Stud. **134**, 13–32 (2020)

Xu, S., Song, F.: Information visualization design based on visual thinking. Packaging Eng. **32**(16), 11–14 (2011)

Empower the Tâi-Gí Teaching Practitioner Through Co-designing the Tâi-Gí Teaching Support Platform

Yi-ping Ma, Wan-Ling Chang(✉), and Min-Yuan Ma

National Cheng Kung University, No.1, University Road, Tainan City 701, Taiwan
{p38111074,WanLingChang}@gs.ncku.edu.tw, mamy@mail.ncku.edu.tw

Abstract. In response to the promotion of the Development of National Languages Act, the Ministry of Education in Taiwan changed the curriculum guidelines of 12-year Basic Education. The high school must have one local language course every week, including Tâi-gí. However, the Tâi-gí teacher are facing the challenges of searching the teaching materials from scattered Tâi-gí literature resources in the internet and limited supports from the education authorities. The Tâi-gí teachers was disadvantaged group in the promotion of Tâi-gí high school education. To empower the teachers who will devoted to the Tâi-gí teaching practices, we in-tend to build a Tâi-gí literature platform to collect Tâi-gí resources in supporting the Tâi-gí teachers preparing their language courses. Instead of applying the top-down approach of building the platform from resources owners, designers and engineers' perspectives, we apply participatory design as the approach to co-create this platform with Tâi-gí teachers in senior high school. In this project, we conducted six workshops for two design stages to exploring their needs of Tâi-gí teaching. We recruited five Tâi-gí teachers to work with the designers and developer throughout the whole project. In this study, we identified two primary challenges in empowering Tâi-gí teachers with design literacy within the PD process. The first challenge pertains to the researchers' ongoing commitment to practicing reflection-in-action throughout the six workshops. The second challenge lies in the Tâi-gí teachers' difficulties in envisioning the future or potential functions of the platform they aspire to use.

1 Introduction

Language is not only the tools for communication but also the representation of the local culture. The Taiwan government intended to celebrate and preserve the diversity of the local cultures and announced the Development of National Languages Act in 2019. In addition to the Mandarin Chinese, which was used officially and pervasively in Taiwan, the law conferring national language status and providing legal protection to over 20 local languages, including Tâi-gí, Hak-kâ-fa, and Zúyǔ of the various indigenous groups [1]. At the same time, in response to the legalization of the law, the Ministry of Education in Taiwan changed the curriculum guidelines of 12-year Basic Education. The high school must have one local language course every week. Tâi-gí, also called as Taiwanese, is one of the most popular local languages taught in the high school. The demands of Tâi-gí

M. Kurosu and A. Hashizume (Eds.): HCII 2024, LNCS 14688, pp. 401–412, 2024.
https://doi.org/10.1007/978-3-031-60449-2_27

teachers greatly increased and many teachers attended the Tâi-gí training program to learn how to teach Tâi-gí in a short period of time. However, there are some problems those new Tâi-gí teachers are encountering. Tâi-gí has developed its own writing for more than one hundred years, but the writing style are varied hugely caused by the historical contexts. In the past two decades, the Tâi-gí literatures are getting to be collected and created digitally and gradually be available in the internet. However, those literatures scatters in different internet sources and written in varied styles. For Tâi-gí teachers, it is always challenging to search for Tâi-gí resources when they prepare the Tâi-gí teaching. The efficacies of Tâi-gí teaching resources and the endangered status of Tâi-gí language leads the Tâi-gí teachers to be disadvantaged and their needs of teaching to support the cultural and language diversity was ignored by the mainstream.

To empower the teachers who will devoted to the Tâi-gí teaching practices, we intend to build a Tâi-gí literature platform to collect Tâi-gí resources in supporting the Tâi-gí teachers preparing their language courses. Instead of applying the top-down approach of building the platform from resources owners, designers and engineers' perspectives, we apply participatory design (PD) as the approach to co-create this platform with Tâi-gí teachers in senior high school. We are not only exploring their needs of Tâi-gí teaching but also empower them with the right to make design decision together with the designers and researchers [2]. We want to transfer the Tâi-gí teachers from passive informants to active designers of this Tâi-gí teaching support platform.

In this project, we conducted six workshops spanning two design stages, comprising five physical sessions and one virtual workshop via Google Meet. From a pool of Tâi-gí teacher training programs, we enlisted five experienced teachers (three females and two males) with over a year of senior high school Tâi-gí teaching. The initial three workshops in Stage 1 aimed to explore Tâi-gí teachers' course preparation needs through mutual learning [3]. We gathered practical issues and potential solutions. Stage 2 centered on collaborative web platform development with the teachers. We not only synthesized Stage 1 results into practical platform functions for discussion but also collaborated on revising the user interface (UI) design of the Tâi-gí teaching support platform. We conclude by summarizing the lessons learned thus far and acknowledging the research's limitations.

2 Background

2.1 Participatory Design

Participatory Design originated in the Scandinavian region, and this research methodology emerged during the vibrant labor movement of the 1960s and 1970s. At that time, the rise of social movements and human rights awareness, particularly prominent in Scandinavia, led to proactive efforts by labor unions to advocate for workers' rights in the workplace [2]. The 1960s and 1970s also marked the early stages of rapid development in computer technology. Many companies had high expectations for computer technology, attempting to introduce computer equipment and software to enhance work and production efficiency. In this context, labor unions demanded a say in the implementation of digital technology, as social activists of that time believed that individuals should have decision-making rights in various aspects of life. They argued that decision outcomes should be achieved through participatory discussions to obtain solutions aligned with everyone's values and interests [4]. This ideology inspired PD, becoming its core principle: users have the right to express their ideas about the products they use, participate in design decisions alongside other stakeholders, and influence the design of the product [2].

2.2 Empowerment Through Co-design

The politically grounded ideology of PD is effectively conveyed through guiding principles such as equalizing power relations, democratic practices, situation-based actions, and mutual learning [2]. Notably, the discourse on PD carries a robust moral and rhetorical stance, placing significant emphasis on user empowerment [5]. Steen [6] identifies virtues in PD, with empowerment standing out as a key value that underpins successful collaboration between designers and users. This underscores the idea that empowerment is not merely an outcome but a guiding principle within the ethos of PD.

Several PD projects align with this emphasis on empowerment. For instance, Kam et al. [7] endeavored to leverage PD in the development of a software platform with the goal of enhancing English language acquisition among children in rural schools and urban slums across India. Byrne and Sahay [8] applied PD to create a community-based health information system in South Africa, highlighting that participation can enhance social development by including the voices of the excluded, who are impacted by development programs. In a case study of Mstów, Poland, Stangel and Szóstek [9] illustrate how PD can empower citizens, showcasing its tangible impact on enhancing the agency and influence of individuals within a community. This example further underscores the transformative potential of PD in fostering empowerment at the grassroots level. User empowerment has played a crucial role in PD studies, emerging as the fundamental essence for achieving greater equality in equitable PD engagements [10]. This study aims to align with the tradition of user empowerment in PD tradition, specifically focusing on amplifying the voices of the marginalized Tâi-gí teacher community during the development of technology tailored to their needs.

3 Methods

3.1 Participants

There was a total of five participants (two males and three females) in this workshop, all of whom were currently teaching at high schools and vocational schools in Taiwan. They exclusively specialized in teaching Tâi-gí, without involvement in other subjects. With teaching experience exceeding one year, they possessed a certain level of expertise in Tâi-gí instruction. Additionally, five designers (all females) participated in the workshop.

3.2 PD Workshops

Within this project, we organized six workshops spanning two design stages – five in a physical setting and one virtually conducted via Google Meet. Each stage encompassed three workshops. Please refer to Fig. 1 for the workshop process.

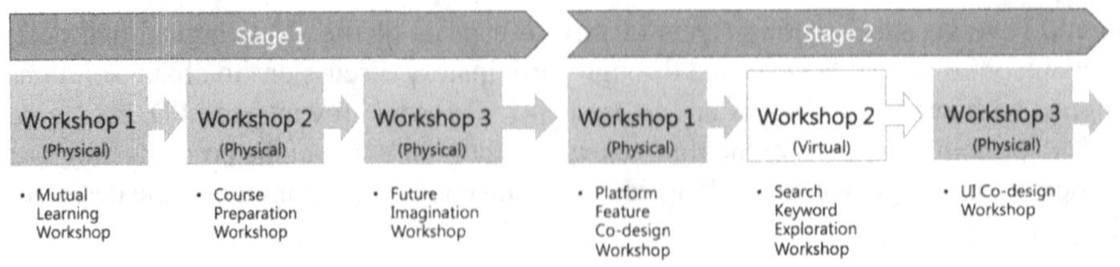

Fig. 1. PD workshop Process

Stage 1 – Workshop 1. In workshop 1, following ice-breaking activities, Tâi-Gí teachers openly discussed the challenges encountered in their teaching processes. Designers undertook the responsibility of keenly observing and documenting these challenges. The subsequent mutual learning session unfolded with two primary themes:

1. Introduction to Tâi-gí Databases: Designers offered insights into the history of Tâi-gí literature. They introduced existing Tâi-gí database resources and engaged in discussions with teachers about the websites they were familiar with and frequently utilized.
2. Introduction to Natural Language Processing (NLP) Technology: Designers presented information about NLP technology and its potential applications in supporting Tâi-gí language teaching platforms. The aim was to encourage Tâi-gí teachers to reflect on their teaching needs and experiences, considering how technology could enhance platform functionality.

In summary, Tâi-gí teachers shared the current challenges they face in searching for course materials, and designers diligently observed and recorded these difficulties. The analysis of challenges in lesson preparation guided the selection of the next workshop's topic. The primary objective of this workshop was to delve into the needs of Tâi-gí teachers, propose relevant technologies for a teaching support platform, and observe pain points and requirements for platform design. This process provided valuable data for future development.

Stage 1 – Workshop 2. The second workshop of the first stage, which focused on lesson preparation session for Tâi-gí teachers, spanned approximately three hours with the participation of five Tâi-gí teachers and five designers. This workshop focused on lesson preparation activities for Tâi-gí teachers. The workshop began with a lesson preparation segment, using a grouping strategy with two groups. One group consisted of three individuals (one male and two females), and the other group comprised two individuals (one male and one female). Designers had created two types of lesson preparation topics, one related to high school curriculum content and the other to vocational high school curriculum content. Tâi-gí teachers drew topics randomly and engaged in lesson preparation. Each group was accompanied by a designer who observed and recorded the preparation process, posing questions as needed. The remaining designers assisted from the sidelines. Finally, each group of Tâi-gí teachers shared their prepared lessons and discussed challenges or discoveries encountered while using databases for lesson preparation (Fig. 2).

Fig. 2. The process of lesson preparation by Tâi-gí teachers and recording by designers.

Stage 1 – Workshop 3. First stage workshop 3 was the Future Imagination Workshop. The third workshop of the first stage spanned approximately three hours with the participation of five Tâi-gí teachers and five designers. The workshop began with designers sharing observations and categorizing issues identified in the previous workshop. Tâi-gí teachers provided additional insights, and both parties jointly reviewed and discussed the results. Participants then collectively discussed potential improvements and features, utilizing brainstorming techniques. Each participant generated 1 to 2 suggestions or requirements for each problem category, sharing their ideas in a rotating fashion. Finally, the suggestions and requirements generated were classified using a cross-axis analysis (categorized as important-not important, urgent-not urgent) to identify priorities for design implementation (Fig. 3).

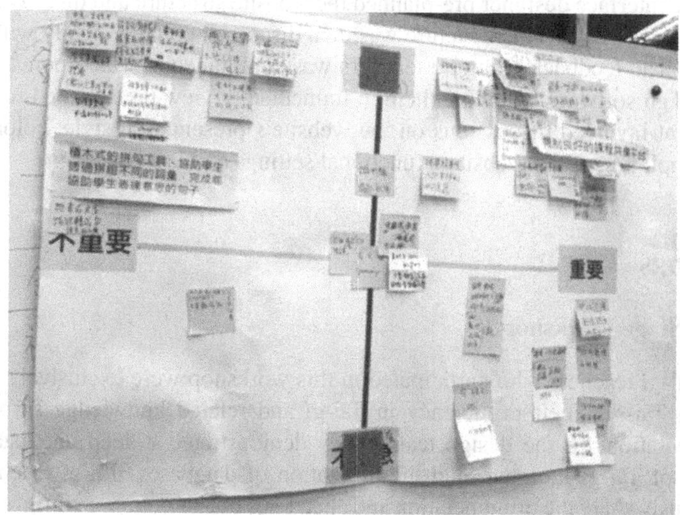

Fig. 3. Using cross-axis analysis to identify priority needs for design.

Stage 2 – Workshop 1. Second stage workshop 1 was the interface feature unwrapping workshop. The first workshop of the second stage spanned approximately three hours with the participation of five Tâi-gí teachers and five designers. The workshop commenced with an explanation of the structure and process of interface design by the interface designer. Subsequently, the designers created two sets of personas – one for a full-time Tâi-gí instructor and another for a part-time Tâi-gí instructor (referring to someone responsible for a specific subject who is additionally assigned as a Tâi-gí instructor). The use of personas aimed to pinpoint the target users of the Tâi-gí teaching support platform. In the final segment, the requirements categorized on the quadrant matrix from the previous workshop were transformed into functional interface elements, completing the functional framework of the website.

Stage 2 – Workshop 2. Second stage workshop 2 was the Keyword Exploration Workshop. The first workshop of the second stage spanned approximately three hours with the participation of five Tâi-gí teachers and five designers. The primary focus was on integrating topics related to Sustainable Development Goals (SDGs) and exploring keywords and categories that Tâi-gí teachers used and needed in the future when searching during lesson preparation. This workshop allowed designers to take inventory of the search needs of Tâi-gí teachers, serving as a reference and direction for classifying website elements.

Stage 2 – Workshop 3. Second stage workshop 3 was the Co-creation of Functional Map and Website Layout Design. The third workshop of the second stage focused on the co-creation of a functional map and the design of the website layout, spanning approximately three hours. Five participants (two males and three females) and four designers attended this workshop. The workshop began with designers sharing the results and discoveries from the previous two workshops in this stage. Building upon these findings, the interface designer pre-planned the website structure and directly presented it during the workshop. This structure was then discussed collaboratively with the Tâi-gí teachers. The feedback from the teachers was simultaneously incorporated into the website design software, allowing them to immediately view the adjusted results. The final segment involved discussions on the website's presentation style, color scheme, and the completion of the website's functional settings and layout design.

4 Findings

4.1 First Stage Workshop 1

The five Tâi-gí teachers who participated in this workshop were exclusively dedicated to teaching Tâi-gí. Their proficiency in Tâi-gí and related knowledge surpassed the initial expectations of the design team. They demonstrated a deep understanding of the history of Tâi-gí literature and the utilization of databases. Tâi-gí teachers could simultaneously share the pronunciation and anecdotes of less common Tâi-gí characters. However, during brainstorming, due to a lack of prior exercises in design thinking, they found it relatively challenging to precisely articulate ideas.

Concerning preparation challenges, Tâi-gí teachers noted that most students possess very basic Tâi-gí skills. To facilitate student absorption, teachers need to adapt and organize the material. The progress of teaching cannot advance rapidly, as it requires catering to diverse student types. This situation resulted in the inability to reuse instructional materials and a necessity to provide supplementary materials and assignments to stimulate student interest. The five teachers unanimously believed that preparatory content needs to be categorized according to the different programs students are enrolled in. For example, high school students might focus on literary materials, while vocational high school students may prioritize practical or skill-based materials. It was challenging to have a one-size-fits-all set of materials, as students vary in their familiarity with Tâi-gí, requiring adjustments in the difficulty of teaching materials.

Furthermore, the Tâi-gí teachers highlighted certain areas that need improvement in the current teaching system's provided materials. Issues include incoherent sentences in textbooks, a lack of contextualization in content, and students' disinterest in the material.

4.2 First Stage Workshop 2

Through observation, it was noted that due to their extensive teaching experience, the five Tâi-gí teachers were very efficient in their preparation speed. They primarily used Google and Wikipedia for information searches, with one teacher consulting book materials. Some teachers conducted life interviews to gather information, such as interviewing elders or seniors who speak Tâi-gí. Each instructor established their website search list, making it relatively easier to find information by categorizing and searching through websites.

Regarding teaching strategies and methods, Tâi-gí teachers mainly focused on course texts. They extended content from the textbook's themes, observed students' levels and conditions, adjusted teaching materials timely, and supplemented with interactive methods (idioms, Taiwanese songs, etc.) to communicate with students. They even designed assignments in interesting formats, such as video editing or introducing unique Tâi-gí culture (e.g., Ba Jia Jiang). All of these approaches tended to successfully pique students' interest in learning.

During the preparation process, teachers encountered challenges such as difficulty searching for specific terms. Sometimes they were unsure which keywords to use, and some search results were overly complex, requiring time to filter and refine. Since various platforms contained duplicate information, many search results were repetitive. Additionally, due to the long history of Tâi-gí, much information had not been digitized, and there were limited online resources for certain data. It was essential to verify the accuracy of information obtained from online searches.

4.3 First Stage Workshop 3

In this workshop, it was discovered that Tâi-gí teachers have specific vocabulary needs related to the workplace, daily life, medical terminology, natural ecology and geographical terms, historical life and customs, industry-specific terminology, and specialized terms in certain fields (such as the periodic table). This indicates that Tâi-gí teachers require a variety of supplementary data beyond textbook content.

For assistance in teaching course texts, Tâi-gí teachers need explanations or examples of Tâi-gí terms, etymology and related background information for vocabulary, and reference materials for extending course content. Additionally, for assistance in teaching extended materials, they require playful and humorous Tâi-gí resources such as recitation of poems, idioms, and tongue twisters, as well as resources related to Tâi-gí history and culture (e.g., Gezaixi).

Regarding platform requirements, the primary focus was on the ability to efficiently find teaching resources and appropriately categorize and guide users to these resources. Teachers also proposed that once the platform is established and stable, an interactive feature for building sentences, such as block-style sentence construction, would be beneficial. They also expressed the desire to establish a well-mechanized collaborative teaching platform in the future, where Taiwanese language teachers can prepare lessons together and exchange resources.

4.4 Second Stage Workshop 1

Regarding the setting of personas, initially, the designer set the persona for part-time teachers as those who were employed at schools and did not need to be responsible for college preparatory courses (e.g., physical education or art teachers). However, through communication with Tâi-gí teachers during the workshop, it was discovered that part-time teachers were more often language teachers (e.g., Chinese or English teachers). Consequently, the characteristics of the persona were directly modified during the workshop, making the subsequent activities smoother. This part differed from the initial setup.

However, in terms of the functional structure, the designer used a structural approach to present the connection between each function and the next. There was a gap in the Tâi-gí teachers' understanding of this structure. They were unable to grasp the logical structure and visualization of the website in their minds, resulting in many communication issues at the beginning. The interface designer immediately visualized the functional structure through drawing during the workshop, allowing Taiwanese language teachers to smoothly participate (Fig. 4).

4.5 Second Stage Workshop 2

Conducted online keyword searches based on the keywords provided by Tâi-gí teachers. Designers categorized the keywords, discovering that some were related to textbook content. Additionally, popular topics (e.g., Demon Slayer, Tokyo Revengers), daily necessities (food, clothing, shelter, transportation, and entertainment), professional terms, sustainable development-related terms, and folk culture-related terms (religion, place names) were all types of keywords searched by Taiwanese language teachers. This result is beneficial for designers as a reference for classification when designing the interface.

4.6 Second Stage Workshop 3

Designers utilized the results and feedback obtained from the previous two workshops, employing interface design software to create a preliminary version during the workshop. Designers and Tâi-gí teachers collaboratively adjusted and modified it on the spot. Since this approach allowed direct visualization of the webpage's design, Tâi-gí teachers could

Fig. 4. The interface designer immediately visualized the functional structure through drawing during the workshop.

provide suggestions based on their existing habits and needs. However, more innovative ideas might not be generated through this process. Designers needed to be keen in identifying issues during the workshop and promptly make corrections.

5 Discussion

5.1 Reflection-In-Action During Workshops

We deeply acknowledge the significance of incorporating reflective practices [11, 12] into the PD workshops throughout the project. Throughout the two-stage PD process conducted in six workshops, we actively engaged in reflection-in-action [13] to refine the workshop flow. We identified two distinct situations that necessitated adjustments to the workshop content: reflection-in-action between workshops and reflection-in-action during workshops.

Reflection-in-action between workshops was crucial to ensure the seamless progression of outcomes from one workshop to the next. For instance, in the initial stage's Workshop 1, we recognized the need to categorize students based on their educational backgrounds, as revealed during the insights shared by Tâi-gí teachers. The disparities in teaching materials and resources between high school and vocational school students significantly impacted teaching methods. Consequently, we adjusted the preparation theme for the second workshop of the first stage based on the insights gathered from the preceding workshop.

In the third workshop of the second stage, the insights gained from the preceding two workshops played a pivotal role in shaping the design of the website interface. This interdependence ensured that the design process was guided by the collective insights accumulated from prior workshops, enhancing the overall cohesion and effectiveness of the PD experience. Another instance involved reflection-in-action within the workshop flow itself. During the first workshop of the second stage, the initially envisioned persona for part-time teachers did not align with the actual situation, prompting real-time adjustments to the persona settings. In the same workshop, when Tâi-gí teachers faced difficulty grasping the logic behind the website's map design, we promptly shifted to a drawing method to aid their understanding of the structural design.

Furthermore, in the third workshop of the second stage, on-site modifications to interface design were implemented based on feedback from Tâi-gí teachers. In both scenarios, participatory designers needed extensive experience in PD workshops and a heightened sensitivity to promptly identify and address issues during the sessions. This real-time reflection, aligned with the reflective practice of PD [11], significantly diverged from retrospective reflection after workshop completion. This approach played a crucial role in ensuring the effectiveness of the workshops and the satisfaction of participants.

5.2 Taiwanese Teachers' Focus on Addressing Current Issues

Throughout the PD workshops, our collaboration with Tâi-gí teachers revealed a predominant focus on addressing immediate teaching challenges, with less emphasis on future needs and imaginative considerations. This observation suggests that Tâi-gí teachers were primarily concerned with resolving known issues during the design process. Their daily teaching experiences, including tasks like preparing teaching materials, guiding student interests, and resource searches, prompted them to express needs that aimed at improving teaching effectiveness and efficiency through technological tools. Despite these efforts, the workshop outcomes did not yield significantly innovative solutions.

It's noteworthy that Tâi-gí teachers presented fewer needs and visions for future occurrences. This might be attributed to their substantial investment of time and effort in daily teaching, resulting in less concern about future changes, or it could indicate a potential lack of imagination when it comes to applying new technologies. In future PD processes, there is a need to guide Tâi-gí teachers to contemplate potential future teaching needs and technological applications actively. Encouraging them to participate more in innovation and imagination during the design process can lead to solutions better aligned with future teaching requirements.

5.3 Constraints and Future Directions

The participants in this workshop were full-time Tâi-gí teachers from high schools and vocational schools. They are pioneers in the teaching field, possessing extensive knowledge of Tâi-gí and teaching experience. In addition to these experienced teachers, the Tâi-gí teaching support platform will also serve newly recruited Tâi-gí teachers, including those who teach other subjects as part-time teachers. With the rise of Tâi-gí education, the number of new teachers will continue to increase. The aim of this workshop was to leverage the experience of these pioneer teachers to construct a lesson preparation platform that provides an operational environment tailored to the needs of Tâi-gí teachers. This platform will establish a database system for Tâi-gí-related resources to assist teachers in improving their lesson preparation efficiency. Future PD workshops for Tâi-gí education will incorporate newly recruited Tâi-gí teachers as participants, making the lesson preparation platform more comprehensive and mature.

6 Conclusion

In response to the promotion of the Development of National Languages Act, the Ministry of Education in Taiwan changed the curriculum guidelines of 12-year Basic Education. However, the Tâi-gí teacher, as the disadvantaged educational practitioners of the policy, are facing the challenges of searching the teaching materials from scattered Tâi-gí literature resources in the internet. To empower the teachers who will devoted to the Tâi-gí teaching practices, we intend to build a Tâi-gí literature platform to collect Tâi-gí resources in supporting the Tâi-gí teachers preparing their language courses. We apply participatory design as the approach to co-create this platform with Tâi-gí teachers in senior high school. In the PD workshops spanning two stages and six sessions, a strong emphasis on reflective practices shaped the project's trajectory. Reflection-in-action was integral both between workshops, ensuring seamless progress, and during workshops themselves. Noteworthy instances included adjusting workshop content based on insights from prior sessions, such as categorizing students in response to teaching disparities. Real-time adjustments, like shifting to a drawing method for understanding website design, underscored the importance of immediate reflection. The collaboration with Tâi-gí teachers revealed a focus on current teaching challenges, potentially linked to their significant daily teaching commitments. This emphasis on known issues during the design process led to less imaginative solutions. Future PD workshops aim to guide Tâi-gí teachers toward contemplating future needs actively, fostering innovation and aligning solutions with evolving teaching requirements. Additionally, the current workshop, attended by experienced Tâi-gí teachers, will evolve to include newly recruited part-time teachers, enhancing the comprehensiveness and maturity of the lesson preparation platform for Tâi-gí education.

Acknowledgments. We thank Dr. Lekun Tan (the Department of Taiwan Literature at National Chen Kung University) and Dr. Wen-Hsiang Lu (the Department of Computer Science and Information Engineering at National Chen Kung University.) for their support in the workshops and valuable discussions, enhancing the progress and quality of our project.

References

1. Huan-Wells, J.: Mandarin-plus to Mandarin-inclusive: conceptualising the New Pluralistic Language Policy in Taiwan. Multiethnica: J. Hugo Valentin Centre **42**, 45–62 (2022). https://doi.org/10.33063/diva-505199
2. Kensing, F., Greenbaum, J.: Heritage: Having a say. In: Routledge International Handbook of Participatory Design. Routledge, pp. 41–56 (2012)
3. Lee, H.R., Šabanović, S., Chang, W.-L., Nagata, S., Piatt, J., Bennett, C., Hakken, D.: Steps toward participatory design of social robots: mutual learning with older adults with depression. In: Proceedings of the 2017 ACM/IEEE International Conference on Human-Robot Interaction, pp. 244–253 (2017)

4. Robertson, T., Simonsen, J.: Participatory Design: an introduction. In: Routledge International Handbook of Participatory Design, pp 1–17. Routledge (2012)
5. Ertner, M., Kragelund, A.M., Malmborg, L.: Five enunciations of empowerment in participatory design. In: Proceedings of the 11th Biennial Participatory Design Conference, pp 191–194 (2010)
6. Steen, M.: Virtues in participatory design: cooperation, curiosity, creativity, empowerment and reflexivity. Sci. Eng. Ethics **19**, 945–962 (2013)
7. Kam, M., Ramachandran, D., Raghavan, A., Chiu, J., Sahni, U., Canny, J.: Practical considerations for participatory design with rural school children in underdeveloped regions: early reflections from the field. In: Proceedings of the 2006 Conference on Interaction Design and Children, pp. 25–32 (2006)
8. Byrne, E., Sahay, S.: Participatory design for social development: a South African case study on community-based health information systems. Inf. Technol. Dev. **13**, 71–94 (2007)
9. Stangel, M., Szóstek, A.: Empowering citizens through participatory design: a case study of Mstów, Poland. Architect. Civil Eng. Environ. **8**, 47–58 (2015)
10. Harrington, C., Erete, S., Piper, A.M.: Deconstructing community-based collaborative design: towards more equitable participatory design engagements. Proc. ACM Human-Comput. Interact. **3**, 1–25 (2019)
11. Bannon, L.J., Ehn, P.: Design matters in participatory design. In: Routledge International Handbook of Participatory Design, pp. 37–63. Routledge, New York (2012)
12. Yoo, D., Huldtgren, A., Woelfer, J.P., Hendry, D.G., Friedman, B.: A value sensitive action-reflection model: evolving a co-design space with stakeholder and designer prompts. In: Proceedings of the SIGCHI Conference on Human Factors in Computing Systems, pp 419–428 (2013)
13. Schön, D.A.: The Reflective Practitioner: How Professionals Think in Action. Routledge (2017)

The Research and Design of an AIGC Empowered Fashion Design Product

Zhuohao Wu[1(✉)], Ritong Tang[1], Ganyu Wang[1], Hailing Li[1], Sibo Yang[1], and Mohammad Shidujaman[2]

[1] School of Animation and Digital Arts, Communication University of China, Beijing, China
HiMrHOW@gmail.com

[2] Department of Computer Science and Engineering, Independent University, Dhaka, Bangladesh

Abstract. This paper explores the transformative potential of Artificial Intelligence Generated Content (AIGC) in the fashion industry, addressing the challenges and opportunities in fashion design. The study examines the current fashion design landscape, which is marked by a focus on trends, cultural diversity, and an increasing demand for personalized products. It identifies the inefficiencies of traditional design processes and proposes AIGC as a solution to enhance creativity, efficiency, and market adaptability.

The research details the application of AIGC across key phases of fashion design, including inspiration, design, manufacturing, and marketing. It showcases how AI can facilitate trend analysis, rapid design iteration, virtual try-ons, and sales prediction, thereby streamlining the design process and reducing costs. A comparative experiment is conducted to assess the impact of AI-assisted design on the productivity and output quality of fashion designers.

Despite the positive outcomes, the study acknowledges the need for advanced AI model training to improve the accuracy of clothing pattern generation, approaches to bridge design to manufacturing, and the importance of objective evaluation methods.

In essence, this paper provides a comprehensive overview of AIGC's role in fashion design, highlighting its current capabilities, limitations, and the path forward for leveraging AI to revolutionize the industry.

Keywords: AIGC · Fashion Design · Product Design · Creativity

1 Introduction

1.1 Design Challenges in the Fashion Industry

The current fashion design in the fashion industry is characterized by its adherence to fashion trends and cultural diversity, with a product focus that directly addresses consumer needs, engages in mass production, and meets the growing demand for higher levels of personalized customization.

M. Kurosu and A. Hashizume (Eds.): HCII 2024, LNCS 14688, pp. 413–429, 2024.
https://doi.org/10.1007/978-3-031-60449-2_28

Industrialized clothing production processes are geared towards mass production. Fast fashion companies meet the ever-evolving needs of consumers by offering a variety of trendy styles and quickly replenishing inventory [1]. Meanwhile, more and more consumers are no longer satisfied with the functionality of clothing, but instead desire personalization. Some fashion companies are using parametric body models, virtual try-on technology, and consumer co-creation platforms to better meet the needs of consumers for personalized customization [2].

Traditional fashion design processes are costly and time-consuming. Some fashion brands and designers are considering AI assistance for enhancing design efficiency and meeting diverse needs, as well as using big data for capturing fashion trends and predicting potential sales.

1.2 AIGC Technologies for Fashion Design

AIGC (Artificial Intelligence Generated Content) has been coming along the way for decades as the fashion industry keeps chasing innovation. Since the 1980s, computer algorithms have been used to design textile [3]. Since the 2010s, style transfer technology has been used to mimic the style of famous artists or historical periods onto new designs [4], GAN (Generative Adversarial Networks) technology has been used to design clothing [5], and 3D garment simulation technology has been used by designers to virtually check their creations on digital models, saving time and resources. Today, the new generative technologies do not only support fashion design [6], replace fashion model [7], but also allow customers to virtually "try on" clothes more realistically than ever [8].

As experiments and demonstrations in 2016, IBM Watson helped human designers to design dresses for pop stars [9]. The process involved information analysis and fashion elements extracting, so to suggest potential design directions. In 2018, Alibaba in collaboration with the Hong Kong Polytechnic University's Textile and Apparel Department and the British Textile Association initiated the FashionAI algorithm competition to explore the application of AI in fashion design [10]. In 2019, more experiments emerged, including Cornell University's AI tool for detecting global fashion trends [11], Facebook AI's Fashion++ for outfit recommendation [12], and DeepBlue Technology's DeepVogue winning the runner-up prize over human designers in a major fashion design competition in China [13]. The Covid-19 pandemic temporarily broke the development [14], but AI for fashion design went back soon with the new powerful generative AI technologies such as diffusion models, large language models and multimodal models since 2021 [15]. In April 2023, the first AI Fashion Week was hosted in New York [16], attracting nearly 400 designers. A lot of experimental products emerged this year, such as Project Primrose by Adobe for creating "wearable, multifunctional, and easy-to-adjust" garments, Style3D by Linctex for incorporating AIGC in its real-time 3D simulation, Weshop AI for generating fashion models and products for ecommerce.

The specialized and unique nature of fashion design creates a professional barrier between typical AI generation methods and the established workflows of traditional fashion design. Conventional AI painting tools are not designed for the specific needs of fashion design. They lack the ability to understand the nuances of fashion, such as the difference between clothing elements and non-clothing elements. This makes it difficult to create professional-grade fashion designs using these tools [17].

To enhance the professionalism and controllability of AI fashion design, the workflow needs to be re-thought. One approach to consider is to use a "big picture first, details later" strategy. This could help to generate design inspiration more efficiently and streamline product design, marketing, and operations. Additionally, designers could skip the traditional process of sampling and photo shoots and submit designs directly to e-commerce sites for user feedback and production decisions. This could lead to more efficient and direct feedback for fashion design.

2 AIGC Empowered Fashion Design Workflow

2.1 Current Fashion Design Workflow

The fashion design process can be divided into four main phases: inspiration, design, manufacturing, and marketing. In the inspiration phase, designers collect creative ideas from a variety of sources, such as fashion trends, social media, art exhibitions, travel etc. These ideas may include new color combinations, unique patterns, or innovative materials. In the design phase, designers develop these ideas into concrete design concepts. This phase includes selecting fabrics, finalizing the design, and creating prototypes. Designers then iterate on these prototypes to ensure that the designs are both aesthetically pleasing and functional. In the manufacturing phase, designers work with manufacturers to turn designs into products. This phase involves considering factors such as production costs, quality control, and time management. Finally, in the marketing phase, designers promote and sell the designs through various channels and campaigns.

2.2 The AIGC Empowerment Potential Throughout the Workflow

In this research, we studied fashion design workflow, explored potential AI applica-tions, designed a prototype for testing and conducted a comparative experiment to validate our hypothesis. We thoroughly went through the fashion design workflow by interviewing professional designers and analyzing their behaviors, so to build up a system of the workflow (see Figs. 1, 2, 5, and 6). We discussed with AI scientists on the feasibility of potential AI applications, and decided to focus on the Inspira-tion, Design and Marketing phases, temporarily skipping the Design-to-Manufacturing phase as it yet requires some technology breakthroughs. We designed a prototype of an AIGC empowered fashion design product (see Figs. 3 and 4) based on our studies, and then tested it with some fashion designers to validate perfor-mance and potential of AIGC in the fashion design workflow. The AI Applications in the Inspiration Phase.

Fashion designers in the traditional industry typically look for inspiration from a variety of sources. On the one hand, they use websites that predict fashion trends. These websites provide information about colors, materials, and patterns that are likely to be popular. This information can help designers understand current market trends and what consumers are interested in. On the other hand, designers also look for inspiration in their everyday lives. This could include activities such as shopping, visiting art galleries, or traveling. They may discover new color combinations, unique pattern designs, interesting material applications, or cultural elements that could be used in their designs. By combining inspiration from these different sources, designers can create designs that are both fashionable and meet the needs of consumers.

AI can be used to crawl and analyze data from fashion information platforms, social media, news websites, and e-commerce platforms. This can be used to predict fashion trends [18, 19] and track online trends [20]. AI's efficient algorithms and powerful computing capabilities allow us to extract valuable information from data, such as popular colors, patterns, and styles. By analyzing user behavior on social media, such as the topics they follow, the content they post, and the frequency of their interactions, AI can help us understand which topics are attracting people's attention, which products or brands are popular, or which may be popular in the future [21]. This information is valuable for brands because it can help them understand consumer needs and preferences, and develop more effective marketing strategies.

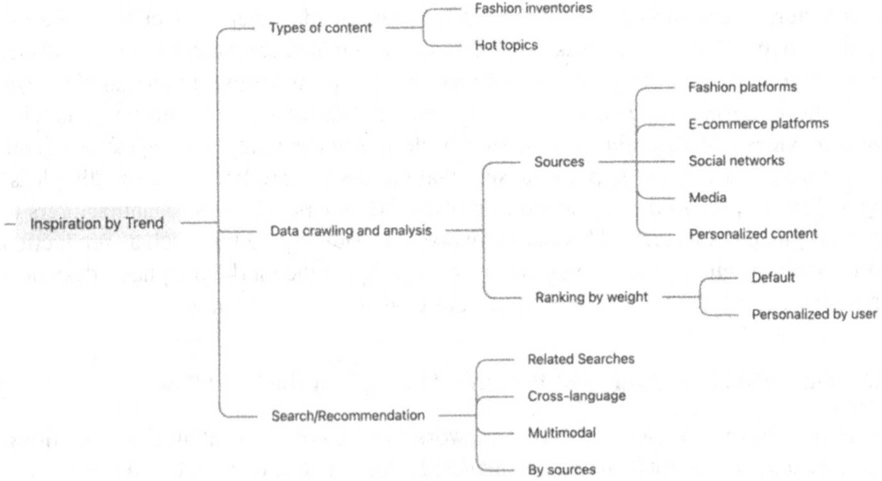

Fig. 1. The trend tracking module of the architecture of our AI fashion design product.

We used user behavior flow analysis to analyze user behavior patterns when using AI fashion design products. Based on this, we conducted a user needs analysis and drew a product architecture diagram. The figure below (see Fig. 1) is the module about fashion trend tracking, showing how trend tracking is achieved by data crawling and analysis. It mainly covers two types of content, fashion inventories and hot topics. It integrates the content from sources including fashion platforms, e-commerce platforms, social networks, media, and personalized content. It presents the content through user search or user recommendations, especially in a cross-language and multimodal format.

2.3 The AI Applications in the Design Phase

Designers use the inspirations collected to develop their design explorations. This process takes into account both artistic creativity and market practicality. Designers collect information from a variety of sources, including fashion trends, color theory, pattern aesthetics, material innovation, and cultural dynamics. They then translate this information into concrete design concepts. The most important thing in this stage is the exploration and experimentation of creativity. Designers use a variety of technical means, such as hand-drawn sketches, digital simulations, or physical samples, to test the feasibility of their designs. The key to their work is to combine creative inspiration with cost-effectiveness, fabric availability, and target market needs to create designs that are both fashionable and meet market demand. The work of designers in this stage is not only about aesthetics, but also about a deep understanding of product practicality and market trends. They ensure that their designs are both in line with brand positioning and attractive to target consumers.

AI technology could drive changes in five perspectives the design phase:

1. AI can generate a large number of designs at low cost and high quality, in assistance to designers. AI uses massive data and algorithms to quickly generate various design schemes, which greatly reduces the time and cost of design, and allows designers to focus more on innovation and optimization of design, rather than repetitive drawing work.
2. AI can simulate the effects of different fabrics and manufacturing processes, helping designers to identify and solve potential problems in the early stage, avoiding waste of resources in the manufacturing phase.
3. AI allows designers to intuitively see the effects of clothing on different types of people, as well as the coordination between single clothing and overall dressing and the scene, helping designers to control the final results from the end to the beginning.
4. AI can quickly modify and iterate designs. For example, when designers want to change the color, pattern, or fabric of a design, they could simply modify the corresponding parameters, and AI will immediately generate a new design. This allows designers to try various design schemes in a short period of time and pick the best results.
5. Because AI can easily generate photo-realistic images, it can even skip traditional prototype making and model shooting, and directly present to users for test outs, and then improve the design and make decision for manufacturing based on user feedback. This can significantly save the time and resources of the overall process, and increase the commercial conversion efficiency.

In general, AI in the design exploration stage can not only improve the efficiency and quality of design, but also provide more innovation space for designers and the business.

After we analyzed user needs in the design phase and planned the design modules (see Fig. 2), we conducted user research based on the product prototype (see Figs. 3 and 4). Through observation and interviews of user behavior, we found that "image-based generation" behavior accounts for the dominant position in the fashion design industry. The core of this mode is to use various reference images as input, including previous work results, fashion trend images recommended by the system, rapid discovery and generation attempts during online browsing or offline shopping and traveling, and then to generate designs based on one or multiple reference images. This mode can work with the basic mode of "text prompt based generation" for more sophisticated control. In addition, our product design focuses on the integration of product functions and AI

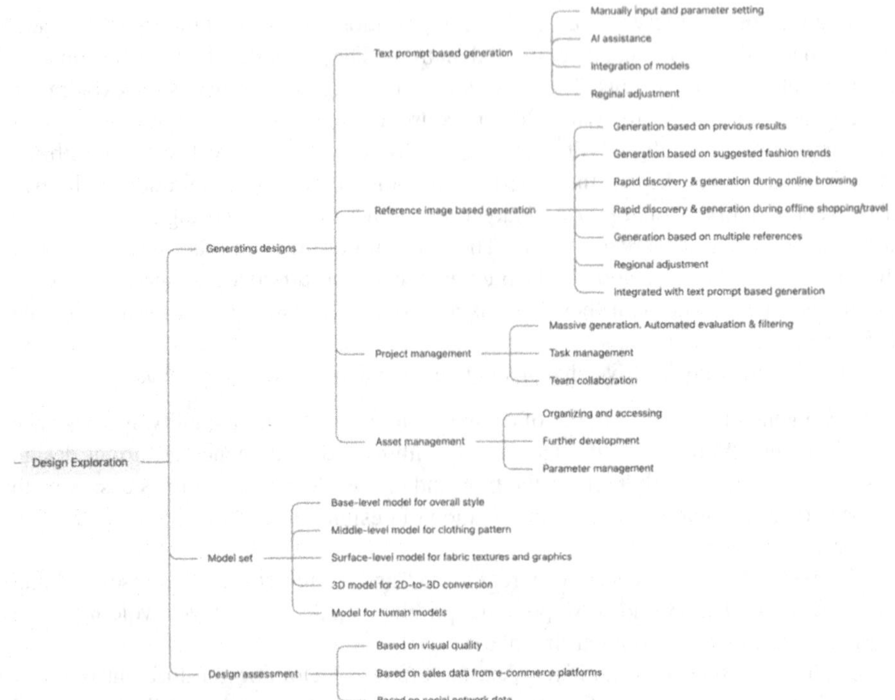

Fig. 2. The design exploration module of the architecture of our AI fashion design product.

technology, especially the use of multiple models, including the base-level model that controls the overall generation style, the middle-level model that controls the clothing pattern, and the surface-level model that controls the generation of fabric textures and graphics.

2.4 AI Application in the Design-To-Manufacturing Phases

In the traditional fashion industry, designers need to carefully consider the fabric and texture treatment of the finished garment when they are designing. This is because the texture of the fabric and the design of the pattern will directly affect the comfort and appearance of the garment. Designers need to ensure that their design can be realized in the actual manufacturing process, not just look good on the design draft. In order to ensure that the details such as cutting and sewing will not have too much deviation in the process of garment pattern making, designers need to work closely with patternmakers to determine the best pattern making scheme. This may require multiple trials and adjustments to ensure that the final result can accurately reflect the designer's innovative ideas. After the design draft is processed into garment pattern by the patternmaker, the designer needs to follow up the making of the prototype, to ensure that the effect can meet the expectation. This requires the designer to establish good communication with the patternmaker and timely solve the problems encountered in the making process.

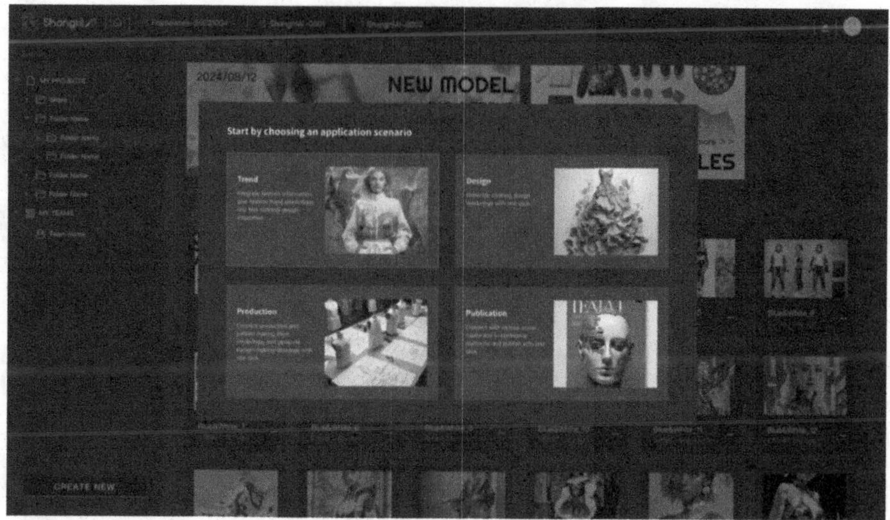

Fig. 3. The Design Exploration Module-1, product prototype of an AI fashion design product.

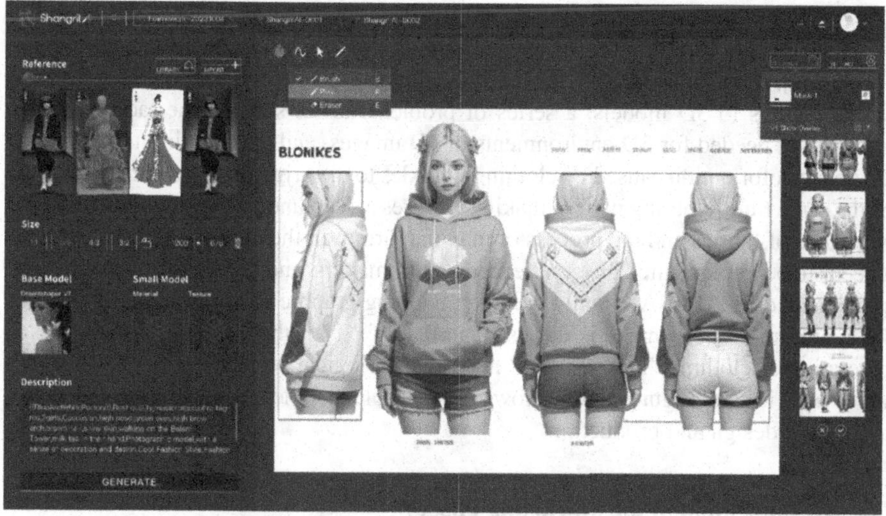

Fig. 4. The Design Exploration Module-2, product prototype of an AI fashion design product.

After the prototype is generally completed, the designer will get real models to try it on, so as to find out the possible problems from the user's perspective and make timely adjustments. This step is essential for ensuring the comfort and suitability of the garment. The manufacturing will be ready when the sampling is done.

AI could play an important role in the manufacturing phase. In the traditional fashion industry, designers need to work with patternmakers to complete the pattern making, which can be time-consuming and error-prone. Theoretically, AI could automate the pattern making process, which can improve efficiency and reduce errors. In the traditional fashion industry, manufacturers need to stock a large amount of fabrics in advance, which can lead to inventory and financial pressures. If they could train various fabrics into models to generate clothing designs, and then purchase fabrics only after manufacturing plan is confirmed, it can effectively reduce pressure, save resources, and improve production efficiency.

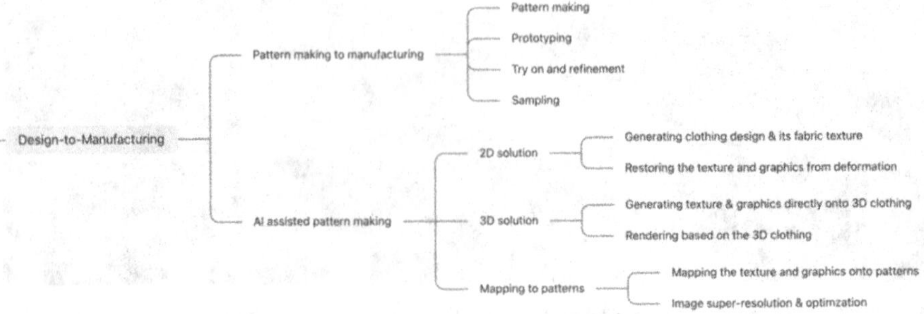

Fig. 5. The Design-to-Manufacturing Module of our AI fashion design product.

However, the current AI technologies have a lot of limitations in generating fashion design [22]. Today's generative AI can only generate 2D renderings. When converting 2D renderings to 3D models, a series of problems arise, such as the lack of all the information needed for 3D environments in 2D images, and the inability to restore the 2D image deformation caused by clothing wrinkles to the original flat texture or graphic. At the same time, clothing pattern making requires a deep understanding of the physical properties of fabrics and the process of manufacturing. In the current clothing industry, it needs to be implemented by experienced patternmakers, and it is not yet possible to be implemented by AI. If AI is only used for mapping graphic generation on 3D models, the contribution it can make is far less than that of AI for the overall and scene-based generation of clothing. This area still needs technological breakthroughs, and we will not discuss it here. Figure 5 only shows the possible technical routes in the process of connecting design and production.

2.5 AI Application in the Marketing Phases

With pretrained AI models, customized text, images, and video materials can be generated for various e-commerce platforms. This not only saves manpower and material resources, but also improves marketing efficiency. It could also lead to a new marketing-to-manufacturing approach, in which AI-generated photorealistic clothing design renderings are directly presented on e-commerce and social platforms, and manufacturing only gets start when purchase orders made. This would effectively reduce upfront investment and lower commercial risks. In addition, the technology of virtual try-on is finally realized after a few decades of development [23]. It not only enhances the shopping experience, but also improves the accuracy of purchases, and reduces the possibility of returns. At the same time, AI analysis of marketing data can help businesses understand market trends and provide a basis for design improvement.

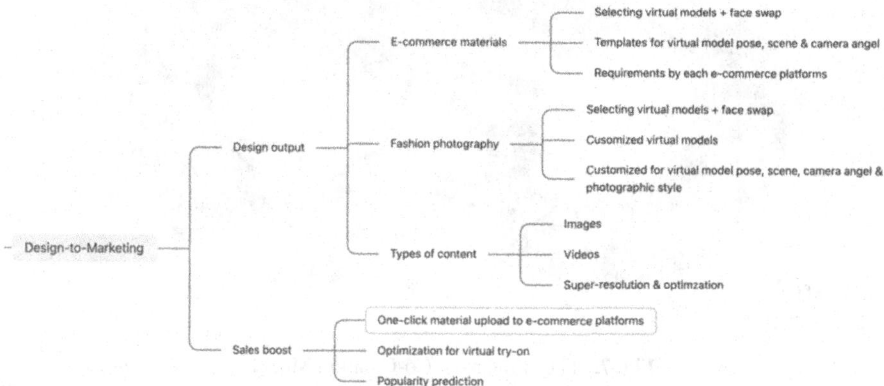

Fig. 6. The Design-to-Manufacturing Module of our AI fashion design product.

In marketing, the key task of design is to process the final clothing renderings, output them as e-commerce materials and fashion photography. E-commerce materials mainly use selected virtual models and templated content, and follow the requirements of different platforms. Fashion photography is more focused on uniqueness and artistic sense, and will customize virtual models, poses, scenes, camera angles, and photographic styles. To better promote sales, it is also possible to provide one-click upload of materials for each e-commerce and social network, and optimize the looking and poses of virtual models for the virtual try-on at e-commerce platforms. The data crawled and analyzed during the training of fashion models includes the user interaction about clothing at e-commerce and social platforms, and can be used to predict the possible popularity of a clothing design at each platform, so to assist in design and manufacturing decision making (See Fig. 6).

3 What Makes Differences and Impact?

3.1 The General Impact of AI on Fashion Design

In Zhuohao W. et al.'s paper "Artificial Intelligence Creativity and the Human-AI Co-Creation Model" [24], "Artificial Intelligence Creativity" is defined as the ability of humans and artificial intelligence to live and create together, achieving greater accomplishments by leveraging each other's strengths. This article provides a detailed description of the role that AI can play in each phase of fashion design. Here is a summary of based on the human-AI Creation Model framework (see Fig. 7). The Inspiration phase of fashion design corresponds to the Human-AI Co-Creation Model's “perception” and “thinking”, where AI provides designers with a large amount of information through big data, and inspires more creativity by supplementing the directions that designers have

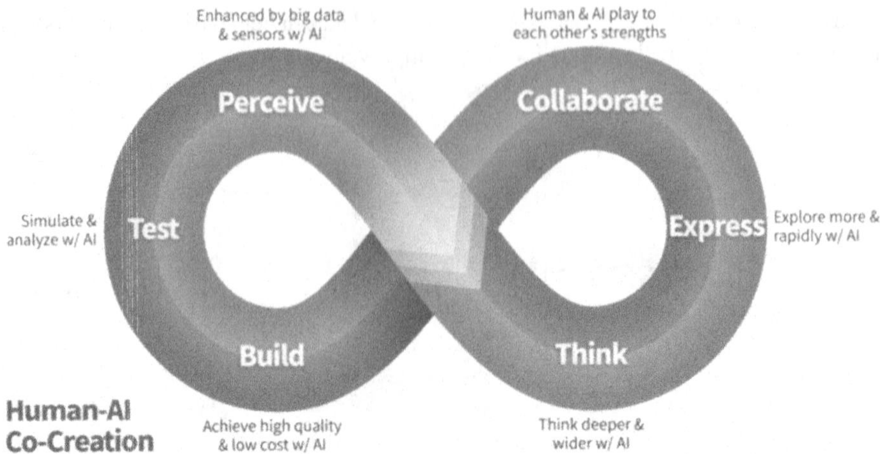

Fig. 7. The Human-AI Co-Creation Model.

not considered. The Design phase of fashion design corresponds to the Human-AI Co-Creation Model's "expression" and "collaboration", where designers and AI collaborate, with AI responsible for conducting rapid and high-quality exploration, and designers responsible for controlling the direction and screening out solutions. The Design-to-Manufacturing and Design-to-Marketing phase of fashion design corresponds to the Human-AI Co-Creation Model's "construction" and "testing", where AI can automatically output materials to each platform's requirements, and evaluate designs based on e-commerce, social media, and industry data to predict their popularity on each platform. It can even obtain user feedback by directly presenting realistic design renderings, which can assist in making design improvements and manufacturing decisions.

3.2 The Model Training and Generation Control in Fashion

In this study, we adopted the Stable Diffusion framework for model training and image generation to simulate the results of our fashion design product, including the overall effects of virtual models, clothing, and scenes, the restoration of the patterns on the clothing, and the consistent presentation of the clothing in multiple views. Here are the process and methods summarized through experiments:

First, the selected textures/graphics were cropped around visual features and then more material images were formed by color transformation, image rotation and flipping. All images were processed by super-resolution and form the training set of basic images (See Fig. 8).

Second, in order to better form the correspondence between the textures/graphics and clothing, a batch of images also needs to be supplemented in the training set, simultaneously displaying the textures/graphics both on clothing and on a flat surface. It is best to use real photos here, or use Photoshop to make some (Fig. 9).

Third, the images were labeled with text to describe the content on the images, to build and strengthen the correspondence between prompts and related visual content in

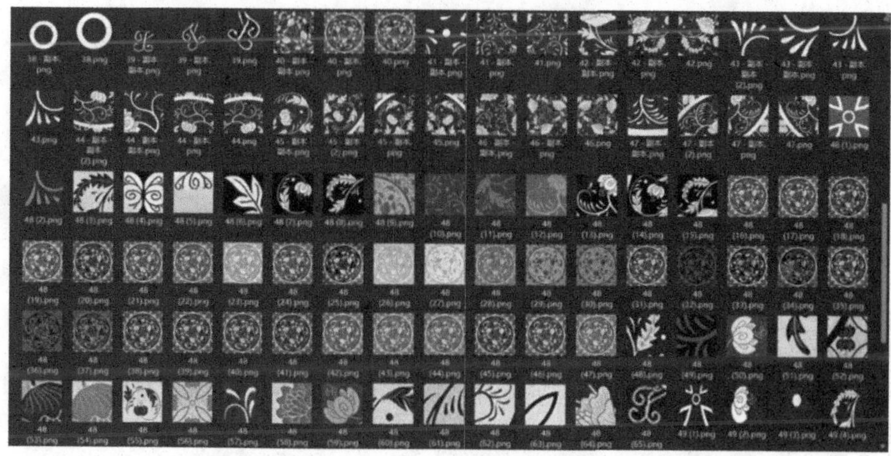

Fig. 8. The training set of basic texture/graphic images.

the AI model, including texture/graphics, clothing winkles, lighting setting, and visual styles.

Through experiments, we trained some models using the above methods and used it to generate clothing designs. 80% of the generated images can meet the requirements, including overall rendering, the correspondent texture/graphics, and the consistency in multiple views (see Fig. 10). The main remaining problem is that AI cannot accurately generate clothing patterns. This can only be achieved by training a specialized clothing pattern model.

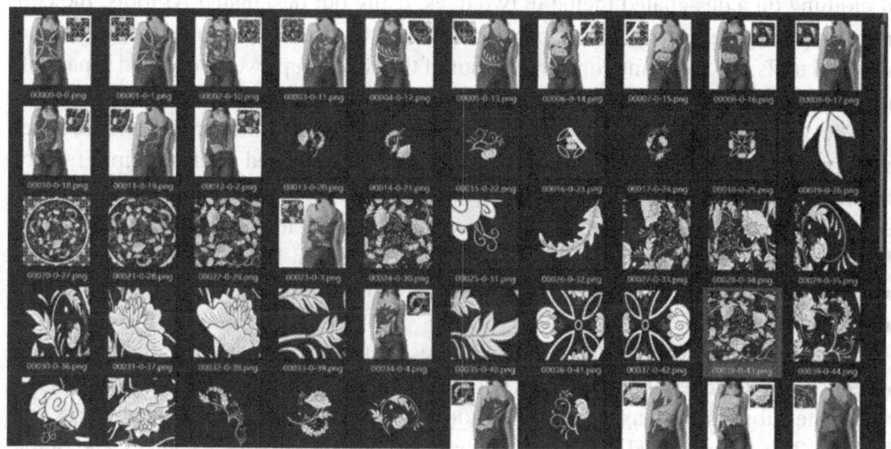

Fig. 9. The training set of the correspondence between the textures/graphics and clothing

Fig. 10. The generated results showing consistency between the clothing design and the texture/graphic in multiple views.

3.3 A Comparative Experiment on AI-Assisted Fashion Design

According to "the creative classification-based creative fashion design method" proposed by Yoon-Kyoung K. and Hye-Won P. [24], the best way to guide design in fashion design is to focus on thinking in a limited space, followed by decomposing the structure into sub-modules and conducting segmented planning. We referred to this theory and divide the fashion design workflow into three sub-modules: inspiration collection, design exploration, and rendering output. We conducted a comparative experiment on AI-assisted fashion design with three participants, as a small sample for future experiments. The participants of the experiment were professional fashion designers and college students majoring in fashion design. The experiment required the participants to design a series of clothing on a designated theme in two days, using our designated AI tools; the control group was the same batch of participants who design for the same theme without using AI tools. The working time and output of the two groups were recorded separately according to the sub-modules of the fashion design workflow.

The experiment task theme was selected based on recent fashion trends and feedback from professionals. The final design schemes can be evaluated from multiple factors, including fabric, colors, design details, clothing silhouette, popular elements, and design expansion space. The participants of the experiment were mainly professional fashion designers and college students majoring in fashion design. Before the experiment, the participants were informed of the experiment conditions and the specific requirements of the output.

The experiment was divided into two phases. In the first phase, the participants were asked to draw sketches and renderings without using AI tools (see Table 1). In the second phase, the subjects were asked to use AI tools to generate sketches and renderings (see Table 2). The AI tools used in the second phase included Midjourney, Dalle·3, and Stable Diffusion for image generation, as well as GPT-4 for text genera-tion. The experiment process and outputs were recorded step by step, with the process unchanged and the time used in each phase unchanged.). The AI tools used in the second phase included Midjourney, Dalle·3, and Stable Diffusion for image generation, as well as GPT-4 for text generation. The experiment process and outputs were recorded step by step, with the process unchanged and the time used in each phase unchanged.

Table 1. Record of the first phase of the experiment

Participant	Time	Task	Output
A	09 December 2023 19:00-20:00	Research	
	09 December 2023 20:00-23:00 09 December 2023 20:00-21:00 10 December 2023 22:30-23:00	Sketch	
	14 December 2023 21:00-23:00	Rendering	
B	09 December 2023 21:00-22:30 10 December 2023 15:00-17:00	Research	
	10 December 2023 19:00-22:00 15 December 2023 19:00-21:00	Rendering	
C	10 December 2023 17:00-18:00	Research	
	10 December 2023 18:00-21:00	Sketch	
	12 December 2023 17:00-18:00	Rendering	

Table 2. Records of the second phase of the experiment

Participant	Time	Task	Output
A	9 December 2023 19:00-20:00	Rendering	
	20 January 2024 16:00-18:00	Rendering	
B	24 December 2023 14:30-16:30	Rendering	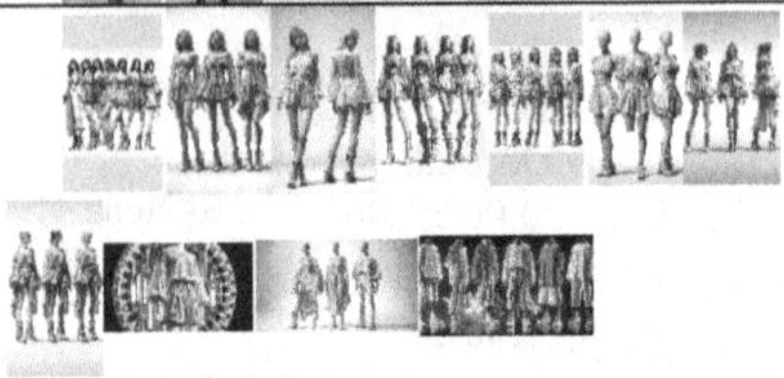
	21 January 2024 15:00-17:00	Rendering	
C	13 December 2023 21:00-22:00	Rendering	
	22 January 2024 21:00-17:00	Rendering	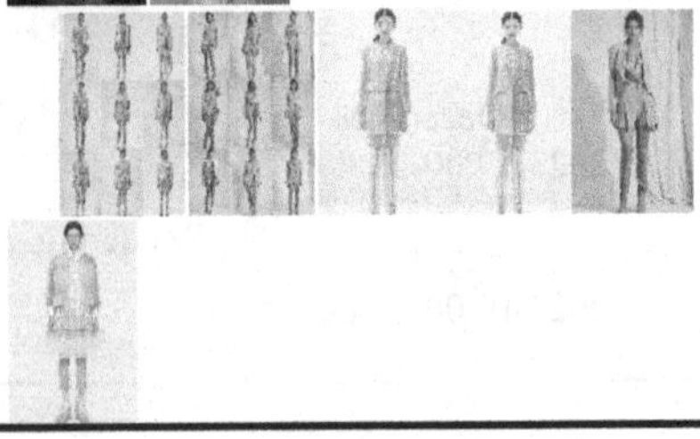

In the inspiration collection phase, all three designers tend to find references from existing products, and then brainstorm. The main reference sources include fashion websites, e-commerce websites, and social networks. Through interviews, we also learned that some designers would like to build up their own image libraries, track news media, and take photos in fashion shows and daily life for references. Designers are used to searching with keywords such as fabrics, clothing styles, design elements, famous designers, or design styles. When collecting reference images, they focus on the design highlights and sources of the reference images. In addition, although the types of clothing silhouette are not used as search keywords, it is also an important factor in screening reference images. The designers spent varying amounts of time on inspiration search, and AI can provide significant assistance in this area.

In the design exploration and rendering output phase, the participants in the control group used their own usual methods to design, while the participants in the experimental group instructed volunteers who were proficient in AI operations to perform the operations, avoiding the impact of operation proficiency on the experiment. We used a questionnaire to ask the participants about their satisfaction with the AI-generated results, referring to the fashion design competition evaluation system, and scored them on 8 dimensions: popularity elements, overall appearance, detailed descriptions, structure ratio, color performance, craftmanship expression, material fabric, and usage scenarios. Although the number of generated results increased significantly with the help of AI, the overall results of the questionnaire showed that the scores of most dimension, except in "detailed description", haven't met the expected results, especially low in "popular elements" and "material fabrics" (see Table 3). We discussed with the participants and all agreed that higher-quality model training is the most promising way to solve these problems.

Table 3. Ratings for AI-assisted design outputs

	Evaluation dimensions (weight)	Mismatched expectations (1)	Barely passing compared to expectations (2)	Achieve well compared to expectations (3)	Achieve expectations (4)	Exceeding expectations (5)	Overall rating
1	Popularity elements	0	2	0	1	0	8
2	Overall appearance	0	1	1	1	0	9
3	Detailed descriptions	0	1	1	0	1	10
4	Structure ratio	0	1	2	0	0	8
5	Color performance	0	1	1	1	0	9
6	Craftmanship expression	0	1	0	2	0	10
7	Material fabric	0	2	0	1	0	8
8	Usage scenarios	0	1	1	1	0	9

3.4 Issues in the Experiment

The experiment in this study used existing tools to build a workflow, simulated to form a product prototype, and achieved an initial experiment. However, there are still many issues to be addressed. First, the sample size of the subjects is too small, and it is necessary to increase the quantity and coverage of the subjects in future experiments. Second, the evaluation of experimental results relies on subjective evaluation, which may affect the accuracy and consistency of the results. Third, AI technologies and tools are rapidly evolving. In this experiment, three tools were used, but the specific functions and use processes of these tools were not standardized, which may lead to inconsistent use of the tools and affect the interpretation and effectiveness of the results.

4 Conclusion and Future Work

This research demonstrated the significant potential and current limitations of AIGC in revolutionizing the fashion industry. The study has explored the integration of AIGC technologies into various phases of the fashion design process, from inspiration to design, manufacturing and marketing, so to enhance design efficiency, reduce costs, and provide a more personalized and innovative approach to fashion creation. However, it also revealed challenges, including the need for higher-quality model training to improve the accuracy of clothing pattern generation and the reliance on subjective evaluation in the assessment of design outputs.

Moving forward, the key technology breakthroughs include refining AI models to better understand and generate complex clothing patterns and textures, building the ability to accurately translate 2D designs into 3D models, and simulating the physical properties of fabrics for bridging design to manufacturing seamlessly. The products for AIGC empowered fashion design are already on the way. The impact is mainly limited in the design exploration, but the potential in inspiration and marketing is about to release, and the barriers of design-to-manufacturing will be overcome as 3D generation technology is developing rapidly.

In conclusion, the future of fashion design is to be significantly influenced by AIGC technologies. By addressing the challenges and building upon the promising results of this study, the fashion industry can harness the power of AI to create more sustainable, personalized, and innovative fashion products that meet the evolving demands of consumers.

References

1. Long, X., Naisry, J.: Sustainability in the fast fashion industry. Manuf. Serv. Oper. Manage. **24**(3), 1276–1293 (2022)
2. Zhao, L., Liu, S., Zhao, X.: Big data and digital design models for fashion design. J. Eng. Fibers Fabrics. **16**, 155892502110190 (2021)
3. Monica, P.S., Alok, S., Samridhi, G.: Artificial Intelligence (AI) in textile industry operational modernization. Res. J. Textile Apparel. **28**(1), 67–83 (2024)
4. Prutha, D., Ashwinkumar, G., Tim, O.: Fashioning with Networks: Neural Style Transfer to Design Clothes. arXiv:1707.09899 (2017)

5. Kato, N., Osone, H., Oomori, K., Ooi, C.W., Ochiai, Y.: GANs-based clothes de-sign: pattern maker is all you need to design clothing. In: 10th Augmented Human International Conference on Proceedings, pp. 1–7, Reims France (2019)
6. Mobarak, I.: GenAI in Fashion | A Segmind Stable Diffusion XL 1.0 Approach. https://www.analyticsvidhya.com/blog/2023/09/genai-in-fashion-a-segmind-stable-diffusion-xl-1-0-approach/. Accessed 31 Dec 2023
7. Bernard, M.: Pixel Perfect: The Rise of AI Fashion Models. https://www.forbes.com/sites/bernardmarr/2023/06/07/pixel-perfect-the-rise-of-ai-fashion-models/. Accessed 31 Dec 2023
8. Lilian, R.: Virtually Try on Clothes with a New AI Shopping Feature. https://blog.google/products/shopping/ai-virtual-try-on-google-shopping/. Accessed 31 Dec 2023
9. Brian, M.: Hot Fashion Designer IBM Watson to Debut Smart Dress at Met Gala. https://www.cnet.com/tech/mobile/marchesa-ibm-watson-to-debut-cognitive-dress-at-met-gala/. Accessed 31 Dec 2023
10. Alibaba Cloud: FashionAI Global Challenge 2018. https://tianchi.aliyun.com/markets/tianchi/FashionAIeng/. Accessed 31 Dec 2023
11. Melanie L.: AI Tool Detects Global Fashion Trends. https://news.cornell.edu/stories/2019/10/ai-tool-detects-global-fashion-trends/. Accessed 31 Dec 2023
12. Facebook AI: Building AI with a Helpful Eye for Fashion. https://tech.facebook.com/artificial-intelligence/2019/9/building-ai-with-a-helpful-eye-for-fashion/. Accessed 31 Dec 2023
13. Mayura J.: An AI "Designer" Just Won Runner-Up in a Major Fashion Design Competition. https://radii.co/article/an-ai-designer-just-won-runner-up-in-a-major-fashion-design-competition/. Accessed 31 Dec 2023
14. Casini, L., Roccetti, M.: Fashion, digital technologies, and AI. Is the 2020 pandemic really driving a paradigm shift? ZoneModa J. **10**(2), 1–10 (2020)
15. Holger, H., Theodora, K., Roger, R., Kimberly, T.: Generative AI: Unlocking the Future of Fashion. https://www.mckinsey.com/industries/retail/our-insights/generative-ai-unlocking-the-future-of-fashion. Accessed 31 Dec 2023
16. Nadine, D.: First-Ever AI Fashion Week Debuts in NYC: 'A New Realm of Creation'. https://nypost.com/2023/04/20/first-ai-fashion-week-coming-to-nyc-new-realm-of-creation/. Accessed 31 Dec 2023
17. Shidong, C., Wenhao C., Shengyu, H., Yanting, Z., Hangyue, C., Gaoang, W.: DiffFashion: Reference-based Fashion Design with Structure-aware Transfer by Diffusion Models. arXiv: 2302.06826 (2023)
18. Shi, M., Chussid, C., Yang, P., et al.: The exploration of artificial intelligence application in fashion trend forecasting. Text. Res. J. **91**(19–20), 2357–2386 (2021)
19. Zhao, L., Min, C.: The rise of fashion informatics: a case of data-mining-based social network analysis in fashion. Cloth. Text. Res. J. **37**(2), 87–102 (2019)
20. Singh, J.: Social media analysis using natural language processing techniques. In: 20th Python in Science Conference on Proceedings, pp. 74–80 (2021)
21. Liu, L., Zhang, H., Ji, Y., Wu, Q.M.J.: Toward AI fashion design: an attribute-GAN model for clothing match. Neurocomputing **341**, 156–167 (2019)
22. Noor, A., Saeed, M.A., Ullah, T., et al.: A review of artificial intelligence applications in apparel industry. J. Textile Inst. **113**(3), 505–514 (2022)
23. Ira, K.: How AI Makes Virtual Try-on More Realistic. https://blog.google/products/shopping/virtual-try-on-google-generative-ai/. Accessed 31 Dec 2023
24. Wu, Z., Ji, D., Yu, K., Zheng, X, Wu, D., Mohammad, S.: AI creativity and the human-AI co-creation model. In: HCII 2021: Human-Computer Interaction. Theory, Methods and Tools, pp. 171–190, July 2021 (2021)
25. Kim, Y.K., Park, H.W.: Study on a creative fashion design development process through idea classification. J. Korean Soc. Costume **60**, 95–105 (2010)

Author Index

M. Kurosu and A. Hashizume (Eds.): HCII 2024, LNCS 14688, pp. 431–432, 2024.
https://doi.org/10.1007/978-3-031-60449-2

Printed in the United States
by Baker & Taylor Publisher Services